my BusinessCourse

FREE WITH NEW COPIES OF THIS TEXTBOOK*

Start using my BusinessCourse **Today: www.mybusinesscourse.com**

my BusinessCourse is a web-based learning and assessment program intended to complement your textbook and faculty instruction.

Student Benefits

- **eLectures**: These videos review the key concepts of each Learning Objective in each chapter.
- **Guided examples**: These videos provide step-by-step solutions for select problems in each chapter.
- **Auto-graded assignments**: Provide students with immediate feedback on select assignments. (**with Instructor-Led course ONLY**).
- **Quiz and Exam preparation**: myBusinessCourse provides students with additional practice and exam preparation materials to help students achieve better grades and content mastery.

You can access my BusinessCourse 24/7 from any web-enabled device, including iPads, smartphones, laptops, and tablets.

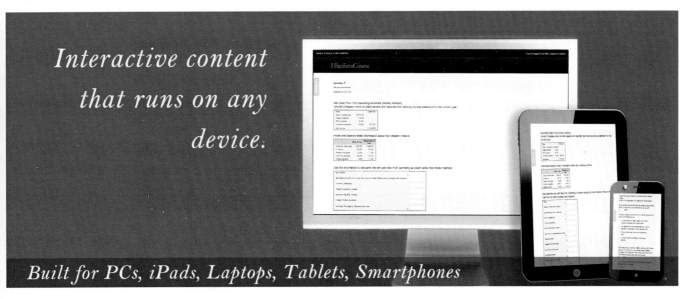

Interactive content that runs on any device.

Built for PCs, iPads, Laptops, Tablets, Smartphones

Managerial Accounting
for Undergraduates

Third Edition

Theodore E. Christensen
Terry College of Business
University of Georgia

L. Scott Hobson
Marriott School of Business
Brigham Young University

James S. Wallace
The Peter F. Drucker and Masatoshi Ito
Graduate School of Management
Claremont Graduate University

Jason W. Matthews
Terry College of Business
University of Georgia

Cambridge
BUSINESS PUBLISHERS

Photo Credits
Chapter 1: © Shutterstock.com
Chapter 2: © Shutterstock.com
Chapter 3: © Shutterstock.com
Chapter 4: © Shutterstock.com
Chapter 5: © Shutterstock.com
Chapter 6: © Shutterstock.com
Chapter 7: © Shutterstock.com
Chapter 8: © Shutterstock.com
Chapter 9: © Shutterstock.com
Chapter 10: © Shutterstock.com
Chapter 11: © Shutterstock.com
Chapter 12: © Shutterstock.com
Chapter 13: © istockphoto.com
Chapter 14: © istockphoto.com

Permissions Statement:

Materials from the Certified Management Accountant Examinations, Copyright © 2015, 2016, 2017, and 2018 by the Institute of Certified Management Accountants, are reprinted and/or adapted with permission.

All Fezzari photos courtesy of Fezzari Bicycles.

AICPA material and logo used with permission from the American Institute of Certified Public Accountants.

Cambridge Business Publishers

MANAGERIAL ACCOUNTING FOR UNDERGRADUATES, Third Edition, by Theodore E. Christensen, L. Scott Hobson, James S. Wallace, and Jason W. Matthews

Student Edition ISBN: 978-1-61853-442-2

Bookstores & Faculty: To order this book, contact the company via email customerservice@cambridgepub.com or call 800-619-6473.

Students & Retail Customers: To order this book, please visit the book's website and order directly online.

Printed in Canada.
10 9 8 7 6 5 4 3 2 1

About the Authors

THEODORE E. CHRISTENSEN is director and Terry Distinguished Chair of Business in the J. M. Tull School of Accounting at the University of Georgia. Prior to coming to UGA, he was on the faculty at Brigham Young University and at Case Western Reserve University. He was a visiting professor at the University of Michigan, the University of Utah, and Santa Clara University. He received a B.S. degree in accounting at San Jose State University, a M.Acc. degree in tax at Brigham Young University, and a Ph.D. in accounting from the University of Georgia. Professor Christensen has authored and coauthored articles published in many journals including *The Accounting Review, Journal of Accounting and Economics, Journal of Accounting Research, Review of Accounting Studies, Contemporary Accounting Research,* and *Accounting Organizations and Society.* He is also the author of an advanced financial accounting textbook. Professor Christensen has taught financial accounting at all levels, financial statement analysis, business valuation, both introductory and intermediate managerial accounting, and corporate taxation. He is the recipient of numerous awards for both teaching and research. He has been active in serving on various committees of the American Accounting Association and is a CPA.

L. SCOTT HOBSON is a Teaching Professor of Accounting (retired) at Brigham Young University (BYU), where he joined the faculty in 2003. He received his B.S. in accounting and Master of Accountancy degrees from BYU. Prior to his career in academics, Professor Hobson was the founder and owner of Hilton Farnkopf & Hobson (now HFH Consultants), a management consulting firm headquartered in Walnut Creek, California, for 14 years. He also worked in public accounting at Price Waterhouse for 5.5 years in both audit and consulting. While at Price Waterhouse, he taught for 2 years as an adjunct faculty at San Jose State University. He has taught accounting at all levels, from principles to M.B.A. courses, including accounting information systems, managerial accounting, financial accounting, governmental and not-for-profit accounting, and management consulting. Professor Hobson is a CMA and is licensed as a CPA in Utah. Professor Hobson has published a case titled "Managing the CPA Firm at Dodge Company" in *Issues in Accounting Education.*

JAMES S. WALLACE is an Associate Professor at The Peter F. Drucker and Masatoshi Ito Graduate School of Management at The Claremont Graduate University. He received his B.A. from the University of California, Santa Barbara, his M.B.A. from the University of California, Davis, and his Ph.D. from the University of Washington. Professor Wallace also holds a CPA certification from the state of California. He previously served on the faculty of the University of California, Irvine and has served as a visiting professor at the University of California, San Diego. Professor Wallace's work has appeared in leading academic journals including the *Journal of Accounting and Economics,* the *Journal of Corporate Finance,* and *Information Systems Research,* along with leading applied journals such as the *Journal of Applied Corporate Finance,* the *Journal of Accountancy, Issues in Accounting Education,* and *Accounting Horizons.* Prior to his career in academics, Professor Wallace worked in public accounting and in industry with a Fortune 500 company. He has done consulting work with numerous companies in multiple industries.

JASON W. MATTHEWS is a Senior Lecturer of Accounting and Director of Undergraduate Programs in the J.M. Tull School of Accounting at the University of Georgia (UGA). He received his B.S. from Missouri State University, his M.Acc. from North Carolina State University, and a Ph.D. from the University of Georgia. Prior to his career in academics, Professor Matthews was the interim Chief Financial Officer at Roark Capital Group, Director and Chief Financial Officer at United Coal Company, and Director and Chief Financial Officer of Oculan Corporation. Professor Matthews has taught across all levels at UGA including undergraduate financial accounting, managerial accounting, cost accounting and auditing; and graduate financial accounting and accounting information systems. He is the recipient of numerous teaching awards, including most recently the 2018 Terry College of Business Instructional Excellence award and the 2021 and 2018 Pearcy B. Yeargin Outstanding Undergraduate Teacher of the Year award. He has been active in serving on committees in the Teaching Learning and Curriculum section of the American Accounting Association and is a CMA.

Preface

Welcome to the third edition of *Managerial Accounting for Undergraduates*. We have written this book to introduce future business professionals to management accounting concepts and decision-making tools that will help them manage their companies in an increasingly competitive global market. While working for both small and large service firms and teaching in a university setting, we observed that some business professionals, although possessing a technically sound knowledge of accounting principles and methods, had difficulty understanding how the "answer" applied in the context of real business issues faced by these firms. Moreover, because the U.S. market is increasingly service oriented, professionals must develop experience in applying these skills to decision-making in a service environment.

Having spent several years supplementing existing textbook problems with more real-world and service industry examples, we saw a need for a new approach. Hence, we focus on helping students to **develop strong analytical skills** and **apply them in realistic decision-making contexts**. Finally, we have written the book with a **heavy emphasis on managerial decisions in service and merchandising enterprises**.

TARGET AUDIENCE

We created *Managerial Accounting for Undergraduates* to satisfy the needs of students taking their first managerial accounting course by providing a **high-quality**, **contemporary**, and **engaging** textbook and online learning system at an **affordable** price. With a suggested retail price of **$85** for the paperback, full-color textbook with **free access** to myBusinessCourse, we challenge faculty to find a better overall value for their students.

Read on to learn why you should use it in your introductory managerial accounting class.

RELEVANCE

Business professionals know that the economy has changed dramatically over the last two decades and that the demands placed on professionals now require an understanding of broad business disciplines, including data analysis, finance, marketing, operations management, and strategy. By exposing students to real-world companies and the challenges that they face, they can begin to understand the need to integrate accounting information with other business information in making good decisions.

One of the authors is a former founder, owner, and chief financial officer of a very successful regional consulting firm, HFH Consultants, LLC. The author was intimately involved in the strategy, marketing, human resource management, finance, and accounting of this service firm from its founding with three partners and an administrative assistant to its growth to include four offices, approximately two dozen professionals and staff, and over $3.5 million in annual revenue. His extensive experience managing this firm for 14 years is reflected throughout the textbook in the form of a continuous problem based on a fictitious service firm. This practical experience is also reflected in other real-world examples and problems based on real companies.

The following features are used throughout the textbook to help students understand how managerial accounting principles are used in real businesses today.

Real Company Examples

Students are more likely to engage in the learning process and retain the concepts taught if the examples used are real companies with which they are familiar. Throughout the textbook, we incorporate a wide range of examples using real companies such as **Apple**, **Microsoft**,

Boeing, and the California State Bar. In addition, the **Service Industry in Focus** section in the assignments of each chapter requires the students to use the financial and operational data of a fictitious consulting company, Environmental Business Consultants, LLC, to address real business issues.

Most chapters also include real-world examples from Fezzari, a custom bike manufacturer.

Environmental Business Consultants

Data Analytics & Excel Skill Development for Career Readiness

The basics of accounting haven't changed much in hundreds of years, but businesses have experienced significant change in the last decade due to the increased use of new technologies ranging from data analytics and Blockchain to machine learning and artificial intelligence. Technology is rapidly altering how accounting is performed and what can be done with the data once they are collected. In response to the changing demands of the business world, the AACSB has incorporated data analytics requirements within its educational framework. More recently, the AICPA and NASBA have underscored the importance of data analytics by making it a significant element in the **CPA Evolution Model Curriculum**. The consensus suggests that today's business students need an understanding and working knowledge of data analytics and data visualization to compete for the best jobs.

In addition to data analytics skills, employers expect prospective employees to be proficient with Excel. In recognition of the increasing importance of data analytics and the need for Excel proficiency, the third edition includes several new features to enhance students' career readiness.

- We include Data Analytics boxes throughout the text to expose students to techniques that are used by businesses in areas related to the topic being discussed. The following box is an example.

DATA ANALYTICS　　　　　**Using Analytics to Improve Cash Flow Management**

Data Analytics

Disney+ may be the new kid in town with the bigger arsenal of big hits relative to Netflix, but Netflix's use of data analytics is keeping it ahead of the competition. Netflix uses predictive analytics to match the preferences of its customer with the shows it produces. Netflix's use of data analytics in its early years came about from necessity.

Netflix started as a DVD rent-by-mail website. The concept proved very popular, but that popularity caused a problem: Netflix did not have enough inventory of new releases to keep up with customer demand. Netflix solved this by developing algorithms, based on its members preferences, that deemphasized popular new releases. Netflix continues to use customer preference data to drive its decisions. It collects data on the summaries you have read, how long you surf through titles, what you watch, and whether you watch the entire show. Then, Netflix uses this data to keep you engaged by suggesting other offerings. It also uses preference data to develop new content.

- Each chapter includes assignments that require students to use **Excel** or **Tableau** to hone data analysis and data visualization skills.

DATA ANALYTICS, DATA VISUALIZATION, AND EXCEL ACTIVITIES

Data Analytics, Data Visualization, and Excel Activities are available in myBusinessCourse. These assignments develop Excel, Tableau, and Data Analytics skills, which will enhance students' career readiness. These exercises are assignable and auto graded by MBC. For an overview of data analytics, see the appendix at the end of this book.

- New **Appendix B**, at the end of the book, provides an overview of data analytics, data visualization, and best practices for the effective display of data.

■ The following excerpt is from **Appendix B**.

DATA ANALYTICS

Data analytics can broadly be defined as the process of examining sets of data with the goal of discovering useful information from patterns found in the data. Increasingly, this process is aided by computers running programs ranging from basic spreadsheet software, such as **Microsoft Excel** and **Google Sheets**, to specialized software, such as **Tableau** or **Power BI**. This technology can reveal trends and insights that would otherwise be lost in the overwhelming amount of data.

LO1 Define Big Data and describe its four attributes.

MBC

Big Data

The concept of data analytics is intertwined with the concept of **big data**. While no precise definition exists for big data, a commonly accepted definition is that big data is a collection of data that is both extremely large and also extremely complex, thus making its analysis beyond the scope of traditional tools. Important attributes of big data commonly referred to as the four

■ MBC now contains a series of short videos that demonstrate the basic functions of Excel. These videos can be accessed within MBC as part of your MBC course.

Environmental, Social, and Governance (ESG)

Increasingly, companies have found that "doing good" leads to a more successful enterprise. Today's students are very engaged in the ESG movement, and we have incorporated ESG boxes to help students understand how ESG is being embraced by forward-thinking enterprises as part of their long-term business models.

ENVIRONMENTAL, SOCIAL, AND GOVERNANCE	Environmental Performance Reporting at Apple

There are probably few companies as secretive as Apple. The company is very careful to control any leaks on its upcoming products. Apple uses this strategy of keeping things secret in order to increase the anticipation before new product announcements. The strategy seems to be working well, based on the excitement surrounding these new product events.

One area that Apple is not secretive about is its environmental responsibility. Apple uses its detailed managerial accounting system to measure the environmental impact of how every product is manufactured. Unlike the secrecy surrounding what the next new product will be, Apple believes in full transparency regarding its environmental performance and reports on this performance in its comprehensive *Product Environmental Reports*. Every Apple product is measured and rated in four categories: climate change, restricted substances, energy efficiency, and material efficiency.

Service Industry in Focus

The service sector is the fastest growing segment of the U.S. economy. The Service Industry in Focus inserts help students understand how managerial accounting is applied to improve the competitiveness of service companies.

SERVICE AND MERCHANDISING

Environmental Business Consultants, LLC (EBC), worked on and completed two projects during June: a review of appropriate rates for solid waste and recycling collection within Klamath County, and a competitive procurement of landfill disposal services for the City of Redding. The following information relates to these two projects:

	Rate Review Project—Klamath	Procurement Project—Redding
WIP Inventory balance at June 1	$46,320	$85,318
Hours worked during June	100	74
Payroll cost per hour:		
Partner	$ 60	$ 60
Manager	$ 38	$ 38
Staff	$ 24	$ 24
Overhead rate per labor hour	$ 25	$ 25

During June, the partner charged 10 hours to the rate review project and 20 hours to the procurement project; the manager charged 30 hours to the rate review project and 24 hours to

Accounting in Practice

These boxed inserts help students bridge the gap between the classroom and what students encounter in the real world. Accounting in Practice illustrations document situations a student will likely encounter and present choices that companies face in making decisions.

ACCOUNTING IN PRACTICE	Factory Supplies versus Indirect Materials

Factory supplies are different from indirect materials. Factory supplies are used in the factory but are not part of the product itself. Lubricant used on the machine that stamps the sheet metal used in a laptop computer would be a factory supply. Indirect materials are part of the product but are difficult to trace to each individual product. Solder used to attach computer chips to a motherboard would be an indirect material. Both factory supplies and indirect materials can become part of manufacturing overhead.

CMA® Examination Questions

The Certified Management Accountant (CMA®) is a professional certification administered by the Institute of Management Accountants (IMA®). The purpose of the CMA certificate is to prepare accountants to be strategic thinkers and to analyze data in order to make better business decisions. We include past CMA questions at the end of each chapter. These questions will help students experience how concepts are applied in realistic business situations and give them an advantage if they choose to pursue a career in management accounting and become a CMA. CMA questions are **identified by a CMA icon in the margin**.

STUDENT SUCCESS

Managerial accounting is often challenging—especially for students lacking business experience or previous exposure to business courses. To help students succeed in the course and better prepare for a career in business management, we include many features that provide direction to students and require them to recall and apply the managerial accounting techniques and tools described in each chapter.

Putting Each Chapter in Context

Often, students lose sight of the big picture. The **Past/Present/Future** feature provides students with an overview of where the chapter fits within the whole course.

PAST

Chapter 1 introduced managerial accounting. It explored career opportunities in managerial accounting, its objectives, and professional certification for m...

PRESENT

Chapter 2 defines basic costing terminology and introduces different types of manufacturing inventories. It illustrates how costs flow

FUTURE

Chapter 3 introduces and explains job costing in more detail for both manufacturing and service industries. It also explains overhead allocation.

Mapping Each Chapter

Each chapter begins with a **Road Map** that outlines each chapter and provides a quick reference table that summarizes the print and digital resources for that chapter.

Road Map

LO	Learning Objective	Page	eLecture	Guided Example	Assignments
LO1	Describe management's use of accounting information in the decision-making process. Define relevant costs and describe the use of differential analysis.	8-3	E8-1	YT8.1	SS1, Q1, Q2, Q3, Q4, Q5, Q6, SE1, E1A, E2A, E3A, E1B, E2B, E3B, PA1, P1B
LO2	Demonstrate when to accept a special order.	8-9	E8-2	YT8.2	SS2, Q7, SE2, SE3, E4A, E5A, E6A, E4B, E5B, E6B, P2A, P2B
LO3	Demonstrate when to make or buy needed parts.	8-10	E8-3	YT8.3	SS3, Q7, SE4, SE5, SE6, E7A, E8A, E9A, E7B, E8B, E9B, P3A, P3B
LO4	Demonstrate when to drop an...	8-12	E8-4	YT8.4	SS4, Q7, SE7, E10A, E10B, P4A, P4B

Your Turn!

Each learning objective concludes with a **Your Turn!** box as a means of reinforcing the material just presented. Solutions are provided at the end of the chapter so students can check their work and a video demonstration of how to solve each **Your Turn!** is included within **myBusinessCourse**, the text's accompanying online learning system.

> **YOUR TURN! 2.3**
> The solution is on page 2-44.
>
> Shea Company reported raw material purchases of $1,400, paid $1,200 in factory labor, and incurred and applied $900 in factory overhead for March. The March 1 inventory balances were $200 for raw materials, $600 for work-in-process inventory, and $400 for finished goods inventory. On March 31, inventory balances were $300 for raw materials, $500 for work-in-process inventory, and $600 for finished goods inventory. What was Shea's cost of goods manufactured for March?

TECHNOLOGY THAT IMPROVES LEARNING AND COMPLEMENTS FACULTY INSTRUCTION

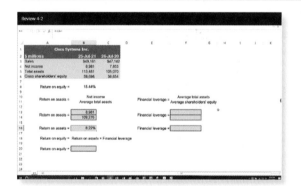

myBusinessCourse is an online learning and assessment program intended to complement your textbook and faculty instruction. Access to **myBusinessCourse** is FREE ONLY with the purchase of a new textbook, but can be purchased separately.

MBC is ideal for faculty seeking opportunities to augment their course with an online component. MBC is also a turnkey solution for online courses. The following are some of the features of MBC.

Increase Student Readiness

- **eLectures** cover each chapter's learning objectives and concepts. Consistent with the text and created by the authors, these videos are ideal for remediation and online instruction.
- **Guided Examples** are narrated video demonstrations created by the authors that show students how to solve select problems from the textbook.
- Immediate feedback with **auto-graded homework**.
- **Test Bank** questions that can be incorporated into your assignments.
- Instructor **gradebook** with immediate grade results.

*In two recent surveys of students who used MBC, 95% responded that MBC helped them learn accounting.**

---

* These statistics are based on the results of two surveys in which 2,330 students participated.

Make Instruction Needs-Based

■ Identify where your students are struggling and customize your instruction to address their needs.

■ Gauge how your entire class or individual students are performing by viewing the easy-to-use gradebook.

■ Ensure your students are getting the additional reinforcement and direction they need between class meetings.

Provide Instruction and Practice 24/7

■ Assign homework from your Cambridge Business Publishers' textbook and have MBC grade it for you automatically.

■ With our eLectures videos, your students can revisit accounting topics as often as they like.

■ Guided Examples videos show students how to solve select problems.

■ Make homework due before class to ensure students enter your classroom prepared.

■ For an additional fee, upgrade MBC to include the eBook and you have all the tools needed for an online course.

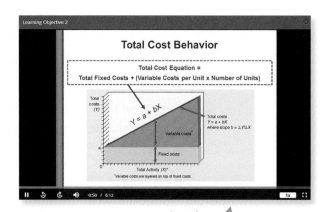

In the same two surveys, **86%** of the students who responded said they would encourage their professor to continue using MBC in future terms.*

Integrate with LMS

^{my}BusinessCourse **integrates** with many learning management systems, including **Canvas**, **Blackboard**, **Moodle**, **D2L**, **Schoology**, and **Sakai**. Your gradebooks sync automatically.

NEW TO THIS EDITION

■ **Expanded Data Analytics:** We have expanded Data Analytics coverage in this edition.

• New Data Analytics boxes have been incorporated to expose students to techniques that are used by businesses in areas related to the topic being discussed.

• Each chapter includes assignments that require students to use **Excel** or **Tableau** to hone data analysis and data visualization skills.

• This edition also includes a new **Appendix B** at the end of the book that provides an overview of data analytics, data visualization, and best practices for the effective display of data. Appendix B also includes additional assignments using **Tableau** and **Excel**.

Data Analytics

 +ableau

■ **Expanded myBusinessCourse Resources:** Additional assignments and Guided Example videos have been added to MBC, so nearly all the textbook assignments are available in the system. In addition, we have increased the overall number of algorithmic assignments and test questions.

■ **Assignable YourTurns!** New in the third edition, the quantitative, in-chapter YourTurns! have been programmed in MBC and can be assigned for a grade.

■ **Gleim CMA Review Questions:** Cambridge Business Publishers has partnered with Gleim to provide students with CMA prep materials within MBC that will give them a competitive advantage as they transition from the accounting classroom to taking the CMA Exam.

GLEIM
CPA REVIEW

---

* These statistics are based on the results of two surveys in which 2,330 students participated.

- **Expanded Excel Resources:** MBC now includes short videos that show students how to use various features and functions in **Excel**. The videos can be accessed within MBC as part of your MBC course.

- **Environmental, Social, and Governance (ESG):** We have incorporated ESG boxes to help students understand how ESG is being embraced by forward-thinking enterprises as part of their long-term business models.

- **New chapter sequencing:** In the third edition, we introduce flexible budgets (now Chapter 10) before the discussion of standard costs and variance analysis (now Chapter 11) to improve the pedagogy and students' learning.

- **Chapter 13:** The statement of cash flows chapter has been revised to be more intuitive for students.

- **Streamlining:** We edited many chapters and exhibits to reduce redundancy and increase clarity. We believe the flow of topics and their presentation have been meaningfully improved this edition.

SUPPLEMENT PACKAGE

For Instructors

BusinessCourse: A web-based learning and assessment program intended to complement your textbook and classroom instruction.

Solutions Manual: Created by the authors, the *Solutions Manual* contains complete solutions to all the assignment material in the text.

PowerPoint: The PowerPoint slides outline key elements of each chapter.

Test Bank: The Test Bank includes multiple-choice items, matching questions, short essay questions, and problems.

Excel Templates: We provide Excel spreadsheets for select assignments. These spreadsheets will save time in data entry and allow students to dedicate additional time to learning the material. The assignments accompanied by Excel spreadsheets are identified by the Excel icon.

Website: All instructor materials are accessible via the book's website (password protected) along with other useful links and marketing information: www.cambridgepub.com

For Students

BusinessCourse: A web-based learning and assessment program intended to complement your textbook and faculty instruction. This easy-to-use program grades homework automatically and provides you with additional help when your instructor is not available. Assignments with the MBC in the margin are available in myBusinessCourse. Access is free with new copies of this textbook (look for the page containing the access code towards the front of the book). If you buy a used copy of the book, you can purchase access at www.mybusinesscourse.com.

Excel Templates: We provide Excel spreadsheets for select assignments. These spreadsheets will save time in data entry and allow students to dedicate additional time to learning the material. The assignments accompanied by Excel spreadsheets are identified by the Excel icon.

Website: Updates and other useful links are available to students free of charge on the book's website.

ACKNOWLEDGMENTS

This text benefited greatly from the valuable feedback of focus group attendees, reviewers, students, and colleagues. We are extremely grateful to them for their help in making this project a success. We extend a special thanks to Colleen Zern at UC Davis for her detailed feedback.

We are particularly grateful for the help of Niels Bybee, our graduate assistant and friend, whose timely and accurate work was so crucial.

Thanks, too, to our families (Ted's wife, Donna, and children, Tyler and Hannah Christensen, Scott and Hannah Christensen, Dallin and Katelyn Christensen, Matthew and Shannon Christensen, Joshua, and Stephanie; Scott's wife, Kay Lani, and children, Ryan and Megan Hobson, Kellie and Callen Bagley, Todd and Chelsea Hobson, Jessica and Kyle Kubal, Morgan, and Kaitlyn; Jason's wife, Pam and children, Jordan, Joshua, Samuel, and Tucker; and Jim's wife, Debra Lester) for their love, encouragement, and support.

Wagdy Abdallah	John Coulter	Jane Jollineau
Ira Abdullah	James Crumbacher	Mark Judd
Nasrollah Ahadiat	Lois Darga	Kathy Kapka
Natalie Allen	Somnath Das	Suzanne Kiess
Michael Alles	Heidi K. Deden	Christine Kloezeman
Bridget Anakwe	Tom Determan	Mehmet Kocakulah
H. Kyle Anderson	Margaret Diaz-Fugetta	Phillip Korb
Dennis Applegate	Patricia Doherty	Anthony Kurek
Lisa Banks	Carleton Donchess	Donald Ladd
Sarah Bee	Amanda Dore	Marco Lam
Erick Bell	Beth Dunn	John Long
Vernon Bell	Raymond Elson	Wenxiang Lu
Jason Bergner	James Emig	Lisa Ludlum
Diane Biagioni	Lili Eng	Susan Lynn
Timothy Biggart	Connie Fajardo	Lois Mahoney
Robert Bowen	Kurt Fanning	Jeff Mankin
John Boyle	Charles Fazzi	Joseph Manzo
Rada Brooks	Kevin Feeney	Annie McGowan
Ann Brooks	Robert Felix	Gwen Meador
Robert Brown	Charlene Foley-Deno	Cathryn Meegan
Jeri Brysch	David Folsom	Michael Meyer
Eugene Bryson	Sheri Geddes	Sue Minke
Patricia Burnett	Dennis George	Anne-Mary Nash-Haruna
Marci Butterfield	Peter Gilbert	Bruce Neumann
Ching-Lih Jan	Brian Gilligan	Wayne Nix
James Cannon	David Golub	Hossein Noorian
Rodney Carmack	Amber Gray	Joe Oliveti
Jackie Casey	Glen Greencorn	Kari Olsen
David Centers	Tom Guarino	Pat Packard
Sandra Cereola	Steven Hansen	Angela Pannell
John Cergnul	Frederick Harmon	Pamela Parker
Julie Chenier	David Harr	Kris Parsons
Yu Chen	Judy Harris	Michael Paz
Gerald Childs	Patricia Hart-Timm	Cynthia Phipps
Dina Clark	Hassan Hefzi	Elizabeth Pierce
Thomas Clausen	Don Heim	Lincoln Pinto
Scott Collins	Cassy Henderson	Claudia Qi
Carolyn Conn	Maggie Houston	Kamala Raghavan
Sue Convery	Connie Hylton	Kathleen Rankin
David Cook	Ron Jastrzebski	Paul Recupero

Andrea Roerdink   Ken Sinclair   Jin Ulmer
Reed Roig   Bhaskar Singh   Jeff Varblow
Francisco Roman   James Smith   Fred Wallace
Pamela Rouse   Liang Song   Robert Walsh
Bernadette Ruf   George Starbuck   Randi Watts
Alison Sawyer   Randall Stone   Lucy Wenxiang Lu
Erica Scheidecker   Bob Strawser   Monica Widdig
Robert Schweikle   Jeff Strawser   Gayle Williams
Barbara Scofield   Kent Swift   Marvin Williams
Daniel Selby   Aida Sy   Valerie Williams
Randy Serrett   Kim Tan   Jim Williamson
Karen Shastri   Lloyd Tanlu   Paula Wilson
Dan Sevall   Jenny Teruya   Maef Woods
Mehdi Sheikholeslami   Kevin Trout   Jia Wu
Whitney Sienko   Eric Typpo   Colleen Zern

In addition, we are extremely grateful to George Werthman, Lorraine Gleeson, Debbie McQuade, Terry McQuade, and the entire team at Cambridge Business Publishers for their encouragement, enthusiasm, and guidance. Feedback is always welcome. Please feel free to contact us with your suggestions or questions.

Ted Christensen   Scott Hobson   Jim Wallace   Jason Matthews

October 2022

Brief Contents

Contents

CHAPTER **12**

Capital Budgeting   12-1

CHAPTER **13**

Statement of Cash Flows   13-1

CHAPTER 14

Analysis and Interpretation of Financial Statements 14-1

APPENDIX A

Accounting and the Time Value of Money A-1

APPENDIX B

Data Analytics B-1

Index I-1

Chapter 1
Overview of Managerial Accounting

Road Maps *summarize each chapter's resources and categorize them by learning objective.*

eLectures *are videos available in MBC that provide 3–5 minute reviews of each learning objective.*

Assignments *reinforce learning and can be completed by hand or within MBC.*

Road Map

LO	Learning Objective	Page	eLecture	Guided Example	Assignments
LO1	Define managerial accounting and describe its objectives.	1-3	E1-1	YT1.1	SS1, SE1, SE2, SE3
LO2	Describe the three types of business entities.	1-5	E1-2	YT1.2	SS2, SE4, SE5, SE6
LO3	Discuss major trends in business and managerial accounting.	1-6	E1-3	YT1.3	SS3, SE7, SE8, SE9
LO4	Describe important characteristics of two companies used throughout the book to illustrate key concepts and processes.	1-8	E1-4		SS4
LO5	Describe career options in managerial accounting.	1-10	E1-5	YT1.4	SS5, SE10, SE11, SE12
LO6	Understand differences between various professional certifications available to managerial accountants.	1-12	E1-6	YT1.5	SS6

Learning Objectives *identify the key learning goals of the chapter.*

YourTurns *follow each learning objective and require students to apply what they have just learned.* **Guided Example** *videos accompany most of the YourTurns and demonstrate how to solve various types of problems. YourTurns are also assignable in MBC.*

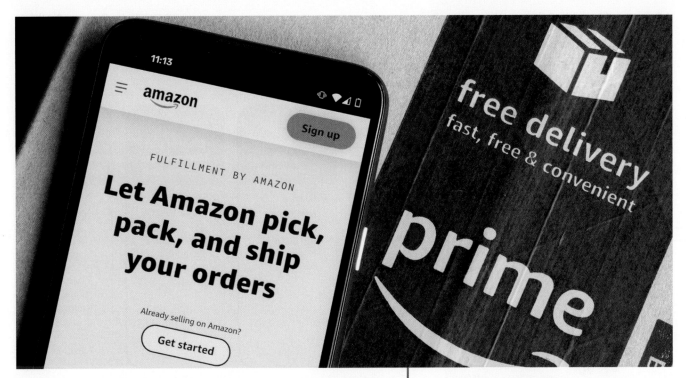

Amazon.com (Amazon) is the world's largest online merchandiser. Amazon seeks to be Earth's most customer-centric company, offering hundreds of millions of unique products through its website. With the acquisition of Whole Foods, these products now include groceries. If you have ever purchased something online, you have most likely visited Amazon's retail website.

What you may not know is that Amazon offers much more than retail consumer products. For example, it is a major provider of cloud computing services, known as "Amazon Web Services." In addition to being a merchandiser and a service provider, Amazon is also a manufacturer. It produces an e-book reader, the Amazon Kindle; a tablet computer, the Kindle Fire HD; and, a smart speaker, the Echo.

This chapter introduces managerial accounting and how management accounting information is used to help business managers in all types of businesses (merchandising, services, and manufacturing) make better decisions regarding future performance.

↑
*A **Focus Company** introduces each chapter and illustrates the relevance of accounting in everyday business.*

PAST

Most students will have taken an introductory financial accounting class. This book builds upon many of the concepts you have likely seen in prior accounting and management courses.

PRESENT

Chapter 1 introduces managerial accounting. Moreover, it presents an overview of two companies used throughout the book to illustrate various concepts and procedures common to managerial accounting and decision-making.

FUTURE

Chapter 2 defines basic costing terminology and introduces different types of manufacturing inventories. It illustrates how costs flow through the inventories and explains the schedule of cost of goods manufactured.

Past/Present/Future provides an overview of where the chapter fits within the context of the whole book.

1-2

Chapter Organization charts *visually depict the key topics and their sequence within the chapter.*

OVERVIEW OF MANAGERIAL ACCOUNTING

Introduction to Managerial Accounting	**Types of Business Entities**	**Major Trends in Business and Managerial Accounting**	**Introducing Two New Companies**	**Careers in Managerial Accounting**	**Professional Certifications**
• Managerial Accounting versus Financial Accounting • Objectives of Managerial Accounting	• Manufacturing Firms • Merchandising Firms • Service Firms	• Big Data and Predictive Analytics • Sustainability • Factory Automation • Customer Profitability	• Fezzari • Environmental Business Consultants	• Alternative Career Paths • Management Accountants' Compensation • Work/Life Balance	• Certified Public Accountant (CPA) • Certified Management Accountant (CMA) • Other Professional Certifications • Ethics in Accounting

Learning Objectives *are repeated at the start of the section covering that topic.*

INTRODUCTION TO MANAGERIAL ACCOUNTING

LO1 **Define** managerial accounting and **describe** its objectives.

eLecture

MBC

eLecture icons denote the availability of an instructional video in **myBusinessCourse** *(MBC). See the Preface for more information on MBC.*

Businesses make decisions every day that impact their competitiveness in the market. What is our target market? What products or services should we offer? How should we price our goods or services to compete effectively with our competitors? How much should we pay our employees to attract and retain great talent? Where should we locate our office or fulfillment center to minimize delivery time and cost? How do we build awareness of our firm and products or services within our target market? How do we achieve our objectives with limited resources? How many employees do we need to hire in the coming year to meet anticipated demand for our products or services? Which employees should we assign to work on this project?

These questions, and many others, require an understanding of broad business disciplines, including finance, marketing, organizational behavior, supply chain management, operations management, and strategy. However, a common element to all of these questions is the need to have a clear understanding of the financial implications of each alternative course of action. For example, in setting the price of a good or service, management needs to understand not only the customers' needs and expectations, competitors' positions in the marketplace, and the anticipated demand for the product or service, but also the business's costs of providing them.

Managerial Accounting versus Financial Accounting

Key Terms *are highlighted in bold, red font.*

This book focuses on **managerial accounting**, which plays a vital role in *internal* decision-making. Many students will have previously taken a **financial accounting** course, which focuses on reporting a company's financial performance to *external* parties. Financial accountants are typically engaged in measuring and reporting the financial results of a business's *past* actions and activities. They report the results of past transactions in accordance with a set of standards known as generally accepted accounting principles (GAAP). Financial accountants typically produce reports such as 10-Qs and 10-Ks (for regulators of publicly traded companies); Annual Reports (for investors and creditors); and, periodic income statements, balance sheets, and cash flow statements (for management).

	Financial Accounting	Management Accounting
Guiding standard	Generally accepted accounting principles (FASB Accounting Standards Codification)	None. Company management's prescribed format.
Purpose	Demonstrate compliance with reporting standards	Help management make informed business decisions
Users of the information	Regulators, investors, creditors, management	Internal management
Types of reports	Annual statements (10-Ks) and quarterly statements (10-Qs) for regulators, audited financial statements for investors and creditors, periodic financial reports for management	Financial and operating budgets, reports on variances from standards, capital budgeting/ resource investment
Reporting periods	Recently concluded quarter or year, often compared to previous quarters or years	Future periods (next year's budget, 10-year capital projection, etc.)
Focus	Financial results of past performance	Financial projections of future performance

Management accountants utilize data from many different sources, such as financial operations, sales, and human resources, to help top management make decisions regarding *future* performance. They provide information to management in a form that is timely, relevant, decision-useful, and in a format that is easily accessible to management but not determined by any external organization. Management accountants might use data gathered from production, marketing, and human resources to prepare a budget for the next operating period; calculate differences between expected and actual results of operations (aka variances) to evaluate production results and revise production standards; or, prepare a net present value or internal rate of return analysis to assist management in selecting from among competing proposed capital investments.

Objectives of Managerial Accounting

Management accountants are professionals who work in business, across all areas of an organization, in decision support, planning, and control functions. They partner with personnel from their firm's executive management to its line employees to make strategic business decisions. Management accountants must capture, analyze, and report critical data in a timely manner. To address important strategic questions like those mentioned previously, management accountants will identify data needed to answer those questions. Such data will usually include financial information but often include non-financial information from both inside and outside the company. If the necessary data aren't readily available, management accountants may help design systems to capture the data. Sometimes, the data are available but must be summarized in a form that is useful to management. Management accountants can use data visualization tools such as Alteryx and Tableau to develop reports that allow management to make sense of the data. They are also proactive in identifying relevant information to help recommend needed improvements in all aspects of their firm's business.

Hints *help explain difficult concepts.*

Hint: Because the information management accountants provide managers is so important, they must ensure that it is both accurate and relevant.

Your Turn! *boxes reinforce the material just presented with self-study questions. To aid learning, solutions are provided at the end of the chapter.*

YOUR TURN! 1.1

Would the following activities be associated with financial accounting or managerial accounting?

1. Issuing a quarterly earnings report to investors.
2. Determining the cost of producing a product.
3. Calculating how many units need to be sold to make a profit.
4. Preparing a report for the Securities and Exchange Commission (SEC).
5. Preparing a sales budget.
6. Preparing a Statement of Cash Flows in accordance with generally accepted accounting principles (GAAP).
7. Choosing among competing capital projects using net present value analysis.

MBC

The solution is on page 1-18.

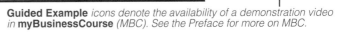

Guided Example *icons denote the availability of a demonstration video in* **myBusinessCourse** *(MBC). See the Preface for more on MBC.*

TYPES OF BUSINESS ENTITIES

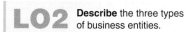

LO2 **Describe** the three types of business entities.

eLecture

MBC

Manufacturing firms are companies that convert materials such as sheets of steel and coils of wire and components such as electric motors and microprocessors into finished products. The manufacturer utilizes human labor; utilities such as electricity, natural gas, and water; and factory assets such as buildings, machinery, and computers to convert the materials and components into sellable products. Manufacturers will normally report three types of inventory on their balance sheets: raw materials inventory, work-in-process inventory, and finished goods inventory.

Merchandising firms are companies that purchase finished products from manufacturers for warehousing, display, and sale to consumers. Wholesalers typically buy finished products in large quantities and store them in large warehouses until they can be sold and shipped in smaller quantities to local retailers. The retailer utilizes human labor or electronic advertising to sell products from a "brick-and-mortar" store or through an online store available through a website. Because merchandising firms purchase finished products for sale, they typically report a single type of inventory on their balance sheets: finished goods or merchandise inventory.

Service firms are companies that provide services to customers. Examples include companies in health care, legal, and accounting services. The types of costs incurred by these firms are generally similar to those of other types of firms except they don't sell a product. Hence, they normally do not carry a raw materials and finished goods inventory. However, if the services provided take many months or years to complete, i.e., project-based services, a service firm could report work-in-process inventory on its balance sheet.

Accounting for manufacturing operations is usually more complex because more activities are involved in producing a product than in purchasing and selling merchandise or providing a service.

Each year, *Forbes* magazine reports the world's "most reputable" companies. The 2021 ranking[1] indicates that roughly 45% of the world's most reputable, and presumably best known, companies are manufacturing firms. You probably recognize most of them and are likely familiar with their products. For example, HP, Procter & Gamble, General Mills, Microsoft, Intel, Nestle, and Apple are among the most reputable manufacturing firms in the world. Interestingly, less than 10% of the most reputable firms are retailers. You are familiar with retailers like Amazon, Walmart, Target, and Best Buy. Notably missing from this list are some of the world's largest retailers, such as Costco and Lowe's. A higher percentage, about 25%, are service companies. This list contains well-known companies like Alphabet, Salesforce.com, FedEx, UPS, and Delta Airlines, whereas foreign airlines are all noticeably absent.

YOUR TURN! 1.2

GuidedExample

MBC

The solution is on page 1-19.

For each of the following companies, identify whether they are a manufacturing, merchandising, or service firm.

Exxon Mobil Co.	Walmart
Southwest Airlines	Hershey Co.
Costco	Boston Consulting Group

TAKEAWAY 1.1   **Concept** ➤ **Method** ➤ **Assessment**

Takeaways summarize the key concepts before proceeding to the next topic.

Concept	Method	Assessment
Can you determine a company's business entity type by looking at its financial statements?	Look at the company's balance sheet or financial statement footnotes for reported inventory accounts.	• If the company reports raw materials, work-in-process, and finished goods inventory, it is a manufacturer. • If the company reports only finished goods inventory, it is a merchandiser. • If the company reports only work-in-process inventory (or no inventory), it is a service firm.

---

[1] Steve Bertoni, "The Just 100: Companies Leading the New Era of Responsible Capitalism," *Forbes*, October 14, 2020.

ENVIRONMENTAL, SOCIAL, AND GOVERNANCE   Choosing a Cost Accounting System

Being a good corporate citizen means more than just providing large returns to a company's shareholders; it means considering all the company's stakeholders. In addition to shareholders, other stakeholders include employees, customers, suppliers, the environment, and the community—essentially, all of society. But does a company have to sacrifice shareholder returns in order to provide for these other stakeholders? Enlightened companies are learning that the answer is no. In fact, providing for all stakeholders can enhance shareholder returns.

Amazon.com, one of the top retailers on Forbes' list of the world's 100 most reputable companies, has learned that being a good corporate citizen is good for business. One example of this is Amazon's Frustration-Free Packaging program that eliminates hard plastic clamshell cases that prove so difficult to open and replaces the plastic cases with 100% recyclable packaging that is not only less frustrating but also better for the planet and less costly to the manufacturer.

As Amazon explains on its website:

At Amazon, if we do our job right, our greatest contribution to the good of society will come from our core business activities: lowering prices, expanding selection, driving convenience, driving frustration-free packaging, creating Kindle, innovating in web services, and other initiatives we'll work hard on in the future.

We also contribute to the communities where our employees and customers live. Our contributions can be seen in many ways—through our donations to dozens of nonprofits across the United States, through the disaster relief campaigns that we host on our homepage, through our employees' volunteer efforts, through the grants that we make to the writing community, and through the Amazon Web Services credits that we provide to educators.

Environmental, Social, and Governance *boxes showcase how forwardthinking companies are embracing ESG as part of their long-term business models.*

MAJOR TRENDS IN BUSINESS AND MANAGERIAL ACCOUNTING

Big Data and Predictive Analytics

Bernard Marr, CEO and Director of Research at Advanced Performance Institute, posted an article in the blog "The Big Data Guru"[2] on Amazon.com's use of customer data to predict who will order what and when. In the article, he notes that Amazon has obtained a patent for what it calls "Anticipatory Shipping." The concept is that Amazon believes that its customer data will allow it to predict what you want and ship it to your door even before you order it. Already, Amazon customizes your online shopping experience by remembering what you bought previously, what you have on your wish list, what you have previously rated and reviewed, and what other customers who searched for similar items bought.

LO3 **Discuss** major trends in business and managerial accounting.

MBC

Data Analytics

Data Analytics *discussions describe how data analytics tools and techniques are used in companies.*

Amazon is not the only company trying to read your mind. The development of new and faster ways of analyzing the data trail that you leave behind following every online search, purchase, and social media interaction is allowing companies of all sizes to anticipate your desires and customize their products and services to better meet those needs.

Data analytics (DA) can broadly be defined as the process of examining sets of data with the goal of discovering useful information from patterns found in the data. Accountants employing data analytics can glean important insights from a company's data and identify areas where opportunities for innovation exist.

Understanding what data analysis is and how it is used are the first steps toward developing marketable skills, so we have included examples at various points in the book and assignments in most chapters that require the use of data analytics tools, including **Excel** and **Tableau**. In addition, **Appendix B** at the end of this book provides a more detailed discussion of data analytics.

© Shutterstock.com

---
[2] http://smartdatacollective.com/bernardmarr/182796/amazon-using-big-data-analytics-read-your-mind.

Sustainability

Sustainability means meeting our needs without compromising the ability of future generations to meet theirs. Recently, companies have begun to pay more attention to the impact their businesses have on the broader economy (profit), society (people), and the environment (planet).

There are many examples of actions companies may take to decrease their impact on the economy, society, and the environment, including decreasing the amount of packaging required for products while increasing the recycled content of the packaging that is used; support of policies that improve access to affordable healthcare, education, housing, etc.; the use of clean, renewable energy (e.g., solar or wind), rotating of crops to prevent the depletion of key nutrients in the soil, or the use of sustainable design and construction principles in the construction of the businesses' facilities.

With an increased emphasis on sustainability, corporations are preparing corporate social responsibility reports, similar to an annual financial report, to disclose and communicate their sustainability goals and the progress they have made toward them. Accountants are often looked to for assistance in collecting accurate and reliable data for these reports.

Factory Automation

Factory automation is a widely recognized trend in modern manufacturing facilities. Factory automation exists in many forms. **Stand-alone automation** incorporates a robot or computer-controlled machine into an existing manufacturing process to perform a single function, such as welding. Stand-alone automation is usually undertaken to reduce both labor and material costs.

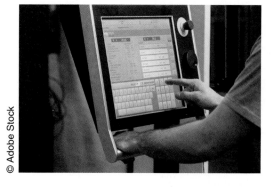

© Adobe Stock

Flexible-manufacturing-system automation involves multiple cells of two or more automated machines. All of the machines in each cell are controlled by a computer. The machines in each cell are interconnected to allow an automated flow of product through the **manufacturing cell**. This type of automated system produces the product from start to finish. The functions performed within the cell can be changed quickly by changing the program in the computer that controls the process.

When deciding whether to automate all or part of a manufacturing process, a manufacturer must compare the costs associated with the automation with the benefits to be derived from the automation. In general, automation should reduce overall costs if it is to be implemented.

Customer Profitability

In the past, companies focused their efforts on the development and standardization of products and services. As discussed previously, management attention was given to wringing all reasonable cost savings from the production process through the automation of manufacturing processes, the modification of product flow to improve efficiencies, the improvement of product quality, and the streamlining of production and delivery systems to minimize inventory on hand.

As markets have become more competitive and available products more homogeneous, companies have shifted to trying to differentiate themselves from their competitors through service. Customers have access to a tremendous amount of information about product features, prices, and quality via the Internet and have become more demanding of quality customer service.

Likewise, companies have a tremendous amount of information about their customers, including the frequency and volume of product purchases by type, their history of change orders, special handling and delivery requests, product returns, and customer service calls. Companies have begun to distinguish among their high-demand and low-demand customers relative to the cost of service to the customer and to focus on ways to increase customer profitability, not just product margin.

Match each term to the appropriate description:

1. Sustainability
2. Factory automation
3. Customer profitability
4. Predictive analytics

a. A large corporate farm rotates its crops among several large plots annually to minimize its impact on the health of the soil.
b. A business with a limited marketing budget uses customer data to forecast which customers have the highest probability of buying its products and sends a 10% discount coupon to only those customers.
c. A car manufacturer installs robots to perform welding and other dangerous tasks previously performed by humans.
d. A company uses a software package to perform algorithmic calculations to determine how to split customers into subcategories based on average order size, number of shipments per order, and number of customer returns for purposes of creating a customer income statement.

INTRODUCING TWO NEW COMPANIES

Throughout the textbook we will highlight two companies to explain key concepts and illustrate how real companies implement different managerial accounting practices. To provide a real-world view of manufacturing and retail sales, we frequently highlight Fezzari Performance Bicycles. Although it is important to understand the manufacture and sale of inventory, the U.S. economy has evolved into a much more service-oriented network of businesses. Hence, we will focus significant attention on how managerial accounting practices are used in the service sector and provide illustrations based on a consulting business, Environmental Business Consultants, LLC. Both of these companies will become very familiar to you throughout the various chapters of the book.

LO4 Describe important characteristics of two companies used throughout the book to illustrate key concepts and processes.

Fezzari—A U.S. Bicycle Manufacturer and Distributor

Fezzari is used throughout the text to provide a real-world view of managerial accounting and how it is applied to a manufacturing business.

Fezzari is a manufacturer and distributor located in Lindon, Utah, that designs, engineers, manufactures, and builds both mountain and road bikes. Fezzari's business model uses primarily a consumer-direct approach, with the vast majority of its sales completed through web-based, direct orders. This direct-order approach allows Fezzari to cut out the middleman (the local bike shop) and provide its customers with a higher-quality product at a lower cost than the brand-name bike manufacturers. Fezzari provides a 23-point custom setup with each bike sold, allowing the company to provide customers with a custom fit.

Fezzari's business model is not without risk. Most cyclists, particularly those who want to purchase a higher-end bike for several thousand dollars, want to be able to see, touch, and even ride the bike before purchase. Almost three-quarters of all bikes are sold in the United States through mass merchandisers (department, discount, and chain toy stores), and local bike shops account for an additional 15% of bike sales. However, according to the National Bicycle Dealers Association, the local bike shops' 13% unit sales is equivalent to 50% of the dollar value of bikes sold in 2015. Fezzari competes primarily with the local bike dealers for sales. By using a consumer-direct, web-based sales model, most Fezzari customers are unable to "kick the tires" before purchase like they can in a mass merchandiser or local bike shop.

Nevertheless, Fezzari's growth has been impressive. Fezzari sold its first bike in 2006 and now sells thousands of bikes each year. The company achieved a 20%

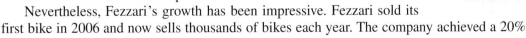

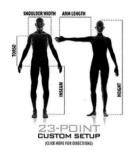

year-over-year annual growth rate and has expanded its initial facility to better service its growing customer base.

Although transactions are typically begun through the company's website, virtually all transactions involve one or more phone calls to gather information from the customer that is needed in the custom-build process. Not only does Fezzari gather body measurements (e.g., height, weight, inseam length, torso length, arm length, etc.), it also asks about the customer's age, the type of riding that the customer plans to do, and injuries that the customer may have experienced that might impact range of motion or flexibility.

Once the specific bike model and components are selected, Fezzari orders the required parts from its suppliers. A minimal quantity of parts is kept in inventory so that the bike assembly can be started without waiting for the parts to arrive. A technician assembles the bike to the customer's specifications, tunes it up, and then test rides it to ensure that it works properly. A second technician then checks the assembly, testing every screw and component, then checks the tune, and performs a second test ride. The bike is then sent to packing to be prepared for shipment by a packer. A second packer checks the pack for completeness. The bike is then sent to the shipping bay, where a final check is performed. The assembly and packaging process can take up to 8 to 12 hours for one of Fezzari's high-end bikes, depending on the degree of customization.

The bicycle manufacturing business is seasonal, with sales picking up in the early spring and not slowing down until the early fall. As a result, Fezzari's employee headcount varies from winter to summer, almost doubling from its low point to its high point.[3]

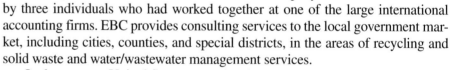

Environmental Business Consultants, LLC—A U.S. Service Firm

Environmental Business Consultants (EBC) is used throughout the text to provide a real-world view of managerial accounting and how it is applied to a service organization.

Environmental Business Consultants, LLC (EBC) is a fictitious management consulting firm headquartered in Los Angeles, California, based on an actual company. It was formed in 1984 by three individuals who had worked together at one of the large international accounting firms. EBC provides consulting services to the local government market, including cities, counties, and special districts, in the areas of recycling and solid waste and water/wastewater management services.

In the western United States, most local governments contract with private companies for garbage, recycling, and water services. Wastewater, or sewer, services are often provided by a regional sewer district created by the local governments utilizing the service. In many cases, the local governments do not have the necessary personnel resources or expertise to manage these services effectively. They frequently turn to outside consultants to assist them. These outside consultants include engineering firms, large international and regional accounting firms, and local consulting firms. Competition is fierce and success is largely based on relationships and reputation.

EBC has performed thousands of consulting projects for hundreds of municipal agencies, assisting them with the procurement, management, and delivery of solid waste, water, and wastewater services. With a focus on west coast agencies, EBC offers its clients a breadth of experience coupled with responsiveness, accountability, and personal commitment. EBC has an excellent reputation within its chosen market.

EBC has grown from the three founders and an administrative assistant in 1984 to six owners located in offices in both northern and southern California with a staff of over 30 accountants, economists, engineers, and management consultants.

---

[3] We are grateful to Fezzari Performance Bicycles for providing significant access to its business model and management philosophy. Moreover, the company has given us access to management and many company resources.

EBC obtains its client work primarily through requests from clients for whom the firm has worked for many years and also by responding to competitive requests for proposals issued by other municipal agencies. In most instances, EBC will meet with the client to discuss the project and gain an understanding of the client's needs. EBC will then prepare a written proposal outlining a scope of work to be performed for a specified fee. Competitive proposals typically require a presentation of the proposal to the client, where the client has the opportunity to ask questions and discuss the details of the proposed approach.

CAREERS IN MANAGERIAL ACCOUNTING

Alternative Career Paths

Some college students believe that graduating with a degree in accounting leads to one thing: a career in public accounting, often with one of the "Big 4" accounting firms. This may be particularly true at one of the top 5 or 10 college accounting programs in the United States, because the Big 4 spend considerable time and money recruiting students from these schools. A 2019 study published by the Association of International Certified Public Accountants reported that nearly 55,000 bachelor's and 22,000 master's students graduated from accounting degree programs in the United States. Approximately 31,000, or 40%, of these students began their careers in public accounting.[4] Regardless of where they begin their careers, it is clear that most accountants will eventually work as management accountants in industry. The U.S. Bureau of Labor Statistics reports that approximately 65% of all U.S. accountants and auditors work in management accounting and academic roles.[5]

LO5 Describe career options in managerial accounting.

eLecture
MBC

A start in public accounting can be advantageous for some students because of the ongoing training and experience that can be obtained as these graduates are exposed to different companies and business functions. Audit or tax attestation experience is often required to be licensed as a certified public accountant (CPA), as discussed further in the next section. Many students want to be certified as CPAs because they believe this professional designation can open doors for future job opportunities. However, upwards of 90% of those who begin their careers in public accounting will leave public accounting and join a company in business or industry within a few years of graduation. Thus, the study of managerial accounting is critical for the success of virtually all accountants.

One of the reasons for this migration from public accounting to private industry is the myriad of opportunities for accountants. Accounting careers may be forged in government, public accounting, private business, and academia. Every business, from the small "mom-and-pop" store to the multinational conglomerate, needs the skills and expertise of an accountant. Accountants fill many roles, with titles such as accounting manager, controller, chief financial officer, treasurer, budget analyst, finance director, internal auditor, forensic accountant, environmental accountant, trustee in bankruptcy, Internal Revenue Service (IRS) criminal investigation special agent, tax consultant, small business owner, and management accountant. A management accountant might:

- be involved in evaluating the relative costs and benefits of outsourcing certain elements of a business;

[4] Association of International Certified Public Accountants, "2019 Trends in the Supply of Accounting Graduates and the Demand for Public Accounting Recruits," 2019, https://www.aicpa.org/content/dam/aicpa/interestareas/accountingeducation/newsandpublications/downloadabledocuments/2019-trends-report.pdf.
[5] Bureau of Labor Statistics, U.S. Department of Labor, *Occupational Outlook Handbook*, Accountants and Auditors, at https://www.bls.gov/ooh/business-and-financial/accountants-and-auditors.htm (visited May 11, 2021).

- be involved in evaluating whether to "insource" services that have previously been outsourced;
- conduct an analysis and help management decide whether or not to automate a manufacturing process;
- be part of the team that determines the appropriate level of safety stock and seasonal inventory required to ensure that the company can meet customer demand;
- be part of the team that helps to implement lean manufacturing at the company;
- be charged with analyzing customer profitability by determining which customers should be offered special incentives to increase the size and reduce the frequency of their orders and which customers are unprofitable and should either be dropped or receive a reduced level of customer service, or
- help to develop a program that implements anticipatory shipping, similar to that which is under development by Amazon.

Management Accountants' Compensation

Management accountants are often integral parts of corporate management, participating in strategic planning, operations management, financial planning, and other key corporate functions. Their compensation reflects the critical contribution they make to their employers' success.

Each year, the Institute of Management Accountants (the IMA) conducts a survey of its members' salaries. The IMA 2021 U.S. Salary Survey reported the 2020 median salary for respondents was $105,000, an increase of about $10,000 since 2018.[6] This is particularly notable given the economic impact of the global pandemic in 2020. Another notable finding was that holding a professional certification had a positive impact on compensation. Certified Management Accountants (CMA) earned 30% higher median compensation ($122,000) than those without a professional certification ($93,900). Certified Public Accountants (CPAs) earned 45% higher median compensation ($136,000) than those without a professional certification. Those with both the CMA and the CPA earned a median compensation of $140,000.

Work/Life Balance

Beginning a career in accounting entails a commitment to client service—although the "clients" may be either internal management or external entities. Because accounting typically involves the reporting of results of operations, accountants are regularly working under a deadline—reports are due by a certain date or within a certain number of days of the end of a period. To make the deadline often requires accountants to work whatever hours are needed, resulting in periods of late nights and weekends from time to time. Certain positions or career choices tend to require more overtime than others, although all accountants should expect to work more than a 40-hour work week on a regular basis.

TAKEAWAY 1.2	Concept ──────▶	Method ──────▶	Assessment
↑ **Takeaways** *summarize the key concepts before proceeding to the next topic.*	What can I do with a degree in accounting?	• Talk to career counselors, professors, professionals, and recruiters about different career options. • Visit your college or university career center to identify firms seeking graduates with an accounting degree.	Consider your career goals in light of available employment opportunities. Evaluate which opportunity provides the best start for where you see yourself in 10 years, recognizing that you will likely change employers once or twice during that time.

---

[6] Shannon Charles and Kip Krumwiede, IMA's 2021 Global Salary Survey, Institute of Management Accountants, 2021

YOUR TURN! 1.4

According to the text, what percentage of accounting students begin their careers in public accounting and what percentage eventually leave for positions outside public accounting?

	Begin in Public Accounting	Leave Public Accounting
a.	75%	50%
b.	100%	90%
c.	40%	90%
d.	49%	65%

MBC

The solution is on page 1-19.

PROFESSIONAL CERTIFICATIONS

Certified Public Accountant (CPA)

The CPA is the most widely recognized and respected professional accounting certification in the United States. The CPA professional certification has been administered by the American Institute of Certified Public Accountants (AIC-PA) or its predecessors since 1887. The AICPA is the largest member association representing the accounting profession. It has more than 650,000 members worldwide. The AICPA administers the CPA exam, a four-part exam that covers Auditing and Attestation, Business Environment and Concepts, Financial Accounting and Reporting, and Regulation.

  Passing the CPA exam is only the first step to obtaining a CPA license. Licensure is handled by each of the 55 State/Territory Boards of Accountancy. Licensure requirements vary slightly from state to state; however, most states require 150 hours of college credit plus a year or more of real-world work experience. Once licensed, CPAs are required to follow a strict Professional Code of Conduct and to complete a certain number of hours of continuing professional education.

LO6 **Understand** differences between various professional certifications available to managerial accountants.

eLecture

MBC

Hint: To find out more about the AICPA's Professional Code of Conduct, see https: //www.aicpa.org /research/standards /codeofconduct.html

Certified Management Accountant (CMA)

The CMA is a professional certification administered by the Institute of Management Accountants (IMA) intended to indicate a level of knowledge and proficiency with accounting and financial management skills, including financial planning, analysis, control, decision support, and professional ethics. CMA candidates are required to hold a bachelor's degree from an accredited college or university, hold membership in the IMA, pass a two-part exam, and have at least two continuous years of professional experience in management accounting or financial management. The exam consists of two four-hour parts, with Part 1 covering Financial Reporting, Planning, Performance, and Control and Part 2 covering Financial Decision-Making. Members of the IMA are required to adhere to the IMA Statement of Ethical Professional Practice.

  The IMA reports that in 2021 more than 70,000 CMA certificates had been awarded to date.

Hint: To find out more about the CMA's Statement of Ethical Professional Practice, see https://www .imanet.org/insights -and-trends/business -leadership-and-ethics /ima-statement-of -ethical-professional -practice?ssopc=1

Other Professional Certifications

There are numerous other professional certifications that indicate specialized skill or experience. These include certified fraud examiner, certified financial planner, certified internal auditor, and enrolled agent.

  Exhibit 1-1 shows the URL where you can find additional information regarding each of these professional certifications.

EXHIBIT 1-1	**Information Regarding Professional Certifications**
Certified Public Accountant	www.aicpa.org
Certified Management Accountant	www.imanet.org
Certified Fraud Examiner	www.acfe.com
Certified Financial Planner	www.cfp.net
Certified Internal Auditor	https://na.theiia.org
Enrolled Agent	https://www.irs.gov/tax-professionals/enrolled-agents/become-an-enrolled-agent

Ethics in Accounting

World markets function on the expectation of the integrity of accounting professionals. Investors make choices among investment alternatives and invest precious capital in companies based on their trust in the accuracy of those companies' financial statements. Creditors provide loans to companies based on the expectation of repayment from resources reported in companies' financial statements. How can investors and creditors have confidence in the financial statements? Because they trust that the accountants who have prepared them have acted with integrity.

Integrity can be defined as "adherence to moral and ethical principles." Because of the fundamental importance of integrity and ethical behavior of accounting professionals to capital markets, professional accounting organizations including the AICPA and IMA have adopted professional codes of conduct. Licensure as a professional accountant typically requires applicants to complete an ethics exam.

For example, the IMA Statement of Ethical Professional Practice is based on four overarching ethical principles: Honesty, Fairness, Objectivity, and Responsibility. The Statement outlines four standards IMA members are expected to uphold: Competence, Confidentiality, Integrity, and Credibility. Visit the IMA website (www.imanet.org) or the AICPA website (www.aicpa.org) to learn more about their ethical standards and the importance of integrity and ethical behavior in the accounting profession.

YOUR TURN! 1.5

MBC

The solution is on page 1-19.

Visit the website of at least two organizations from Exhibit 1-1, or another organization that provides a professional certification, and learn the minimum education requirement to take the exam.

Summaries review key bullet points for each Learning Objective and summarize each section's Takeaway.

SUMMARY OF LEARNING OBJECTIVES

LO1   **Define managerial accounting and describe its objectives. (p. 1-3)**
- Managerial accounting focuses on internal decision-making.
- Managerial accounting utilizes both financial and operational information.
- Managerial accounting provides information that is timely, relevant, decision-useful, and in a format that is easily accessible to management.
- Management accountants partner with personnel to plan, manage, and make strategic business decisions.

LO2   **Describe the three types of business entities. (p. 1-5)**
- Manufacturing firms convert materials into finished products.
- Merchandising firms purchase finished products from manufacturers for warehousing, display, and sale to consumers.
- Service firms are companies that perform services for customers.

Discuss major trends in business and managerial accounting. (p. 1-6)   **LO3**

■ With an increased emphasis on sustainability, corporations are preparing corporate social responsibility reports, similar to an annual financial report, to disclose and communicate their sustainability goals and the progress they have made toward them.

■ Stand-alone automation of a factory incorporates a robot or computer-controlled machine into an existing manufacturing process. Flexible-manufacturing-system automation of a factory operation involves the use of multiple cells of two or more automated machines. Each cell produces a product from start to finish.

■ Traditional manufacturing inventories are used as buffers against unforeseen delays.

■ Just-in-time inventory systems (rather than just-in-case inventory systems) minimize the amount of inventory that is on hand.

■ Lean manufacturing focuses on the flow of the entire production process and uses customer demand to "pull" the product through production, thereby reducing setup times and inventory costs.

■ Managerial accounting can help companies distinguish between high-demand and low-demand customers relative to their cost of service. This allows them to focus on ways to increase customer profitability.

■ The development of new and faster ways of analyzing the data trail that customers leave behind following every online search, purchase, and social media interaction is allowing companies of all sizes to anticipate customers' desires and customize company products and services to better meet those needs.

Describe important characteristics of two companies used throughout the book to illustrate key concepts and processes. (p. 1-8)   **LO4**

■ Fezzari is a manufacturer and distributor of bikes.

■ Fezzari primarily sells direct to the customer through web-based transactions.

■ Environmental Business Consultants (EBC) is a fictitious management consulting firm.

■ EBC provides services to local government clients in California.

Describe career options in managerial accounting. (p. 1-10)   **LO5**

■ Careers in managerial accounting might lead to or include titles such as management accountant, accounting manager, controller, chief financial officer, treasurer, budget analyst, finance director, internal auditor, forensic accountant, environmental accountant, trustee in bankruptcy, IRS criminal investigation special agent, tax consultant, and small business owner.

■ Almost 90% of those accountants who begin their careers in public accounting will leave for a position in business or industry.

Understand differences between various professional certifications available to managerial accountants. (p. 1-12)   **LO6**

■ The CPA is the most widely recognized and respected professional accounting certification in the United States.

■ The CPA is administered by the American Institute of Certified Public Accountants (AICPA).

■ The CMA is a professional certification intended to indicate a level of knowledge and proficiency with accounting and financial management skills, including financial planning, analysis, control, decision support, and professional ethics.

■ The CMA is administered by the Institute of Management Accountants (IMA).

■ There are numerous other professional certifications that indicate specialized skill or experience.

Concept ➡	Method ➡	Assessment	**SUMMARY**
Can you determine a company's business entity type by looking at its financial statements?	Look at the company's balance sheet or financial statement footnotes for reported inventory accounts.	• If the company reports raw materials, work-in-process, and finished goods inventory, it is a manufacturer. • If the company reports only finished goods inventory, it is a merchandiser. • If the company reports only work-in-process inventory (or no inventory), it is a service firm.	**TAKEAWAY 1.1**

continued

continued

SUMMARY	Concept ➤	Method ➤	Assessment
TAKEAWAY 1.2	What can I do with a degree in accounting?	• Talk to career counselors, professors, professionals, and recruiters about different career options. • Visit your college or university career center to identify firms seeking graduates with an accounting degree.	Consider your career goals in light of available employment opportunities. Evaluate which opportunity provides the best start for where you see yourself in 10 years, recognizing that you will likely change employers once or twice during that time.

Key Terms *are listed for each chapter with references to page numbers within the chapter.*

KEY TERMS

Data analytics (DA) (p. 1-6)

Financial accounting (p. 1-3)

Flexible-manufacturing-system automation (p. 1-7)

Integrity (p. 1-13)

Managerial accounting (p. 1-3)

Manufacturing cell (p. 1-7)

Manufacturing firms (p. 1-5)

Merchandising firms (p. 1-5)

Service firms (p. 1-5)

Stand-alone automation (p. 1-7)

Sustainability (p. 1-7)

Self-Study Questions *in multiple-choice format with answers provided at the end of each chapter.*

Assignments with the (MBC) logo in the margin are available in BusinessCourse.
See the Preface of the book for details.

LOs link assignments to the Learning Objectives of each chapter.

SELF-STUDY QUESTIONS

(Answers to Self-Study Questions are at the end of this chapter.)

LO1 1. **Which of the following group of terms best describes the role of managerial accounting?**
  a. Internal decision-making, future-focused
  b. Internal decision-making, past-focused
  c. External reporting, future-focused
  d. External reporting, past-focused

LO2 2. **A company that sells finished products that it has acquired from a manufacturer to consumers is a**
  a. Manufacturer
  b. Merchandiser
  c. Service firm

LO3 3. **Using estimates of miles driven based on past customer service records, an auto repair shop sends customers reminders of services due to be performed. This is an example of**
  a. customer profitablilty analysis
  b. factory automation
  c. predictive analytics
  d. corporate sustainability

LO4 4. **What business model does Fezzari follow to sell its products to its customers?**
  a. Sales through local bike shops.
  b. Sales through large mass merchandisers.
  c. Sales direct to customers through web-based orders.
  d. Sales of bike components to other bike manufacturers.

LO5 5. **Approximately what percentage of accountants who begin their careers in public accounting will leave for positions in businesses and corporations?**
  a. 50%
  b. 75%
  c. 90%
  d. 95%

LO6 6. **Which of the following is the professional certification intended to indicate a level of knowledge and proficiency with accounting and financial management skills, including financial planning, analysis, control, decision support, and professional ethics?**
  a. CPA
  b. CMA
  c. CFE
  d. CIA

Homework *icons indicate which assignments are available in* **myBusinessCourse** *(MBC). This feature is only available when the instructor incorporates MBC in the course.*

QUESTIONS

LO1 1. How does managerial accounting differ from financial accounting?

LO1 2. Which type of accounting would produce reports relevant to stockholders?

3. A business owner plans to introduce a new product in the next year and needs to prepare a budget that reflects the increased sales, production costs, equipment, and personnel that will be required. Which of her two accountants, the financial accountant or the management accountant, would she most likely ask to help with the budget and why?   **LO1**

4. Name the three types of business entities and briefly describe the nature of each.   **LO2**

5. In what way do manufacturing firms and merchandising firms work together to provide end consumers with products?   **LO2**

6. Pick any large company and identify which type of business entity it is.   **LO2**

7. What are three main areas of concern in sustainability reporting?   **LO3**

8. Describe a manufacturing cell and contrast a cell to the equipment arrangement in a traditional manufacturing operation.   **LO3**

9. Describe and contrast stand-alone automation and flexible-manufacturing-system automation.   **LO3**

10. Explain the relationship between safety stock and just-in-time inventory systems.   **LO3**

11. What is lean manufacturing?   **LO3**

12. Which type of business model does Fezzari use?   **LO4**

13. What are the advantages of Fezzari's business model?   **LO4**

14. From where does Environmental Business Consultants, LLC, primarily obtain its client work?   **LO4**

15. List five job titles that an individual with an accounting degree may have during a career.   **LO5**

16. Why is managerial accounting relevant to accounting majors and their future careers?   **LO5**

17. Do most accountants work in public accounting or in industry, and why?   **LO5**

18. Describe the process an accounting graduate takes to obtain the CPA certification.   **LO6**

19. Can an individual with an accounting degree obtain only one professional certification?   **LO6**

20. Use the Internet to explore different career paths that an individual with the CMA certification can take.   **LO6**

SHORT EXERCISE

SE1-1.   Managerial accounting   **LO1**
   a.   reports financial results of past performance.
   b.   reports results in accordance with generally accepted accounting principles.
   c.   helps management make decisions regarding future performance.
   d.   focuses on external users.

SE1-2.   Managerial accounting activities include all the following except   **LO1**
   a.   issuing a quarterly earnings report to investors.
   b.   preparing a budget.
   c.   choosing among competing capital projects.
   d.   performing a variance analysis of budgeted versus actual results of operations.

SE1-3.   Which of the following are the principal users of managerial accounting information?   **LO1**
   a.   Regulators   *c.*   Internal management
   b.   Investors   *d.*   Creditors

SE1-4.   Amazon is a   **LO2**
   a.   merchandiser.   *c.*   manufacturer.
   b.   service provider.   *d.*   all of the above.

SE1-5.   A _____ would typically report three inventories: raw materials, work-in-process, and finished goods.   **LO2**
   a.   manufacturer   *c.*   merchandiser
   b.   wholesaler   *d.*   service provider

SE1-6.   Which type of inventory might a service provider report?   **LO2**
   a.   raw materials   *d.*   two or more of *a*, *b*, and *c*.
   b.   work-in-process   *e.*   a service provider never reports inventory
   c.   finished goods

LO3   **SE1-7.** An on-line merchandiser analyzes demographic data to identify the states with the highest birth rates to determine which regional fulfillment centers should store the most diapers and baby formula. This is an example of

    a. customer profitability analysis.   *c.* factory automation.
    b. sustainability.   *d.* predictive analytics.

LO3   **SE1-8.** A manufacturer decided to reduce the amount of packaging required for its products by investing in a machine that makes custom cardboard shipping boxes based on a scan of the finished products dimensions. This is an example of

    a. customer profitability analysis.   *c.* factory automation.
    b. sustainability.   *d.* more than one of the above.

LO3   **SE1-9.** A management accountant is asked to determine each customer's annual number of orders, average order size, annual number of returns, and number of contacts with the customer service department. The accountant is most likely assisting the company with

    a. customer profitability analysis.   *c.* a factory automation study.
    b. a sustainability analysis.   *d.* a report to the SEC.

LO5   **SE1-10.** A management accountant might be involved in which of the following activities?

    a. a cost-benefit analysis   *c.* a corporate sustainability study
    b. a customer profitability analysis   *d.* all the above

LO5   **SE1-11.** Which of the following professional certifications require licensure by individual states?

    a. CPA   *c.* Both the CPA and CMA
    b. CMA   *d.* Neither the CPA nor CMA

LO5   **SE1-12.** Professional certifications available to individuals with a background in accounting include

    a. IRS Enrolled Agent   *c.* Certified Management Accountant
    b. Certified Fraud Examiner   *d.* All of the above

DATA ANALYTICS, DATA VISUALIZATION, AND EXCEL ACTIVITIES

Data Analytics, Data Visualization, and Excel Activities are available in myBusinessCourse. These assignments develop Excel, Tableau, and Data Analytics skills, which will enhance students' career readiness. These exercises are assignable and auto graded by MBC. For an overview of data analytics, see the appendix at the end of this book.

Extending Your Knowledge *assignments require use of the real-world financial information and critical thinking skills.*

EXTENDING YOUR KNOWLEDGE

EYK1-1. **Model Manufacturing** is a company that specializes in producing model cars, trains, and airplanes for customers of all ages. Model has been in business for over 50 years and has provided generations of detailed models that can be customized by color, type of metal, size, and numerous other features. The company sells its completed models to merchandising companies, which then advertise and sell the products to the end consumer. Because Model produces mass quantities of models, it requires efficient operations to ensure timely delivery of quality products to merchandisers.

    a. Model can obtain varying qualities of metal and other materials that it uses to produce models. Why would the company choose to spend more for materials of higher quality when it can produce cheaper, similar models with lower-quality materials?

    b. Model's customers are mainly merchandising companies. Is Model more or less likely to enter into long-term contracts with these companies than Model would with an end consumer? Why?

EYK1-2. **Masterful Merchandising** is a company that specializes in obtaining large quantities of products from multiple manufacturing companies and sells these products to end consumers. Its products include clothing, athletic equipment, electronics, home and kitchen products, groceries, and many other products. It prides itself in being a one-stop-shop where consumers can fill all their shopping needs without having to travel to multiple stores.

a. Masterful receives daily shipments of goods from manufacturers to stock its shelves. From a cost perspective, is it cheaper to buy manufactured goods in small or large quantities? What incentives would a manufacturer provide in order to facilitate ordering large quantities?

b. Why would a merchandiser choose to operate online instead of through a brick-and-mortar store? Do you think an online presence eliminates the need to have a physical store for consumer shopping?

> **Service and Merchandising** *icons denote assignments related to the service and merchandising industry.*
>
>

EYK1-3. Superior Services is a firm that provides audit, tax, and advisory services to over 100 companies in the western United States. It employs thousands of professionals who have obtained accounting, finance, economics, and business degrees and who focus on providing value and enhancing the operations of their clients. The firm has been in existence for nearly 70 years, and many of its clients are loyal to Superior and look nowhere else for services.

a. Superior does not sell physical products, but it does need to consider how to price its services in order to make a profit. What costs will the company consider when deciding how much to charge clients for its services?

b. How is accounting for Superior's operations different from accounting for Model's (see EYK1-1) and Masterful's (see EYK1-2) operations? Are there costs that Superior will incur that the other two will not?

EYK1-4. Peach Inc. is a manufacturer of consumer electronic devices, including computers, tablets, and phones. Peach has earned a reputation of providing reliable high-quality products at affordable prices. The company has also earned a reputation of being a good corporate citizen with many environmental and social initiatives. For example, the company uses far more recycled materials in its products than any of its competitors. The company is also known for its charity work with educational institutions.

In an effort to control costs, Peach outsources manufacturing of its hardware to many overseas factories; however, it closely monitors each facility to make sure quality is maintained. Tom Peach, the company CEO, was recently approached by Young, Inc., a company that asserts it can significantly reduce Peach's manufacturing costs by overseeing Peach's manufacturing. Young will find factories that it claims can maintain the same level of quality at lower costs. In addition, Young will do all the monitoring so that Peach can save the costs of monitoring and auditing the manufacturing facilities.

Jorge Workman, Peach's director of accounting, became quite concerned when he learned of the potential deal with Young. Jorge immediately went to Tom with his concerns. In particular, Jorge did not want to turn over the responsibility of monitoring the facilities to another company. Tom, however, feels that the quality control testing done locally is enough to ensure that quality can be maintained, and the cost savings are very important to the company's efforts to keep its prices affordable. In addition, Tom felt that under this arrangement, anything that might go wrong at one of the facilities would be Young's responsibility and not the responsibility of Peach.

Jorge was still not convinced. He knew how labor problems in the supply chain of Nike in the 1990s had caused significant reputational and financial damage to Nike, and he did not want to risk the same thing happening to Peach.

What do you think Peach should do?

ANSWERS TO SELF-STUDY QUESTIONS:

1. a   2. b   3. c   4. c   5. c   6. b

YOUR TURN! SOLUTIONS

Solution 1.1

1. Financial
2. Managerial
3. Managerial
4. Financial
5. Managerial
6. Financial
7. Managerial

Solution 1.2

Exxon Mobil Co.	Manufacturing
Walmart	Merchandising
Southwest Airlines	Service
Hershey Co.	Manufacturing
Costco	Merchandising
Boston Consulting Group	Service

Solution 1.3

1. *a.*   2. *c.*   3. *d.*   4. *b.*

Solution 1.4

c.

Solution 1.5

CPA: Bachelor's degree (equivalent of 120 credit hours) plus 30 additional credit hours

CMA: Bachelor's degree or professional accounting certification

CFE: Bachelor's degree or two years of fraud-related professional experience for each year of academic study

CFP: College-level program of study in personal financial planning

CIA: Associate's degree or seven years of verified experience in internal audit

EA: None

Chapter 2
Managerial Accounting Concepts and Cost Flows

Road Map

LO	Learning Objective	Page	eLecture	Guided Example	Assignments
LO1	Identify the key objectives of a managerial accounting system and define product costs and period costs; variable, fixed, and mixed costs; direct and indirect costs; and cost control.	2-3	E2-1	YT2.1	SS1, SS2, Q1, Q2, Q3, SE1, SE2, SE3, SE4, E1A, E2A, E1B, E2B
LO2	Describe the three manufacturing inventories—materials, work-in-process, and finished goods—and discuss the categories of manufacturing costs and how these costs flow among the inventories and cost of goods sold.	2-8	E2-2	YT2.2	SS2, Q4, Q5, Q6, Q7, SE5, SE6, E3A, E4A, E5A, E3B, E4B, E5B
LO3	Define total manufacturing costs, cost of goods manufactured, and cost of goods sold, and illustrate the schedule of cost of goods manufactured and sold and the income statement.	2-14	E2-3	YT2.3	SS3, SS4, Q8, Q9, Q10, Q11, SE7, SE8, SE9, E3A, E5A, E6A, E7A, E8A, E9A, E10A, E3B, E5B, E6B, E7B, E8B, E9B, E10B, P1A, P2A, P3A, P1B, P2B, P3B
LO4	Illustrate the journal entries to record product cost flows using a perpetual inventory system.	2-18	E2-4	YT2.4	SS5, Q12, Q13, Q14, Q15, SE10, E11A, E12A, E11B, E12B, P4A, P5A, P4B, P5B

At 46 years old, **Apple Inc.** is the world's largest information technology company by sales revenue ($275 billion in 2020)[1] and the largest publicly traded corporation by market capitalization ($2,256 billion in 2021).[2] Although it started as a seller of personal computers (PCs), it has expanded its products to include consumer electronics, consumer software, and commercial servers.

How did Apple grow from a garage-based start-up to overtake companies like Commodore, Tandy, IBM, Microsoft, Sun Microsystems, and Xerox? Perhaps as important as talented employees, innovative products, and strategic alliances, one key was the development of managerial accounting systems to capture, summarize, and report critical data to be used in making strategic business decisions.

This chapter discusses the types of cost data used in management accounting and how these costs flow through the accounting records.

PAST

Chapter 1 introduced managerial accounting. It explored career opportunities in managerial accounting, its objectives, and professional certifications for managerial accountants.

PRESENT

Chapter 2 defines basic costing terminology and introduces different types of manufacturing inventories. It illustrates how costs flow through the inventories and explains the schedule of cost of goods manufactured.

FUTURE

Chapter 3 introduces and explains job costing in more detail for both manufacturing and service industries. It also explains overhead allocation.

---

[1] 2020 Apple Form 10-K.
[2] https://companiesmarketcap.com/

MANAGERIAL ACCOUNTING CONCEPTS AND COST FLOWS

Key Objectives of a Managerial Accounting System	Inventories and Cost Categories	Product Cost Flows	Illustration of Product Cost Accumulation	Illustration of Product Cost Journal Entries
• Product Costing in a Manufacturing Environment • Product Costing in a Service and Merchandising Environment	• Inventories • Manufacturing Product Cost Categories	• Raw Materials • Labor • Manufacturing Overhead • Cost of Goods Manufactured • Cost of Goods Sold	• Introduction of T-Accounts • Real-World Manufacturing Example • Schedule of Cost of Goods Manufactured • Calculating Cost of Goods Sold • Income Statement for a Manufacturing Firm	• Cost Flows • Financial Statements

KEY OBJECTIVES OF A MANAGERIAL ACCOUNTING SYSTEM

LO1 **Identify** the key objectives of a managerial accounting system and **define** product costs and period costs; variable, fixed, and mixed costs; direct and indirect costs; and cost control.

eLecture

MBC

Hint: A cost object is anything to which costs may be traced. Examples for Apple include everything from an mp3 file to a tablet PC to a service department.

Business operations vary widely in complexity. However, all managerial accounting systems have the objective of providing management with financial and other business information that is useful in analyzing and making business decisions.

Product Costing in a Manufacturing Environment

Business managers need information about the cost of their products and services in order to control costs and set prices that will result in a profit to the owners and provide the ability to grow the business. For example, Apple is clearly interested in knowing its costs and market share for its manufactured products (e.g., the iPhone and the iPad) for determining merchandise prices.

Product costing involves gathering and assigning the costs of all inputs in the manufacturing or acquisition process to individual products. The individual products represent a type of **cost object**, which may be anything for which business managers must determine a cost. The manufacturer must know its product costs in order to measure inventory values and calculate the profitability of its products for reporting on its financial statements. Using product costing information, management can also determine which products to continue producing and which products to drop. This chapter introduces product costing.

Product versus Period Costs

Exhibit 2-1 indicates that costs can be classified into two broad categories for companies that sell products. **Product costs** include all costs necessary to bring a product to completion. For a manufacturer, product costs include materials and components, human labor, utilities, and the use of factory assets. These costs are all recorded initially in inventory accounts.

Period costs are recognized as an expense on the income statement in the period incurred and not assigned to products. The benefits associated with these costs are assumed to expire in the period incurred rather than in the period in which the product is sold. For manufacturers, selling expenses and non-factory administrative

EXHIBIT 2-1   **Cost Classifications**

Costs

Product
- Sheet metal in an automobile
- Lumber for a furniture manufacturer
- Factory worker hourly wages
- Factory equipment depreciation
- Factory utilities

Period
- Sales force salaries
- General liability insurance premiums
- Advertising expenses
- Legal expenses
- CEO's salary and benefits

expenses are considered period costs. In summary, product costs are matched with the asso-ciated sales revenue in the period of the sale and period costs are matched with the period in which the cost is incurred.

Exhibit 2-2 presents Apple's partial income statement for its 2020 fiscal year, illustrating its product and period costs:

Hint: Some departments in a manufacturing firm, such as personnel, may benefit both factory and non-factory activities. The costs of these departments are therefore partly product cost and partly period cost.

EXHIBIT 2-2	Apple's Partial Income Statement

APPLE INC.
Income Statement
For the Year Ended September 26, 2020
(in $millions)

This is a product cost.

Net sales.		$274,515
Less cost of goods sold		169,559
Gross profit on sales.		104,956
Operating expenses		
Research and development	$18,752	
Selling, general, and administrative	19,916	38,668
Operating income.		66,288

These are period costs.

A.K.A. Cost of sales is another term for cost of goods sold.

A.K.A. Gross margin is also referred to as gross profit.

Concept ➡	Method ➡	Assessment	TAKEAWAY 2.1
A founder of a new consulting firm is trying to determine the firm's cost of service.	• Identify the cost object. • Classify the firm's expenses as product costs vs. period costs relative to that cost object. • Sum the product costs.	• Costs associated with completion of specific consulting projects, such as consultant labor and project supplies, would be considered product costs. • Costs not directly related to projects but related to operating the business, such as general liability insurance premiums, office rent, and marketing costs, would be considered period costs.	

Variable, Fixed, and Mixed Costs

Another way to classify costs that can be helpful to decision-makers is to classify them based on their behavior (see **Exhibit 2-3**). A **variable cost** is a cost that *varies in total but is fixed per unit* for a certain period of time and range of activity. In total, variable costs change proportionately with changes in the volume of activity. The cost of a microprocessor chip used in an iPad and the hourly wage paid to the iPad assembly employees are variable costs. To illustrate, assume the cost of the microprocessor chip used in producing one Apple iPad is approximately $30. If Apple produces 100,000 iPads during a period, the total cost of the chips used would be $3,000,000. Alternatively, if Apple produces 1,000,000 iPads, the total cost of the chips would be $30,000,000, still $30 per iPad. In **Exhibit 2-4**, total variable costs increase by $30 for each additional iPad produced. Yet, the cost per iPad is a constant $30 per unit.

A **fixed cost** is *fixed in total but variable on a per-unit basis* for a particular period of

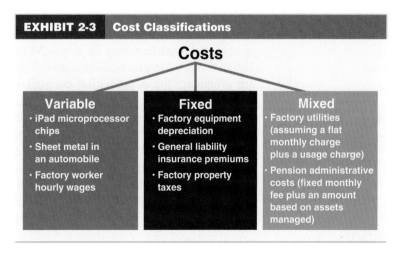

EXHIBIT 2-3	Cost Classifications

Costs

Variable	Fixed	Mixed
• iPad microprocessor chips • Sheet metal in an automobile • Factory worker hourly wages	• Factory equipment depreciation • General liability insurance premiums • Factory property taxes	• Factory utilities (assuming a flat monthly charge plus a usage charge) • Pension administrative costs (fixed monthly fee plus an amount based on assets managed)

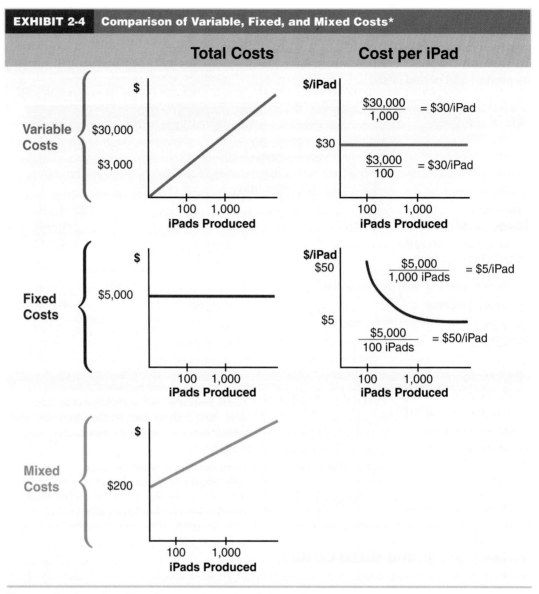

EXHIBIT 2-4   Comparison of Variable, Fixed, and Mixed Costs*

*Assumes all costs are linear; All numbers, except per-unit, are in thousands.

time and range of activity. Fixed costs do not change when the volume of activity changes. Examples are depreciation on buildings and property taxes. Assume that the depreciation on the iPad manufacturing facility is $5 million per month, as shown in **Exhibit 2-4**. If only 100,000 iPads are produced in a month, the depreciation per unit is $50. If 1,000,000 iPads are produced, the depreciation per unit is $5. As we will discuss later, making decisions based on fixed costs per unit can be problematic.

Mixed costs—sometimes called **semi-variable costs**—have both fixed and variable components. A mixed cost changes linearly with changes in activity, but there is still a positive cost when the activity level is zero, as shown in **Exhibit 2-4**. As an example of a mixed cost, consider Apple's utility expense at the factory that produces the iPad. Assume that even if Apple shuts down production for one month, it still incurs a minimum amount for utilities, say $200,000. When production resumes, the costs of heating, air conditioning, lighting, and water increase with usage as production increases. We discuss how to determine the variable and fixed portions of a mixed cost in Chapter 6. **Exhibit 2-4** presents a graphic illustration of these three different types of costs.

Concept ➜	Method ➜	Assessment	TAKEAWAY 2.2
How can one determine whether a cost is variable, fixed, or mixed?	• Observe cost behavior as production levels change. • Use the high-low method or least squares regression analysis (see Chapter 6).	• If costs increase proportionately with production, the cost is variable. • If costs remain unchanged as production changes, the cost is fixed. • If costs change, but not proportionately, as production changes, the cost is mixed.	

Direct and Indirect Costs

Finally, costs can also be classified as *direct* or *indirect* (see **Exhibit 2-5**). A **direct cost** is a cost that can be easily and cost-effectively traced to a specific cost object, such as a unit of product. In a manufacturing company, two obvious direct costs are the main materials and the labor used to produce a unit of product. However, other costs may be directly traced as well. For example, in determining the cost of an iPad, Apple would attempt to trace as many costs as possible directly to each iPad unit. Clearly, the main materials, such as the liquid crystal display (LCD) screen and the microprocessor, and the labor involved in assembly would be traced directly to each iPad. However, in a highly automated process, it is possible that Apple could also trace some robotic assembly costs directly to each iPad.

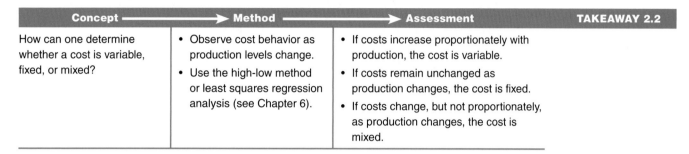

EXHIBIT 2-5 Cost Classifications

Classification is dependent on the definition of the cost object.

Costs

Direct
• iPad microprocessor chips
• Factory worker hourly wages
• Shipping costs

Indirect
• Factory equipment depreciation
• Factory property taxes
• Raw materials warehouse supervisor salary

An **indirect cost**, therefore, is a cost that cannot be easily and cost-effectively traced to a specific cost object. If Apple were interested in the cost of one of the thousands of products shipped from one of its warehouses, the depreciation expense for that warehouse would be an indirect cost because it is not easily traced to any one unit of product that passes through the warehouse. It would be considered a common cost for all products of the warehouse. As noted in the previous examples, a particular cost may be considered direct or indirect, depending on the cost object.

Concept ➜	Method ➜	Assessment	TAKEAWAY 2.3
The CEO of a local medical center has asked you to identify the costs of the urgent care, family medicine, and orthopedic practices for purposes of evaluating each area's performance.	• Identify the cost object. • Classify expenses as either direct or indirect relative to that cost object. • Sum the direct costs by cost object.	• Expenses that are specific and limited to one practice (i.e., can be traced to an individual practice) are direct costs. • Expenses that are incurred for the benefit of or are used by more than one practice (i.e., cannot be easily traced to an individual practice) are indirect costs.	

Product Costing in a Service and Merchandising Environment

SERVICE AND MERCHANDISING

Product versus Period Costs

Like manufacturers, service firms need to understand the cost of providing their services to customers. Although these firms do not produce a tangible product, they must know the cost of their services to determine the proper fee for those services and ensure a return to their owners. Service firms may include labor and other directly traceable costs in determining the **cost of jobs or projects**. Merchandising companies record the cost of acquired inventory as a product cost, whereas items such as salaries and wages, utilities, and depreciation are recorded immediately as operating expenses.

Service firms and merchandisers expense **period costs** in the period the costs are incurred. The benefits associated with these costs are assumed to expire in the period incurred rather than in the period in which the product is sold. Like manufacturers, selling expenses and non-factory administrative expenses are considered period costs.

Variable, Fixed, and Mixed Costs

The definitions of variable, fixed, and mixed costs are the same for service and merchandise firms as those given previously for manufacturers. An example of a variable cost in a consulting firm would be office supplies expense, which would increase with the number of consulting projects performed. The consulting firm's office lease expense would be considered a fixed cost because it would not vary with the number of projects performed. The firm's contribution to the employee 401(k) profit-sharing retirement plan would be a mixed cost assuming that the plan required a minimum contribution of 3% and that additional contributions would be made based on the level of profit earned in a year. Wages and salaries costs for a merchandising company with a brick and mortar physical location might be a fixed cost because some employees would be required during operating hours regardless of the level of sales. However, commissions expense would be a variable costs because it will vary with the level of sales.

Direct and Indirect Costs

Again, the definitions of direct and indirect costs are the same as given previously for a manufacturing firm. In a service or merchandising company, wages or salaries are the most common direct cost. However, service company costs such as photocopying, postage, and travel that can be traced to a particular job could also be considered direct costs. Service and merchandising companies would typically consider marketing costs and costs associated with employee continuing education or training classes as indirect costs.

YOUR TURN! 2.1

The solution is on page 2-44.

MBC

Classify each of the following costs relative to the cost object "Apple iPad":

	Product or Period	Variable, Fixed, or Mixed	Direct or Indirect
Assembly labor....................................			
iPad case			
CEO salary.......................................			
Microprocessor...................................			
Depreciation on Apple corporate headquarters			
Health insurance for factory workers			
Touch screen			
Adhesive on the serial number label			

INVENTORIES AND COST CATEGORIES

Inventories

Manufacturing Firms

At any point in time, manufacturing operations typically have units of product at various stages of completion. Three inventories are usually maintained on a perpetual basis to reflect these stages—materials, work-in-process, and finished goods.

The **materials inventory** includes factory materials and components that have been purchased but not yet placed into production. Some of the items in the materials inventory, such as sheets of steel or microprocessors, were finished products to the supplying company but are materials and components to the purchasing company. All items in the materials inventory account are recorded at their net delivered cost (i.e., product cost plus inbound shipping).

The **work-in-process inventory** of a manufacturing firm includes units of product that have been placed in production but have not yet been completed. All the costs of materials and components, direct human labor, utilities, and use of factory assets (overhead costs) are included in the work-in-process inventory. All items in the work-in-process inventory account are recorded at cost.

The **finished goods inventory** of a manufacturing firm includes all units of product that have been completed but have not been sold. These items are stored in a warehouse until they are sold and shipped to the customer. All items in the finished goods inventory account were recorded at cost in the work-in-process inventory account and transferred to the finished goods inventory account.

Many manufacturing firms also maintain an inventory of factory and office supplies for the manufacturing operation. **Factory supplies** are consumable items, such as cleaning supplies and machinery lubricants, used in the factory but not incorporated into the product; **office supplies** include copy paper, toner, and paper clips, items used in the office but not charged to a particular job. The inventory of factory and office supplies is usually maintained on a periodic basis, so the cost of factory and office supplies used during a period is determined at period-end after the supplies on hand are counted.

LO2 **Describe** the three manufacturing inventories—materials, work-in-process, and finished goods—and **discuss** the categories of manufacturing costs and how these costs flow among the inventories and cost of goods sold.

eLecture

MBC

ACCOUNTING IN PRACTICE   **Factory Supplies versus Indirect Materials**

Factory supplies are different from indirect materials. Factory supplies are used in the factory but are not part of the product itself. Lubricant used on the machine that stamps the sheet metal used in a laptop computer would be a factory supply. Indirect materials are part of the product but are difficult to trace to each individual product. Solder used to attach computer chips to a motherboard would be an indirect material. Both factory supplies and indirect materials can become part of manufacturing overhead.

Merchandising and Service Firms

Merchandising firms have only one inventory account—merchandise inventory. This is similar to the finished goods inventory account at a manufacturer because it contains finished products that are available for immediate sale. As discussed previously, manufacturing firms usually have three primary inventory accounts: materials, work-in-process, and finished goods.

SERVICE AND MERCHANDISING

Service firms typically have only one inventory account—work-in-process inventory. This account represents the service firm's partially completed projects. Service firms would include the cost of direct labor and overhead in work-in-process inventory. Although service firms may utilize office supplies on their projects, these costs are usually immaterial and not considered a materials inventory. Because completed projects are billed to the customer immediately upon completion, there is no need for a finished goods inventory. These inventories are reported in the current assets section of the balance sheet, as illustrated in **Exhibit 2-6**.

EXHIBIT 2-6	Comparison of Merchandising, Service, and Manufacturing Inventories	
Merchandising Firm	**Service Firm**	**Manufacturing Firm**
Cash . . . . $ 10,000	Cash . . . . $ 10,000	Cash . . . . $ 10,000
Short-term investments . . . 20,000	Short-term investments 20,000	Short-term investments . . . 20,000
Receivables 45,000	Receivables 45,000	Receivables 45,000
Merchandise inventory 80,000	Work-in-process inventory . . 80,000	Inventories:
Prepaid expenses 15,000	Prepaid expenses 15,000	Materials 35,000
Total current assets $170,000	Office supplies 5,000	Work-in-process 55,000
	Total current assets $175,000	Finished goods 25,000
		Prepaid expenses 15,000
		Factory supplies 5,000
		Total current assets $210,000

Inventory accounts include all costs necessary to bring the inventory to completion—all product costs.

Manufacturing Product Cost Categories

Product costs in a manufacturing setting can be classified into three subcategories (see **Exhibit 2-7**):

1. **Direct materials** include all the important materials and components that physically make up the product (such as sheets of steel and electric motors). Incidental material items, such as glue and fasteners, are considered **indirect materials** and are included in manufacturing overhead. Both direct material items and indirect material items are included in the materials inventory. Therefore, all items in the materials inventory will be used as either direct materials or indirect materials.

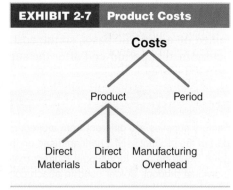

EXHIBIT 2-7   Product Costs

Hint: "Manufacturing product costs" include all direct materials, direct labor, and manufacturing overhead for a period of time and represent the additions to work-in-process inventory. "Manufacturing costs" should not be confused with "manufacturing overhead costs," although both terms have the word "manufacturing" in them.

A.K.A.
Manufacturing overhead has several other names that are commonly used in practice, such as **factory overhead**, factory burden, and indirect manufacturing costs.

2. **Direct labor** includes the salary and wage cost of factory employees who work directly on the product (such as machine operators, assemblers, and painters). The salary and wage cost of factory employees who do not work directly on the product (e.g., supervisors, inspectors, and material handlers) is considered **indirect labor**, which is included in manufacturing overhead. The total amount of factory labor (direct and indirect) is identified on a manufacturing firm's factory payroll.

3. **Manufacturing overhead** consists of all manufacturing costs not included in direct materials and direct labor. Manufacturing overhead includes indirect materials, indirect labor, factory supplies used, factory payroll tax and fringe benefits costs, factory utilities, and factory building and machinery costs (such as depreciation, insurance, property taxes, and repairs and maintenance). Manufacturing overhead specifically *excludes* selling and non-factory administrative expenses because these expenses are not incurred in the manufacturing process.

Apple Inc. Corporate Headquarters   iPad Factory

Combined Costs

Manufacturing Firms

Manufacturing cost categories are frequently combined for convenience. As illustrated in **Exhibit 2-8**, the sum of direct materials and direct labor for a particular product is known as prime cost. **Prime cost** is made up of the elements of product cost that are easily and directly traceable to individual products. **Conversion cost** is the sum of direct labor and manufacturing overhead. Conversion cost represents the elements of product cost necessary to convert the materials and components to the final finished products.

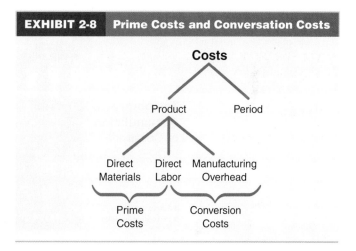

EXHIBIT 2-8   **Prime Costs and Conversation Costs**

Service Firms

Prime cost and conversion cost can also apply to a service firm. A service firm's prime cost is limited to direct labor cost (because no direct materials are typically used). A service firm's conversion cost is the sum of direct labor and applied general overhead.

> **SERVICE AND MERCHANDISING**

Although Apple is not primarily a service firm, it has a technical support department that assists customers with hardware and software questions that arise in the normal operation of Apple products. Prime costs for the technical support department would simply include the wages and salaries of support personnel because the service department would have no direct materials. Conversion costs for the technical support department would include both the wages and the salaries of support personnel in addition to overhead costs, such as depreciation on office equipment, employee health insurance premiums, the costs associated with janitorial services, and utilities.

PRODUCT COST FLOWS

Raw Materials

The materials inventory frequently contains both direct and indirect materials. As direct materials are used in production, they are traced directly to specific units of product. Thus, the cost of direct materials flows from raw materials inventory directly into work-in-process inventory. On the other hand, indirect materials cannot be traced to particular units of product. As a result, as they are used in the production process, their cost is transferred from raw materials inventory to manufacturing overhead. **Exhibit 2-9a** illustrates the flow of both direct and indirect materials from raw materials inventory to the work-in-process and manufacturing overhead, respectively.

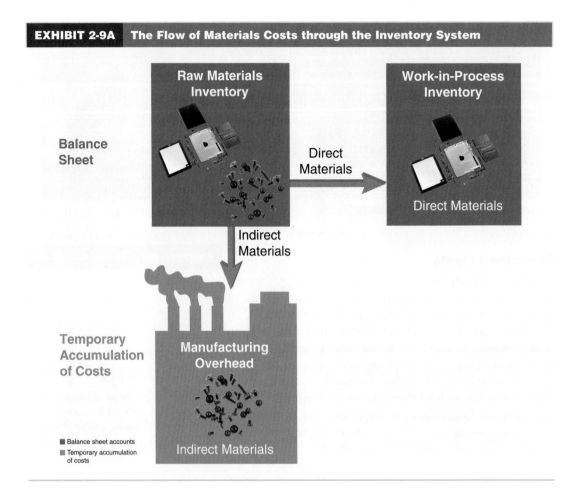

EXHIBIT 2-9A   The Flow of Materials Costs through the Inventory System

Labor

Both direct and indirect labor costs are incurred in the manufacturing process. The wages of employees who work directly on units of product are traced directly to specific units. Therefore, when these labor costs are incurred, they are recorded in work-in-process inventory. On the other hand, the wages of factory employees not working directly on the product cannot be traced directly to particular units. They are recorded as manufacturing overhead. **Exhibit 2-9b** illustrates how both direct and indirect labor flow into work-in-process and manufacturing overhead, respectively.

EXHIBIT 2-9B   The Flow of Labor Costs through the Inventory System

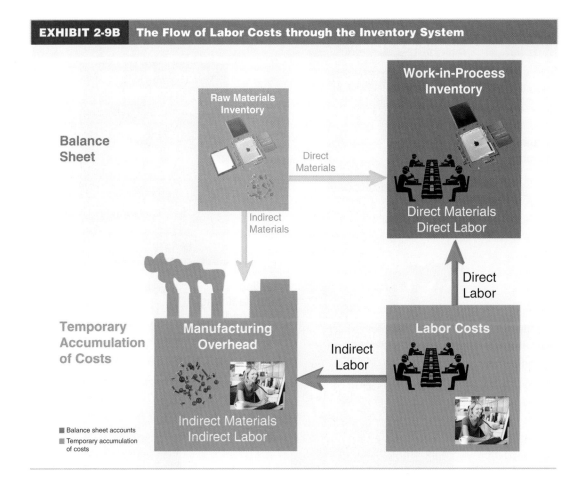

Manufacturing Overhead

Because overhead costs are, by definition, indirect costs that cannot be traced to a particular unit of product, they are accumulated in manufacturing overhead during the accounting period. Indirect materials and indirect labor are just two examples of indirect costs accumulated in manufacturing overhead. Other examples include costs that cannot be traced to a particular unit of product, such as depreciation on the factory and factory equipment, factory utilities, insurance on production facilities, property taxes related to the factory, and so forth. The problem accountants face is that it is impossible to know with certainty how much manufacturing overhead will accumulate during a particular period. Rather than waiting until the end of the period to divide the actual manufacturing overhead costs by the number of units actually produced to allocate the costs to jobs passing through the production process, accountants use their knowledge from past periods to calculate an estimated overhead rate at the beginning of the period to allocate overhead to jobs as they pass through the production process. We discuss the process for estimating and allocating manufacturing overhead in more detail in Chapter 3. However, **Exhibit 2-9c** illustrates the flow of overhead costs from manufacturing overhead to the work-in-process inventory.

Hint: Actual indirect costs are recorded on the debit side of the manufacturing overhead account, whereas overhead applied to units produced is recorded on the credit side because overhead is allocated to jobs (in the work-in-process inventory account).

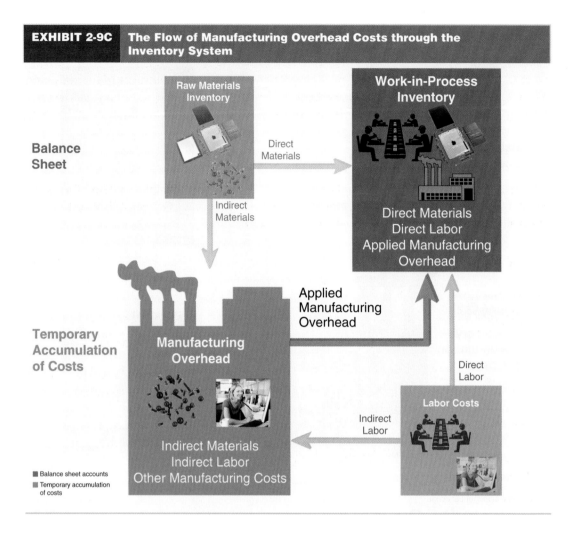

EXHIBIT 2-9C   The Flow of Manufacturing Overhead Costs through the Inventory System

Cost of Goods Manufactured

Total manufacturing costs consist of direct materials, direct labor, and manufacturing overhead. **Exhibit 2-9d** summarizes how all of these costs flow into work-in-process inventory.

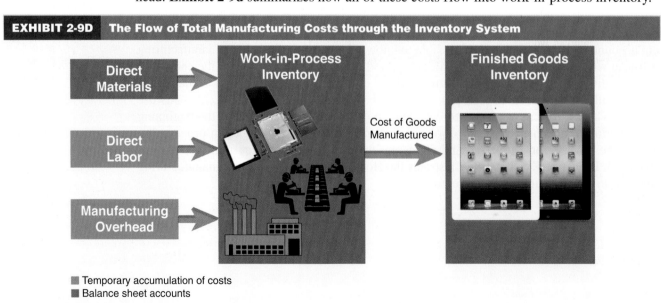

EXHIBIT 2-9D   The Flow of Total Manufacturing Costs through the Inventory System

The product costs that flow from work-in-process to the finished goods during an accounting period are known as **cost of goods manufactured (COGM)**. The schedule of cost of goods manufactured (which we demonstrate in the next section) summarizes all of the different costs incurred in the production of inventory: (1) direct materials, (2) labor costs, and (3) manufacturing overhead. All of these costs flow into work-in-process inventory. The total cost of goods manufactured is transferred to finished goods inventory, as illustrated in **Exhibit 2-9d**.

Cost of Goods Sold

Exhibit 2-9e illustrates the flow of all product costs through the inventory system of a manufacturing firm. All costs that are accumulated in work-in-process eventually flow to finished goods and, when the products are sold, are recognized as **cost of goods sold (COGS)**.

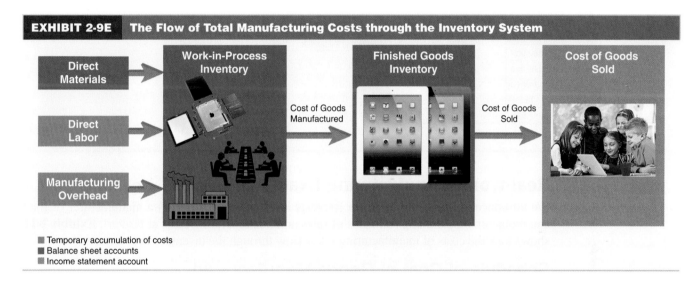

EXHIBIT 2-9E   The Flow of Total Manufacturing Costs through the Inventory System

■ Temporary accumulation of costs
■ Balance sheet accounts
■ Income statement account

Which of the following represents the correct sequence of the flow of costs in a typical manufacturing company?

   a. Direct materials, cost of goods sold, work-in-process inventory, finished goods inventory

   b. Direct materials, work-in-process inventory, cost of goods sold, finished goods inventory

   c. Direct materials, work-in-process inventory, finished goods inventory, cost of goods sold

   d. Work-in-process inventory, direct materials, finished goods inventory, cost of goods sold

YOUR TURN! 2.2

The solution is on page 2-44.

GuidedExample

MBC

ILLUSTRATION OF PRODUCT COST ACCUMULATION

Introduction of T-Accounts

Exhibit 2-9e illustrates the flow of all product costs through the inventory accounts. As you learn in financial accounting, each account can be represented by a T-account, which is a visual illustration of the flow of dollars into and out of the account. **Exhibit 2-10** illustrates the T-accounts associated with each item in **Exhibit 2-9e**.

LO3   **Define** total manufacturing costs, cost of goods manufactured, and cost of goods sold, and **illustrate** the schedule of cost of goods manufactured and sold and the income statement.

eLecture

MBC

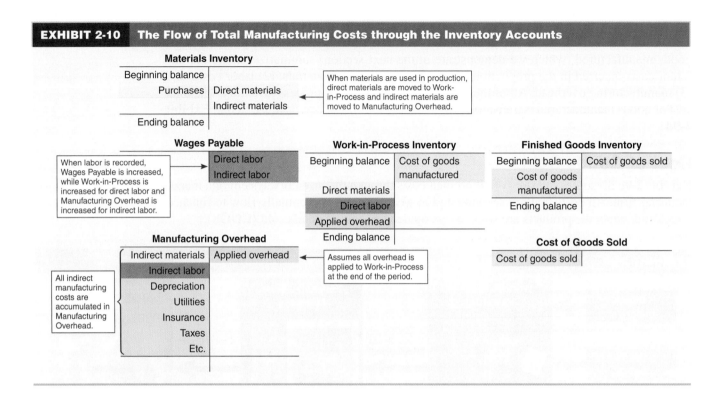

EXHIBIT 2-10   The Flow of Total Manufacturing Costs through the Inventory Accounts

Real-World Manufacturing Example

We introduced Fezzari Performance Bicycles in Chapter 1. Fezzari is a manufacturer of road and mountain bikes. Using estimates of sales and manufacturing costs at Fezzari, **Exhibit 2-11** shows how the costs of manufacturing bikes flow through the inventory accounts.

Schedule of Cost of Goods Manufactured

Although **Exhibit 2-11** is helpful in visualizing the flow of costs through Fezzari's accounts, it is not very useful for management decision-making. The schedule of cost of goods manufactured presents information about an entity's product cost for a particular accounting period in a format that is more suitable for decision-making. **Exhibit 2-12** presents Fezzari's schedule of cost of goods manufactured. The schedule has two sections. The first section summarizes the **total manufacturing costs** for the year: direct materials, direct labor, and manufacturing overhead incurred in the manufacturing process during the year. These are all of the costs that flow into the work-in-process inventory account during the year. In the calculation of direct materials used during the year, the net delivered cost of materials purchased is added to the beginning materials inventory to determine the cost of materials available during the year. The cost of materials not used (ending materials inventory) is then subtracted to identify the cost of all materials used during the year. This total represents both direct materials used and indirect materials used. We subtract indirect materials used to determine the direct materials used. Direct labor is presented on a single line. The detail of manufacturing overhead is calculated by summing all of the individual components of manufacturing overhead.

Exhibit 2-11 shows how the costs of manufacturing bikes flow through the inventory accounts on the balance sheet and into the cost of goods sold account on the income statement. Review each transaction in the exhibit, then trace its impact through the related T-accounts. The balances at the beginning of the period are as follows (all numbers are in thousands): Materials Inventory, $25; Work-in-Process Inventory, $10; and Finished Goods Inventory, $12.

EXHIBIT 2-11   The Flow of Fezzari's Costs through the Inventory Accounts

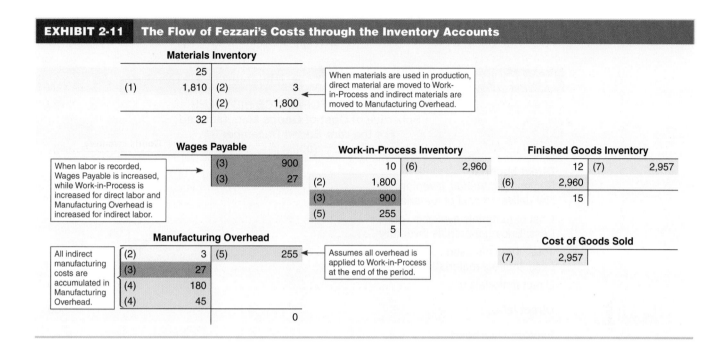

Accounting for Materials

(1) Materials inventory of $1,810 is purchased and received.

(2) Materials inventory is used in the production process. Direct materials of $1,800 are used and transferred to Work-in-Process Inventory. Indirect materials of $3 are used and transferred to and accumulated in Manufacturing Overhead.

Accounting for Labor

(3) Manufacturing wages are incurred in the production process. Direct labor of $900 is incurred and recorded in both Work-in-Process Inventory and Wages Payable. Indirect labor of $27 is incurred and recorded in both Manufacturing Overhead and Wages Payable.

Accounting for Manufacturing Overhead

(4) Additional indirect manufacturing costs are incurred during the production process and accumulated in Manufacturing Overhead. These costs include the lease on the factory of $180 and depreciation on factory machinery of $45.

(5) At the end of the period, the $255 of costs accumulated in Manufacturing Overhead is applied to Work-in-Process Inventory.

Accounting for Finished Goods and Cost of Goods Sold

(6) As bikes are completed, their total manufacturing costs of $2,960 are transferred from Work-in-Process Inventory to Finished Goods Inventory.

(7) When bikes are sold, their total manufacturing costs of $2,957 are transferred out of Finished Goods Inventory and recognized as a cost of goods sold expense. This entry is recorded along with the related sales entry.

The second section of the schedule of cost of goods manufactured determines the cost of goods manufactured—the cost of goods completed during the year and transferred to finished goods. In this section, total manufacturing costs for the year are added to the amount representing the work-in-process at the beginning of the year to determine the total cost of work-in-process during the year. The cost of incomplete units (ending work-in-process inventory) is then subtracted to determine the cost associated with the completed units (cost of goods manufactured). These are all of the numbers that appear in the work-in-process inventory account.

EXHIBIT 2-12	Schedule of Cost of Goods Manufactured

FEZZARI PERFORMANCE BICYCLES
Schedule of Cost of Goods Manufactured
For the Year Ended December 31
(000s)

Direct Material		
Beginning materials inventory	$ 25	
Net delivered cost of materials purchased	1,810	
Cost of materials available	1,835	
Less: Ending materials inventory	(32)	
Total materials used	1,803	
Less: Indirect materials used	(3)	
Direct materials used		$1,800
Direct labor		900
Factory Overhead		
Indirect materials	3	
Indirect labor	27	
Lease—factory	180	
Depreciation—factory machinery	45	
Total factory overhead		255
Total manufacturing costs for the year		2,955
Add: Beginning work-in-process inventory		10
Total cost of work-in-process during the year		2,965
Less: Ending work-in-process inventory		(5)
Cost of goods manufactured		$2,960

Total manufacturing costs include the amounts of direct materials used, direct labor, and applied overhead for the period reported.

Cost of goods manufactured is total manufacturing costs plus or minus the change in the work-in-process inventory balance.

Calculating Cost of Goods Sold

Exhibit 2-13 presents Fezzari's cost of goods sold summary. The calculation of cost of goods manufactured is an important step in determining cost of goods sold. The cost of the beginning finished goods inventory is added to cost of goods manufactured to report the cost of goods available for sale during the year. The cost of unsold units (ending finished goods inventory) is then subtracted to identify the cost associated with the units that were sold during the year (cost of goods sold).

EXHIBIT 2-13	Cost of Goods Sold Calculation

FEZZARI PERFORMANCE BICYCLES
Schedule of Cost of Goods Sold
For the Year Ended December 31
(000s)

Cost of goods manufactured	$2,960
Add: Beginning finished goods inventory	12
Cost of goods available for sale	$2,972
Less: Ending finished goods inventory	(15)
Cost of goods sold	$2,957

This amount will be reported on Fezzari's income statement and matched against the related sales revenue.

The schedule of cost of goods manufactured and the calculation of cost of goods sold provide useful information about product costs in support of the income statement. They are not, however, required financial statements.

Income Statement for a Manufacturing Firm

Exhibit 2-14 presents the income statement for Fezzari. Fezzari uses the perpetual inventory system for finished goods, so its cost of goods sold amount is reported in the general ledger account. The schedule of cost of goods manufactured (see **Exhibit 2-12**) and the cost of goods sold calculation (see **Exhibit 2-13**) tie to the cost of goods sold amount in the income statement.

EXHIBIT 2-14	Income Statement

FEZZARI PERFORMANCE BICYCLES
Income Statement
For the Year Ended December 31
(000s)

Sales.		$4,500
Cost of goods sold		2,957
Gross profit on sales.		$1,543
Operating expenses:		
Selling expenses.	$ 400	
Non-factory administrative expenses	340	740
Income from operations		$ 803
Other income and expense:		
Interest expense		5
Income before income tax		$ 798
Income tax expense		279
Net income		$ 519

> Represents all product costs of products sold during the period identified in the summary of costs of goods sold in Exhibit 2-13.

Shea Company reported raw material purchases of $1,400, paid $1,200 in factory labor, and incurred and applied $900 in factory overhead for March. The March 1 inventory balances were $200 for raw materials, $600 for work-in-process inventory, and $400 for finished goods inventory. On March 31, inventory balances were $300 for raw materials, $500 for work-in-process inventory, and $600 for finished goods inventory. What was Shea's cost of goods manufactured for March?

YOUR TURN! 2.3

The solution is on page 2-44.

GuidedExample

MBC

ILLUSTRATION OF PRODUCT COST JOURNAL ENTRIES

The following illustration for **Apple Inc.** presents hypothetical summary transactions and adjustment entries for 2021 related to the accounts used to accumulate product costs. Assume that Apple Inc. uses the perpetual inventory system and had the following manufacturing inventory account balances (in millions) at October 1, 2019 (the beginning of its 2020 fiscal year):

LO4 Illustrate the journal entries to record product cost flows using a perpetual inventory system.

eLecture

MBC

Materials inventory	$ 800
Work-in-process inventory	1,300
Finished goods inventory	2,000

When a manufacturing firm uses the perpetual inventory system for Materials Inventory, Work-in-Process Inventory, and Finished Goods Inventory, cost of goods sold can be determined directly by reference to the Cost of Goods Sold account in the general ledger. Total manufacturing costs and cost of goods manufactured, however, are not directly available in a general ledger account. Assume Apple's subsidiary records for 2020 contain the following data:

1. Net delivered cost of materials purchased was $50,000.

2. The cost of direct materials used in production was $44,400.

3. Direct labor totaled $17,500.

4. Manufacturing overhead consists of the following:

Indirect materials	$ 5,000
Indirect labor.	4,000
Various costs	62,500
Year-end adjustments.	10,000*
	$81,500

*This is composed of $2,000 for manufacturing supplies and $8,000 for depreciation on factory machinery.

Based on this information, assume Apple records the following entries for 2020:

1. Acquisition of materials

Materials inventory	49,300	
Accounts payable		49,300
To record the delivered cost of materials purchased.		

2. Use of direct materials and indirect materials

Work-in-process inventory	44,400	
Manufacturing overhead	5,000	
Materials inventory		49,400
To record the transfer of direct materials ($44,400) to the work-in-process inventory and the transfer of indirect materials ($5,000) to manufacturing overhead.		

3. Incurrence of factory payroll

Work-in-process inventory	17,500	
Manufacturing overhead	4,000	
Wages payable		21,500
To record the factory payroll as direct labor ($17,500) to the work-in-process inventory and as indirect labor ($4,000) to manufacturing overhead.		

4. Incurrence of manufacturing overhead costs during year

Manufacturing overhead	62,500	
Accounts payable or cash		62,500
To record various factory costs incurred during the year as manufacturing overhead.		

5. Recognition of certain manufacturing overhead costs with year-end adjustments

Manufacturing overhead	36,159	
Manufacturing supplies		4,000
Accumulated depreciation—factory machinery		32,159
To record cost of supplies used for and depreciation on factory machinery.		

6. Application of manufacturing overhead

Work-in-process inventory	107,659	
Manufacturing overhead		107,659

To record the application of manufacturing overhead to the work-in-process inventory. (The procedures for determining this application will be described in a subsequent chapter.)

Cost Flows

Exhibit 2-15 presents T-accounts to which these summary entries have been posted. The arrows in **Exhibit 2-15** indicate the flows of product cost. Direct material flows from Materials Inventory to Work-in-Process Inventory, whereas indirect material flows from Materials Inventory to Manufacturing Overhead. Direct labor flows from Wages Expense to Work-in-Process Inventory, whereas indirect labor flows from Wages Payable to Manufacturing Overhead. Actual manufacturing overhead comes from several sources, and manufacturing overhead applied flows to Work-in-Process Inventory.

Hint: In practice, applied manufacturing overhead rarely equals the actual manufacturing overhead incurred during a period, as illustrated in this example. Chapter 3 explains how to deal with over- or underapplied overhead.

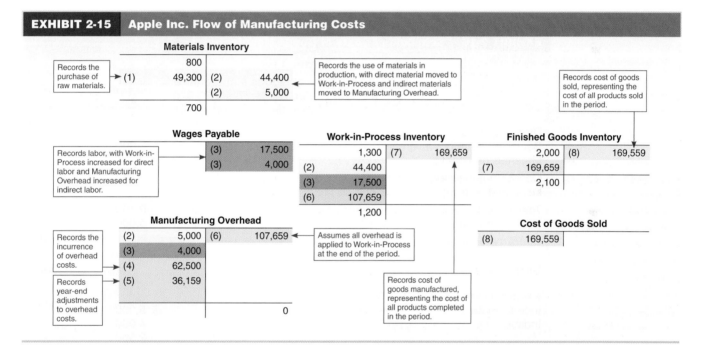

EXHIBIT 2-15   Apple Inc. Flow of Manufacturing Costs

Cost of goods manufactured (the product cost of goods completed during the accounting period) flows from Work-in-Process Inventory to Finished Goods Inventory. The cost of goods sold flows from Finished Goods Inventory to the Cost of Goods Sold account. These cost flows are represented by the following journal entries:

7. Recognition of cost of goods manufactured

Finished goods inventory	169,659	
Work-in-process inventory		169,659

To record the transfer of the cost associated with goods completed from the work-in-process inventory to the finished goods inventory.

8. Recognition of cost of goods sold

Cost of goods sold	169,559	
Finished goods inventory		169,559

To record the transfer of the cost associated with goods sold to customers from the finished goods inventory to cost of goods sold— recorded with the related sales entry.

TAKEAWAY 2.4	Concept ⟶	Method ⟶	Assessment
	What amount should be reported as cost of goods sold in the annual financial statements?	• Accumulate the costs of direct materials, direct labor, and manufacturing overhead for all products produced in a period. • Report the cost of goods sold in the period of the sale.	• If the ending balance in finished goods inventory is less than the beginning balance, then cost of goods sold will be greater than cost of goods manufactured. • If the ending balance in finished goods inventory is greater than the beginning balance, then cost of goods sold will be less than cost of goods manufactured.

Based on the information in these journal entries and as summarized in the T-accounts in **Exhibit 2-15**, **Exhibit 2-16** presents Apple Inc.'s schedule of cost of goods manufactured for 2017.

EXHIBIT 2-16	Schedule of Costs of Goods Manufactured

APPLE INC.
Schedule of Cost of Goods Manufactured
For the Year Ended September 26, 2020
(in $millions)

Direct Material		
Beginning materials inventory	$ 800	
Materials purchased	49,300	
Cost of materials available	$50,100	
Less: Ending materials inventory	700	
Total materials used	$49,400	
Less: Indirect materials used	5,000	
Direct materials used		$ 44,400
Direct labor		$ 17,500
Factory Overhead		
Indirect materials	$ 5,000	
Indirect labor	4,000	
Various costs	62,500	
Year-end adjustments	36,159	
Total factory overhead		$107,659
Total manufacturing costs for the year		$169,559
Add: beginning work-in-process inventory		$ 1,300
Total cost of work-in-process during the year		170,859
Less: Ending work-in-process inventory		1,200
Cost of goods manufactured		$169,659

Total Manufacturing Cost includes all direct materials, direct labor, and applied overhead for **work done** during the period.

Cost of Goods Manufactured reflects the total manufacturing costs for the **products completed** during the period.

Financial Statements

Exhibit 2-17 presents Apple Inc.'s 2020 income statement.

EXHIBIT 2-17	Income Statement

APPLE INC.
Income Statement
For Year Ended September 26, 2020

(in millions)	2020
Net sales	$274,515
Less cost of goods sold	169,559
Gross profit on sales	104,956
Operating expenses	
Research and development expenses	18,752
Selling, general, and administrative	19,916
Total operating expenses	38,668
Income from operations	66,288
Other income and expenses	803
Income before income taxes	67,091
Income tax expense	9,680
Net income	$ 57,411

> Cost of Goods Sold reflects the total manufacturing costs for the **products sold** during the period.

Exhibit 2-18 presents the September 26, 2020, balance sheet for Apple, Inc. Note that the multiple inventory accounts are combined into a single line in the current assets section for presentation purposes.

EXHIBIT 2-18	Balance Sheet

APPLE INC.
Balance Sheet
September 26, 2020

(in millions)	2020
Assets	
Current assets:	
Cash	$ 38,016
Short-term investments	52,927
Accounts receivable	16,120
Inventory	4,061
Other current assets	32,589
Total current assets	143,713
Long-term assets:	
Marketable securities	100,887
Property, plant, and equipment	36,766
Other noncurrent assets	42,522
Total long-term assets	180,175
Total assets	$323,888
Liabilities	
Current liabilities:	
Accounts payable	$ 42,296
Other current liabilities	63,096
Total current liabilities	105,392

> All inventory accounts are combined into one line item for presentation purposes.

continued

continued from previous page

EXHIBIT 2-18	Balance Sheet

APPLE INC.
Balance Sheet
September 26, 2020

(in millions)	2020
Long-term liabilities:	153,157
Total liabilities	258,549
Stockholders' Equity	
Common stock	50,779
Retained earnings	14,966
Other equity	(406)
Total stockholders' equity.	65,339
Total liabilities and stockholders' equity	$323,888

YOUR TURN! 2.4	

The solution is on
page 2-44.

MBC

Shea Company reported raw material purchases of $1,400, paid $1,200 in factory labor, and incurred and applied $900 in factory overhead for March. The March 1 inventory balances were $200 for raw materials, $600 for work-in-process inventory, and $400 for finished goods inventory. On March 31, inventory balances were $300 for raw materials, $500 for work-in-process inventory, and $600 for finished goods inventory. What are the March journal entries to record Shea's

a. Raw materials purchase
b. Raw materials usage
c. Direct labor
d. Application of manufacturing overhead
e. Cost of goods manufactured
f. Cost of goods sold

ENVIRONMENTAL, SOCIAL, AND GOVERNANCE	Environmental Performance Reporting at Apple

There are probably few companies as secretive as Apple. The company is very careful to control any leaks on its upcoming products. Apple uses this strategy of keeping things secret in order to increase the anticipation before new product announcements. The strategy seems to be working well, based on the excitement surrounding these new product events.

One area that Apple is not secretive about is its environmental responsibility. Apple uses its detailed managerial accounting system to measure the environmental impact of how every product is manufactured. Unlike the secrecy surrounding what the next new product will be, Apple believes in full transparency regarding its environmental performance and reports on this performance in its comprehensive *Product Environmental Reports*. Every Apple product is measured and rated in four categories: climate change, restricted substances, energy efficiency, and material efficiency.

As stated on Apple's website, "We strive to create products that are the best they can be in every way. . . . The same passion for innovation goes into how we think about environmental responsibility. It's why we work tirelessly to reduce our impact on climate change, find ways to use greener materials, and conserve the resources we all need to thrive."

A famous expression in business is that you can't manage what you can't measure. For Apple to be a leader in both product development and environmental responsibility, the company depends on its managerial accounting systems to provide the information needed to properly manage everything the company does.

SERVICE INDUSTRY IN FOCUS

Environmental Business Consultants, LLC (EBC), is a consulting firm that specializes in the areas of recycling and solid waste and water/wastewater management services. The firm has offices located in northern and southern California. EBC has serviced hundreds of municipal agencies since 1984. Both the firm's executives and consultants work on client projects. EBC's adjusted trial balance is shown below.

SERVICE AND MERCHANDISING

Description	Trial Balance	
	Debit	**Credit**
Cash	390,000	
Accounts receivable	474,000	
Allowance for uncollectible accounts		—
Work-in-process inventory	247,000	
Other current assets	32,000	
Furniture and fixtures	150,000	
Accumulated depreciation—furniture		150,000
Office equipment	277,000	
Accumulated depreciation—equipment		198,000
Accounts payable		—
Other current liabilities		37,500
Noncurrent liabilities		3,000
Owners' capital		90,000
Retained earnings		573,000
Sales		4,146,000
Reimbursable costs	431,000	
Executive salaries	844,500	
Clerical salaries	217,500	
Consultant salaries	1,050,000	
Employee benefits	145,500	
Payroll taxes	123,000	
Employee bonuses	126,000	
Marketing expenses	48,000	
Employee continuing education expenses	27,000	
Office lease expense	202,500	
Office supplies expense	64,500	
Other general administrative expenses	355,500	
Other income/(expense)		7,500
	5,205,000	5,205,000

Required

1. Classify each of the expense line items in the trial balance as:

   a. Direct or indirect. Assume that the cost object is a consulting project.

   b. Fixed or variable. Assume that the cost object is one of EBC's two offices.

   c. Product or period. Assume that the cost object is a consulting project.

2. Prepare a schedule of cost of services for EBC for the year ended December 31. Assume that the beginning Work-in-Process Inventory balance was $223,000. Regardless of your classification in requirement 1, assume that all executive and consultant salaries, benefits, and taxes are product costs and that EBC treats all bonuses and continuing education expenses as period costs.

3. Prepare an income statement for EBC for the year ended December 31.

Solution

1*a.*

Line Item	Direct Cost	Indirect Cost
Reimbursable costs	X	
Executive salaries.	X	X
Clerical salaries		X
Consultant salaries.	X	
Employee benefits	X	X
Payroll taxes	X	X
Employee bonuses.	X	X
Marketing expenses		X
Employee continuing education expenses		X
Office lease expense		X
Office supplies expense		X
Other general administrative expenses		X

1*b.*

Line Item	Fixed Cost	Variable Cost
Reimbursable costs		X
Executive salaries.	X	
Clerical salaries	X	
Consultant salaries.	X	
Employee benefits	X	
Payroll taxes	X	
Employee bonuses.		X
Marketing expenses		X
Employee continuing education expenses		X
Office lease expense	X	
Office supplies expense		X
Other general administrative expenses	X	X

1*c.*

Line Item	Product Cost	Period Cost
Reimbursable costs	X	
Executive salaries.	X	
Clerical salaries		X
Consultant salaries.	X	
Employee benefits	X	X
Payroll taxes	X	X
Employee bonuses.		X
Marketing expenses		X
Employee continuing education expenses		X
Office lease expense	X	
Office supplies expense	X	X
Other general administrative expenses	X	X

2.

Environmental Business Consultants, LLC Schedule of Cost Services As of December 31		
Direct labor.		$2,380,500
General Overhead:		
Office lease expense	$202,500	
Office supplies expense	64,500	
Total general overhead.		267,000
Total manufacturing costs for the year		2,647,500
Add: beginning work-in-process inventory		223,000
Total cost of work-in-process during the year.		2,870,500
Less: ending work-in-process inventory		(247,000)
Cost of services		$2,623,500

3.

Environmental Business Consultants, LLC Income Statement For the Year Ended December 31		
Gross sales.		$4,146,000
Less: Reimbursable costs.		$ (431,000)
Net sales.		$3,715,000
Cost of services		2,623,500
Gross profit on sales.		1,091,500
Operating Expenses:		
Employee bonuses	126,000	
Marketing expenses	48,000	
Employee continuing education expenses	27,000	
Other general administrative expenses.	355,500	
Total operating expenses		556,500
Income from operations		535,000
Other income/(expense).		7,500
Net income.		$ 542,500

DATA ANALYTICS	**Data analytics and the management accountant**

It is an exciting time to be a management accountant. Their role in strategic management, planning, decision-making, and control is moving beyond traditional transactional-based accounting toward the world of big data and analytics. In the past, companies primarily used internal sources of data ranging from spreadsheets to ERP systems to conduct their analyses. A key characteristic of this data is that they are structured in ways that traditional software can understand and analyze. More recently, management accountants, with the help of data analytics software such as **Tableau**, have increased their sources of data to analyze. Data Analytics tools and machine learning technologies can process unstructured data from websites, emails, tweets, and sensors. Combining structured and unstructured data in their analyses provides management accountants with a more complete picture of a company's operations and performance.

Data Analytics

COMPREHENSIVE PROBLEM

MBC

At December 31, the end of its fiscal year, Perez Manufacturing Corporation collected the following data:

Materials inventory, January 1	$ 80,000
Materials inventory, December 31	60,000
Work-in-process inventory, January 1	100,000
Work-in-process inventory, December 31	140,000
Finished goods inventory, January 1	120,000
Finished goods inventory, December 31	110,000
Net delivered cost of materials purchased	180,000
Direct labor	280,000
Indirect materials	15,000
Indirect labor	75,000
Factory supplies used	16,000
Factory depreciation	30,000
Factory repairs and maintenance	22,000
Selling expenses	64,000
Non-factory administrative expenses	58,000

Required

Prepare a schedule of cost of goods manufactured and sold for Perez Manufacturing Corporation for the year ended December 31, assuming that there were no other manufacturing overhead items than those listed above.

Solution

PEREZ MANUFACTURING CORPORATION
Schedule of Cost of Goods Manufactured and Sold
For the Year Ended December 31

Direct materials:		
Beginning materials inventory	$ 80,000	
Net delivered cost of materials purchased	180,000	
Cost of materials available	$260,000	
Less: Ending materials inventory	60,000	
Total materials used	$200,000	
Less: Indirect materials used	15,000	
Direct materials used		$185,000
Direct labor		280,000
Manufacturing overhead:		
Indirect materials	$ 15,000	
Indirect labor	75,000	
Manufacturing supplies used	16,000	
Manufacturing depreciation	30,000	
Manufacturing repairs and maintenance	22,000	
Total manufacturing overhead		158,000
Total manufacturing costs for the year		**$623,000**
Add: Beginning work-in-process inventory		100,000
Total Cost of work-in-process during the year		$723,000
Less: Ending work-in-process inventory		140,000
Cost of goods manufactured		**$583,000**
Add: Beginning finished goods inventory		120,000
Cost of goods available for sale		$703,000
Less: Ending finished goods inventory		110,000
Cost of goods sold		**$593,000**

SUMMARY OF LEARNING OBJECTIVES

Identify the key objectives of a managerial accounting system and define product costs and period costs; variable, fixed, and mixed costs; and direct and indirect costs; and cost control. (p. 2-3)   **LO1**

- The primary objectives of managerial accounting systems are to provide management with financial and other business information that is useful in analyzing and making business decisions.
- Product costs include all costs necessary to bring a product to completion.
- Period costs are expensed in the period incurred and not assigned to products.
- A variable cost varies in total but is fixed per unit for a certain range of activity. A fixed cost is fixed in total but varies per unit for a certain range of activity. Mixed costs have both fixed and variable cost components.
- A direct cost can easily be traced to a cost object. An indirect cost cannot be easily traced to a cost object.

Describe the three manufacturing inventories—materials, work-in-process, and finished goods—and discuss the categories of manufacturing costs and how these costs flow among the inventories and cost of goods sold. (p. 2-8)   **LO2**

- Materials inventory includes all factory materials and components that have been purchased but not yet placed into production.
- Work-in-process inventory includes all units of product that have been placed into production but not yet completed.
- Finished goods inventory includes all units of product that have been completed but not yet sold.
- Total product costs consist of direct materials, direct labor, and manufacturing overhead (which includes indirect materials and indirect labor).
- Prime cost is direct materials plus direct labor. Product costs are easily and directly traceable to individual products. Conversion cost is direct labor plus manufacturing overhead. Conversion cost represents the elements of product cost necessary to convert the materials and components to the final finished products.
- Product cost flows from the Materials Inventory account to the Work-in-Process Inventory account to the Finished Goods Inventory account and finally to the Cost of Goods Sold account.

Define total manufacturing costs, cost of goods manufactured, and cost of goods sold, and illustrate the schedule of cost of goods manufactured and sold and the income statement. (p. 2-14)   **LO3**

- Total manufacturing costs is the sum of direct materials, direct labor, and manufacturing overhead incurred during the accounting period.
- Cost of goods manufactured (cost of product transferred to finished goods inventory during the accounting period) is total manufacturing costs plus beginning work-in-process inventory minus ending work-in-process inventory.
- Cost of goods sold is cost of goods manufactured plus beginning finished goods inventory minus ending finished goods inventory.
- The schedule of cost of goods manufactured and sold has subtotals that reveal total manufacturing costs, cost of goods manufactured, and cost of goods sold.

Illustrate the journal entries to record product cost flows using a perpetual inventory system. (p. 2-18)   **LO4**

- Direct materials, direct labor, and manufacturing overhead costs are accumulated in the Work-in-Process Inventory account.
- When manufacturing is completed, product costs are transferred from the Work-in-Process Inventory account to the Finished Goods Inventory account.
- When goods are sold, product costs are transferred from the Finished Goods Inventory account to Cost of Goods Sold.

SUMMARY	Concept ⟶	Method ⟶	Assessment
TAKEAWAY 2.1	A founder of a new consulting firm is trying to determine the firm's cost of service.	• Identify the cost object. • Classify the firm's expenses as product costs vs. period costs relative to that cost object. • Sum the product costs.	• Costs associated with completion of specific consulting projects, such as consultant labor and project supplies, would be considered product costs. • Costs not directly related to projects but related to operating the business, such as general liability insurance premiums, office rent, and marketing costs, would be considered period costs.
TAKEAWAY 2.2	How can one determine whether a cost is variable, fixed, or mixed?	• Observe cost behavior as production levels change. • Use the high-low method or least squares regression analysis (see Chapter 6).	• If costs increase proportionately with production, the cost is variable. • If costs remain unchanged as production changes, the cost is fixed. • If costs change, but not proportionately, as production changes, the cost is mixed.
TAKEAWAY 2.3	The CEO of a local medical center has asked you to identify the costs of the urgent care, family medicine, and orthopedic practices for purposes of evaluating each area's performance.	• Identify the cost object. • Classify expenses as either direct or indirect relative to that cost object. • Sum the direct costs by cost object.	• Expenses that are specific and limited to one practice (i.e., can be traced to an individual practice) are direct costs. • Expenses that are incurred for the benefit of or are used by more than one practice (i.e., cannot be easily traced to an individual practice) are indirect costs.
TAKEAWAY 2.4	What amount should be reported as cost of goods sold in the annual financial statements?	• Accumulate the costs of direct materials, direct labor, and manufacturing overhead for all products produced in a period. • Report the cost of goods sold in the period of the sale.	• If the ending balance in finished goods inventory is less than the beginning balance, then cost of goods sold will be greater than cost of goods manufactured. • If the ending balance in finished goods inventory is greater than the beginning balance, then cost of goods sold will be less than cost of goods manufactured.

KEY TERMS

Conversion cost (p. 2-10)

Cost object (p. 2-3)

Cost of goods manufactured (COGM) (p. 2-14)

Cost of goods sold (COGS) (p. 2-14)

Cost of jobs or projects (p. 2-7)

Direct cost (p. 2-6)

Direct labor (p. 2-9)

Direct materials (p. 2-9)

Factory overhead (p. 2-9)

Factory supplies (p. 2-8)

Finished goods inventory (p. 2-8)

Fixed cost (p. 2-4)

Indirect cost (p. 2-6)

Indirect labor (p. 2-9)

Indirect materials (p. 2-9)

Manufacturing overhead (p. 2-9)

Materials inventory (p. 2-8)

Mixed costs (p. 2-5)
Office supplies (p. 2-8)
Period costs (p. 2-3, 2-7)
Prime cost (p. 2-10)

Product costing (p. 2-3)
Product costs (p. 2-3, 2-9)
Semi-variable costs (p. 2-5)
Tableau (p. 2-26)

Total manufacturing
  costs (p. 2-13, 2-15)
Variable cost (p. 2-4)
Work-in-process
  inventory (p. 2-8)

Assignments with the 🌐 logo in the margin are available in BusinessCourse.
See the Preface of the book for details.

SELF-STUDY QUESTIONS

(Answers to Self-Study Questions are at the end of this chapter.)

1. **Which of the following is never an element of product cost?** **LO1**
   a. Insurance
   b. Utilities
   c. Advertising
   d. Supplies

2. **Which of the following is not an element of manufacturing overhead?** **LO1, 2**
   a. Factory office salaries
   b. Plant manager's salary
   c. Product inspector's salary
   d. Company president's salary

3. **The sum of direct materials, direct labor, and manufacturing overhead plus beginning work-in-process inventory minus ending work-in-process inventory computes** **LO3**
   a. total manufacturing costs.
   b. cost of goods manufactured.
   c. cost of goods sold.
   d. total cost of work-in-process.

4. **A manufacturer incurred $20,000 of direct material, $10,000 of direct labor, and $15,000 of manufacturing overhead during 2019. Beginning work-in-process inventory was $8,000. If cost of goods manufactured was $47,000, what was the amount of the ending work-in-process inventory?** **LO3**
   a. $55,000
   b. $6,000
   c. $10,000
   d. $53,000

5. **The journal entry to record the distribution of the factory payroll requires** **LO4**
   a. a debit to Work-in-Process Inventory for direct labor.
   b. a debit to Work-in-Process Inventory for indirect labor.
   c. a debit to Manufacturing Overhead for direct labor.
   d. a credit to Manufacturing Overhead for direct labor.

QUESTIONS

1. Describe how the per-unit amount of a variable and fixed cost changes as production increases over time. **LO1**
2. Explain the difference between a direct cost and an indirect cost of production. **LO1**
3. How are product costs accounted for differently from period costs? Give examples of each. **LO1**
4. Name the three inventory accounts maintained by manufacturing firms and briefly describe the nature of each. **LO2**
5. Name and briefly describe the three major categories used to account for manufacturing costs. **LO2**
6. Define prime cost and conversion cost. **LO2**
7. List six examples of manufacturing overhead costs. **LO2**
8. What is the basic format of the income statement of a manufacturing firm? **LO3**
9. In what way is total manufacturing cost different from cost of goods manufactured? **LO3**
10. If the cost of work-in-process during the year is $480,000 and ending work-in-process inventory is $50,000, what is the amount of cost of goods manufactured? **LO3**
11. If beginning and ending finished goods inventories are $55,000 and $45,000, respectively, and the cost of goods sold is $420,000, what is the cost of goods manufactured? **LO3**
12. What journal entry would be made to record the transfer of $12,000 of direct materials and $2,500 of indirect materials from the materials inventory? **LO4**

LO4 13. What journal entry would be made to record the distribution of a factory payroll consisting of $11,000 of direct labor and $4,000 of indirect labor?

LO4 14. What journal entry would be made to record the payment of $1,500 cash for factory utilities?

LO4 15. What journal entry would be required to record the transfer of completed products costing $15,000?

SHORT EXERCISES

LO1 **SE2-1.** Which one of the following refers to a cost that remains the same as the volume of activity decreases within the relevant range?

   a. Average cost per unit   *c.* Unit fixed cost

   b. Variable cost per unit   *d.* Total variable cost

LO1 **SE2-2.** Taylor Corporation is determining the cost behavior of several items in order to budget for the upcoming year. Past trends have indicated the following dollars were spent at three different levels of output.

	Unit Levels		
	10,000	12,000	15,000
Cost A......................	$25,000	$29,000	$35,000
Cost B......................	10,000	15,000	15,000
Cost C......................	15,000	18,000	22,500

In establishing a budget for 14,000 units, Taylor should treat Costs A, B, and C, respectively, as

   a. mixed, fixed, and variable.   *c.* mixed, mixed, and mixed.

   b. variable, fixed, and variable.   *d.* variable, mixed, and mixed.

LO1 **SE2-3.** Claire Corporation's trial balance includes the following expenses:

Raw materials used in production	$ 5,500
Raw materials purchased.............................	6,500
General manager salary..............................	50,000
Sales manager salary................................	30,000
Direct labor incurred................................	130,000
General liability insurance premium	3,000
Factory rent	24,000
Office lease.......................................	18,000
Factory utilities	12,000
Depreciation on factory equipment....................	14,000

Assuming that this list represents all expenses for the year, what amount should Claire report as a period (non-product) expense?

   a. $74,000

   b. $83,000

   c. $101,000

   d. $107,500

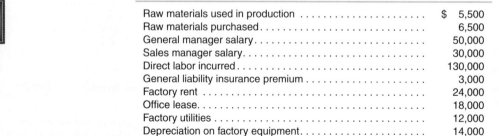

LO1 **SE2-4.** Claire Corporation's trial balance includes the following expenses:

Raw materials used in production	$ 5,500
Raw materials purchased.............................	6,500
General manager salary..............................	50,000
Sales manager salary................................	30,000
Direct labor incurred................................	130,000
General liability insurance premium	3,000
Factory rent	24,000
Office lease.......................................	18,000
Factory utilities	12,000
Depreciation on factory equipment....................	14,000

Assuming no change in the work-in-process and finished goods inventory balances for the year, what total amount should Claire report as a product expense?

a. $171,500   c. $186,500
b. $185,500   d. $236,500

SE2-5. Which one of the following items would not be considered a manufacturing cost?

a. Cream for an ice cream maker
b. Sales commissions for a car manufacturer
c. Plant property taxes for an ice cream maker
d. Tires for an automobile manufacturer

SE2-6. Carson Company reported the following amounts for December:

Beginning raw materials inventory	$10,000
Beginning work-in-process inventory	20,000
Beginning finished goods inventory	45,000
Raw materials purchases	75,000
Wages paid	13,000
Applied manufacturing overhead	92,000
Ending raw materials inventory	8,000
Ending work-in-process inventory	14,000
Ending finished good inventory	50,000

What amount of raw materials was used in production in December?

a. $71,000   c. $77,000
b. $73,000   d. $85,000

SE2-7. All of the following would appear on a schedule of cost of goods manufactured except for

a. ending work-in-process inventory.   c. the cost of raw materials used.
b. beginning finished goods inventory.   d. applied manufacturing overhead.

SE2-8. Given the following data for Scurry Company, what is the cost of goods sold?

Beginning inventory of finished goods	$100,000
Cost of goods manufactured	700,000
Ending inventory of finished goods	200,000
Beginning work-in-process inventory	300,000
Ending work-in-process inventory	50,000

a. $500,000   c. $800,000
b. $600,000   d. $950,000

SE2-9. Carson Company reported the following amounts for December:

Beginning raw materials inventory	$10,000
Beginning work-in-process inventory	20,000
Beginning finished goods inventory	45,000
Raw materials purchases	75,000
Wages paid	13,000
Applied manufacturing overhead	92,000
Ending raw materials inventory	8,000
Ending work-in-process inventory	14,000
Ending finished good inventory	50,000

What is cost of goods manufactured for December?

a. $176,000   c. $186,000
b. $182,000   d. $188,000

SE2-10. The journal entry to record the application of manufacturing overhead to production would include a debit to which account?

a. Cost of goods sold   c. Work-in-process inventory
b. Manufacturing overhead   d. Cost of goods manufactured

DATA ANALYTICS, DATA VISUALIZATION, AND EXCEL ACTIVITIES

Data Analytics, Data Visualization, and Excel Activities are available in myBusinessCourse. These assignments develop Excel, Tableau, and Data Analytics skills, which will enhance students' career readiness. These exercises are assignable and auto graded by MBC. For an overview of data analytics, see the appendix at the end of this book.

EXERCISES—SET A

LO1   **E2-1A.   Cost Classification** Classify each of the following costs relative to the cost object "client project" for a CPA firm that specializes in audit:

	Product or Period	Variable, Fixed, or Mixed	Direct or Indirect
Staff auditor salaries..................................			
Receptionist salary....................................			
Depreciation on staff auditor laptop computers			
Health insurance for administrative staff.................			
Subscription to cloud backup service for project files.......			
Office lease expense			
Travel to client location			

LO1   **E2-2A.   Cost Classification** Classify each of the following costs relative to the cost object "customer" for a clothing retailer:

	Product or Period	Variable, Fixed, or Mixed	Direct or Indirect
Salesperson wages			
Store manager salary................................			
Depreciation on furniture and fixtures			
Cost of merchandise			
Online advertising...................................			
Cost of discount coupon.............................			
Store lease expense.................................			

LO2, 3   **E2-3A.   Product Cost Flows** Complete the following T-accounts:

Materials Inventory

320	
?	?
	18,120
250	

Wages Payable

| | 9,000 |
| | 300 |

Work-in-Process Inventory

1,000	?
?	
9,000	
?	
500	

Manufacturing Overhead

50	?
?	
18,000	
4,500	
	0

Cost of Goods Sold

| ? | |

E2-4A. Prime Cost and Conversion Cost Piper Consulting Company incurred the following:

Direct labor	$ 45,000
Overhead	90,000
Selling expenses	40,000
Administrative expenses	100,000

Calculate prime cost and conversion cost for Piper Consulting Company.

E2-5A. Product Cost Flows Number the following activities from 1 to 5 in the order corresponding to the typical flow of cost in a manufacturing company:

___ Record the transfer of raw materials into production.

___ Record cost of goods sold.

___ Record the completion of production of inventory.

___ Record the application of manufacturing overhead.

___ Record the purchase of raw materials.

E2-6A. Schedule of Cost of Goods Manufactured and Sold At December 31, the end of its fiscal year, Lederman Manufacturing Corporation collected the following data:

Materials inventory, January 1	$ 25,000
Materials inventory, December 31	15,000
Work-in-process inventory, January 1	30,000
Work-in-process inventory, December 31	41,000
Finished goods inventory, January 1	51,000
Finished goods inventory, December 31	36,000
Net delivered cost of materials purchased	150,000
Direct labor	148,000
Indirect materials	12,000
Indirect labor	37,000
Factory supplies used	10,000
Factory depreciation	65,000
Factory repairs and maintenance	21,000
Selling expenses (total)	62,000
Non-factory administrative expenses (total)	58,000

Prepare a schedule of cost of goods manufactured and sold for Lederman Manufacturing Corporation for the year ended December 31, assuming that there were no other manufacturing overhead items than those listed above.

E2-7A. Schedule of Cost of Goods Manufactured Sydney Company reported the following amounts for October:

Beginning raw materials inventory	$ 80,000
Beginning work-in-process inventory	140,000
Beginning finished goods inventory	500,000
Raw materials purchases	570,000
Wages paid	310,000
Applied manufacturing overhead	900,000
Ending raw materials inventory	100,000
Ending work-in-process inventory	200,000
Ending finished good inventory	450,000

Use Excel to prepare a schedule of cost of goods manufactured for October.

LO3   **E2-8A.   Schedule of Cost of Goods Sold** Sydney Company reported the following amounts for October:

Beginning raw materials inventory	$ 80,000
Beginning work-in-process inventory	140,000
Beginning finished goods inventory	500,000
Raw materials purchases	570,000
Wages paid	310,000
Applied manufacturing overhead	900,000
Ending raw materials inventory	100,000
Ending work-in-process inventory	200,000
Ending finished good inventory	450,000

Use Excel to prepare a schedule of cost of goods sold for October.

LO3   **E2-9A.   Cost of Goods Manufactured and Cost of Goods Sold** For each of the following unrelated companies, compute the cost of goods manufactured and the cost of goods sold:

	A	B	C
Selling expenses	$ 500	$ 800	$ 600
Factory insurance	260	245	140
Ending finished goods inventory	810	750	515
Non-factory administrative expenses	250	450	350
Direct labor	2,560	2,760	2,120
Beginning materials inventory	520	670	350
Beginning work-in-process inventory	1,120	840	1,070
Indirect materials used	390	420	230
Factory utilities	240	275	150
Factory depreciation	730	760	380
Ending work-in-process inventory	1,360	790	950
Ending materials inventory	440	710	410
Indirect labor	425	280	160
Beginning finished goods inventory	850	725	480
Factory repairs and maintenance	215	230	175
Net delivered cost of materials purchased	3,140	4,410	2,870
Factory supplies used	330	310	210

LO3   **E2-10A.   Income Statement** Lederman Manufacturing Corporation (see E2-6A) sold 14,000 units of product for $45 each during the year. During the year, 5,000 shares of common stock were outstanding. Prepare an income statement for the year (ignore income taxes). Calculate earnings per share.

LO4   **E2-11A.   Entries for Product Cost Flow** The following transactions occurred during January for Richards Manufacturing Company:

Jan.   5   Acquired $4,500 of materials on account that will be used to produce product for resale.

11   Requisitioned $3,750 of materials for use as direct materials in the factory.

16   Completed the manufacturing of products with a total product cost of $15,000 and transferred them to the warehouse.

Record these transactions in general journal form. Assume that Richards Manufacturing Company uses the perpetual inventory system.

LO4   **E2-12A.   Entries for Product Cost Flow** Record the following transactions that occurred during March for Harris Manufacturing Company, which uses the perpetual inventory system:

Mar.   12   Transferred $5,000 of completed goods from the factory to the warehouse.

15   Requisitioned $3,000 of materials for use in the factory as direct materials and $500 for indirect materials.

18   Sold goods costing $4,000 for $6,000 on account.

EXERCISES—SET B

E2-1B. Cost Classification Classify each of the following costs relative to the cost object "patient" for a medical office:

LO1

	Product or Period	Variable, Fixed, or Mixed	Direct or Indirect
Nurse salaries.			
Receptionist salary			
Depreciation on exam room computers			
Health insurance for administrative staff.			
Subscription to patient management software service.			
Office lease expense			
Gloves, swabs, and other medical supplies			

E2-2B. Cost Classification Classify each of the following costs relative to the cost object "customer" for a new car dealer:

LO1

	Product or Period	Variable, Fixed, or Mixed	Direct or Indirect
Salesperson wages			
Dealership manager salary			
Depreciation on showroom furniture.			
Cost of automobiles			
Online advertising.			
Cost of new car prep			
Showroom lease expense			

E2-3B. Product Cost Flows Complete the following T-accounts:

LO2, 3

Materials Inventory

?	
20,000	?
	19,900
300	

Wages Payable

| | 15,000 |
| | ? |

Work-in-Process Inventory

2,000	?
?	
?	
32,000	
5,000	

Manufacturing Overhead

300	?
?	
27,000	
3,900	
	0

Cost of Goods Sold

| 65,900 | |

E2-4B. Prime Cost and Conversion Cost Benton Engineering Services Company incurred the following during the year:

LO2

Direct labor.	$ 60,000
Overhead	110,000
Selling expenses	56,000
Administrative expenses.	95,000

Calculate prime cost and conversion cost for Benton Engineering Services Company.

LO2, 3 **E2-5B.** **Service Cost Flows** Number the following activities from 1 to 3 in the order corresponding to the typical flow of cost in a CPA firm.

____ Record the time worked on a client project by professional staff.

____ Record the completion of a client project.

____ Record the application of office overhead.

LO3 **E2-6B.** **Schedule of Cost of Goods Manufactured and Sold** At December 31, the end of its fiscal year, Kelly Metal Products Corporation collected the following data:

Materials inventory, January 1	$ 32,000
Materials inventory, December 31	22,000
Work-in-process inventory, January 1	34,000
Work-in-process inventory, December 31	45,000
Finished goods inventory, January 1	21,000
Finished goods inventory, December 31	18,000
Net delivered cost of materials purchased	210,000
Direct labor	190,000
Indirect materials	13,000
Indirect labor	25,000
Factory supplies used	12,000
Factory depreciation	78,000
Factory repairs and maintenance	28,000
Selling expenses (total)	63,000
Non-factory administrative expenses (total)	57,000

Required

Prepare a schedule of cost of goods manufactured and sold for Kelly Metal Products Corporation for the year ended December 31, assuming that there were no other manufacturing overhead items than those listed above.

LO3 **E2-7B.** **Schedule of Cost of Goods Manufactured** Brooklyn Company reported the following amounts for October:

Beginning raw materials inventory	$ 40,000
Beginning work-in-process inventory	70,000
Beginning finished goods inventory	250,000
Raw materials purchases	285,000
Wages paid	155,000
Applied manufacturing overhead	450,000
Ending raw materials inventory	50,000
Ending work-in-process inventory	100,000
Ending finished goods inventory	225,000

Use Excel to prepare a schedule of cost of goods manufactured for October.

LO3 **E2-8B.** **Schedule of Cost of Goods Sold** Brooklyn Company reported the following amounts for October:

Beginning raw materials inventory	$ 40,000
Beginning work-in-process inventory	70,000
Beginning finished goods inventory	250,000
Raw materials purchases	285,000
Wages paid	155,000
Applied manufacturing overhead	450,000
Ending raw materials inventory	50,000
Ending work-in-process inventory	100,000
Ending finished goods inventory	225,000

Use Excel to prepare a schedule of cost of goods sold for October.

E2-9B. Cost of Goods Manufactured and Cost of Goods Sold For each of the following unrelated columns of data for the year, compute the cost of goods manufactured and the cost of goods sold: **LO3**

	A	B	C
Selling expenses	$ 600	$ 700	$ 900
Factory insurance	180	270	300
Ending finished goods inventory	620	660	930
Non-factory administrative expenses	300	400	800
Direct labor	2,130	2,850	3,160
Beginning materials inventory	425	575	850
Beginning work-in-process inventory	840	920	1,290
Indirect materials used	270	325	520
Factory utilities	350	360	500
Factory depreciation	820	740	965
Ending work-in-process inventory	790	985	1,425
Ending materials inventory	385	610	820
Indirect labor	225	410	365
Beginning finished goods inventory	565	680	950
Factory repairs and maintenance	330	250	415
Net delivered cost of materials purchased	2,780	3,620	8,170
Factory supplies used	210	230	260

E2-10B. Income Statement Kelly Metal Products Corporation (see E2-6B) sold 18,000 units of product for $40 each. During the year, 10,000 shares of common stock were outstanding. Prepare an income statement for the year (ignore income taxes). Calculate earnings per share.   **LO3**

E2-11B. Entries for Product Cost Flow The following transactions occurred during February for Thompson Manufacturing Company: **LO4**

Feb. 10 Acquired $10,000 of materials on account that will be used to produce product for resale.

    11 Requisitioned $8,000 of materials for use as direct materials in the factory.

    16 Completed the manufacturing of products with a total product cost of $48,000 and transferred them to the warehouse.

Record these transactions in general journal form. Assume that Thompson Manufacturing Company uses the perpetual inventory system.

E2-12B. Entries for Product Cost Flow Record the following transactions that occurred during April for Boyd Manufacturing Corporation, which uses the perpetual inventory system: **LO4**

Apr. 21 Transferred $160,000 of completed goods from the factory to the warehouse.

    25 Requisitioned $90,000 of materials for use in the factory as direct materials and $20,000 for indirect materials.

    28 Sold goods costing $60,000 for $100,000 on account.

PROBLEMS—SET A

P2-1A. Schedule of Cost of Goods Manufactured and Sold The following amounts are available for Bourne Manufacturing Company: **LO3**

Administrative salaries (non-factory)	$ 70,000
Administrative rent (non-factory)	35,000
Advertising and promotion expense	41,000
Depreciation—administrative	22,000
Depreciation—factory	30,000
Depreciation—selling	17,000
Direct labor	175,000
Factory rent	18,000
Factory supplies used	12,000
Finished goods inventory (January 1)	57,000
Finished goods inventory (December 31)	50,000
Indirect materials used	14,000
Indirect labor	19,000
Materials inventory (January 1)	15,000
Materials inventory (December 31)	20,000
Net delivered cost of materials purchased	138,000
Other factory overhead	26,000
Sales	845,000
Sales salaries expense	72,000
Work-in-process inventory (January 1)	18,000
Work-in-process inventory (December 31)	20,000

Required
Using the above data, prepare a schedule of cost of goods manufactured and sold.

LO3

P2-2A. Cost of Goods Manufactured and Sold The following data relate to three independent production periods of Riverside Manufacturing Company. Missing data are indicated by question marks.

	A	B	C
Materials:			
Beginning inventory	$ 52	$ 164	$110
Purchases	?	700	500
Ending inventory	74	100	?
Total materials used	330	?	440
Direct labor	580	960	800
Manufacturing overhead:			
Indirect materials	96	?	120
Indirect labor	160	150	350
Other	?	200	340
Total manufacturing overhead	520	480	?
Work-in-process inventories:			
Beginning	?	90	260
Ending	70	?	100
Finished goods inventories:			
Beginning	?	400	80
Ending	335	120	330
Cost of goods manufactured	1,384	?	?
Cost of goods sold	1,339	2,324	?

Required
Using the above data, determine the missing amounts. (You should set up a schedule of cost of goods manufactured and sold, fill in the known data, and calculate the missing amounts.)

LO3

P2-3A. Total Manufacturing Cost, Income Statement, Unit Cost, and Selling Price Two inventors, recently organized as Innovation, Inc., consult you regarding a planned new product. They have estimates of the annual costs of materials, labor, overhead, and other expenses but need to know how much to charge for each unit to earn a profit equal to 15% of their estimated total long-term investment of $400,000 (ignore income taxes). Their plans indicate that each unit of the new product requires the following:

Direct materials	4 lbs. of a material costing $5/lb.
Direct labor	2 hrs. of a metal former's time at $11/hr.
	0.6 hr. of an assembler's time at $8/hr.

Major items of production overhead would be annual rent of $46,460 for a factory building, $28,660 rent for machinery, and $21,700 of indirect materials. Other production overhead is estimated to be $233,280. Selling expenses are an estimated 30% of total sales, and non-factory administrative expenses are 20% of total sales.

The consensus at Innovation is that during the year, 10,000 units of product should be produced for selling and another 2,000 units should be produced for the next year's beginning inventory. Also, an extra 3,000 pounds of materials will be purchased as beginning inventory for the next year. Because of the nature of the manufacturing process, all units started must be completed, so work-in-process inventories are negligible.

Required

a. Incorporate the above data into a schedule of estimated total manufacturing costs and compute the unit production cost for the year.
b. Prepare an estimated income statement that would provide the target amount of profit for the year.
c. What unit sales price should Innovation charge for the new product?

P2-4A. Journal Entries Taylor Manufacturing Company uses the perpetual inventory system to record transactions related to its manufacturing inventories. The following transactions occurred during March: **LO4**

Mar. 6 Recorded the payroll: $5,000 of direct labor and $1,000 of indirect labor.
8 Received $7,000 of materials and components that had been ordered on account.
10 Completed product costing $11,000 and transferred it to the warehouse. Requisitioned $2,500 of materials for use in the factory; $2,000 was used as direct materials and the remainder was used as indirect materials.
12 Sold on account product costing $1,500 for $2,250.
15 Applied $3,000 of manufacturing overhead cost to the product currently being worked on.
21 Paid $250 cash for a special material component that was shipped via overnight delivery.
27 Sold product costing $1,450 for $2,500 cash.

Required
Prepare general journal entries to record these transactions.

P2-5A. Journal Entries Paulson Manufacturing Company uses the perpetual inventory system to account for its manufacturing inventories. The following are Paulson's transactions during July: **LO4**

July 5 Received materials costing $3,000 from a supplier. The materials were purchased on account.
9 Requisitioned $9,000 of materials for use in the factory, consisting of $7,500 of direct materials and $1,500 of indirect materials.
11 Recorded the factory payroll: $20,250 of direct labor and $2,250 of indirect labor.
17 Incurred various overhead costs totaling $21,000. (Credit Accounts Payable.)
20 Applied $30,000 of manufacturing overhead to the products being manufactured.
23 Completed product costing $20,000 and moved it to the warehouse.
26 Sold goods with a product cost of $4,500 on account for $7,500.

Required

a. Set up T-accounts for the following four accounts and post the July 1 balances: Materials Inventory, $10,500; Work-in-Process Inventory, $37,500; Finished Goods Inventory, $15,000; and Cost of Goods Sold, $45,000.
b. Record the transactions listed above in general journal form, post relevant portions to the four T-accounts, and balance the four accounts.

PROBLEMS—SET B

LO3   **P2-1B.   Schedule of Cost of Goods Manufactured and Sold** The following amounts are available for Bishop Manufacturing Company:

Administrative salaries (non-factory)	$ 85,000
Administrative rent (non-factory)	47,000
Advertising and promotion expense	93,000
Depreciation—administrative	77,000
Depreciation—factory	95,000
Depreciation—selling	36,000
Direct labor	325,000
Factory rent	68,000
Factory supplies used	23,000
Finished goods inventory (January 1)	61,000
Finished goods inventory (December 31)	65,000
Indirect materials used	27,000
Indirect labor	44,000
Materials inventory (January 1)	22,000
Materials inventory (December 31)	27,000
Net delivered cost of materials purchased	210,000
Other factory overhead	55,000
Sales	938,000
Sales salaries expense	71,000
Work-in-process inventory (January 1)	33,000
Work-in-process inventory (December 31)	25,000

Required

Using the above data, prepare a schedule of cost of goods manufactured and sold.

LO3   **P2-2B.   Cost of Goods Manufactured and Sold** The following data relate to three independent production periods of Randolph Manufacturing Company. Missing data are indicated by question marks.

	A	B	C
Materials:			
Beginning inventory	$ 78	$ 410	$ 220
Purchases	?	1,750	1,000
Ending inventory	111	250	?
Total materials used	495	?	880
Direct labor	870	2,400	1,600
Manufacturing overhead:			
Indirect materials	144	?	110
Indirect labor	240	375	700
Other	?	500	680
Total manufacturing overhead	780	1,100	?
Work-in-process inventories:			
Beginning	?	225	520
Ending	105	?	200
Finished goods inventories:			
Beginning	?	1,000	160
Ending	495	300	660
Cost of goods manufactured	2,076	?	?
Cost of goods sold	2,016	5,275	?

Required

Using the above data, determine the missing amounts. (You should set up a schedule of cost of goods manufactured and sold, fill in the known data, and calculate the missing amounts.)

LO3   **P2-3B.   Total Manufacturing Costs, Income Statement, Unit Cost, and Selling Price** You are consulted by Investors, Inc., a group of investors planning a new product. They have estimates of the costs of materials, labor, overhead, and other expenses for the year but need to know how much to charge

for each unit to earn a profit equal to 10% of their estimated investment of $500,000 (ignore income taxes).

Their plans indicate that each unit of the new product requires the following:

Direct Materials	4 lbs. of a material costing $6/lb.
Direct Labor	3 hrs. of a die cutter's time at $9/hr.
	2 hrs. of an assembler's time at $8/hr.

Major items of production overhead would be annual rent of $40,000 on the factory building and $25,000 on machinery as well as indirect materials of $21,000. Other production overhead is an estimated 60% of total direct labor costs. Selling expenses are an estimated 20% of total sales, and nonfactory administrative expenses are 10% of total sales.

The consensus at Investors is that 4,000 units of product should be produced for selling and another 1,000 units should be produced for the next year's beginning inventory. Also, an extra 6,000 pounds of materials will be purchased as beginning inventory for the next year. Because of the nature of the manufacturing process, all units started must be completed, so work-in-process inventories are negligible.

Required
a. Incorporate the above data into a schedule of estimated total manufacturing costs and compute the unit production cost.
b. Prepare an estimated income statement that would provide the target amount of profit.
c. What unit sales price should Investors charge for the new product?

P2-4B. Journal Entries Travis Manufacturing Company uses the perpetual inventory system to record transactions related to its manufacturing inventories. The following transactions occurred during August: **LO4**

Aug. 5 Received $4,500 of materials and components that had been ordered on account.
    7 Recorded the payroll: $3,250 of direct labor and $750 of indirect labor.
   11 Sold on account product costing $1,750 for $2,600.
   16 Completed product costing $8,000 and transferred it to the warehouse.
   20 Requisitioned $3,500 of materials for use in the factory; $2,950 was used as direct materials and the remainder was used as indirect materials.
   25 Applied $5,000 of manufacturing overhead cost to the product currently being worked on.
   29 Paid $200 cash for a special material component that was shipped via overnight delivery.
   31 Sold product costing $500 for $850 cash.

Required
Prepare general journal entries to record these transactions.

P2-5B. Journal Entries Porter Manufacturing Company uses the perpetual inventory system to account for its manufacturing inventories. The following are Porter's transactions during September: **LO4**

Sept. 5 Received materials costing $4,500 from a supplier. The materials were purchased on account.
   9 Requisitioned $10,500 of materials for use in the factory, consisting of $8,400 of direct materials and $2,100 of indirect materials.
   11 Recorded the factory payroll: $21,000 of direct labor and $3,000 of indirect labor.
   17 Incurred various overhead costs totaling $22,500. (Credit Accounts Payable.)
   20 Applied $31,500 of manufacturing overhead to the products being manufactured.
   23 Completed product costing $25,500 and moved it to the warehouse.
   26 Sold goods with a product cost of $6,000 on account for $8,000.

Required
a. Set up a T-account for the following four accounts and post the September 1 balance listed after the account title: Materials Inventory, $8,000; Work-in-Process Inventory, $26,000; Finished Goods Inventory, $11,000; and Cost of Goods Sold, $32,000.
b. Record the transactions listed above in general journal form, post relevant portions to the four T-accounts, and balance the four accounts.

EXTENDING YOUR KNOWLEDGE

LO3   **EYK2-1. Business Decision Case** James Alvarez, an engineer, needs some accounting advice. In their spare time during the past year, Alvarez and his college-aged son, Robert, have manufactured a small weed-trimming sickle in a rented building near their home. Robert, who has had one accounting course in college, keeps the books.

Alvarez is pleased about the results of their first year's operations. He asks you to look over the following income report prepared by Robert before they leave on a well-deserved vacation to Hawaii, after which they plan to expand their business significantly.

Sales (34,000 units at $10 each)		$340,000
Costs of producing 35,000 units:		
Materials:		
Precast blades at $1.50 each	$ 57,000	
Preturned handles at $1 each	40,000	
Labor costs of hired assemblers	26,600	
Labor costs of hired painters	33,000	
Rent on building	14,900	
Rent on machinery	7,100	
Utilities for production	8,000	
Other production costs	11,900	
Advertising expense	26,200	
Sales commissions	35,700	
Delivery of products to customers	14,350	
Total costs	$274,750	
Less: Ending inventory of 1,000 units at average production		
costs of $7.85 (or $274,750/35,000 units)	7,850	
Cost of goods sold		266,900
Net income		$ 73,100

After you examine the income report, Alvarez responds to your questions and assures you that (1) no theft or spoilage of materials has occurred, (2) no partially completed units are involved, and (3) he and his son Robert have averaged 30 hours each per week in the business for 50 weeks (ignore income taxes).

Required
a.   Identify any apparent discrepancy in the income report in the cost of materials used.
b.   Recalculate the cost of goods manufactured, the average cost per unit produced, and the net income for the year.
c.   What factors should James consider regarding the profitability of his venture before deciding to expand it significantly?

LO2   **EYK2-2. Apple's 2021 Environmental Responsibility Report can be found at the following link:**

https://www.apple.com/environment/pdf/Apple_Environmental_Progress_Report_2021.pdf

Skim this report. Why do you think Apple is so transparent with regard to its environmental activity but so secretive regarding its product development?

LO2   **EYK2-3. Ethics Case** Great Cakes is a large bakery known for its quality "boxed cake" products. Its motto

is "We Use Only the Best Ingredients." Ralph Sands, the purchasing supervisor, is responsible for ordering the ingredients for all the bakery products. He is being considered for a promotion based on his proven ability to purchase ingredients at the best price available.

The cost of all the ingredients has risen substantially over the past few months. Sands decides to purchase 25% of the ingredients at a lower quality than Great Cakes normally uses because the cost is significantly less. Without relying on the company's test kitchens, he believes this substitution will not be noticed by the customers and the lower cost will counterbalance the increased costs of the other ingredients.

Sands explains this decision to his friend, Lynn Pall, the company's accountant, one day at lunch. He also tells her that he does not intend to inform management of the inclusion of the lower-quality ingredients in the bakery's products.

Required
What ethical considerations arise from Ralph Sands' decisions? What problems face Lynn Pall because of his actions?

ANSWERS TO SELF-STUDY QUESTIONS:

1. c   2. d   3. b   4. b   5. a

YOUR TURN! SOLUTIONS

Solution 2.1

	Product or Period	Variable, Fixed, or Mixed	Direct or Indirect
Assembly labor	Product	Variable	Direct
iPad case	Product	Variable	Direct
CEO salary	Period	Fixed	Indirect
Microprocessor	Product	Variable	Direct
Depreciation on Apple corporate headquarters	Period	Fixed	Indirect
Health insurance for factory workers	Product	Fixed	Indirect
Touch screen	Product	Variable	Direct
Adhesive on the serial number label	Product	Variable	Indirect

Solution 2.2

c.

Solution 2.3

Direct materials:		
Beginning balance	$ 200	
Purchases	1,400	
Cost of materials available	$1,600	
Less ending inventory	300	
Direct materials used		$1,300
Direct labor		1,200
Manufacturing overhead		900
Total manufacturing cost		$3,400
Add beginning work-in-process inventory		$ 600
Total cost of work-in-process		$4,000
Less ending work-in-process inventory		($500)
Cost of goods manufactured		**$3,500**

Solution 2.4

a.	Raw materials inventory	1,400	
	Cash or accounts payable		1,400
b.	Work-in-process inventory	1,300	
	Raw materials inventory		1,300
c.	Work-in-process inventory	1,200	
	Wages payable		1,200
d.	Work-in-process inventory	900	
	Manufacturing overhead		900
e.	Finished goods inventory	3,500	
	Work-in-process inventory		3,500
f.	Cost of goods sold	3,300	
	Finished goods inventory		3,300

Chapter 3
Cost Accounting Systems: Job Order Costing

Road Map

LO	Learning Objective	Page	eLecture	Guided Example	Assignments
LO1	Describe the two basic types of cost accounting systems, discuss how they may be used in both manufacturing and nonmanufacturing environments, and explain the need for the timely determination of product costs.	3-3	E3-1	YT3.1	SS1, Q1, Q2, Q3, Q4, SE1
LO2	Explain the need for a predetermined overhead rate and demonstrate its calculation.	3-5	E3-2	YT3.2	SS2, Q5, Q6, Q7, Q8, Q9, SE2, SE3, SE4, E1A, E2A, E3A, E6A, E7A, E1B, E2B, E3B, E6B, E7B, P1A, P2A, P1B, P2B
LO3	Describe and explain a job order costing system, identify types of records used in job order costing, and demonstrate the journal entries that accompany the flow of product costs.	3-7	E3-3	YT3.3	SS3, SS4, Q10, Q11, Q12, E4A, E5A, E4B, E5B, P1A, P3A, P4A, P5A, P6A, P7A, P1B, P3B, P4B, P5B, P6B, P7B
LO4	Discuss the procedures and journal entries used to account for finished goods and the sale of finished goods.	3-13	E3-4	YT3.4	SS4, SS5, Q13, Q14, Q15, SE5, SE6, SE7, E6A, E7A, E8A, E9A, E10A, E11A, E12A, E6B, E7B, E8B, E9B, E10B, E11B, E12B, P2A, P4A, P5A, P6A, P7A, P2B, P4B, P5B, P6B, P7B
LO5	Contrast plant-wide overhead rates and departmental overhead rates.	3-18	E3-5	YT3.5	SS6, Q16, Q17, SE8

CH2M is a U.S.-based consulting, design, construction, operation, and program management service firm that provides services to clients worldwide. CH2M has performed thousands of projects on six continents and in more than 180 countries. CH2M Hill's projects are typically very large and complex. These have included the Panama Canal Expansion Program, a project to replace the entire sanitary sewer system for the country of Singapore, and the deconstruction of the Maine Yankee Atomic Power Company.

As you think about the massive scale of these projects, you might wonder how CH2M Hill keeps track of all of the costs (materials, labor, and overhead) incurred over weeks, months, and even years. To properly track the costs and customer billings associated with each of its projects, CH2M Hill must use some very sophisticated job order costing systems.

This chapter describes one of two basic types of cost accounting systems—called job order costing.

PAST

Chapter 2 defined basic costing terminology and introduced different types of manufacturing inventories. It illustrated how costs flow through the inventories and explained the schedule of cost of goods manufactured.

PRESENT

Chapter 3 introduces and explains job costing in more detail for both manufacturing and service industries. It also explains overhead allocation.

FUTURE

Chapter 4 introduces process costing and how it differs from job order costing. It illustrates equivalent units and the flow of costs through the inventory accounts, as well as introduces the production cost report.

COST ACCOUNTING SYSTEMS: JOB ORDER COSTING

Cost Accounting Systems	Predetermined Overhead Rates	Job Order Costing Systems	Departmental Overhead Rates
• Two Basic Types of Cost Accounting Systems • Timely Product Costing	• Calculation of Predetermined Overhead Rate	• Illustration of Job Order Costing for a Manufacturer • Illustration of Job Order Costing for a Service Firm	• Departmental Rates

COST ACCOUNTING SYSTEMS

LO1 **Describe** the two basic types of cost accounting systems, **discuss** how they may be used in both manufacturing and nonmanufacturing environments, and **explain** the need for the timely determination of product costs.

eLecture

MBC

Virtually all manufacturing and service firms have a cost accounting system consisting of forms, procedures, and records used to develop and report timely information about product and service costs. Any orderly method of developing product or service cost information constitutes a cost accounting system. Typically, some amount of cost is accumulated and related to some unit of activity or accomplishment. Examples include accumulating the cost of cutting and forming materials, assembling parts, and painting the final product that results in a completed unit of product such as a lawnmower, a computer, or a custom-designed executive jet aircraft, or the costs associated with CH2M Hill's overseeing the widening of the Panama Canal. Although a cost accounting system could be maintained independently of a firm's formal accounting system, most comprehensive cost accounting systems are integrated into the formal accounting system.

Cost accounting systems are usually illustrated for manufacturing situations involving product costs per unit. Note, however, that reliable cost-per-unit-of-production information is vital to managerial decision-making in all types of entities, including service firms and governmental units. For example, a hospital may need to know the cost per patient of providing a specific surgical procedure, an insurance company may want to know the cost of providing health care insurance to a particular group, and a city may need to know the cost per ton of trash removal. Many of the cost accounting concepts and techniques that we discuss in this and subsequent chapters therefore apply to nonmanufacturing as well as manufacturing entities.

Two Basic Types of Cost Accounting Systems

Job order costing systems and process costing systems are designed to develop timely information about product and job costs, manufacturing inventories, and per-unit costs.

A **job order costing system** is used for *customized* products and services. Therefore, job order costing is characterized by a series of *unique products* or *jobs* undertaken either to fill specific orders from customers or to produce a general stock of products from which future customer orders are filled. In a job order costing system, the costs of direct materials, direct labor, and manufacturing overhead are accumulated separately for each job or product, as illustrated in **Exhibit 3-1**.

Job order costing is used by construction companies (to accumulate the cost of each construction project), printing companies (to track the cost of each printing job), manufacturers of custom products (to determine the cost per unit of each product manufactured), and

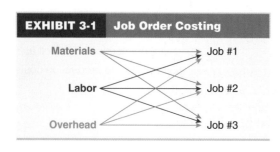

EXHIBIT 3-1   Job Order Costing

hospitals (to determine the cost per patient). For example, CH2M Hill keeps track of the costs associated with its Singapore project separately from those associated with its Panama project.

A **process costing system** (**Exhibit 3-2**) lends itself to the production of a *large volume* of *homogenous products* manufactured in a continual flow operation, such as the distillation of fuels or manufacture of paint or wire. In these manufacturing contexts, the materials and operations are involved repetitively during each manufacturing period. Direct materials, direct labor, and manufacturing overhead are accumulated by a production department or process for a period and then divided by the units produced during that period to calculate a per-unit cost. Assembly-line operations of entities such as breweries or flour mills and mass-production operations such as power plants and chemical companies would use process costing.

EXHIBIT 3-2   Process Costing

Job order costing and process costing are two extremes along the spectrum of costing systems. A company will design its own accounting system to fit its particular needs. Many companies blend ideas from both job order costing and process costing systems.

ACCOUNTING IN PRACTICE   Choosing a Cost Accounting System

Both job order and process costing systems allocate materials, labor, and overhead costs to determine unit costs. In a job order system, costs are identified with specific jobs or products, but a process costing system identifies costs with production processes and averages them over all jobs completed or products made during the period. The type of cost accounting system used by a particular company depends on the nature of the company's operations. One company may, in fact, use job order costing to account for one part of its operation and use process costing to account for another part of its operation. For example, Fezzari Performance Bicycles (introduced in Chapter 1) uses job costing for each unique bike order received. Yet, the manufacture of bicycle frames is accounted for using process costing because each frame of a particular size and model is identical.

Timely Product Costing
Manufacturing Firms

A cost accounting system—either job order costing or process costing—must provide for the timely determination of product costs. Companies need to calculate product costs to determine work-in-process and finished goods inventory balances, which they report in periodic financial statements. In order to accurately calculate income, companies must develop a way to identify product costs for products sold and for products that remain on hand, either finished or unfinished. Product costing is also used to develop budgets and control production costs.

To identify costs with a product or group of products, a manufacturer must trace production costs—direct materials, direct labor, and manufacturing overhead—to products. To account for materials used, a company may keep track of the costs of materials requisitioned for production by job, product, or department. Labor costs can similarly be accounted for based on timekeeping records or by identifying a particular product or job with total payroll costs of personnel in the factory production departments. A manufacturing firm cannot, however, directly determine the amount of manufacturing overhead that should be identified with particular products or a group of products. The reason is quite simple: Overhead costs are accumulated during a particular accounting period, but it is impossible to know exactly how much overhead cost will accumulate until the *end* of the period. The problem is that companies need to assign product costs *during* the period *before* total overhead costs can be determined for the period. It isn't feasible to wait until the end of the period to determine total product costs to bill customers for jobs completed during the period. Consequently, firms typically assign manufacturing overhead costs to products during the period based on estimates by using predetermined overhead rates.

SERVICE AND MERCHANDISING

Service Firms

The same principles apply to a service company like CH2M Hill. CH2M Hill is also interested in the timely determination of the costs of its projects (or jobs) in order to prepare periodic financial reports and determine income or loss on each project.

Because CH2M Hill's projects typically extend more than a year in length, it is likely that it will have many projects that are in process at the end of each reporting period. Project managers may help to establish budgets, compare budgets to actual results, and take action to control project costs.

For example, the Panama Canal Expansion Program required CH2M Hill to trace labor costs for assigned project managers, engineers, and other consultants to this project over the course of several years. These individuals' salaries and benefits were assigned directly to the project for the period of their involvement on the project team. In addition, CH2M Hill traced other direct project costs to the project, such as team member travel, lodging, and meals incurred while working on the project. Corporate overhead was assigned to the project on a monthly basis to allow management to determine project profitability at any point in time.

ENVIRONMENTAL, SOCIAL, AND GOVERNANCE	Shortage of Highly Trained Engineers

As was noted in the opening vignette, CH2M Hill manages some massive engineering projects. Projects of this size and complexity involve many highly trained engineers. A problem that companies like CH2M Hill face is the acute shortage of engineering talent, especially among women, Hispanics, and African Americans, groups that will comprise a large percentage of the future workforce. As part of its corporate responsibility initiative, CH2M Hill is doing something about this pressing problem.

CH2M Hill believes that "today's children are tomorrow's leaders" is a core tenet of sustainability. The company also understands how important it is to invest in future generations and to mentor them toward careers in engineering and science. CH2M Hill offers summer programs at no cost to the families that introduce their children to these important fields of study. As John Madia, CH2M Hill's chief human resources officer, states, "For most kids, particularly children of color and girls, STEM [Science, Technology, Engineering, and Mathematics] learning opens minds and doors where they have few role models. In helping to grow a diverse pool of future talent, our firm benefits by putting into practice our values of creating partnerships to help sustain and build better communities."

Source: CH2M Hill 2014 Sustainability and Corporate Citizenship Report

---

YOUR TURN! 3.1

The solution is on page 3-40.

GuidedExample

MBC

Which costing system (job order or process) would most likely be used by the following industries?
   Production of chemicals in large batches
   Custom printing of wedding announcements or marketing materials
   Construction of commercial aircraft
   Refining of crude oil into gas and other products for retail sale
   Production of exterior or interior paint for the DIY market
   Production of glass windows for use in residential construction
   Construction of custom furniture
   Construction of large machinery used for producing integrated circuits for the computer industry

---

PREDETERMINED OVERHEAD RATES

LO2 Explain the need for a predetermined overhead rate and **demonstrate** its calculation.

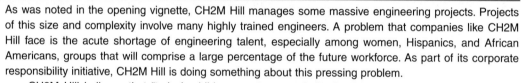

eLecture

MBC

Predetermined manufacturing overhead rates are so named because (1) they are calculated prior to the beginning of each accounting period; (2) they deal with production overhead, that is, all production costs other than direct materials and direct labor; and (3) they are usually stated in terms of a rate, such as $20 per direct labor hour. Recall that the purpose of calculating the predetermined overhead rate is to allow management to estimate total product costs in a timely manner to allow for the establishment of appropriate prices and the evaluation of operating results. Before the beginning of each year, management normally prepares budgets. Included in the total budget is a production budget, which estimates utilization of the firm's productive capacity in terms of a common measure of activity. Traditionally, firms have used volume measures that are already being recorded for other purposes, such as direct labor hours (recorded for payroll) and machine hours (recorded for depreciation). More recently, more sophisticated and detailed measures have been implemented by some firms, as discussed briefly later in this chapter and in more detail in Chapter 5. Also included in the total budget is an estimate of overhead costs for the year.

Calculation of Predetermined Overhead Rate

A **predetermined manufacturing overhead rate** is computed by dividing the budgeted or estimated total overhead cost for the year by the budgeted or estimated level of the application base.

$$\text{Predetermined overhead rate} = \frac{\text{Estimated overhead cost}}{\text{Estimated level of the application base}}$$

The estimated overhead cost is usually computed from the annual budget. The application base is simply the activity used to assign overhead. This application base is generally the **cost driver** most closely related to the accumulation of overhead costs. This cost driver is typically the utilization of the facility's productive capacity for the year (such as total estimated direct labor hours or total estimated machine hours). Calculations of predetermined rates are typically based on one-year production periods, but they could be calculated based on shorter horizons, such as quarterly or monthly production periods. Companies should choose the application base that corresponds to the period over which activity decisions are typically made.

Using a predetermined overhead rate, management can estimate the overhead costs of any job at any stage of production, computing "costs to date" both for control purposes and for inventory costing. This method also eliminates wide fluctuations in unit costs that might result if actual recorded overhead costs were assigned to products during short interim periods when production departed markedly from normal levels.

Assume that the most appropriate measure of activity for applying overhead at CH2M Hill is direct labor hours. If CH2M's management estimates 50 million direct labor hours in a year and the estimated total annual manufacturing overhead cost is $2,200 million, the overhead rate may be calculated as follows:

$$\text{Predetermined overhead rate} = \frac{\text{Estimated overhead cost}}{\text{Estimated direct labor hours}}$$

$$= \frac{\$2,200 \text{ million}}{50 \text{ million hours}}$$

$$= \$44 \text{ per direct labor hour}$$

Hint: Applied overhead is a product of the predetermined overhead rate and actual hours for that job, not budgeted hours.

If, during March, a particular project requires 1,000 direct labor hours, $44,000 of manufacturing overhead (1,000 × $44) would be assigned to this project.

Before selecting the allocation base for applying overhead to products or projects, a firm should carefully analyze the relationship between overhead incurred and various alternative measures of activity. Direct labor hours or direct labor costs would be used as the measure of activity in a service company that has labor-intensive projects. However, in a factory in which automation has replaced many of the production workers, machine hours may be a more appropriate measure.

ACCOUNTING IN PRACTICE   **Multiple Predetermined Overhead Rates**

Often, companies calculate more than one predetermined manufacturing overhead rate for a given period. For example, some firms will calculate a predetermined variable overhead rate and a predetermined fixed overhead rate. Why? Doing so allows management to evaluate a production department's control of costs that are expected to vary with the level of production (often within the control of local management) separately from those costs that are related to the capacity to do work (often fixed in nature and largely out of local management's hands).

TAKEAWAY 3.1	**Concept**	**Method**	**Assessment**
	You have been asked to calculate the predetermined overhead rate for the next operating period.	• Forecast expected total overhead for the period. • Select an application base or cost driver. • Estimate total activity for the cost driver for the period.	Predetermined overhead rate = total estimated overhead divided by the total estimated activity level of the application base (such as machine hours or direct labor hours).

YOUR TURN! 3.2

The solution is on page 3-41.

GuidedExample

MBC

Assume you own a manufacturing company that budgets an estimated $250,000 in overhead for the coming year and 10,000 direct labor hours. Also assume your manufacturing overhead application base is direct labor hours. Actual overhead during the year amounts to $216,000, and employees work 9,000 actual direct labor hours. Compute the predetermined overhead rate and the amount of overhead that is applied to work-in-process inventory.

JOB ORDER COSTING SYSTEMS

LO3   **Describe** and **explain** a job order costing system, **identify** types of records used in job order costing, and **demonstrate** the journal entries that accompany the flow of product costs.

eLecture

MBC

Job order costing systems are designed to accumulate product costs—direct materials, direct labor, and manufacturing overhead—by job and in total. **Exhibit 3-3** illustrates the flow of the documents in a job order costing system that might be used by Fezzari for an order of a high-end triathlon/time-trial bike.

When the customer places the order for the bike, Fezzari would create a **sales order** specifying the bike model and customer-specified options. Based on this sales order, the assembly department would create a **production order** directing the assembly employees to build the bike in accordance with the customer's specifications. Before assembly can begin, the assembly technician must gather the correct parts together. This is done based on a **bill of materials**, or list of each required part for the particular bike model. The technician creates a **materials requisition**, requesting that the bike components on the bill of materials be pulled from inventory and brought to the assembly station. As the technician assembles the bike, she would keep track of her time on a **time record**, either in written form on a timesheet or electronically through a time clock. As the job progresses, the materials used, labor expended, and overhead applied would be accumulated on a **job order cost sheet**. A job order cost sheet is a record of the materials, labor, and overhead for each job and serves as a subsidiary record or subset of the work-in-process account. When the bike is finished, the job order cost sheet would be closed.

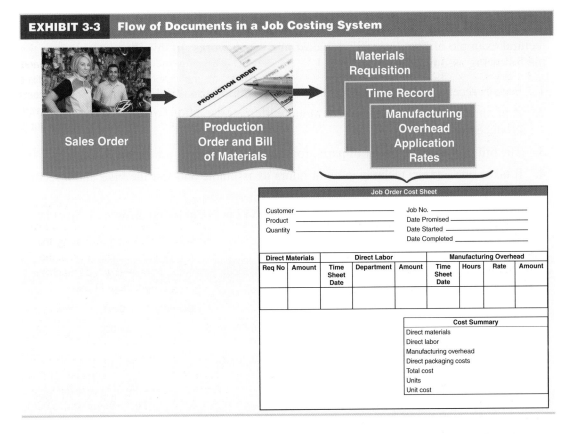

EXHIBIT 3-3   Flow of Documents in a Job Costing System

Illustration of Job Order Costing for a Manufacturer

The U.S. bicycle industry has been remarkably stable at $6 billion in sales since 2003, with a slight dip in 2013 due to the U.S. recession.[1] However, recent events had significant impacts on the sale of bicycles in the U.S. in 2019 and 2020. The first was the imposition of tariffs (Section 301 tariffs) on bicycles and bicycle components imported from China. The second was the surge in demand for bicycles as a result of the COVID-19 pandemic. These events resulted in a severe shortage of bicycles, which continued into 2021. Approximately 15 to 20 million bicycles are sold in the U.S. each year, with about 95% imported from China and Taiwan. Domestic bike manufacturers, over 100 in all, produce approximately 500,000 units per year. The recent surge in demand for bicycles suggests they will continue to be a critical component of America's transportation and recreation future.[2]

Fezzari Performance Bicycles is a U.S. bike manufacturer that builds both mountain bikes and road bikes. Located in Lindon, Utah, it sells a few thousand bikes per year, from a $500 entry-level mountain and hybrid bike to a high-end full-suspension mountain bike and triathlon bike that sells for over $10,000. As described in Chapter 1, once a customer selects a specific bike model and components, Fezzari orders the required parts from its suppliers. Fezzari maintains a minimal quantity of parts in inventory so that the bike assembly can be started without waiting for ordered parts to arrive. A technician assembles the bike to the customer's specifications, tunes it up, and then test rides it to ensure that it works properly. A second technician then checks the assembly, testing every screw and component, then checks the tune-up and performs a second test ride. The bike is then sent to packing to be prepared for shipment.

---

[1] https://nbda.com/articles/industry-overview-2015-pg34.htm
[2] https://wsd-pfb-sparkinfluence.s3.amazonaws.com/uploads/2020/12/2021_tradeagenda_booklet_reducedv1.pdf

We now turn to a comprehensive illustration of job order costing, which provides a conjectural example of how Fezzari's job costing system works. In this illustration, we make the following assumptions:

Hint: A bill of materials is a list of all parts or components needed for the manufacture of the finished product.

1. Fezzari receives a sales order for a high-end triathlon/time-trial bike, the T5.

2. A production order is then issued, along with the related bill of materials necessary to produce the T5.

3. The bill of materials, or list of parts, for the T5 is as shown in **Exhibit 3-4**.

4. It takes one Fezzari technician eight hours to assemble and test the bike and a second technician two hours to perform a quality check.

5. Fezzari uses a predetermined overhead rate of $12 per hour based on annual direct labor hours to assign overhead to products.

EXHIBIT 3-4	**Bill of Materials—T5**			
A	B	C	D	E
Item	**Description**	**Quantity**	**Cost**	**Extension**
Frame	Fezzari Racing Design FA1 3K Monocoque Carbon Aero TT Frame	1	$4,000	$4,000
Fork	Fezzari Racing XrA 3K Aero Fork, Carbon Steerer Tube	1	integrated	
Headset	Cane Creek Orbit IS-2 7075/T6 Crown Race, 1 1/8" Steerer Tube	1	integrated	
Seatpost	Fezzari Racing Design XrTT Aero 3K Carbon	1	integrated	
Shifters, derailleurs, cables	Shimano Dura-Ace 9000, 22 Speed	1	$ 900	$ 900
Cassette	Shimano Dura-Ace 9000	1	$ 170	$ 170
Crank	Vision Trimax Carbon	1	$ 300	$ 300
Chainrings	FSA BB30 Trimax 54/39t	1	$ 60	$ 60
Bottom bracket	FSA BB30 Ceramic	1	$ 30	$ 30
Chain	Shimano Dura-Ace 9000	1	$ 20	$ 20
Handlebars, stem, tape	Vision Trimax Carbon	1	$ 290	$ 290
Saddle	Fizik Arione Tri 2	1	$ 100	$ 100
Wheels	Reynolds 90 Areo, Carbon Clinchers	2	$1,200	$2,400
Tires, including tubes	Maxxis Xenith Hors Categorie M-201, 700 x 23c, race tire	2	$ 90	$ 180
Brakes, levers, cables	Shimano Dura-Ace 9000	2	$ 75	$ 150
				$8,600

Accounting for Materials

For a high-end bike like the T5, Fezzari orders the frame from its Taiwanese supplier and the tires and other components from other local suppliers upon receipt of the order. Thus, the first transaction to record is the *purchase* of materials. Fezzari purchased parts listed on the bill of materials for a total cost of $8,600. Following is the entry to record this purchase:

1	Materials inventory	8,600	
	Accounts payable		8,600
	To record the purchase of materials.		

The next transaction is the *requisition* of the following materials from the materials inventory for use in the production of the T5: $4,000 for the frame, $900 for the shifters, derailleurs, and cables, $170 for the cassette, and so forth. **Exhibit 3-5** shows a sample requisition for a Fezzari T5.

Assume that in addition to the direct materials listed on the bill of materials, the assembly of the T5 requires $30 of indirect materials (lubricants, bar end plugs, etc.). The entry to record the requisitioning and use of both direct and indirect materials is as follows:

2	Work-in-process inventory	8,600	
	Manufacturing overhead	30	
	Materials inventory		8,630
	To record the requisitioning of materials—both direct and indirect.		

EXHIBIT 3-5	Materials Requisition Form				
	A	B	C	D	E
1	Date 8/5	Job. No. 372		Requisition No. 567	
2		Quantity			
3	**Item**	**Authorized**	**Issued**	**Unit Price**	**Amount**
4	Frame	1	1	$4,000	$4,000
5	Fork	1	1	integrated	
6	Headset	1	1	integrated	
7	Seatpost	1	1	integrated	
8	Shifters, derailleurs, cables	1	1	$ 900	$ 900
9	Cassette	1	1	$ 170	$ 170
10	Crank	1	1	$ 300	$ 300
11	Chainrings	1	1	$ 60	$ 60
12	Bottom Bracket	1	1	$ 30	$ 30
13	Chain	1	1	$ 20	$ 20
14	Handlebars, stem, tape	1	1	$ 290	$ 290
15	Saddle	1	1	$ 100	$ 100
16	Wheels	2	2	$1,200	$2,400
17	Tires, including tubes	2	2	$ 90	$ 180
18	Brakes, levers, cables	2	2	$ 75	$ 150
19	Total				$8,600
20	Authorized by: TC Issued by: GAP Received by: CB				

Hint: A materials requisition form is a list of items to be pulled from inventory for use in manufacturing a product.

The effect of the various postings of these transactions is shown in **Exhibit 3-6**. The amount of direct materials used would also be recorded on the job order cost sheet for Job 372 (see **Exhibit 3-10**).

EXHIBIT 3-6	Entries for Recording the Acquisition and Use of Materials

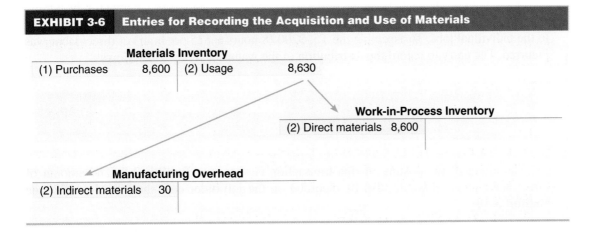

Accounting for Labor

Manufacturing firms (including Fezzari) typically use **time clocks** or time records to collect the total amount of time that each employee worked during a particular pay period. **Exhibit 3-7** shows a sample time record for a Fezzari employee.

Time clocks collect only total time worked; time records collect hours worked on particular jobs. Time clocks and computer time records are used to prepare the payroll recorded in Wages Payable.

Hint: A time record is a method of recording and organizing time spent on a product or job.

EXHIBIT 3-7	**Time Record**						
Employee Name: Robert ....Employee No. 42							
Skill Specification:		Technician		Date:			8/5
Time Started	**Time Stopped**	**Total Time**	**Hourly Labor Rate**	**Department**		**Job No.**	**Total Cost**
8:00	12:00	4	$25	Assembly		372	$100
1:00	5:00	4	$25	Assembly		372	$100
Total		8					$200
Approved by *LSH*							

ACCOUNTING IN PRACTICE	**Tracking Time**

In practice, companies use various methods to track employees' time. Where employees are paid on an hourly-rate basis for hours worked, time clocks are used. In some firms, employees place a small paper card in the time clock at the beginning and end of their work shift, and the card is imprinted (or "punched") with the date and time. More commonly, employees slide or wave an employee ID card through or in front of a card reader that records the date and time information. The most recent innovation in tracking employees' time involves a device that recognizes an employee's fingerprint, iris, or face, eliminating the need for a physical card of any kind. Where employees are salaried, but there is a need to attribute hours worked to a particular job or product for costing purposes, time records are used. Employees record the amount of time that they spend each day working on a particular job or jobs so that customers can be billed the appropriate amount for labor.

Assume that Fezzari uses time records to identify labor costs with specific jobs. Hourly wage rates are used to compute the labor costs for the various products assembled. The sum of the amounts calculated using the time records should equal the total wages payable for the period. In fact, the amounts calculated from the time records are used to distribute the wages payable to the individual jobs. To assemble the T5, $200 (8 hours × $25 per hour) of direct labor was incurred. The entry to record the distribution of the wages payable is as follows:

3	Work-in-process inventory	200	
	Wages payable		200
	To distribute the wages payable.		

The effect of the posting of this transaction is shown in **Exhibit 3-8**. The amount of direct labor incurred would also be recorded on the job order cost sheet for Job 372 (see **Exhibit 3-10**).

EXHIBIT 3-8   **Entries for Recording and Distributing Labor**

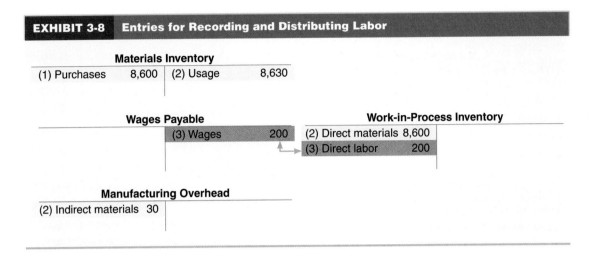

Accounting for Manufacturing Overhead

Factory costs are routinely charged to manufacturing overhead as incurred or through adjusting entries at the end of the accounting period. One of the elements of manufacturing overhead—indirect materials—has already been recorded through the transactions related to materials. Other general manufacturing overhead costs incurred by Fezzari during the period are recorded as they are incurred: indirect labor, $28,000; factory utilities, $31,000; factory lease, $100,000; factory insurance, $68,000; factory property taxes, $12,000; and other manufacturing overhead, $13,000. Manufacturing overhead to be recorded as a year-end adjustment is depreciation on the factory equipment of $45,000. The following are the journal entries to record these items:

4	Manufacturing overhead	252,000	
	Cash, Accounts payable, or Wages payable		252,000
	To record elements of manufacturing overhead as incurred.		

5	Manufacturing overhead	45,000	
	Accumulated depreciation—factory equipment		45,000
	To record depreciation on factory equipment.		

As explained previously, actual manufacturing overhead costs are not assigned directly to individual jobs. Instead, through the use of a predetermined overhead rate, the work-in-process inventory account is charged with manufacturing overhead applied. During the budgeting process, Fezzari determined its predetermined overhead rate to be $12 per direct labor hour. The T5 order accumulated 8 hours of direct labor. As a result, $96 of manufacturing overhead is applied to the job.

The journal entry to record the application of manufacturing overhead to Job 372 is as follows:

6	Work-in-process inventory	96	
	Manufacturing overhead		96
	To record the application of manufacturing overhead to the work-in-process inventory using the predetermined overhead rate.		

The effect of the various postings of these transactions is shown in **Exhibit 3-9**. The amount of overhead applied would also be recorded on the job order cost sheet for Job 372 (see **Exhibit 3-10**).

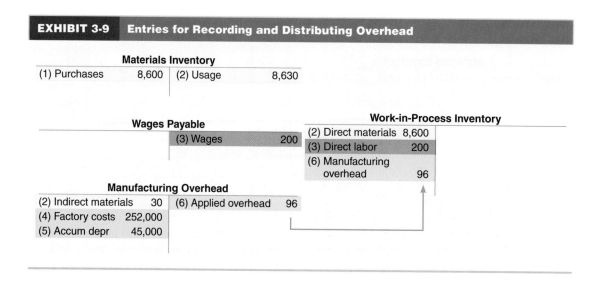

EXHIBIT 3-9   Entries for Recording and Distributing Overhead

Materials Inventory

(1) Purchases	8,600	(2) Usage	8,630

Wages Payable

		(3) Wages	200

Manufacturing Overhead

(2) Indirect materials	30	(6) Applied overhead	96
(4) Factory costs	252,000		
(5) Accum depr	45,000		

Work-in-Process Inventory

(2) Direct materials	8,600
(3) Direct labor	200
(6) Manufacturing overhead	96

YOUR TURN! 3.3

The solution is on page 3-41.

MBC

Match the account that should be debited with the recorded activity. (The accounts may be used more than once.)

Activity

____ Apply manufacturing overhead
____ Record direct labor incurred
____ Record purchase of raw materials
____ Record indirect labor incurred
____ Record use of indirect materials
____ Record use of direct materials

Account

1. Work-in-process inventory
2. Materials inventory
3. Manufacturing overhead
4. Wages payable

Accounting for Packaging and Finished Goods

LO4 Discuss the procedures and journal entries used to account for finished goods and the sale of finished goods.

eLecture

MBC

When products are finished, they are transferred from Work-in-Process Inventory to Finished Goods Inventory. The costs transferred from Work-in-Process to Finished Goods Inventory include all manufacturing costs. However, these costs also include packaging costs.

ACCOUNTING IN PRACTICE   **Treatment of Packaging Costs**

A product is not complete or finished until it is packaged in the container in which it will be sold. Packaging costs are part of the product cost transferred to the Finished Goods Inventory account.

Fezzari spends two hours to inspect, partially dissemble, and package the T5 for shipment to the customer. The two hours of inspecting are recorded in a time record at a pay rate of $25 per hour. Approximately $75 is required for the shipment container and packing materials. The packing materials are purchased on account and immediately placed into Work-in-Process. Remember that Fezzari applies overhead based on direct labor hours. Thus, Fezzari would also record $24 (2 hours × $12 per hour) to Work-in-Process Inventory. The total packaging costs applied to Work-in-Process are $149.

7	Work-in-process inventory	50	
	Cash and wages payable		50
	To record the packaging labor for Job 372.		

continued

continued from previous page

8	Work-in-process inventory	75	
	Accounts payable		75
	To record the cost of packing materials for Job 372.		
9	Work-in-process inventory	24	
	Manufacturing overhead		24
	To record the application of manufacturing overhead to the work-in-process inventory using the predetermined overhead rate.		

When the T5 bike order is completed, the unit cost of the T5 is obtained by summing the costs charged to the job. **Exhibit 3-10** shows the completed job cost sheet for Fezarri's Job 372. The job cost sheet accumulates all product costs for the job, including direct materials, direct labor, manufacturing overhead, and packaging. The report also identifies the total unit cost of $9,045. Notice that this amount also matches the total of the debits to the work-in-process inventory account in **Exhibit 3-11**. The accountant credits Work-in-Process Inventory and debits Finished Goods Inventory for the total cost of the job completed. The journal entry to record the completion of the T5 is as follows:

10	Finished goods inventory	9,045	
	Work-in-process inventory		9,045
	To record the completion of Job 372.		

EXHIBIT 3-10	Fezzari's Job Cost Sheet for Job No. 372

Fezzari Job Cost Sheet

Customer	Ryan Hobson		Job No.	372
Product	T5		Date Promised	5/15
Quantity	1		Date Started	8/1
			Date Completed	8/6

Direct Materials		Direct Labor			Manufacturing Overhead			
Req No	Amount	Time Sheet Date	Department	Amount	Time Sheet Date	Hours	Rate	Amount
567	$8,600	8/5	Assembly	$200	8/5	8	$12/DLH	$96

Cost Summary	
Direct materials	$8,600
Direct labor	$ 200
Manufacturing overhead	$ 96
Total packaging costs	$ 149*
Total cost	**$9,045**
Units	1
Unit cost	$9,045

*Total packaging costs include materials of $75, labor of $50, and overhead of $24.

When the T5 is delivered to the customer, the cost of the bike is removed from the finished goods subaccount. Two journal entries are recorded. The first entry is a debit to Accounts Receivable and a credit to Sales for the selling price of the bike. The second entry is a debit to Cost of Goods Sold and a credit to Finished Goods Inventory for the cost of the bike. The entries to record the sale of the T5 are as follows:

11	Accounts receivable	10,500	
	Sales		10,500
	To record the sale of Job 372.		

12	Cost of goods sold	9,045	
	Finished goods inventory		9,045
	To record the cost of Job 372.		

The effect of the various postings of these transactions is shown in **Exhibit 3-11**. Note that entry 11 is not shown in this exhibit because it involves the revenue associated with the sale, not the cost of the job. The job order cost sheet for Job 372 would also be closed.

EXHIBIT 3-11   Entries for Completing the Job and Recording the Sale

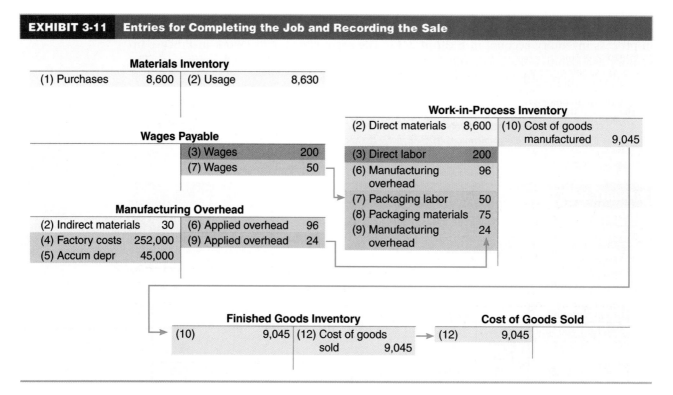

Disposition of Under- and Overapplied Overhead

As introduced in Chapter 2 and described earlier in this chapter, overhead costs are accumulated in the manufacturing overhead account during an accounting period (usually a year). During the same period, overhead costs are being applied to products or jobs based on a predetermined overhead rate. It is not until the end of the period, after all actual overhead costs have been recorded and all overhead has been applied to products and jobs, that management determines whether the amount of overhead applied to products and jobs is greater or less than the amount of actual overhead costs recorded. If more has been applied than recorded, overhead is said to be **overapplied**. If less has been applied than recorded, overhead is said to be **underapplied**.

At year-end, a journal entry is made to dispose of the underapplied or overapplied amount of manufacturing overhead. If the amount of underapplied or overapplied overhead is insignificant, an entry is made to transfer the amount to the cost of goods sold account. The under- or overapplied overhead is almost always immaterial in practice. An overapplied amount is transferred by debiting Manufacturing Overhead and crediting Cost of Goods Sold. An underapplied amount is transferred by debiting Cost of Goods Sold and crediting Manufacturing Overhead.

When the under- or overapplied amount is significant, it should be allocated to all of the jobs that were worked on during the year. The amount transferred is allocated proportionately among Work-in-Process Inventory, Finished Goods Inventory, and Cost of Goods Sold based on the amount of Applied Overhead that is in each of the three accounts at the end of the year. This is accomplished by a journal entry that transfers the amount to Work-in-Process Inventory, Finished Goods Inventory, and Cost of Goods Sold. An overapplied amount is transferred by debiting Manufacturing Overhead and crediting Work-in-Process Inventory, Finished Goods Inventory, and Cost of Goods Sold. An underapplied amount is transferred by debiting Work-in-Process Inventory, Finished Goods Inventory, and Cost of Goods Sold sold and crediting Manufacturing Overhead.

Hint: After the disposition of over- or underapplied overhead, the balance in the overhead account should be $0.

Concept ⟶	Method ⟶	Assessment	TAKEAWAY 3.2
Your company applies overhead based on a predetermined overhead rate. The CEO has asked you to determine actual cost of goods sold for the year just ended for an emergency management meeting. Historically, the amount of over- or underapplied overhead has not been significant.	• Determine actual overhead costs incurred for the year (sum the additions to manufacturing overhead). • Determine the amount of applied overhead for the year (sum the additions to work-in-process inventory for overhead). • Subtract applied overhead from actual overhead.	• If the difference is positive (underapplied), add the difference to the amount of cost of goods sold in the general ledger account. • If the difference is negative (overapplied), subtract the difference from the amount of cost of goods sold in the general ledger account.	

Exhibit 3-12 reflects the various postings of the journal entries related to manufacturing overhead. Items from entries 4, 5, 6, and 9 are highlighted in bold type. Assume that Fezzari has recorded a total of $3,000 of indirect materials for the period. In addition, assume that an additional $295,200 in manufacturing overhead was applied to other jobs throughout the year. Note that the sum of the debits in manufacturing overhead is $300,000 but that the sum of the credits is $295,320. In other words, actual factory costs were $300,000, but only $295,320 of manufacturing overhead was applied to the work-in-process inventory account. Therefore, overhead was underapplied by $4,680. Assume that this amount is insignificant.

The journal entry to record the transfer of the underapplied overhead is as follows:

13	Cost of goods sold	4,680	
	Manufacturing overhead		4,680
	To record the disposition of underapplied overhead.		

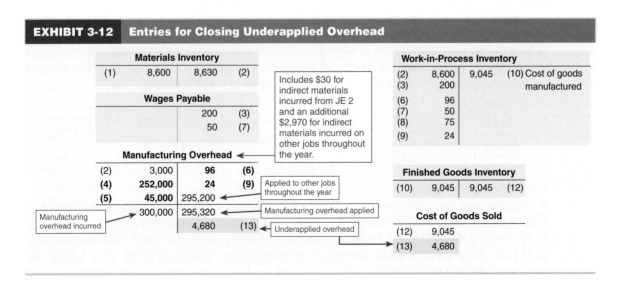

EXHIBIT 3-12   **Entries for Closing Underapplied Overhead**

As illustrated in the Fezzari example in Exhibits 2-12, 13, and 14 of Chapter 2, the entries shown in the accounts in **Exhibit 3-12** could be used to create a Schedule of Cost of Goods Manufactured and a Schedule of Cost of Goods Sold for the T5. Together with other information about sales and costs of Fezzari's other products and selling and administrative expenses, Fezzari management could then prepare an Income Statement for the period.

Illustration of Job Order Costing for a Service Firm

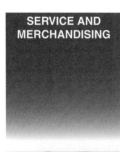

Job order costing is also used by service companies. An abbreviated illustration using a CH2M Hill project will demonstrate the use of job order costing in a service environment.

One of the services that CH2M Hill provides to clients is assistance with implementation of lean enterprise solutions. Essentially, CH2M Hill utilizes proven approaches and methods to streamline client manufacturing and office processes. One such client was the Perrier Group of America. The objective of the CH2M Hill project was to determine the optimal location for a new bottling facility needed for projected five-year sales growth in the company's Northeast Region. CH2M Hill evaluated Perrier's entire supply chain, from the spring to the customer. The result of the project was the determination of new raw materials requirements to support projected growth, the optimal location of the bottling facility, and the number and location of additional warehouse facilities to support increased sales during peak periods of the year.

Accounting for Materials

Because this project was for services, no materials were used. This is typical of service projects.

Accounting for Labor

CH2M Hill's project manager, engineers, and consultants recorded their time working on the Perrier project on a time record or timesheet. These employees also worked on other projects during the same period and recorded the time worked on those projects separately. Assume that during one period, the assigned employees worked a total of 40 hours on the Perrier project and that the portion of their salaries associated with the time spent on the Perrier project was $5,000. This would have been recorded as follows:

Work-in-process—Perrier	5,000	
Salaries payable		5,000
To record salaries on the Perrier project.		

Accounting for Overhead

Assume that CH2M Hill uses a predetermined overhead rate for consulting engagements of $150 per hour. Because 40 hours of labor was charged to the Perrier project for the period, a total of $6,000 ($150 × 40 hours) of overhead would have been applied to the project. The entry to record the application of overhead is the same as shown earlier for Fezzari:

Work-in-process—Perrier	6,000	
Overhead		6,000
To record the application of overhead to the Perrier project using the		
predetermined overhead rate.		

Recording the Sale

Recall that with the completion of a product, the accumulated cost of the product is moved from work-in-process inventory to finished goods inventory. However, service companies do not have a finished goods inventory. Instead, when a project is completed, the accumulated cost of the service is removed from work-in-process inventory as the final project invoice is prepared. In our illustration, assume that when CH2M Hill completed the project, the Work-in-Process—Perrier account had a total balance of $245,000 and that the contract between CH2M Hill and Perrier was for $300,000. CH2M Hill would have recorded the following journal entries in its financial records:

Accounts receivable	300,000	
Sales		300,000
To record the final billing for the Perrier project.		
Cost of goods sold	245,000	
Work-in-process—Perrier		245,000
To record the cost of the Perrier project.		

You are a junior accountant at Angel Manufacturing. The controller has asked you to prepare the journal entries associated with a special order (#144) recently completed for a new customer. She hands you the following information from which to prepare the journal entries, including the cost of goods sold entry:

YOUR TURN! 3.4

The solution is on page 3-41.

Materials purchased.	$2,000
Direct materials used for #144	2,600
Indirect materials used for #144	350
Direct labor incurred for #144.	1,650
Overhead applied to #144	3,300

DEPARTMENTAL OVERHEAD RATES

LO5 Contrast plant-wide overhead rates and departmental overhead rates.

Manufacturing companies that use traditional overhead rates typically use either a plant-wide (or company-wide) overhead rate or departmental overhead rates. A **plant-wide (or company-wide) overhead rate** is determined by dividing estimated total plant (or company) overhead for the year by estimated utilization of the total plant (or company) productive capacity for the year. The discussions and illustration in this chapter have incorporated a plant-wide overhead rate. When a plant-wide overhead rate is adopted, the cost accounting system uses a single predetermined rate for applying overhead to work done in all the producing departments, such as bending, drilling, welding, assembling, and painting.

Departmental Overhead Rates

Some manufacturing companies have adopted a cost accounting system that uses **departmental overhead rates**. When departmental overhead rates are used, a separate overhead rate is predetermined for each producing department in the factory by dividing the estimated overhead associated with each department by the estimated utilization of the capacity of that department.

A manufacturer would use departmental overhead rates for two primary reasons. First, the predetermined overhead rate in one department may be significantly different from the rate in another department. For instance, in department 1, the overhead rate might be $5 per direct labor hour, whereas the overhead rate in department 2 might be $20 per direct labor hour. Second, the capacity measure in one department may be different from the capacity measure in another department. For example, if department 1 is highly automated, then machine hours would be an appropriate measure of capacity for department 1. However, if department 2 is direct-labor intensive, then direct labor hours would be an appropriate measure of capacity for department 2.

When departmental overhead rates are used, the manufacturer accumulates the appropriate measure of capacity for each department for each job so that the appropriate overhead rates can be applied. Assume that a particular manufacturer has three producing departments: machining, painting, and assembling.

The capacity measure for machining and painting is machine hours, whereas the capacity measure for assembly is direct labor hours. For Job 368, the factory accumulated 30 machine hours of machining, 20 machine hours of painting, and 40 direct labor hours of assembling.

Machining has a predetermined overhead rate of $4 per machine hour, painting has a predetermined overhead rate of $3 per machine hour, and assembling has a predetermined overhead rate of $2 per direct labor hour. Manufacturing overhead would be applied to Job 368 as follows:

Machining (30 machine hours × $4)	$120
Painting (20 machine hours × $3)	60
Assembling (40 direct labor hours × $2)	80
Total manufacturing overhead applied to Job 368	$260

Departmental overhead rates usually provide a more equitable application of manufacturing overhead to individual jobs than do plant-wide rates. However, when there are significant variations in volume or complexity among the individual jobs, neither plant-wide nor departmental overhead rates may provide an equitable application of manufacturing overhead among the individual jobs. Instead, **activity-based costing** may be more appropriate. Activity-based costing is discussed in detail in Chapter 5.

YOUR TURN! 3.5

The solution is on page 3-41.

MBC

Assume that a manufacturer has three producing departments: molding, machining, and painting. The capacity measure for molding and machining is machine hours, whereas the capacity measure for painting is direct labor hours. For Job #59, the factory accumulated 20 machine hours of molding, 10 machine hours of machining, and 5 direct labor hours of painting. Molding has a predetermined overhead rate of $10 per machine hour, machining has a predetermined overhead rate of $8 per machine hour, and painting has a predetermined overhead rate of $4 per direct labor hour. How much overhead should be applied to Job #59?

SERVICE INDUSTRY IN FOCUS

SERVICE AND MERCHANDISING

Environmental Business Consultants, LLC (EBC), worked on and completed two projects during June: a review of appropriate rates for solid waste and recycling collection within Klamath County, and a competitive procurement of landfill disposal services for the City of Redding. The following information relates to these two projects:

	Rate Review Project—Klamath	Procurement Project—Redding
WIP Inventory balance at June 1	$46,320	$85,318
Hours worked during June	100	74
Payroll cost per hour:		
Partner	$ 60	$ 60
Manager	$ 38	$ 38
Staff	$ 24	$ 24
Overhead rate per labor hour	$ 25	$ 25

During June, the partner charged 10 hours to the rate review project and 20 hours to the procurement project; the manager charged 30 hours to the rate review project and 24 hours to the procurement project; and the staff charged 60 hours to the rate review project and 30 hours to the procurement project.

On June 30, EBC billed its clients for the completed projects. The invoice for the rate review project was for $60,000 and for the procurement project was $105,000.

Required

1. Prepare the journal entry to distribute the payroll to the projects during June. (Assume that the correct entry was made when the payroll was paid.)

2. Prepare the journal entry to apply the overhead to the projects during June.

3. Prepare the journal entry(ies) to record the completion of the projects as of the end of June. (*Hint:* Don't forget the work that was performed on the jobs prior to June, which is reflected in the beginning WIP balance. Also, don't forget that there is no finished goods inventory in a service firm—once the project is complete, it is billed to the client.)

4. Determine the amount of profit or loss that EBC earned on each of the two projects.

Solution

1.

WIP—Klamath	3,180	
WIP—Redding	2,832	
Payroll expense		6,012

Klamath: ($60 × 10 hours) + ($38 × 30 hours) +
($24 × 60 hours) = $3,180
Redding: ($60 × 20 hours) + ($38 × 24 hours) +
($24 × 30 hours) = $2,832

2.

WIP—Klamath	2,500	
WIP—Redding	1,850	
Overhead		4,350

Klamath: (10 + 30 + 60) × $25 = 2,500
Redding: (20 + 24 + 30) × $25 = 1,850

3.

Accounts receivable—Klamath	60,000	
Sales revenue		60,000
Cost of sales	52,000	
WIP—Klamath		52,000

(46,320 + 3,180 + 2,500)

Accounts receivable—Redding	105,000	
Sales revenue		105,000
Cost of sales	90,000	
WIP—Klamath		90,000

(85,318 + 2,832 + 1,850)

4.

Klamath:	Sales revenue	$ 60,000
	Cost of goods sold	52,000
	Gross profit	$ 8,000

Redding:	Sales revenue	$105,000
	Cost of goods sold	90,000
	Gross profit	$ 15,000

DATA ANALYTICS   The data science behind successful chocolate promotions

Data Analytics

Kilwins has opened nearly 100 chocolate franchises since the first shop opened in Petoskey, Michigan, in 1947. The stores offer plenty of sweets to choose from, including fudge, ice cream, and its signature Tuttle treat. Until recently, however, one thing was missing: cutting-edge business intelligence.

    To understand how the company was performing, the management team at Kilwins would have to cut and paste spreadsheets together, which was a very time-consuming process. Things have changed since the business began using **Tableau**. Not only has the data analytics software helped management save time, but it has also provided them with better insights that result in better decision-making. For example, Jeff Hall, Kilwins's Director of Marketing, notes how much easier it is to plan seasonal promotions. "I can very easily go back year over year to look at a promotional period. I can show accurate sales data for what was in that promotion." Tableau's analysis tools help ensure successful promotions based on past experience. Definitely a sweet result!

COMPREHENSIVE PROBLEM

MBC

The annual budget for Diamond Corporation included the following costs and expenses:

Direct materials.	$ 30,000
Direct labor ($8 per hour)	120,000
Sales commissions.	28,000
Factory supervision	16,000
Indirect labor.	27,000
Factory depreciation.	25,000
Factory taxes	7,000
Factory insurance.	6,000
Factory utilities	9,000

Required

a. Compute the plant-wide predetermined manufacturing overhead rate using direct labor hours as the activity measure.

b. Determine the amount of manufacturing overhead that would be applied to jobs during March when 1,100 direct labor hours were actually incurred.

Solution

a. Budgeted manufacturing overhead:

Factory supervision	$16,000
Indirect labor.	27,000
Factory depreciation.	25,000
Factory taxes	7,000
Factory insurance.	6,000
Factory utilities	9,000
Budgeted manufacturing overhead.	$90,000

Budgeted direct labor hours:

$$\frac{\$120,000}{\$8/hour} = 15,000 \text{ budgeted direct labor hours}$$

Predetermined overhead rate:

$$\frac{\text{Budgeted manufacturing overhead}}{\text{Budgeted direct labor hours}} = \frac{\$90,000}{15,000} = \$6 \text{ per direct labor hour}$$

b. 1,100 hours × $6 = $6,600 applied manufacturing overhead

SUMMARY OF LEARNING OBJECTIVES

LO1   Describe the two basic types of cost accounting systems, discuss how they may be used in both manufacturing and nonmanufacturing environments, and explain the need for the timely determination of product costs. (p. 3-3)

- A costing system is an orderly process for tracking product or service cost information.
- In a manufacturing environment, materials, labor, and overhead costs are accumulated and assigned to specific jobs and products.
- In a nonmanufacturing (service) setting, labor and overhead costs are accumulated and assigned to specific customers.
- A job order costing system is used when production is characterized by a series of unique products or jobs undertaken either to fill specific orders from customers or to produce a general stock from which future orders will be filled.
- A process costing system lends itself to the production of a large volume of homogeneous products manufactured in a continual flow operation.
- A cost accounting system must trace, on a timely basis, direct materials, direct labor, and manufacturing overhead to products or jobs.

Explain the need for a predetermined overhead rate and demonstrate its calculation. (p. 3-5)   **LO2**

■ The predetermined overhead rate is calculated by dividing the estimated total manufacturing overhead cost for the year by the estimated utilization of the factory productive capacity during the upcoming year.

■ Companies should choose the application base that corresponds to the period over which activity decisions are typically made.

Describe and explain a job order costing system, identify types of records used in job order costing, and   **LO3**
demonstrate the journal entries that accompany the flow of product costs. (p. 3-7)

■ Materials requisitions authorize issuance from the materials inventory.

■ Time records document the labor time by job.

■ The *job order cost sheet* summarizes the product costs—direct materials, direct labor, and manufacturing overhead applied—for one job; the predetermined overhead rate is used to apply manufacturing overhead.

■ When material is requisitioned from the materials inventory, the Work-in-Process Inventory account is debited for the cost of direct materials and the Manufacturing Overhead account is debited for the cost of indirect materials.

■ When the wages payable is distributed, the Work-in-Process Inventory account is debited for the cost of direct labor and the Manufacturing Overhead account is debited for the cost of indirect labor.

■ Actual manufacturing overhead costs are recorded by debiting the Manufacturing Overhead account.

■ Manufacturing overhead is applied to jobs by debiting the Work-in-Process Inventory account and crediting the Manufacturing Overhead account.

Discuss the procedures and journal entries used to account for finished goods and the sale of finished   **LO4**
goods. (p. 3-13)

■ A product is not complete or finished until it is packaged in the container in which it will be sold. Packaging costs are part of the product cost transferred to the Finished Goods Inventory account.

■ The cost of finished goods is recorded by debiting the Finished Goods Inventory account and crediting the Work-in-Process Inventory account.

■ The sale of finished goods is recorded by debiting the Cost of Goods Sold account and crediting the Finished Goods Inventory account for the cost of the goods sold and by debiting the Accounts Receivable account and crediting the Sales account for the selling price.

■ At year-end, a journal entry is made to dispose of the **underapplied** or **overapplied** amount of manufacturing overhead. If the amount of underapplied or overapplied overhead is insignificant, an entry is made to transfer the amount to the cost of goods sold account. When the amount is significant, it should be allocated to all of the jobs that were worked on during the year. This is accomplished by a journal entry that transfers the amount to Work-in-Process Inventory, Finished Goods Inventory, and Cost of Goods Sold.

Contrast plant-wide overhead rates and departmental overhead rates. (p. 3-18)   **LO5**

■ When departmental overhead rates are used, a separate rate is calculated for each producing department in the factory.

■ A plant-wide (or company-wide) overhead rate is determined by dividing estimated total plant (or company) overhead for the year by estimated utilization of the total plant (or company) productive capacity for the year.

Concept ➝	Method ➝	Assessment	SUMMARY
You have been asked to calculate the predetermined overhead rate for the next operating period.	• Forecast expected total overhead for the period. • Select an application base or cost driver. • Estimate total activity for the cost driver for the period.	Predetermined overhead rate = total estimated overhead divided by the total estimated activity level of the application base (such as machine hours or direct labor hours). Assign the predetermined overhead rate to each unit of cost driver during the period.	TAKEAWAY 3.1

continued

continued from previous page

SUMMARY	Concept ⟶	Method ⟶	Assessment
TAKEAWAY 3.2	Your company applies overhead based on a pre-determined overhead rate. The CEO has asked you to determine actual cost of goods sold for the year just ended for an emergency management meeting. Historically, the amount of over- or underapplied overhead has not been significant.	• Determine actual overhead costs incurred for the year (sum the additions to manufacturing overhead) • Determine the amount of applied overhead for the year (sum the additions to work-in-process inventory for overhead) • Subtract applied overhead from actual overhead	• If the difference is positive (under-applied), add the difference to the amount of cost of goods sold in the general ledger account. • If the difference is negative (over-applied), subtract the difference from the amount of cost of goods sold in the general ledger account.

KEY TERMS

Activity-based costing (p. 3-19)	Job order cost sheet (p. 3-7)	Process costing system (p. 3-4)
Bill of materials (p. 3-7)	Materials requisition (p. 3-7)	Production order (p. 3-7)
Cost driver (p. 3-6)	Overapplied (p. 3-15)	Sales order (p. 3-7)
Departmental overhead rates (p. 3-18)	Plant-wide (or company-wide) overhead rate (p. 3-18)	Time clocks (p. 3-11)
Job order costing system (p. 3-3)	Predetermined manufacturing overhead rate (p. 3-6)	Time record (p. 3-7)
		Underapplied (p. 3-15)

Assignments with the ⓜ logo in the margin are available in 𝐁usinessCourse.
See the Preface of the book for details.

SELF-STUDY QUESTIONS

(Answers to Self-Study Questions are at the end of this chapter.)

LO1
1. **Which product costing system would most likely be used to account for a home builder building custom homes for its customers?**
   - a. Job order costing
   - b. Process costing
   - c. Normal costing
   - d. Standard costing

LO2
2. **Predetermined manufacturing overhead rates should be**
   - a. higher than actual manufacturing overhead rates.
   - b. lower than actual manufacturing overhead rates.
   - c. based on monthly budgets.
   - d. based on annual budgets.

LO3
3. **Which account is debited to record the issuance of material to production for incorporation into the product?**
   - a. Direct Materials
   - b. Materials Inventory
   - c. Work-in-Process Inventory
   - d. Factory Supplies

LO3, 4
4. **Which of the following is usually *not* found on a job order cost sheet?**
   - a. Manufacturing overhead
   - b. Finished units currently on hand
   - c. Direct materials
   - d. Unit cost

LO4
5. **When should the balance of the manufacturing overhead account be zero?**
   - a. At the end of each month
   - b. After year-end closing
   - c. Never
   - d. Each time a job is completed

LO5
6. **Which of the following would be a reason for choosing to use departmental overhead rates, instead of a single company-wide overhead rate?**
   - a. Each department's overhead is structured very differently from other departments, resulting in very different rates.
   - b. The logical capacity measure of each department is different from the other departments.
   - c. Neither *a* nor *b*
   - d. Both *a* and *b*

QUESTIONS

1. Briefly describe a cost accounting system.   **LO1**

2. What types of entities, other than manufacturers, use cost accounting systems?   **LO1**

3. Contrast a job order costing system and a process costing system.   **LO1**

4. Give three examples of types of companies that would use job order costing.   **LO1**

5. Why do we name it a *predetermined* manufacturing overhead rate?   **LO2**

6. How is a predetermined manufacturing overhead rate determined?   **LO2**

7. Briefly justify the use of an annual predetermined manufacturing overhead rate as opposed to actual   **LO2**
   monthly manufacturing overhead.

8. Wesley Manufacturing Company uses a predetermined plant-wide manufacturing overhead rate of $25 per   **LO2**
   direct labor hour. During April, Job 541 had $3,000 of direct materials assigned to it; 60 hours of direct labor
   at $10 per hour were incurred for the job. What is the total product cost accumulated on Job 541 during April?

9. Parker Manufacturing, Inc., employs an overhead rate of 140% of direct labor cost. The Job 783 cost sheet   **LO2**
   shows that $5,000 in direct materials has been used and that $8,000 in direct labor has been incurred. If
   1,000 units of product have been produced on Job 783, what is the unit cost of the product?

10. Briefly explain the sequential flow of product costs through a cost accounting system.   **LO3**

11. What type of records would be used or maintained for the following manufacturing activities?   **LO3**

    a. Determining the amount of a specific material on hand
    b. Issuing direct materials for production
    c. Assigning the direct labor costs for a particular worker
    d. Accumulating the cost of a particular product or batch of products

12. Explain the general format and give examples of the data that would appear on (a) a sales order, (b) a bill **LO3**
    of materials, and (c) a job order cost sheet.

13. Why can we say that the sale of a manufactured product is recorded at two different amounts?   **LO4**

14. Slaton Company records both actual overhead and applied overhead in one account, Manufacturing Over-   **LO4**
    head. On January 31, the account has a credit balance. Has overhead been under- or overapplied during
    January?

15. Lyle Manufacturing Company applies manufacturing overhead at the rate of 150% of direct labor cost.   **LO4**
    During October, Lyle incurred $82,000 of direct labor costs and $120,000 of manufacturing overhead
    costs. What is the amount of over- or underapplied manufacturing overhead for October?

16. Why would a company use a departmental overhead rate rather than a plant-wide overhead rate?   **LO5**

17. A company with four production departments that had been using a plant-wide overhead rate based on   **LO5**
    direct labor hours changes to a departmental overhead rate. Product A's total allocated overhead increases
    as a result. Why might this have happened?

SHORT EXERCISES

SE3-1.   A process costing system would most likely be used for all of the following except   **LO1**

    a. a manufacturer of plywood sheets.   *c.* a tailor.

    b. a men's barbershop.   *d.* a hay farmer.

SE3-2.   Henry Manufacturing, which uses direct labor hours to apply overhead to its product line, undertook **LO2**
an extensive renovation and modernization program two years ago. Manufacturing processes were
reengineered, considerable automated equipment was acquired, and 60% of the company's nonunion
factory workers were terminated.

    Which of the following statements would apply to the situation at Henry?

    I. The company's factory overhead rate has likely increased.
    II. The use of direct labor hours seems to be appropriate.
    III. Henry will lack the ability to properly determine labor variances.
    IV. Henry has likely reduced its ability to quickly cut costs in order to respond to economic
        downturns.

    a. I, II, III, and IV.   *c.* II and IV only.
    b. I and IV only.   *d.* I and III only.

LO2   SE3-3. Using the following budget data for Valley Corporation, which produces only one product, calculate the company's predetermined manufacturing overhead application rate for variable overhead. *Hint:* The factory supervisor's salary is direct labor, since it is incurred regardless of production. SG&A expenses relate to the entire operations of Valley Corporation and not just related to manufacturing.

Units to be produced	11,000
Units to be sold.	10,000
Indirect materials, varying with production	$ 1,000
Indirect labor, varying with production	10,000
Factory supervisor's salary, incurred regardless of production.	20,000
Depreciation on factory building and equipment	30,000
Utilities to operate factory machines.	12,000
Security lighting for factory	2,000
Selling, general, and administrative (SG&A) expenses	5,000

a.	$2.09	*c.*	$4.73
b.	$2.30	*d.*	$5.00

LO2   SE3-4. Baldwin Printing Company uses a job order costing system and applies overhead based on machine hours. A total of 150,000 machine hours have been budgeted for the year. During the year, an order for 1,000 units was completed and incurred the following:

Direct materials costs.	$1,000
Direct labor costs	1,500
Actual overhead	1,980
Machine hours	450

The accountant calculated the inventory cost of this order to be $4.30 per unit. The annual budgeted overhead in dollars was

a.	$577,500.	*c.*	$645,000.
b.	$600,000.	*d.*	$660,000.

LO4   SE3-5. As the staff accountant at Diablo Manufacturing, you have been asked to prepare the journal entries associated with a recently completed custom order (#720). You have the following information from which to prepare the journal entries:

Materials purchased.	$1,500
Direct materials used for #720	1,200
Indirect labor used for #720	250
Direct labor incurred for #720.	850
Overhead applied to #720	1,000

What would be the account and amount of the debit in the journal entry to record Cost of Goods Manufactured for order #720?

a.	Work-in-process inventory, $3,050	*c.*	Work-in-process inventory, $3,300
b.	Finished goods inventory, $3,050	*d.*	Finished goods inventory, $3,300

LO4   SE3-6. Sanchez Consulting applies overhead to consulting projects based on the direct labor hours charged by employees to each job. Selected data for the firm follow:

Budgeted overhead for the year.	$150,000
Budgeted direct labor cost for the year (@ $25/hour)	375,000
Actual overhead for November.	10,000
Actual direct labor cost for November (1,100 hours)	28,000

What is the amount of over- or underapplied overhead for the month of November?

a.	$1,000 underapplied	*c.*	$1,200 underapplied
b.	$1,000 overapplied	*d.*	$1,200 overapplied

SE3-7. Given the following data for Scurry Company, what is the cost of goods sold?

LO4

Beginning inventory of finished goods	$100,000
Cost of goods manufactured	700,000
Ending inventory of finished goods	200,000
Beginning work-in-process inventory	300,000
Ending work-in-process inventory	50,000

 a. $500,000.   *c.* $800,000.
 b. $600,000.   *d.* $950,000.

SE3-8. John Sheng, cost accountant at Starlet Company, is developing departmental manufacturing overhead application rates for the company's tooling and fabricating departments. The budgeted overhead for each department and the data for one job are shown below.

LO5

	Departments	
	Tooling	**Fabricating**
Supplies	$ 850	$ 200
Supervisors' salaries	1,500	2,000
Indirect labor	1,200	4,880
Depreciation	1,000	5,500
Repairs	4,075	3,540
Total budgeted manufacturing overhead	$8,625	$16,120
Total direct labor hours	460	620
Direct labor hours on Job #231	12	3

Using the departmental overhead application rates, total overhead applied to Job #231 in the Tooling and Fabricating Departments will be

 a. $225.   *c.* $537.
 b. $303.   *d.* $671.

DATA ANALYTICS, DATA VISUALIZATION, AND EXCEL ACTIVITIES

Data Analytics, Data Visualization, and Excel Activities are available in myBusinessCourse. These assignments develop Excel, Tableau, and Data Analytics skills, which will enhance students' career readiness. These exercises are assignable and auto graded by MBC. For an overview of data analytics, see the appendix at the end of this book.

EXERCISES—SET A

E3-1A. **Calculate and Use Overhead Rate** Bagley Corporation expects to incur $450,000 of factory overhead and $600,000 of general and administrative costs next year. Direct labor costs at $20 per hour are expected to total $200,000. If factory overhead is to be applied per direct labor hour, how much overhead will be applied to a job incurring 40 hours of direct labor?

LO2

E3-2A. **Calculate and Use Overhead Rate** Bagley Corporation expects to incur $450,000 of factory overhead and $600,000 of general and administrative costs next year. Direct labor costs at $20 per hour are expected to total $200,000. If factory overhead is to be applied per direct labor dollar, how much overhead will be applied to a job incurring $1,000 of direct labor?

LO2

E3-3A. **Calculate and Use Overhead Rate** During the coming accounting year, Baker Manufacturing, Inc., anticipates the following costs, expenses, and operating data:

LO2

Direct material (16,000 lb.)	$ 80,000
Direct labor (@ $10/hr.)	200,000
Indirect materials	12,000
Indirect labor	22,000
Sales commissions	34,000
Factory administration	16,000
Nonfactory administrative expenses	20,000
Other manufacturing overhead*	80,000

*Provides for operating 40,000 machine hours.

a. Calculate the predetermined manufacturing overhead rate for the coming year for each of the following application bases: (1) direct labor hours, (2) direct labor costs, and (3) machine hours.

b. For each item in requirement *a*, determine the proper application of manufacturing overhead to Job 63, to which 16 direct labor hours, $150 of direct labor cost, and 40 machine hours have been charged.

LO3   **E3-4A.   Flow of Product Costs through Accounts**   Assuming a routine manufacturing activity, present journal entries (account titles only) for each of the following transactions:

a. Purchased materials on account.
b. Recorded wages payable (for indirect labor) earned but not paid.
c. Requisitioned both direct materials and indirect materials.
d. Assigned direct and indirect labor costs.
e. Recorded factory depreciation and accrued factory property tax.
f. Applied manufacturing overhead to production.
g. Completed work on products.
h. Sold finished goods on account.
i. Paid wages

LO3   **E3-5A.   Job Order Cost Sheets**   For each of the manufacturing transactions or activities indicated in Exercise E3-4A, briefly identify the detailed forms, records, or documents (if any) that would probably underlie each journal entry.

LO2, 4   **E3-6A.   Calculate and Use Overhead Rate**   Selected data for the consulting department of Austin Consulting, Inc., follow:

Estimated consulting overhead cost for the year	$360,000
Estimated direct labor cost for the year (@ $9/hr.)	180,000
Actual manufacturing overhead cost for January	19,500
Actual direct labor cost for January (1,200 hours)	11,000

Assuming that direct labor cost is the basis for applying consulting overhead,

a. Calculate the predetermined overhead rate.
b. Prepare a journal entry that applies consulting overhead for January.
c. By what amount is consulting overhead over- or underapplied in January?

LO2, 4   **E3-7A.   Calculate and Use Overhead Rate**   Using the data in Exercise 3-6A, but assuming that the basis for applying consulting overhead is direct labor hours, complete requirements (a) through (c).

LO4   **E3-8A.   Applied vs. Actual Manufacturing Overhead**   Kubal Inc. applies overhead based on machine hours. Kubal reports the following for the year just ended:

Budgeted overhead for the year	$250,000
Budgeted machine hours	2,000
Actual overhead for the year	275,000
Actual machine hours	2,400

What is the amount of over- or underapplied overhead for the year?

E3-9A.   Applied vs. Actual Manufacturing Overhead Davis Manufacturing Corporation applies manufactur- **LO4**
ing overhead on the basis of 140% of direct labor cost. An analysis of the related accounts and job order
cost sheet indicates that during the year total manufacturing overhead incurred was $315,000 and that
at year-end Work-in-Process Inventory, Finished Goods Inventory, and Cost of Goods Sold included
$40,000, $20,000, and $140,000, respectively, of direct labor incurred during the current year.

 a.   Determine the underapplied manufacturing overhead at year-end. (Assume it is significant.)
 b.   Prepare a journal entry to record the disposition of the underapplied manufacturing overhead.

E3-10A. Perpetual Inventories The following summary data are from the job order cost sheets of Hampton **LO4**
Company:

	Dates			Total Costs Assigned at April 30	Total Production Costs Added in May
Job	Started	Finished	Shipped		
1	4/10	4/20	5/9	$7,300	
2	4/18	4/30	5/20	5,400	
3	4/24	5/10	5/25	2,900	$5,700
4	4/28	5/20	6/3	3,600	4,800
5	5/15	6/10	6/20		2,600
6	5/22	6/18	6/28		3,800

Using the above data, compute (a) the finished goods inventory at May 1 and May 31, (b) the work-
in-process inventory at May 1 and May 31, and (c) the cost of goods sold for May. Hampton began
operations with Job 1.

E3-11A. Finished Goods and Cost of Goods Sold Before the completed production for June is recorded, the **LO4**
work-in-process inventory account for James Company appears as follows:

Work-in-Process Inventory	
Balance June 1.	20,000
Direct materials.	45,000
Direct labor.	32,000
Manufacturing overhead applied	34,000

Assume that completed production for June includes Jobs 107, 108, and 109 with total costs of $28,000,
$55,000, and $25,000, respectively.
 a.   Determine the cost of unfinished jobs at June 30 and prepare a journal entry to record completed
       production.
 b.   Using general journal entries, record the sale of Job 107 for $40,000 on account.

E3-12A. Preparing a Job Order Cost Sheet Riverwood Accounting Company has the following account in **LO4**
its cost records:

SERVICE AND MERCHANDISING

Work-in-Process—Jones Audit			
Direct labor.	20,000	Services completed	42,253
Project overhead	27,000		

Riverwood applies overhead to projects at a predetermined rate based on direct labor costs. Assume that
Riverwood uses a job order costing system and that Jones Audit is the only job in process at the end of
the period. Complete the following cost sheet for services still in process for Jones Audit.

Job Order Cost Sheet—Jones Audit (Services in Process)	
Direct labor.	_____
Project overhead	_____
Total cost	_____

EXERCISES—SET B

LO2   **E3-1B.**   **Calculate and Use Overhead Rate**   Chipman Corporation expects to incur $300,000 of factory overhead and $500,000 of general and administrative costs next year. Direct labor costs at $25 per hour are expected to total $500,000. If factory overhead is to be applied per direct labor hour, how much overhead will be applied to a job incurring 100 hours of direct labor?

LO2   **E3-2B.**   **Calculate and Use Overhead Rate**   Chipman Corporation expects to incur $300,000 of factory overhead and $500,000 of general and administrative costs next year. Direct labor costs at $25 per hour are expected to total $500,000. If factory overhead is to be applied per direct labor dollar, how much overhead will be applied to a job incurring $3,000 of direct labor?

LO2   **E3-3B.**   **Calculate and Use Manufacturing Overhead Rate**   During the coming accounting year, Ester Manufacturing, Inc., anticipates the following costs, expenses, and operating data:

Direct materials (15,000 lb.)	$45,000
Direct labor (@ $12/hr.)	120,000
Indirect materials	7,000
Indirect labor.	12,000
Sales commissions.	18,000
Factory administration	13,000
Nonfactory administrative expenses. . . .	14,000
Other manufacturing overhead*	28,000

*Machine hours are 30,000 hours.

a.   Calculate the predetermined manufacturing overhead rate for the coming year for each of the following application bases: (1) direct labor hours, (2) direct labor costs, and (3) machine hours.

b.   For each item in requirement (a), determine the proper application of manufacturing overhead to Job 128, to which 9 direct labor hours, $100 of direct labor cost, and 32 machine hours have been charged.

LO3   **E3-4B.**   **Flow of Product Costs through Accounts**   The following T accounts present a cost flow in which all or part of typical manufacturing transactions are indicated by parenthetical letters on the debit or credit side of each account.

Materials Inventory			Wages Payable			Manufacturing Overhead	
(a)	(c)		(i)	(b)		(b)	(f)
				(d)		(c)	
						(d)	
						(e)	

Work-in-Process Inventory			Finished Goods Inventory			Cost of Goods Sold	
(c)	(g)		(g)	(h)		(h)	
(d)							
(f)							

For each parenthetical letter, present a general journal entry with explanation indicating the apparent transaction or procedure that has occurred. (Disregard amounts.)

LO3   **E3-5B.**   **Job Order Cost Sheets**   For each of the manufacturing transactions or activities indicated by the parenthetical letters in Exercise E3-4B, briefly identify the detailed forms or documents (if any) that would probably underlie each journal entry.

LO2, 4   **E3-6B.**   **Calculate and Use Overhead Rate**   Selected data for the consulting department of Kingman Consulting, Inc., follow:

SERVICE AND
MERCHANDISING

Estimated consulting overhead cost for the year	$486,000
Estimated direct labor cost for the year (@ $9/hr.).	324,000
Actual consulting overhead cost for May	29,000
Actual direct labor cost for May (2,400 hrs.).	22,000

Assuming that direct labor cost is the basis for applying consulting overhead,

a.   Calculate the predetermined overhead rate.

b.   Prepare a journal entry that applies consulting overhead for May.

c.   By what amount is consulting overhead over- or underapplied in May?

E3-7B. Calculate and Use Overhead Rate Using the data in Exercise E3-6B, but assuming that the basis for applying consulting overhead is direct labor hours, complete requirements (a) through (c).

LO2, 4

E3-8B. Applied vs. Actual Manufacturing Overhead Harrison Inc. applies overhead based on machine hours. Harrison reports the following for the year just ended:

LO4

Budgeted overhead for the year	$500,000
Budgeted machine hours	25,000
Actual overhead for the year.	$505,000
Actual machine hours.	24,000

What is the amount of over- or underapplied overhead for the year?

E3-9B. Applied vs. Actual Manufacturing Overhead Sloan Manufacturing Corporation applies manufacturing overhead on the basis of 130% of direct labor cost. An analysis of the related accounts and job order cost sheets indicates that during the year total manufacturing overhead incurred was $210,000 and that at year-end Work-in-Process Inventory, Finished Goods Inventory, and Cost of Goods Sold included $30,000, $20,000, and $150,000, respectively, of direct labor incurred during the current year.

LO4

a. Determine the manufacturing overapplied overhead at year-end. (Assume it is significant.)
b. Prepare a journal entry to record the disposition of the overapplied overhead.

E3-10B. Perpetual Inventories The following summary data are from the job order cost sheets of Castle Company:

LO4

	Dates			Total Assigned Costs at September 30	Total Production Costs Added in October
Job	Started	Finished	Shipped		
1	9/10	9/20	10/11	$9,000	
2	9/17	9/29	10/22	6,600	
3	9/25	10/11	10/27	3,500	$7,100
4	9/27	10/19	11/4	4,400	5,700
5	10/14	11/10	11/18		3,200
6	10/23	11/17	11/29		4,900

Using the data provided, compute (a) the finished goods inventory at October 1 and October 31, (b) the work-in-process inventory at October 1 and October 31, and (c) the cost of goods sold for October. Castle began operations with Job 1.

E3-11B. Finished Goods and Cost of Goods Sold Before the completed production for August is recorded, the work-in-process inventory account for Bayfield Company appears as follows:

LO4

Work-in-Process Inventory	
Balance, August 1.	17,000
Direct materials.	33,000
Direct labor	20,000
Manufacturing overhead applied	20,000

Assume that completed production for August includes Jobs 317, 318, and 319 with total costs of $31,000, $18,000, and $29,000, respectively.

a. Determine the cost of unfinished jobs at August 31 and prepare a journal entry to record completed production.
b. Using general journal entries, record the sale of Job 317 for $45,000 on account.

E3-12B. Job Order Cost Sheet Everglade Accounting Company has the following account in its cost records:

LO4

Work-in-Process—Davis Audit				
Direct labor	38,400	Services completed		84,000
Project overhead	57,600			

Everglade applies overhead to projects at a predetermined rate based on direct labor costs. Assume that Everglade uses a job order costing system and that Davis Audit is the only job in process at the end of the period. Complete the following cost sheet for services still in process for Davis Audit.

Job Order Cost Sheet—Davis Audit (Services in Process)	
Direct labor	_____
Project overhead	_____
Total cost	_____

PROBLEMS—SET A

Note: In both problem sets, assume perpetual inventory procedures, a single Manufacturing Overhead account, first-in, first-out (FIFO) costing of inventories, and that the Materials Inventory account is the control account for both direct materials and indirect materials.

LO2, 3

P3-1A. **Determine and Use Overhead Rate** Cortez Consulting, Inc., expects the following costs and expenses during the coming year:

Direct labor (@ $12/hr.)	$162,000
Sales commissions	37,000
Overhead	202,500

Required

a.   Compute a predetermined overhead rate applied on the basis of direct labor hours.

b.   Prepare a general journal entry to apply overhead during an interim period when 1,500 direct labor hours were worked.

c.   What amount of overhead would be assigned to Job 466, to which $180 in direct labor had been charged?

LO2, 4   **P3-2A.**   **Determine and Use Overhead Rate** The following selected ledger accounts of Cameron Company are for February (the second month of its accounting year):

MATERIALS INVENTORY

Feb. 1 balance	31,500	February credits	105,000
February debits	104,000		

MANUFACTURING OVERHEAD

February debits	163,350	Feb. 1 balance	11,600
		February credits	166,650

WORK-IN-PROCESS INVENTORY

Feb. 1 balance	22,400	February credits	375,000
February debits:			
Direct materials	95,000		
Direct labor	151,500		
Manufacturing overhead	166,650		

WAGES PAYABLE

February debits	193,500	Feb. 1 balance	45,000
		February credits	185,000

FINISHED GOODS INVENTORY

Feb. 1 balance	76,500	February credits	386,000
February debits	375,000		

Required

a.   Determine the amount of indirect materials requisitioned for production during February.

b.   How much indirect labor cost was apparently incurred during February?

c.   Calculate the manufacturing overhead rate based on direct labor cost.

d.   Was manufacturing overhead for February under- or overapplied, and by what amount?

e. Was manufacturing overhead for the first two months of the year under- or overapplied, and by what amount?

f. What is the cost of production completed in February?

g. What is the cost of goods sold in February?

P3-3A. **Job Cost Journal Entries** Holiday Manufacturing had the following inventories at December 31, Year 1, the end of its fiscal year: **LO3**

Materials inventory	$19,000
Work-in-process inventory	20,000
Finished goods inventory	13,000

During January of Year 2 the following transactions occurred:

1. Purchased materials on account, $126,000.
2. Requisitioned direct materials of $110,000 and indirect materials of $20,000.
3. Incurred wages payable, $61,000.
4. Assigned total wages payable, of which $11,000 was considered indirect labor.
5. Incurred other manufacturing overhead, $32,800. (Credit Accounts Payable.)
6. Applied manufacturing overhead on the basis of 120% of direct labor costs.
7. Determined completed production, $206,000. Use this information to determine the amount of WIP transferred to finished goods inventory.
8. Determined cost of goods sold, $203,000. Use this information to determine the reduction to finished goods inventory.

Required

a. Prepare general journal entries to record these transactions.

b. If the above transactions covered a full year's operations, prepare a journal entry to dispose of the overhead account balance. Assume that the balance is significant. Also assume that the following accounts contained the indicated amounts of manufacturing overhead applied during Year 2:

Work-in-process inventory	$ 6,000
Finished goods	4,000
Cost of goods sold	50,000

P3-4A. **Job Cost Journal Entries** Prior to the beginning of Year 1, Lowe Company estimated that it would incur $176,000 of manufacturing overhead cost for the year, using 16,000 direct labor hours to produce the desired volume of goods. On January 1, Year 1, beginning balances of Materials Inventory, Work-in-Process Inventory, and Finished Goods Inventory were $28,000, $-0-, and $43,000, respectively.   **LO3, 4**

Required

Prepare general journal entries to record the following for the year:

a. Purchased materials on account, $39,000.

b. Of the total dollar value of materials used, $31,000 represented direct materials and $11,000 indirect materials.

c. Determined total factory labor, $135,000 (15,000 hrs. @ $9/hr.).

d. Of the factory labor, 80% was direct and 20% indirect.

e. Applied manufacturing overhead based on direct labor hours to work-in-process.

f. Determined actual manufacturing overhead other than those items already recorded, $92,000. (Credit Accounts Payable.)

g. Ending inventories of work-in-process and finished goods were $32,000 and $57,000, respectively. Determine the cost of finished goods (credit WIP) and the cost of goods sold (credit FG inventory). Make separate entries.

h. Transferred the balance in Manufacturing Overhead to Cost of Goods Sold.

LO3, 4   P3-5A.   Job Cost Journal Entries and T Accounts Following are certain operating data for Durango Manufacturing Company for January:

	Materials Inventory	Work-in-Process Inventory	Finished Goods Inventory
Beginning inventory	$57,000	$24,000	$75,000
Ending inventory.	33,000	40,500	48,000

Total sales were $1,800,000, on which the company earned a 40% gross profit. Durango uses a predetermined manufacturing overhead rate of 120% of direct labor costs. Manufacturing overhead applied was $360,000. Exclusive of indirect materials used, total manufacturing overhead incurred was $243,000; it was overapplied by $22,500.

Required

Compute the following items. (Set up T accounts for Materials Inventory, Work-in-Process Inventory, Finished Goods Inventory, and Manufacturing Overhead; fill in the known amounts; and then use the normal relationships among the various accounts to compute the unknown amounts.)

a.   Cost of goods sold.   d.   Direct materials used.
b.   Cost of goods manufactured.   e.   Indirect materials used.
c.   Direct labor incurred.   f.   Total materials purchased.

LO3, 4   P3-6A.   Job Cost Journal Entries and T Accounts Summarized data for the first month's operations of Dobson Welding Foundry are presented below. A job order costing system is used.

1.   Materials purchased on account, $58,000.
2.   Amounts of materials requisitioned and foundry labor used:

Job	Materials	Foundry Labor
1	$ 4,400	$2,600
2	7,000	5,000
3	3,200	2,400
4	12,000	4,600
5	4,800	2,800
6	1,400	1,200
Indirect materials	6,200	
Indirect labor.		3,400

3.   Foundry overhead is applied at the rate of 200% of direct labor costs.
4.   Miscellaneous foundry overhead incurred:

Prepaid foundry insurance written off.	$ 1,480
Property taxes on foundry building accrued.	2,360
Foundry utilities payable accrued.	5,280
Depreciation on foundry equipment	7,440
Other costs incurred on account.	10,320

5.   Ending work-in-process consisted of Jobs 4 and 6.
6.   Jobs 1 and 3 and one-half of Job 2 were sold on account for $20,000, $17,400, and $14,400, respectively.

Required

a.   Open general ledger T accounts for Materials Inventory, Wages Payable, Foundry Overhead, Work-in-Process Inventory, Finished Goods Inventory, and Cost of Goods Sold. Also set up subsidiary T accounts as job order cost sheets for each job.

b.   Prepare general journal entries to record the summarized transactions for the month, and post appropriate entries to any accounts listed in requirement (a). Key each entry parenthetically to the related number in the problem data.

c.   Determine the balances of any accounts necessary and prepare schedules of jobs in ending work-in-process and jobs in ending finished goods to confirm that they agree with the related control accounts.

P3-7A. **Complex Job Cost Journal Entries and Analysis** During June, its first month of operations, Weston   **LO3, 4**
Manufacturing Company completed the transactions listed below. Weston uses a job order costing
system. Materials requisitions and the wages payable summary are analyzed on the 15th and the last
day of each month, and charges for direct materials and direct labor are entered directly on specific
job order cost sheets. Manufacturing overhead at the rate of 140% of direct labor costs is recorded on
individual job order cost sheets when a job is completed and at month-end for any job then in process.
At month-end, entries to the general ledger accounts summarize materials requisitions, distribution of
wages, payable costs, and the application of manufacturing overhead for the month. All other entries
to general ledger accounts are made as they occur.

1. Purchased materials on account, $130,000.
2. Paid miscellaneous manufacturing overhead costs, $32,600.
3. An analysis of materials requisitions and the wages payable summary for June 1–15 indicates the
   following cost distribution:

Job	Materials	Factory Labor
1	$21,600	$36,800
2	10,400	16,000
3	4,400	10,800
Indirect materials	7,600	
Indirect labor.		35,400
	$44,000	$99,000

4. Jobs 1 and 2 were completed on June 15 and transferred to finished goods inventory on the next
   day. (Enter the appropriate manufacturing overhead amounts on the job order cost sheets, mark
   them completed, and make a general journal entry transferring the appropriate amount of cost to
   the Finished Goods Inventory account.)
5. Paid miscellaneous manufacturing overhead costs, $23,400.
6. Sold Job 1 on account, $185,600 (recognized its cost of sales in the general journal).
7. An analysis of materials requisitions and wages payable summary for June 16–30 indicates the
   following cost distribution:

Job	Materials	Factory Labor
3	$22,800	$16,800
4	18,000	32,400
5	7,800	13,000
6	3,000	4,600
Indirect materials	6,800	
Indirect labor.		29,400
	$58,400	$96,200

8. Jobs 3 and 4 were completed on June 30 and transferred to finished goods inventory on the same
   day. (See transaction 4.)
9. Sold Job 3 on account, $155,600 (recognized its cost of sales in the general journal).
10. Recorded the following additional manufacturing overhead:

Depreciation on factory building.	$26,000
Depreciation on factory equipment.	15,200
Expiration of prepaid factory insurance	4,200
Accrual of factory property taxes payable.	7,000
	$52,400

11. Recorded monthly general journal entry for the costs of all materials used.
12. Recorded monthly general journal entry for the distribution of wages payable costs.
13. Recorded manufacturing overhead on the job order cost sheets for jobs in ending work-in-process
    and in the general journal for all manufacturing overhead applied during the month.

Required

    a.   Set up the following general ledger T accounts: Materials Inventory, Wages Payable, Manufacturing Overhead, Work-in-Process Inventory, Finished Goods Inventory, Cost of Goods Sold, and Sales.

    b.   Set up T accounts for each of Jobs 1–6 as job order cost sheets.

    c.   Noting the accounting procedures described in the first paragraph of the problem, do the following:

        i.   Record general journal entries for all transactions. Note that general journal entries are not required in transactions 3 and 7. Post only those portions of these entries affecting the general ledger accounts set up in requirement (a).

        ii.   Enter the applicable amounts directly on the appropriate job order cost sheets for transactions 3, 4, 7, 8, and 13. Note parenthetically the nature of each amount entered.

    d.   Present a brief analysis showing that the general ledger accounts for Work-in-Process Inventory and for Finished Goods Inventory agree with the related job order cost sheets.

    e.   Explain in one sentence each what the balance of each general ledger account established in requirement (a) represents.

PROBLEMS—SET B

LO2, 3

P3-1B.   **Determine and Use Consulting Rate** Oxford Consulting, Inc., expects the following costs and expenses during the coming year:

Direct labor (@ $14/hr.)	$336,000
Sales commissions.	72,000
Overhead	312,000

Required

    a.   Compute a predetermined overhead rate applied on the basis of direct labor hours.

    b.   Prepare a general journal entry to apply overhead during an interim period when 3,500 direct labor hours were worked.

    c.   What amount of overhead would be assigned to Job 325, to which $532 in direct labor had been charged?

LO2, 4

P3-2B.   **Determine and Use Manufacturing Overhead Rate** The following selected ledger accounts of the Lakewood Manufacturing Company are for May (the fifth month of its accounting year):

Materials Inventory			
May 1 balance	40,000	May credits	145,000
May debits	125,000		

Factory Overhead			
May debits	160,000	May 1 balance	14,000
		May credits	171,000

Work-in-Process Inventory			
May 1 balance	28,000	May credits	480,000
May debits:			
Direct materials.	129,000		
Direct labor	180,000		
Manufacturing overhead . . .	171,000		

Factory Payroll Payable			
May debits	200,000	May 1 balance	50,000
		May credits	196,000

Finished Goods Inventory			
May 1 balance	102,000	May credits	500,000
May debits	480,000		

Required

a. Determine the amount of indirect materials requisitioned for production during May.

b. How much indirect labor cost was apparently incurred during May?

c. Calculate the manufacturing overhead rate based on direct labor cost.

d. Was manufacturing overhead for May under- or overapplied, and by what amount?

e. Was manufacturing overhead for the first five months of the year under- or overapplied, and by what amount?

f. What is the cost of production completed in May?

g. What is the cost of goods sold in May?

P3-3B. Job Cost Journal Entries Dillon Manufacturing had the following inventories at December 31, Year 1, the end of its fiscal year: **LO3**

Materials inventory	$15,000
Work-in-process inventory	17,000
Finished goods inventory	30,000

During January Year 2, the following transactions occurred:

1. Purchased materials on account, $125,000.

2. Requisitioned total materials of $130,000, of which $8,000 was considered indirect materials.

3. Incurred wages payable, $105,000.

4. Assigned total wages payable, of which $15,000 was considered indirect labor.

5. Incurred other manufacturing overhead, $57,000. (Credit Accounts Payable.)

6. Applied manufacturing overhead on the basis of 100% of direct labor costs.

7. Determined ending work-in-process, $14,000. Use this information to calculate the amount of WIP transferred to finished goods inventory (credit WIP).

8. Determined ending finished goods, $26,000. Use this information to calculate the cost of goods sold (credit FG inventory).

Required

a. Prepare general journal entries to record these transactions.

b. If the above transactions covered a full year's operations, prepare a journal entry to dispose of the overhead account balance. Assume that the balance is significant. Also assume that the following accounts contained the indicated amounts of manufacturing overhead applied during Year 2:

Work-in-process inventory	$ 3,000
Finished goods inventory	7,000
Cost of goods sold	80,000

P3-4B. Job Cost Journal Entries Prior to the beginning of the year, Stapleton Company estimated that it would incur $153,000 of manufacturing overhead cost for the year, using 17,000 direct labor hours to produce the desired volume of goods. On January 1, beginning balances of Materials Inventory, Work-in-Process Inventory, and Finished Goods Inventory were $48,000, $-0-, and $87,000, respectively.   **LO3, 4**

Required

Prepare general journal entries to record the following:

a. Purchased materials on account, $316,000.

b. Of the total dollar value of materials used, $284,000 represented direct materials and $35,000 indirect materials.

c. Determined total factory labor, $189,000 (18,000 hrs. @ $10.50/hr.).

d. Of the factory labor, 15,800 were direct labor hours.

e. Applied manufacturing overhead based on direct labor hours to work-in-process.

f. Determined actual manufacturing overhead other than those items already recorded, $83,000. (Credit Accounts Payable.)

g. Ending inventories of work-in-process and finished goods were $57,000 and $71,800, respectively. Determine the cost of finished goods (credit WIP) and the cost of goods sold (credit FG inventory). Make separate entries.

h. Transferred the balance in Manufacturing Overhead to Cost of Goods Sold.

LO3, 4   P3-5B.   Job Cost Journal Entries and T Accounts Following are certain operating data for Redwood Manufacturing Company for January:

	Materials Inventory	Work-in-Process Inventory	Finished Goods Inventory
Beginning inventory	$40,000	$50,000	$80,000
Ending inventory.	70,000	60,000	56,000

Total sales were $2,000,000, on which the company earned a 40% gross profit. Redwood uses a predetermined manufacturing overhead rate of 110% of direct labor costs. Manufacturing overhead applied was $396,000. Exclusive of indirect materials used, total manufacturing overhead incurred was $300,000; it was underapplied by $24,000.

Required

Compute the following items. (Set up T accounts for Materials Inventory, Work-in-Process Inventory, Finished Goods Inventory, and Manufacturing Overhead; fill in the known amounts; and then use the normal relationships among the various accounts to compute the unknown amounts.)

a. Cost of goods sold.   d. Direct materials used.
b. Cost of goods manufactured.   e. Indirect materials used.
c. Direct labor incurred.   f. Total materials purchased.

LO3, 4   P3-6B.   Job Cost Journal Entries and T Accounts Summarized data for the first month's operations of Slater Foundry are presented below. A job order costing system is used.

1. Materials purchased on account, $88,000.
2. Amounts of materials requisitioned and foundry labor used:

Job	Materials	Foundry Labor
1	$ 4,600	$ 3,600
2	5,200	6,000
3	3,800	8,800
4	13,400	12,000
5	6,400	7,200
6	4,000	2,000
Indirect materials	11,000	
Indirect labor.		18,000

3. Foundry overhead is applied at the rate of 150% of direct labor costs.
4. Miscellaneous foundry overhead incurred:

Prepaid foundry insurance written off.	$ 1,880
Property taxes on foundry building accrued	3,760
Foundry utilities payable accrued	4,400
Depreciation on foundry equipment	8,400
Other costs incurred on account.	14,640

5. Ending work-in-process consisted of Jobs 4 and 6. Jobs 1 and 3 and one-half of Job 2 were sold on account for $25,200, $31,600, and $18,920, respectively.

Required

a. Open general ledger T accounts for Materials Inventory, Wages Payable, Foundry Overhead, Work-in-Process Inventory, Finished Goods Inventory, and Cost of Goods Sold. Also set up subsidiary T accounts as job order cost sheets for each job.
b. Prepare general journal entries to record the summarized transactions for the month, and post appropriate entries to any accounts listed in requirement (a). Key each entry parenthetically to the related number in the problem data.
c. Determine the balances of any accounts necessary and prepare schedules of jobs in ending work-in-process and jobs in ending finished goods to confirm that they agree with the related control accounts.

P3-7B. **Complex Job Cost Journal Entries and Analysis** During June, its first month of operations, Logan   **LO3, 4**
Manufacturing Company completed the transactions listed below. Logan uses a job order costing
system. Materials requisitions and the wages payable summary are analyzed on the 15th and the last
day of each month, and charges for direct materials and direct labor are entered directly on specific
job order cost sheets. Manufacturing overhead at the rate of 160% of direct labor costs is recorded on
individual job order cost sheets when a job is completed and at month-end for any job then in process.
At month-end, entries to the general ledger accounts summarize materials requisitions, distribution of
wages payable costs, and the application of manufacturing overhead for the month. All other entries to
general ledger accounts are made as they occur.

1. Purchased materials on account, $210,000.
2. Paid miscellaneous manufacturing overhead costs, $52,000.
3. An analysis of materials requisitions and the wages payable summary for June 1–15 indicates the
   following cost distribution:

Job	Materials	Factory Labor
1	$34,000	$60,000
2	16,000	26,000
3	8,000	18,000
Indirect materials	14,000	
Indirect labor.		56,000
Total	$72,000	$160,000

4. Jobs 1 and 2 were completed on June 15 and transferred to finished goods inventory on the next
   day. (Enter the appropriate manufacturing overhead amounts on the job order cost sheets, mark
   them completed, and make a general journal entry transferring the appropriate amount of cost to
   the Finished Goods Inventory account.)
5. Paid miscellaneous manufacturing overhead costs, $38,000.
6. Sold Job 1 on account, $300,000 (recognized its cost of sales in the general journal).
7. An analysis of materials requisitions and wages payable summary for June 16–30 indicates the
   following cost distribution:

Job	Materials	Factory Labor
3	$36,000	$28,000
4	30,000	54,000
5	12,000	20,000
6	6,000	8,000
Indirect materials	10,000	
Indirect labor.		46,000
Total	$94,000	$156,000

8. Jobs 3 and 4 were completed on June 30 and transferred to finished goods inventory on the same
   day. (See transaction 4.)
9. Sold Job 3 on account, $250,000 (recognized its cost of sales in the general journal).
10. Recorded the following additional manufacturing overhead:

Depreciation on factory building.	$42,000
Depreciation on factory equipment.	24,000
Expiration of prepaid factory insurance	7,000
Payable.	13,000
	$86,000

11. Recorded monthly general journal entry for the costs of all materials used.
12. Recorded monthly general journal entry for the distribution of wages payable costs.
13. Recorded manufacturing overhead on the job order cost sheets for jobs in ending work-in-process
    and in the general journal for all manufacturing overhead applied during the month.

Required

a. Set up the following general ledger T accounts: Materials Inventory, Wages Payable, Manufacturing Overhead, Work-in-Process Inventory, Finished Goods Inventory, Cost of Goods Sold, and Sales.

b. Set up T accounts for each of Jobs 1–6 as job order cost sheets.

c. Noting the accounting procedures described in the first paragraph of the problem, do the following:

    1. Record general journal entries for all transactions. Note that general journal entries are not required in transactions 3 and 7. Post only those portions of these entries affecting the general ledger accounts set up in requirement (a).

    2. Enter the applicable amounts directly on the appropriate job order cost sheets for transactions 3, 4, 7, 8, and 13. Note parenthetically the nature of each amount entered.

d. Present a brief analysis showing that the general ledger accounts for work-in-process inventory and for finished goods inventory agree with the related job order cost sheets.

e. Explain in one sentence each what the balance of each general ledger account established in requirement (a) represents.

EXTENDING YOUR KNOWLEDGE

EYK3-1. Business Decision Case Elizabeth Flanigan and Associates is an engineering and design firm that specializes in developing plans for recycling plants for municipalities. The firm uses a job costing system to accumulate the cost associated with each design project. Flanigan employs three levels of employee: senior engineers, associate engineers, and clerical staff. The salary cost of the senior engineers and the associate engineers is assigned to each project as direct labor. The salary cost of the clerical staff is included in overhead, along with the cost of engineering supplies, automobile travel, and equipment depreciation. The cost of airline travel, motels, building permits, and fees from other consultants is charged to each project as direct materials. Overhead is applied to projects using a predetermined overhead rate based on total engineering hours. The rate is $5 per hour.

The six different salary levels for the employees of Elizabeth Flanigan and Associates are listed below. The hourly rate is determined by dividing the yearly salary by 2,000 hours per year.

Senior engineer
Level 1: $44,000 per year ($22 per hour)
Level 2: $36,000 per year ($18 per hour)
Associate engineer
Level 3: $30,000 per year ($15 per hour)
Level 4: $24,000 per year ($12 per hour)
Clerical staff
Level 5: $16,000 per year ($8 per hour)
Level 6: $14,500 per year ($7.25 per hour)

The billings that are sent to the municipalities for engineering services utilize cost-plus billing. Typically, the total costs accumulated for a project (direct materials, direct labor, and overhead) are multiplied by 140% to determine the amount of the billing. The difference between the billed amount and the accumulated cost is the "plus" in cost plus.

During March, Flanigan accumulated the following information related to Job 295 for Johnson Creek City:

Senior engineer hours	
Level 1	52
Level 2	84
Associate engineer hours	
Level 3	106
Level 4	44
Clerical hours	
Level 5	20
Level 6	66
Building permits	$1,500
Airline travel and motel	$865

Required
a. What amount should be billed to Johnson Creek City for March?
b. How much profit was earned on Job 295 during March?

EYK3-2. **Environmental, Social, and Governance** The ESG box in this chapter discusses CH2M Hill's efforts to offer summer programs at no cost introducing underrepresented groups to STEM education. The company's stated goal is twofold: to increase the pool of future engineering talent and to build better communities.

Some would look at these efforts as costly programs with no tangible financial benefit. There is certainly no guarantee that these children will work for CH2M Hill in the future, or even that they will choose careers in engineering. In fact, these efforts may end up supplying talent for CH2M Hill's competitors and driving up future engineering wages.

What do you think?

EYK3-3. **Ethics Case** Metal Creations, Inc., is a custom manufacturer that uses a job order costing system. Currently, Metal Creations has 35% excess capacity in its factory. Charlie Rollins, the president, has instituted a campaign to obtain new customers. Rollins has offered the salespeople a bonus equal to 25% of the gross profit on work for new customers. The average gross profit rate has been 30% of the contract price.

Steve Starling, the sales manager for Metal Creations, wants to submit a proposal to a new customer that undercuts the usual pricing structure by 30%. As a result, this job would have no gross profit using the regular job order costing system. Instead, Starling suggests that the overhead rate applied to this job should be only 40% of the normal overhead rate, resulting in a gross profit of 28%. Starling suggests that the controller should handle this contract herself and that no one else in the organization should know about it, especially the other salespeople, because the creative approach to overhead application might create problems.

Required
Does taking an order at a significantly reduced price create an ethical problem? Does altering the accounting for a particular order create an ethical problem? Does asking the controller to handle the contract and keep the accounting confidential create an ethical problem?

ANSWERS TO SELF-STUDY QUESTIONS:

1. a   2. d   3. c   4. b   5. b   6. d

YOUR TURN! SOLUTIONS

Solution 3.1

Industry	Cost System
Chemicals	Process
Printing	Job order
Aircraft	Job order
Oil refining	Process
Paints	Process
Glass	Process
Furniture	Job order
Machinery	Job order

Solution 3.2

Estimated manufacturing overhead	$250,000
Divided by budgeted direct labor hours	10,000
Predetermined overhead rate per direct labor hour	$ 25
Actual direct labor hours.	$ 9,000
Multiplied by predetermined overhead rate	× 25
Applied overhead	$225,000

Solution 3.3

1, 1, 2, 3, 3, 1

Solution 3.4

Materials inventory	2,000	
Cash or Accounts Payable		2,000
WIP inventory—#144	2,600	
Materials inventory		2,600
Manufacturing overhead	350	
Materials inventory		350
WIP inventory—#144	1,650	
Wages payable or cash		1,650
WIP inventory—#144	3,300	
Manufacturing overhead		3,300
Finished goods inventory	7,550	
WIP inventory—#144		7,550
Cost of goods sold	7,550	
Finished goods inventory		7,550

Solution 3.5

Molding (20 hours × $10)	$200
Machining (10 hours × $8)	80
Painting (5 hours × $4)	20
Total	$300

Chapter 4

Cost Accounting Systems: Process Costing

Road Map

LO	Learning Objective	Page	eLecture	Guided Example	Assignments
LO1	Compare and contrast job order costing and process costing.	4-3	E4-1		Q1, Q2
LO2	Describe the basic concepts of process costing.	4-5	E4-2		SS1, SS2, Q2, Q3
LO3	Explain techniques for determining unit costs when process costing is used.	4-7	E4-3	YT4.1, YT4.2, YT4.3, YT4.4, YT4.5	SS1, Q3, Q4, Q5, Q6, Q7, Q8, SE1, SE2, SE3, SE4, SE5, E1A, E2A, E3A, E4A, E5A, E1B, E2B, E3B, E4B, E5B, P1A, P2A, P3A, P4A, P5A, P1B, P2B, P3B, P4B, P5B
LO4	Explain the procedures used to prepare the product cost report using the weighted average method in a process costing system.	4-15	E4-4		SE1, SE2, SE5, E3A, E4A, E5A, E3B, E4B, E5B, P1A, P2A, P3A, P4A, P5A, P1B, P2B, P3B, P4B, P5B
LO5	Illustrate the journal entries used with process costing.	4-16	E4-5	YT4.6	E6A, E6B, P5A, P5B
LO6	Appendix 4A: Explain techniques for determining unit costs when the FIFO method for process costing is used.	4-21	E4-6	YT4.7, YT4.8, YT4.9, YT4.10, YT4.11	SS3, Q9, SE6, SE7, E7A, E8A, E9A, E10A, E11A, E7B, E8B, E9B, E10B, E11B, P6A, P7A, P6B, P7B
LO7	Appendix 4A: Explain the procedures used to prepare the product cost report using the FIFO method in a process costing system.	4-28	E4-7		Q9, E9A, E10A, E11A, E9B, E10B, E11B, P6A, P7A, P8A, P6B, P7B, P8B
LO8	Appendix 4A: Illustrate the journal entries used with FIFO process costing.	4-29	E4-8	YT4.12	Q9

General Mills Inc. is a Fortune 500 company based in Golden Valley, Minnesota. Consumers know General Mills best for its ready-to-eat cereal products, of which they consume 60 million servings per day. The quality of these cereal products can be traced back to Gold Medal flour in 1880, which today remains the number-one-selling brand of flour in the United States. General Mills's brand portfolio includes more than 100 leading U.S. brands and numerous category leaders around the world. Some of the top-selling brands include Betty Crocker, Yoplait, Totinos, Pillsbury, Cheerios, Trix, and Lucky Charms. One unique manufacturing feature these brands share is that they are produced in mass quantities, with little to distinguish one cupful of cereal or yogurt from another.

Manufacturers like General Mills that produce massive quantities of inventory that are indistinguishable from one another rely on process costing to track inventory costs. Rather than track the cost of each piece of cereal, General Mills tracks the total costs of inventory produced over a given period and divides these total costs by the pounds of inventory produced to obtain an average price per pound for each product. This costing system stands in stark contrast to industries such as custom cabinet manufacturing, in which costs are tallied on a job cost record for each unique custom cabinet rather than spreading them over multiple identical units of inventory.

This chapter examines how companies like General Mills utilize process costing in order to properly value their inventory. We focus on how the weighted average method of process costing provides useful information to managers and illustrates the journal entries required throughout the manufacturing process. We also introduce the concept of equivalent units and their application to process costing.

PAST

Chapter 3 introduced and explained job costing in more detail for both manufacturing and service industries. It also explained overhead allocation.

PRESENT

Chapter 4 introduces process costing and how it differs from job order costing. It illustrates equivalent units and the flow of costs through the inventory accounts, as well as introduces the product cost report.

FUTURE

Chapter 5 explores activity-based costing and its benefits relative to traditional plant-wide and departmental overhead allocation, and contrasts it with activity-based management.

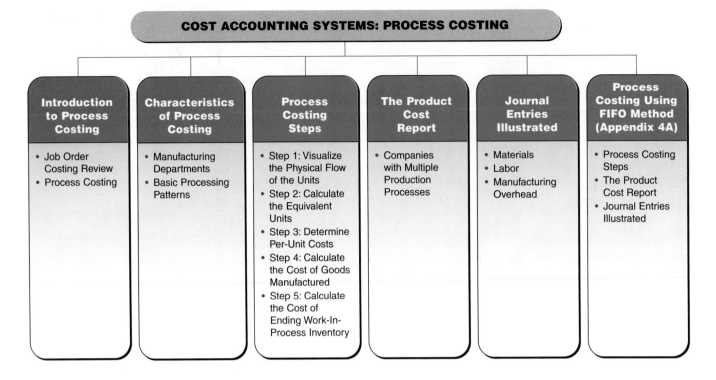

INTRODUCTION TO PROCESS COSTING

LO1

Compare and **contrast** job order costing and process costing.

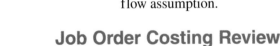

The early sections of this chapter explain and illustrate the concepts and procedures that are typical in a process costing system that involves only one processing department using the weighted average cost flow assumption. Appendix 4A illustrates the procedures and differences under the first-in, first-out (FIFO) cost flow assumption.

Job Order Costing Review

Prior chapters have introduced and discussed the concepts used in job order costing. Recall that job order costing accumulates costs for each specific job in a separate work-in-process inventory account dedicated to that unique job. **Exhibit 4-1** presents the typical flow of product costs in a job order costing system for Job 372. Direct materials and direct labor are traced to each specific job, whereas indirect overhead costs are allocated to each job.

EXHIBIT 4-1	**Product Cost Flows in a Job Order Costing System**

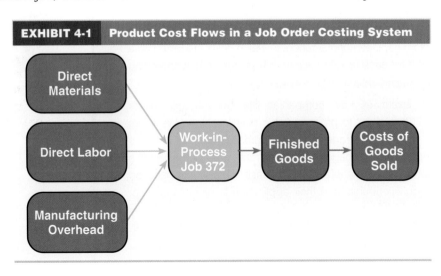

Although production costs are tracked separately for each job, companies also need to understand their total costs. Hence, costs for all of the individual jobs are accumulated in the work-in-process control account, which represents the overall cost summary of all jobs currently in production. For example, **Exhibit 4-2** lists four individual jobs that are currently in process. The work-in-process inventory control account represents the sum of all jobs that are currently in process. Overhead costs are accumulated and applied to the work-in-process inventory control account based on an annual predetermined overhead rate. Specifically, actual overhead costs, including indirect materials and indirect labor, are accumulated in the manufacturing overhead account as debits, and the applied overhead is transferred to Work-in-Process Inventory with a credit. Perpetual inventory techniques are typically used to move product cost from Work-in-Process Inventory to Finished Goods Inventory and finally to Cost of Goods Sold, as illustrated in **Exhibit 4-2**.

EXHIBIT 4-2   **Job Order Costing Summary (Accumulating Costs by Job)**

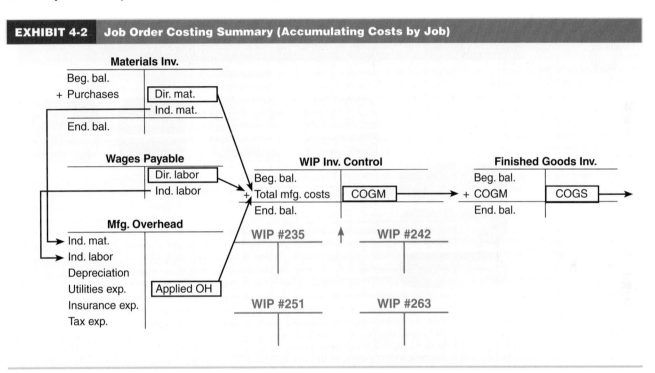

Job order costing is appropriate when products or services are characterized by customization to meet the customer's specifications. Job order costing can result when products are produced or jobs are undertaken to (1) fill specific customer orders or (2) produce a stock of products from which future orders can be filled.

Process Costing

Process costing, however, is used when large volumes of identical (homogeneous) products are manufactured in a continuous-flow operation, such as the production of fuels, chemicals, small appliances, building materials, and electricity. In process costing, product costs are accumulated by department, not by job or product. We note at the outset that although it is possible to use process costing in a service environment, it is not common. For example, a service agency that provides identical services to each customer could calculate an average cost per customer. However, most of the examples in this chapter focus on manufacturing companies because process costing is much more common in a manufacturing setting. We provide a detailed service example at the end of the chapter.

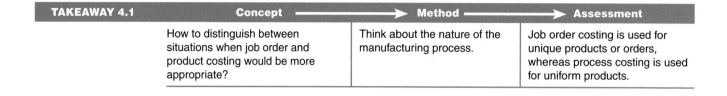

TAKEAWAY 4.1	Concept	→	Method	→	Assessment
	How to distinguish between situations when job order and product costing would be more appropriate?		Think about the nature of the manufacturing process.		Job order costing is used for unique products or orders, whereas process costing is used for uniform products.

CHARACTERISTICS OF PROCESS COSTING

LO2 Describe the basic concepts of process costing.

eLecture

MBC

Exhibit 4-3 presents the typical flow of product cost in a **process costing system**. The following process costing characteristics are evident in **Exhibit 4-3**:

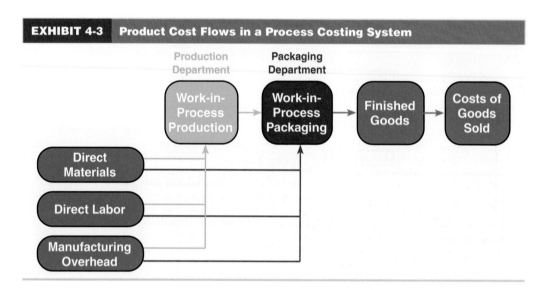

EXHIBIT 4-3   Product Cost Flows in a Process Costing System

1. Each manufacturing department has a separate work-in-process inventory account. **Exhibit 4-3** assumes a company with two manufacturing departments: production and packaging. Costs are accumulated for each department in a separate work-in-process inventory account.

Hint: A process can be defined as a step in the manufacture of a product. In a process costing system, materials, labor, and overhead are charged to processing departments rather than to specific jobs.

2. **Exhibit 4-4** shows how the costs in this process flow through the accounts. Direct materials, direct labor, and manufacturing overhead costs can be added to the work-in-process inventory account in each department. **Exhibit 4-4** shows all three elements of product cost being added to both work-in-process inventory accounts.

3. Products physically move through the process on a first-in, first-out (FIFO) basis. That is, the unfinished units in work-in-process are assumed to be completed first in the subsequent period before new units are started.

A.K.A. The product cost report is also known as a "cost of production report" or a "process cost summary."

4. Under process costing, managers use a **product cost report** to accumulate costs by process or department. These costs are then allocated to specific units of product that pass through that process or department using either the weighted average or FIFO allocation method. In this chapter, we focus on the weighted average costing method, and Appendix 4A explains the FIFO costing method.

EXHIBIT 4-4   **Process Costing Summary (Accumulating Costs by Process or Department)**

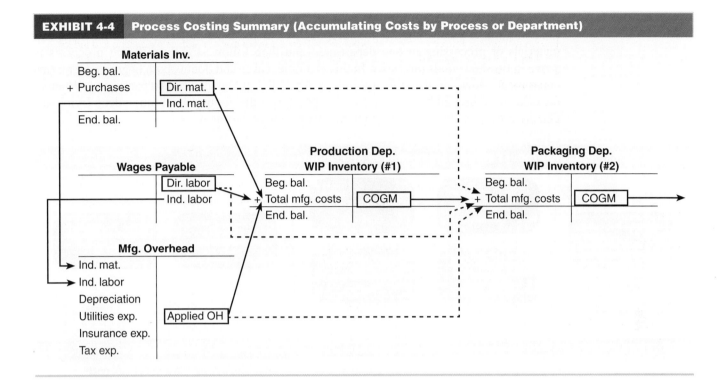

Manufacturing Departments

Typically, multiple manufacturing departments are identified when process costing is used. Products will flow through these departments at different stages of the manufacturing process. For example, a baked good product might be processed through three departments: mixing, baking, and packaging. In a particular bakery, some products may go through many departments or processes, and other products may go through only a few departments or processes, depending on the nature of the product being baked. Regardless, the work in any department must be performed uniformly on all units, and the output of the department must be uniform in nature.

Basic Processing Patterns

There are two basic patterns for arranging the departments in a process costing setting: sequential and parallel processing. **Exhibit 4-5** presents a **sequential product processing** pattern, in which all baked products follow a single path through the manufacturing process to finished goods inventory.

EXHIBIT 4-5   **Sequential Product Processing**

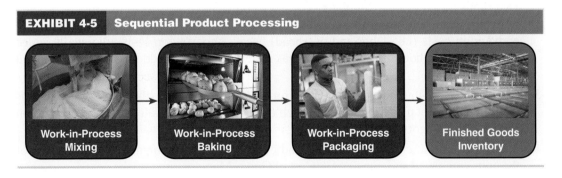

Exhibit 4-6 presents a simple example of **parallel product processing**. Numerous variations of parallel processing are possible, but similar products may begin with the same raw materials or processing in one department and then follow slightly different processes to arrive in finished goods inventory. In this example, cakes and donuts both begin in the mixing department. However, they undergo different parallel processes prior to packaging. Whereas the cake goes through baking and frosting processes, the donut goes through deep frying and glazing processes. Finally, both go to the packaging department.

EXHIBIT 4-6	Parallel Product Processing for Cakes and Donuts

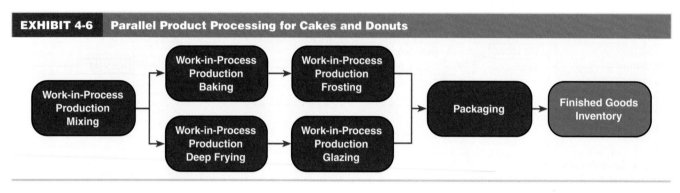

TAKEAWAY 4.2	Concept ⟶	Method ⟶	Assessment
	How are departments that use process costing different from those that use job order costing?	Think about the work that is being performed in each department.	When process costing is appropriate, each processing department has two essential features: 1. The activity is performed uniformly on all products passing through it. 2. The output is homogeneous.

PROCESS COSTING STEPS

LO3 Explain techniques for determining unit costs when process costing is used.

eLecture

MBC

The techniques described in this chapter require the calculation of unit costs to facilitate the end-of-period transfer of product cost from one work-in-process inventory account to another, from the final work-in-process inventory account to the finished goods inventory account, and from the finished goods inventory account to the cost of goods sold account. In process costing, unit costs are usually calculated on a monthly basis. These unit costs can be compared to unit costs of prior accounting periods to determine when additional cost control measures are necessary.

Process costing requires five steps or calculations:

1. Visualize or chart the physical flow of the units through the system.

2. Determine the equivalent whole units of work completed (or **equivalent units** of production) during the period. This calculation is usually performed separately for materials and **conversion costs** (i.e., labor and overhead) because conversion costs are usually added uniformly throughout the process, whereas materials are often added at a particular point in the process.

3. Compute the per-unit cost of production for the period for materials and conversion costs by dividing the total costs incurred in each category by the equivalent units of production for that cost category.

4. Using the per-unit costs for materials and conversion costs, compute the dollar value of the units completed and transferred (Cost of Goods Manufactured) to the next department.

5. Using the same per-unit costs, compute the dollar value of the unfinished units that remain in the department. (These ending work-in-process units will usually be completed in the following period.)

There are two primary methods for allocating costs: weighted average and FIFO. We illustrate the **weighted average method** here and the **FIFO method** in **Appendix 4A**. The objective of each step is the same for both the weighted average and FIFO methods of cost allocation. However, the execution of the steps is slightly different between the two methods. We discuss these steps in more detail for the weighted average method in the following sections. For illustration purposes, assume that the Big G division of General Mills uses process costing to account for its cereal production (measured in tons) and that it has the results for January as illustrated in **Exhibit 4-7**.

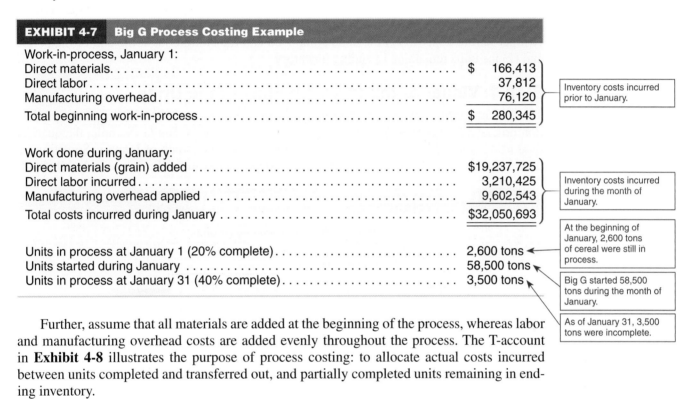

EXHIBIT 4-7   Big G Process Costing Example

Work-in-process, January 1:
Direct materials...	$ 166,413
Direct labor..	37,812
Manufacturing overhead................................	76,120
Total beginning work-in-process........................	$ 280,345

Inventory costs incurred prior to January.

Work done during January:
Direct materials (grain) added	$19,237,725
Direct labor incurred..................................	3,210,425
Manufacturing overhead applied	9,602,543
Total costs incurred during January	$32,050,693

Inventory costs incurred during the month of January.

Units in process at January 1 (20% complete)...........	2,600 tons
Units started during January	58,500 tons
Units in process at January 31 (40% complete).........	3,500 tons

At the beginning of January, 2,600 tons of cereal were still in process.

Big G started 58,500 tons during the month of January.

As of January 31, 3,500 tons were incomplete.

Further, assume that all materials are added at the beginning of the process, whereas labor and manufacturing overhead costs are added evenly throughout the process. The T-account in **Exhibit 4-8** illustrates the purpose of process costing: to allocate actual costs incurred between units completed and transferred out, and partially completed units remaining in ending inventory.

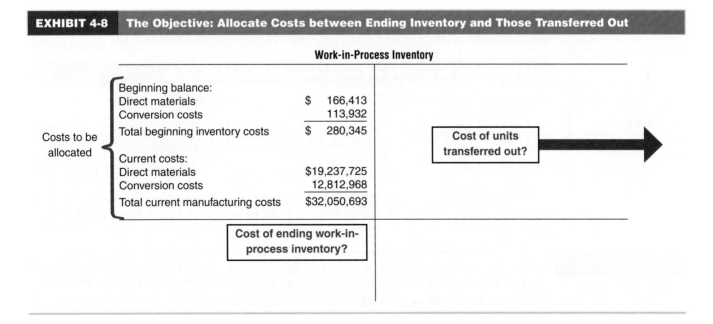

EXHIBIT 4-8   The Objective: Allocate Costs between Ending Inventory and Those Transferred Out

Work-in-Process Inventory

Costs to be allocated

Beginning balance:
Direct materials	$ 166,413
Conversion costs	113,932
Total beginning inventory costs	$ 280,345

Current costs:
Direct materials	$19,237,725
Conversion costs	12,812,968
Total current manufacturing costs	$32,050,693

Cost of units transferred out?

Cost of ending work-in-process inventory?

We know the costs associated with the beginning work-in-process inventory on January 1 ($280,345). We also know the costs incurred during the month of January for direct materials ($19,237,725), direct labor ($3,210,425), and manufacturing overhead ($9,602,543). For simplicity, because we assume both direct labor and manufacturing overhead costs are applied uniformly during the production process, we combine them and simply refer to them as "conversion costs." Because we started the period with partially completed inventory, during the period we will first finish the previously started units and then begin work on new units. We also end the period with partially completed units. We don't know how much of these costs should be applied to units transferred out at the end of the period and how much should remain with the partially complete ending inventory. Process costing helps us calculate an average cost per unit to apply to (1) the units completed and transferred out at the end of the period and (2) the units remaining in ending inventory.

Step 1: Visualize the Physical Flow of the Units

The starting point in process costing is to visualize how the units flow through the production process, as illustrated in **Exhibit 4-9**. In the General Mills Big G example, the quantity produced is measured in tons of cereal processed during the month of January. Sometimes it is useful to visualize how the units correspond to the dollars in the T-account in **Exhibit 4-8**.

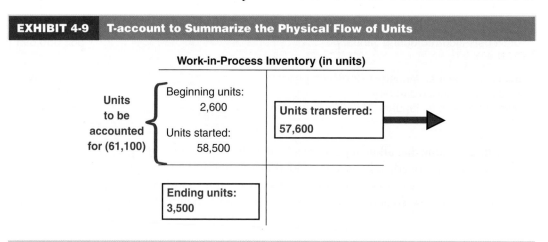

EXHIBIT 4-9   T-account to Summarize the Physical Flow of Units

Work-in-Process Inventory (in units)

Units to be accounted for (61,100)

Beginning units: 2,600

Units started: 58,500

Units transferred: 57,600

Ending units: 3,500

Another way to visualize the flow of the cereal produced during January is by asking where the units come from and where they end up, as shown in **Exhibit 4-10**.

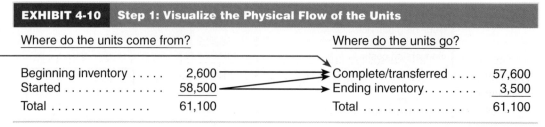

EXHIBIT 4-10   Step 1: Visualize the Physical Flow of the Units

The complete/transferred inventory is composed of the 2,600 units in the beginning inventory (which were completed first) as well as 55,000 of the units that were started this period (leaving 3,500 unfinished units in the ending inventory).

Where do the units come from?		Where do the units go?	
Beginning inventory	2,600	Complete/transferred	57,600
Started	58,500	Ending inventory	3,500
Total	61,100	Total	61,100

We assume that all of the beginning inventory is completed first. Of the 58,500 units started this month, 55,000 are complete by the end of the month, and 3,500 remain partially complete.

YOUR TURN! 4.1

The solution is on page 4-47.

Beginning work-in-process is composed of 100 units. Also assume that 700 units are started and completed during the period, and ending work-in-process includes 90 units. Summarize "Where do the units come from" and "Where do the units go."

GuidedExample

MBC

Step 2: Calculate the Equivalent Units

Introduction to Equivalent Units

The average cost per unit is calculated by dividing total costs by the total number of units produced. The work-in-process accounts described in **Exhibits 4-5** and **4-6** illustrate how total costs are accumulated and tracked through the system. Accountants are good at keeping track of costs. However, cost accountants face a major problem in allocating costs in continuous-flow manufacturing processes because it is difficult to estimate how units are complete. **Equivalent units** are the equivalent number of *whole units* completed during the period. At any given point in time, units of product are at various stages of completion. Hence, it is difficult to determine the number of equivalent complete units to use in the average cost per unit calculation:

Hint: Instead of tracking specific costs incurred to produce each unit of product as in job order costing, process costing accumulates costs by department and then calculates an average cost per unit to be assigned to all units of product produced during that period.

$$\frac{\text{Average}}{\text{cost per unit}} = \frac{\text{Total costs incurred}}{\text{\# of equivalent units}} \quad \longleftarrow \quad \text{We know this.}$$
$$\longleftarrow \quad \text{We don't know this.}$$

The notion of equivalent units of production is a key concept in process costing. When units of product are produced in a continuous process, engineers and manufacturing supervisors must estimate the average percentage completion of units in a given department at the end of each period. Accountants use this information to estimate the number of equivalent *complete* units of product. For example, the following illustration shows eight glasses of water that are *half* full. How many *full* glasses of water is this equivalent to?

8 Glasses ½ Full = 4 Full Glasses

The eight half-full glasses are approximately equivalent to four full glasses. This example illustrates what accountants do each period in determining the average cost per unit in a given department.

To properly determine per-unit costs, we must first calculate equivalent units of production to be used in the denominator of the average cost per unit calculation. Again, equivalent units are the equivalent number of *whole units* completed during the period. In the previous illustration, the eight partially full glasses of water are equivalent to four full glasses (similar to four equivalent complete units of production). The calculation of equivalent units of production requires accountants to (1) track the *actual quantity* of products at each stage of production and (2) estimate the *average amount of work completed* on each unit of product in terms of conversion costs and direct material costs.

Engineers or production experts estimate the percentage of work completed in terms of conversion costs, on average. As illustrated in **Exhibit 4-11**, because the 2,600 tons of cereal on hand on January 1 is 20% complete (based on work completed during December),

Big G only has to complete the remaining 80% of the processing during the month of January. During January, Big G begins work on 55,000 tons of cereal that is both started and completed during the month of January. Finally, Big G begins work on an additional 3,500 tons of cereal that is not completed by the end of the month. Engineers determine that only 40% of the processing is complete on this batch of cereal by January 31.

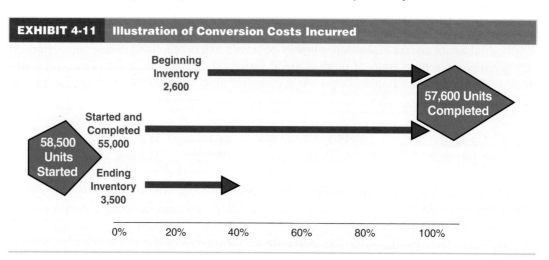

EXHIBIT 4-11	Illustration of Conversion Costs Incurred

We assume that all direct materials are added at the beginning of the process; therefore, the average amount of work completed on each unit of product related to direct materials is 100%.

Calculating equivalent units can be performed using either the weighted average or the FIFO cost flow assumption. A key difference between the two cost allocation methods is that the weighted average method mixes inventory layers, whereas the FIFO method keeps inventory layers separate. To keep these layers separate, the FIFO method tracks costs incurred during December separate from those incurred during January. The weighted average method averages all costs incurred in the production of a batch of units, regardless of when those costs were incurred. Thus, the FIFO method asks "What costs were incurred during THIS PERIOD?" whereas the weighted average method simply asks "How much work is complete (regardless of when the work was done)?"

Equivalent Unit Calculation for Direct Materials—Weighted Average
Because materials are added at the beginning of the process, all units that have been started (61,100) are 100% complete with respect to materials. **Exhibit 4-12** illustrates the calculation of equivalent units in terms of direct materials based on the weighted average cost flow assumption.

EXHIBIT 4-12	Step 2: Calculate the Equivalent Units—Direct Materials

	Physical Units (tons)		Proportion Completed		Equivalent Units (tons)
Complete and transferred............	57,600	×	100%	=	57,600
Ending inventory...................	3,500	×	100%	=	3,500
Total	61,100				61,100

Equivalent Unit Calculation for Conversion Costs—Weighted Average
When considering conversion costs (direct labor and manufacturing overhead), it is often useful to visualize the amount of work done during the period on each unique set of inventory

passing through the production process, as previously illustrated in **Exhibit 4-11**. Despite the fact that some of the units were started during December, the weighted average method simply asks what percentage of the work has been completed by the end of January, as illustrated in **Exhibit 4-13**. The units that were completed and transferred out are 100% complete with respect to conversion costs, while the units that were started but remaining in ending inventory are only 40% complete with respect to conversion costs.

EXHIBIT 4-13	Step 2: Calculate the Equivalent Units—Conversion Costs					
	Physical Units (tons)		Proportion Completed		Equivalent Units (tons)	
Complete and transferred.........	57,600	×	100%	=	57,600	
Ending inventory.................	3,500	×	40%	=	1,400	
Total	61,100				59,000	

We can summarize the flow of the units worked on during the period and how the amount of work completed translates them into equivalent units, as illustrated in **Exhibit 4-14**.

EXHIBIT 4-14	Summary of Step. 4-1 and 2: Unit Flows and Equivalent Units Calculations

Step 2: Calculate the Equivalent Units

Step 1: Visualize the Physical Flow of the Units

					Equivalent Units			
Where do the units come from?		Where do the units go?			% Work Done?	Dir. Mat.	% Work Done?	Conv. Costs
Beginning inventory	2,600 →	Complete/transferred	57,600		100%	57,600	100%	57,600
Started	58,500 →	Ending inventory........	3,500		100%	3,500	40%	1,400
Total	61,100	Total	61,100			61,100		59,000

Concept ——→	Method ——→	Assessment	TAKEAWAY 4.3
How many full glasses of water are equivalent to this number of partially full glasses?	Multiply the percentage of completion by the number of units being worked on.	An equivalent unit is the amount of work necessary to produce one complete physical unit of product.	

Assume all materials are added at the beginning of the production process, and conversion costs are added uniformly throughout the process. Beginning work-in-process is composed of 100 units, which are 35% complete with respect to conversion costs. Also assume that 700 units are started and completed during the period, and ending work-in-process includes 90 units that are 70% complete with respect to conversion costs. Compute equivalent units of production for direct materials and conversion costs under the weighted average cost flow assumption.

YOUR TURN! 4.2

The solution is on page 4-48.

Step 3: Determine the Per-Unit Costs

The product cost report summarizes where the costs come from and where they go (i.e., where they are allocated). In order to calculate an average cost per unit of direct materials and conversion costs, we first need to summarize the total costs incurred for direct materials and conversion costs. These numbers were illustrated in the T-account in **Exhibit 4-8**. The top part of our product cost report simply asks where the costs come from and organizes them into categories: Direct Materials and Conversion Costs, as illustrated in **Exhibit 4-15**.

EXHIBIT 4-15	Product Cost Report: Where Do the Costs Come From?			

Product Cost Report
General Mills Big G Division
January Production

Where do the costs come from?	Total	Direct Materials	Conversion Costs
Beginning inventory	$ 280,345	$ 166,413	$ 113,932
Current	32,050,693	19,237,725	12,812,968
Total costs to account for	$32,331,038	$19,404,138	$12,926,900

We then calculate the average cost per unit for materials and conversion costs by dividing total costs in each category by total equivalent units in each category from Step 2. In other words, we divide total materials costs by total equivalent units of materials ($19,404,138/61,100 equivalent units) to get an average cost per unit of $317.58. Similarly, we divide total conversion costs by total equivalent units of conversion costs ($12,926,900/59,000 equivalent units) to get an average cost per unit of $219.10. **Exhibit 4-16** summarizes this calculation.

EXHIBIT 4-16	Step 3: Product Cost Report: Determine Per-Unit Costs			

Product Cost Report
General Mills Big G Division
January Production

Where do the costs come from?	Total	Direct Materials	Conversion Costs
Beginning inventory	$ 280,345	$ 166,413	$ 113,932
Current	32,050,693	19,237,725	12,812,968
Total costs to account for	$32,331,038	$19,404,138	$12,926,900
÷ Total equivalent units		61,100	59,000
Average cost/unit		$ 317.58	$ 219.10

Note that the weighted average method includes *all* costs incurred on units worked on during the month, whereas the FIFO method only includes costs incurred during the *current* period. Hence, both the numerator (costs incurred) and the denominator (equivalent units) will differ between the weighted average and FIFO methods.

YOUR TURN! 4.3	Assume that you have 890 total equivalent units of materials and 863 total equivalent units of conversion costs. Also assume that your beginning inventory is composed of $3,390 of materials and $1,493 of conversion costs and that you use $19,750 of materials and incur $14,904 of conversion costs during the current period. Calculate the average cost per unit of materials and conversion costs assuming the weighted average cost flow assumption.

The solution is on page 4-48.

MBC

Step 4: Calculate the Cost of Goods Manufactured

At the end of each month and for each department, we calculate the cost of goods manufactured (illustrated in **Exhibit 4-17**), which is composed of the cost of the goods that are completed and transferred to the finished goods inventory. Under the weighted average cost flow assumption, the Big G division's cost of goods manufactured during January consists of

57,600 equivalent units of materials and conversion costs (shown in **red** in **Exhibit 4-14**) multiplied by their respective per-unit costs computed in Step 3 (shown in **green** in **Exhibit 4-16**).

EXHIBIT 4-17	Step 4: Cost of Goods Manufactured Calculation	
Materials..............................	[**57,600** EU × **$317.58**]	$18,292,608
Conversion costs	[**57,600** EU × **$219.10**]	12,620,160
Total cost of goods manufactured...........		$30,912,768

Assume that you have completed and transferred 800 units out of your department during the period and that you have determined your average cost per equivalent unit of direct materials to be $26.00 and your average cost per equivalent unit of conversion costs to be $19.00. Determine your cost of goods manufactured.

YOUR TURN! 4.4

The solution is on page 4-48.

MBC

Step 5: Calculate the Cost of Ending Work-in-Process Inventory

Exhibit 4-18 illustrates the final step, which is to calculate the **cost of goods remaining** in ending work-in-process. Assuming all materials are added at the beginning and conversion costs are added evenly throughout the process, we multiply the equivalent units of materials and conversion costs in ending inventory (denoted in **red** in **Exhibit 4-14**) by their respective unit costs (shown in **green** in **Exhibit 4-16**) computed in Step 3, as shown in **Exhibit 4-18**.

EXHIBIT 4-18	Step 5: Calculate Cost of Ending Work-in-Process Inventory	
Materials..............................	[**3,500** EU × **$317.58**]	$1,111,530
Conversion costs	[**1,400** EU × **$219.10**]	306,740
Total cost of ending inventory..............		$1,418,270

Assume that your ending inventory is composed of 90 equivalent units of materials and 63 equivalent units of conversions costs and that you have determined your average cost per equivalent unit of direct materials to be $26.00 and your average cost per equivalent unit of conversion costs to be $19.00. Determine the cost of your ending inventory.

YOUR TURN! 4.5

The solution is on page 4-48.

MBC

ENVIRONMENTAL, SOCIAL, AND GOVERNANCE	General Mills Tries to Make a Difference

If you read the current popular media reports, you are likely to get the idea that the only stakeholders a corporation cares about are its shareholders. **General Mills** thinks differently. The goal of General Mills is to stand among the world's most socially responsible food companies. The company believes that being a good corporate citizen means considering all its stakeholders. To do this, General Mills seeks to create long-term economic, social, and environmental value.

General Mills also recognizes that it makes good business sense to behave in a manner that considers other stakeholders. One of those stakeholders is the planet itself. General Mills, a company rooted in agriculture, is aware that the ability of the earth's natural resources to sustain agriculture has declined, while at the same time the earth's growing population's need for food has increased. The company is working to make a meaningful difference through regenerative agriculture, a process they define as a "holistic, principles-based approach to farming and ranching that seeks to strengthen ecosystems and community resilience." The six core principles of regenerative agriculture are (1) understand the context of farm operation, (2) minimize disturbance, (3) maximize diversity, (4) keep the soil covered, (5) maintain living roots year-round, and (6) integrate livestock. The outcomes of regenerative agriculture include biodiversity, water management, soil health, cow and herd well-being, and farmer livelihood and community resilience.

Source: https://globalresponsibility.generalmills.com/HTML1/general_mills-global_responsibility_2022_0030.htm

THE PRODUCT COST REPORT

LO4 **Explain** the procedures used to prepare the product cost report using the weighted average method in a process costing system.

Using the Big G example, the product cost report illustrated in **Exhibit 4-19** summarizes all of the steps in the total cost allocation process from (1) visualizing the physical flow of the units, to (2) calculating equivalent units, to (3) calculating unit costs, to (4) calculating cost of goods manufactured, to (5) calculating the cost of ending work-in-process inventory. Moreover, **Exhibit 4-19** also provides Big G's product cost report. Note that in this illustration, the equivalent units of production for materials and conversion costs (the numbers in **red**) are multiplied by the corresponding cost per unit figures for materials and conversion costs (the numbers in **green**) to calculate the cost allocation to cost of goods manufactured and ending inventory.

EXHIBIT 4-19	Summary of the Five Process Costing Steps

Flow of the Units and Equivalent Units Calculation

				Step 2: Calculate the Equivalent Units			
Step 1: Visualize the Physical Flow of the Units					Equivalent Units		
Where do the units come from?		Where do the units go?		% Work Done?	Dir. Mat.	% Work Done?	Conv. Costs
Beginning inventory...	2,600	Compl./transferred	57,600	100%	57,600	100%	57,600
Started	58,500	Ending inventory.	3,500	100%	3,500	40%	1,400
Total	61,100	Total	61,100		61,100		59,000

Product Cost Report
General Mills Big G Division
January Production

Step 3: Determine Per-Unit Costs

Where do the costs come from?	Total		Dir. Mat.	Conv. Costs
Beginning inventory	$ 280,345		$ 166,413	$ 113,932
Current	32,050,693		19,237,725	12,812,968
Total costs to account for	$32,331,038		$19,404,138	$12,926,900
÷ Total equivalent units			**61,100**	**59,000**
Average cost/equivalent unit..............			$ 317.58	$ 219.10

Where do the costs go?

Step 4: Calculate the Cost of Goods Manufactured

Complete/transferred:			
Materials	$18,292,608	[57,600 × $317.58]	
Conversion costs....................	12,620,160	[57,600 × $219.10]	
Cost of goods manuactured	$30,912,768 ⌐		

Step 5: Calculate the Cost of the Ending Work-in-Process Inventory

Ending inventory:			
Materials	$ 1,111,530	[3,500 × $317.58]	
Conversion costs....................	306,740	[1,400 × $219.10]	
Cost of ending inventory	1,418,270 ⌐		
Total costs allocated	$32,331,038 ◄		

As a final check to see that we have performed all of the calculations correctly, the sum of the Cost of Goods Manufactured ($30,912,768) and the ending Working Process Inventory balance ($1,418,270) should equal the total costs that we determined at the outset needed to be allocated (Beginning balance $280,345 + Current costs $32,050,693 = $32,331,038).

Specifically, the T-account in **Exhibit 4-20** summarizes the process costing allocation of costs between the cost of goods manufactured transferred out and costs remaining in ending inventory.

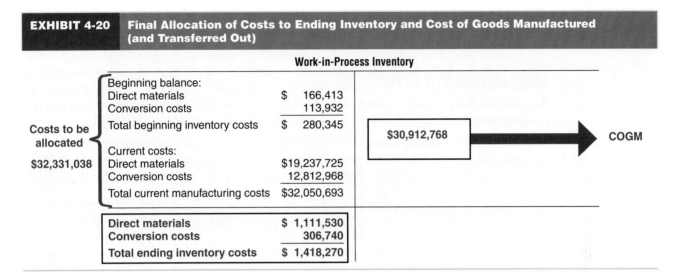

EXHIBIT 4-20   **Final Allocation of Costs to Ending Inventory and Cost of Goods Manufactured (and Transferred Out)**

Companies with Multiple Production Processes

At the outset of this chapter, we described situations in which a company produces its products through a long series of production processes. So far, we have illustrated process costing in a single department. When a company's production process involves a series of different departments, costs are accumulated by production process. The costs transferred out of one department are transferred into the next department. Hence, as units of product move from one department or process to the next, they carry the costs from all prior processes with them. From a practical perspective, the only thing that changes in the product costing process is that an extra column is added for transferred-in costs. For example, the $30,912,768 transferred out of the production process described in the previous section would become the transferred-in costs for the next department.

Hint: For companies with multiple production processes, their product costing process will include transferred-in costs. These costs will be part of their cost of goods manufactured and ending inventory.

JOURNAL ENTRIES ILLUSTRATED

After computing these amounts, Big G would record the following journal entries related to January production. ***These entries assume that materials are added at the beginning of the process, and that labor and overhead are added evenly over the month of January.***

LO5 Illustrate the journal entries used with process costing.

MBC

Materials

During January, assume that Big G purchased $20,000,000 of grain on account. The following is a summary journal entry for the January purchases:

1	Materials inventory	20,000,000	
	Accounts payable		20,000,000
	To record January materials purchases.		

The direct materials requisitioned during January for the processing department are shown in the following entry:

2	Work-in-process	19,237,725	
	Materials inventory		19,237,725
	To record direct materials used during January.		

Labor

During January, Big G accrued $3,210,425 of direct labor expense. The journal entry to record this payroll would be as follows:

3	Work-in-process	3,210,425	
	Wages payable		3,210,425
	To record the payroll for January.		

Manufacturing Overhead

Assume that Big G has recorded $10,000,000 of actual manufacturing overhead costs (such as maintenance, depreciation, and utilities) in Manufacturing Overhead as incurred.

4	Manufacturing overhead	10,000,000	
	Maintenance wages payable		2,000,000
	Accumulated depreciation		7,000,000
	Utilities payable		1,000,000

Also assume that Big G applies manufacturing overhead costs to Work-in-Process using pre-determined overhead rates. The following entry records $9,602,543 of applied manufacturing overhead for the processing department:

5	Work-in-process	9,602,543	
	Manufacturing overhead		9,602,543
	To apply manufacturing overhead to work-in-process inventory.		

As a result of the journal entries recorded during the month, the Work-in-Process account contains the following balance as of the end of the month:

	Work-in-Process
Beginning balance	$ 280,345
Direct materials	19,237,725
Direct labor	3,210,425
Manufacturing overhead	9,602,543
Balance before month-end adjustments	$32,331,038

At the end of the month, an additional journal entry is needed to transfer product costs from the processing department to Finished Goods (the amount of Cost of Goods Manufactured). The following entry records the Cost of Goods Manufactured:

6	Finished goods	30,912,768	
	Work-in-process		30,912,768
	To transfer the cost of completed product from work-in-process inventory.		

YOUR TURN! 4.6

The solution is on page 4-49.

MBC

Assume the following cost information related to May production, and only one manufacturing department. What journal entries would be made to capture May production?

Direct materials	$19,750
Direct labor	9,500
Manufacturing overhead applied	5,404

SERVICE INDUSTRY IN FOCUS

Environmental Business Consultants, LLC (EBC), has a contract with Terrabean Coffee, a large retail coffee company with 5,000 shops across North America, to manage the company's waste disposal and recycling services. Under the contract with Terrabean, EBC is responsible for negotiating, monitoring, and servicing contracts with dozens of garbage and recycling collection companies in major cities throughout the United States and Canada. These contracts generally require the garbage and recycling collection companies to collect both garbage and recyclables on a daily basis from between 10 and 30 shops, 365 days per year. When collection is missed, invoices are questioned, service is changed, new shops are opened, or other issues arise, the shop managers call EBC for assistance.

EBC maintains a call center to receive these calls and coordinate the appropriate response. The call center employees record each call and refer the issue to the EBC manager responsible for that location for follow-up. Locations are assigned to one of five geographic regions: Northeast (includes major metropolitan areas in eastern Canada), Southeast, Midwest, Southwest, and Northwest (includes major metropolitan areas in western Canada). EBC uses process costing with a weighted average cost flow assumption to assign the call center cost to each geographic region on a per-call unit cost. Overhead is applied per labor hour worked. Thus, the percentage complete can be applied to both labor and overhead. Because some questions/complaints take more than a day or two to resolve, there are typically some "unfinished" calls at the end of each period.

For the fiscal year ended September 30, Year 2, the EBC call center reported the following information regarding calls handled:

Work-in-process, October 1, Year 1:	$350
Work done during fiscal Year 2:	
Direct labor incurred	$262,480
Overhead applied	247,947
Total costs incurred during fiscal Year 2	$510,427
Calls in process at October 1, Year 1 (30% complete)	50 calls
Calls started and finished during fiscal Year 2	35,200 calls
Calls in process at September 30, Year 2 (40% complete)	40 calls

Required

1. Determine the equivalent number of calls completed during fiscal Year 2.
2. Determine the per-unit cost of each call.
3. Determine the cost of the calls completed.
4. Determine the cost of ending work-in-process inventory at September 30, Year 2.

Solution: Exhibit 4-21 shows the solution.

> The first 50 calls (on October 1, Year 1) were all completed. Plus, 35,160 of the calls started during the year (35,200 – 40) were also completed, leaving 40 unfinished calls at the end of the year.

EXHIBIT 4-21	Service Industry In Focus Solution

Flow of the Units and Equivalent Units Calculation

Where do the units come from?		Where do the units go?		% Work Done?	Conv. Costs
Calls in process (10/1/Year 1)	50	Calls complete	35,210	100%	**35,210**
Calls started and finished	35,200	Calls in process (9/30/Year 2)	40	40%	**16**
Total	35,250	Total	35,250		35,226

continued

continued from previous page

Product Cost Report Environmental Business Consultants, LLC Fiscal Year 2 Service Calls		
Where do the costs come from?		Conv. Costs
Beginning WIP	$ 350	$ 350
Current period costs	510,427	510,427
Total costs to account for	$510,777	$510,777
÷ Total equivalent units		35,226
Average cost/equivalent unit		$14.50
Where do the costs go?		
Cost of calls completed	510,545	[35,210 × $14.50]
Cost of ending inventory	232	[16 × $14.50]
Total costs allocated	$510,777	

Data Analytics

+ableau

DATA ANALYTICS   **Tableau introduces the new Racial Equity Data Hub**

Many people think of Tableau as just a tool for businesses to gain insight into their customers or their costs, but it can be so much more. At the heart of visualization software is data, and as Tableau states on their blog, "Data is a critical tool in the fight against racism and for justice and equality." The **Tableau Foundation** launched the **Racial Equity Hub** to help democratize the types of data needed by those working toward equity and justice. In the words of the Tableau Foundation, "The Racial Equity Data Hub has been designed as a platform for local organizations and advocates doing the work of addressing institutionalized racism in their communities. It is being built to connect them with relevant data, analyses, tools from experts, and each other to advance the use of data in this work." The hub is meant to combine Tableau's strength in helping people see and understand data with the expertise of researchers and advocates working toward a more equitable and just society.

COMPREHENSIVE PROBLEM (INCLUDING TRANSFERRED-IN COSTS)

MBC

Kensington Corp. makes gourmet brownies. Brownies are produced in a three-stage process. In the Baking Department, the raw materials for the brownies are mixed, poured into large trays, and baked. In the Finishing Department, frosting is applied to the brownies and they are sliced while still in the baking trays. Finally, in the Packing Department, the brownies are divided into smaller packages containing 12 brownies per package and prepared for shipping. Kensington has tracked the following information for the Baking and Finishing Departments during October:

	Baking	Finishing
Trays in beginning inventory	200	100
Trays started / transferred in	5,100	?
Trays in ending inventory	100	300
Total cost of brownies transferred out in October	$18,200	?

The beginning inventory in the Finishing Department included $350 of transferred-in costs from the Baking Department incurred during September, $25 of materials, and $80 of conversion costs. During October, the Finishing Department incurred $1,075 for materials and $4,221 for conversion costs. The Finishing Department's beginning inventory was estimated to be 60% complete, and the ending inventory was estimated to be 20% complete. The frosting (the only new materials added in the Finishing Department) is added when the brownies are 25% through the production process.

One purpose of this comprehensive problem is to illustrate a more realistic example of how costs flow through a process with multiple departments or processes. Therefore, because this problem focuses on the second of three departments (the Finishing Department), we must consider transferred-in costs in addition to the direct materials costs and conversion costs incurred in the current department. Transferred-in costs merely represent the costs transferred from one department to the next and are therefore considered 100% complete as they are carried forward to the next department. In this problem, the costs incurred in the Baking Department stay with the trays of baked brownies as they come into the Finishing Department. The 100 trays in the beginning inventory (transferred in during September) carried $350 of costs from the Baking department, whereas the units transferred in during October carried $18,200 of costs from the Baking Department.

Required

1. Assuming Kensington uses the weighted average cost flow assumption, prepare the October product cost report for the Finishing Department. Be sure to include your equivalent units calculations.
2. Give the journal entry to transfer completed brownies from the Finishing Department to the Packing Department.

Solution to Comprehensive Problem

Before preparing the solution for the Finishing Department, it is important to first determine the number of trays transferred out of the Baking Department. The 5,200 trays transferred OUT of the Baking Department are the trays transferred IN to the Finishing Department. Obviously, Kensington would need to prepare a product cost report to determine the cost of the brownie trays transferred out. Because this problem focuses on the second department in the production process, the costs incurred to bake these 5,200 trays is simply given ($18,200). This number is used in the Finishing Department as the cost of trays transferred in.

1. We first illustrate the percentage complete and T-accounts (in units and dollars) that are helpful in preparing the product cost report. Note that each arrow in the timeline represents the conversion costs incurred in the Finishing Department during October for each inventory group: (1) the beginning inventory balance, (2) the trays transferred in and finished during the period, and (3) the trays transferred in and remaining in ending inventory.

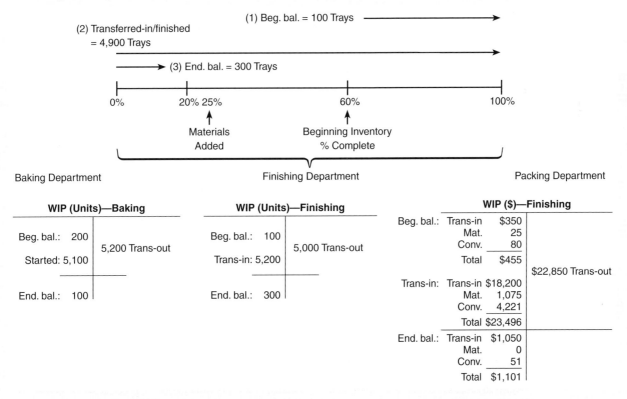

We then calculate equivalent units and prepare the product cost report.

	Finishing Department				Equivalent Units			
Where do the units come from?	**Where do the units go?**	**% Trans-in**	**Trans-in**	**% Work Done?**	**Dir. Mat.**	**% Work Done?**	**Conv. Costs**
Beg. inv. 100	Compl./transf. 5,000	100%	5,000	100%	5,000	100%	5,000
Started 5,200	End. inv. 300	100%	300	0%	0	20%	60
Total 5,300	Total 5,300		5,300		5,000		5,060

	Product Cost Report		
Where do the costs come from?	**Trans-in**	**Dir. Mat.**	**Conv. Costs**
Beg. inv. .... $ 455	$ 350	$ 25	$ 80
Current 23,496	18,200	1,075	4,221
Total costs to account for $23,951	$18,550	$ 1,100	$ 4,301
÷ Total equivalent units......	5,300	5,000	5,060
Average cost/equiv. unit	$3.5000	$0.2200	$ 0.850

Where do the costs go?				
Compl./transf.:				
Trans-in $17,500		[5,000 × $3.500]		
Direct materials 1,100			[5,000 × $0.2200]	
Conversion costs 4,250				[5,000 × $0.85]
COGM	$22,850			
End. inv.:				
Trans-in 1,050		[300 × $3.500]		
Direct materials .... —				
Conversion costs 51				[60 × $0.85]
Cost of ending inv.	1,101			
Total costs allocated.......	$23,951			

2.

	WIP—Packing Department	22,850	
	WIP—Finishing Department		22,850

APPENDIX 4A: Process Costing Using FIFO Method

This appendix illustrates the use of process costing and the first-in, first-out (FIFO) method to assign product costs to the goods transferred out and to the ending work-in-process inventory. In this appendix, we will repeat the same Big G example introduced in the chapter, but this time using the FIFO cost allocation method.

PROCESS COSTING STEPS

LO6 **Explain** techniques for determining unit costs when the FIFO method for process costing is used.

In this chapter, we discussed process costing and the use of the weighted average cost allocation method to transfer product costs from one work-in-process inventory account to another, from the final work-in-process inventory account to the finished goods inventory account, and from the finished goods inventory account to the cost of goods sold account. In this appendix, we will accomplish the same task, but we will use the FIFO cost allocation method to assign and transfer product costs. The following steps are the same as those used for the weighted average method. However, the execution of these steps is slightly different.

Recall that process costing requires five steps or calculations:

1. Visualize or chart the physical flow of the units through the system.
2. Determine the equivalent whole units of work completed (or equivalent units of production) during the period. This calculation is usually performed separately for materials and conversion costs (i.e., labor and overhead) because conversion costs are usually added uniformly throughout the process, whereas materials are often added at a particular point in the process.
3. Compute the per-unit cost of production for the period for materials and conversion costs by dividing the total costs incurred in each category by the equivalent units of production for that cost category.
4. Using the per-unit costs for materials and conversion costs, compute the dollar value of the units completed and transferred (Cost of Goods Manufactured) to the next department.
5. Using the same per-unit costs, compute the dollar value of the unfinished units that remain in the department. (These ending work-in-process units will usually be completed in the following period.)

We discuss these steps in more detail with respect to the FIFO cost allocation method in the following sections. Recall that the Big G division of General Mills uses process costing to account for its cereal production and that it had the results for January as illustrated in **Exhibit 4-1A**.

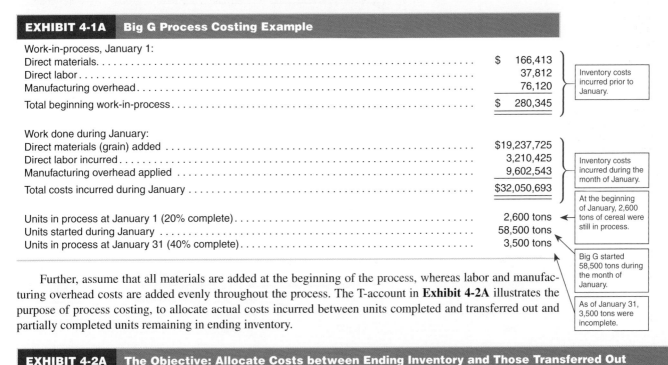

EXHIBIT 4-1A   **Big G Process Costing Example**

Work-in-process, January 1:	
Direct materials.	$ 166,413
Direct labor	37,812
Manufacturing overhead	76,120
Total beginning work-in-process	$ 280,345

Inventory costs incurred prior to January.

Work done during January:	
Direct materials (grain) added	$19,237,725
Direct labor incurred	3,210,425
Manufacturing overhead applied	9,602,543
Total costs incurred during January	$32,050,693

Inventory costs incurred during the month of January.

Units in process at January 1 (20% complete)	2,600 tons
Units started during January	58,500 tons
Units in process at January 31 (40% complete)	3,500 tons

At the beginning of January, 2,600 tons of cereal were still in process.

Big G started 58,500 tons during the month of January.

As of January 31, 3,500 tons were incomplete.

Further, assume that all materials are added at the beginning of the process, whereas labor and manufacturing overhead costs are added evenly throughout the process. The T-account in **Exhibit 4-2A** illustrates the purpose of process costing, to allocate actual costs incurred between units completed and transferred out and partially completed units remaining in ending inventory.

EXHIBIT 4-2A   **The Objective: Allocate Costs between Ending Inventory and Those Transferred Out**

Work-in-Process Inventory

Costs to be allocated		
Beginning balance:		
Direct materials	$ 166,413	
Conversion costs	113,932	
Total beginning inventory costs	$ 280,345	**Cost of units transferred out?**
Current costs:		
Direct materials	$19,237,725	
Conversion costs	12,812,968	
Total current manufacturing costs	$32,050,693	

Cost of ending work-in-process inventory?

We know the costs associated with the beginning work-in-process inventory on January 1 ($280,345). We also know the costs incurred during the month of January for direct materials ($19,237,725), direct labor ($3,210,425), and manufacturing overhead ($9,602,543). For simplicity, because we assume both direct labor and manufacturing overhead costs are applied uniformly during the production process, we combine them and simply refer to them as "conversion costs." Because we started the period with partially completed inventory, during the period we will finish the previously started units and begin work on new units. We also end the period with partially completed units. We don't know how much of these costs should be applied to units transferred out at the end of the period and how much should remain with the partially complete ending inventory. Process costing helps us calculate an average cost per unit to apply to (1) the units completed and transferred out at the end of the period and (2) the units remaining in ending inventory.

Step 1: Visualize the Physical Flow of the Units

The starting point in process costing is to visualize how the units flow through the production process, as illustrated in **Exhibit 4-3A**. In the General Mills Big G example, the quantity produced is measured in tons of cereal processed during the month of January. Sometimes it is useful to visualize how the units correspond to the dollars in the T-account in **Exhibit 4-2A**.

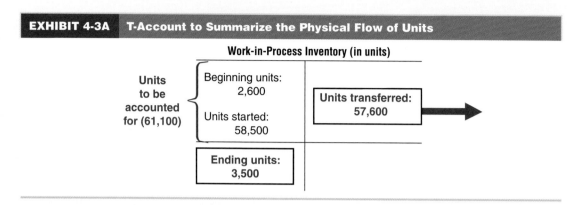

EXHIBIT 4-3A   **T-Account to Summarize the Physical Flow of Units**

Work-in-Process Inventory (in units)

Units to be accounted for (61,100)

Beginning units: 2,600

Units started: 58,500

Units transferred: 57,600

Ending units: 3,500

Another way to visualize the flow of the cereal produced during January is by asking where the units come from and where they end up, as shown in **Exhibit 4-4A**.

Hint: Under the weighted average cost flow assumption, the costs of beginning inventory and costs incurred in the current period are "averaged" together. However, under the FIFO method, the inventory "layers" are kept separate. Thus, we do not mix costs incurred in different periods.

EXHIBIT 4-4A   **Step 1: Visualize the Physical Flow of the Units**

Where do the units come from?

Where do the units go?

Beginning inventory	2,600	
Started	58,500	
Total	61,100	

Complete/transferred:

Beginning inventory	2,600
Started and complete	55,000
Ending inventory	3,500
Total	61,100

We assume that all 2,600 units in beginning inventory are completed first. Then, of the 58,500 units started this month, 55,000 are complete by the end of the month, and 3,500 remain partially complete. Unlike the weighted average method, which mixes inventory layers (i.e., not distinguishing between work done in each period), the FIFO method keeps the beginning inventory separate from units started during the period and accounts for each inventory layer separately. Whereas the weighted average method does not distinguish between work done in different periods, the FIFO method does not mix costs incurred in different periods.

YOUR TURN! 4.7

The solution is on page 4-50.

MBC

Beginning work-in-process is composed of 100 units. Also assume that 700 units are started and completed during the period, and ending work-in-process includes 90 units. Summarize "Where do the units come from" and "Where do the units go."

Step 2: Calculate the Equivalent Units

Introduction to Equivalent Units

The average cost per unit is calculated by dividing total costs by the total number of units produced. The work-in-process accounts previously described in **Exhibits 4-5** and **4-6** illustrate how total costs are accumulated and tracked through the system. Accountants are good at keeping track of costs. However, cost accountants face a major problem in allocating costs in continuous-flow manufacturing processes because it is difficult to estimate how units are complete. **Equivalent units** are the equivalent number of *whole units* completed during the period. At any given point in time, units of product are at various stages of completion. Hence, it is difficult to determine the number of equivalent complete units to use in the average cost per unit calculation:

$$\frac{\text{Average cost}}{\text{per unit}} = \frac{\text{Total costs incurred}}{\text{\# of equivalent units}} \quad \begin{array}{l} \longleftarrow \quad \textbf{We know this.} \\ \longleftarrow \quad \textbf{We don't know this.} \end{array}$$

The notion of equivalent units of production is a key concept in process costing. When units of product are produced in a continuous process, engineers and manufacturing supervisors must estimate the average percentage completion of units in a given department at the end of each period. Accountants use this information to estimate the number of equivalent *complete* units of product. For example, the following illustration shows eight glasses of water that are *half* full. How many *full* glasses of water is this equivalent to?

8 Glasses ½ Full = 4 Full Glasses

The eight half-full glasses are approximately equivalent to four full glasses. This example illustrates what accountants do each period in determining the average cost per unit in a given department.

To properly determine per-unit costs, we must first calculate equivalent units of production to be used in the denominator of the average cost per unit calculation. Again, equivalent units are the equivalent number of *whole units* completed during the period. In the previous illustration, the eight partially full glasses of water are equivalent to four full glasses (similar to four equivalent complete units of production). The calculation of equivalent units of production requires accountants to (1) track the *actual quantity* of products at each stage of production and (2) estimate the *average amount of work completed* on each unit of product in terms of conversion costs and direct material costs.

Engineers or production experts estimate the percentage of work completed in terms of conversion costs, on average. As illustrated in **Exhibit 4-5A**, because the 2,600 tons of cereal on hand on January 1 is 20% complete (based on work completed during December), Big G only has to complete the remaining 80% of the processing during the month of January. During January, Big G begins work on 55,000 tons of cereal that is both started and completed during the month of January. Finally, Big G begins work on an additional 3,500 tons of cereal that is not completed by the end of the month. Engineers determine that only 40% of the processing is complete on this batch of cereal by January 31. We assume that all direct materials are added at the beginning of the process; therefore, the average amount of work completed on each unit of product related to direct materials is 100%.

EXHIBIT 4-5A	Illustration of Conversion Costs Incurred

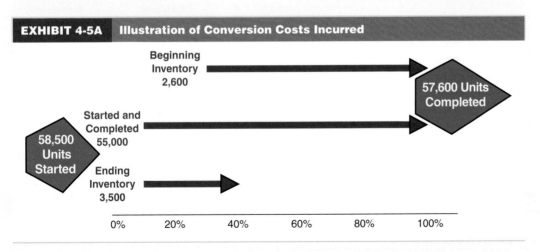

A key difference between the weighted average method and the FIFO method is that the weighted average mixes costs across inventory layers, whereas the FIFO method keeps costs incurred across inventory layers (i.e., incurred in different periods) separate. Whereas the weighted average method averages all costs incurred in the production of a batch of units, regardless of when those costs were incurred, the FIFO method keeps costs incurred during December separate from those incurred during January. Thus, the weighted average method asks "How much work is complete (regardless of when the work was done)?" whereas the FIFO method asks "What costs were incurred during THIS PERIOD?" A critical feature of the FIFO method is that because materials are added at the *beginning* of the process in this example, the beginning inventory units moved beyond the point of adding materials during the last period. Thus, NO materials are added THIS PERIOD. Because the beginning inventory was started last month, the materials for the beginning inventory were actually added during December. Thus, no new materials are added to these 2,600 units during January.

Equivalent Unit Calculation for Direct Materials—FIFO

The materials for the units started and completed during the month and for the ending inventory are added during this period. **Exhibit 4-6A** illustrates the calculation of equivalent units based on the FIFO cost flow assumption. The units in each "layer" of inventory are multiplied by the percentage of materials added during the CURRENT period (January) to calculate the equivalent units of materials added during THIS PERIOD, as shown in **Exhibit 4-6A**.

Hint: The 2,600 units of direct materials inventory were started last month. Thus, they will not be counted during the current period.

EXHIBIT 4-6A	**Step 2: Calculate the Equivalent Units—Direct Materials**					
		Physical Units (tons)		**Proportion Completed**		**Equivalent Units (tons)**
Beginning inventory		2,600	×	0%	=	0
Started and finished during January.		55,000	×	100%	=	55,000
Ending inventory.		3,500	×	100%	=	3,500
Total		61,100				58,500

Equivalent Unit Calculation for Conversion Costs—FIFO

When considering conversion costs (direct labor and manufacturing overhead), it is often useful to visualize the amount of work done during the period on each unique set of inventory passing through the production process, as previously illustrated in **Exhibit 4-5A**, which summarizes the work performed in the Big G division during the month of January. Because materials are added at the beginning of the period, the arrows only represent the amount of conversion costs applied to the process during the *current* period. We can then calculate the number of equivalent units with respect to conversion costs incurred during January, as illustrated in **Exhibit 4-7A**.

Hint: Notice that the equivalent units for direct materials are lower under the FIFO cost flow assumption than they were under the weighted average method. The difference is due to the fact that the FIFO method only allocates CURRENT costs. This is why the equivalent units for beginning inventory are zero (under the FIFO method) because these costs were incurred last period.

EXHIBIT 4-7A	**Step 2: Calculate the Equivalent Units—Conversion Costs**					
		Physical Units (tons)		**Proportion Completed This Month**		**Equivalent Units (tons)**
Beginning inventory		2,600	×	80%	=	2,080
Started and finished during January.		55,000	×	100%	=	55,000
Ending inventory.		3,500	×	40%	=	1,400
Total		61,100				58,480

Again, we calculate equivalent units of production by multiplying the number of units in each "layer" of inventory by the percentage of conversion costs added during the current period.

We can then summarize the flow of the units worked on during the period and how the amount of work completed during the period translates them into equivalent units, as illustrated in **Exhibit 4-8A**.

EXHIBIT 4-8A	**Summary of Step. 4-1 and 2: Unit Flows and Equivalent Units Calculations**

Step 2: Calculate the Equivalent Units

Step 1: Visualize the Physical Flow of the Units

Where do the units come from?			Where do the units go?		Equivalent Units			
					% in Jan.?	Materials	% in Jan.?	Conv. Costs
			Complete/transferred:					
Beginning inventory . . .	2,600	→	Beginning inventory	2,600	0%	0	80%	2,080
			Started and completed	55,000	100%	55,000	100%	55,000
Started	58,500		Ending inventory.	3,500	100%	3,500	40%	1,400
Total	61,100		Total	61,100		58,500		58,480

Concept	→	Method	→	Assessment	TAKEAWAY 4.3A
How many full glasses of water are equivalent to this number of partially full glasses?		Multiply the percentage of completion by the number of units being worked on.		An equivalent unit is the amount of work necessary to produce one complete physical unit of product.	

YOUR TURN! 4.8

The solution is on page 4-50.

MBC

Assume all materials are added at the beginning of the production process, and conversion costs are added uniformly throughout the process. Beginning work-in-process is composed of 100 units, which are 35% complete with respect to conversion costs. Also assume that 700 units are started and completed during the period, and ending work-in-process includes 90 units that are 70% complete with respect to conversion costs. Compute equivalent units of production for direct materials and conversion costs under the FIFO cost flow assumption.

Step 3: Determine the Per-Unit Costs

The product cost report summarizes where the costs come from and where they go (i.e., where they are allocated). The FIFO method differs from the weighted average method in an important way. The FIFO method does not mix "layers" of costs incurred during different periods. The $280,345 of costs in beginning inventory at the start of the month were incurred during December. When we calculate the average cost per unit, we calculate the average cost per unit of costs incurred during the CURRENT PERIOD. Hence, the costs incurred last month to help the inventory to reach the 20% point stay with those beginning inventory units and are NOT ALLOCATED across the units started during THIS PERIOD. In order to calculate an average cost per unit of materials and conversion costs incurred during THIS PERIOD, we first need to separate the current-period costs into their materials and conversion cost components. These numbers were illustrated in the T-account in **Exhibit 4-2A**. **Exhibit 4-9A** illustrates two important points. First, the beginning inventory costs incurred in the prior period are carried down and assigned to stay with the beginning inventory units. Second, only the costs incurred during the current period are allocated and used subsequently in the average cost per unit calculation.

EXHIBIT 4-9A	Product Cost Report: Where Do the Costs Come From?

Product Cost Report
General Mills Big G Division
January Production

Where do the costs come from?	Total	Direct Materials	Conversion Costs
Beginning inventory	$ 280,345		
Current	32,050,693	$19,237,725	$12,812,968
Total costs to account for	$32,331,038		

Carry to Step 4

We then calculate the average cost per unit by dividing current-period costs in each category by total equivalent units in each category from Step 2. In other words, we divide current materials costs by total equivalent units of materials ($19,237,725/58,500 equivalent units) to get an average cost per unit of $328.85. Similarly, we divide current conversion costs by total equivalent units of conversion costs ($12,812,968/58,480 equivalent units) to get an average cost per unit of $219.10. **Exhibit 4-10A** summarizes this calculation.

EXHIBIT 4-10A	Step 3: Determine Per-Unit Costs

Product Cost Report
General Mills Big G Division
January Production

Where do the costs come from?	Total	Direct Materials	Conversion Costs
Beginning inventory	$ 280,345		
Current	32,050,693	$19,237,725	$12,812,968
Total costs to account for	$32,331,038		
÷ Total equivalent units		58,500	58,480
Average cost/unit		$ 328.85	$ 219.10

Carry to Step 4

Note that under the FIFO cost flow assumption, the costs from the prior period associated with the beginning inventory stay with the beginning inventory and are not allocated to any other units. The costs incurred during the current period are allocated across all work incurred during the current period. Hence, under the FIFO cost flow assumption, the accountant keeps the "layers" of inventory separate. In the Big G example, note that the per-unit costs of materials and conversions costs only include costs incurred during January.

YOUR TURN! 4.9

The solution is on page 4-50.

MBC

Assume that you have 790 total equivalent units of materials and 828 total equivalent units of conversion costs. Also assume that your beginning inventory is composed of $3,390 of materials and $1,493 of conversion costs and that you use $19,750 of materials and incur $14,904 of conversion costs during the current period. Calculate the average cost per unit of materials and conversion costs assuming the FIFO cost flow assumption.

Step 4: Calculate the Cost of Goods Manufactured

At the end of each month and for each department, we calculate the cost of goods manufactured and transferred out (illustrated in **Exhibit 4-11A**). Under the FIFO cost flow assumption, the Big G division's product completed and transferred out during January consists of (1) the product in beginning work-in-process (2,080 equivalent tons) and (2) the product started and completed during the period (55,000 equivalent tons). Specifically, it is composed of all costs to manufacture the beginning inventory (both this period and last period) and the cost of units started and finished this period. To determine the dollar cost value of the product transferred to finished goods (called Cost of Goods Manufactured), we multiply the equivalent units of materials and conversion costs transferred (shown in **red** in **Exhibit 4-8A**) by their respective per-unit costs computed in Step 3 (shown in **green** in **Exhibit 4-10A**) and add these costs to the cost value of the beginning work-in-process, as shown in **Exhibit 4-11A**.

EXHIBIT 4-11A	Step 4: Cost of Goods Manufactured Calculation

		Carry from Step 3
Beginning inventory:		
Costs incurred in December		$ 280,345
Conversion costs incurred in January.	[**2,080** EU × **$219.10**]	455,728
Started and finished:		
Materials	[**55,000** EU × **$328.85**]	18,086,750
Conversion costs.	[**55,000** EU × **$219.10**]	12,050,500
Total cost of goods manufactured		$30,873,323

YOUR TURN! 4.10

The solution is on page 4-51.

MBC

Assume that you had beginning inventory costs incurred last period of $14,883 and that you added 65 equivalent units of conversion costs to complete your beginning inventory. Moreover, you started and completed 700 units during the current period. Finally, assume you have determined your average cost per equivalent unit of direct materials to be $25.00 and your average cost per equivalent unit of conversion costs to be $18.00. Determine your cost of goods manufactured assuming the FIFO cost flow assumption.

Step 5: Calculate the Cost of Ending Work-in-Process Inventory

Exhibit 4-12A illustrates the final step, which is to calculate the cost of goods remaining in ending work-in-process inventory. Assuming all materials are added at the beginning and conversion costs are added evenly through the process, we multiply the equivalent units of materials and conversion costs in ending inventory (denoted in **red** in **Exhibit 4-8A**) by their respective unit costs (shown in **green** in **Exhibit 4-10A**) computed in Step 2, as follows:

EXHIBIT 4-12A	Step 5: Calculate Cost of Ending Work-in-Process Inventory

Materials.	[**3,500** EU × **$328.85**]	$1,150,975
Conversion costs	[**1,400** EU × **$219.10**]	306,740
Total cost of goods remaining in ending inventory		$1,457,715

Cost of goods manufactured and transferred out (**Exhibit 4-11A**)	$30,873,323
Cost of ending inventory (**Exhibit 4-12A**)	1,457,715
Total cost to account for (**Exhibit 4-10A**)	$32,331,038

YOUR TURN! 4.11

Assume that your ending inventory is composed of 90 equivalent units of materials and 63 equivalent units of conversions costs and that you have determined your average cost per equivalent unit of direct materials to be $25.00 and your average cost per equivalent unit of conversion costs to be $18.00. Determine the cost of your ending inventory assuming the FIFO cost flow assumption.

The solution is on page 4-51.

MBC

THE PRODUCT COST REPORT

The product cost report in **Exhibit 4-13A** summarizes the last three steps in the cost allocation process. The report calculates the cost of goods manufactured and transferred out of work-in-process and into finished goods. The report also calculates the cost of the remaining ending balance in work-in-process. Using the Big G example, **Exhibit 4-13A** also summarizes all of the steps in the total cost allocation process from (1) visualizing the physical flow of the units, to (2) calculating equivalent units, to (3) calculating per-unit costs, to (4) calculating cost of goods manufactured, to (5) calculating the cost of ending work-in-process inventory.

LO7 **Explain** the procedures used to prepare the product cost report using the FIFO method in a process costing system.

eLecture

MBC

EXHIBIT 4-13A **Summary of the Five Process Costing Steps**

Flow of the Units and Equivalent Units Calculation

Step 2: Calculate the Equivalent Units

Step 1: Visualize the Physical Flow of the Units

Where do the units come from?		Where do the units go?		% in Jan.?	Materials	% in Jan.?	Conversion Costs
					Equivalent Units		
		Complete/transferred:					
Beginning inventory	2,600 →	Beginning inventory	2,600	0%	0	80%	2,080
	↗	Started and completed . .	55,000	100%	55,000	100%	55,000
Started	58,500 ↗	Ending inventory	3,500	100%	3,500	40%	1,400
Total	61,100	Total	61,100		58,500		58,480

Product Cost Report
General Mills Big G Division
January Production

Step 3: Determine Per-Unit Costs

Where do the costs come from?	Total		Direct Materials	Conversion Costs
Beginning inventory	$ 280,345			
Current	32,050,693		$19,237,725	$12,812,968
Total costs to account for	$32,331,038			
÷ Total equivalent units			58,500	58,480
Average cost/unit			$328.85	$219.10

Where do the costs go?

Step 4: Calculate the Cost of Goods Manufactured

Beginning inventory:				
Costs incurred in December	$ 280,345		[0 × $328.85] +	[2,080 × $219.10]
Costs incurred in January	455,728		[55,000 × $328.85] +	[55,000 × $219.10]
Started and finished	30,137,250			
Cost of goods manufactured		$30,873,323		

Step 5: Calculate the Cost of the Ending Work-in-Process Inventory

Ending inventory:				
Materials	$ 1,150,975		[3,500 × $328.85]	
Conversion costs	306,740			[1,400 × $219.10]
Cost of ending inventory		1,457,715		
Total costs allocated		$32,331,038		

Finally, **Exhibit 4-13A** provides Big G's product cost report. Note that in this illustration, the equivalent units of production for materials and conversion costs (the numbers in **red**) are multiplied by the corresponding cost per unit figures for materials and conversion costs (the numbers in **green**) to calculate the cost allocation amounts used to assign costs to cost of goods manufactured and ending inventory.

As a final check to see that we have performed all of the calculations correctly, the sum of Cost of Goods Manufactured ($30,873,323) and the ending work-in-process balance ($1,457,715) should equal the total costs that we determined at the outset needed to be allocated (Beginning Balance $280,345 + Current Costs $32,050,693 = $32,331,038). Specifically, the T-account in **Exhibit 4-14A** summarizes the process costing allocation of costs between costs transferred out and costs remaining in ending inventory.

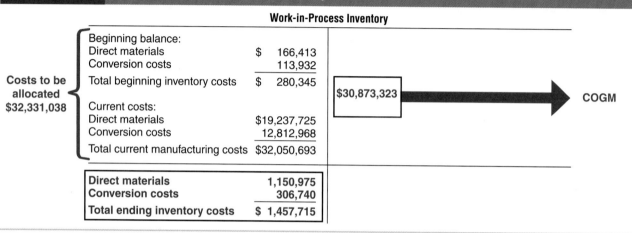

EXHIBIT 4-14A   Final Allocation of Costs to Ending Inventory and Cost of Goods Manufactured (and Transferred Out)

Work-in-Process Inventory

Costs to be allocated $32,331,038

Beginning balance:	
Direct materials	$ 166,413
Conversion costs	113,932
Total beginning inventory costs	$ 280,345
Current costs:	
Direct materials	$19,237,725
Conversion costs	12,812,968
Total current manufacturing costs	$32,050,693

$30,873,323 → COGM

Direct materials	1,150,975
Conversion costs	306,740
Total ending inventory costs	$ 1,457,715

Companies with Multiple Production Processes

At the outset of this chapter, we described situations in which a company produces its products through a long series of production processes. So far, we have illustrated process costing in a single department. When a company's production process involves a series of different departments, costs are accumulated by production process. The costs transferred out of one department are transferred into the next department. Hence, as units of product move from one department or process to the next, they carry the costs from all prior processes with them. From a practical perspective, the only thing that changes in the product costing process is that an extra column is added for transferred-in costs. For example, the $30,873,323 transferred out of the production process described in the previous section would become the **transferred-in costs** for the next department.

JOURNAL ENTRIES ILLUSTRATED

LO8

Illustrate the journal entries used with FIFO process costing.

After computing these amounts, Big G would record the following journal entries related to January production. *These entries assume that materials are added at the beginning of the process and that labor and overhead are added evenly over the month of January.*

eLecture

MBC

Materials

During January, assume that Big G purchased $20,000,000 of grain on account. The following is a summary journal entry for the January purchases:

1	Materials inventory	20,000,000	
	Accounts payable		20,000,000
	To record January materials purchases.		

The direct materials requisitioned during January for the processing department is shown in the following entry:

2	Work-in-process	19,237,725	
	Materials inventory		19,237,725
	To record direct materials used during January.		

Labor

During January, Big G accrued $3,210,425 of direct labor expense. The journal entry to record this payroll would be as follows:

3	Work-in-process	3,210,425	
	Wages payable		3,210,425
	To record the payroll for January.		

Manufacturing Overhead

Assume that Big G has recorded its manufacturing overhead costs (such as maintenance, depreciation, and utilities) in Manufacturing Overhead as incurred. Also assume that Big G applies manufacturing overhead costs to Work-in-Process using predetermined overhead rates. The following entry records the amount of applied manufacturing overhead for the processing department:

4	Work-in-process	9,602,543	
	Manufacturing overhead		9,602,543
	To apply manufacturing overhead to work-in-process		
	inventory.		

As a result of the journal entries recorded during the month, the Work-in-Process account contains the following balance as of the end of the month:

	Work-in-Process
Beginning balance	$ 280,345
Direct materials.	19,237,725
Direct labor.	3,210,425
Manufacturing overhead.	9,602,543
Balance before month-end adjustments.	$32,331,038

At the end of the month, an additional journal entry is needed to transfer product costs from the processing department to Finished Goods (the amount of Cost of Goods Manufactured). The following entry records the Cost of Goods Manufactured:

5	Finished goods	30,873,323	
	Work-in-process		30,873,323
	To transfer the cost of completed product from work-in-process		
	inventory.		

YOUR TURN! 4.12

Assume the following cost information for May production and only one manufacturing department. What journal entries would be made to capture May production?

Direct materials.	$19,750
Direct labor.	9,500
Manufacturing overhead applied	5,404

The solution is on page 4-52.

GuidedExample

MBC

SUMMARY OF LEARNING OBJECTIVES

Compare and contrast job order costing and process costing. (p. 4-3)   **LO1**

- Job order costing is used when production consists of a variety of different products or unique customer orders.
- Process costing is used when production consists of a large volume of the same (homogeneous) product produced in a continual flow.

LO2   **Describe the basic concepts of process costing. (p. 4-5)**

- There is a separate work-in-process account for each department under a process costing system, whereas there is only one work-in-process control account in a job order costing system.

- In a process costing environment, products flow through multiple departments that are arranged in either a sequential pattern or a parallel pattern.

LO3   **Explain techniques for determining unit costs when process costing is used. (p. 4-7)**

- Visualize or chart the physical flow of the units through the system.

- Determine the equivalent whole units of work completed (or equivalent units of production) during the period. This calculation is usually performed separately for materials and conversion costs (i.e., labor and overhead) because conversion costs are usually added uniformly throughout the process, whereas materials are often added at a particular point in the process.

- Compute the per-unit cost of production for the period for materials and conversion costs by dividing the total costs incurred in each category by the equivalent units of production for that cost category.

- Using the per-unit costs for materials and conversion costs, compute the dollar value of the units completed and transferred (cost of goods manufactured) to the next department.

- Using the same per-unit costs, compute the dollar value of the unfinished units that remain in the department. (These ending work-in-process units will usually be completed in the following period.)

LO4   **Explain the procedures used to prepare the product cost report using the weighted average method in a process costing system. (p. 4-15)**

- The product cost report and its supporting calculations include all of the five steps in the process costing procedure.

- The weighted average method mixes inventory layers and asks the question "how much work has been completed?" in calculating equivalent units of production.

LO5   **Illustrate the journal entries used with process costing. (p. 4-16)**

- At each stage of the manufacturing process, costs are added to the work-in-process account of the department where the work is completed. The journal entries are identical to those illustrated under a job order costing system.

- Direct materials are added to the materials inventory account when they are purchased.

- Materials used in the manufacturing process are transferred from the materials inventory account with a credit and debited to the appropriate work-in-process account.

- Labor and overhead are recorded as debits to the appropriate work-in-process account.

LO6   **Appendix 4A: Explain techniques for determining unit costs when the FIFO method for process costing is used. (p. 4-21)**

- The five process costing steps are the same under the FIFO method as under the weighted average method.

- In assigning manufacturing costs, one must consider three batches (or layers) of product: units from beginning work-in-process, units started and finished during this period, and units remaining in the ending work-in-process. Instead of mixing the layers (as in the weighted average method), the FIFO method keeps these three layers of inventory separate.

- The key difference between the weighted average and FIFO methods is that under the FIFO method, costs per equivalent unit are calculated by dividing current costs by current equivalent units; prior period costs and equivalent units are excluded from these calculations but are included in the total costs to be accounted for.

LO7   **Appendix 4A: Explain the procedures used to prepare the product cost report using the FIFO method in a process costing system. (p. 4-28)**

- When work-in-process inventories exist at the beginning and the end of the accounting period, the measurement of work accomplished requires that partially finished units be converted to equivalent units for accounting purposes.

- When materials are added at a different rate than conversion work is accomplished, equivalent units must be computed separately for materials and conversion costs.

- The product cost report and its supporting calculations include all of the five steps in the process costing procedure.

■ The FIFO method keeps inventory layers separate and asks the question "how much work was completed during THIS PERIOD?" in calculating equivalent units of production.

Appendix 4A: Illustrate the journal entries used with FIFO process costing. (p. 4-29)   **LO8**

■ At each stage of the manufacturing process, costs are added to the work-in-process account of the department where the work is completed. The journal entries are identical to those illustrated under a job order costing system.

■ Direct materials are added to the materials inventory account when they are purchased.

■ Materials used in the manufacturing process are transferred from the materials inventory account with a credit and debited to the appropriate work-in-process account.

■ Labor and overhead are recorded as debits to the appropriate work-in-process account.

Concept ⟶	Method ⟶	Assessment	SUMMARY
How to distinguish between situations when job order and product costing would be more appropriate?	Think about the nature of the manufacturing process.	Job order costing is used for unique products or orders, whereas process costing is used for uniform products.	TAKEAWAY 4.1
How are departments that use process costing different from those that use job order costing?	Think about the work that is being performed in each department.	When process costing is appropriate, each processing department has two essential features: 1. The activity is performed uniformly on all products passing through it. 2. The output is homogeneous.	TAKEAWAY 4.2
How many full glasses of water are equivalent to this number of partially full glasses?	Multiply the percentage of completion by the number of units being worked on.	An equivalent unit is the amount of work necessary to produce one complete physical unit of product.	TAKEAWAY 4.3A

KEY TERMS

Conversion costs (p. 4-7)

Cost of goods
    remaining (p. 4-14)

Equivalent units (p. 4-7, 4-10,
    4-23)

FIFO method (p. 4-8)

Parallel product
    processing (p. 4-7)

Process costing (p. 4-4)

Process costing system (p. 4-5)

Product cost report (p. 4-5)

Sequential product
    processing (p. 4-6)

Transferred-in costs (p. 4-29)

Weighted average
    method (p. 4-8)

Assignments with the ⊛ logo in the margin are available in BusinessCourse.
See the Preface of the book for details.

SELF-STUDY QUESTIONS

(Answers to Self-Study Questions are at the end of this chapter.)

1. **Which of the following costs will not be part of product cost when using a process costing system?**   **LO2, 3**
    a. Prior department cost   c. Byproduct cost
    b. Conversion cost   d. Materials cost

2. **For which of the following will there be multiple accounts in the general ledger when using process**   **LO2**
    costing?
    a. Finished goods   c. Materials
    b. Work-in-process   d. Wages payable

LO6
(Appendix 4A)

3. **Which of the following will not influence the calculation of equivalent units when the FIFO cost flow assumption is used?**
   a. Units processed in prior departments
   b. Ending inventory units
   c. Beginning inventory units
   d. Units sold

QUESTIONS

LO1

1. What are the important differences between job order and process costing systems?

LO1, 2

2. How are all manufacturing costs for a series of processing departments accumulated into finished goods inventory?

LO2, 3

3. Why do unit cost computations in a manufacturing process require equivalent unit computations?

LO3

4. Why do we say that process cost accounting is basically an averaging computation?

LO3

5. What is meant by the term *equivalent unit*?

LO3

6. What are conversion costs?

LO3

7. Why must we sometimes compute equivalent units separately for materials and for conversion costs?

LO3

8. Why is it true that in each department's work-in-process inventory account all beginning inventory and current-period costs must end up either being transferred out or in ending work-in-process inventory?

LO6, 7, 8
(Appendix 4A)

9. Describe the three "layers" of inventory that are typically involved in a period's production under the FIFO accounting method. In what special situation are there only two layers?

SHORT EXERCISES

LO3, 4

SE4-1. During December, Krause Chemical Company had the following selected data concerning the manufacture of Xyzine, an industrial cleaner.

Production Flow	Physical Units	
Completed and transferred to the next department	100	
Add: Ending work-in-process inventory	10	(40% complete as to conversion)
Total units to account for.	110	
Less: Beginning work-in-process inventory	20	(60% complete as to conversion)
Units started during December.	90	

All materials are added at the beginning of processing in this department, and conversion costs are added uniformly during the process. The beginning work-in-process inventory had $120 of raw materials and $180 of conversion costs incurred. Materials added during December was $540 and conversion costs of $1,484 were incurred. Krause uses the weighted-average process-costing method. The total raw materials costs in the ending work-in-process inventory for December are

a. $120.
b. $72.
c. $60.
d. $36.

LO3, 4

SE4-2. Mack Inc. uses a weighted-average process costing system. Direct materials and conversion costs are incurred evenly during the production process. During the month of October, the following costs were incurred:

Direct materials.	$39,700
Conversion costs	70,000

The work-in-process inventory as of October 1 consisted of 5,000 units, valued at $4,300, that were 20% complete. During October, 27,000 units were transferred out. Inventory as of October 31 consisted of 3,000 units that were 50% complete. The weighted-average inventory cost per unit completed in October was

a. $3.51.
b. $3.88.
c. $3.99.
d. $4.00.

SE4-3. Colt Company uses a weighted-average process cost system to account for the cost of producing a chemical compound. As part of production, Material B is added when the goods are 80% complete. Beginning work-in-process inventory for the current month was 20,000 units, 90% complete. During the month, 70,000 units were started in process, and 65,000 units were completed. There were no lost or spoiled units. If the ending inventory was 60% complete, the total equivalent units for Material B for the month were

a. 65,000 units.   *c.* 85,000 units.
b. 70,000 units.   *d.* 90,000 units.

SE4-4. San Jose Inc. uses a weighted-average process costing system. All materials are introduced at the start of manufacturing, and conversion costs are incurred evenly throughout production. The company started 70,000 units during May and had the following work-in-process inventories at the beginning and end of the month:

May 1	30,000 units, 40% complete
May 31	24,000 units, 25% complete

Assuming no spoilage or defective units, the total equivalent units used to assign costs for May are

	Materials	**Conversion Cost**
a.	70,000	70,000.
b.	82,000	82,000.
c.	100,000	70,000.
d.	100,000	82,000.

SE4-5. During December, Krause Chemical Company had the following selected data concerning the manufacture of Xyzine, an industrial cleaner:

Production Flow	**Physical Units**	
Completed and transferred to the next department	100	
Add: Ending work-in-process inventory	10	(40% complete as to conversion)
Total units to account for.	110	
Less: Beginning work-in-process inventory	20	(60% complete as to conversion)
Units started during December.	90	

All materials are added at the beginning of processing in this department, and conversion costs are added uniformly during the process. The beginning work-in-process inventory had $120 of raw materials and $180 of conversion costs incurred. Materials added during December were $540 and conversion costs of $1,484 were incurred. Krause uses the weighted-average process-costing method. The total conversion costs assigned to units transferred to the next department in December were

a. $1,664.   *c.* $1,513.
b. $1,600.   *d.* $1,484.

SE4-6. During December, Krause Chemical Company had the following selected data concerning the manufacture of Xyzine, an industrial cleaner:

Production Flow	**Physical Units**	
Completed and transferred to the next department	100	
Add: Ending work-in-process inventory	10	(40% complete as to conversion)
Total units to account for.	110	
Less: Beginning work-in-process inventory	20	(60% complete as to conversion)
Units started during December.	90	

All materials are added at the beginning of processing in this department, and conversion costs are added uniformly during the process. The beginning work-in-process inventory had $120 of raw materials and $180 of conversion costs incurred. Materials added during December were $540 and conversion costs of $1,484 were incurred. Krause uses the first-in, first-out (FIFO) process-costing method. The equivalent units of production used to calculate conversion costs for December were

a.   110 units.   c.   100 units.
b.   104 units.   d.   92 units.

LO6
(Appendix 4A)

SE4-7.   Jones Corporation uses a first-in, first-out (FIFO) process costing system. Jones has the following unit information for the month of August:

	Units
Beginning work-in-process inventory, 100% complete	
for materials, 75% complete for conversion cost.	10,000
Units completed and transferred out.	90,000
Ending work-in-process inventory, 100% complete	
for materials, 60% complete for conversion costs.	8,000

The number of equivalent units of production for conversion costs for the month of August is

a.   87,300.   c.   92,300.
b.   88,000.   d.   92,700.

DATA ANALYTICS, DATA VISUALIZATION, AND EXCEL ACTIVITIES

Data Analytics, Data Visualization, and Excel Activities are available in myBusinessCourse. These assignments develop Excel, Tableau, and Data Analytics skills, which will enhance students' career readiness. These exercises are assignable and auto graded by MBC. For an overview of data analytics, see the appendix at the end of this book.

EXERCISES—SET A

LO3

E4-1A.   **Equivalent Units Calculations—Weighted Average Method** Ferris Corporation makes a powdered rug shampoo in two sequential departments, Compounding and Drying. Materials are added at the beginning of the process in the Compounding Department. Conversion costs are added evenly throughout each process. Ferris uses the weighted average method of process costing. In the Compounding Department, beginning work-in-process was 6,000 pounds (70% processed), 38,000 pounds were started in process, 36,000 pounds transferred out, and ending work-in-process was 60% processed.
Calculate equivalent units for March for the Compounding Department.

LO3

E4-2A.   **Equivalent Units Calculations—Weighted Average Method** The following are selected operating data for Jackson Company's Blending Department for April. Tinting and packaging operations are carried out subsequently in other departments.

Beginning inventory	4,000 units, 60% complete
Started and completed	68,000 units
Ending inventory	6,000 units, 30% complete

Calculate the equivalent units completed using the weighted average method, assuming that the materials are added at the beginning of the process and conversion costs are incurred evenly throughout.

LO3, 4

E4-3A.   **Equivalent Units and Product Cost Report—Weighted Average Method** In its first month's operations (January), Schramski Company's Department 1 incurred charges of $120,000 for direct materials (10,000 units), $29,875 for direct labor, and $58,000 for manufacturing overhead. At month-end, 9,000 units had been finished and transferred out. The remaining units were finished with respect to materials but only 25% complete with respect to conversion costs.
Assuming Schramski uses the weighted average method and that materials are added at the beginning of the process and conversion costs occur evenly, compute the following:

a.   The equivalent units of materials and conversion costs.
b.   The cost per equivalent unit of materials and conversion costs.
c.   The total cost assigned to the units transferred out.
d.   The total cost assigned to the ending inventory.
e.   Prove that your solutions to requirements (c) and (d) sum to the total costs to be accounted for.

E4-4A. Equivalent Units and Product Cost Report—Weighted Average Method The following data (and annotations) are for the work-in-process account of the first of Johnson Company's four departments used in manufacturing its only product for October.

LO3, 4

Work-in-Process—Department 1	
Beginning balance (2,000 units, 70% complete)	
Direct materials.	$ 15,500
Conversion costs.	9,600
Transferred to department 2: (20,000 units)	(a)
Direct materials (21,000 units)	157,000
Direct labor.	145,200
Manufacturing overhead.	48,135
Ending balance [(b) units, 25% complete].	(c)

Assuming that Johnson uses the weighted average method and that materials are added at the beginning of the process and conversion costs are incurred evenly throughout, solve for the three missing numbers.

E4-5A. Equivalent Units and Product Cost Report—Weighted Average Method The following data (and annotations) are for Joyner Company's processing department work-in-process account for the month of June:

LO3, 4

Beginning inventory (700 units, 40% complete)	
Direct materials.	$ 2,905
Conversion costs.	7,942
Current period	
Direct materials (5,000 units)	35,000
Direct labor	59,600
Manufacturing overhead applied.	37,800

Joyner uses the weighted average method. Materials are added at the beginning of the process and conversion costs are incurred evenly throughout. Ending work-in-process is composed of 900 units, 70% complete. Compute the following:

a. Equivalent units for materials and conversion costs.
b. Cost per equivalent unit for materials and conversion costs.
c. Total cost assigned to the units transferred out.

E4-6A. Cost Flows Through Journal Entries The Mixing Department performs a series of processes in which a fluid chemical is concentrated. Records indicate that the Mixing Department has been charged with $64,000 of direct labor costs. The manufacturing overhead rate is 150% of direct labor costs. Beginning work-in-process was $224,000, and ending work-in-process totaled $34,000. One-half of this period's completed products is sold on account at a price equal to 160% of its cost.

LO5

Prepare journal entries to record (1) various costs charged to the Mixing Department this period, (2) transfer of this period's completed product, and (3) sale of one-half of this period's production.

E4-7A. Equivalent Units Calculations—FIFO Method Ferris Corporation makes a powdered rug shampoo in two sequential departments: Compounding and Drying. Materials are added at the beginning of the process in the Compounding Department. Conversion costs are added evenly throughout each process. Ferris uses the FIFO method of process costing. In the Compounding Department, beginning work-in-process was 6,000 pounds (70% processed), 38,000 pounds were started in process, 36,000 pounds transferred out, and ending work-in-process was 60% processed.

LO6
(Appendix 4A)

Calculate equivalent units for March for the Compounding Department.

E4-8A. Equivalent Units Calculations—FIFO Method The following selected operating data are for Jackson Company's Blending Department for the month of April. Tinting and packaging operations are carried out subsequently in other departments.

LO6
(Appendix 4A)

Beginning inventory	4,000 units, 60% complete
Started and completed	68,000 units
Ending inventory.	6,000 units, 30% complete

Calculate the equivalent units accomplished using the FIFO method, assuming that the materials are added at the beginning of the process and conversion costs are incurred evenly throughout.

E4-9A.   Equivalent Units and Product Cost Report—FIFO Method In its first month's operations (January), Allred Company's Department 1 incurred charges of $120,000 for direct materials (10,000 units), $33,000 for direct labor, and $58,000 for manufacturing overhead. At month-end, 8,800 units had been finished and transferred out. The remaining units were finished with respect to materials but only 25% complete with respect to conversion costs.

Assuming Allred uses the FIFO method and that materials are added at the beginning of the process and conversion costs occur evenly, compute the following:

a.   The equivalent units for material and conversion costs.
b.   The cost per equivalent unit for materials and conversion costs.
c.   The total cost assigned to the units transferred out.
d.   The total cost assigned to the ending inventory.
e.   Prove that your solutions to requirements (c) and (d) sum to the total costs to be accounted for.

E4-10A. Equivalent Units and Product Cost Report—FIFO Method The following data (and annotations) are for the work-in-process account of the first of Crocker Company's four departments used in manufacturing its only product for October.

Work-in-Process—Department 1	
Beginning balance (2,000 units, 70% complete)	$ 25,100
Transferred to department 2: (20,000 units)	(a)
Direct materials (21,000 units)	157,500
Direct labor	145,200
Manufacturing overhead	48,300
Ending balance [(b) units, 25% complete]	(c)

Assuming that Crocker uses the FIFO method and that materials are added at the beginning of the process and conversion costs are incurred evenly throughout, solve for the three missing numbers.

E4-11A. Equivalent Units and Product Cost Assignment—FIFO Method The following data (and annotations) are related to the June charges appearing in the work-in-process account for Sutter Company's first processing department:

Beginning inventory (700 units, 40% complete)	
Direct materials	$ 5,780
Conversion costs	5,000
Current period	
Direct materials (5,000 units)	50,000
Direct labor	59,600
Manufacturing overhead applied	22,800

Sutter uses the FIFO method. Direct materials are added at the beginning of the process, and conversion costs are incurred evenly throughout. Ending work-in-process totals 900 units, 70% complete. Compute the following:

a.   Equivalent units for direct materials and conversion costs.
b.   Cost per equivalent unit for direct materials and conversion costs.
c.   Total cost assigned to the units transferred out.

EXERCISES—SET B

E4-1B.   Equivalent Units Calculations—Weighted Average Method Terrace Corporation makes an industrial cleaner in two sequential departments: Compounding and Drying. All materials are added at the beginning of the process in the Compounding Department. Conversion costs are added evenly throughout each process. Terrace uses the weighted average method of process costing. In the Compounding Department, beginning work-in-process was 2,000 pounds (60% processed), 36,000 pounds were started, 34,000 pounds were transferred out, and ending work-in-process was 70% processed.

Calculate equivalent units for the Compounding Department for August.

E4-2B. **Equivalent Units Calculations—Weighted Average Method** The following are selected operating data for Jackson Company's Blending Department for November. Painting and packaging operations are carried out subsequently in other departments.

LO3

Beginning inventory	5,000 units, 70% complete
Started and completed	62,000 units
Ending inventory	3,000 units, 40% complete

Calculate the equivalent units finished for the month of November using the weighted average method, assuming that the materials are added at the beginning of the process and conversion costs are incurred evenly throughout.

E4-3B. **Equivalent Units and Product Cost Assignment—Weighted Average Method** In its first month of operations (May), Holland Company's Department 1 incurred charges of $72,000 for direct materials (9,000 units), $38,700 for direct labor, and $13,950 for manufacturing overhead. At month-end, 7,500 units had been finished and transferred out. Those remaining were finished with respect to materials but only 40% finished with respect to conversion costs.

LO3, 4

Assuming Holland uses the weighted average method and that materials are added at the beginning of the process and conversion occurs evenly, compute the following:

a. The equivalent units for materials and conversion costs.
b. The cost per equivalent unit for materials and conversion costs.
c. The total cost assigned to the units transferred out.
d. The total cost assigned to the ending inventory.
e. Prove that your solutions to requirements (c) and (d) sum to the total costs to be accounted for.

E4-4B. **Equivalent Units and Product Cost Report—Weighted Average Method** The following data (and annotations) for March are for the work-in-process account of the first of Eyring Company's four departments used in manufacturing its only product.

LO3, 4

Work-in-Process—Department 1	
Beginning balance (3,000 units, 40% complete)	
Direct materials	$13,350
Conversion costs	5,600
Transferred to Department 2: (23,000 units)	(a)
Direct materials (24,000 units)	96,000
Direct labor	77,300
Manufacturing overhead	34,700
Ending balance [(b) units, 25% complete]	(c)

Assuming that Eyring uses the weighted average method, that materials are added at the beginning of the process, and that conversion costs are incurred evenly throughout, solve for the three missing numbers.

E4-5B. **Equivalent Units and Product Cost Report—Weighted Average Method** The following data (and annotations) are for Nelson Company's processing department work-in-process account for the month of September:

LO3, 4

Beginning inventory (1,500 units, 70% complete)	
Direct materials	$22,000
Conversion costs	10,000
Current period	
Direct materials (6,000 units)	50,000
Direct labor	41,000
Manufacturing overhead applied	65,440

Nelson uses the weighted average method. Materials are added at the beginning of the process and conversion costs are incurred evenly throughout. Ending work-in-process is composed of 1,000 units, 60% complete. Compute the following:

a. Equivalent units for direct materials and conversion costs.
b. Cost per equivalent unit for direct materials and conversion costs.
c. Total cost assigned to the units transferred out.

LO5   **E4-6B.   Cost Flows Through Journal Entries** The Mixing Department performs a series of processes
            in which a fluid chemical is concentrated. Records indicate that the Mixing Department has been
             charged with $50,000 of direct labor costs. The manufacturing overhead rate is 170% of direct labor
             costs. Beginning work-in-process was $170,000, and ending work-in-process totaled $36,000. One-
             half of this period's completed products is sold on account at a price equal to 150% of its cost.

             Prepare journal entries to record (1) various costs charged to the Mixing Department this period,
             (2) transfer of this period's completed product, and (3) sale of one-half of this period's production.

LO6   **E4-7B.   Equivalent Units Calculations—FIFO Method** Terrace Corporation makes an industrial cleaner
(Appendix 4A)   in two sequential departments: Compounding and Drying. All materials are added at the beginning
            of the process in the Compounding Department. Conversion costs are added evenly throughout each
             process. Terrace uses the FIFO method of process costing. In the Compounding Department, begin-
             ning work-in-process was 2,000 pounds (60% processed), 36,000 pounds were started, 34,000 pounds
             were transferred out, and ending work-in-process was 70% processed.

             Calculate equivalent units for the Compounding Department for August.

LO6   **E4-8B.   Equivalent Units Calculations—FIFO Method** The following are selected operating data for Jack-
(Appendix 4A)   son Company's Blending Department for November. Painting and packaging operations are carried
         out subsequently in other departments.

Beginning inventory	5,000 units, 70% complete
Started and completed	62,000 units
Ending inventory	3,000 units, 40% complete

Calculate the equivalent units finished for the month of November using the FIFO method, assuming
that the materials are added at the beginning of the process and conversion costs are incurred evenly
throughout.

LO6, 7   **E4-9B.   Equivalent Units and Product Cost Report—FIFO Method** In its first month of operations (May
(Appendix 4A)   of Year 1), Allred Company's Department 1 incurred charges of $72,000 for direct materials (9,000
            units), $38,700 for direct labor, and $13,500 for manufacturing overhead. At month-end, 8,500 units
             had been finished and transferred out. Those units remaining were finished with respect to materials
             but only 40% finished with respect to conversion costs.

             Assuming Allred uses the FIFO method and that materials are added at the beginning of the process
             and conversion costs are incurred evenly throughout the period, compute the following:

             a.   The equivalent units for materials and conversion costs.
             b.   The cost per equivalent unit for materials and conversion costs.
             c.   The total cost assigned to the units transferred out.
             d.   The total cost assigned to the ending inventory.
             e.   Prove that your solutions to requirements (c) and (d) sum to the total costs to be accounted for.

LO6, 7   **E4-10B. Equivalent Units and Product Cost Report—FIFO Method** The following data (and annotations)
(Appendix 4A)   for March are for the work-in-process account of the first of Olympus Company's four departments
             used in manufacturing its only product.

Work-in-Process—Department 1	
Beginning balance (3,000 units, 40% complete)	$18,200
Transferred to Department 2: (23,000 units)	(a)
Direct materials (24,000 units)	96,000
Direct labor	77,300
Manufacturing overhead	36,700
Ending balance [___(b)___ units, 25% complete]	(c)

Assuming that Olympus uses the FIFO method, that materials are added at the beginning of the process,
and that conversion costs are incurred evenly throughout, solve for the three missing numbers.

LO6, 7   **E4-11B. Equivalent Units and Product Cost Report—FIFO Method** Following are the September charges
(Appendix 4A)   (and certain annotations) appearing in the work-in-process account for Empire Company's processing
            department:

Beginning inventory (1,500 units, 70% complete)	
Direct materials.	$21,950
Conversion costs.	10,000
Current period	
Direct materials (6,000 units)	72,000
Direct labor	32,500
Manufacturing overhead applied.	52,200

Empire uses the FIFO method. Materials are added at the beginning of the process and conversion costs are incurred evenly throughout. Ending work-in-process is composed of 1,000 units, 60% complete. Compute the following:

a.   Equivalent units for direct materials and conversion costs.
b.   Cost per equivalent unit or units transferred in and conversion costs.
c.   Total cost assigned to the units transferred out.

PROBLEMS—SET A

P4-1A.   **Calculate Equivalent Units, Unit Costs, and Transferred Costs—Weighted Average Method**
Canfield Manufacturing, Inc., operates a plant that produces its own regionally marketed Spicy Steak Sauce. The sauce is produced in two processes: blending and bottling. In the Blending Department, all materials are added at the start of the process, and labor and overhead are incurred evenly throughout the process. Canfield uses the weighted average method. The following data from the Work-in-Process— Blending Department account for January are missing a few items:

Work-in-Process—Blending Department	
January 1 inventory (5,000 gallons, 60% processed)	
Direct materials.	$ 12,000
Conversion costs.	5,900
Transferred to Bottling Department (60,000 gallons)	_____
January charges:	
Direct materials (61,000 gallons)	153,000
Direct labor.	73,600
Manufacturing overhead.	42,480
January 31 inventory (_____ gallons, 70% processed)	_____

Required
Assuming Canfield uses the weighted average method in process costing, calculate the following amounts for the Blending Department:

a.   Number of units in the January 31 inventory.
b.   Equivalent units for materials and conversion costs.
c.   January cost per equivalent unit for materials and conversion costs.
d.   Cost of the units transferred to the Bottling Department.
e.   Cost of the incomplete units in the January 31 inventory.

P4-2A.   **Calculate Equivalent Units, Unit Costs, and Transferred Costs—Weighted Average Method**   Monroe Company processes a food seasoning powder through its Compounding and Packaging departments. In the Compounding Department, direct materials are added at the beginning of the process, and direct labor and manufacturing overhead are incurred evenly throughout the process. Monroe uses the weighted average method. Costs in the Compounding Department can be summarized as follows:

Inventory, August 1 (2,000 units, 40% complete)	
Direct materials.	$ 980
Conversion costs.	4,100
Current period (31,000 units started)	
Direct materials.	33,010
Direct labor	62,560
Manufacturing overhead	75,789
	$171,359

LO3, 4

LO3, 4

At August 31, 3,000 units were in process, 30% complete with respect to conversion costs.

Required

Calculate the following for the Compounding Department:

a.   Equivalent units for materials and conversion costs during August.
b.   Costs per equivalent unit for materials and conversion costs.
c.   Total cost of units transferred to the Packaging Department.
d.   Inventory cost at August 31.

LO3, 4   P4-3A.   Product Cost Report—Weighted Average Method Riley Manufacturing Corporation produces a cosmetic product in three consecutive processes. The costs of Department 1 for May were as follows:

Cost of beginning inventory		
Direct materials.		$ 9,800
Conversion costs.		16,480
Costs added in Department 1:		
Direct materials.	$295,120	
Direct labor	298,550	
Manufacturing overhead	203,130	796,800

Department 1 handled the following units during May:

Units in process, May 1	2,000
Units started in Department 1	40,000
Units transferred to Department 2	39,000
Units in process, May 31	3,000

On average, the May 1 units were 30% complete. The May 31 units were 60% complete. Materials are added at the beginning of the process, and conversion costs occur evenly throughout the process in Department 1. Riley uses the weighted average method for process costing.

Required

Prepare the product cost report for Department 1 for May.

LO3, 4   P4-4A.   Product Cost Report—Weighted Average Method Bath Manufacturing Company uses the weighted average method for process costing. Bath produces processed food products that pass through three sequential departments. The costs for Department 1 for September were as follows:

Cost of beginning inventory:	
Materials	$ 11,850
Conversion costs.	20,544
	$ 32,394
Costs added in Department 1 during September:	
Direct materials.	$340,150
Direct labor	341,370
Manufacturing overhead	245,990
	$927,510
Department 2 handled the following units during September:	
Units in process, September 1	2,000
Units started in Department 1.	48,000
Units transferred out to Department 2.	46,000
Units in process, September 30	4,000

On average, the September 1 units were 30% complete, and the September 30 units were 60% complete. Materials are added at the beginning of the process and conversion costs occur evenly throughout the process in Department 1.

Required

Prepare the product cost report for September for Department 1.

LO3, 4, 5   P4-5A.   Two Departments, Journal Entries with Supporting Calculations—Weighted Average Method (Note: This problem includes two departments. The second department may be beyond the scope of most classes. Instructors may choose to assign only the requirements related to Department 1.)

Patterson Laboratories, Inc., produces one of its products in two successive departments. All materials are added at the beginning of the process in Department 1; no materials are used in Department 2. Conversion costs are incurred evenly in both departments. Patterson uses the weighted average method for process costing. January 1 inventory account balances are as follows:

Materials inventory	$30,000
Work-in-process—Department 1 (3,000 units, 30% complete)	
Direct materials	4,560
Conversion costs	10,640
Work-in-process—Department 2 (3,550 units, 40% complete)	43,439
Finished goods inventory (2,000 units @ $16)	32,000

During January, the following transactions occurred:

1. Purchased materials on account, $90,000.
2. Placed $84,000 of materials into process in Department 1. This $84,000 represents 24,000 units of materials.
3. Distributed total payroll costs: $108,116 of direct labor to Department 1, $62,700 of direct labor to Department 2, and $51,000 of indirect labor to Manufacturing Overhead.
4. Incurred other actual manufacturing overhead costs, $81,000. (Credit Other Accounts.)
5. Applied overhead to the two processing departments: $88,000 to Department 1 and $43,900 to Department 2.
6. Transferred 25,000 completed units from Department 1 to Department 2. The 2,000 units remaining in Department 1 were 20% completed with respect to conversion costs.
7. Transferred 26,000 completed units from Department 2 to finished goods inventory. The 2,550 units remaining in Department 2 were 70% completed with respect to conversion costs.
8. Sold 20,000 units on account at $27 per unit. Patterson uses weighted average inventory costing procedures for the finished goods inventory.

Required

a. Record the January transactions in general journal form for Department 1 and Department 2.
b. Prepare a product cost report (with its supporting calculations) for Department 1.
c. Prepare a product cost report (with its supporting calculations) for Department 2.
d. Determine the balances remaining in the Materials Inventory account, in each work-in-process account, and in the Finished Goods Inventory account.

P4-6A. Calculate Equivalent Units, Unit Costs, and Transferred Costs—FIFO Method Gaston Manufacturing, Inc., operates a plant that produces its own regionally marketed Spicy Steak Sauce. The sauce is produced in two processes: blending and bottling. In the Blending Department, all materials are added at the start of the process, and labor and overhead are incurred evenly throughout the process. Gaston uses the FIFO method. The following data from the Work-in-Process—Blending Department account for January are missing a few items:

LO6, 7
(Appendix 4A)

Work-in-Process—Blending Department	
January 1 inventory (5,000 gallons, 60% processed)	$17,900
Transferred to Bottling Department (65,000 gallons)	_____
January charges:	
Direct materials (66,000 gallons)	161,700
Direct labor	79,400
Manufacturing overhead	53,000
January 31 inventory (_____ gallons, 70% processed)	_____

Required

Assuming Gaston uses the FIFO method in process costing, calculate the following amounts for the Blending Department:

a. Number of units in the January 31 inventory.
b. Equivalent units for materials and conversion costs.
c. January cost per equivalent unit for materials and conversion costs.
d. Cost of the units transferred to the Bottling Department.
e. Cost of the incomplete units in the January 31 inventory.

LO6, 7   **P4-7A.**   **Calculate Equivalent Units, Unit Costs, and Transferred Costs—FIFO Method** Commodore
(Appendix 4A)   Company processes a food seasoning powder through its Compounding and Packaging departments.
                            In the Compounding Department, direct materials are added at the beginning of the process, and direct
                            labor and manufacturing overhead are incurred evenly throughout the process. Arrow uses the FIFO
                            method. August costs in the Compounding Department can be summarized as follows:

Inventory, August 1 (2,000 units, 40% complete)	$ 5,080
Direct materials (31,000 units)	32,550
Direct labor.	62,560
Manufacturing overhead.	75,900
	$176,090

At August 31, 3,000 units were in process, 30% complete with respect to conversion costs.

Required

Calculate the following for the Compounding Department:

a.   Equivalent units during August.

b.   Costs per equivalent unit.

c.   Total cost of units transferred to finished goods inventory.

d.   Inventory cost at August 31.

LO7   **P4-8A.**   **Product Cost Report—FIFO Method** Reston Manufacturing Corporation produces a cosmetic
(Appendix 4A)   product in three consecutive processes. The costs of Department 1 for May were as follows:

Cost of beginning inventory		$606,390
Costs added in Department 1:		
Direct materials.	$80,400	
Direct labor	81,550	
Manufacturing overhead	55,130	217,080

Department 1 handled the following units during May:

Units in process, May 1	2,000
Units started in Department 1	40,000
Units transferred to Department 2	39,000
Units in process, May 31	3,000

On average, the May 1 units were 30% complete; the May 31 units were 60% complete. Materials
are added at the beginning of the process and conversion costs occur evenly throughout the process in
Department 1. Reston uses the FIFO method for process costing.

Required

Prepare the product cost report for Department 1 for May.

PROBLEMS—SET B

LO3, 4   **P4-1B.**   **Calculate Equivalent Units, Unit Costs, and Transferred Costs—Weighted Average Method**
                            Chelsea Manufacturing, Inc., operates a plant that produces its own regionally marketed Super
                            Salad Dressing. The dressing is produced in two processes: blending and bottling. In the Blend-
                            ing Department, all materials are added at the beginning of the process, and labor and overhead are
                            incurred evenly throughout the process. Chelsea uses the weighted average method. The Work-in-
                            Process—Blending Department account for January follows:

Work-in-Process—Blending Department	
January 1 inventory (4,000 gallons, 75% finished)	
Direct materials.	$ 31,200
Conversion costs.	8,800
Transferred to Bottling Department (70,000 gallons)	
January charges:	
Direct materials (71,000 gallons)	568,800
Direct labor	164,000
Manufacturing overhead	184,900
January 31 inventory (_____ gallons, 60% processed)	

Required

Calculate the following amounts for the Blending Department:

a.   Number of units in the January 31 inventory.
b.   Equivalent units for materials cost and conversion costs.
c.   January cost per equivalent unit for materials and conversion costs.
d.   Cost of the units transferred to the Bottling Department.
e.   Cost of the incomplete units in the January 31 inventory.

P4-2B. **Calculate Equivalent Units, Unit Costs, and Transferred Costs—Weighted Average Method** Evans Company processes a scouring powder through its Compounding Department and Packaging Department. In the Compounding Department, direct materials are added at the beginning of the process, and direct labor and manufacturing overhead are incurred evenly throughout the process. Evans uses the weighted average method. Costs charged to the Compounding Department in October follow:

LO3, 4

Inventory, October 1 (5,000 units, 25% complete)	
Direct materials.	$ 2,400
Conversion costs.	1,850
Current period (82,000 units started):	
Direct materials.	171,600
Direct labor	67,440
Manufacturing overhead	71,470
	$310,510

At October 31, 7,000 units were in process, 40% completed.

Required

Calculate the following for the Compounding Department:

a.   Equivalent units during October.
b.   Costs per equivalent unit.
c.   Total cost of units transferred to the Packaging Department.
d.   Inventory cost at October 31.

P4-3B. **Product Cost Report—Weighted Average Method** Salanger Manufacturing Corporation produces a dandruff shampoo in three consecutive processes. The costs of Department 1 for June were as follows:

LO3, 4

Cost of beginning inventory		
Direct materials.		$ 5,500
Conversion costs.		12,740
Costs added in Department 1:		
Direct materials.	$223,390	
Direct labor	358,300	
Manufacturing overhead	155,269	736,959

Department 1 handled the following units during June:

Units in process, June 1	2,000
Units started in Department 1	45,000
Units transferred to Department 2	46,000
Units in process, June 30	1,000

On average, the June 1 units were 40% complete; the June 30 units were 70% complete. Direct materials are added at the beginning of the process, and conversion costs occur evenly throughout the process in Department 1. Salanger uses the weighted average method for process costing.

Required
Prepare the product cost report for Department 1 for June.

LO3, 4   **P4-4B.**   **Equivalent Units and Product Cost Report—Weighted Average Method** Summers Manufacturing Corporation produces chemical products using a continual process. Summers uses the weighted average method for process costing. All manufacturing is accomplished in one department. Materials are added at the beginning of the process while conversion costs are incurred evenly throughout the process.

The work-in-process inventory at the beginning of February consisted of 10,000 gallons that were 20% complete. The work-in-process at the end of February consisted of 15,000 gallons that were 40% complete. During February 195,000 gallons were transferred to finished goods.

The beginning inventory contained $90,000 of materials and $30,000 of conversion costs. Product costs incurred during February consisted of $2,010,000 of materials and $3,186,000 of conversion costs.

Required
Calculate equivalent units, cost per equivalent unit, and prepare the product cost report for Summers Manufacturing Corporation for the month of February.

LO3, 4, 5   **P4-5B.**   **Two Departments, Journal Entries with Supporting Calculations—Weighted Average Method** (Note: This problem includes two departments. The second department may be beyond the scope of most classes. Instructors may choose to assign only the requirements related to Department 1.)

Parker Laboratories, Inc., produces one of its products in two successive departments. All materials are added at the beginning of the process in Department 1. No materials are used in Department 2. Conversion costs are incurred evenly in both departments. August 1 inventory account balances are as follows:

Materials inventory	$15,000
Work-in-process—Department 1 (6,000 units, 25% finished)	
Direct materials.	11,500
Conversion costs.	18,750
Work-in-process—Department 2 (3,500 units, 35% finished)	41,000
Finished goods inventory (4,000 units @ $12.50)	50,000

During August, the following transactions occurred:

1. Purchased materials on account, $58,000.
2. Placed $63,300 (16,000 units) of materials into process in Department 1.
3. Distributed total payroll costs: $83,770 of direct labor to Department 1, $42,300 of direct labor to Department 2, and $19,100 of indirect labor to Manufacturing Overhead.
4. Incurred other actual manufacturing overhead costs, $21,200. (Credit Other Accounts.)
5. Applied overhead to the two processing departments: Department 1, $21,080, Department 2, $17,900.
6. Transferred 20,000 completed units from Department 1 to Department 2. The 2,000 units remaining in Department 1 were 30% completed with respect to conversion costs.
7. Transferred 15,000 completed units from Department 2 to Finished Goods Inventory. The 8,500 units remaining in Department 2 were 40% completed with respect to conversion costs.
8. Sold 13,000 units on account at $24 per unit. Parker uses weighted average inventory costing for finished goods inventory.

Required
a.   Record the August transactions in general journal form for Department 1 and Department 2.
b.   Prepare a product cost report (with its supporting calculations) for Department 1.
c.   Prepare a product cost report (with its supporting calculations) for Department 2.
d.   Determine the balances remaining in the Materials Inventory account, in each work-in-process account, and in the Finished Goods Inventory account.

P4-6B.   Calculate Equivalent Units, Unit Costs, and Transferred Costs—FIFO Method Kipling Manufacturing, Inc., operates a plant that produces its own regionally marketed Super Salad Dressing. The dressing is produced in two processes: blending and bottling. In the Blending Department, all materials are added at the beginning of the process, and labor and overhead are incurred evenly throughout the process. Kipling uses the FIFO method. The Work-in-Process—Blending Department account for January follows:

LO6, 7
(Appendix 4A)

Work-in-Process—Blending Department	
January 1 inventory (4,000 gallons, 75% finished)	$ 40,000
Transferred to Bottling Department (70,000 gallons)	
January charges:	
Direct materials (71,000 gallons)	568,000
Direct labor	164,000
Manufacturing overhead	186,000
January 31 inventory (_____ gallons, 60% processed)	

Required

Calculate the following amounts for the Blending Department:

 a.   Number of units in the January 31 inventory.
 b.   Equivalent units for materials cost and conversion costs.
 c.   January cost per equivalent unit for materials and conversion costs.
 d.   Cost of the units transferred to the Bottling Department.
 e.   Cost of the incomplete units in the January 31 inventory.

P4-7B.   Calculate Equivalent Units, Unit Costs, and Transferred Costs—FIFO Method Kipper Company processes a scouring powder through its Compounding Department and Packaging Department. In the Compounding Department, direct materials are added at the beginning of the process, and direct labor and manufacturing overhead are incurred evenly throughout the process. Kipper uses the FIFO method. Costs charged to the Compounding Department in October follow:

LO6, 7
(Appendix 4A)

Inventory, October 1 (5,000 units, 25% complete)	$ 4,250
Direct material (82,000 units)	246,000
Direct labor	31,770
Manufacturing overhead	33,470
	$315,490

At October 31, 7,000 units were in process, 40% completed.

Required

Calculate the following for the Compounding Department:

 a.   Equivalent units during October.
 b.   Costs per equivalent unit.
 c.   Total cost of units transferred to the Packaging Department.
 d.   Inventory cost at October 31.

P4-8B.   Product Cost Report—FIFO Method Chauncer Manufacturing Corporation produces a dandruff shampoo in three consecutive processes. The costs of Department 1 for June were as follows:

LO7
(Appendix 4A)

Cost of beginning inventory		$ 18,240
Costs added in Department 1:		
Direct material.	$219,600	
Direct labor	361,300	
Manufacturing overhead	155,993	736,893

Department 1 handled the following units during June:

Units in process, June 1	2,000
Units started in Department 1	45,000
Units transferred to Department 2	46,000
Units in process, June 30	1,000

On average, the June 1 units were 40% complete. The June 30 units were 70% complete. Materials are added at the beginning of the process and conversion costs occur evenly throughout the process in Department 1. Chauncer uses the FIFO method for process costing.

Required

Prepare the product cost report for Department 1 for June.

EXTENDING YOUR KNOWLEDGE

EYK4-1.   Ethics Case Sweet Fragrances Company uses process costing to account for the manufacture of its perfume. The factory consists of three departments: Blending, Bottling, and Packaging.

The production manager of the Bottling department, Janine Post, has recommended that her department not be charged for new labels that are more elaborate and expensive than those used in previous years. The new labels were designed as a tie-in for the marketing and advertising campaigns. Post recommends that the costs of the labels be charged to advertising expense. This would result in slightly lower product costs charged to the Bottling department than last year.

The company has instituted a bonus plan for all managers based on keeping costs within a range of previous years' costs.

Sam Block, the accounting manager, reviews all recommendations by all managers before they are presented to top management.

Required

What ethical considerations may arise from Janine Post's recommendation? What alternative recommendations might be made?

ANSWERS TO SELF-STUDY QUESTIONS:

1. c   2. b   3. a

YOUR TURN! SOLUTIONS

Solution 4.1

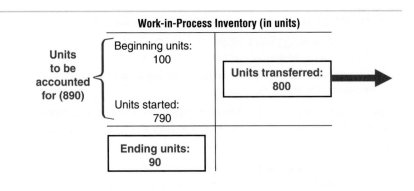

Where do the units come from?		Where do the units go?	
Beginning inventory . . .	100	Complete/transferred . . .	800
Started	790	Ending inventory.	90
Total	890	Total	890

Solution 4.2

Remember that when using the weighted average method, the question is "what percentage of the work has been completed?"

Where do the units come from?		Where do the units go?		% Work Done?	Direct Materials	% Work Done?	Conversion Costs
					Equivalent Units		
Beginning inventory . . .	100	Complete/transferred . . .	800	100%	**800**	100%	**800**
Started	790	Ending inventory	90	100%	**90**	70%	**63**
Total	890	Total	890		890		863

Solution 4.3

Where do the costs come from?	Total	Direct Materials	Conversion Costs
Beginning inventory	$ 4,883	$ 3,390	$ 1,493
Current	34,654	19,750	14,904
Total costs to account for	$39,537	$23,140	$16,397
÷ Total equivalent units		890	863
Average cost/unit		$ 26.00	$ 19.00

Solution 4.4

Materials	[800 EU × $26.00]	20,800
Conversion costs	[800 EU × $19.00]	15,200
Total cost of goods manufactured		$36,000

Solution 4.5

Materials	[90 EU × $26.00]	2,340
Conversion costs	[63 EU × $19.00]	1,197
Total cost of goods manufactured		$3,537

Comprehensive Solution to Your Turn 4.1–4.5.

Flow of the Units and Equivalent Units Calculation

Step 1: Visualize the Physical Flow of the Units

Step 2: Calculate the Equivalent Units

Where do the units come from?		Where do the units go?		Equivalent Units			
				% Work Done?	Direct Materials	% Work Done?	Conversion Costs
Beginning inventory...	100	Compl./transferred ...	800	100%	800	100%	800
Started	790	Ending inventory.	90	100%	90	70%	63
Total	890	Total	890		890		863

Product Cost Report
January Production

Step 3: Determine Per-Unit Costs

Where do the costs come from?	Total		Dir. Mat.	Conv. Costs
Beginning inventory	$ 4,883		$ 3,390	$ 1.493
Current	34,654		19,750	14,904
Total costs to account for	$39,537		$23,140	$16,397
÷ Total equivalent units			890	863
Average cost/equivalent unit..........			$ 26.00	$ 19.00

Where do the costs go?

Step 4: Calculate the Cost of Goods Manufactured

Complete/transferred:			
Materials	$20,800	[800 EU × $26.00]	
Conversion costs.................	15,200		[800 EU × $19.00]
Cost of goods manufactured........	$36,000		

Step 5: Calculate the Cost of the Ending Work-in-Process Inventory

Ending inventory:			
Materials	$ 2,340	[90 EU × $26.00]	
Conversion costs.................	1,197		[63 EU × $19.00]
Cost of ending inventory	3,537		
Total costs allocated	$39,537		

Solution 4.6

Work-in-process	19,750	
Materials inventory		19,750
Work-in-process	9,500	
Wages payable		9,500
Work-in-process	5,404	
Manufacturing overhead		5,404

Solution 4.7

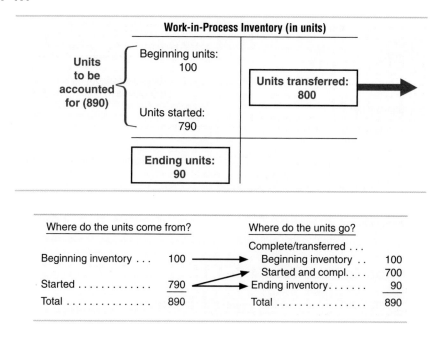

Where do the units come from?		Where do the units go?	
		Complete/transferred . . .	
Beginning inventory . . .	100	Beginning inventory . .	100
		Started and compl. . . .	700
Started	790	Ending inventory.	90
Total	890	Total	890

Solution 4.8

Remember that when using the FIFO method, the question is "what percentage of the work was completed during THIS PERIOD?"

Where do the units come from?		Where do the units go?		% in Jan.?	Direct Materials	% in Jan.?	Conversion Costs
						Equivalent Units	
		Complete/transferred:					
Beginning inventory	100	Beginning inventory	100	0%	0	65%	65
		Started and completed . . .	700	100%	700	100%	700
Started	790	Ending inventory	90	100%	90	70%	63
Total	890	Total	890		790		828

Solution 4.9

Where do the costs come from?	Total	Direct Materials	Conversion Costs
Beginning inventory	$ 4,883		
Current	34,654	$19,750	$14,904
Total costs to account for	$39,537		
÷ Total equivalent units		790	828
Average cost/unit		$ 25.00	$ 18.00

Solution 4.10

Beginning inventory:		
Costs incurred last period....................................		$ 4,883
Costs incurred this period..................................	[65 EU × $18.00]	1,170
Started and finished:		
Materials..	[700 EU × $25.00]	17,500
Conversion costs..	[700 EU × $18.00]	12,600
Total cost of goods manufactured............................		$36,153

Solution 4.11

Materials...	[90 EU × $25.00]	2,250
Conversion costs	[63 EU × $18.00]	1,134
Total cost of goods manufactured............................		$3,384

Comprehensive Solution to Your Turn 4.7–4.11.

Flow of the Units and Equivalent Units Calculation							

					Step 2: Calculate the Equivalent Units		
Step 1: Visualize the Physical Flow of the Units						Equivalent Units	
Where do the units come from?		Where do the units go?		% in Jan.?	Materials	% in Jan.?	Conversion Costs
		Compl./transferred					
Beginning inventory...	100 →	Beginning inventory ..	100	0%	**0**	65%	**65**
		Started and compl....	700	100%	**700**	100%	**700**
Started	790 ⤳	Ending inventory.	90	100%	**90**	70%	**63**
Total	890	Total	890		790		828

Product Cost Report **January Production**				

Step 3: Determine Per-Unit Costs

Where do the costs come from?	Total	Dir. Mat.	Conv. Costs
Beginning inventory	$ 4,883		
Current	34,654	$19,750	$14,904
Total costs to account for	$39,537		
÷ Total equivalent units		790	828
Average cost/equivalent unit..........		$ 25.00	$ 18.00

Where do the costs go?

Step 4: Calculate the Cost of Goods Manufactured

Beginning inventory:			
Costs incurred last period..........	$4,883		
Costs incurred this period..........	1,170	[0 × $329.06]	[65 EU × $18.00]
Started and finished................	30,100	[700 EU × $25.00]	[700 EU × $18.00]
Cost of goods manufactured.........	$36,153		

Step 5: Calculate the Cost of the Ending Work-in-Process Inventory

Ending inventory:			
Materials.......................	$ 2,250	[90 EU × $25.00]	
Conversion costs.................	1,134		[63 EU × $18.00]
Cost of ending inventory...........	3,384		
Total costs allocated................	$39,537		

Solution 4.12

Work-in-process	19,750	
Materials inventory		19,750
Work-in-process	9,500	
Wages payable		9,500
Work-in-process	5,404	
Manufacturing overhead		5,404

Chapter 5
Activity-Based Costing

Road Map

LO	Learning Objective	Page	eLecture	Guided Example	Assignments
LO1	Explain the changes in the modern production environment that have affected cost structures.	5-3	E5-1		SS1, SE1
LO2	Understand the concept of activity-based costing (ABC) and how it is applied.	5-4	E5-2	YT5.1	SS2, Q1, Q2, Q3, Q4, Q5, SE2, E1A, E2A, E3A, E4A, E5A, E1B, E2B, E3B, E4B, E5B, P3A, P4A, P5A, P6A, P1B, P2B, P3B, P4B, P5B, P6B, P7B
LO3	Explain the difference between traditional company-wide and departmental overhead methods and ABC.	5-8	E5-3	YT5.2	SS3, Q6, SE3, SE4, SE5, SE6, SE7, SE8, SE9, E5A, E5B, P1A, P2A, P5A, P6A, P7A, P1B, P2B, P3B, P5B, P6B, P7B
LO4	Describe the implementation of an ABC system.	5-13	E5-4	YT5.3	SS4, Q7, P7A
LO5	Explain customer profitability analysis based on ABC.	5-14	E5-5	YT5.4	SS5, Q8, SE10, E6A, E6B, P8A, P9A, P8B
LO6	Explain the difference between ABC and activity-based management.	5-17	E5-6	YT5.5	SS6, Q9

THE STATE BAR OF CALIFORNIA
A Judicial Branch Agency

Among its several responsibilities, the **California State Bar Association** regulates the professional conduct of the state's lawyers. The State Bar's discipline system is designed to protect the public from lawyers who violate the state's ethical code of professional conduct. The state's Business and Professions Code authorizes the State Bar to recover a portion of the costs of pursuing action against disciplined lawyers, including "charges determined by the State Bar to be 'reasonable costs' of investigation, hearing, and review." What constitutes "reasonable costs"?

To answer this question, the State Bar used activity-based costing (ABC) to determine the amount of "reasonable costs." Each of the State Bar offices (Office of Investigation, Office of Trials, etc.) is a "cost pool" that is allocated to a "product" (a type of case) based on a "cost driver" (a task performed). Although ABC is traditionally used to determine the cost of products, it can have application in a service setting as well.

This chapter explains how activity-based costing can be used as a more precise method of measuring the overhead cost of products and services.

PAST

Chapter 4 introduced process costing and how it differs from job order costing. It illustrated equivalent units and the flow of costs through the inventory accounts, as well as introduced the production cost report.

PRESENT

Chapter 5 explores activity-based costing, explains its benefits relative to traditional company-wide and departmental overhead allocation, and contrasts it with activity-based management.

FUTURE

Chapter 6 utilizes our understanding of cost behavior to determine break-even and make planning and budgeting decisions.

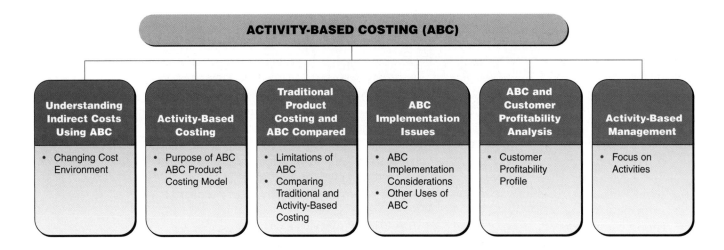

UNDERSTANDING INDIRECT COSTS USING ACTIVITY-BASED COSTING

LO1 **Explain** the changes in the modern production environment that have affected cost structures.

Effective management of costs is a hallmark of sound financial management, and indirect costs (commonly referred to as overhead) are the most challenging costs to measure and manage. Direct costs, including direct materials and direct labor, can be readily traced to a job, product, or other unit of work. Indirect costs, which are typically incurred for the benefit of several different products or cost objects, are not as easily traced to specific units or projects. Managing indirect costs is a major concern of managers because this broad category of costs has become increasingly more significant over time.

Many companies that once thrived have failed, arguably, because they did not manage effectively a growing pool of indirect costs. You might say they failed because they did not fully understand their business or their business model. If a business's actual cost of producing and selling products is more than the revenues generated by those products, the business will not succeed in the long term.

It is well documented that for many years the **U.S. Postal Service (USPS)**, a service entity, has struggled with mounting losses while its competitors, **UPS** and **FedEx**, have thrived in a highly competitive marketplace. At a meeting of the President's Commission on the United States Postal Service (created to examine the problems of the USPS), the discussion focused on differences in the cost systems at the USPS and UPS. It was reported that the USPS cost system attributes only 58% of its operating costs to it various products, whereas UPS attributes 100% of its costs to its products. The UPS representative on the panel stated that UPS does not price any product below its full cost. With only 58% of its costs attributed to products, the USPS cannot know whether any of its products, individually, is making a profit.[1]

As global competition puts increasing pressure on companies to price products more competitively, cost management is increasingly important. Organizations and entities such as UPS, **Coca-Cola**, **IBM**, the **City of Indianapolis**, and **Toronto's Hospital for Sick Children** have benefited greatly from a type of cost system referred to as **activity-based costing (ABC)**. In this chapter we will define and discuss ABC systems, compare ABC with traditional costing systems, and demonstrate how ABC can be used to analyze customer profitability. Finally, we will introduce the notion of **activity-based management (ABM)**, which uses ABC information to better manage processes and activities within an organization.

---

[1] James A. Johnson and Harry J. Pearce, Co-chairs, "Minutes of Meeting of the President's Commission on the U.S. Postal Service," May 28, 2003, p3, http://www.ustreas.gov/offices/domestic-finance/usps/pdf/may_28_minutes.pdf.

Changing Cost Environment

As technology has advanced over the last century, there has been a fundamental shift in manufacturing organizations from labor-intensive to automated assembly processes. These changes have had a profound influence on the activities performed to meet customer needs and, consequently, the costs of producing goods and services.

At the beginning of the twentieth century, products had long life cycles, production procedures were relatively straightforward, production was labor intensive, and only limited numbers of related products were produced in a single plant. It was said of the Model T Ford that "you could have any color you wanted, as long as it was black." The largest cost elements of most manufactured goods were the cost of raw materials and the wages paid to production employees. Manufacturing overhead was a relatively small portion of the overall cost of manufacturing products.

The twentieth century saw an accelerating shift from traditional labor-based activities to production procedures requiring large investments in automated equipment. In the past, production employees used equipment to assist them in performing their jobs. Now employees spend considerable time scheduling, setting up, maintaining, and moving materials to and from equipment. They spend relatively little time on actual production. The equipment does the work, and the employees keep it running efficiently. Increased com-

plexity of production procedures and an increase in the variety of products produced in a single facility have also caused a shift toward more support personnel and fewer production employees. The result is a significant increase in manufacturing overhead as a percentage of total product cost. This change in the typical production cost structure over the past century is illustrated in **Exhibit 5-1**.

In the "low-tech," labor-intensive manufacturing environment, factors related to direct labor were often the primary drivers of manufacturing overhead costs; however, in today's "high-tech" automated environment there are many other factors that drive manufacturing overhead costs, and the specific set of cost drivers differs from organization to organization.

Chapter 3 on product costing illustrates a simplified traditional system for allocating manufacturing overhead to products using a single, volume-based cost driver, such as direct labor hours. The following section introduces ABC, which recognizes the multiple activities that drive manufacturing overhead costs in today's production environment.

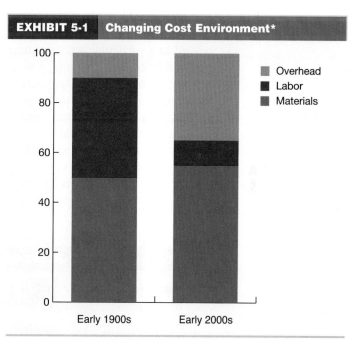

* James F. Cox, III and Michael S. Spencer, *The Constraints Management Handbook* (CRC Press, 1997), p. 5-54.

ACTIVITY-BASED COSTING

The manufacturing overhead cost account has been referred to as a "bucket" of common costs. The constant growth of costs classified as overhead has forced us to search for increasingly detailed methods to analyze these costs. If overhead costs are low in comparison with materials and labor costs and if factories produce few products in large production runs, the use of a single overhead rate based on direct labor hours or machine hours may be adequate. However, as the amount of overhead costs grows, as manufacturing facilities produce a wider variety of products, and

LO2 Understand the concept of activity-based costing (ABC) and how it is applied.

MBC

as competition intensifies, the inadequacies of a single overhead rate based on a single cost driver such as direct labor hours become evident.

Fortunately, advances in information technology and the declining costs of computerized information systems have facilitated the development and maintenance of increasingly detailed databases. The increased complexity of the production environment, coupled with faster and cheaper computing technology, gave rise to the emergence and development of ABC during the 1980s and 1990s.

ABC involves determining the cost of **activities** (discrete tasks or steps in a manufacturing or service process) and tracing those costs to cost objects based on their proportionate usage of the activities. ABC is generally implemented through a series of steps:

1. Identify activities that cause the company to incur costs.
2. Determine the total resources (or cost pool) for each activity for a period.
3. Select a cost driver (or allocation base) for each cost pool.
4. Calculate a cost allocation rate for each cost pool by dividing the total cost pool dollars (Step 2) by the total cost driver (Step 3).
5. Assign costs from each cost pool to the cost objects based on the cost driver units used by the cost object.

It might be helpful to review a few terms used in the discussion of activity-based costing. A **resource** is simply a cost or expense incurred by a company. These expenses are recorded in the company's general ledger of accounts. A **cost pool** represents the sum of resources related to a particular activity undertaken in response to a customer request or need. A cost pool might contain the sum of several different resources that are incurred as a result of the activity. A **cost object** is typically a product or customer service supplied by the company in response to a customer demand or need.

The California State Bar vignette from the beginning of the chapter can be used to illustrate these concepts. As illustrated in **Exhibit 5-2**, the State Bar incurs various costs in response to customer needs. For example, a client may complain that a lawyer has broken his fiduciary responsibility to the client in mismanaging the client's trust fund. The client's complaint causes the State Bar to incur costs (or use resources) in several ways. It must receive and document the client's complaint (referred to as "intake"), investigate the complaint (referred

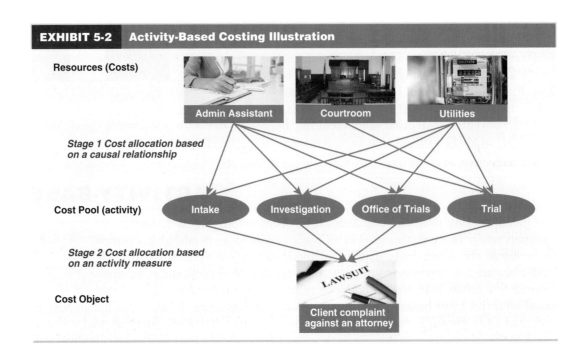

EXHIBIT 5-2   Activity-Based Costing Illustration

Resources (Costs): Admin Assistant, Courtroom, Utilities

Stage 1 Cost allocation based on a causal relationship

Cost Pool (activity): Intake, Investigation, Office of Trials, Trial

Stage 2 Cost allocation based on an activity measure

Cost Object: Client complaint against an attorney

to as "the investigation"), prepare and prosecute the complaint (handled by the Office of Trials), and conduct a trial in a courtroom (the State Bar Court). These are examples of activities that incur costs (Step 1). The costs of (or resources demanded by) each of these activities are accumulated into cost pools (the intake cost pool, the investigation cost pool, the Office of Trials cost pool, and the State Bar Court cost pool) (Step 2). Each client complaint may differ significantly in terms of total resource demand, depending on the type of complaint and the lawyer's response. There should be a logical and causal relationship between the resource and the cost pool. In our State Bar example, the investigation cost pool would logically include the salaries of the lawyers who investigate the clients' claims.

The cost pools should be assigned to cost objects on the basis of the units of activity (machine hours, number of purchase orders, number of product returns, number of invoice line items, etc.) (Step 3) consumed by the cost object. In the State Bar example, assume the investigation cost pool is driven by the number of hours spent by investigators. Dividing the total investigation cost by the total number of investigation hours yields a cost per hour (Step 4). If a typical malpractice complaint takes 20 hours to investigate, the equivalent 20-hour cost of the investigator should be assigned to the complaint.

The cost object is typically a product or service provided to a customer. In our example, the cost object is the client's complaint—that is, we want to know what it costs to follow up on each client complaint so that we can recover the appropriate cost from the wayward attorney. Depending on the information needs of decision-makers, as we will discuss later in this chapter, the cost object could be the customer.

To summarize, ABC is a system of analysis that identifies (Step 1) and summarizes (Step 2) the cost of key activities into cost pools, and then traces these cost pools to products or other cost objects (Step 5) based on the quantity of the cost pools consumed by the cost objects (Steps 3 and 4). ABC is based on the premise that activities drive costs and that costs should be assigned to products (or other cost objects) in proportion to the volume of activities they consume. Although activity cost analysis is most often associated with product costing, it offers many benefits for controlling and managing costs, as we will see later in this chapter. As the Accounting in Practice box (page 5-7) explains, ABC was actually used to improve cost management before it was used for product costing.

ENVIRONMENTAL, SOCIAL, AND GOVERNANCE   **Standards of Professionalism**

The opening vignette of this chapter discusses how the California State Bar Association determines the reasonable costs of pursuing action against disciplined lawyers. Because of the extraordinary responsibility society places upon the attorneys within our democracy, it is critical that groups such as the California State Bar Association maintain the highest ethical standards for its members. Just how does the Association see this responsibility? The following is quoted from the California Attorney Guidelines of Civility and Professionalism:

> As officers of the court with responsibilities to the administration of justice, attorneys have an obligation to be professional with clients, other parties and counsel, the courts, and the public. This obligation includes civility, professional integrity, personal dignity, candor, diligence, respect, courtesy, and cooperation, all of which are essential to the fair administration of justice and conflict resolution.

ABC Product Costing Model

Traditional costing considers the cost of a product to be its direct costs for materials and labor plus some allocated portion of manufacturing overhead, using overhead rates typically based on direct labor or machine hours. ABC is based on the notion that companies incur costs because of the activities they conduct in pursuit of their goals and objectives. For example, various activities take place to produce a particular product, such as setting up, maintaining, or monitoring the machines to make the product, physically moving raw materials and work-in-process, and so forth. Each of these activities has a cost; therefore, the total cost of producing a product using ABC is the sum of the direct materials and direct labor costs of that product, plus the cost of other activities conducted to produce that product.

Exhibit 5-2 illustrates the general two-stage ABC product cost model. The first stage includes the assignment of overhead resource costs, such as indirect labor, depreciation, and utilities, to activity cost pools for the key activities identified. Typical activity cost pools in a manufacturing environment include pools for machine setup, material movement, and engineering. The second stage assigns those activity cost pools to cost objects.

Remember that **Exhibit 5-2** is focused solely on overhead costs—the direct product or service costs, such as direct materials and direct labor, are directly assigned to cost objects and are excluded from the activity cost pools. Only indirect product costs (overhead) are assigned to products via activity cost pools.

Hint: If an increase in an activity does not cause a measurable increase in a particular cost, there is not a logical causal relationship.

Probably the most critical step in ABC is identifying **cost drivers**. The activity cost driver for a particular cost (or cost pool) is the characteristic selected for measuring the quantity of the activity for a particular period of time. In the example shown in **Exhibit 5-2**, if an activity cost pool is established for a trial, it is necessary to select some basis for measuring the quantity of trial activity associated with the costs in the pool. The quantity of trial activity could be measured by the number of trials held, the amount of time the courtroom is in use, the number of staff working in the courtroom, or some other measure. It is critical that the activity measure used has a logical causal relationship to the costs in the pool and that the quantity of the activity is highly correlated with the amount of cost in the pool. Statistical methods, such as regression analysis and correlation analysis, can be very useful in selecting activity cost drivers.

Once the budgeted cost in the activity pool and the budgeted activity cost driver have been determined, the cost per unit of activity is calculated as the total cost divided by the total amount of activity. This is the predetermined rate that will be used to apply costs to products or services during the period. For example, if total costs assigned to the trial activity pool in July were $100,000 and 100 hours of courtroom time were available in July, the cost per courtroom hour for the month would be $1,000. If during July a particular trial took eight hours of courtroom time, the total courtroom cost that would be assigned to the trial would be $8,000 ($1,000 × 8 hours).

ACCOUNTING IN PRACTICE   Development of ABC

ABC came to the forefront in the 1980s and 1990s; however, it was beginning to evolve as early as the 1960s when finance and accounting staff at **General Electric** (GE) attempted to improve the usefulness of accounting information in controlling ever-increasing indirect costs. The GE staff noted that indirect costs were often the result of "upstream" decisions, such as engineering design and change orders, which were made long before the costs were actually incurred. Frequently, the engineering department was not informed of the consequences its actions had on the other parts of the organization.

The second phase of the development of ABC was accomplished by business consultants, professors, and manufacturing companies during the 1970s and early 1980s. By generating more accurate cost and profitability measures for the various products offered by companies, these consultants and professors hoped to improve product cost information used in pricing and product mix decisions. ABC has since been extended to assess customer profitability.

In the late 1980s and 1990s, ABC was being promoted by many of the leading consulting firms, and it almost became a fad, much as total quality management (TQM) and just-in-time (JIT) systems had before it. Consequently, many companies that jumped on the ABC bandwagon early in its life later determined that it was not for them. Most of the companies that abandoned ABC probably adopted it initially for the wrong reasons.

Knowledge of the historical development of ABC is important in order to clearly understand what ABC analysis was intended to accomplish, as well as what it was not intended to accomplish.

Concept	→	Method	→	Assessment	TAKEAWAY 5.1
Can a company that has traditionally allocated overhead on a single, company-wide rate improve its understanding of its product costs by using a different approach?		• Choose a cost object (typically a product or service). • Identify the activities required to complete and deliver that cost object. • Determine the costs incurred for each activity. • Assign the costs to the activity cost pool(s). • Choose an activity driver for each cost pool. • Allocate the cost pools to each cost object based on the proportion of the activity driver used by each cost object.		Cost objects that require more of a particular activity will receive a greater portion of that activity's costs, leading to a better understanding of the cost object's real cost.	

Only Chips specializes in making two types of chip cookies—semi-sweet and butterscotch—and delivering them to customers while they are still warm from the oven. The butterscotch cookies tend to be preferred by those living downtown, while the semi-sweet cookies are more popular in the suburbs. Most bakers assess a product's profitability by comparing revenues to the cost of goods sold. However, due to its unique business model, Jessy Baker, the firm's new accountant, wants to use an activity-based costing system that takes into consideration the cost of the delivery person. Listed below are activity and cost information for Only Chips's two products.

YOUR TURN! 5.1

The solution is on page 5-43.

MBC

	Semi-Sweet	Butterscotch
Revenue	$200,000	$140,000
Cost of goods sold	$112,000	$ 84,000
Delivery activity:		
Number of deliveries	15,000	10,500
Average length of delivery	18 Minutes	12 Minutes
Cost per hour for delivery	$15.00	$15.00

Using activity-based costing, which one of the products is more profitable?

TRADITIONAL PRODUCT COSTING AND ABC COMPARED

Recall that in Chapter 3, Fezzari Performance Bicycles applied overhead using a company-wide overhead rate of $12.00 per direct labor hour. This may seem to be a very low overhead rate until you remember that Fezzari is primarily assembling parts that have been manufactured by other suppliers. Fezzari's factory doesn't have large, expensive manufacturing equipment that you might associate with other types of manufacturers.

LO3 Explain the difference between traditional company-wide and departmental overhead methods and ABC.

eLecture

MBC

We assumed that each hour of labor worked on a project caused $12.00 of overhead to be incurred. In that case, all overhead costs were associated with one factor: direct labor hours. As discussed at the beginning of this chapter, such an assumption is often not appropriate with modern methods of producing goods or services where manufacturing overhead is related to a diverse set of activities and cost drivers.

Where overhead costs or capacity measures vary significantly from one department to the next, a separate overhead rate may be calculated for each department. Chapter 3 introduced the concept of departmental overhead rates, where a separate overhead rate is predetermined for each producing department in a factory. In most multiproduct manufacturing environments, this approach represents a cost system improvement over using a single, company-wide overhead rate, and it reduces the likelihood of cost cross-subsidization, which occurs when one product is assigned too much cost as a result of another being assigned too little cost.

Assume that Fezzari has two production departments—Assembly and Packaging—and that these departments have overhead costs of $240,000 and $60,000, respectively. Assume, further, that Fezzari management determined that the Assembly Department overhead costs should be allocated to bicycles on the basis of direct labor hours and that the Packaging Department overhead costs should be allocated to bicycles on the basis of units produced. **Exhibit 5-3** shows that the resulting department predetermined overhead rates would be $9.60 per direct labor hour for the Assembly Department and $12.63 per unit for the Packaging Department.

EXHIBIT 5-3	Computing Department Overhead Rates		
	A	B	C
1	**Overhead costs per unit**	**Assembly**	**Packaging**
2	Total department manufacturing overhead (direct department costs plus allocated costs)	$240,000	$60,000
3	Quantity of overhead application base			
4	Direct labor hours	25,000	
5	Units produced		4,750
6	Department manufacturing overhead rates	$ 9.60	$ 12.63
7		*per direct labor hour*	*per unit*

Department overhead rates may improve product costing results for many organizations, and in fact may be satisfactory. However, this method does not attempt to reflect the actual activities used in producing the different products.

Applying Overhead with Activity-Based Costing

An even more precise method of measuring the cost of products than company-wide or departmental rates is the ABC method. As stated earlier, ABC typically involves two stages of cost allocation. The first stage is identifying and measuring the cost of activities used to produce the various products. The second stage is summing the cost of those activities to determine the ultimate cost of the products.

The overhead rates for each Fezzari department were determined in the last section as $9.60 and $12.63, respectively. The easiest way to assign these costs to products is by using one base and one rate for all products going through a given process (e.g., assembly). However, different products typically use different amounts of resources from a given process, and using the same base and overhead rate for all may distort the cost for some or all products.

Overhead costs in the Assembly and Packaging Departments consisted of two types of costs: **production department costs** and support department costs. Production department overhead costs are costs that are incurred by the production department, such as indirect labor, indirect materials, depreciation on equipment, supervisory wages, and so forth. Support department costs are costs allocated from other departments (for the Fezzari example, the support departments include Design, Receiving/Inventory, and Building) that provide services to both Assembly and Packaging. Fezzari's accountant determined that the production department overhead costs in Assembly were driven primarily by labor hours, whereas support department overhead costs in Packaging were driven primarily by units produced. It was also determined that each component of design, receiving/inventory, and building represents a separate activity cost pool, and that these costs should be assigned to the products based on specific cost drivers rather than a single cost driver for the entire department.

Exhibit 5-4 presents a detailed analysis of overhead cost data for July's operations.

EXHIBIT 5-4	ABC Stage One: Assign Costs to Cost Pools (Activities)				
	A	B	C D	E	F
1	Overhead Cost Pool	Total Cost	Cost Pool Driver (number of)	Driver Quantity	Unit Rates*
2	Direct departmental overhead costs:				
3	Assembly	$200,000	Direct labor hours	25,000	$8.00
4	Packaging	21,500	Units produced	4,750	$4.53
5	Allocated support costs:				
6	Receiving/Inventory	28,500	Units produced	4,750	$6.00
7	Design	50,000	Change orders	20,000	$2.50
8	Total	$300,000			
9					
10	* Rounded				

Each cost is taken from the general ledger.

The selected driver should have a causal relationship to the cost pool such that changes in the driver would cause changes in the cost.

The total cost is divided by the driver quantity to compute the per-unit rate.

Data for each driver should be readily available from the financial or operational systems.

ACCOUNTING IN PRACTICE   **Benefits of ABC**

According to a presentation entitled "Activity Based Costing at UPS," UPS developed its ABC system to link its operating behavior to its business segment costs, support pricing decisions, and report consistent and reliable profitability by product. The UPS ABC system was created by cross-functional teams from Finance and Accounting, Engineering, IT, and Operations.

UPS operations are extremely complex, involving numerous service options, operating conditions, and supporting activities. However, because UPS has an extensive database of work measurement and package movement information, it is able to precisely measure a package's movement from location to location and measure product cost. UPS uses data mining techniques to analyze tens of millions of records to determine profits by package and by customer.

The UPS ABC system produces reports at multiple levels (corporate, operational business unit, customer, and product). Reports are generated monthly in an electronic format that can be viewed across periods. The information in the ABC system is updated continuously.

Using their ABC system allows UPS to focus on improving operations in high-impact areas, change shipping behavior, modify their distribution network, and integrate logistic solutions over the entire value chain. By measuring their financial performance more accurately, UPS is able to make better decisions about pricing, cost control, quality improvement, reengineering, forecasting, and customer relationship management.

Source: http://govinfo.library.unt.edu/usps/offices/domestic-finance/usps/pdf/Holsen.pdf

---

Assume that Fezzari management wants to compare the use of a company-wide, departmental, and ABC overhead allocation method on the cost of two road bikes: the top-end T5 (from Chapter 3) and the entry-level Catania. The T5 is typically purchased by serious triathletes who are very particular about the setup and customization of their bikes, whereas the Catania is typically purchased by fitness newbies who know little about bike components and fit and are primarily driven by price in the selection of their bikes. For simplicity, assume that these are the only two bikes produced by Fezzari. The amounts of activity attributed to the T5 and Catania and the overhead cost per unit based on ABC costs are shown in **Exhibit 5-5**.

5-11 Chapter 5 Activity-Based Costing

© Cambridge Business Publishers

EXHIBIT 5-5	ABC Stage Two: Assign Activities to Cost Objects							
	A	B	C	D	E	F	G	H
1	Bicycle Model				T5		Catania	
2	Activity	Cost Driver	Cost per unit of activity	Quantity of Activity	Cost of Activity		Quantity of Activity	Cost of Activity
3	Assembly	Direct labor hours	$8.00	12,000	$ 96,000.00		13,000	$104,000.00
4	Packaging	Units produced	4.53	1,500	6,795.00		3,250	14,722.50
5	Receiving/Inventory	Units produced	6.00	1,500	9,000.00		3,250	19,500.00
6	Design	Change orders	2.50	18,000	45,000.00		2,000	5,000.00
7	Total overhead product cost				$156,795.00			$143,222.50
8	Units produced				1,500.00			3,250.00
9	Overhead per unit of product				$ 104.53			$ 44.07
10								
11								

These rates were calculated in Exhibit 5-4.

The sum of each driver quantity line should equal the total driver quantity on Exhibit 5-4.

Exhibit 5-6 summarizes the allocated overhead costs for Fezzari's two products using the three different overhead cost assignment methods.

EXHIBIT 5-6	Overhead Cost per Unit Using Various Overhead Methods	T5	Catania
Company-wide overhead rate*		$ 96.00	$48.00
Departmental overhead rates**		89.43	51.03
ABC		104.53	44.07

The ABC method is more precise and more accurately reflects the T5 overhead cost. This is important for determining pricing and inventory valuation.

*Direct labor hours per unit × $12.00 = (12,000/1,500) × $12 = $96 (T5); = (13,000/3,250) × $12 = $48 (Catania)

**(Direct labor hours per unit × $9.60) + $12.63 per unit = ((12,000/1,500) × $9.60) + $12.63 = $89.43 (T5); = ((13,000/3,250) × $9.60) + $12.63 = $51.03 (Catania)

ABC product costing reveals a different cost picture. Using either a company-wide overhead rate or departmental rates, the Catania bike is bearing more than its share of total overhead costs.

Using either of these methods could lead the company into pricing the Catania too high in the market. With a more accurate overhead cost of $44.07, rather than $51.03 or $48.00, the company clearly has the ability to compete on price with other companies in this market. In Fezzari's case, overhead is a relatively minor cost relative to the cost of the direct materials, as shown in Chapter 3. This is due to the fact that Fezzari is mainly an assembler of parts, rather than a manufacturer of those parts. However, in other industries, the effect of adopting ABC may be much more significant.

However, regardless of the differences among the various cost methods, inaccurate costing can affect management's assessment of product profitability and its decisions regarding which products to continue to produce and which products to discontinue. Flawed product costing information can cause management mistakenly to decide to keep products that are losing money, while deciding to discontinue products that are profitable. Using a company-wide or departmental overhead allocation method could have led Fezzari management to shift its emphasis from the low-end bike to the high-end bike market, a decision that could have been damaging to the company.

Limitations of ABC Illustration

Several limitations of the Fezzari illustration should be mentioned. For the sake of simplicity, the example was limited to manufacturing cost considerations. A complete analysis would also require considerations of nonmanufacturing costs, such as marketing, distribution, and customer service, before a final determination of product profitability could be made. Finally, in calculating the activity cost per unit of activity, it is necessary to decide how to measure the total quantity of activity. For example, for Fezzari, the receiving/inventory cost per unit was calculated as $6.00 based on the actual quantity of 4,750 bicycles produced for the period. Alternatively, the receiving cost could have been calculated based on **practical capacity**, which is the maximum possible volume of activity, while allowing for normal downtime for repairs and maintenance. If the plant has a practical capacity to produce 5,000 bicycles per period, the cost per bike based on the practical capacity is $5.70 per purchase order. Using this overhead rate in costing products, only $27,075 would have been assigned to the two products, which required only 4,750 bicycles, and the remaining $1,425 for the 250 bicycles of excess (or idle) capacity not used would be written off as an operating expense of the period as underapplied overhead. Practical capacity is generally regarded as better than actual capacity for calculating activity costs because it does not hide the cost of idle capacity within product costs, and it gives a truer cost of the activities used to produce the product.

Comparing Traditional and Activity-Based Costing

Procedurally, ABC is not a new method for assigning costs to cost objectives. Traditional costing systems have used a two-stage allocation model (similar to the ABC model) to assign costs to cost pools (such as departments) and subsequently assign those cost pools to products using an allocation base. In most traditional costing systems, overhead is assigned to one or more cost pools based on departments and functional characteristics (such as labor-related, machine-related, and space-related costs) and then reassigned to products using a general allocation base such as direct labor hours or machine hours. ABC is different in that it divides the overall manufacturing processes into activities. ABC accumulates costs in cost pools for the major activities and then assigns the costs of these activities to products or other cost objectives that benefit from these activities. *Conceptually,* ABC is different because of the way it views the operations of the company; *procedurally,* it uses a methodology that has been around for a long time.

The challenge in using ABC is specifying the model—that is, determining how many activity pools should be established for a given cost measurement purpose, which costs should be assigned to each activity pool, and the appropriate activity driver for each pool. Specifying the model also includes determining the resource cost drivers for assigning indirect resource costs to the various activity cost pools.

Concept ⟶	Method ⟶	Assessment	TAKEAWAY 5.2
Why might a company choose to calculate its overhead rates based on practical capacity instead of budgeted capacity?	• Total overhead cost pool/ **budgeted** activity driver = predetermined overhead rate • Total overhead cost pool/ **practical** activity driver = predetermined overhead rate	If budgeted (and actual) activity is less than practical activity, the company has excess capacity. Using practical capacity to calculate overhead rates will highlight this idle capacity in the form of under-applied overhead.	

Assume you are a controller for a manufacturing company that uses a traditional product costing system but is looking to transition to ABC. The CEO has asked you why this would be a useful transition. What would you tell him regarding the benefits of activity-based costing?

YOUR TURN! 5.2

The solution is on page 5-44.

MBC

ABC IMPLEMENTATION ISSUES

LO4 Describe the implementation of an ABC system.

eLecture

MBC

The distortion in product costs for Fezzari from using traditional cost systems based on company-wide or departmental rates, although hypothetical, is not uncommon. Studies have shown that distortions of this type occur regularly in traditional systems in which a significant variation exists in the volume and complexity of products and services produced. Traditional systems tend to over-cost high-volume, low-complexity products, and they tend to under-cost low-volume, high-complexity products. These studies indicate that the typical amount of over-costing is up to 200% for high-volume products with low complexity and that the typical under-costing can be more than 1,000% for low-volume, highly complex products. In companies with a large number of different products, traditional costing can show that most products are profitable. After changing to ABC, however, these companies might find that 10% to 15% of the products are profitable while the remainder are unprofitable. Adopting ABC often leads to increased profits merely by changing the product mix to minimize the number of unprofitable products.[2]

ABC Implementation Considerations

Most companies initially do not abandon their traditional cost system and move to a system that uses ABC for management and financial reporting purposes because financial statements must withstand the scrutiny of auditors and tax authorities. This scrutiny typically implies more demands on the cost accounting system for consistency, objectivity, and uniformity than required when the system is used only for management purposes. In addition, ABC systems must be built facility by facility rather than being embedded in a software program that can be used by all facilities within the company.[3] Often, companies maintain traditional costing for external reporting purposes and ABC for pricing and other internal decision-making purposes.

Once an ABC system has been developed for a production facility, including an activities list (sometimes called an activities dictionary), identification of activity cost drivers, and calculation of cost per unit of driver activity, the activity costs of a current or proposed product can be readily determined. In ABC, as illustrated for Fezzari, manufacturing a product is viewed simply as the combination of activities selected to make it; therefore, the activity cost of a product or service is the sum of the costs of those activities. This approach to viewing a product enables management to evaluate the importance of each of the activities consumed in making a product. Possibly some activities can be eliminated or a lower-cost activity substituted for a more costly one without reducing the quality or performance of the product.

ACCOUNTING IN PRACTICE	Results of ABC

In the 1980s, the **Coca-Cola Company** used ABC to determine that it was less costly—and thus more profitable—to deliver soft drink concentrate to some fountain drink retailers (such as fast-food restaurants) in nonreturnable, disposable containers rather than in returnable stainless steel containers, which had been standard in the industry for many years.

Although an ABC system may be complex, it merely mirrors the complexity of an organization's design, manufacturing, and distribution systems. If a firm's products are diverse and its production and distribution procedures complex, the ABC system will also be complex; however, if its products are homogeneous and its production environment relatively simple, its ABC system should also be relatively simple. Even in highly complex manufacturing environments, ABC systems usually have no more than 10 to 20 cost pools. Many ABC experts in practice have observed that creating a large number of activity cost pools for a given costing

---

[2] Gary Cokins, Alan Stratton, and Jack Helbling, *An ABC Manager's Primer* (Montvale, NJ: Institute of Management Accountants, 1993).

[3] Robert S. Kaplan and Robin Cooper, *Cost and Effect* (Boston: Harvard Business School Press, 1998), p. 5-105.

application normally does not significantly improve cost accuracy above that of a smaller number of cost pools. As with any information system design, the costs of developing and maintaining the system must not exceed its benefits; hence, although adding more activity cost pools may result in some small amount of increased accuracy, it may be so small as not to be cost effective.

Other Uses of ABC

In addition to using ABC for product costing purposes, other important uses for ABC have also been found. One of the most useful applications for ABC discussed in the next section is in evaluating customer costs and distribution channel costs. Other applications include costing administrative functions such as processing accounts receivable or accounts payable; costing the process of hiring and training employees; and costing such menial tasks as processing a letter or copying a document. As illustrated by the California State Bar illustration at the beginning of the chapter, any process, function, or activity performed in an organization, whether it is related to production, marketing and sales, finance and accounting, human resources, or even research and development, is a candidate for ABC analysis. In short, almost any cost objective that has more than an insignificant amount of indirect costs can be more effectively measured using ABC.

YOUR TURN! 5.3

The solution is on page 5-44.

A company has a significantly varied product and service mix, with many high-volume, homogeneous products and many low-volume, complex products. Historically, the company has used a single, company-wide overhead rate. After implementing an activity-based costing system, the company is likely to find that

   a. The high-volume products were under-costed previously.
   b. The high-volume products were over-costed previously.
   c. The low-volume products were over-costed previously.
   d. The costs of both low- and high-volume products will be unchanged.

ABC AND CUSTOMER PROFITABILITY ANALYSIS

One of the most beneficial applications of activity-based costing is in the analysis of the profitability of customers. Companies that have a large number of diverse customers also usually have widely varied profits from serving those customers. Many companies never attempt to calculate the profit earned from individual customers. They merely assume that if they are selling products above their costs, and that overall the company is earning a profit, then each of the customers must be profitable. Unfortunately, the cost incurred to sell goods and services, and to provide services, to individual customers is not usually proportionate with the gross profits generated by those sales. Customers with high sales volume are not necessarily the most profitable. Profitability of individual customers depends on whether the gross profits from sales to those customers exceed the customer-specific costs of serving those customers. Some customers are simply more costly than others, and some may even be unprofitable, and the unprofitable customers are eating away at the total profits of the company. In an ideal world, only profitable customers would be retained, and unprofitable customers would be either converted to a profitable status or dropped as customers.

LO5 Explain customer profitability analysis based on ABC.

Customer Profitability Profile

If a company knows the amount of profits (or losses) generated by each of its customers, a customer profitability profile can be prepared, as illustrated in the following section.

ABC Customer Profitability Analysis Illustrated

Let's assume that Pure Water Company is a "green" company located in the West that manufactures and sells all-natural compounds for purifying water distributed through large public water systems. Let's also assume that Ron James, the CEO and founder of Pure Water, personally developed the compounds using natural materials obtained from remote regions of the world. He knows that he has a product that is far superior to the traditional processes based on synthetic chemicals that have been used for generations to purify water. After five years in business, Pure Water has built a solid and growing customer base, but it has to invest significant time and expense servicing customers, especially those that have recently embraced its approach to water purification. Some customers require a lot of "hand-holding," with frequent visits and telephone calls, and they tend to purchase frequently in small amounts, often requiring repackaging. Other customers require little attention and support, and many of them purchase in large amounts once a year.

Although the company is making money, there is concern that profits could be higher if sales and other customer-related costs could be decreased. Ron James decided to ask Environmental Business Consultants (EBC; introduced in Chapter 1) to conduct a customer profitability analysis using activity-based costing. As a first step, EBC determined that there were five primary activities related to serving customers: visits of customers by sales representatives, remote contacts (phone, email, fax), processing and shipping of customer orders, repackaging, and billing and collection. After extensive analysis, including numerous interviews and statistical analyses of activity and cost data, EBC determined the cost drivers and cost per unit of activity for the five customer-related activities, shown in **Exhibit 5-7**.

EXHIBIT 5-7	Pure Water's Customer Service Activity Per-Unit Costs	
Activity	**Activity Cost Driver**	**Cost per Unit of Driver Activity**
Visits to customers	Number of visits	$800
Remote contacts.	Number of contacts	75
Processing & shipping	Number of customer orders	450
Repackaging.	Number of requests	250
Billing and collection.	Number of invoices.	90

After collecting activity driver data on each of these activities for Pure Water's major customers, EBC prepared the customer activity cost and profitability analysis presented in **Exhibit 5-8** for its five largest customers (in terms of sales dollars) in the order of greatest to least profit for the most recent year.

Because Pure Water is selling only one product to all of its customers and has the same pricing policy for all customers, there is a constant 40% gross profit ratio across all customers, and the combined net profitability of these customers is 11.6% of sales. However, all customers are not equally profitable. The high level of support required by Manhattan and Great Lakes resulted in a net customer loss from sales to Great Lakes and only a 6.8% customer profitability ratio for Manhattan.

Armed with the information in the customer activity cost and profitability analysis, Pure Water can take proactive steps to increase its overall profitability ratio. An obvious option would be to try to terminate its relationship with Great Lakes because the company is clearly losing money on that customer. If Great Lakes were terminated as a customer, and assuming that all of the activity costs associated with Great Lakes could be avoided by the termination, Pure Water's total sales would drop to $68,750 (or $80,750 minus $12,000), but its total profit would increase to $11,785 (or $9,335 plus $2,450), resulting in a profitability ratio on the remaining four customers of 17.1%.

A more proactive approach would be to work with Great Lakes and Manhattan, which have high support requirements, such as repackaging, frequent visits, and phone contacts, to try to lower the level of high-cost support activities without reducing sales to those customers.

EXHIBIT 5-8	Pure Water Customer Activity Cost and Profitability Analysis					
	A	B	C	D	E	F	G

	A	Consolidated Water, Inc.	West Coast Utilities	Seattle Water District	Manhattan Water Authority	Great Lakes Utility	Total
1	These activity counts would come from Pure Water's customer management, operations, and financial systems.						
2	**Customer Activity Cost Analysis:**						
3	*Activity Cost Driver Data*						
4	Visits to customers	1	1	3	5	4	
5	Remote contacts	3	2	5	7	8	
6	Processing & shipping	1	4	3	3	5	
7	Repackaging	0	0	0	2	3	
8	Billing & collection	1	4	3	3	5	
9	*Customer Activity Cost*						
10	Visits to customers	$ 800	$ 800	$ 2,400	$ 4,000	$ 3,200	
11	Remote contacts	225	150	375	525	600	
12	Processing & shipping	450	1,800	1,350	1,350	2,250	
13	Repackaging	0	0	0	500	750	
14	Billing & collection	90	360	270	270	450	
15	Total activity cost	$ 1,565	$ 3,110	$ 4,395	$ 6,645	$ 7,250	
16							
17	**Customer Profitability Analysis**						
18	Customer sales	$16,250	$15,000	$17,500	$20,000	$12,000	$80,750
19	Less cost of goods sold	9,750	9,000	10,500	12,000	7,200	48,450
20	Gross profit on sales	$ 6,500	$ 6,000	$ 7,000	$ 8,000	$ 4,800	$32,300
21	Less activity cost	1,565	3,110	4,395	6,645	7,250	22,965
22	Customer profitability	$ 4,935	$ 2,890	$ 2,605	$ 1,355	$(2,450)	$ 9,335
23	Customer profitability ratio*	30.4%	19.3%	14.9%	6.8%	–20.4%	11.6%
24							
25	** Customer profitability ÷ Sales*						

Callouts:
- These amounts are computed by multiplying the activity counts by the per-unit costs computed in Exhibit 5-7.
- Customer activity costs are subtracted from customer gross profit to determine customer profitability.
- Customer gross profit percentage (gross profit/sales) is the same for all customers at 40%.

This could result in maintaining the current level of gross profit but generating a significantly higher level of total net customer profitability.

Once a company has profitability data on each of its customers (or categories of customers), only then can it proceed to try to convert them to profitability, or seek to terminate the relationships with those customers. Just as we saw that ABC provided a model for producing more accurate product cost data, ABC is also a valuable tool for generating customer profitability data.

Two caveats should be considered when using activity cost data to manage customer profitability. First, there may be justifiable reasons (such as having a new customer that requires a high level of early-stage support, trying to penetrate a new geographic market, or existing relationships with other more profitable customers) for keeping customers that have lower profitability, or even customers that are not profitable. If so, these customers should be managed intensely to attempt to reduce the activities devoted to their support. Second, eliminating a customer may not immediately translate into an immediate reduction of activity costs. Some activity costs may not have a variable cost behavior pattern, and eliminating customers may merely create excess capacity in the short term.

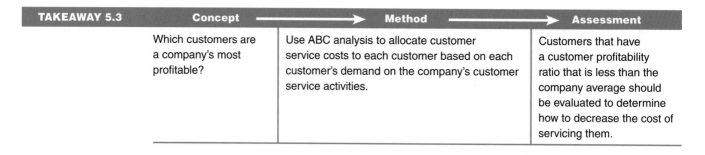

TAKEAWAY 5.3	Concept	→	Method	→	Assessment
	Which customers are a company's most profitable?		Use ABC analysis to allocate customer service costs to each customer based on each customer's demand on the company's customer service activities.		Customers that have a customer profitability ratio that is less than the company average should be evaluated to determine how to decrease the cost of servicing them.

YOUR TURN! 5.4

The solution is on page 5-44.

Guided Example

MBC

Quality Meats provides standard cuts of beef, lamb, and pork to restaurant chains for use in preparing customer meals. The price and cost of the beef, lamb, and pork is the same for all customers, with an average gross profit of 15%. However, the sales manager has recently been complaining that a particular customer is too "picky" and would like to drop them as a customer. As the corporate controller, you have gathered the following information about this customer and the costs of performing certain activities. The cost of these activities would be avoided if they were dropped as a customer.

Total sales.	$100,000
Total cost of meat	$ 85,000
Number of returns	50
Number of visits	25
Number of calls.	120
Cost per return	$100
Cost per visit.	$150
Cost per call	$30

Based on this information, should Quality Meats drop this customer?

ACTIVITY-BASED MANAGEMENT

LO6 Explain the difference between ABC and activity-based management.

eLecture

MBC

Activity-based costing has been highly touted as a technique for improving the measurement of the cost and profitability of products, customers, and other cost objectives. In the early development of ABC, it was discovered that a by-product of accurately measuring costs using ABC is that management invariably gains a much better understanding of the processes and activities that are used to create cost objects, such as products. Although ABC could be justified on the basis of its value as a tool in helping produce more accurate cost measurements for various cost objectives, its greatest potential value may be in its by-products. The access to ABC data enables managers to engage in **activity-based management (ABM)**, defined as the identification and selection of activities to maximize the value of the activities while minimizing their cost from the perspective of the final consumer. In other words, ABM is concerned with how to efficiently and effectively manage activities and processes to provide value to the final consumer.

Focus on Activities

Defining processes and identifying key activities help management better understand the business and evaluate whether activities being performed add value to the customer. ABM focuses managerial attention on what is most important among the activities performed to create value for customers.

A helpful analogy in understanding what ABC can do for a company is to compare a company's operations with a large retail store, such as a **Home Depot** store. In a Home Depot store there is a clearly marked price on each of the tens of thousands of individual items that customers may decide to purchase. Similarly, every activity that takes place in

Hint: It is often not feasible to perform a cost analysis on every activity, so management must exercise judgment in choosing activities to track costs for.

any organization has a cost that can be determined and that management can use to make a judgment about the activity's value. In an ideal world, a manager could walk through the business and evaluate the cost of every activity being performed—maybe thousands of different activities—and then decide which ones are worth the cost and which ones are not adding value. But because generating ABC data has a cost, management must decide which ABC data are likely to be useful and cost beneficial. Our discussion here is only an introduction to activity-based costing and some of its applications. As the following Accounting in Practice points out, over the past quarter of a century, ABC has matured well beyond merely accurately measuring costs of products and customers. More advanced ABC topics and methods are covered in advanced managerial accounting (or cost accounting) courses.

ACCOUNTING IN PRACTICE   Current Status of ABC

One of the leading thinkers and authors on the topic of activity-based costing over the past 25 years has been Peter B. B. Turney. He recently traced the evolution of ABC within the context of a product life cycle, showing how ABC functionality has expanded since it was first introduced in the 1980s. Turney asserts that ABC is now in its fourth generation, where it has become "an integral part of business performance management solutions, including profitability management, performance measurement, financial management, sustainability, and human capital management." In its current state of development, a single ABC model can support a number of needs, including historical cost measurement, resource planning, performance measurement, and other analyses.

YOUR TURN! 5.5

In using activity-based management techniques, management would be most likely to try to eliminate or reduce which of the following activities? (Hint: Which activity adds the least value from the customer's perspective?)

a. Inspection of the final product before transfer to finished goods inventory.

b. Engineering design to improve product ergonomics.

c. Movement of materials from the raw materials storeroom to the production floor.

d. Operation of robots in the manufacturing process.

The solution is on page 5-44.

MBC

SERVICES INDUSTRY IN FOCUS

Customer Profitability Analysis

Environmental Business Consultants (EBC) serves three different sizes of clients (large, medium, and small). EBC's solid waste rate review projects are fairly standardized and routine; hence, the pricing is also standardized for all clients. Although the company is profitable overall, the CFO thinks the net margins should be higher. She is concerned that customer support costs are eating up some of the margin and has decided to do a customer profitability analysis based on the three different sizes of clients to see if some of the client groups may actually be less profitable than others. The following data for the most recent period have been collected to support the analysis:

SERVICE AND MERCHANDISING

Support Activity	Driver	Cost per Driver Unit
A. Scope change requests	Number of requests	$150
B. Visits to client	Number of visits	$200
C. Communication	Number of calls	$ 50

Customer Group	Activity A	Activity B	Activity C	Profit Before Support Costs
Large	36	72	180	$390,000
Medium.	75	150	205	100,500
Small.	21	42	80	52,000

Required

1. Calculate the customer profitability for each customer group, taking into account the support activity required for each customer group.

2. Comment on the usefulness of this type of analysis. What reasonable actions might the CEO take as a result of this analysis?

Solution

1. Activity A—Scope change requests

   Activity B—Visits to client

   Activity C—Communication

Activity	Large	Medium	Small
A (@ $150)...................................	$ 5,400	$ 11,250	$ 3,150
B (@ $200)...................................	14,400	30,000	8,400
C (@ $50)...................................	9,000	10,250	4,000
Total support costs	$ 28,800	$ 51,500	$15,550
Profit before support costs	390,000	100,500	52,000
Customer profits.............................	$361,200	$ 49,000	$36,450
Ratio of support costs to profit before support costs:..	7.4%	51.2%	29.9%

2. This analysis is beneficial to EBC because it shows that large clients consume the lowest amount in terms of support services required. Medium clients are a significantly larger consumer of activities for all three of the support activities. Calculating the ratio of total support costs to profit before support costs provides additional insight into the relative profitability of the client groups. All three client groups are profitable; however, this analysis provides useful information for improving profits by working with the medium and small client groups to control support activities and related costs and attempt to bring their support costs in line with the large client group.

Data Analytics

DATA ANALYTICS   Advances to data analytics technology revives ABC

The use of activity-based costing (ABC) has had peaks and valleys over the years. Stories of huge cost savings by some companies resulting from improved product costing persuaded countless manufacturers and other businesses to try to implement ABC. The trouble with ABC, however, was that without adequate technology to capture costs, ABC proved too expensive and costly for most companies. By the early 2000s, many companies abandoned their use of ABC. Thanks to recent technological advances, the data analytics required for an ABC system is now more affordable. Manual work necessary in the early days of ABC has been replaced by systems automation. For instance, modern general ledger systems can tag and track the activity data, resulting in informative dashboards and reports to support an ABC system. The advances in data analytics tools has made ABC more feasible for more companies.

SUMMARY OF LEARNING OBJECTIVES

Explain the changes in the modern production environment that have affected cost structures. (p. 5-3)   **LO1**

- Manufacturing organizations have shifted from labor-intensive to automated assembly processes.
- Activity-based costing recognizes that multiple activities drive manufacturing overhead costs in today's production environment.

Understand the concept of activity-based costing (ABC) and how it is applied. (p. 5-4)   **LO2**

- ABC involves determining the cost of activities and tracing those costs to cost objects based on their proportionate usage of the activities.
- ABC is based on the premise that activities drive costs and that costs should be assigned to products in proportion to the volume of activities they consume.

Explain the difference between traditional company-wide and departmental overhead methods and ABC. (p. 5-8)   **LO3**

- Company-wide and departmental overhead methods base overhead costs on one cost driver, whereas ABC allocates overhead based on a diverse set of activities and cost drivers.
- ABC divides the overall manufacturing processes into activities, accumulates costs in cost pools for the major activities, and then assigns the costs of these activities to products or other cost objectives that benefit from these activities.
- The challenge in using ABC is determining how many activity pools should be established for a given cost measurement purpose, which costs should be assigned to each activity pool, and the appropriate activity driver for each pool.
- A complete ABC analysis would require considerations of nonmanufacturing costs, such as marketing, distribution, and customer service, before a final determination of product profitability could be made.
- Practical capacity, the maximum possible volume of activity, is generally regarded as better than actual capacity for calculating activity costs because it does not hide the cost of idle capacity within product costs, and it gives a truer cost of the activities used to produce the product.
- Procedurally, ABC is not a new method for assigning costs to objects. Traditional costing systems have used a two-stage allocation model similar to ABC to assign costs to cost pools and subsequently assign those cost pools to products using an allocation base.

Describe the implementation of an ABC system. (p. 5-13)   **LO4**

- Most companies initially do not abandon their traditional cost system and move to a system that uses ABC for management and financial reporting purposes because financial statements must withstand the scrutiny of auditors and tax authorities.
- Often, companies maintain traditional costing for external reporting purposes and ABC for pricing and other internal decision-making purposes.
- Although an ABC system may be complex, it merely mirrors the complexity of an organization's design, manufacturing, and distribution systems. If a firm's products are diverse and its production and distribution procedures complex, the ABC system will also be complex; however, if its products are homogeneous and its production environment relatively simple, its ABC system should also be relatively simple.
- One of the most useful applications for ABC is evaluating customer costs and distribution channel costs.

Explain customer profitability analysis based on ABC. (p. 5-14)   **LO5**

- A customer profitability profile can be prepared if a company knows the amount of profits (or losses) generated by each of its customers.
- Even if the company is making a profit overall, individual customers may be sold to at a loss.
- If customers have low profitability, there may be justifiable reasons for keeping them, but they should be managed intensely to attempt to reduce the activities devoted to their support.

Explain the difference between ABC and activity-based management. (p. 5-17)   **LO6**

- The access to ABC data enables managers to engage in activity-based management (ABM), which is the identification and selection of activities to maximize the value of the activities while minimizing their cost from the perspective of the final consumer.
- ABM focuses managerial attention on what is most important among the activities performed to create value for customers.

SUMMARY	Concept	➡ Method	➡ Assessment
TAKEAWAY 5.1	Can a company that has traditionally allocated overhead on a single, company-wide rate improve its understanding of its product costs by using a different approach?	• Choose a cost object (typically a product or service). • Identify the activities required to complete and deliver that cost object. • Determine the costs incurred for each activity. • Assign the costs to the activity cost pool(s). • Choose an activity driver for each cost pool. • Allocate the cost pools to each cost object based on the proportion of the activity driver used by each cost object.	Cost objects that require more of a particular activity will receive a greater portion of that activity's costs, leading to a better understanding of the cost object's real cost.
TAKEAWAY 5.2	Why might a company choose to calculate its overhead rates based on practical capacity instead of budgeted capacity?	• Total overhead cost pool/**budgeted** activity driver = predetermined overhead rate • Total overhead cost pool/**practical** activity driver = predetermined overhead rate	If budgeted (and actual) activity is less than practical activity, the company has excess capacity. Using practical capacity to calculate overhead rates will highlight this idle capacity in the form of under-applied overhead.
TAKEAWAY 5.3	Which customers are a company's most profitable?	Use ABC analysis to allocate customer service costs to each customer based on each customer's demand on the company's customer service activities.	Customers that have a customer profitability ratio that is less than the company average should be evaluated to determine how to decrease the cost of servicing them.

KEY TERMS

Activities (p. 5-5)

Activity-based costing (ABC) (p. 5-3)

Activity-based management (ABM) (p. 5-3, 5-17)

Cost drivers (p. 5-7)

Cost object (p. 5-5)

Cost pool (p. 5-5)

Practical capacity (p. 5-12)

Production department costs (p. 5-9)

Resource (p. 5-5)

Assignments with the (MBC) logo in the margin are available in BusinessCourse.
See the Preface of the book for details.

SELF-STUDY QUESTIONS

(Answers to Self-Study Questions are at the end of this chapter.)

LO1

1. **Which of the following statements most accurately describes the current production environment and its effect on manufacturers' cost structures?**

   a. Due to the relatively high cost of technology and normal resistance to change by employees, production remains relatively labor-intensive.

   b. As more and more of the earth's resources are consumed, some raw materials are growing scarce, driving up their cost and making raw materials cost the most significant production cost for most companies.

   c. Technological advances have led to a shift from labor-intensive operations to automated operations, reducing the need for production employees while increasing the level of support, or overhead costs, as a percentage of manufacturing costs.

   d. None of the above.

Chapter 5   Activity-Based Costing   **5-22**

2. **Which of the following is not an element of ABC?**   **LO2**
   a. Tracing costs to cost objects
   b. Calculating a predetermined rate
   c. Identifying the cost drivers
   d. All are elements of ABC.

3. **ABC differs from traditional product costing in which of the following ways?**   **LO3**
   a. Overhead is allocated to products in ABC.
   b. Estimated costs are used.
   c. Diverse cost drivers are used.
   d. It is completely accurate.

4. **Implementation of ABC costing in a company that has been using a plant-wide overhead rate would typically be expected to result in all of the following except:**   **LO4**
   a. More accurate product costing
   b. Elimination of traditional cost accounting systems used for financial reporting purposes
   c. Increased profitability from the elimination or reduction of unprofitable products or services
   d. Greater insight into the production activities that add value to the company's products

5. **Which of the following is not a benefit of customer profitability analysis?**   **LO5**
   a. Identifies unprofitable customers
   b. Helps track cost spent on customers
   c. Helps managers identify actions to improve specific customer profitability
   d. Speeds up production process

6. **Activity-based management (ABM) is defined as:**   **LO6**
   a. The implementation of an activity-based costing system in a service company, such as a management consulting firm.
   b. The identification and selection of activities to minimize the value of the activities while maximizing their cost from the perspective of the final consumer of the product or service.
   c. The process of identifying the cost drivers to be used in calculating the per-activity rate for each cost pool in an activity-based costing system.
   d. The identification and selection of activities to maximize the value of the activities while minimizing their cost from the perspective of the final consumer of the product or service.

QUESTIONS

1. Summarize the concepts underlying activity-based costing in two sentences.   **LO2**
2. What steps are required to implement the two-stage activity-based costing model?   **LO2**
3. Define activity cost pool, activity cost driver, and cost per unit of activity.   **LO2**
4. Name two possible activity cost drivers for each of the following activities: maintenance, materials movement, machine setup, inspection, materials purchases, and customer service.   **LO2**
5. What is the premise of activity-based costing for product costing purposes?   **LO2**
6. In what ways does ABC product costing differ from traditional product cost methods?   **LO3**
7. Explain why ABC often reveals that low-volume products are over-costed and high-volume products are under-costed.   **LO4**
8. How can ABC be used to improve customer profitability analysis?   **LO5**
9. Explain activity-based management and how it differs from activity-based costing.   **LO6**

SHORT EXERCISES

SE5-1. Product costs in a complex organization are likely to be distorted if a traditional volume-based cost driver is used and   **LO1**
   a. raw materials costs are a significant percentage of total production costs.
   b. direct labor costs are a significant percentage of total production costs.
   c. manufacturing overhead costs are a significant percentage of total production costs.
   d. direct costs are a significant percentage of total production costs.

SE5-2. All of the following are likely to be used as a cost allocation base in activity-based costing **except** the   **LO2**
   a. number of different materials used to manufacture the product.
   b. units of materials used to manufacture the product.
   c. number of vendors supplying the materials used to manufacture the product.
   d. cost of materials used to manufacture the product.

LO3   **SE5-3.**   A profitable company with five departments uses plant-wide overhead rates for its highly diversified operation. The firm is studying a change to either allocating overhead by using departmental rates or using activity-based costing (ABC). Which one of these two methods will likely result in the use of a greater number of cost allocation bases and more accurate costing results?

	Greater Number of Allocation Bases	More Accurate Costing Results
a.	Departmental	Departmental
b.	Departmental	ABC
c.	ABC	Departmental
d.	ABC	ABC

LO3   **SE5-4.**   Pelder Products Company manufactures two types of engineering diagnostic equipment used in construction. The two products are based upon different technologies—x-ray and ultra-sound—but are manufactured in the same factory. Pelder has computed the manufacturing cost of the x-ray and ultra-sound products by adding together direct materials, direct labor, and overhead cost applied based on the number of direct labor hours. The factory has three overhead departments that support the single production line that makes both products. Budgeted overhead spending for the departments is as follows.

	Department		
Engineering Design	Materials Handling	Setup	Total
$6,000	$5,000	$3,000	$14,000

Pelder's budgeted manufacturing activities and costs for the period are as follows.

	Product	
Activity	X-Ray	Ultra-Sound
Units produced and sold.	50	100
Direct materials used	$5,000	$ 8,000
Direct labor hours used	100	300
Direct labor cost	$4,000	$12,000
Number of parts used.	400	600
Number of engineering changes	2	1
Number of product setups	8	7

The budgeted cost to manufacture one ultra-sound machine using the activity-based costing method is

a. $225.
b. $264.
c. $293.
d. $305.

LO3   **SE5-5.**   The Chocolate Baker specializes in chocolate baked goods. The firm has long assessed the profitability of a product line by comparing revenues to the cost of goods sold. However, Barry White, the firm's new accountant, wants to use an activity-based costing system that takes into consideration the cost of the delivery person. Listed below are activity and cost information relating to two of Chocolate Baker's major products.

	Muffins	Cheesecake
Revenue.	$53,000	$46,000
Cost of goods sold	26,000	21,000
Delivery Activity		
Number of deliveries.	150	85
Average length of delivery	10 Minutes	15 Minutes
Cost per hour for delivery	$20.00	$20.00

Using activity-based costing, which one of the following statements is correct?

a.   The muffins are $2,000 more profitable.
b.   The cheesecakes are $75 more profitable.
c.   The muffins are $1,925 more profitable.
d.   The muffins have a higher profitability as a percentage of sales and, therefore, are more advantageous.

SE5-6.   Atmel Inc. manufactures and sells two products. Data with regard to these products are given below.   **LO3**

	Product A	Product B
Units produced and sold.	30,000	12,000
Machine hours required per unit.	2	3
Receiving orders per product line.	50	150
Production orders per product line	12	18
Production runs	8	12
Inspections	20	30

Total budgeted machine hours are 100,000. The budgeted overhead costs are shown below.

Receiving costs	$ 450,000
Engineering costs	300,000
Machine setup costs	25,000
Inspection costs	200,000
Total budgeted overhead costs	$ 975,000

Using activity-based costing, the per unit overhead cost allocation of receiving costs for product A is

a. $3.75.
b. $10.75.
c. $19.50.
d. $28.13.

SE5-7.   TC Company makes four types of patio sets: wood, plastic, wicker, and aluminum. Data regarding the four products follows: **LO3**

	DLHs/unit	Annual Production
Wood	2.0	1,000 units
Plastic	1.0	2,000 units
Wicker	5.0	5,000 units
Aluminum	3.0	10,000 units

Additional information about the company follows:

- Wood sets require $40 in direct materials per unit, plastic sets require $20, wicker sets require $60, and aluminum sets require $50.
- The direct labor wage rate for all production except for the aluminum sets is $15 per hour. Aluminum sets are more difficult to produce, so the wage rate for direct labor is $20 per hour.
- Wood and wicker sets go through a special painting process.
- Wood, plastic, and wicker sets all go through the sanding process.

The ABC system used for allocating Manufacturing Overhead Costs has the following activity pools:

			Level of Activity			
Activity Cost Pool	Activity Measure	Estimated Cost	Wood	Plastic	Wicker	Aluminum
Mach setups	# of setups	$136,000	100	100	500	1,000
Painting	# pints used	$ 30,000	250	—	1,250	—
Sanding	# machine hrs	$ 17,500	250	500	1,000	—
Gen. factory	# DLHs	$354,000	2,000	2,000	25,000	30,000

What is the total cost per unit under the ABC system for wicker patio sets?

a. $45.00   c. $147.50
b. $135.00   d. $180.00

LO3   SE5-8. Curry Company has two divisions: Eastern Division and Western Division. Curry Company has been allocating overhead based on direct labor hours. For the most recent year, the predetermined overhead rate was $70 per direct labor hour.

An activity-based costing analysis of Curry's operations has identified three different cost pools. Data about the cost drivers for each pool for the most recent year are given below.

Cost Pool	Number of Events per Year	Cost Pool
A.............	2,000	$100,000
B.............	1,000	200,000
C.............	50	50,000
Total		$350,000

The following data relate to cost driver event activity within the two divisions during the most recent year.

	Eastern Division	Western Division	Total
Cost Driver A events......	1,500	500	2,000
Cost Driver B events......	200	800	1,000
Cost Driver C events......	30	20	50
Direct labor hours........	2,000	3,000	5,000

Which of the following statements is *correct*?

If the activity-based costing system had been used in the most recent year in place of the traditional overhead allocation technique,

a. profit for Eastern Division would have increased by $5,000.
b. profit for Western Division would have increased by $5,000.
c. profit for Eastern Division would have decreased by $145,000.
d. profit for Western Division would have decreased by $205,000.

LO3   SE5-9. The controller for Tamale Cooking Oil Co. established the following overhead cost pools and cost drivers:

Overhead Cost Pool	Budgeted Overhead	Cost Driver	Estimated Cost Driver Level
Machine setup	$14,300	# of setups	11 setups
Materials handling	$12,480	# of barrels	780 barrels
Quality control................	$31,620	# of inspections......	102 inspections
Machine utilities/ maintenance ...	$17,250	# of machine hours...	1,150 machine hours

An order of 80 finished barrels of cooking oil used:

Machine setups	1 setup
Materials handling	82 barrels
Quality inspections	10 inspections
Machine hours	??? machine hours

If the company uses activity-based costing and the total overhead charged to the order was $7,182, how many machine hours were used to complete the order?

a. 98   c. 118
b. 109   d. 479

LO5   SE5-10. ClearView, Inc. provides quarterly commercial window cleaning services for three high-rise commercial buildings, Sequoia, Tower Plaza, and Cornwall, and it uses a job costing system for determining the costs for completing each job. ClearView guarantees its customers' satisfaction and will return to reclean windows that do not meet the customer's requirements at no additional charge to the customer.

The job cost system does not capture any cost incurred by ClearView for return touchups. ClearView cleans each building on a square footage contract price, which includes the initial cleaning as well as all required touchups. Each year, the company generates about one-third of its total revenues and gross profits from each of the three buildings. The ClearView owner has observed that the buildings, however, require substantially different levels of support following the initial completion of jobs. The following data have been gathered:

Support Activity	Driver	Cost per Driver Unit
Major touchups........	Hours on jobs.....	$ 40
Minor touchups........	Number of visits ...	$160
Communication........	Number of calls....	$ 20

Customer	Major Touchups	Minor Touchups	Communication
Sequoia	48	12	50
Tower Plaza	16	24	48
Cornwall	0	40	120

Assuming that each of the three customers produces gross profits of $50,000, which customer is the most profitable, after taking into account the support activity required for each building?

a. Sequoia

b. Tower Plaza

c. Cornwall

d. Can't determine from the information given.

DATA ANALYTICS, DATA VISUALIZATION, AND EXCEL ACTIVITIES

Data Analytics, Data Visualization, and Excel Activities are available in myBusinessCourse. These assignments develop Excel, Tableau, and Data Analytics skills, which will enhance students' career readiness. These exercises are assignable and auto graded by MBC. For an overview of data analytics, see the appendix at the end of this book.

Data Analytics Data Visualization

EXERCISES—SET A

E5-1A. **Activities and Cost Drivers** For each of the following activities, select the most appropriate cost driver. Each cost driver may be used only once.

LO2

Activity	Cost Driver
1. Pay vendors	a. Number of different kinds of raw materials
2. Evaluate vendors	b. Number of classes offered
3. Inspect raw materials	c. Number of tables
4. Plan for purchases of raw materials	d. Number of employees
5. Packaging	e. Number of operating hours
6. Supervision	f. Number of units of raw materials received
7. Employee training	g. Number of moves
8. Clean tables	h. Number of vendors
9. Machine maintenance	i. Number of checks issued
10. Move in-process product from one work station to the next	j. Number of customer orders

E5-2A. **Stage One ABC for Machine Shop: Assigning Costs to Activity** As the chief engineer of a small fabrication shop, Brenda Tolliver refers to herself as a "jack-of-all-trades." When an order for a new product comes in, Brenda must do the following:

LO2

1. Design the product to meet customer requirements.

2. Prepare a bill of materials (a list of materials required to produce the product).

3. Prepare an operations list (a sequential list of the steps involved in manufacturing the product).

Each time the foundry manufactures a batch of the product, Brenda must perform these activities:

1. Schedule the job.
2. Supervise the setup of machines that will work on the job.
3. Inspect the first unit produced to verify that it meets specifications.

Brenda supervises the production employees who perform the actual work on individual units of product. She is also responsible for employee training, ensuring that production facilities are in proper operating condition, and attending professional meetings. Brenda's estimates (in percent) of time spent on each of these activities last year are as follows:

Unit level activities:	
Supervising production	25%
Batch level activities:	
Scheduling jobs.	18%
Supervising setups	7%
Inspecting first units	1%
Product level activities:	
Designing product.	15%
Preparing bills of materials	5%
Preparing operations lists	8%
Facility level activities:	
Training employees	14%
Maintaining facility.	5%
Attending professional meetings.	2%
	100%

Required

Assuming Brenda Tolliver's salary is $132,000 per year, determine the dollar amount of her salary assigned to unit-, batch-, product-, and facility-level activities.

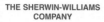

LO2   E5-3A. Stage Two ABC for Manufacturing: Reassigning Costs to Cost Objectives National Technology, LTD. has developed the following activity cost information for its manufacturing activities:

Activity	Activity Cost
Machine setup	$60.00 per batch
Movement.	15.00 per batch
	0.10 per pound
Drilling.	3.00 per hole
Welding.	4.00 per inch
Shaping	25.00 per hour
Assembly	18.00 per hour
Inspection	2.00 per unit

Filling an order for a batch of 50 fireplace inserts that weighed 100 pounds each required the following:

- Four batch moves
- Two sets of inspections
- Drilling ten holes in each unit
- Completing 100 inches of welds on each unit
- Forty-five minutes of shaping for each unit
- One hour of assembly per unit

Required

Determine the activity cost of converting the raw materials into 50 fireplace inserts.

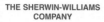

LO2   E5-4A. Stage Two ABC for Manufacturing Assume **The Sherwin-Williams Company**, a large paint manufacturer, has determined the following activity cost pools and cost driver levels for the latest period:

THE SHERWIN-WILLIAMS
COMPANY

Activity Cost Pool	Activity Cost	Activity Cost Driver
Machine setup	$900,000	2,500 setup hours
Materials handling	820,000	4,000 materials moves
Machine operation	400,000	20,000 machine hours

The following data are for the production of single batches of two products: Mirlite and Subdue:

	Mirlite	Subdue
Gallons produced	60,000	25,000
Direct labor hours	400	250
Machine hours	800	250
Direct labor cost	$ 10,000	$ 7,500
Direct materials cost	$360,000	$150,000
Setup hours	15	12
Materials moves	60	35

Required
Determine the batch and unit costs per gallon of Mirlite and Subdue using ABC.

E5-5A. **Activity-Based Costing** Steampunk Corporation has the following predicted indirect costs and cost drivers for the coming year for the given activity cost pools:

LO2, 3

	Fabrication Department	Finishing Department	Cost Driver
Maintenance	$ 30,000	$15,000	Machine hours
Materials handling	45,000	22,500	Material moves
Machine	105,000	7,500	Machine setups
Inspections	—	37,500	Inspection hours
Total	$180,000	$82,500	

The following activity predictions were also made for the year:

	Fabrication Department	Finishing Department
Machine hours	5,000	2,500
Materials moves	1,500	750
Machine setups	350	25
Inspection hours	—	500

It is assumed that the cost per unit of activity for a given activity does not vary between departments.

Steampunk's president, Abner Punk, is trying to evaluate the company's product mix strategy regarding two of its product models: SW100 and SG150. The company has been using a company-wide overhead rate based on machine hours but is considering switching to either department rates or activity-based rates. The production manager has provided the following data for the production of a batch of 100 units for each of these models:

	SW100	SG150
Direct materials cost	$10,000	$15,000
Direct labor cost	$ 4,000	$ 3,000
Machine hours (Fabrication)	250	350
Machine hours (Finishing)	100	50
Materials moves	20	40
Machine setups	5	10
Inspection hours	15	30

Required
a. Determine the cost of one unit each of SW100 and SG150, assuming a company-wide overhead rate is used based on total machine hours.
b. Determine the cost of one unit of SW100 and SG150, assuming department overhead rates are used. Overhead is assigned based on machine hours in both departments.
c. Determine the cost of one unit of SW100 and SG150, assuming activity-based overhead rates are used for maintenance, materials handling, machine setup, and inspection activities.
d. Comment on the results of these cost calculations.

LO5

E5-6A. Customer Profitability Analysis HyStandard Services, Inc. provides residential painting services for three home building companies—Alpine, Blue Ridge, and Pineola—and it uses a job costing system for determining the costs for completing each job. The job cost system does not capture any cost incurred by HyStandard for return touchups and refinishes after the homeowner occupies the home. HyStandard paints each house on a square footage contract price, which includes painting as well as all refinishes and touchups required after the homes are occupied. Each year, the company generates about one-third of its total revenues and gross profits from each of the three builders. The HyStandard owner has observed that the builders, however, require substantially different levels of support following the completion of jobs. The following data have been gathered:

Support Activity	Driver	Cost per Driver Unit
Major refinishes	Hours on jobs	$ 60
Touchups	Number of visits	$100
Communication.	Number of calls	$ 40

Builder	Major Refinishes	Touchups	Communication
Alpine	80	150	260
Blue Ridge	35	110	105
Pineola	42	115	90

Required
Assuming that each of the three customers produces gross profits of $100,000, calculate the profitability from each builder after taking into account the support activity required for each builder.

EXERCISES—SET B

LO2

E5-1B. Developing List of Activities for Baggage Handling at an Airport As part of a continuous improvement program, you have been asked to determine the activities involved in the baggage-handling process of a major airline at one of the airline's hubs. Prior to conducting observations and interviews, you decide that a list of possible activities would help you to better observe key activities and ask meaningful questions.

Required
For incoming aircraft only, develop a sequential list of baggage-handling activities. Your list should contain between 8 and 10 activities.

LO2

E5-2B. Stage One ABC at a College: Assigning Costs to Activities An economics professor at Prince Town University devotes 60% of her time to teaching, 35% of her time to research and writing, and 5% of her time to service activities such as committee work and student advising. The professor teaches two semesters per year. During each semester, she teaches one section of an introductory economics course (with a maximum enrollment of 50 students) and one section of a graduate economics course (with a maximum enrollment of 30 students). Including course preparation, classroom instruction, and appointments with students, each course requires an equal amount of time. The economics professor is paid $250,000 per year.

Required
Determine the activity cost of instruction per student in both the introductory and the graduate economics courses.

LO2

E5-3B. Stage Two ABC for a Wholesale Company Information is presented for the activity costs of Oxford Wholesale Company:

Activity Cost per Unit of Activity Driver	
Customer relations per month	$100.00 per customer
Selling	0.06 per sales dollar
Accounting	5.00 per order
Warehousing	0.50 per unit shipped
Packing	0.25 per unit shipped
Shipping	0.20 per pound shipped

The following information pertains to Oxford Wholesale Company's activities in Massachusetts for the month of March:

Number of orders	200
Sales revenue	$160,000
Cost of goods sold	$95,000
Number of customers	25
Units shipped	5,400
Pounds shipped	90,000

Required
Determine the profitability of sales in Massachusetts for March.

E5-4B. Stage Two ABC for Manufacturing Detroit Foundry, a large manufacturer of heavy equipment components, has determined the following activity cost pools and cost driver levels for the year: **LO2**

Activity Cost Pool	Activity Cost	Activity Cost Driver
Machine setup	$720,000	12,000 setup hours
Materials handling	120,000	3,000 tons of materials
Machine operation	680,000	10,000 machine hours

The following data are for the production of single batches of two products—C23 Cams and U2 Shafts—during the month of August:

	C23 Cams	U2 Shafts
Units produced	500	300
Machine hours	4	5
Direct labor hours	200	400
Direct labor cost	$ 5,000	$10,000
Direct materials cost	$20,000	$15,000
Tons of materials	13	8
Setup hours	3	7

Required
Determine the unit costs of C23 Cams and U2 Shafts using ABC.

E5-5B. Activity-Based Costing Slack Corporation has the following predicted indirect costs and cost drivers for the most recent year for the given activity cost pools: **LO2, 3**

	Fabrication Department	Finishing Department	Cost Driver
Maintenance	$ 20,000	$10,000	Machine hours
Materials handling	30,000	15,000	Material moves
Machine setups	70,000	5,000	Machine setups
Inspections	—	25,000	Inspection hours
	$120,000	$55,000	

The following activity predictions were also made for the year:

	Fabrication Department	Finishing Department
Machine hours	10,000	5,000
Materials moves	3,000	1,500
Machine setups	700	50
Inspection hours	—	1,000

It is assumed that the cost per unit of activity for a given activity does not vary between departments.

Slack's president, Charles Slack, is trying to evaluate the company's product mix strategy regarding two of its five product models: ZX300 and SL500. The company has been using a company-wide overhead rate based on machine hours but is considering switching to either department rates or activity-based rates. The production manager has provided the following data for the production of a batch of 100 units for each of these models:

	ZX300	SL500
Direct materials cost.	$12,000	$18,000
Direct labor cost	$ 5,000	$ 4,000
Machine hours (Fabrication).	500	700
Machine hours (Finishing)	200	100
Materials moves	30	50
Machine setups	5	9
Inspection hours	30	60

Required

a. Determine the cost of one unit each of ZX300 and SL500, assuming a company-wide overhead rate is used based on total machine hours.

b. Determine the cost of one unit of ZX300 and SL500, assuming department overhead rates are used. Overhead is assigned based on machine hours in both departments.

c. Determine the cost of one unit of ZX300 and SL500, assuming activity-based overhead rates are used for maintenance, materials handling, machine setup, and inspection activities.

d. Comment on the results of these cost calculations.

LO5   E5-6B. Customer Profitability Analysis FanGear, Inc. produces metal products for universities and colleges, including items such as trailer hitch covers and license plate holders with the institutions' logos and mascot likenesses, for sale by the institutions to their alumni and sports fans. FanGear produces these products in batches and uses a job costing system for determining the costs for completing each job. Each new batch requires a unique design, reconfiguring of dies and machinery to produce the product, and cleaning and maintenance of the machinery following the production run in preparation for the next batch. FanGear's CFO wants to implement an activity-based costing system for allocating overhead costs to each job. The accounting department staff have gathered the following activity cost pools and per-activity rates for the latest period:

Support Activity	Driver	Cost per Driver Unit
Product design	Change orders	$100
Batch setup.	Setup hours	$ 50
Machine maintenance	Machine hours	$ 40

For the latest period, FanGear produced products for three new major university customers.

Customer	Change Orders	Setup Hours	Machine Hours
Southern Utah	10	4	32
Utah Valley	6	8	48
Utah State.	4	6	40

Assuming that the production run for each of the three universities results in gross profits of $10,000, calculate the profitability from each university customer after taking into account the support activity required for each university customer.

PROBLEMS—SET A

P5-1A. Calculating Manufacturing Overhead Rates Glassman Company accumulated the following data for the current year.

LO3

Milling Department manufacturing overhead	$484,000
Finishing Department manufacturing overhead	$260,000
Machine hours used	
Milling Department	10,000 hours
Finishing Department	2,000 hours
Labor hours used	
Milling Department	1,000 hours
Finishing Department	1,000 hours

Required
a. Calculate the company-wide manufacturing overhead rate using machine hours as the allocation base.
b. Calculate the company-wide manufacturing overhead rate using direct labor hours as the allocation base.
c. Calculate department overhead rates using machine hours in Milling and direct labor hours in Finishing as the allocation bases.
d. Calculate department overhead rates using direct labor hours in Milling and machine hours in Finishing as the allocation bases.
e. Which of these allocation systems seems to be more appropriate? Explain.

P5-2A. Calculating Activity-Based Costing Overhead Rates Assume that manufacturing overhead for Glassman Company in the previous exercise consisted of the following activities and costs:

LO3

Setup (1,000 setup hours)	$288,000
Production scheduling (400 batches).............................	60,000
Production engineering (60 change orders).......................	180,000
Supervision (2,000 direct labor hours)	56,000
Machine maintenance (12,000 machine hours)	168,000
Total activity costs..	$752,000

The following additional data were provided for Job 845:

Direct materials costs	$7,000
Direct labor cost (5 Milling direct labor hours;	
35 Finishing direct labor hours).............................	$1,000
Setup hours	5 hours
Production scheduling	1 batch
Machine hours used (25 Milling machine hours;	
5 Finishing machine hours)................................	30 hours
Production engineering.......................................	3 change orders

Required
a. Calculate the cost per unit of activity driver for each activity cost category.
b. Calculate the cost of Job 845 using ABC to assign the overhead costs.
c. Calculate the cost of Job 845 using the company-wide overhead rate based on machine hours calculated in P5-1A(a).
d. Calculate the cost of Job 845 using a machine hour departmental overhead rate for the Milling Department and a direct labor hour overhead rate for the Finishing Department (see P5-1A (c)).

P5-3A. ABC—A Service Application Grand Haven is a senior living community that offers a full range of services including independent living, assisted living, and skilled nursing care. The assisted living division provides residential space, meals, and medical services (MS) to its residents. The current costing system adds the cost of all of these services (space, meals, and MS) and divides it by total resident days to get a cost per resident day for each month. Recognizing that MS tends to vary significantly among the residents, Grand Haven's accountant recommended that an ABC system be designed

LO2

to calculate more accurately the cost of MS provided to residents. She decided that residents should be classified into four categories (A, B, C, D) based on the level of services received, with group A representing the lowest level of service and D representing the highest level of service. Two cost drivers being considered for measuring MS costs are number of assistance calls and number of assistant contacts. A contact is registered each time an assistance professional provides medical services or aid to a resident. The accountant has gathered the following data for the most recent annual period:

Resident Classification	Annual Resident Days	Annual Assistance Hours	Number of Assistance Contacts
A...............	8,760	15,000	60,000
B...............	6,570	20,000	52,000
C...............	4,380	22,500	52,000
D...............	2,190	32,500	52,000
	21,900	90,000	216,000

Other data:	
Total cost of medical services for the period......................	$5,000,000
Total cost of meals and residential space	$3,280,000

Required (Round Answers and Intermediate Calculations to the Nearest Dollar)

a. Determine the ABC cost of a resident day for each category of residents using assistance hours as the cost driver.

b. Determine the ABC cost of a resident day for each category of residents using assistance contacts as the cost driver.

c. Which cost driver do you think provides the more accurate measure of the cost per day for a Grand Haven resident?

LO2   **P5-4A.   Stage Two ABC for Manufacturing** Merlot Company has determined its activity cost pools and cost drivers to be the following:

Cost Pools	
Setup.	$ 59,500
Materials handling.	16,000
Machine operation	300,000
Packing	60,000
Total indirect manufacturing costs.	$435,500

Cost drivers	
Setups.	350
Materials moves	640
Machine hours	20,000
Packing orders	1,000

One product made by Merlot, metal casements, used the following activities during the period to produce 500 units:

Setups	20
Materials moves	80
Machine hours	1,900
Packing orders	150

Required

a. Calculate the cost per unit of activity for each activity cost pool for Merlot Company.

b. Calculate the manufacturing overhead cost per metal casement manufactured during the period.

LO2, 3   **P5-5A.   Traditional Product Costing Versus Activity-Based Costing** Assume that Panasonic Company has determined its estimated total manufacturing overhead cost for one of its plants to be $204,000, consisting of the following activity cost pools for the current month:

PANASONIC COMPANY

Activity Centers	Activity Costs	Cost Drivers	Activity Level
Assembly setups	$ 45,000	Setup hours	1,500
Materials handling	15,000	Number of moves	300
Assembly	120,000	Assembly hours	12,000
Maintenance.	24,000	Maintenance hours.	1,200
Total	$204,000		

Total direct labor hours used during the month were 8,000. Panasonic produces many different electronic products, including the following two products produced during the current month:

	Model X301	Model Z205
Units produced	1,000	1,000
Direct materials costs	$15,000	$15,000
Direct labor costs	$12,500	$12,500
Direct labor hours	500	500
Setup hours	50	100
Materials moves	25	50
Assembly hours	800	800
Maintenance hours	10	40

Required

a. Calculate the total per-unit cost of each model using direct labor hours to assign manufacturing overhead to products.

b. Calculate the total per-unit cost of each model using activity-based costing to assign manufacturing overhead to products.

c. Comment on the accuracy of the two methods for determining product costs.

d. Discuss some of the strategic implications of your answers to the previous requirements.

P5-6A. Activity-Based Costing in a Service Organization Red River Banking Company has ten automatic teller machines (ATMs) spread throughout the city maintained by the ATM Department. You have been assigned the task of determining the cost of operating each machine. Management will use the information you develop, along with other information pertaining to the volume and type of transactions at each machine, to evaluate the desirability of continuing to operate each machine and/or changing security arrangements for a particular machine.

LO2, 3

SERVICE AND MERCHANDISING

The ATM Department consists of a total of six employees: a supervisor, a head cashier, two associate cashiers, and two maintenance personnel. The associate cashiers make between two and four daily trips to each machine to collect and replenish cash and to replenish supplies, deposit tickets, and so forth. Each machine contains a small computer that automatically summarizes and reports transactions to the head cashier. The head cashier reconciles the activities of the two associate cashiers to the computerized reports. The supervisor, who does not handle cash, reviews the reconciliation. When an automatic teller's computer, a customer, or a cashier reports a problem, the two maintenance employees and one cashier are dispatched immediately. The cashier removes all cash and transaction records, and the maintenance employees repair the machine.

Maintenance employees spend all of their time on maintenance-related activities. The associate cashiers spend approximately 50% of their time on maintenance-related activities and 50% on daily trips. The head cashier's time is divided, with 75% directly related to daily trips to each machine and 25% related to supervising cashiers on maintenance calls. The supervisor devotes 20% of the time to daily trips to each machine and 80% to the equal supervision of each employee. Cost information for a recent month follows:

Salaries	
Supervisor.	$ 4,000
Head cashier.	3,000
Other ($1,800 each)	7,200
Lease and operating costs	
Cashiers' service vehicle.	1,200
Maintenance service vehicle.	1,400
Office rent and utilities	2,300
Machine lease, space rent, and utilities ($1,500 each).	15,000
Total	$34,100

Related monthly activity information for this month follows:

Machine	Routine Trips	Maintenance Hours
1	30	5
2	90	17
3	60	15
4	60	30
5	120	15
6	30	10
7	90	25
8	120	5
9	60	20
10	60	18
Total	720	160

Additional information follows:

- The office is centrally located with about equal travel time to each machine.
- Maintenance hours include travel time.
- The cashiers' service vehicle is used exclusively for routine visits.
- The office space is divided equally between the supervisor and the head cashier.

Required

a.   Determine the monthly operating costs of machines 7 and 8 when cost assignments are based on the number of machines.

b.   Determine the activity cost of a routine trip and a maintenance hour for the month given. Round answers to the nearest cent.

c.   Determine the operating costs assigned and reassigned to machines 7 and 8 when activity-based costing is used.

d.   How can ABC cost information be used by Red River Banking Company to improve the overall management of monthly operating costs?

LO3, 4   P5-7A.   Product Costing: Company-Wide Overhead Versus ABC LaMesa produces machine parts as a contract provider for a large manufacturing company. LaMesa produces two particular parts: shafts and gears. The competition is keen among contract producers, and LaMesa's top management realizes how vulnerable its market is to cost-cutting competitors. Hence, having a very accurate understanding of costs is important to LaMesa's survival.

LaMesa's president, Jose Rodriguez, has observed that the company's current cost to produce shafts is $21.35, and the current cost to produce gears is $12.36. He indicated to the controller that he suspects some problems with the cost system because LaMesa is suddenly experiencing extraordinary competition on shafts, but it seems to have a virtual corner on the gears market. He is even considering dropping the shaft line and converting the company to a one-product manufacturer of gears. He asked the controller, Felix Bernhardt, to conduct a thorough cost study and to consider whether changes in the cost system are necessary. The controller collected the following data about the company's costs and various manufacturing activities for the most recent month:

	Shafts	Gears
Production units	50,000	10,500
Selling price	$31.86	$24.00
Overhead per unit (based on direct labor hours)	$12.82	$ 6.10
Materials and direct labor cost per unit.	$ 8.53	$ 6.26
Number of production runs.	10	20
Number of purchasing and receiving orders processed.	40	100
Number of machine hours	12,750	6,000
Number of direct labor hours	25,000	2,500
Number of engineering hours.	5,000	5,000
Number of material moves	50	40

The controller was able to summarize the company's total manufacturing overhead into the following pools:

Setup costs.	$ 30,000
Machine cost	175,000
Purchasing and receiving costs	210,000
Engineering costs.	200,000
Materials handling costs.	90,000
Total	$705,000

Required
a. Calculate LaMesa's current company-wide overhead rate based on direct labor hours.
b. Verify LaMesa's calculation of overhead cost per unit of $12.82 for shafts and $6.10 for gears.
c. Calculate the manufacturing overhead cost per unit for shafts and gears using activity-based costing, assuming each of the five cost pools represents a separate activity pool. Use the most appropriate activity driver for assigning activity costs to the two products.
d. Comment on LaMesa's current cost system and the reason the company is facing fierce competition for shafts but little competition for gears.

P5-8A. **Customer Profitability Analysis** Gonalong, Inc., has 10 customers that account for all of its $4,500,000 of net income. Its activity-based costing system is able to assign all costs, except for $650,000 of general administrative costs, to key activities incurred in connection with serving its customers. A customer profitability analysis based on activity costing produced the following customer profits and losses:

LO5

Customer #1.	$ 346,000
#2	624,000
#3	(257,000)
#4	969,000
#5	1,040,000
#6	872,000
#7	628,000
#8	322,000
#9	(105,000)
#10	711,000
Total	$5,150,000

Required
Prepare a customer profitability profile graph. Sort the customers in order of profitability from most profitable to least profitable, then plot the cumulative profit with total profits along the y-axis and customers along the x-axis. What is the maximum amount of profit that Gonalong could achieve if it were to eliminate its unprofitable customers?

P5-9A. **Customer Profitability Analysis** Refer to the previous exercise P5-8A for Gonalong, Inc.

LO5

Required
a. If Gonalong were to notify customers 3 and 9 that it will no longer be able to provide them services in the future, will that increase company profits by $362,000? Why or why not?
b. What is the primary benefit of preparing a customer profitability analysis?

PROBLEMS—SET B

LO2, 3   **P5-1B.**   **Activity-Based Costing and Conventional Costs Compared** Hickory Grill Company manufactures two types of cooking grills: the Gas Cooker and the Charcoal Smoker. The Cooker is a premium product sold in upscale outdoor shops; the Smoker is sold in major discount stores. Following is information pertaining to the manufacturing costs for the current month.

	Gas Cooker	Charcoal Smoker
Units	1,000	4,000
Number of batches	50	10
Number of batch moves	80	20
Direct materials	$40,000	$90,000
Direct labor	$20,000	$25,000

Manufacturing overhead follows:

Activity	Cost	Cost Driver
Materials acquisition and inspection	$52,000	Amount of direct materials cost
Materials movement	17,450	Number of batch moves
Scheduling	30,000	Number of batches
	$99,450	

Required

a.   Determine the total and per-unit costs of manufacturing the Gas Cooker and Charcoal Smoker for the month, assuming all manufacturing overhead is assigned on the basis of direct labor dollars.

b.   Determine the total and per-unit costs of manufacturing the Gas Cooker and Charcoal Smoker for the month, assuming manufacturing overhead is assigned using activity-based costing.

LO2, 3   **P5-2B.**   **Activity-Based Costing Versus Conventional Costing** Refer to the previous exercise in P5-1B for Hickory Grill.

Required

a.   Comment on the differences between the solutions to requirements (a) and (b). Which is more accurate? What errors might managers make if all manufacturing overhead costs are assigned on the basis of direct labor dollars?

b.   Comment on the adequacy of the preceding data to meet management's needs.

LO2, 3   **P5-3B.**   **Traditional Product Costing Versus Activity-Based Costing** High Country Outfitters, Inc., makes backpacks for large sporting goods chains that are sold under the customers' store brand names. The accounting department has identified the following overhead costs and cost drivers for next year:

Overhead Item	Expected Costs	Cost Driver	Maximum Quantity
Setup costs	$ 828,000	Number of setups	7,200
Ordering costs	252,000	Number of orders	60,000
Maintenance	1,360,000	Number of machine hours	80,000
Power	210,000	Number of kilowatt hours	600,000

Total predicted direct labor hours for next year is 60,000. The following data are for two recently completed jobs:

	Job 201	Job 202
Cost of direct materials	$13,500	$15,000
Cost of direct labor	$19,125	$71,250
Number of units completed	1,125	915
Number of direct labor hours	270	330
Number of setups	18	22
Number of orders	24	45
Number of machine hours	540	450
Number of kilowatt hours	270	360

Required

a. Determine the unit cost for each job using a traditional company-wide overhead rate based on direct labor hours.

b. Determine the unit cost for each job using ABC. (Round answers to two decimal places.)

c. As the manager of High Country, is there additional information that you would want to help you evaluate the pricing and profitability of Jobs 201 and 202?

d. Assuming the company has been using the method required in part *a*, how should management react to the findings in part *b*?

P5-4B. Stage Two ABC for Manufacturing with Variances Montreat Manufacturing has developed the following activity cost pool information for its manufacturing activities:

LO2

	Budgeted Activity Cost	Activity Cost Driver at Practical Capacity
Purchasing and materials handling	$675,000	900,000 kilograms
Setup	700,000	1,120 setups
Machine operations	954,000	12,000 hours
First unit inspection	50,000	1,000 batches
Packaging	250,000	312,500 units

Actual production information for the most recent year is as follows:

	Standard Product A	Standard Product B	Specialty Products
Units	150,000	100,000	50,000
Batches	100	80	600
Setups*	300	160	900
Machine operations (hours)	6,000	3,000	2,000
Kilograms of raw materials	400,000	300,000	200,000
Direct materials costs	$900,000	$600,000	$820,000

*Some products require setups on two or more machines.

Required

a. Determine the unit cost of each product for Montreat Manufacturing.

b. Explain why the unit cost of the specialty products is so much higher than the unit cost of Standard Product A or Standard Product B.

P5-5B. ABC Costing for a Service Organization Fairfield Mortgage Company is a full-service residential mortgage company in the Atlanta area that operates in a very competitive market. The CEO, Richard Sissom, is concerned about operating costs associated with processing mortgage applications and has decided to install an ABC costing system to help him get a handle on costs. Although labor hours seem to be the primary driver of the cost of processing a new mortgage, the labor cost for the different activities involved in processing new loans varies widely. The Accounting Department has provided the following data for the company's five major cost pools for the latest year:

LO2, 3

SERVICE AND MERCHANDISING

Activity Cost Pools		Activity Drivers	
Taking customer applications	$ 300,000	Time—assistant managers	12,000 hours
Conducting credit investigations	450,000	Time—credit managers	16,500 hours
Underwriting	525,000	Time—Underwriting Department	10,000 hours
Preparing loan packages	200,000	Time—Processing Department	8,000 hours
Closing loans	600,000	Time—Legal Department hours	6,000 hours
	$2,075,000		52,500 hours

During the year, the company processed and issued 5,000 new mortgages, two of which are summarized here with regard to activities used to process the mortgages:

	Loan 5066	Loan 5429
Application processing hours	1.50	2.75
Credit investigating hours........................	4.00	3.00
Underwriting hours	2.50	4.75
Processing hours	3.50	3.00
Legal processing hours	1.50	1.50
Total hours	13.00	15.00

Required

a. Determine the cost per unit of activity for each activity cost pool.

b. Determine the cost of processing loans 5066 and 5429.

c. Determine the cost of preparing loans 5066 and 5429 assuming that an average cost per hour for all activities is used.

d. Compare and discuss your answers to requirements (b) and (c).

LO2, 3   P5-6B.   Product Costing: Department Versus ABC for Overhead Advertising Technologies, Inc. (ATI) specializes in providing both published and online advertising services for the business marketplace. The company monitors its costs based on the cost per column inch of published space printed in print advertising media and based on the cost per minute of telephone advertising time delivered on "The AD Line," a computer-based, online advertising service. ATI has one new competitor, Tel-a-Ad, in its local teleadvertising market; and with increased competition, ATI has seen a decline in sales of online advertising in recent years. ATI's president, Robert Beard, believes that predatory pricing by Tel-a-Ad has caused the problem. The following is a recent conversation between Robert and Jane Minnear, director of marketing for ATI.

> *Jane:* I just received a call from one of our major customers concerning our advertising rates on "The AD Line" who said that a sales rep from another firm (it had to be Tel-a-Ad) had offered the same service at $1 per minute, which is $1.50 per minute less than our price.
>
> *Robert:* It's costing about $1.27 per minute to produce that product. I don't see how they can afford to sell it so cheaply. I'm not convinced that we should meet the price. Perhaps the better strategy is to emphasize producing and selling more published ads, which we're more experienced with and where our margins are high and we have virtually no competition.
>
> *Jane:* You may be right. Based on a recent survey of our customers, I think we can raise the price significantly for published advertising and still not lose business.
>
> *Robert:* That sounds promising; however, before we make a major recommitment to publishing, let's explore other possible explanations. I want to know how our costs compare with our competitors. Maybe we could be more efficient and find a way to earn a good return on teleadvertising.

After this meeting, Robert and Jane requested an investigation of production costs and comparative efficiency of producing published versus online advertising services. The controller, Tim Gentry, indicated that ATI's efficiency was comparable to that of its competitors and prepared the following cost data:

	Published Advertising	Online Advertising
Estimated number of production units	200,000	10,000,000
Selling price	$200	$2.50
Direct product costs	$21,000,000	$5,000,000
Overhead allocation*	$9,800,000	$7,700,000
Overhead per unit......................................	$49	$0.77
Direct costs per unit	$105	$0.50
Number of customers.....................................	180,000	25,000
Number of salesperson days	32,000	5,500
Number of art and design hours............................	35,000	5,000
Number of creative services subcontract hours	100,000	25,000
Number of customer service calls	72,000	8,000

*Based on direct labor costs

Upon examining the data, Robert decided that he wanted to know more about the overhead costs because they were such a high proportion of total production costs. He was provided the following list of overhead costs and told that they were currently being assigned to products in proportion to direct labor costs.

Selling costs	$7,500,000
Visual and audio design costs	3,000,000
Creative services costs.	5,000,000
Customer service costs	2,000,000

Required

Using the data provided by the controller, prepare analyses to help Robert and Jane in making their decisions. (*Hint:* Prepare cost calculations for both product lines using ABC to see whether there is any significant difference in their unit costs.) Should ATI switch from the fast-growing, online advertising market back into the well-established published advertising market? Does the charge of predatory pricing seem valid? Why are customers likely to be willing to pay a higher price to get published services? Do traditional costing and activity-based costing lead to the same conclusions?

P5-7B.   Unit-Level and Multiple-Level Cost Assignments CarryAll Company produces briefcases from leather, fabric, and synthetic materials in a single production department. The basic product is a standard briefcase made from leather and lined with fabric. CarryAll has a good reputation in the market because the standard briefcase is a high-quality item that has been produced for many years.

LO2, 3

Last year, the company decided to expand its product line and produce specialty briefcases for special orders. These briefcases differ from the standard in that they vary in size, contain both leather and synthetic materials, and are imprinted with the buyer's logo. (The standard briefcase is simply imprinted with the CarryAll name in small letters.) The decision to use some synthetic materials in the briefcase was made to hold down the materials cost. To reduce the labor costs per unit, most of the cutting and stitching on the specialty briefcases is done by automated machines, which are used to a much lesser degree in the production of the standard briefcases. Because of these changes in the design and production of the specialty briefcases, CarryAll management believed that they would cost less to produce than the standard briefcases. However, because they are specialty items, they were priced slightly higher; standards are priced at $30 and specialty briefcases at $32.

After reviewing last month's results of operations, CarryAll's president became concerned about the profitability of the two product lines because the standard briefcase showed a loss while the specialty briefcase showed a greater profit margin than expected. The president is wondering whether the company should drop the standard briefcase and focus entirely on specialty items. Units and cost data for last month's operations as reported to the president are as follows:

	Standard	Specialty
Units produced	10,000	2,500
Direct materials		
Leather (1 sq. yd. × $15.00; ½ sq. yd. × $15.00).	$15.00	$ 7.50
Fabric (1 sq. yd. × $5.00; 1 sq. yd. × $5.00)	5.00	5.00
Synthetic.		5.00
Total Materials	20.00	17.50
Direct Labor (½ hr. × $12.00; ¼ hr. × $12.00).	6.00	3.00
Manufacturing Overhead (½ hr. × $8.98; ¼ hr. × $8.98)	4.49	2.25
Cost per unit.	$30.49	$22.75

Manufacturing overhead is applied on the basis of direct labor hours. The rate of $8.98 per direct labor hour was calculated by dividing the total overhead ($50,500) by the direct labor hours (5,625). As shown in the table, the cost of a standard briefcase is $0.49 higher than its $30 sales price; the specialty briefcase has a cost of only $22.75, for a gross profit per unit of $9.25. The problem with these costs is that they do not accurately reflect the activities involved in manufacturing each product. Determining the costs using ABC should provide better product costing data to help gauge the actual profitability of each product line.

The manufacturing overhead costs must be analyzed to determine the activities driving the costs. Assume that the following costs and cost drivers have been identified:

- The Purchasing Department's cost is $6,000. The major activity driving these costs is the number of purchase orders processed. During the month, the Purchasing Department prepared the following number of purchase orders for the materials indicated:

Leather	20
Fabric	30
Synthetic materials	50

- The cost of receiving and inspecting materials is $7,500. These costs are driven by the number of deliveries. During the month, the following number of deliveries were made:

Leather	30
Fabric	40
Synthetic materials	80

- Production line setup cost is $10,000. Setup activities involve changing the machines to produce the different types of briefcases. Each setup for production of the standard briefcases requires one hour; each setup for specialty briefcases requires two hours. Standard briefcases are produced in batches of 200, and specialty briefcases are produced in batches of 25. During the last month, there were 50 setups for the standard item and 100 setups for the specialty item.
- The cost of inspecting finished goods is $8,000. All briefcases are inspected to ensure that quality standards are met. However, the final inspection of standard briefcases takes very little time because the employees identify and correct quality problems as they do the hand cutting and stitching. A survey of the personnel responsible for inspecting the final products showed that 150 hours were spent on standard briefcases and 250 hours on specialty briefcases during the month.
- Equipment-related costs are $6,000. Equipment-related costs include repairs, depreciation, and utilities. Management has determined that a logical basis for assigning these costs to products is machine hours. A standard briefcase requires 1/2 hour of machine time, and a specialty briefcase requires two hours. Thus, during the last month, 5,000 hours of machine time relate to the standard line and 5,000 hours relate to the specialty line.
- Plant-related costs are $13,000. These costs include property taxes, insurance, administration, and others. For the purpose of determining average unit costs, they are to be assigned to products using machine hours.

Required

a. Using activity-based costing concepts, what overhead costs should be assigned to the two products?
b. What is the unit cost of each product using activity-based costing concepts?
c. Reevaluate the president's concern about the profitability of the two product lines.
d. Discuss the merits of activity-based management as it relates to CarryAll's ABC cost system.

LO5   P5-8B.   Customer Profitability Analysis Rogers Aeronautics, LTD, is a British aeronautics subcontract company that designs and manufactures electronic control systems for commercial airlines. The vast majority of all commercial aircraft are manufactured by Boeing in the U.S. and Airbus in Europe; however, there is a relatively small group of companies that manufacture narrow-body commercial jets. Assume for this exercise that Rogers does contract work for the two major manufacturers plus three companies in the second tier.

Because competition is intense in the industry, Rogers has always operated on a fairly thin 20% gross profit margin; hence, it is crucial that it manage non-manufacturing overhead costs effectively in order to achieve an acceptable net profit margin. With declining profit margins in recent years, Rogers Aeronautics's CEO, Len Rogers, has become concerned that the cost of obtaining contracts and maintaining relations with its five major customers may be getting out of hand. You have been hired to conduct a customer profitability analysis.

Rogers Aeronautics's non-manufacturing overhead consists of $2.5 million of general and administrative (G&A) expense (including, among other expenses, the CEO's salary and bonus and the cost of operating the company's corporate jet) and selling and customer support expenses of $3 million (including 5% sales commissions and $1,050,000 of additional costs).

The accounting staff determined that the $1,050,000 of additional selling and customer support expenses related to the following four activity cost pools:

Activity	Activity Cost Driver	Cost per Unit of Activity
1. Sales visits	Number of visit days	$ 800
2. Product adjustments	Number of adjustments	1,300
3. Phone and email contacts	Number of calls/contacts	50
4. Promotion and entertainment events	Number of events	2,000

Financial and activity data on the five customers follows (Sales and Gross Profit data in millions):

Customer	Sales	Gross Profit	Quantity of Sales and Support Activity			
			Activity 1	Activity 2	Activity 3	Activity 4
#1	$17	$3.40	106	23	220	82
#2	12	2.4	130	36	354	66
#3	3	0.6	52	10	180	74
#4	4	0.8	34	6	138	18
#5	3	0.6	16	5	104	10
	$39	$7.80	338	80	996	250

In addition to the above, the sales staff used the corporate jet at a cost of $800 per hour for trips to customers as follows:

Customer #1...	24 hours
Customer #2...	36 hours
Customer #3...	5 hours
Customer #4...	0 hours
Customer #5...	6 hours

The total cost of operating the airplane is included in general and administrative expense; none is included in selling and customer support costs.

Required

a.   Prepare a customer profitability analysis for Rogers Aeronautics that shows the gross profits less all expenses that can reasonably be assigned to the five customers.

b.   Now assuming that the remaining general and administrative costs are assigned to the five customers based on relative sales dollars, calculate net profit for each customer.

c.   Discuss the merits of the analysis in part *a* versus part *b*.

EXTENDING YOUR KNOWLEDGE

EYK5-1.   Business Decision Case   The Reserve Club is a traditional private golf and country club that has three different categories of memberships: golf, tennis & swimming, and social. Golf members have access to all amenities and programs in the club, Tennis & Swimming members have access to all amenities and programs except use of the golf course, and Social members have access to only the social activities of the club, excluding golf, tennis, and swimming. All members have clubhouse privileges, including use of the bar and restaurant, which is operated by an outside contractor. During the past year, the average membership in each category, along with the number of club visits during the year, was

	Members	Visits
Golf.	260	9,360
Tennis & Swimming	50	1,500
Social	120	2,160

Some members of the club have been complaining that heavy users of the club are not bearing their share of the costs through their membership fees. Dess Rosmond, General Manager of the Reserve Club, agrees that monthly fees paid by the various member groups should be based on the annual average amount of cost-related activities provided by the club for the three groups, and he intends to set fees on that basis for the coming year. The annual direct costs of operating the golf course, tennis courts, and swimming pool have been calculated by the club's controller as follows:

Golf course	$900,000
Swimming pool	50,000
Tennis courts	25,000

The operation of the bar and restaurant and all related costs, including depreciation on the bar and restaurant facilities, are excluded from this analysis. In addition to the above costs, the club incurs general overhead costs in the following amounts for the most recent (and typical) year:

General Ledger Overhead Accounts	Amounts
Indirect labor for the club management staff (the general manager, assistant general manager, membership manager, and club controller)	$250,000
Utilities (other than those directly related to golf, swimming, and tennis)	24,000
Website maintenance	2,000
Postage	5,000
Computers and information systems maintenance	7,500
Clubhouse maintenance and depreciation	30,000
Liability insurance	4,000
Security contract	12,000
	$334,500

Dess believes that the best way to assign most of the overhead costs to the three membership categories is with an activity-based system that recognizes four key activities that occur regularly in the club:

- Recruiting and providing orientation for new members
- Maintaining the membership roster and communicating with members
- Planning, scheduling, and managing club events
- Maintaining the financial records and reporting for the club

Required

a. Identify and explain which overhead costs can reasonably be assigned to one or more of the four key activities, and suggest a basis for making the assignment.

b. Identify a cost driver for each activity cost pool that would seem to be suitable for assigning the activity cost pool to the three membership categories.

c. Suggest a method for assigning any overhead costs to the three membership categories that cannot reasonably be assigned to activity pools.

d. Comment on the suitability of ABC to this cost assignment situation.

ANSWERS TO SELF-STUDY QUESTIONS:

1. c   2. d   3. c   4. b   5. d   6. d

YOUR TURN! SOLUTIONS

Solution 5.1

The butterscotch cookies are $4,000 more profitable, as shown below:
Cost of semi-sweet cookie delivery: [(15,000 × 18) ÷ 60] × $15 = $67,500
Cost of butterscotch cookie delivery: [(10,500 × 12) ÷ 60] × $15 = $31,500
Semi-sweet cookie profit: $200,000 − $112,000 − $67,500 = $20,500
Butterscotch cookie profit: $140,000 − $84,000 − $31,500 = $24,500
Profit difference: $4,000

Solution 5.2

Your response might include the following major points:

1. An ABC costing system would help the company to more completely identify all of the activities that cause the company to incur the overhead cost in the first place.
2. An ABC costing system would provide for more accurate tracing of overhead costs to products because the overhead costs are more closely associated with the related activity (or cost driver).
3. Having a better understanding of the costs of each product will help management set production priorities, sales targets, and prices to maximize company profits.

Solution 5.3

b. Traditional cost systems that utilize a single overhead rate tend to over-cost high volume products.

Solution 5.4

No. Despite the customer's large number of returns and high demand for visits and calls, a customer profitability analysis shows that they are still profitable:

Sales − cost of sales − (cost of returns + cost of visits + cost of calls) = customer profit

$100,000 − $85,000 − (50*$100 + 25*$150 + 120*$30) = $2,650

Solution 5.5

c. Movement of materials does not add value from the customer's perspective. The company might arrange for the vendor to deliver the raw materials directly to the production floor as needed, eliminating or reducing the need for a raw materials storehouse.

Chapter **6**
Cost-Volume-Profit Relationships

Road Map

LO	Learning Objective	Page	eLecture	Guided Example	Assignments
LO1	Develop an understanding of how specific types of costs change in response to volume changes.	6-3	E6-1	YT6.1	SS1, Q1, Q2, Q3, Q4, Q7, SE2, E1A, E18A, E18B, P2A, P7A, P2B, P7B
LO2	Define the concept of relevant range.	6-6	E6-2	YT6.2	SS2, Q1, Q6, E3A, P2A, P3A, P4A, P7A, P2B, P3B, P4B, P7B
LO3	Outline the approach to developing cost formulas.	6-7	E6-3	YT6.3	SS3, Q4, Q5, Q7, Q8, SE2, E2A, E3A, E4A, E5A, E6A, E1B, E2B, E3B, E4B, E5B, E6B, P2A, P3A, P4A, P5A, P6A, P7A, P2B, P3B, P4B, P5B, P6B, P7B
LO4	Present a discussion of and a formula for calculating the break-even point.	6-13	E6-4	YT6.4	SS4, Q9, Q10, Q11, Q12, SE4, E7A, E13A, E14A, E7B, E8B, E9B, E10B, E12B, E13B, E14B, E15B, P1A, P8A, P9A, P10A, P11A, P1B, P8B, P9B, P10B, P11B
LO5	Define contribution margin and contribution margin ratio and present alternate break-even formulas and examples of their application.	6-15	E6-5	YT6.5	SS5, Q13, E8A, E9A, E10A, E11A, E13A, E14A, E15A, E8B, E9B, E10B, E11B, E12B, E13B, E14B, E15B, P1A, P8A, P9A, P10A, P11A, P1B, P8B, P9B, P10B, P11B
LO6	Discuss approaches to planning net income using cost-volume-profit analyses.	6-18	E6-6	YT6.6	SS6, Q14, Q15, Q16, SE1, SE3, SE5, E12A, E13A, E14A, E15A, E16A, E17A, E9B, E10B, E12B, E13B, E14B, E15B, E16B, E17B, P3A, P8A, P9A, P10A, P11A, P3B, P8B, P9B, P10B, P11B

In 2019, **Disney**'s then-CEO Bob Iger called Disney+ a "bet on the future of this [Disney's] business."[1] The streaming service Disney+ was launched on November 12, 2019, in the United States, Canada, and the Netherlands. In large part due to its affordable pricing and its extensive library of beloved Disney content, 10 million users had subscribed to the service by the end of its first day of business. By mid-2021, the streaming platform had expanded to 59 different countries and had over 100 million subscribers. But Disney+'s overall success is tempered by the investment costs associated with it. One research media firm estimated that Disney+ lost approximately $2.1 billion in 2020 and predicts peak losses in 2022, as rollout costs and content development expenses continue to be very high.[2] To that end, Disney has acknowledged that its flagship streaming service won't break-even until 2024.

How is Disney able to predict a break-even point or marginal profitability 3 to 4 years in the future? They have forecast the inputs that impact future revenues and costs and, therefore, profitability! Disney+ executives forecasted between $230–260 million total paid subscribers in fiscal year 2024. Additionally, they estimate that Disney+ will incur between $8–9 billion in content spending in fiscal year 2024.[3] Though they have not announced any future pricing strategies, current subscriber prices for Disney+ range from $79.99–$119.99 annually. (These prices are highly dependent on the country where the subscriber is located and whether they've chosen a monthly subscription or an annual membership.) This suggests a business generating potentially $20–30 billion in annual sales. Each of these items play an important role in forecasting break-even points and future profitability.

This chapter explores how cost-volume-profit analysis can help a company like Disney determine the number of subscribers it would need to break-even on its business or help Fezzari predict the number of bikes it must produce and sell to achieve a particular profit level.

---

[1] https://www.cnn.com/2019/11/11/media/disney-launch/index.html

[2] https://www.nytimes.com/2020/11/12/business/media/disney-plus-73-million-subscribers.html

[3] https://deadline.com/2020/12/disney-will-be-spending-14-16-billion-on-all-streaming-content-by-2024-as-it-ramps-up-production-1234654652/

PAST

Chapter 5 explored activity-based costing and its benefits relative to traditional company-wide and departmental overhead allocation, and contrasted it with activity-based management.

PRESENT

Chapter 6 advances our understanding of cost behaviors (introduced in Chapter 2) to assist in the development of cost formulas. We also use cost behaviors to determine break-even points, target profit volumes, and make planning and budgeting decisions.

FUTURE

Chapter 7 will use the cost formula approach and contribtion margin statement developed in Chapter 6 to prepare a variable income statement. We will also discuss reporting for segments of businesses.

6-2

COST-VOLUME-PROFIT RELATIONSHIPS

Cost Behavior Analysis	Relevant Range	Analyzing Cost Behavior	Cost-Volume-Profit Analysis	Planning for Profit
• Selecting the Activity Basis • Cost-Volume Graphs • Classifications of Cost Behavior Patterns	• Define Relevant Range of Activity	• Scattergraph Method • High-Low Method • Least Squares Regression Method • Analyzing Costs in Practice	• Break-Even Analysis • Contribution Margin Analysis	• Desired Profit • Margin of Safety • Operating Leverage • Using Cost-Volume-Profit Relationships • Break-Even Analysis and Multiple Products • Cost-Volume-Profit Analysis for Retail Businesses

"We lose money on every sale—but make up the difference in volume."

—ANONYMOUS

A.K.A. Cost-volume-profit analysis is often referred to in practice by its abbreviation, CVP, or break-even analysis.

Management must study a number of factors when planning the future course for an organization. One of the most important factors is the relationship among sales (revenue), costs (expenses), and profit (net income). **Cost-volume-profit (CVP) analysis** is used to study these relationships.

CVP analysis is appropriately used by for-profit organizations as well as not-for-profit (NFP) organizations. NFPs use the analysis with a target profit of zero. All of the relationships studied in the analysis are equally valid for both types of organizations.

COST BEHAVIOR ANALYSIS

LO1 **Develop** an understanding of how specific types of costs change in response to volume changes.

eLecture
MBC

Recall from Chapter 2 that classifying costs based on their behavior is incredibly useful to decision makers. We briefly revisit these concepts in Chapter 6 because the foundation for CVP analysis is a thorough understanding of cost behavior. **Cost behavior analysis** is the study of how specific costs respond to changes in the volume of business activity. Each specific cost incurred by an organization may be affected differently by changes in the volume of business activity. Some costs will increase proportionately as volume increases, some costs will change disproportionately, and some costs will remain the same. Other factors besides volume can also cause changes in specific costs. For example, an increase in the assessment rate can increase property tax expense, whereas a decrease in electricity rates can lower total utility expense. These types of changes, however, are not typically caused by changes in business activity volume.

Selecting the Activity Basis

For meaningful managerial analysis, costs must be associated to some measure of business activity. As we introduced in Chapter 3 and discussed further in Chapter 5, this measure of business activity is referred to as a cost driver. Cost drivers can include units of product, direct labor hours, machine hours, or the percentage of capacity. A critical aspect is that the activity measure used must have a logical causal relation with costs, and the quantity of the activity must be highly correlated with the level of costs. Management must consider the objective of the analysis when selecting the most relevant and useful cost driver. For example, if Disney+ managers want to analyze the total cost of their streaming service for budget purposes, they might choose the number of countries where the streaming service has been launched or the total number of worldwide subscribers. CVP analysis can often use several bases, depending on the objectives of the analysis.

To help demonstrate various cost behaviors, we return to the Fezzari example. Fezzari produces a carbon water bottle cage that can be used on both road and mountain bikes. In the first part of this chapter, we explore several examples related to the various costs associated with producing Fezzari's water bottle cages. We discuss various types of cost behaviors and graph those behaviors in cost-volume graphs. Later in the chapter, we further analyze those costs and how they relate to profits.

Cost-Volume Graphs

One of the most useful tools for analyzing the relationship between changes in cost and volume is the **cost-volume graph**. A cost-volume graph illustrates the relationship between costs and volume. These graphs typically plot total costs on the vertical *y*-axis and either volume or activity level on the horizontal *x*-axis. Recall from Chapter 2 that companies typically have both variable and fixed costs. **Exhibits 6-1** and **6-2** are examples of cost-volume graphs, plotting total cost on the *y*-axis and the number of water bottle cages on the *x*-axis. Keep in mind that the total cost line in **Exhibits 6-1** and **6-2** is composed of both fixed and variable costs. Point A in **Exhibit 6-1** indicates that at a volume level of 5,000 units the associated cost is $7,500. Similarly, point B in **Exhibit 6-1** represents a cost of $22,500 for a volume level of 35,000 units.

Cost-volume graphs are particularly valuable when available cost-volume data are plotted on the same graph and other cost-volume relationships are estimated by fitting a line to the known points. In **Exhibit 6-1**, for example, we use three known data points (an increased number of known data points should be used to develop a more reliable graph). The known data points, represented by solid points, are as follows:

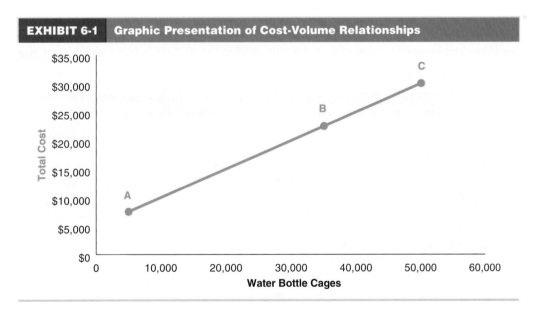

EXHIBIT 6-1   Graphic Presentation of Cost-Volume Relationships

By connecting the known data points with a straight line, we can estimate the costs associated with other volume levels. For example, as illustrated in **Exhibit 6-2**, the open points indicate that for volumes of 22,500, 42,500, and 59,000 units, the related costs would be $16,250, $26,250, and $34,500, respectively. We discuss important limitations to using the cost-volume relationship to estimate costs later in the chapter.

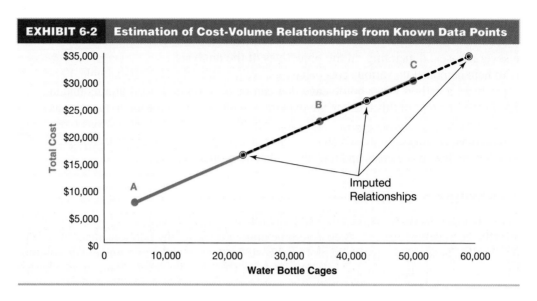

EXHIBIT 6-2 | **Estimation of Cost-Volume Relationships from Known Data Points**

Classifications of Cost Behavior Patterns

To better analyze cost behavior patterns, we typically classify costs (based on the definitions discussed in Chapter 2) as *variable, fixed,* or *mixed.*

Hint: The variable cost per unit is the slope of the line, commonly referred to as "rise over run."

Total variable costs change proportionately with changes in the volume of activity. For example, the cost of each water bottle cage is a variable cost in producing either a road or mountain bike. **Exhibit 6-3** is a typical variable cost graph. As illustrated here, a purely variable cost pattern always passes through the origin, because zero cost is associated with zero volume. Also, because variable costs respond in direct proportion to changes in volume, a variable cost line always slopes upward to the right. The steepness of the slope depends on the amount of cost associated with each unit of volume—the greater the unit cost, the steeper the slope. Assume that the variable cost associated with each water bottle cage is $0.50 per unit. **Exhibit 6-3** shows that if Fezzari produces 20,000 bikes, it will spend a total of $10,000 on water bottle cages for those bikes. Additionally, if Fezzari doubles its production to 40,000 bikes, the cost of water bottle cages also doubles to $20,000.

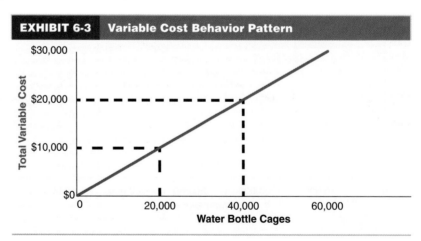

EXHIBIT 6-3 | **Variable Cost Behavior Pattern**

Fixed costs do not change when the volume of activity changes. Depreciation on manufacturing machinery is an example of a fixed cost.

Because fixed costs do not respond to changes in volume, they are represented by horizontal lines on a cost-volume graph. In **Exhibit 6-4**, fixed costs are $5,000 regardless of the volume level considered. Note in **Exhibit 6-4** that whether Fezzari uses 0, 20,000, or 40,000 water bottle cages in the production of bikes, total fixed costs remain $5,000.

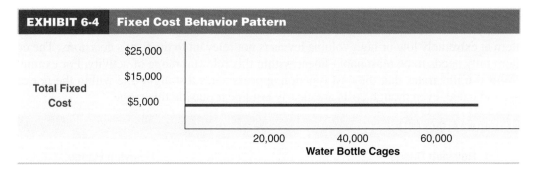

EXHIBIT 6-4   Fixed Cost Behavior Pattern

Total Fixed Cost — $25,000 / $15,000 / $5,000

Water Bottle Cages — 20,000 / 40,000 / 60,000

Mixed costs—sometimes called *semi-variable costs*—can be described as having both fixed and variable components. Mixed costs respond to volume changes but less than proportionately. For example, assume that Fezzari's process for installing a water bottle cage on each bike manufactured uses the labor of an employee. The employee is paid a fixed monthly salary, but is also paid a monthly bonus for each water bottle cage installed beyond some base level (e.g., a monthly base salary of $1,500 for the first 500 water bottle cages installed but an additional $5 for every water bottle cage installed beyond 500). Because the cost of installing a water bottle cage is composed of both a fixed and variable component, the cost would be considered a mixed cost.

Hint: The fixed portion of a mixed service cost represents the basic charge for a service. The variable portion represents the charge for the use of the service.

A mixed cost is a single cost containing both a fixed and variable component. For analysis and planning purposes, mixed costs are typically broken down into their fixed and variable components. Total costs are then the sum of all of a company's fixed and variable costs over a period of time. As shown in **Exhibit 6-5**, total costs are composed of both fixed and variable costs.

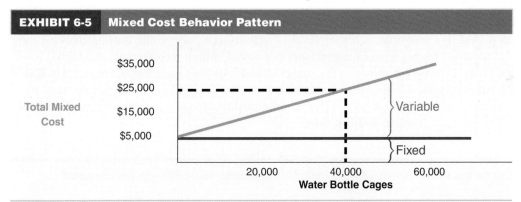

EXHIBIT 6-5   Mixed Cost Behavior Pattern

Total Mixed Cost — $35,000 / $25,000 / $15,000 / $5,000

Variable

Fixed

Water Bottle Cages — 20,000 / 40,000 / 60,000

Using the cost assumptions in **Exhibit 6.5**, what are the total costs Fezzari will incur to mount water bottle cages on 40,000 bikes?

YOUR TURN! 6.1

The solution is on page 6-51.

GuidedExample

MBC

RELEVANT RANGE

The cost behavior illustrations provided thus far are oversimplified because they portray linear cost behavior over the entire range of possible activity. Actually, plotting costs against volume may not always produce a single straight line. For example, certain costs may increase abruptly at intervals in a "step" pattern. Others may exhibit a curvilinear pattern when plotted over a wide range of activity. We present examples graphically of these cost patterns in **Exhibit 6-6**.

LO2   Define the concept of *relevant range*.

eLecture

MBC

The **relevant range** is the range of activity over which the behavior of a cost acts consistently. Clearly, an assumption of linear costs over the entire scale on either axis in these two cases causes some degree of error. The significance of this error is often minimized by the fact that many of the firm's decisions involve relatively small changes in volume. The actual cost pattern at extremely low or high volume levels is not relevant to the firm's decisions. The cost pattern only needs to be reasonably linear within this relevant range of activity. For example, **Exhibit 6-6** illustrates that the cost function approximates a straight line within the relevant range indicated, even though costs are clearly not linear outside this range.

EXHIBIT 6-6   Illustrations of Relevant Ranges

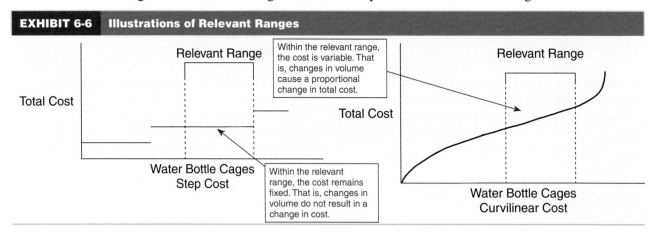

The cost-volume relationships for fixed cost, variable cost, and mixed cost typically remain the same for only one range of activity and for only one time period (frequently 1 year). Therefore, fixed, variable, and mixed costs are assumed to have a consistent relationship in terms of volume within this relevant range during the given time period. The cost relationships, however, may change when moving to a different range of activity or a different time period. For example, a higher level of activity (i.e., above the current relevant range) could require a higher level of supervisory personnel, which would result in a higher level of fixed salary expense (as shown in the step cost Water Bottle Cages Step Cost graph in **Exhibit 6-6**). Alternatively, a higher direct materials cost due to significantly higher demand for the direct materials could lead to a different relationship (as shown in the Water Bottle Cages Curvilinear Cost graph in **Exhibit 6-6**).

YOUR TURN! 6.2

The solution is on page 6-51.

Can the concept of relevant range be applied to mixed costs, fixed costs, and variable costs?

ANALYZING COST BEHAVIOR

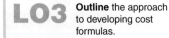 **Outline** the approach to developing cost formulas.

Managers often have detailed information about costs. Nevertheless, in order to perform CVP analysis to make better decisions, they need to break total costs into fixed and variable components. Although some costs are easy to classify as variable or fixed costs, it isn't always easy to split mixed (semi-variable) costs into variable and fixed components. We illustrate three approaches for better understanding the nature of a company's costs using (1) the scattergraph method, (2) the high-low method, and (3) the least squares regression method. We note at the outset that these methods differ both in their ease of application and in their accuracy. For example, the scattergraph method is fast and easy, but it isn't very accurate. On the other extreme, the least squares regression method may take a little more effort, but it is much more accurate. Managers need to weigh costs and benefits in determining which approach will be most useful.

Scattergraph Method

For purposes of cost analysis, a mixed cost is divided into its fixed and variable components. We accomplish this by using any one of several approaches that vary in their degree of sophistication. One simple method entails plotting the observed cost at several levels of volume on a graph. If cost behavior in actual situations were perfectly correlated, the observations (i.e., points) would form a straight line (see **Exhibit 6-1** for an example). More realistically, however, we expect only a discernible pattern.

Assume that Fezzari purchases its carbon water bottle cages from a company in Taiwan that produces similar products for companies around the world. **Exhibit 6-7** reports the supplier's manufacturing costs for various levels of production over the past eight months (sorted by production volume):

Cost	Water Bottle Cages
$27,000	44,000
$29,500	48,000
$30,000	51,000
$31,500	52,000
$32,500	54,000
$32,000	55,000
$36,000	63,000
$38,000	66,000

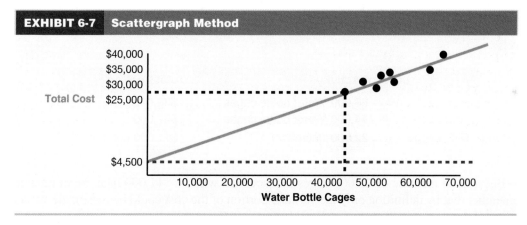

EXHIBIT 6-7   Scattergraph Method

HINT: Where the scattergraph plot line intersects the y-axis represents the fixed cost component (i.e., the cost level at an activity level of zero).

After plotting the actual costs relative to volume over the past eight months, the individual performing the analysis would simply draw a line that places approximately half of the dots above and half below the line. The line in **Exhibit 6-7** has been subjectively determined to approximate the pattern of data points on this scattergraph. Extending this line to the y-axis intercept indicates that $4,500 of total costs are fixed costs. To determine the approximate formula for the total cost line at a volume level of 44,000 water bottle cages, we subtract the $4,500 in fixed costs from the approximate total cost of $27,000 at 44,000 water bottle cages to get total variable costs of $22,500. Therefore, the variable cost per water bottle cage is $22,500/44,000 cages, or approximately $0.51 per water bottle cage. In summary, we describe the mixed cost as $4,500 in fixed costs plus variable costs of $0.51 per water bottle cage and quantify the mixed cost using the following cost formula:

Total cost = $4,500 + ($0.51 × number of water bottle cages)

High-Low Method

When too few cost observations are available to plot a graph, or when the analyst wishes to avoid visually fitting a subjective line to the data points, the high-low method can be used to approximate the position and slope of the cost line. This relatively simple method compares costs at the highest and lowest levels of activity for which representative cost data are available. The line is drawn between the highest- and lowest-volume data points, as shown in **Exhibit 6-8**. The variable cost per activity unit (here, per water bottle cage) is determined by dividing the difference in costs at these two levels by the difference in activity. The fixed element of cost is then isolated by multiplying the variable cost per unit by either the top or bottom level of activity, and then subtracting the resulting product from the total cost at the selected activity level.

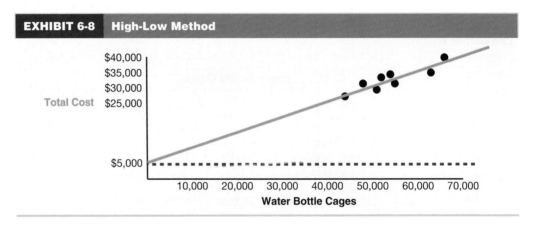

EXHIBIT 6-8   High-Low Method

Using the same data from the prior example, the lowest and highest levels of activity are 44,000 and 66,000 cages, respectively, and the following are the total costs for these two levels:

	Level of Activity		Total Cost
High	66,000	Water bottle cages	$38,000
Low.	44,000	Water bottle cages	$27,000
Difference	22,000	(increase)	$11,000 (increase)

Because an increase of 22,000 cages is associated with an $11,000 increase in total cost (remember that by definition only the variable portion of the cost could increase), the variable portion of the total mixed cost must be $11,000/22,000 water bottle cages, or $0.50 per water bottle cage. Subtracting the total variable portion from the total mixed cost at the high- and low-activity levels gives us the fixed portion of total cost as follows:

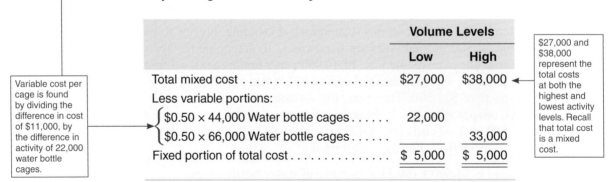

	Volume Levels	
	Low	High
Total mixed cost	$27,000	$38,000
Less variable portions:		
$0.50 × 44,000 Water bottle cages	22,000	
$0.50 × 66,000 Water bottle cages		33,000
Fixed portion of total cost	$ 5,000	$ 5,000

Variable cost per cage is found by dividing the difference in cost of $11,000, by the difference in activity of 22,000 water bottle cages.

$27,000 and $38,000 represent the total costs at both the highest and lowest activity levels. Recall that total cost is a mixed cost.

The high-low analysis tells us that any volume level has $5,000 of fixed cost plus a variable portion of $0.50 per water bottle cage, which can be formulated as follows:

Total cost = $5,000 + ($0.50 × water bottle cages)

In other words, we can now easily compute the total cost for varying levels of production. However, if either the high or low value used in this method is not representative of the actual cost behavior (i.e., the value is an outlier), the resulting cost formula lacks precision.

Least Squares Regression Method

The most accurate method of fitting a line to the cost data points is the least squares regression method, or regression analysis. The least squares regression method is a statistical tool that uses all the data points to separate a mixed cost into its variable and fixed components. A regression line is fitted to the data points so that the distance from each point to the line is minimized for all points. Although regression analysis can be relatively challenging to do by hand, it is a very simple task to complete using Microsoft Excel. Using the same data used for the scattergraph and high-low methods, **Exhibit 6-9** illustrates the regression analysis output provided by Microsoft Excel.

In an Excel spreadsheet, type in your data as pictured in the table above **Exhibit 6-7**. Put the volume data in one column and the associated cost data in the adjacent column. Click on the "Data" tab on the menu bar. Next, click on "Data Analysis" (if you do not see the Data Analysis option, it will need to be added, see HINT in the margin). From the list of data analysis tools, select "Regression," then "OK." Follow the three instructions on the screen:

i. Highlight (or type in) the *y*-axis data range (this is your cost data).

ii. Highlight (or type in) the *x*-axis data (this is your volume data).

iii. Click "OK."

Excel provides the output shown in **Exhibit 6-9**.

HINT: If you don't see "Data Analysis" in your Excel menu bar, follow these directions for add-ins:

i. Click on the "File" tab on the menu bar. Then select "Options" on the left-hand side of the screen.

ii. Click "Add-ins."

iii. In the "Manage" selection box at the bottom of the screen, select "Excel Add-ins" and click "GO."

iv. In the "Add-ins available" box, select the "Analysis Toolpak" check box, and then click "OK."

v. If asked, click "Yes" to install.

vi. Excel may need to be closed and relaunched for the Analysis Toolpak to become active.

EXHIBIT 6-9	Least Squares Regression Excel Output					
	A	B	C	D	E	F	G

	A	B	C	D	E	F	G
1	SUMMARY OUTPUT						
2							
3	*Regression Statistics*						
4	Multiple R	0.99228					
5	**R Square**	**0.98461**					
6	Adjusted R Square	0.98205					
7	Standard Error	474.33286					
8	Observations	8					
9							
10	ANOVA						
11		*df*	*SS*	*MS*	*F*	*Significance F*	
12	Regression	1	86368800.017	86368800.017	383.8755558	1.14564E-06	
13	Residual	6	1349949.983	224991.664			
14	Total	7	87718750				
15							
16		**Coefficients**	**Standard Error**	**t Stat**	**P-value**	**Lower 95%**	**Upper 95%**
17	**Intercept**	**6082.86**	1336.546	4.551	0.004	2812.452	9353.270
18	**Water Bottle Cages**	**0.48**	0.024	19.593	0.000	0.420	0.540

The intercept represents the total fixed cost component of the mixed cost.

The X-variable, Water Bottle Cages, represents the variable cost per water bottle cage component of the mixed cost.

Although Exhibit 6.9 may seem overwhelming, only three figures from the Microsoft Excel output are needed to develop and evaluate the cost formula estimated by the least squares regression method:

1. The coefficient for "Intercept" (Y-intercept) represents fixed costs of $6,082.86.

2. The coefficient for "Water Bottle Cages" (X-variable) is the slope of the line and represents variable costs per unit of $0.48 per cage.

3. The R-Square value measures how well the least square line fits the data points = 0.985 (rounded).

The resulting cost equation would be written as:

Total cost = $6,082.86 + ($0.48 × number of water bottle cages produced)

Further explanation of these three figures provides valuable insight into the cost formula.

■ First, the "Intercept" coefficient represents where the mixed cost line intercepts the *y*-axis. This intercept is the fixed cost component of the mixed cost. Thus, the fixed cost component of the mixed cost is approximately $6,083. Note that this amount is different than the $5,000 we found using the high-low method and $4,500 we approximated using the scattergraph method. As opposed to the high-low method, which only uses two data points, regression analysis uses every data point to fit the line. Additionally, instead of subjectively fitting a line using the scattergraph method, regression analysis mathematically minimizes the distances of each point from the line to calculate the "line of best fit."

■ Second, the "Water Bottle Cages" coefficient is the slope of the line and represents the variable cost per unit. Thus, the manufacturer incurs $0.48 in variable costs on each water bottle cage that it installs. This is slightly lower than the $0.50 per water bottle cage that we calculated using the high-low method.

■ Last, the R-Square value is a statistic that can range in value from zero to one, and is often referred to as a "goodness of fit" measure. The R-Square measures how well the *x*-values predict the *y*-values. That is, how well do the number of water bottle cages predict total costs? If the *x*-values perfectly predict the *y*-values, then the R-Square value would be one. In our case, the number of water bottle cages explains approximately 98.5% of the total cost, which is a very strong relationship. An R-Square over 0.80 generally means that the cost equation provided by the regression analysis can reliably predict costs within the relevant range.

Looking back, we can see how each method arrives at a somewhat different result:

Scattergraph equation: **Total cost = $4,500 + ($0.51 × water bottle cages)**
High-low equation: **Total cost = $5,000 + ($0.50 × water bottle cages)**
Least squares regression equation: **Total cost = $6,083 + ($0.48 × water bottle cages)**

Although the scattergraph and high-low methods are the easiest to implement, they are also less accurate. They work well for quick estimates. However, with the availability of desktop computers and programs that can compute least squares regressions, and given the limitations of the scattergraph and high-low methods, managers generally prefer to use the least squares regression method to estimate the fixed and variable portions of a mixed cost.

Analyzing Costs in Practice

SERVICE AND MERCHANDISING

How might we use this understanding of cost behavior as business managers? The budget for a business, which is discussed in detail in Chapter 9, is a financial plan that reflects anticipated or planned amounts of items such as revenue, costs, cash balances, and net income. Underlying most aspects of budgeting is some assumed number of units or dollars of sales, as well as an analysis of the total cost incurred for that level of operation.

For example, assume that management is preparing the budget for the next fiscal year. Because of uncertainty regarding the continued economic recovery from a recent recession, management wants to prepare a budget that will enable it to quickly determine expected costs if they vary significantly from anticipated levels. Based on the previous year, total fixed costs are $2.0 billion, mixed costs have a fixed portion of $250 million and a variable portion of $0.50 per Disney+ subscriber, and variable costs are $3.50 per Disney+ subscriber. The formula for budgeting the total cost is as follows:

Total cost = Total fixed cost + (Variable cost per subscriber × # of subscribers)
Total cost = $2.25 billion fixed cost + ($0.40 Variable cost × # of subscribers)

By using this formula, Disney+ management can forecast costs at different levels of activity. **Exhibit 6-10** illustrates how each type of cost behavior pattern is considered in the formula.

EXHIBIT 6-10	Disney+ Cost Factors Example						
Type of Cost	**Total Cost (in millions)**		**Total Fixed Cost (in millions)**		**Variable Cost per Subscriber**	×	**Number of Subscribers (in millions)**
Variable Costs	$ 105	=	$ —	+	$3.50	×	30
Mixed Costs:							
Variable Portion. . . .	15	=	—	+	0.50	×	30
Fixed Portion.	250	=	250	+	0	×	30
Fixed Costs.	2,000	=	2,000	+	0	×	30
Total cost.	**$2,370**	=	**$2,250**	+	**$4.00**	×	**30**

Notice in **Exhibit 6-10** that by combining the various cost factors into the aggregate formula, Disney+ management can determine expected costs not only at the 30 million subscribers level but also at other levels simply by inserting the appropriate volume figure in the final formula. For example, total budgeted cost at 75 million subscribers is $2.55 billion ($2.25 billion + [$4.00 × 75 million subscribers]) and at 100 million subscribers, the total budgeted cost is $2.65 billion ($2.25 billion + [$4.00 × 100 million subscribers]).

A word of caution is appropriate here. Because the cost formula relies so heavily on cost analysis, all the limitations of cost analysis (assumed linearity, relevant ranges, and so on) apply. Also, categorizing many costs into fixed and variable components is often quite complex and imprecise. All these limitations to some degree affect the potential usefulness of managerial cost analysis. It is important to note that these models provide data that can be used to help managers make decisions. However, managers should not blindly follow the outputs from their models. Managers ultimately need to evaluate all relevant information to make sound decisions. In some cases, the simple analytical approach presented here is sufficient, but it cannot be followed blindly.

Concept →	Method →	Assessment	TAKEAWAY 6.1
Can a firm determine the variable and fixed components of a mixed cost?	Three different techniques are used to determine the variable and fixed elements of mixed costs: • Scattergraph method • High-low method • Least squares regression method	Each method provides an estimated cost function formula with the variable cost per unit and total fixed cost. Both the scattergraph and high-low methods rely on just two observations to estimate the cost function. Least square regression analysis uses all available data and does not rely on subjective judgment to draw a cost line.	

YOUR TURN! 6.3
The solution is on page 6-51.

Given the following cost and volume levels, calculate the variable cost per unit and fixed cost within this relevant range using

a. the high-low method and
b. least squares regression method.

MBC

Cost	Volume	Cost	Volume
$15,000	5,000 units	$24,500	9,750 units
$13,000	4,000 units	$18,000	6,500 units
$19,300	7,150 units	$21,000	8,000 units

COST-VOLUME-PROFIT (CVP) ANALYSIS

LO4 **Present** a discussion of and a formula for calculating the break-even point.

eLecture
MBC

Break-Even Analysis

Management frequently wants to know the sales level (in dollars), or the number of units that must be sold, in order to cover its costs. The level at which total revenues equal total costs is called the **break-even point**. The break-even point can be expressed in dollars or in units sold. As an example, we illustrate several important calculations for one of Fezzari's medium-range road bikes, the Foré CR1, using the condensed income statement data shown in **Exhibit 6-11**.

EXHIBIT 6-11 **Fezzari Foré CR1 Operating Income**		
Sales (3,000 units @ $1,500)		$4,500,000
Costs:		
Variable cost (3,000 units @ $1,138)	$3,414,000	
Fixed cost	595,000	
Total cost.		$4,009,000
Net operating income		$ 491,000

Any mixed costs are divided into their fixed or variable component.

Revenue   Cost

This information assumes that all mixed costs have been accurately divided into their fixed and variable components and combined with other fixed and variable costs. We now examine some of the uses of this information.

The Cost-Volume-Profit Chart

To prepare a cost-volume-profit (CVP) chart for the Foré CR1, we use the same basic graph employed previously to explain and portray cost behavior patterns. In **Exhibit 6-12** the vertical axis measures both total revenues and total costs. As in previous exhibits, volume is measured along the horizontal axis. In this Fezzari product line, the activity basis is the number of Foré CR1s manufactured and sold. Total revenues and total costs are measured in thousands of dollars along the vertical axis.

With zero revenue for zero units sold, the graph of total revenues always passes through the origin. We draw the total revenue line by connecting the origin with any other point that represents total revenue for some volume amount. For Fezzari's CR1, total revenue for 3,000 units is $4,500,000, point **A** in **Exhibit 6-12**. To construct the total revenue line, we simply draw a straight line from the origin to **A** and extend it beyond **A**.

We now construct the total cost line in the same manner. With fixed costs of $595,000, the total cost line must intersect the vertical axis at the fixed costs level, $595,000. To produce 3,000 bicycles, Fezzari incurs total costs of $4,009,000. Given this information, we can plot point **B** and draw the total cost line connecting the intersection of the fixed cost line and the vertical axis with **B** as shown in **Exhibit 6-12**. After constructing the total cost line, its intersection with the total revenue line marks the break-even point.

Extending the dashed horizontal and vertical lines from the break-even point, we find that Fezzari's break-even point can be described as either (1) 1,644 units of production, or (2) $2,466,000 of total sales revenue. (We explain the calculation of these numbers next.) Note that all levels of sales below the break-even point indicate a loss, and levels of sales above the break-even point result in a profit. In other words, Fezzari earns a profit from its CR1 product line when the total revenue line is above the total cost line, and it incurs a loss when the reverse is true. **Exhibit 6-12** indicates the profit and loss areas. The amount of profit or loss at any volume level is determined by measuring the vertical distance between the total cost and total revenue lines. For example, the difference between points **A** and **B** indicates the profit of $491,000 for selling 3,000 CR1 road bikes.

EXHIBIT 6-12   Fezzari Foré CR1 Cost-Volume-Profit Chart

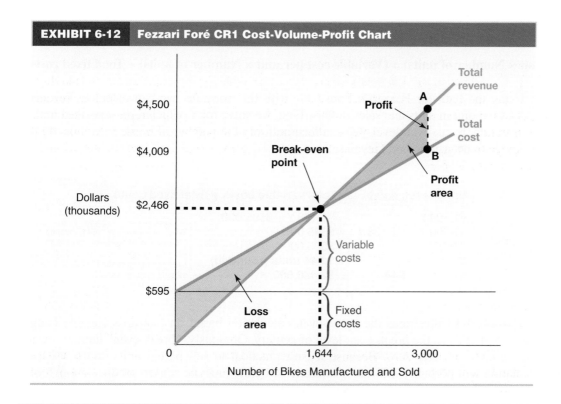

The Basic Assumptions of Break-Even Analysis

In our construction of a break-even chart, we assumed linear relationships over a wide range of activity. This approach implies the following:

1. Total fixed cost and total variable cost per unit are constant over the entire range of analysis.

2. Selling price per unit remains the same regardless of the volume of sales.

3. When more than one product is involved and sales volume varies, each product's percentage of total sales (i.e., the sales mix) does not change.

Even though these assumptions somewhat limit the usefulness of break-even analysis, it is still a convenient method of measuring the effect of changes in sales, costs, volumes, and profits.

Break-Even Formula

The following formula reflects the basic relationship between the break-even point and costs; the break-even point is that point at which total revenue equals total cost:

Break-even sales = Total variable costs + Total fixed costs

Break-even sales and total variable costs can be expressed as follows:

(Selling price per unit × Number of units) = (Variable cost per unit × Number of units) + Total fixed costs

Using the data for Fezzari's Foré CR1 with this formula, we can calculate Fezzari's break-even point in units and sales dollars. First, we solve for Y, which represents the number of units at the break-even level. We can then multiply the number of break-even units by the sales price to determine break-even sales.

Hint: When total sales are approximately $2,466,000, Fezzari is generating just enough sales dollars to cover its variable and fixed operating costs. Therefore, operating income will be very close to $0.

Break-even sales	= Total variable costs + Total fixed costs
$1,500 Y	= $1,138 Y + $595,000
$1,500 Y – $1,138 Y	= $595,000
$362 Y	= $595,000
Y	= **1,644 units (rounded)**
$1,500 × 1,644	= **$2,466,000** ◄

> When unit sales are 1,644, revenue equals $2,466,000. At this level, sales dollars are just enough to cover all variable and fixed operating costs. Therefore, operating income approximates $0.

Exhibit 6-13 illustrates the break-even calculation based on Fezzari's flexible budget using 1,644 units as the break-even level of activity. Obviously, "break-even" literally means a net profit of exactly zero. Because it isn't practical to sell partial units, the break-even calculation will normally indicate how many full units must be sold to produce enough of a contribution margin to cover fixed costs. In this example, 1,644 CR1 road bikes sold enable the company to "break-even," with $128 left over, whereas selling 1,643 units would have resulted in a small loss. Hence, we round to the number of complete units that enable the company to just exceed the zero-profit threshold.

EXHIBIT 6-13	Fezzari Performance Bicycles	
	A	B
1	Sales (1,644 units @ $1,500)	$2,466,000 ◄
2	Variable cost (1,644 units @ $1,138)	1,870,872
3	Contribution margin	$ 595,128
4	Fixed cost	595,000
5	Net operating income	$ 128

YOUR TURN! 6.4	Sam runs his own sandwich truck on the U of C campus. The monthly cost of the truck and necessary campus permit is $595. Sam spends $2.10 on each sandwich sold, including all of the ingredients, condiments, and paper products. He sells each sandwich for $3.50.
The solution is on page 6-51.	

a. How many sandwiches does Sam have to sell each month to break even?
b. Predict operating income for a month in which Sam sell 1,200 sandwiches.

LO5 Define *contribution margin* and *contribution margin ratio* and **present** alternate break-even formulas and examples of their application.

Contribution Margin Analysis

Because total variable costs change proportionately with changes in total revenue, each time additional revenue is generated, additional variable costs are also generated. The difference between the revenue generated and the variable costs generated is called the **contribution margin**. The restructured **variable**

operating income statement for Fezzari's CR1 shown in **Exhibit 6-14** illustrates the importance of contribution margin.

EXHIBIT 6-14	Fezzari Foré CR1 Operating Income	
	A	B
1	Sales (3,000 units @ $1,500)	$4,500,000
2	Variable cost (3,000 units @ $1,138)	3,414,000
3	**Contribution margin**	**$1,086,000** ◄
4	Fixed cost	595,000
5	Net operating income	$ 491,000

The contribution margin tells us how much money is left over after subtracting out variable costs.

The contribution margin of $1,086,000 "contributes" to covering fixed costs of $595,000 and earning operating income of $491,000.

When using the variable format for the income statement, we first deduct all variable costs from sales to calculate the contribution margin. We then deduct fixed costs from the contribution margin to calculate operating income. Thus, contribution margin can be viewed as a measure of what is left over after covering variable costs to go toward covering fixed costs and generating profits. At 3,000 units, the total contribution margin is $1,086,000. The contribution margin per unit is calculated as the selling price per unit minus the variable cost per unit. In the Fezzari CR1 example, the contribution margin per unit of $362 would be calculated as the selling price per unit of $1,500 minus the $1,138 variable cost per unit. The contribution margin per unit means that for each additional CR1 sold beyond the break-even point, $362 of additional contribution margin is generated to help produce additional profit.

Contribution Margin Ratio

A related concept often used in break-even analysis is the **contribution margin ratio**, which is the ratio of the contribution margin to sales. The formula to calculate the contribution margin ratio can use either *total* amounts:

$$\text{Contribution margin ratio} = \frac{\text{Contribution margin}}{\text{Sales}}$$

or *per-unit* amounts:

$$\text{Contribution margin ratio} = \frac{\text{Unit contribution margin}}{\text{Unit sales price}}$$

In the Fezzari CR1 example:

$$\text{Contribution margin ratio} = \frac{\$1,086,000}{\$4,500,000} = 0.24 \text{ (rounded)}$$

or

$$\text{Contribution margin ratio} = \frac{\$362}{\$1,500} = 0.24 \text{ (rounded)}$$

The contribution margin ratio is easier to work with than the unit contribution margin if a company has more than one product line. The contribution margin ratio allows comparisons among product lines, which we illustrate later in the chapter.

Hint: The contribution margin is defined as the amount of sales revenue after variable expenses are deducted that is used to cover fixed costs and provide a profit. At the break-even point, the contribution margin equals fixed costs (i.e., profit is zero).

Alternative Break-Even Formulas

Two alternative break-even formulas[4] can be directly derived from our previous break-even formula. You can calculate the break-even point either in *units:*

$$\text{Break-even units} = \frac{\text{Total fixed cost}}{\text{Unit contribution margin}}$$

or in *sales dollars:*

$$\text{Break-even sales dollars} = \frac{\text{Total fixed cost}}{\text{Contribution margin ratio}}$$

In the Fezzari CR1 example, we can calculate the break-even point using these two formulas. Using the first formula (expressed in units):

$$\text{Break-even units} = \frac{\$595,000}{\$362} = 1,644 \text{ units}$$

Using the second formula (expressed in sales dollars):

$$\text{Break-even sales} = \frac{\$595,000}{0.24} = \$2,479,167^{5}$$

The results obtained from any of the break-even formulas can be verified by placing the amounts in an income statement format and verifying that the net income equals zero.

TAKEAWAY 6.2	**Concept** ➜	**Method** ➜	**Assessment**
	Can management determine how many units or how many sales dollars must be generated to break even?	• Break-even point in units = Total fixed costs/Unit contribution margin • Break-even point in sales dollars = Total fixed costs/Contribution margin ratio	Knowing the point at which unit sales or sales dollars results in zero income provides managers valuable information. For example, if the break-even point in units is higher than the projected demand, managers could either increase the sales price or reduce variable costs per unit, or both. This would increase the contribution margin and decrease the break-even point in units.

YOUR TURN! 6.5

The solution is on page 6-51.

MBC

Sam runs his own sandwich truck on the U of C campus. The monthly cost of the truck and necessary campus permit is $595. Sam's contribution margin per unit is $1.40, and the contribution margin ratio is 40%.

a. How many sandwiches does Sam have to sell each month to break even?
b. Predict the total variable costs for a month in which Sam sell 1,400 sandwiches.

_____

[4] These formulas can be derived from the general break-even formula provided previously:

Break-even sales = Total variable cost + Total fixed cost

(Selling price per unit × Number of units) = (Variable cost per unit × Number of units) + Total fixed costs

(Selling price per unit × Number of units) – (Variable cost per unit × Number of units) = Total fixed costs

(Selling price per unit – Variable cost per unit) × Number of units = Total fixed costs

(Contribution margin per unit) × Number of units = Total fixed costs

$$\text{Number of units} = \frac{\text{Total fixed costs}}{\text{Contribution margin per unit}}$$

The second formula can be derived simply by multiplying both sides of this equation by the selling price per unit.

[5] This solution differs from the sales revenue computed previously because the contribution margin used has been rounded to the nearest hundredth.

PLANNING FOR PROFIT

Desired Profit

Target Profits without Taxes

With an understanding of the cost-volume-profit relationship, business managers can develop plans for desired levels of profit. Rather than making the calculations for breakeven, where profit is equal to zero, they use formulas that include a *desired profit*. These formulas are similar to the previous CVP break-even formula and take into consideration the additional desired net income (or profit):

LO6 **Discuss** approaches to planning net income using cost-volume-profit analyses.

eLecture

MBC

$$\textbf{Desired sales = Total variable costs + Total fixed costs + Desired profit}\quad{}^{6}$$

Recall that the definition of contribution margin is what is left over from sales, after covering variable costs, to cover fixed costs and generate profits. Using the contribution margin approach, we can then rearrange our CVP formula to solve for the level of units and sales to achieve our desired net income:

A.K.A. The desired profit is also referred to as *desired net income*. These terms are also referred to as *target profit* or *target income*.

$$\textbf{Desired units} = \frac{\textbf{Total fixed costs + Desired net income}}{\textbf{Unit contribution margin}}$$

And

$$\textbf{Desired sales} = \frac{\textbf{Total fixed costs + Desired net income}}{\textbf{Contribution margin ratio}}$$

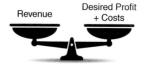
Revenue   Desired Profit + Costs

Assume that Fezzari wants to attain a net income of $1,000,000 before income tax on its CR1 line. Using these formulas, we can determine the level of output in sales dollars or units.
Using the CVP equation:

$$\$1,500 \times Y = \$1,138Y + \$595,000 + \$1,000,000$$
$$\$1,500Y - \$1,138Y = \$1,595,000$$
$$\$362Y = \$1,595,000$$
$$Y = 4,406 \text{ units}$$
$$4,406 \text{ units} \times \$1,500 = \$6,609,000$$

Using the contribution margin approach:

$$\textbf{Desired units} = \frac{\$595,000 + \$1,000,000}{\$362}$$
$$= 4,406 \text{ units}$$

$$\textbf{Desired sales} = \frac{\$595,000 + \$1,000,000}{0.24}$$
$$= \$6,645,833\,{}^{7}$$

---

[6] Note that the desired net income in these formulas is pre-tax net income. When taxes are applicable, managers need to adjust the formulas to account for taxes in order to determine a desired after-tax net income.

[7] This calculation differs from the sales revenue computed using the first formula because the contribution margin used has been rounded to the nearest hundredth.

Target Profits with Taxes

Fezzari's management might want to develop plans using net income (after tax) rather than net income before income taxes. In this case, net income (after tax) must be converted to net income before income tax so the formulas presented previously can be used:

$$\text{Net income before income tax} = \frac{\text{Net income}}{1 - \text{Income tax rate}}$$

Assume that Fezzari's management wants to attain an after-tax net income of $700,000 when the income tax rate is 30%. Net income before income tax can be calculated as follows:

$$\text{Net income before income tax} = \frac{\$700,000}{1 - 0.3} = \frac{\$700,000}{0.7} = \$1,000,000$$

A brief income statement verifies the calculations made in the preceding sections:

Sales (4,406 units × $1,500)	$6,609,000
Less: Variable cost (4,406 units × $1,138)	5,014,028
Contribution margin	$1,594,972
Less: Fixed cost	595,000
Net operating income	$ 999,972
Income tax ($999,972 × 0.30)	299,992
Net income	$ 699,980[8]

ACCOUNTING IN PRACTICE   CVP Disclosure

The Securities and Exchange Commission requires all publicly held companies to include a "management discussion and analysis (MD&A) of the results of operations" in quarterly and annual reports. This analysis may include cost-volume-profit data. For example, in Amazon's 2017 annual report, the MD&A section addresses several items that impact its target profitability—including variations in the sales mix of its products and services, increases in the cost of packing materials, shipping costs incurred, the rate of vendor returns, and its significant capital investments that result in future fixed costs. Management's focus on these items indicates extensive use of CVP analysis and its sensitivity to their impact on profitability.

TAKEAWAY 6.3	Concept ⟶	Method ⟶	Assessment
	Do income taxes impact the break-even and desired profit calculations?	Income taxes have no impact on the break-even calculations because at the break-even point operating income is equal to zero. Income taxes are only paid when operating income is greater than $0. Income taxes impact both the desired sales and the desired units calculations. The desired income figure must be converted to a pre-tax figure using the following formula: • Net income before income tax = Net income after income tax/(1 – income tax rate) • Once net income before income tax has been calculated, the formulas for desired sales and desired units can be used. • Desired units = (Total fixed costs + Desired net income before income tax)/Unit contribution margin • Desired sales = (Total fixed costs + Desired net income before income tax)/Contribution margin ratio	Income taxes are an important expense for all for-profit companies and the expense impacts the desired units and desired sales calculations. Regardless of the tax rate faced by a company, income taxes will increase the desired unit and desired sales figures.

---

[8] Difference from target net income after tax of $700,000 due to rounding.

Margin of Safety

The **margin of safety** is the amount by which the actual sales level of a company exceeds the break-even sales level. It represents the company's "breathing room" in which it will remain profitable. If sales decrease by more than the margin of safety, then the company will incur an operating loss. The formula for calculating the margin of safety follows:

$$\text{Margin of safety} = \text{Actual sales} - \text{Break-even sales}$$

In the Fezzari CR1 example, **Exhibit 6-13** indicates that Fezzari needs sales of $2,466,000 (i.e., 1,644 CR1s) to break even. Assume Fezzari achieves sales of $3,000,000 in a given year. Its margin of safety for that year would be calculated as:

$$\text{Margin of safety} = \$3,000,000 - \$2,466,000 = \$534,000$$

In other words, Fezzari could decrease sales by up to $534,000 and still achieve a profit.

Another way of looking at the "breathing room" beyond break-even sales is on a ratio (or percentage) basis, referred to as the margin-of-safety ratio. It is calculated as follows:

$$\text{Margin-of-safety ratio} = \frac{\text{Margin of safety}}{\text{Actual sales}}$$

For example, continuing the previous Fezzari example (and assuming sales of $3,000,000), the margin-of-safety ratio would be calculated as:

$$\text{Margin-of-safety ratio} = \frac{\$534,000}{\$3,000,000} = 17.8\%$$

In other words, Fezzari could decrease CR1 sales by up to 17.8% and still achieve a profit.

Operating Leverage

Apple's Disney + division and Fezzari have relatively low fixed costs. On the other hand, other companies or industries are characterized by relatively high fixed costs, including utilities (e.g., Pacific Gas and Electric Co. and Florida Power & Light) and auto manufacturers (e.g., General Motors Company and Toyota Motor Corporation). One measure of a firm's relative level of fixed costs is **operating leverage**. Operating leverage is computed as follows:

$$\text{Operating leverage} = \frac{\text{Contribution margin}}{\text{Net operating income}}$$

Note that the difference between the numerator (contribution margin) and the denominator (net operating income) is the amount of fixed costs (look back at the variable income statement in **Exhibit 6-14** to confirm this). Thus, this ratio is really a measure of a company's operating cost structure, or its level of fixed costs (relative to variable costs). If two companies have the same level of sales and costs, but the cost structure (i.e., the mix between variable and fixed costs) is different, the company with relatively higher fixed costs will have the higher operating leverage. At one extreme, a company that has no fixed costs (i.e., all costs are variable) will have an operating leverage of 1.0 because its contribution margin and net operating income will be the same. **Exhibit 6-15** illustrates graphically a company with an operating leverage of 1.0. Note that because there are no fixed costs, as long as the per-unit sales price of the product is greater than the cost of the product, each sale generates an operating profit equal to the unit contribution margin.

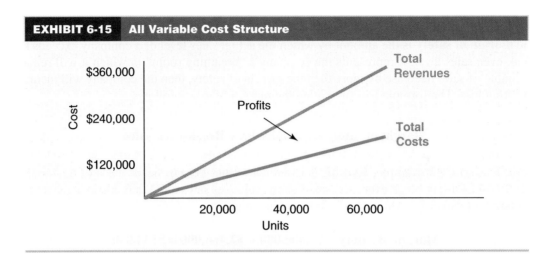

EXHIBIT 6-15   All Variable Cost Structure

The company illustrated in **Exhibit 6-15** sells its products for $6 per unit, and the variable costs to produce a unit of product amount is $2 per unit. Thus, the contribution margin per unit is $4 ($6 – $2 = $4). Because the company has no fixed costs, when it sells its first unit of product to a customer, it will generate $4 of operating profit. Each additional unit of product sold will likewise result in additional operating profits of $4 per unit.

Because a world without fixed costs isn't reasonable, knowing the operating leverage is important to help managers assess how their cost structure (i.e., their unique mix of variable and fixed costs) influences their break-even point. The higher a company's fixed costs, the more units it will need to sell in order to break even. Hence, a company struggling to break even would want to avoid fixed costs in order to lower its break-even point.

As a company's relative mix of costs shifts more toward fixed costs, its operating leverage increases, suggesting greater risk. **Exhibit 6-16** graphically illustrates a company with an operating leverage greater than 1.0 (i.e., with both fixed and variable costs). Assume the company has fixed costs of $120,000, variable costs of $2 per unit, and a selling price of $6 per unit.

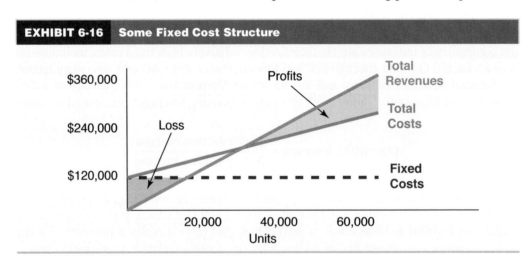

EXHIBIT 6-16   Some Fixed Cost Structure

Breakeven for this company would be computed as follows:

$$\text{Break-even units} = \frac{\text{Total fixed cost}}{\text{Unit contribution margin}}$$

$$\text{Break-even units} = \frac{\$120,000}{\$4/\text{unit}} = 30,000 \text{ units}$$

Note that because the company has $120,000 of fixed costs, it must sell 30,000 units before making a profit. What happens as a company's fixed costs increase? It will need to sell more units to break even. For example, if the company in this example were to increase its fixed costs to $160,000, its break-even point would shift up to 40,000 units. Because it would be harder for the company to break even with this higher level of fixed costs, its risk would increase. Operating leverage can be a useful metric to help managers assess the risk associated with their fixed costs.

An important thing to remember about operating leverage is that a firm's operating leverage changes with its level of output and sales. For example, assume that the company in **Exhibit 6-16** is operating at a level of sales above breakeven where it achieves a profit. Compare the company's performance if the company sells 50,000 units or 60,000 units; its operating income would be calculated as follows:

	Sales Volume	
	50,000	60,000
Sales ($6/unit)	$300,000	$360,000
Less: Variable cost ($2/unit)	(100,000)	(120,000)
Contribution margin	200,000	240,000
Less: Fixed cost	(120,000)	(120,000)
Net operating income	$ 80,000	$120,000

Operating leverage at the 50,000 level of sales would be 2.5, computed as follows:

$$\textbf{Operating leverage} = \frac{\textbf{Contribution margin}}{\textbf{Net operating income}}$$

$$= \frac{\$200,000}{\$80,000}$$

$$= 2.5$$

and operating leverage at the 60,000 level would change to 2.0:

$$\textbf{Operating leverage} = \frac{\textbf{Contribution margin}}{\textbf{Net operating income}}$$

$$= \frac{\$240,000}{\$120,000}$$

$$= 2.0$$

Thus, when fixed costs stay at a given level (e.g., at a level of $120,000), a corresponding higher level of sales results in a lower operating leverage ratio. Conversely, a corresponding lower level of sales results in a higher operating leverage ratio. So when sales are at 60,000 units or $360,000, the degree of operating leverage is 2.0, and when sales are lower, at a level of 50,000 units or $300,000, the degree of operating leverage is 2.5. The greater the degree of operating leverage, the more that changes in sales will affect operating income. The degree of operating leverage can be used to determine how a percentage change in the level of sales will impact net operating profit:

% Increase in operating income = % Increase in sales × Operating leverage

Fezzari's CR1 example illustrates this concept. Assume that Fezzari's management anticipates a 20% increase in sales in the coming year. What should the resulting operating income be? From **Exhibit 6-17**, we can calculate Fezzari's operating leverage as follows:

$$\text{Operating leverage} = \frac{\textbf{Contribution margin}}{\textbf{Net operating income}}$$

$$\text{Operating leverage} = \frac{\$1,086,000}{\$491,000} = 2.2118 \text{ (rounded)}$$

If sales increase by 20%, operating income should be $708,200, calculated as follows:

% Increase in operating income = % Increase in sales × Operating leverage

$$44.236\% = 20\% \times 2.2118$$

$$\$708,200^* = \$491,000 \times (1 + 0.44236)$$

* Difference due to rounding.

Exhibit 6-17 proves this calculation.

EXHIBIT 6-17	Fezzari Foré CR1 Operating Income Comparison		
	A	B	C	D
1			Sales Increase	
2	Sales (3,000 units @ $1,500)	$4,500,000	20%	$5,400,000
3	Variable cost (3,000 units @ $1,138)	3,414,000	20%	$4,096,800
4	Contribution margin	$1,086,000		$1,303,200
5	Fixed cost	595,000		595,000
6	Net operating income	$ 491,000		$ 708,200

Note that operating leverage for the CR1 product line is not a constant, but is computed for each level of sales. For example, Fezzari's new operating leverage (following the 20% increase in sales) would be:

$$\text{Operating leverage} = \frac{\$1,303,200}{\$708,200} = 1.8402 \text{ (rounded)}$$

ENVIRONMENTAL, SOCIAL, AND GOVERNANCE	**Break-even Analysis for Disposable Cups**

Sometimes, the socially responsible choice is not obvious. Consider a restaurant that wants to make the best environmental choice and must choose between using reusable or disposable cups. Many may think selecting reusable cups is the obvious choice. However, reusable cups require vastly more energy to produce, and they also require more energy for the cleaning process between uses. Based on a study done by chemistry professor, Martin Hocking, the break-even point for a ceramic cup versus a disposable foam cup is over a thousand uses.

Source: Hocking, Martin B. "Reusable and Disposable Cups: An Energy-Based Evaluation." *Environmental Management* 18(6), 1994, pp. 889–899.

Using Cost-Volume-Profit Relationships

Cost-volume-profit relationships can be used in a number of ways during planning and budgeting sessions to test possible courses of action. The following three independent situations, based on Fezzari's operating income presented in **Exhibit 6-11**, reveal ways that Fezzari might use cost-volume-profit relationships to make business decisions.

Situation 1

Assume that Fezzari's managers are considering reducing the average price of the CR1 (on a per-unit basis) from $1,500 to $1,300. *How would this change affect the break-even point in units?*

$$\text{Break-even units} = \frac{\text{Total fixed cost}}{\text{Unit contribution margin}}$$

$$= \frac{\$595,000}{(\$1,300 - \$1,138)}$$

$$= 3,673 \text{ units}$$

The $200 price decrease would cause the break-even point to increase from 1,644 units (previously calculated) to 3,673 units.

Situation 2

Assume that Fezzari's managers are considering an advertising campaign that would increase the CR1's fixed costs by $50,000 to $645,000 and allow a price increase from $1,500 to $1,600 per unit. *How would this change affect the break-even point in units* for the CR1 product line?

$$\text{Break-even units} = \frac{\text{Total fixed cost}}{\text{Unit contribution margin}}$$

$$= \frac{\$645,000}{(\$1,600 - \$1,138)}$$

$$= 1,396 \text{ units}$$

The $50,000 advertising campaign and the related $100 price increase would cause the CR1 break-even point to decrease from 1,644 units to 1,396 units.

Situation 3

Assume that Fezzari's managers are considering eliminating the sales commission program and increasing the sales force base salaries. This change would decrease the CR1 unit variable cost from $1,138 to $1,088 and would increase fixed costs from $595,000 to $695,000. Average unit sales price would remain at $1,500. If the company wants to achieve an after-tax net income for the CR1 product line of $700,000, and if the income tax rate is 30%, *what would the impact be on desired units sold of eliminating the sales commission program?*

$$\text{Desired units} = \frac{\text{Total fixed cost} + \text{Desired net income before income tax}}{\text{Unit contribution margin}}$$

With the current sales commissions program:

$$\text{Desired units} = \frac{\$595,000 + \dfrac{\$700,000}{(1 - 0.30)}}{\$1,500 - \$1,138} = 4,406 \text{ units}$$

Without the current sales commissions program:

$$\text{Desired units} = \frac{\$695,000 + \dfrac{\$700,000}{(1 - 0.30)}}{\$1,500 - \$1,088} = 4,114 \text{ units}$$

The elimination of the sales commission program would decrease the desired CR1 volume from 4,406 units to 4,114 units. As a result, Fezzari would be able to sell 292 fewer CR1s at the same price and still attain the same desired after-tax net income.

Break-Even Analysis and Multiple Products

As indicated previously, we must assume in break-even analysis that only one product is involved or that the product mix (i.e., the ratio of units of each product sold to the total units sold) is constant. Break-even sales can be computed for a sales mix of two or more products by calculating the weighted average unit contribution margin.

Assume that a company sells three units of product A for every unit of B (note that this information indicates that the sales mix is 75% A and 25% B) and has fixed costs of $88,000. Also assume the following relationships between selling price and variable costs:

	Product A	Product B
Unit selling price	$14.00	$7.00
Less: Unit variable cost.	8.00	3.00
Unit contribution margin	$ 6.00	$4.00

The weighted average unit contribution margin can be calculated as follows:

Product A: $6.00 × 0.75 =	$4.50
Product B: $4.00 × 0.25 =	1.00
Weighted average unit contribution margin	$5.50

The break-even volume can then be calculated:

$$\text{Break-even units} = \frac{\textbf{Total fixed cost}}{\textbf{Weighted average contribution margin}}$$

$$= \frac{\$88,000}{\$5.50}$$

$$= 16{,}000 \text{ Weighted average units}$$

The 16,000 weighted average units include a mix of units A and B, based on their relative sales mix. The exact mix and related contribution margin are calculated as illustrated in **Exhibit 6-18**.

EXHIBIT 6-18	Multiple Product Break-Even Analysis				
	A	B	C	D	E
1	Product	Product Mix	Units Sold	Unit Contribution Margin	Total Contribution Margin
2	A	0.75	12,000	$6.00	$72,000
3	B	0.25	4,000	$4.00	16,000
4	Total		16,000		$88,000

Recall that the sales mix was 75% of unit A and 25% of unit B.
16,000 × 75% = 12,000 units of A
16,000 × 25% = 4,000 units of B

These concepts could be applied to any product mix or number of products.

Cost-Volume-Profit Analysis for Retail Businesses

SERVICE AND MERCHANDISING

Most retailing industries have developed relationships between product costs and retail price that need to be maintained in order to be profitable. Each segment of each industry has its own ideal relationship. For example, a men's clothing store would typically have a lower ratio of retail price to product cost than a custom tailor, whereas a downhill ski shop would typically have a higher ratio than a general sports retail store. In this example, assume Joe's

Food Shack, located on a Southern California beach, wants
to maintain a retail price ratio of 2.5 times the cost of the
food used in each menu item.

Retail establishments also have varying staffing needs.
The number of employees on duty will change, for example,
depending on the time of day. For instance, assume Joe's
Food Shack has one cook and one cashier working from
11:00 A.M. to 2:00 P.M., two cooks and three cashiers working
from 2:00 P.M. to 5:00 P.M., and two cooks and two cashiers
working from 5:00 P.M. to 9:00 P.M. The number and type of
employees on duty must be predetermined. Therefore, the
cost to employ these servers and cooks is fixed over a given
shift. They are typically paid the same amount regardless of
how many meals are served. Customer tips (which are not
an expense of the company) would vary, depending in part on the number of meals served.

These concepts should be incorporated in cost-volume-profit analysis for a restaurant.
Assume Joe's Food Shack serves only three food choices: hamburgers, hot dogs, and nachos,
with food costs per item of $5.00, $4.00, and $3.00, respectively. Because Joe's is the only
establishment on the entire beach, Joe's can charge monopoly prices for its food items. Using
the 2.5 ratio, the related prices are $12.50, $10.00, and $7.50, respectively. If 20% of the
items sold are hamburgers, 50% are hot dogs, and 30% are nachos, then the average revenue
per food item sold would be $9.75 and the average food cost would be $3.90, as illustrated in
Exhibit 6-19.

EXHIBIT 6-19	Cost and Pricing Analysis for Joe's Food Shack				
	A	B	C	D	E	F
1	Food Type	Proportion	Cost per Unit	Weighted Average Cost	Price per Unit	Weighted Average Price
2	Hamburger	20%	$5.00	$1.00	$12.50	$2.50
3	Hot dog	50%	4.00	2.00	10.00	5.00
4	Nachos	30%	3.00	0.90	7.50	2.25
5	Total			$3.90		$9.75

The weighted average unit contribution margin, therefore, is $9.75 − $3.90 = $5.85.

If the total fixed costs, including personnel, are $64,350 for a typical 30-day month when
the restaurant is open every day for the scheduled hours, the break-even volume would be
calculated as follows:

$$\frac{\$64,350}{\$5.85} = 11,000 \text{ food items per month}$$

Thus, this sales mix is composed of 2,200 hamburgers (11,000 × 0.20), 5,500 hot dogs (11,000
× 0.50), and 3,300 nachos (11,000 × 0.30).

ACCOUNTING IN PRACTICE   **Management Perspective on Cost Analysis**

Managing costs is a prevailing concern for managers. The concepts introduced in this chapter underlie
most efforts to analyze and project cost in a variety of decision situations. In practice, because projections
of future costs are subject to many complicating factors, for most companies they are *estimates of probable costs* rather than precise determinations. Properly used—with full recognition of their limitations—cost
behavior analyses can be highly useful to management.

YOUR TURN! 6.6

The solution is on page 6-52.

GuidedExample

MBC

Hungry Hikers buys nutrition bars for $1.25 each and sells them for $5.00. Management budgets monthly fixed expenses of $12,675 for sales volumes between 0 and 10,000 bars.

Requirements:

1. Use the contribution margin ratio approach to compute monthly break-even sales in revenue (dollars).
2. Use the unit contribution margin approach to compute monthly break-even sales in units.
3. Compute the monthly sales level (in units) required to earn a pre-tax target operating profit of $15,000.
4. Assume Hungry Hikers wants to earn an after-tax monthly net income of $18,000 when the income tax rate is 25%. Compute the monthly sales level (in units) to acheive the after-tax net income target.
5. Assuming a no-tax environment, calculate the margin of safety in dollars at sales level of 7,400 units.

SERVICE INDUSTRY IN FOCUS

SERVICE AND MERCHANDISING

Environmental Business Consultants (EBC) has two offices, one in Northern California and one in Southern California. EBC provides three basic services to its clients: rate reviews, contract procurement and negotiations, and operational studies. EBC management wants to determine how many projects of each service would need to be performed in the current year to achieve a before-tax profit of $650,000. EBC managers have gathered the following information from the prior year for the analysis.

The proportion of projects done in each office was as follows:

	Northern California	Southern California
Rate reviews.	30%	50%
Contract procurements. . .	60%	30%
Operational studies.	10%	20%

The average contribution margin for each project type was as follows:

	Northern California	Southern California
Rate reviews.	$ 5,100	$24,124
Contract procurements. . .	28,000	37,000
Operational studies.	10,035	20,000

In the prior year, EBC budgeted fixed expenses to be $2,251,159 and $644,341 in the Northern and Southern California offices, respectively.

Required

1. How many projects of each type must EBC perform in the Northern California office if managers expect the office to generate $450,000 of the desired total income?

2. How many projects of each type must EBC perform in the Southern California office if managers expect the office to generate $200,000 of the desired total income?

Solution

1. The weighted average contribution margin for the Northern California office is:

$ 5,100 × 0.30 =	$ 1,530
$28,000 × 0.60 =	16,800
$10,035 × 0.10 =	1,004
Weighted average contribution margin	$19,334

The number of total projects needed is:

$$\text{Needed projects} = \frac{\$2,251,159 + \$450,000}{\$19,334}$$

$$= 140 \text{ projects (rounded)}$$

The number of projects by type is:

Rate reviews............	(140 × 0.30)	42
Contract procurements....	(140 × 0.60)	84
Operational studies.......	(140 × 0.10)	14

2. The weighted average contribution margin for the Southern California office is:

$24,124 × 0.50 =	$12,062
$37,000 × 0.30 =	11,100
$20,000 × 0.20 =	4,000
Weighted average contribution margin	$27,162

The number of total projects needed is:

$$\text{Needed projects} = \frac{\$644,341 + \$200,000}{\$27,162}$$

$$= 31 \text{ projects (rounded)}$$

The number of projects by type is:

Rate reviews............	(31 × 0.50)	16 (rounded)
Contract procurements....	(31 × 0.30)	9 (rounded)
Operational studies.......	(31 × 0.20)	6 (rounded)

DATA ANALYTICS   **Using Analytics to Improve Cash Flow Management**

Data Analytics

Disney+ may be the new kid in town with the bigger arsenal of big hits relative to Netflix, but Netflix's use of data analytics is keeping it ahead of the competition. Netflix uses predictive analytics to match the preferences of its customer with the shows it produces. Netflix's use of data analytics in its early years came about from necessity.

Netflix started as a DVD rent-by-mail website. The concept proved very popular, but that popularity caused a problem: Netflix did not have enough inventory of new releases to keep up with customer demand. Netflix solved this by developing algorithms, based on its members preferences, that deemphasized popular new releases. Netflix continues to use customer preference data to drive its decisions. It collects data on the summaries you have read, how long you surf through titles, what you watch, and whether you watch the entire show. Then, Netflix uses this data to keep you engaged by suggesting other offerings. It also uses preference data to develop new content.

COMPREHENSIVE PROBLEM

Maricopa Corporation has developed the budget for its next year of operations. The budget included the following:

GuidedExample
MBC

Sales of 100,000 units at $5	
Units sold will equal units produced	
Variable costs for 100,000 units:	
Direct materials..................	$125,000
Direct labor	100,000
Variable overhead	30,000
Selling and administrative expense....	45,000
Total fixed cost	120,000
Income tax rate of 30%	

Required

a. What is Maricopa's break-even point, in units and in dollars, for next year?

b. Demonstrate that the unit amount reconciles with the dollar amount.

c. What amount of sales revenue would Maricopa need to realize next year in order to generate a net income of $63,000 after tax?

d. Demonstrate the correctness of the calculations in requirement (c) by constructing an income statement.

Solution

a. Variable costs:

Direct materials.	$125,000
Direct labor.	100,000
Variable overhead.	30,000
Selling and administrative.	45,000
Total variable cost at 100,000 units. . . .	$300,000

$$\frac{\$300,000}{100,000 \text{ units}} = \$3 \text{ per unit}$$

$$\text{Unit contribution margin} = \$5 - \$3 = \$2$$

$$\text{Contribution margin ratio} = \frac{\$2}{\$5} = 0.4$$

$$\text{Break-even units} = \frac{\text{Total fixed cost}}{\text{Unit contribution margin}}$$
$$= \frac{\$120,000}{\$2}$$
$$= 60,000 \text{ units}$$

$$\text{Break-even sales} = \frac{\text{Total fixed cost}}{\text{Contribution margin ratio}}$$
$$= \frac{\$120,000}{0.4}$$
$$= \$300,000$$

b. 60,000 units × $5 unit selling price = $300,000

c.

$$\text{Desired sales} = \frac{\text{Total fixed cost} + \dfrac{\text{Net income}}{1 - \text{Income tax}}}{\text{Contribution margin ratio}}$$

$$= \frac{\$120,000 + \dfrac{\$63,000}{1 - 0.3}}{0.4}$$

$$= \$525,000$$

d.

Sales.	$525,000
Variable cost ([1 − 0.4] × $525,000)	315,000
Contribution margin	$210,000
Fixed cost.	120,000
Net income before income tax	$ 90,000
Income tax at 30%	27,000
Net income.	$ 63,000

SUMMARY OF LEARNING OBJECTIVES

Develop an understanding of how specific types of costs change in response to volume changes. (p. 6-3)   **LO1**

- For meaningful managerial analysis, costs must be related to some measure of business activity or cost driver. A critical aspect is that the activity measure used must have a logical causal relation with costs, and the quantity of the activity must be highly correlated with the level of costs.

- One of the most useful tools for analyzing the relationship between changes in cost and volume is the *cost-volume graph*. Such graphs typically plot total costs on the vertical axis and either volume or activity level on the horizontal axis. Cost-volume graphs are particularly valuable when available cost-volume data are plotted on the same graph and other cost-volume relationships are estimated by fitting a line to the known points.

- The behavior of total cost in response to volume changes is divided into three basic categories within a relevant range:
  - Variable, which responds proportionately, with zero cost at zero volume
  - Fixed, which is constant
  - Mixed, which responds but less than proportionately, due to the fixed component

- Total cost for most entities is best represented by the mixed cost pattern.

Define the concept of *relevant range*. (p. 6-6)   **LO2**

- We can assume linearity of cost because it is approximately true within the range of volume relevant to the analysis.

- The relevant range is the range of activity over which the behavior of a cost behaves consistently.

- Within the relevant range, *per-unit* costs behave as follows when volume is increased:
  - Variable costs remain constant.
  - Fixed costs decrease proportionately.
  - Variable plus fixed cost decreases but not proportionately.

Outline the approach to developing cost formulas. (p. 6-7)   **LO3**

- In order to perform CVP analysis to make better decisions, total costs need to be broken into fixed and variable components. We illustrate three approaches for accomplishing this: (1) the scattergraph method, (2) the high-low method, and (3) the least squares regression method.

- The scattergraph method entails plotting the observed cost at several levels of volume on a graph, then drawing a line that places approximately half of the dots above and half below the line.

- The high-low method is relatively simple and compares costs at the highest and lowest levels of activity for which representative cost data are available. A line is then drawn between the highest- and lowest-volume data points.

- The least squares regression method is a statistical tool that uses all of the data points to separate a mixed cost into its variable and fixed components. A regression line is fitted to the data points so that the distance from each point to the line is minimized for all points. Although regression analysis can be relatively challenging to do by hand, it is a very simple task to complete using Microsoft Excel.

- A general formula for planning total cost is as follows: Total cost = Total fixed cost + (Variable cost per unit × Number of units).

Present a discussion of and a formula for calculating the break-even point. (p. 6-13)   **LO4**

- The break-even point (where Revenues = Costs) can be derived by graph, formula, or contribution margin analysis.

- Assumptions underlying break-even analysis include the following:
  - Total fixed cost and per-unit variable cost are constant over the entire relevant range.
  - Selling price per unit remains the same regardless of the volume of sales.
  - When more than one product is involved and sales volume varies, each product's percentage of total sales (i.e., sales mix) does not change.

LO5   Define *contribution margin* and *contribution margin ratio* and present alternate break-even formulas and examples of their application. (p. 6-15)

- Contribution margin = Revenue − Variable cost

- Contribution margin ratio = $\dfrac{\text{Contribution margin}}{\text{Sales}}$

  or

- Contribution margin ratio = $\dfrac{\text{Unit contribution margin}}{\text{Unit selling price}}$

- Formulas used in break-even analysis include the following:

  - Break-even units = $\dfrac{\text{Total fixed cost}}{\text{Unit contribution margin}}$

  - Break-even sales = $\dfrac{\text{Total fixed cost}}{\text{Contribution margin ratio}}$

LO6   Discuss approaches to planning net income using cost-volume-profit analyses. (p. 6-18)

- Formulas used in planning net income include the following:

  - Desired sales = Total variable cost + Total fixed cost + Desired net income

  - Desired units = $\dfrac{\text{Total fixed cost + Desired net income}}{\text{Unit contribution margin}}$

  - Desired sales = $\dfrac{\text{Total fixed cost + Desired net income}}{\text{Contribution margin ratio}}$

- Often management wants to develop plans using net income after tax instead of net income. The relationship between net income before income tax and net after-tax income is demonstrated by the following formula:

  - Net income before income tax = $\dfrac{\text{Net after-tax income}}{1 - \text{Income tax rate}}$

- Margin of safety = Actual sales − Break-even sales
- One measure of a firm's relative level of fixed costs is operating leverage. Operating leverage is computed as follows:

  - Operating leverage = $\dfrac{\text{Contribution margin}}{\text{Net operating income}}$

- Break-even and net income planning computations involving multiple products incorporate the concept of weighted average unit contribution margin.

SUMMARY	Concept ⟶	Method ⟶	Assessment
TAKEAWAY 6.1	Can a firm determine the variable and fixed components of a mixed cost?	Three different techniques are used to determine the variable and fixed elements of mixed costs: • Scattergraph method • High-low method • Least squares regression method	Each method provides an estimated cost function formula with the variable cost per unit and total fixed cost. Both the scattergraph and high-low methods rely on just two observations to estimate the cost function. Least square regression analysis uses all available data and does not rely on subjective judgment to draw a cost line.

Concept ⟶	Method ⟶	Assessment	SUMMARY
Can management determine how many units or how many sales dollars must be generated to break even?	• Break-even point in units = Total fixed costs/Unit contribution margin • Break-even point in sales dollars = Total fixed costs/Contribution margin ratio	Knowing the point at which unit sales or sales dollars result in zero income provides managers valuable information. For example, if the break-even point in units is higher than the projected demand, managers could either increase the sales price, reduce variable costs per unit, or both. This would increase the contribution margin and decrease the break-even point in units.	TAKEAWAY 6.2
Do income taxes impact the break-even and desired profit calculations?	Income taxes have no impact on the break-even calculations because at the break-even point operating income is equal to zero. Income taxes are only paid when operating income is greater than $0. Income taxes impact both the desired sales and the desired units calculations. The desired income figure must be converted to a pre-tax figure using the following formula: • Net income before income tax = Net income after income tax/(1 − income tax rate) • Once net income before income tax has been calculated, the formulas for desired sales and desired units can be used. • Desired units = (Total fixed costs + Desired net income before income tax)/Unit contribution margin • Desired sales = (Total fixed costs + Desired net income before income tax)/Contribution margin ratio	Income taxes are an important expense for all for-profit companies, and the expense impacts the desired units and desired sales calculations. Regardless of the tax rate faced by a company, income taxes will increase the desired unit and desired sales figures.	TAKEAWAY 6.3

KEY TERMS

Break-even point (p. 6-13)

Contribution margin (p. 6-15)

Contribution margin ratio (p. 6-16)

Cost behavior analysis (p. 6-3)

Cost-volume graph (p. 6-4)

Cost-volume-profit (CVP) analysis (p. 6-3)

Fixed costs (p. 6-5)

Margin of safety (p. 6-20)

Mixed costs (p. 6-6)

Operating leverage (p. 6-20)

Relevant range (p. 6-6)

Total variable costs (p. 6-5)

Variable operating income statement (p. 6-15)

Assignments with the 🔵 logo in the margin are available in **BusinessCourse**.
See the Preface of the book for details.

SELF-STUDY QUESTIONS

(Answers to Self-Study Questions are at the end of this chapter.)

1. **A(n) _____ cost is a cost whose total amount changes in direct proportion to a change in volume.**

   LO1

   a. variable

   b. fixed

   c. mixed

   d. irrelevant

2. **When moving from the low end to the high end of a relevant range, straight-line depreciation expense per unit**

   LO2

   a. increases.

   b. decreases.

   c. remains the same.

   d. changes unpredictably.

LO3 3. **In a typical cost formula**
  a. fixed costs are per unit, and variable costs are per unit.
  b. fixed costs are per unit, and variable costs are in total.
  c. fixed costs are in total, and variable costs are in total.
  d. fixed costs are in total, and variable costs are per unit.

LO4 4. **At the break-even point**
  a. contribution margin = fixed costs.   c. sales = contribution margin.
  b. variable costs = fixed costs.   d. contribution margin = 0.

LO5 5. **Contribution margin ratio iS**
  a. unit sales price/unit contribution margin.   c. total contribution margin/sales.
  b. I/margin of safety.   d. variable cost/fixed cost.

LO6 6. **Net income before income tax is**
  a. net income/(1 – income tax rate).   c. net income + contribution margin.
  b. income tax rate/net income.   d. net income/income tax rate.

QUESTIONS

LO1, 2 1. Define the terms *cost behavior* and *relevant range.*

LO1 2. Identify some common activity bases in terms of which the volume of a manufacturing operation might be stated. What general criterion might be used in choosing an activity base?

LO1 3. Name and define briefly the three most widely recognized cost behavior patterns.

LO1, 3 4. Explain (a) how a mixed cost can be considered "partly fixed and partly variable," and (b) why a firm's total cost is best represented by the mixed cost pattern.

LO3 5. Briefly describe the two most straightforward techniques for dividing a mixed cost into its fixed and variable components.

LO2 6. "Actual costs often behave in a nonlinear fashion. Therefore, assumptions of linearity invalidate most cost behavior analyses." Do you agree or disagree with this statement? Briefly defend your position.

LO1, 3 7. Describe how fixed and variable costs per unit respond to volume increases.

LO3 8. Present a formula based on units for planning total cost, and explain how mixed costs are incorporated into the formula.

LO4 9. Define and briefly explain three approaches to break-even analysis.

LO4 10. Patrick's Bakery Shop has fixed costs per month of $3,600, and variable costs are 55% of sales. What amount of monthly sales allows the shop to break even?

LO4 11. Quality Car Wash has fixed costs per month of $16,800, and variable costs are 20% of sales. The average amount collected per car washed during the past year has been $5. How many cars must be washed per month to break even?

LO4 12. You have graphed the cost-volume-profit relationships for a company on a break-even chart after being informed of certain assumptions. Explain how the lines on the chart would change if (a) fixed costs increased over the entire range of activity, (b) selling price per unit decreased, and (c) variable costs per unit increased.

LO5 13. Define *contribution margin.* Is it best expressed as a total amount or as a per-unit amount? In what way is the term descriptive of the concept it represents?

LO6 14. Explain the approach to break-even analysis that is used for a mix of two or more products.

LO6 15. Explain how break-even formulas can provide income-planning analyses.

LO6 16. In planning net income, how can (post tax) net income be incorporated into the planning formula?

SHORT EXERCISES

SE6-1. All of the following are assumptions of cost-volume-profit analysis **except**

LO1, 3

    a.   total fixed costs do not change with a change in volume.
    b.   revenues change proportionately with volume.
    c.   variable costs per unit change proportionately with volume.
    d.   sales mix for multi-product situations do not vary with volume changes.

SE6-2. Break-even quantity is defined as the volume of output at which revenues are equal to

LO4

    a.   marginal costs.   *c.*   variable costs.
    b.   total costs.   *d.*   fixed costs.

SE6-3. Bolger and Co. manufactures large gaskets for the turbine industry. Bolger's per unit sales price and variable costs for the current year are as follows:

Sales price per unit $300
Variable costs per unit   210

Bolger's total fixed costs aggregate $360,000. As Bolger's labor agreement is expiring at the end of the year, management is concerned about the effect a new agreement will have on its unit break-even point. The controller performed a sensitivity analysis to ascertain the estimated effect of a $10 per unit direct labor increase and a $10,000 reduction in fixed costs. Based on these data, it was determined that the break-even point would

    a.   decrease by 1,000 units.   *c.*   increase by 375 units.
    b.   decrease by 125 units.   *d.*   increase by 500 units.

SE6-4. Carson Inc. manufactures only one product and is preparing its budget for next year based on the following information:

LO6

Selling price per unit.	$100
Variable costs per unit	75
Fixed costs	250,000
Effective tax rate.	35%

If Carson wants to achieve a net income of $1.3 million next year, its sales must be

    a.   62,000 units.   *c.*   80,000 units.
    b.   70,200 units.   *d.*   90,000 units.

SE6-5. Ticker Company sells two products. Product A provides a contribution margin of $3 per unit, and Product B provides a contribution margin of $4 per unit. If Ticker's sales mix shifts toward Product A, which one of the following statements is **correct**?

LO6

    a.   The total number of units necessary to break even will decrease.
    b.   The overall contribution margin ratio will increase.
    c.   Operating income will decrease if the total number of units sold remains constant.
    d.   The contribution margin ratios for Products A and B will change.

DATA ANALYTICS, DATA VISUALIZATION, AND EXCEL ACTIVITIES

Data Analytics, Data Visualization, and Excel Activities are available in myBusinessCourse. These assignments develop Excel, Tableau, and Data Analytics skills, which will enhance students' career readiness. These exercises are assignable and auto graded by MBC. For an overview of data analytics, see the appendix at the end of this book.

Data Analytics *Data Visualization*

EXERCISES—SET A

LO1

E6-1A. **Cost-Volume Graphs** Set up a cost-volume graph. Volume should range from 0 to 24,000 units (in 4,000-unit increments), and cost should range from $0 to $35,000 (in $5,000 increments). Plot each of the following groups of cost data using different marks for each group. After completing the graph, indicate the type of cost behavior exhibited by each group.

Volume (applicable to each group)	Group A Costs	Group B Costs	Group C Costs
2,000	$ 2,600	$ 1,000	$2,400
12,000	12,600	6,000	2,400
16,000	16,600	8,000	2,400
20,000	20,600	10,000	2,400

LO3

E6-2A. **High-Low Method** Apply the high-low method of cost analysis to the three cost data groups in E6-1A. What cost behavior patterns are apparent? Express each as a cost formula.

LO2, 3

E6-3A. **Relevant Range and High-Low Method** The following selected data relate to the major cost categories experienced by Shaw Company at varying levels of operating volumes. Assuming that all operating volumes are within the relevant range, calculate the appropriate costs in each column in which blanks appear.

	Total Cost (@ 3,000 units)	Total Cost (@ 4,000 units)	Variable Cost per Unit	Total Fixed Cost	Total Cost (@ 5,000 units)
Direct labor (variable).	$90,000	$120,000	_____	_____	_____
Factory supervision (semivariable). . .	60,000	72,000	_____	_____	_____
Factory depreciation (fixed)	40,000	40,000	_____	_____	_____

LO3

E6-4A. **Total Cost Formula** Davis Company has analyzed its overhead costs and derived a general formula for their behavior: $65,000 + $16 per direct labor hour employed. The company expects to use 80,000 direct labor hours during the next accounting period. What overhead rate per direct labor hour should be applied to jobs worked during the period?

LO3

E6-5A. **Interpreting Cost Formula** Wylie Enterprises's controller, Josh Senior, estimated the following formula, based on monthly data, for total overhead cost:

$$\text{Overhead costs} = \$167,500 + (\$42.50 \times \text{Direct labor hours})$$

Required

1. Link each term in Column A to the corresponding term in Column B.

Column A	Column B
Overhead cost	Fixed cost (intercept)
$167,500	*y*-axis variable
$42.50	*x*-axis variable
Direct labor hours	Variable rate (slope)

2. If next month's budgeted direct labor hours equal 8,000 and are within the relevant range, what is the budgeted overhead cost?
3. If next quarter's budgeted direct labor hours equal 26,000 and are within the relevant range, what is the budgeted overhead cost?
4. If next year's budgeted direct labor hours equal 101,250 and are within the relevant range, what is the budgeted overhead cost?

E6-6A. Interpreting Regression Output Rikki Bake, the controller for XYZ Incorporated, suspects that factory overhead costs are driven by the number of machine hours used. Using Excel, Ms. Bake input 12 months of historical data for total factory overhead costs and machine hours used. The summary output information is provided below. Use the output information provided to develop a cost formula for overhead cost. Round the fixed and variable costs to the nearest penny. **LO3**

	A	B	C	D	E	F	G	H	I
1	SUMMARY OUTPUT								
2									
3	*Regression Statistics*								
4	Multiple R	0.963809718							
5	R Square	0.928929173							
6	Adjusted R Square	0.92182209							
7	Standard Error	56.42709871							
8	Observations	12							
9									
10	ANOVA								
11		*df*	*SS*	*MS*	*F*	*Significance F*			
12	Regression	1	416166.0753	416166.0753	130.7047086	4.6008E-07			
13	Residual	10	31840.17469	3184.017469					
14	Total	11	448006.25						
15									
16		*Coefficients*	*Standard Error*	*t Stat*	*P-value*	*Lower 95%*	*Upper 95%*	*Lower 95%*	*Upper 95%*
17	Intercept	$970.12	415.4592475	2.335045169	0.0416902	44.41521808	1895.816999	44.41521808	1895.816999
18	Machine Hours	36.138	3.160962926	11.432616	4.6008E-07	29.09501101	43.18113962	29.09501101	43.18113962

E6-7A. Break-Even Chart Set up a break-even chart similar to the one in **Exhibit 6-12** with proportional scales from $0 to $72,000 (in $12,000 increments) on the vertical axis and from 0 to 12,000 units of production (in 2,000-unit increments) on the horizontal axis. Prepare the break-even chart for Morton Company, assuming total fixed costs of $24,000, and unit selling price and unit variable cost for the company's one product of $8 and $5, respectively. Label the total revenue line and the total cost line. Indicate the break-even point in units and dollars. **LO4**

E6-8A. Cost-Volume Profit Analysis Incline Company generated $1,400,000 in revenue selling 800 units of its only product. Each unit has a contribution margin of $280. The company has fixed costs of $125/unit at the current production volume (assume unit production volume equals unit sales volume). **LO5**
   a. What is the contribution margin ratio for Incline's product?
   b. Calculate the break-even point in revenue for Incline?

E6-9A. Cost-Volume Profit Analysis Recline Company is planning to produce and sell 11,250 units of its only product at a unit price of $106. At this sales level, Recline Company will generate $405,000 in total contribution margin and incur fixed costs of $25/unit. **LO5**
   a. Calculate Recline's contribution margin ratio.
   b. Calculate the break-even point in sales dollars for Recline?

E6-10A. Break-Even (Units) Parker & Associates, LLC has budgeted the following amounts for its next fiscal year: **LO5**

Total fixed expenses.	$980,000
Selling price per unit.	$ 48
Variable expenses per unit	$ 23

If fixed expenses increase by 10%, the selling price per unit would need to increase by what percentage in order to maintain the original break-even sales in units (round to the nearest tenth of a percent)?

E6-11A. Break-Even (Sales Dollars) Fixed expenses total $28,678, the break-even sales in dollars is $92,512, and the selling price per unit is $98. Calculate the variable expense per unit (round to the nearest cent). **LO5**

LO6 **E6-12A. Net Income Planning** Nolden Company has charged a selling price of $24 per unit, incurred variable costs of $15 per unit, and total fixed costs of $108,000. What unit sales volume is necessary to earn the following related amounts of net income before income tax?

a. $18,000;

b. $27,000; or

c. Equal to 20% of sales revenue.

LO4, 5, 6 **E6-13A. Cost-Volume Profit Analysis** Hailstorm Company sells a single product for $28 per unit. Variable costs are $22 per unit, and fixed costs are $60,000 at an operating level of 7,000 to 15,000 units.

a. What is Hailstorm Company's break-even point in units?

b. How many units must be sold to earn $12,000 before income tax?

c. How many units must be sold to earn $14,500 after income tax, assuming a 35% tax rate?

LO4, 5, 6 **E6-14A. Break-Even with Multiple Products** Wagner Enterprise sells two products, large tractors and small tractors. A large tractor sells for $62,000 per unit with variable costs of $28,520 per unit. Small tractors sell for $34,000 per unit with variable costs of $16,320 per unit. Total fixed costs for the company are $1,560,000. Wagner Enterprises typically sells two large tractors for every three small tractors. Assuming the sales mix remains constant, how many large and small tractors are sold (in units) at Wagner's break-even point?

LO5 **E6-15A. Break-Even with Multiple Products** McDoogle Farms has $240,340 of total fixed costs and sells products A and B with a product mix of 30% A and 70% B. Selling prices and variable costs for A and B result in contribution margins per unit of $8 and $14, respectively. Compute the break-even point.

LO6 **E6-16A. Margin of Safety** Yellow Sticker Company's variable expenses are 40% of sales. The company has monthly fixed expenses of $15,000 and sells each unit for $0.50. The monthly target operating income is $3,750.

a. What is the monthly margin of safety in dollars if Yellow Sticker Company achieves its operating income goal?

b. What is the monthly margin of safety in units if Yellow Sticker Company achieves its operating income goal?

LO6 **E6-17A. Operating Leverage** PB&J Eatery has a monthly target operating income of $8,400. Variable expenses are 60% of sales and monthly fixed expenses are $12,600. What is PB&J Eatery's operating leverage factor at the target level of operating income?

LO1 **E6-18A. Cost Patterns** The graphs below represent approximations of cost behavior patterns. The horizontal axis of each graph represents units and the vertical axis represents dollars of total cost.

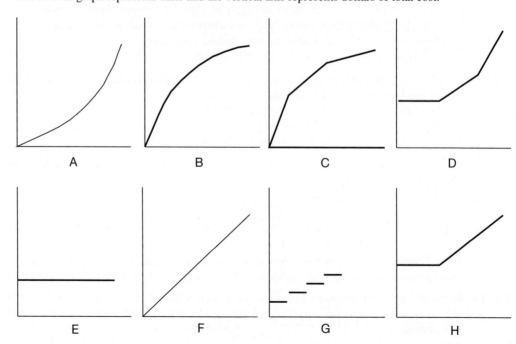

Select the graph that best matches each of the situations described below. Each graph may be selected more than once.

a. Straight-line depreciation of a factory building

b. Utility bill for electricity that includes a fixed charge per month plus a constant usage rate per hour for hours in excess of 100

c. Cost of microchip incorporated into a product

d. Labor cost of machine operators who become more productive as they gain experience

e. Water bill that includes a flat fee for the first 10,000 gallons used, plus an increasing usage charge for each additional 10,000 gallons used

f. Cost of factory supplies when increasing quantities bring cost discounts as each price break level is attained

g. Salaries of quality inspectors when one additional inspector is hired for each 20,000 units produced

h. Cost of an advertising campaign

EXERCISES—SET B

E6-1B. **High-Low Method** The highest and lowest levels of activity for the Felton Company were 58,000 direct labor hours and 42,000 direct labor hours, respectively. If maintenance costs were $420,000 at the 58,000-hour level and $380,000 at the 42,000-hour level, what cost might we expect at an operating level of 52,000 direct labor hours?

LO3

E6-2B. **High-Low Method** During the past year, Gutter Corp., operated within the relevant range of its fixed costs. Monthly production volume during the year ranged from 30,000 to 50,000 units of product and corresponding total manufacturing costs ranged from $5.75 to $4.75 per unit. Determine the total cost behavior pattern experienced by Gutter Corp.

LO3

E6-3B. **Relevant Range and High-Low Method** The following selected data relate to the major cost categories experienced by Silver & Company at varying levels of operating volumes. Assuming that all operating volumes are within the relevant range, calculate the appropriate costs in each column in which blanks appear (some blanks can be $0):

LO3

	Total Cost (@ 2,000 units)	Total Cost (@ 3,000 units)	Variable Cost per Unit	Total Fixed Cost	Total Cost (@ 4,000 units)
Direct labor (variable).	$120,000	$150,000	—	—	—
Factory supervision (semivariable). . .	54,000	66,000	—	—	—
Factory depreciation (fixed)	35,000	35,000	—	—	—

E6-4B. **Cost Formula** The following amounts of various cost categories are experienced by Patton Manufacturing in producing and selling its only product:

LO3

Direct materials.	$14 per unit of product
Direct labor.	$12 per direct labor hour*
Manufacturing overhead.	$15,000 + $3.50 per direct labor hour
Selling expenses	$17,000 + $2.75 per unit of product
Administrative.	$9,000 + $0.40 per unit of product

*Each unit of product requires 1.5 direct labor hours.

Combine the various cost factors into a general total cost formula for Patton Manufacturing and determine the total cost of producing and selling 25,000 units.

E6-5B. **Least Squares Regression Analysis** Bogota Corporation has gathered data on its overhead activities and associated costs for the past 12 months. Josh Hopper, from the accounting department, has convinced management that overhead costs can be better estimated and controlled if the fixed and variable components of each overhead activity are known. One such area is the purchasing department (receiving and reviewing purchase requisitions, issuing purchase orders, and managing vendor relationships), which he believes is driven by the number of purchase orders issued. Twelve months of data have been gathered for the purchasing activity and are as follows:

LO3

Month	Purchase Orders Issued	Purchasing Cost
1	1,050	$18,100
2	750	$15,100
3	1,550	$28,100
4	1,250	$17,100
5	1,350	$25,100
6	1,150	$21,100
7	1,650	$29,100
8	1,450	$24,100
9	1,750	$27,100
10	950	$16,100
11	1,250	$18,100
12	1,500	$18,600

Assume Josh has used the method of least squares regression (i.e., regression analysis) on the purchasing data and has gotten the following results:

Intercept	$3,231
Slope	$13.99

Required

a. Using the results from the method of least squares regression, prepare a cost formula for the purchasing activity.

b. Using the formula for Requirement A, what is the predicted cost of purchasing for a month in which 1,525 purchase orders are processed? (Note: Round your answer to the nearest dollar.)

LO3   **E6-6B.** **Least Squares Regression Analysis** Bogota Corporation has gathered data on its overhead activites and associated costs for the past 12 months. Josh Hopper, from the accounting department, has convinced management that overhead costs can be better estimated and controlled if the fixed and variable components of each overhead activity are known. One such area is the purchasing department (receiving and reviewing purchase requisitions, issuing purchase orders, and managing vendor relationships), which he believes is driven by the number of purchase orders issued. Twelve months of data have been gathered for the purchasing activity and are as follows:

Month	Purchase Orders Issued	Purchasing Cost
1	1,050	$23,738
2	750	16,788
3	1,550	35,113
4	1,250	27,263
5	1,350	27,463
6	1,150	27,988
7	1,650	34,388
8	1,450	29,213
9	1,750	38,663
10	950	21,938
11	1,250	25,688
12	1,500	34,200

a. Run a regression using Excel or a similar computer spreadsheet program. Provide the intercept, slope, and R_2 for the regression.

b. Using the results from requirement *a*, prepare a cost formula for the purchasing activity.

c. Using the formula from requirement *b*, what is the predicted cost of purchasing for a month in which 1,375 purchase orders are issued? (Note: Round your answer to the nearest dollar.)

E6-7B. **Break-Even Calculations** Compute the break-even point in units for each of the following independent situations:

LO4

SERVICE AND MERCHANDISING

	Unit Selling Price	Unit Variable Cost	Total Fixed Cost
a.	$12.00	$8.00	$ 87,000
b.	15.00	11.00	146,000
c.	8.75	2.50	52,000

Using the break-even point in units, calculate the break-even point in revenue. Confirm the break-even point in revenue using the contribution margin ratio.

E6-8B. **Break-Even Analysis** Feet-First Industries plans to sell 7,750 sleds at $80 each in the coming year. Variable cost is 60 percent of the sales price. Fixed factory overhead equals $49,540, and fixed selling and administrative expense equals $34,780.

LO4, 5

a. Calculate the units that Feet-First must sell in order to break even.
b. Calculate the sales revenue that Feet-First must earn to break even by using the contribution margin.
c. Confirm your answer in requirement *b,* by muliplying the number of break-even units in requirement *a,* by the unit sales price.

E6-9B. **Net Income Planning** Holland Corporation earned an after-tax net income of $182,000 last year. Fixed costs were $750,000. The selling price per unit of its product was $130, of which $60 was a contribution to fixed cost and net income. The income tax rate was 35%.

LO4, 5, 6

a. How many units of product were sold last year?
b. What was the break-even point in units last year?
c. The company wishes to increase its after-tax net income by 20% this year. If selling prices and the income tax rate remain unchanged, how many units must be sold?

E6-10B. **Cost-Volume-Profit Analysis** Gannon Company sells a single product for $18.75 per unit. Variable costs are $9 per unit, and fixed costs are $134,940 at an operating level of 12,000 to 25,000 units.

LO4, 5, 6

SERVICE AND MERCHANDISING

a. What is Gannon Company's break-even point in units?
b. How many units must be sold to earn $20,000 before income tax?
c. How many units must be sold to earn $30,000 after income tax, assuming a 40% tax rate?

E6-11B. **Break-Even Analysis** Pinnacle Party Inflatables, a supplier of inflatable bouncy houses, has budgeted the following amounts for its next fiscal year:

LO5

Total fixed expenses	$236,250
Selling price per unit	$ 300
Variable expenses per unit	$ 125

If Pinnacle Party Inflatables can reduce fixed expenses by $47,250, by how much can variable expenses per unit increase and still allow the company to maintain the original break-even sales in units?

E6-12B. **Multiple Product Break-Even Analysis** Wynn Company has $141,360 total fixed cost and sells products A and B with a product mix of 70% A and 30% B. Selling prices and variable costs for A and B result in contribution margins per unit of $9 and $7, respectively. Compute the break-even point in units of A and B.

LO4, 5, 6

SERVICE AND MERCHANDISING

E6-13B. **Break-Even with Multiple Products** We Scream For Ice Cream sells ice cream in three flavors: chocolate, strawberry, and vanilla. It sold 28,000 gallons last year, but it is still losing money. For every five gallons of ice cream sold, one gallon is strawberry and the remainder is split evenly between chocolate and vanilla. Fixed costs for We Scream For Ice Cream are $55,056 and additional information follows:

LO4, 5, 6

	Chocolate	Vanilla	Strawberry
Sales price per gallon	$5.25	$5.25	$5.25
Variable cost per gallon	$2.75	$3.75	$3.95

     a.   Assuming the sales mix remains constant, how many total gallons of ice cream must be sold to break even?

     b.   How many gallons of strawberry ice cream will be sold at the break-even point?

     c.   What will total revenue equal at the break-even point?

LO4, 5, 6   **E6-14B. Break-Even with Multiple Products** Wylie's Watering Hole sells fruit smoothies. Last year, Wylie sold a total of 24,000 fruit smoothies. Pineapple smoothies outsold coconut smoothies 2 to 1. Sales of mango smoothies were the same as sales of pineapple. Fixed costs for the company are $18,189 and additional information follows:

Product	Unit Sales Prices	Unit Variable Cost
Pineapple	$2.50	$0.80
Coconut	$3.75	$1.35
Mango	$3.20	$1.40

     a.   Calculate the sales mix percentage of all three products (based upon the number of smoothies).

     b.   Calculate the weighted average contribution margin for all three types of drinks.

     c.   Calculate the break-even volume in number of total smoothies.

     d.   Calculate the break-even point in revenue.

LO4, 5, 6   **E6-15B. Break-Even with Multiple Products** Pippy's Tasty Treats sells muffins, scones, and cookies. It sold a total of 19,000 dozens last year. Cookies and muffins each represent 40% of unit sales. Scones represent the remaining 20% of unit sales. Fixed costs for Pippy's Tasty Treats are $154,601 and additional information follows:

Product	Sales Prices	Variable Cost
1 dozen muffins	$36.00	$28.00
1 dozen scones	$45.00	$32.00
1 dozen cookies	$33.00	$21.00

     a.   Calculate the weighted average contribution margin for all three types of dozens.

     b.   Calculate the break-even volume in number of dozens.

     c.   Calculate the break-even sales in dollars.

LO6   **E6-16B. Margin of Safety** Jake's Sub Shop sells large sub sandwiches for $8.75. Unit variable expenses total $3.85. The break-even sales in units is 5,250, and budgeted sales in units is 9,500. What is the margin of safety in dollars? What are Jake's fixed costs?

LO6   **E6-17B. Operating Leverage** Jordan's Bake Shop has a monthly target operating income of $10,500. Variable expenses are 50% of sales, and the bakery must sell 3,500 units to break even. Jordan sells her product for $4.50 per unit. What is the operating leverage factor for Jordan's Bake Shop at the target level of operating income?

LO1   **E6-18B. Cost Patterns** The following graph depicts cost-volume relationships for Tallmadge Company:

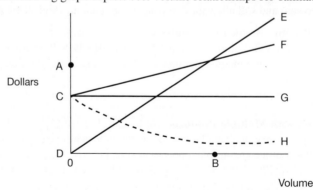

Choose a labeled point *or* line on the graph that *best* represents the behavior of each of the following items as operating volume is increased. Answers may be the same for more than one item. Answer each item independently.

a. Total sales revenue	*d.* Total fixed costs
b. Total costs	*e.* Total mixed cost
c. Total variable costs	*f.* Break-even point

PROBLEMS—SET A

P6-1A.   Net Income Planning Selected operating data for Oakbrook Company in four independent situations are shown below.

LO5

SERVICE AND
MERCHANDISING

MBC

	A	B	C	D
Sales.	$525,000	$ c.	$ e.	$300,000
Variable expense	$ a.	$405,000	$ f.	$ g.
Fixed expense	$ b.	$98,000	$47,000	$140,000
Net income before tax (loss).	$ 22,000	$307,000	$28,000	$ (20,000)
Units sold	35,000	d.		
Unit contribution margin	$ 8.25	$ 9.00		
Contribution margin ratio			0.25	h.

Required

Fill in the blanks for each independent situation. Show your calculations.

P6-2A.   Graphing Mixed Cost During a recent six-month period, Wade Corporation had the following monthly production volume and total monthly maintenance expense:

LO1, 2, 3

	Units Produced	Maintenance Expense
March	21,000	$140,000
April	15,000	112,000
May	30,000	184,000
June	27,000	172,000
July	35,000	208,000
August	25,000	160,000

Required

Assume that all volumes are in the relevant range.

a.   Explain why the data indicate that the maintenance expense is neither a fixed nor a variable expense.

b.   Construct a graph similar to the one in **Exhibit 6-7** and plot the maintenance expense data.

c.   Fit a line (by sight) to the cost observation points and estimate the cost formula.

d.   Confirm your answer in requirement (c) with high-low analysis.

P6-3A.   Cost Formulas Longboat Manufacturing produces a single product requiring the following direct materials and direct labor:

LO2, 3, 6

MBC

Description	Cost per Unit of Input	Required Amount per Unit of Product
Material A	$ 9/pound	20 ounces
Material B	7/pound	4 ounces
Material C	25/gallon	0.4 gallon
Cutting labor	12/hour	45 minutes
Shaping labor	15/hour	15 minutes
Finishing labor	14/hour	75 minutes

Manufacturing overhead consists of indirect materials, $0.60 per unit of product; indirect labor, $1,000 per month plus $0.75 per unit of product; factory maintenance, $17,000 per year plus $0.65 per unit of product; factory depreciation, $18,000 per year; and annual factory property taxes, $10,000. Selling and administrative expenses include the salaries of a sales manager, $40,000 per year; an office manager, $22,000 per year; and two salespersons, each of whom is paid a base salary of $15,000 per year and a commission of $4 per unit sold. Advertising and promotion of the product are done through a year-round media package program costing $1,500 per week.

Required

a.   Analyze all cost and expense factors to determine a general formula (based on units of production) for total cost.

b.   Assuming a relevant range of 10,000 to 30,000 units, what is the estimated unit cost for producing and selling 10,000 units? 25,000 units? Explain the variation in unit cost at the two levels of production.

c.   If 22,000 units are produced and sold in a year, what selling price results in a net income before income tax of $75,000?

LO2, 3   **P6-4A.**   **High-Low and Cost Formula** Harrison Company has accumulated the following total manufacturing overhead costs for two levels of activity (within the relevant range):

	Low	High
Activity (direct labor hours)	90,000	130,000
Total manufacturing overhead	$484,000	$628,000

The total overhead cost includes variable, fixed, and mixed costs. At 130,000 direct labor hours, the total cost breakdown is as follows:

Variable cost	$286,000
Fixed cost	85,000
Semi-mixed cost	257,000

Required

a.   Using the high-low method of cost analysis, determine the variable portion of the semi-variable cost per direct labor hour. Determine the total fixed cost component of the mixed cost.

b.   What should the total planned overhead cost be at 115,000 direct labor hours?

LO3   **P6-5A.**   **Least Squares Regression Analysis** The controller for TG Enterprises is trying to determine whether direct labor hours or machine hours is driving the company's overhead cost. He collected the following data on the number of direct labor hours, the number of machine hours, and the associated factory overhead cost for the year 2018:

Month	Machine Hours	Direct Labor Hours	Overhead Cost
January.	132	724	$5,750
February.	130	730	$5,685
March	131	715	$5,790
April	126	685	$5,480
May.	128	695	$5,590
June	123	585	$5,430
July	135	775	$5,790
August	130	680	$5,705
September	132	725	$5,804
October.	138	840	$5,976
November.	128	775	$5,487
December.	143	825	$6,108

Required

a.   Using Excel, run a regression on these data using machine hours as the independent variable. Provide the cost formula for overhead cost. Round fixed and variable costs to the nearest cent.

b.   Using Excel, run a regression on these data using direct labor hours as the independent variable. Provide the cost formula for overhead cost. Round the fixed and variable costs to the nearest cent.

c.   What is the R^2 for the regression in requirement *a*? What is the R^2 for the regression in requirement *b*? Which independent variable, direct labor hours or machine hours, is a better predictor of
factory overhead cost?

d.   Assuming that expected January 2019 machine hours are 150, what is expected factory overhead
cost using the cost formula in requirement *a*? (*Note:* Round to the nearest dollar.)

P6-6A.   Least Squares Regression Analysis   The management of Digger Inc., is trying to develop a cost **LO3**
formula for its major manufacturing overhead activities. Digger's manufacturing process is highly automated and power costs are a significant manufacturing cost. Cost analysts have decided that power
costs are mixed. The costs must be separated into their fixed and variable components so that the cost
behavior of the power usage activity can be better understood. Analysts have determined that machine
hours drive power usage; thus, machine hours are the cost driver for power costs. Nine months of data
have been collected and are presented in the chart below:

Period	Machine Hours	Power Cost
January.	24,000	$32,500
February.	30,000	47,500
March	36,000	53,125
April	26,400	46,250
May.	25,200	42,500
June	21,600	36,250
July.	28,800	45,000
August	33,600	50,000
September	31,200	40,000

Note: For the following requirements, round the variable cost per unit to the nearest cent and the total
fixed cost to the nearest dollar.

Required

a.   Use the high and low points to estimate a power cost formula.

b.   Use the method of least squares in Excel (or a similar computer program) to estimate a power
cost formula.

c.   Evaluate R_2 from requirement *b*. Are machine hours a good predictor of power costs?

P6-7A.   Cost Formula   Princeton Manufacturing Company summarizes the following total cost data for the **LO1, 2, 3**
month of March. Princeton has a normal capacity per month of 25,000 units of product that sell for
$40 each. For the foreseeable future, sales volume should equal normal capacity of production.

Direct materials.	$295,000
Direct labor.	165,000
Variable overhead.	85,000
Fixed overhead (Note 1).	140,000
Selling expense (Note 2)	80,000
Administrative expense (fixed)	56,000
	$821,000

Notes:

1.   Beyond normal capacity, fixed overhead cost increases $6,350 for each 1,000 units *or fraction
thereof until* a maximum capacity of 30,000 units is reached.

2.   Selling expenses are a 5% sales commission plus shipping costs of $1.20 per unit.

Required

a.   Using the information available, prepare a formula to estimate Princeton's total cost at various
production volumes up to normal capacity.

b.   Prove your answer in requirement (a) relative to the total cost figure for 25,000 units.

c.   Calculate the planned total cost at 20,000 units, and explain why total cost did not decrease in
proportion to the reduced volume.

d.   If Princeton were operating at normal capacity and accepted an order for 500 more units, what
would it have to charge for the order to earn a net income before income tax of $8 per unit on the
new sale?

LO4, 5, 6

SERVICE AND
MERCHANDISING

MBC   X

P6-8A. **Net Income Planning** Superior Corporation sells a single product for $75 per unit, of which $42 is contribution margin. Fixed costs total $100,800 and the net income before income tax is $28,800.

Required
Determine the following (show key computations):
a. The present sales volume in dollars
b. The break-even point in units
c. The sales volume in units necessary to attain a net income before income tax of $39,000
d. The sales volume in units necessary to attain a net income before income tax equal to 20% of sales revenue
e. The sales volume in units necessary to attain an after-tax net income of $43,720 if the tax rate is 40%

LO4, 5, 6

MBC

P6-9A. **Break-Even and Net Income Planning** The controller of Grafton Company is preparing data for a conference call concerning certain *independent* aspects of its operations.

Required
Prepare answers to the following questions for the controller:
a. Total fixed cost is $1,440,000 and a unit of product is sold for $12 in excess of its unit variable cost. What is the break-even in units?
b. The company will sell 60,000 units of product—each having a unit variable cost of $22—at a price that will enable the product to absorb $600,000 of fixed cost. What minimum unit sales price must be charged to break even?
c. A net income before income tax of $320,000 is desired after covering $1,200,000 of fixed costs. What minimum contribution margin ratio must be maintained if total sales revenue is to be $3,800,000?
d. Net income before income tax is 10% of sales revenue, the contribution margin ratio is 30%, and the break-even dollar sales is $640,000. What is the amount of total revenue?
e. Fixed costs total $1,000,000, the variable cost per unit is $30, and selling price per unit is $80. What dollar sales volume will generate an after-tax net income of $84,000 when the income tax rate is 40%?

LO4, 5, 6

MBC

P6-10A. **Break-Even and Net Income Planning** Hank Company has recently leased facilities for the manufacture of a new product. Based on studies made by its accounting personnel, the following data are available:
Estimated annual sales: 20,000 units.

Estimated Costs	Amount	Unit Cost
Direct materials.	$345,000	$17.25
Direct labor.	328,000	16.40
Manufacturing overhead.	196,000	9.80
Administrative expenses.	124,000	6.20
	$993,000	$49.65

Selling expenses are expected to be 10% of sales, and the selling price is $71 per unit. Ignore income tax in this problem.

Required
a. Compute a break-even point in dollars and in units. Assume that manufacturing overhead and administrative expenses are fixed, but that other costs are variable. (Round contribution margin ratio computation to three decimal places.)
b. What would net income before income tax be if 30,000 units were sold?
c. How many units must be sold to earn a net income before income tax of 10% of sales?

LO4, 5, 6

MBC

P6-11A. **Multiple Product Break-Even and Net Income Planning** Grand Company manufactures and sells the following three products:

	Economy	Standard	Deluxe
Unit sales	10,000	6,000	4,000
Unit sales price.	$48	$56	$68
Unit variable cost	$30	$32	$36

Required

Assume that the total fixed cost is $339,000.

a. Compute the net income before income tax based on the sales volumes shown above.

b. Compute the break-even point in total dollars of revenue and in units for each product.

c. Prove your break-even calculations by computing the total contribution margin related to your answer in requirement (b).

PROBLEMS—SET B

P6-1B. **Net Income Planning** Selected operating data for Verona Company in four independent situations is shown below.   **LO4, 5**

SERVICE AND
MERCHANDISING

	A	B	C	D
Sales.	$320,000	$ c.	$ e.	$280,000
Variable expense	$ a.	$48,000	$ f.	$ g.
Fixed expense	$ b.	$56,000	$240,000	$120,000
Net income before tax	$ 40,000	$16,000	$ 96,000	$ (8,000)
Units sold	7,000	d.		
Unit contribution margin	$ 20	$ 9		
Contribution margin ratio			0.70	h.

Required

Fill in the blanks for each independent situation above. Show your calculations.

P6-2B. **Graphing Mixed Cost** During the past operating year, Davenport Corporation had the following monthly volume of production and total monthly maintenance expense: **LO1, 2, 3**

	Units Produced	Maintenance Expense		Units Produced	Maintenance Expense
January.	123,000	$28,600	July	127,000	$29,000
February.	147,000	31,600	August	157,000	32,800
March	159,000	33,000	September	131,000	29,600
April	133,000	29,400	October.	163,000	33,400
May.	143,000	31,200	November.	155,000	32,600
June	153,000	32,600	December.	159,000	33,000

Required

Assume that all volumes are in the relevant range.

a. Explain why the data indicate that the maintenance expense is neither a fixed nor a variable expense.

b. Construct a graph similar to the one in **Exhibit 6-7** and plot the maintenance expense data.

c. Fit a line (by sight) to the cost observation points and estimate the cost formula.

d. Confirm your answer in requirement (c) with high-low analysis.

P6-3B. **Cost Formulas** Colonial Manufacturing produces a single product requiring the following direct materials and direct labor: **LO2, 3, 6**

Description	Cost per Unit of Input	Required Amount per Unit of Product
Material A.	$12/pound	24 ounces
Material B.	8/pound	8 ounces
Material C.	15/gallon	0.6 gallon
Cutting labor.	14/hour	45 minutes
Shaping labor	12/hour	30 minutes
Finishing labor	16/hour	90 minutes

Manufacturing overhead consists of indirect materials, $0.40 per unit of product; indirect labor, $900 per month plus $0.80 per unit of product; factory maintenance, $18,000 per year plus $0.75 per unit of product; factory depreciation, $22,000 per year; and annual factory property taxes, $12,000. Selling and administrative expenses include the salaries of a sales manager, $45,000 per year; an office manager, $24,000 per year; and two salespersons, each of whom is paid a base salary of $18,000 per year and a commission of $3 per unit sold. Advertising and promotion of the product are done through a year-round media package program costing $1,000 per week.

Required

a. Analyze all cost and expense factors to determine a general formula (based on units of production) for total cost.

b. Assuming a relevant range of 10,000 to 30,000 units, what is the estimated unit cost for producing and selling 12,000 units? 24,000 units? Explain the variation in unit cost at the two levels of production.

c. If 28,000 units are produced and sold in a year, what selling price results in a net income before taxes of $75,000?

LO2, 3   P6-4B. High-Low and Cost Formula Harrison Company has accumulated the following total manufacturing overhead costs for two levels of activity (within the relevant range):

	Low	High
Activity (direct labor hours)...	120,000	180,000
Total manufacturing overhead	$963,500	$1,251,500

The total overhead cost includes variable, fixed, and mixed costs. At 120,000 direct labor hours, the total cost breakdown is as follows:

Variable cost..	$318,000
Fixed cost...	260,500
Semi-variable cost	385,000

Required

a. Using the high-low method of cost analysis, determine the variable portion of the mixed cost per direct labor hour. Determine the total fixed cost component of the mixed cost.

b. What should the total planned overhead cost be at 140,000 direct labor hours?

LO3   P6-5B. Least Squares Regression Analysis The controller for TG Enterprises is trying to determine whether direct labor hours or machine hours is driving the company's overhead cost. He collected the following data on the number of direct labor hours, the number of machine hours, and the associated factory overhead cost for the year 2018:

Month	Machine Hours	Direct Labor Hours	Overhead Cost
January..........	198	1810	$17,610
February.........	195	1825	17,410
March...........	197	1788	17,735
April	189	1713	16,780
May.............	192	1738	17,240
June	185	1463	16,635
July.............	203	1938	17,700
August	195	1700	17,500
September	198	1813	17,775
October..........	207	2100	18,400
November........	192	1938	16,805
December........	215	2063	18,895

Required

a. Using Excel, run a regression on these data using machine hours as the independent variable. Provide the cost formula for overhead cost. Round fixed and variable costs to the nearest cent.

b. Using Excel, run a regression on these data using direct labor hours as the independent variable. Provide the cost formula for overhead cost. Round the fixed and variable costs to the nearest cent.

c. What is the R_2 for the regression in requirement *a*? What is the R_2 for the regression in requirement *b*? Which independent variable, direct labor hours or machine hours, is a better predictor of factory overhead cost?

d. Assuming that expected January 2019 machine hours are 212, what is expected factory overhead cost using the cost formula in requirement *a*? (Note: Round to the nearest dollar.)

P6-6B.   Least Squares Regression Analysis The management of Digger Inc., is trying to develop a cost formula for its major manufacturing overhead activities. Digger's manufacturing process is highly automated and power costs are a significant manufacturing cost. Cost analysts have decided that power costs are mixed. The costs must be separated into their fixed and variable components so that the cost behavior of the power usage activity can be better understood. Analysts have determined that machine hours drive power usage, thus machine hours are the cost driver for power costs. Nine months of data have been collected and are presented in the chart below:

LO3

Period	Machine Hours	Power Cost
January..............	36,000	$45,000
February.............	45,000	60,300
March	54,000	67,500
April	39,600	53,064
May................	37,800	47,250
June	32,400	43,416
July................	43,200	54,000
August	50,400	67,536
September	46,800	58,500

Note: For the following requirements, round the variable cost per unit to the nearest cent and the total fixed cost to the nearest dollar.

Required
a. Use the high and low points to estimate a power cost formula.
b. Use the method of least squares regression in Excel (or a similar computer program) to estimate a power cost formula.
c. Evaluate R_2 from requirement *b*. Are machine hours a good predictor of power costs?
d. Using the cost formula from requirement *b*, estimate power costs when 55,800 machine hours are used.

P6-7B.   Cost Formula The following total cost data are for Phoenix Manufacturing Company, which has a normal capacity per period of 40,000 units of product that sell for $60 each. For the foreseeable future, sales volume should equal normal capacity of production.

LO1, 2, 3

Direct materials.	$ 640,000
Direct labor.	400,000
Variable overhead.	200,000
Fixed overhead (Note 1).	216,000
Selling expense (Note 2)	280,000
Administrative expense (fixed)	88,000
	$1,824,000

Notes:
1. Beyond normal capacity, fixed overhead cost increases $6,240 for each 2,000 units *or fraction thereof* until a maximum capacity of 50,000 units is reached.
2. Selling expenses are a 10% sales commission, plus shipping costs of $1 per unit.

Required
a. Using the information available, prepare a formula to estimate Phoenix's total cost at various production volumes up to normal capacity.
b. Prove your answer in requirement (a) against the above total cost figure at 40,000 units.

    c.   Calculate the planned total cost at 30,000 units, and explain why total cost did not decrease in proportion to the reduced volume.

    d.   If Phoenix were operating at normal capacity and accepted an order for 600 more units, what would it have to charge for the order to earn a net income before tax of $8 per unit on the new sale?

LO4, 5, 6   **P6-8B.**   **Net Income Planning** Night Hawk Corporation sells a single product for $150 per unit, of which $60 is contribution margin. Total fixed cost is $240,000, and net income before income tax is $54,000.

Required
Determine the following (show key computations):
a.   The present sales volume in dollars
b.   The break-even point in units
c.   The sales volume in units necessary to attain a net income before income tax of $75,000
d.   The sales volume in units necessary to attain a net income before income tax equal to 10% of sales revenue
e.   The sales volume in units necessary to attain a net income of $54,000 if the tax rate is 20%

LO4, 5, 6   **P6-9B.**   **Break-Even and Net Income Planning** The controller of Wright Company is preparing data for a conference concerning certain *independent* aspects of its operations.

Required
Prepare answers to the following questions for the controller:

a.   Total fixed cost is $720,000, and a unit of product is sold for $10 in excess of its unit variable cost. What is the break-even unit volume?

b.   The company will sell 30,000 units of product—each having a unit variable cost of $14—at a price that will enable the product to absorb $360,000 of fixed cost. What minimum unit sales price must be charged to break even?

c.   A net income before income tax of $150,000 is desired after covering $410,000 of fixed cost. What minimum contribution margin ratio must be maintained if total sales revenue is to be $1,600,000?

d.   A net income before income tax is 20% of sales revenue, the contribution margin ratio is 60%, and the break-even dollar sales is $200,000. What is the amount of total revenue?

e.   The total fixed cost is $350,000, the variable cost per unit is $26, and the unit sales price is $50. What dollar sales volume will generate an after-tax net income of $60,000 when the income tax rate is 40%?

LO4, 5, 6   **P6-10B.**   **Break-Even and Net Income Planning** Venice Company has recently leased facilities for the manufacture of a new product. Based on studies made by its accounting personnel, the following data are available:

Estimated annual sales . . . . 60,000 units

Estimated Costs	Amount	Unit Cost
Direct materials.	$ 870,000	$14.50
Direct labor.	750,000	12.50
Manufacturing overhead.	384,000	6.40
Administrative expenses.	228,000	3.80
	$2,232,000	$37.20

Selling expenses are expected to be 20% of sales, and the selling price is $82 per unit. Ignore income tax in this problem.

Required
a.   Compute a break-even point in dollars and in units. Assume that manufacturing overhead and administrative expenses are fixed, but that other costs are variable.
b.   What would net income before income tax be if 40,000 units were sold?
c.   How many units must be sold to earn a net income before an income tax of 10% of sales?

P6-11B. Multiple Product Break-Even and Net Income Planning Madison Company manufactures and sells the following three products:

LO4, 5, 6

SERVICE AND
MERCHANDISING

X   MBC

	Red	Blue	Green
Unit sales	20,000	30,000	50,000
Unit sales price.....................................	$30	$62	$18
Unit variable cost	$18	$38	$14

Required

Assume that total fixed cost is $324,800.

a. Compute the net income before income tax based on the sales volumes shown above.
b. Compute the break-even point in total dollars of revenue and in specific unit sales volume for each product.
c. Prove your break-even calculations by computing the total contribution margin related to your answer in requirement (b).

EXTENDING YOUR KNOWLEDGE

EYK6-1. Business Decision Case The following total cost data are for Ralston Manufacturing Company, which has a normal capacity per period of 400,000 units of product that sell for $18 each. For the foreseeable future, regular sales volume should continue at normal capacity of production.

LO6

Direct materials.........................	$1,720,000
Direct labor............................	1,120,000
Variable overhead......................	560,000
Fixed overhead (Note 1).................	880,000
Selling expense (Note 2)	720,000
Administrative expense (fixed)	200,000
	$5,200,000

Notes:

1. Beyond normal capacity, fixed overhead cost increases $30,000 for each 20,000 units *or fraction thereof* until a maximum capacity of 640,000 units is reached.
2. Selling expenses are a 10% sales commission. Ralston pays only one-half of the regular sales commission rates on any sale of 20,000 or more units.

Ralston's sales manager has received a special order for 48,000 units from a large discount chain at a special price of $16 each, F.O.B. factory. The controller's office has furnished the following additional cost data related to the special order:

1. Changes in the product's construction will reduce direct materials by $1.80 per unit.
2. Special processing will add 25% to the per-unit direct labor costs.
3. Variable overhead will continue at the same proportion of direct labor costs.
4. Other costs should not be affected.

Required

a. Present an analysis supporting a decision to accept or reject the special order. Assume Ralston's regular sales are not affected by this special order.
b. What is the lowest unit sales price Ralston could receive and still make a before-tax profit of $39,600 on the special order?

EYK6-2. Ethics Case Gina DeMarc, a partner in a large CPA firm, has been approached by Bruce Jonas, a manager, with the following recommendation for incentive bonuses for staff members. Jonas recommends that the firm continue to pay each staff member a straight annual salary (which has been traditionally the only payment made), plus a bonus based on the staff member's ability to achieve a 10% reduction in time spent on each client's work. The firm would also pay a 5% finder's fee for any new client the staff member brings into the firm.

Jonas believes this will motivate the staff to work more efficiently, to sell the firm to new clients, and to service more clients in any given time period. This should also generate more revenue for the firm.

Required

How would you advise Gina DeMarc? What ethical issues should she consider?

ANSWERS TO SELF-STUDY QUESTIONS:

1. a   2. b   3. d   4. a   5. c   6. a

YOUR TURN! SOLUTIONS

Solution 6.1

y-intercep. ± = Total fixed costs of $5.000

Slop. ± = Variable cost per unit of approximately $0.50 per water bottle cage

Total cost = ($0.50 × # of water bottle cages) + $5,000

$25,000 = $0.50 × 40,000 + $5,000

Solution 6.2

The concept of relevant range can be applied to variable, fixed, and mixed costs. The assumption of a linear pattern is sufficiently accurate within a range of probable operations (i.e., the relevant range), where fixed costs remain unchanged and the addition of each additional unit is accompanied by a proportional increase in total cost.

Solution 6.3

a. Mixed cost: $2 per unit plus $5,000

$$\frac{\$24,500 - \$15,000}{9,750 - 5,000} = \$2 \text{ per unit}$$

$24,500 − ($2 × 9,750) = $5,000 fixed cost

or

$15,000 − ($2 × 5,000) = $5,000 fixed cost

b. From the Excel output:

Intercep. = $5,000
X-variable (Volume) = $2.00
Mixed cost = ($2 × Volume) + $5,000

Solution 6.4

Contribution margin = $3.50 − $2.10 = $1.40 per sandwich
Fixed cost = $595

a. Break-even point = $595/$1.40 per sandwich = 425 sandwiches
b. Total contribution margin = 1,200 sandwiches × $1.40 = $1,680
Operating income = $1,680 − $595 in fixed cost = $1,085

Solution 6.5

Sales price = $1.40/40% = $3.50 per sandwich

a. Break-even point in sales dollars = $595/40% = $1,487.50
$1,487.50/$3.50 per sandwich = 425 sandwiches must be sold to break even

b. Variable cost per unit = \$3.50 − \$1.40 = \$2.10 per unit
   1,400 sandwiches × \$2.10 = \$2,940 OR
   Variable cost % = 1 − Contribution margin % so 1 − 40% = 60%
   \$3.50 × 60% = \$2.10 in variable cost per unit
   1,400 sandwiches × \$2.10 = \$2,940

Solution 6.6

Contribution margin per unit = \$5.00 − \$1.25 = \$3.75 per unit
Contribution margin % = \$3.75/\$5.00 = 75%
Total fixed costs = \$12,675

1. \$12,675/75% = \$16,900
2. From part (1) \$16,900 in break-even point revenue. \$16,900/\$5.00 per unit = 3,380 units to break-even
3. [\$12,675 + \$15,000]/\$3.75 unit contribution margin = 7,380 desired units
4. Pre-tax operating profit = \$18,000/(1 − 25%) = \$24,000
   [\$12,675 + \$24,000]/\$3.75 unit contribution margin = 36,675 desired units
5. At 7,400 units, sales dollars = 7,400 × \$5 per unit = \$37,000
   From part (1), at breakeven sales dollars are \$16,900
   Margin of safety = \$37,000 − \$16,900 = \$20,100
   Check: 7,400 units − 3,380 units at breakeven = 4,020 units
   4,020 units × \$5 per unit = \$20,100

Chapter 7

Variable Costing: A Tool for Decision-Making

Road Map

LO	Learning Objective	Page	eLecture	Guided Example	Assignments
LO1	Describe the difference in the treatment of product costs between variable costing and absorption costing.	7-3	E7-1	YT7.1	SS1, SS6, Q1, Q2, SE1, SE2
LO2	Prepare an income statement under both variable costing and absorption costing methods.	7-5	E7-2	YT7.2	SS2, SS3, SE3, SE4, E1A, E2A, E1B, E2B, P1A, P2A, P3A, P1B, P2B, P3B
LO3	Explain why net income differs between absorption costing and variable costing. Reconcile the two different income amounts.	7-7	E7-3	YT7.3	SS3, SS4, SS5, Q3, Q4, SE5, SE6, SE7, SE8, SE9, E2A, E3A, E4A, E2B, E3B, E4B, P3A, P4A, P3B, P4B
LO4	Describe the advantages and disadvantages of the variable costing methods.	7-10	E7-4	YT7.4	SS6, Q5, SE10

General Motors (GM) designs, manufactures, and sells cars, trucks, and automobile parts worldwide. In North America, they are recognized by their Buick, Cadillac, Chevrolet, and GMC brands. GM operates in a highly competitive global marketplace.

The automotive industry has relatively high fixed costs and significant limitations on their ability to reduce these costs. Automobile manufacturers typically respond to these relatively high fixed costs by attempting to sell more vehicles by adding vehicle options, providing financing programs, offering marketing incentives, or reducing vehicle prices. In 2020, GM reported that its inventories declined from $10.4 billion to $10.2 billion.[1] Because a significant portion of GM's costs are fixed, this means that fixed manufacturing costs incurred in previous years (that had been recorded as part of inventories) were expensed in 2020, reducing GAAP income from what it would have been had GM sold fewer vehicles!

This chapter describes the difference in treatment of product costs between variable costing (useful for internal reporting) and absorption costing (required by GAAP).

PAST

Chapter 6 utilized our understanding of cost behavior to determine break-even and make planning and budgeting decisions.

PRESENT

Chapter 7 discusses the preparation of a variable income statement.

FUTURE

Chapter 8 describes some of the tools and techniques that management can use in making strategic business decisions.

---

[1] General Motors 10-K Report dated February 10, 2021.

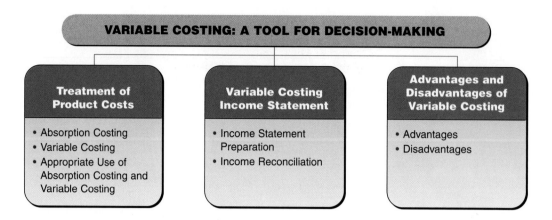

TREATMENT OF PRODUCT COSTS

LO1 **Describe** the difference in the treatment of product costs between variable costing and absorption costing.

![eLecture MBC]

A.K.A. Absorption costing is also referred to as *full costing* because it includes both variable and fixed components of product costs.

Includes fixed manufacturing overhead costs associated with the units sold, associating all manufacturing costs with the related sales revenue.

Absorption Costing

In **Chapter 2**, we define product costs as **all** manufacturing costs: direct materials, direct labor, and variable and fixed manufacturing overhead. These costs are capitalized as inventory during the production period and recognized as expense (cost of goods sold) only when the related merchandise is sold. This method of attaching all manufacturing costs to the product is known as **absorption costing**. **Exhibit 7-1a** presents the absorption costing income statement for Fezzari.

EXHIBIT 7-1A	Absorption Costing Income Statement for Fezzari

FEZZARI PERFORMANCE BICYCLES
Absorption Costing Income Statement
For the Year Ended December 31
(000's)

Sales.		$4,500
Cost of goods sold		2,957
Gross profit on sales.		$1,543
Operating expenses:		
Selling expenses.	$400	
Non-factory administrative expenses	340	740
Income from operations		$ 803
Other Income and Expense:		
Interest expense		5
Income before income tax		$ 798
Income tax expense		279
Net income		$ 519

A.K.A. Variable costing is also referred to as *direct costing*. The latter is a misnomer, however, because variable costs—not direct costs—are capitalized under direct costing.

Variable Costing

In contrast, for internal reporting purposes, some companies use **variable costing** to determine the cost of their manufactured products. Under variable costing, only *variable* manufacturing costs are capitalized as inventory. This includes direct materials, direct labor, and the variable portion of manufacturing overhead. All fixed manufacturing overhead costs are expensed in the period incurred. These fixed manufacturing costs are treated as a period cost in the same manner as selling, general, and administrative expenses. As a result, under variable costing, variable manufacturing cost amounts do not include the fixed portion of manufacturing overhead. **Exhibit 7-1b** presents the variable costing income statement for Fezzari.

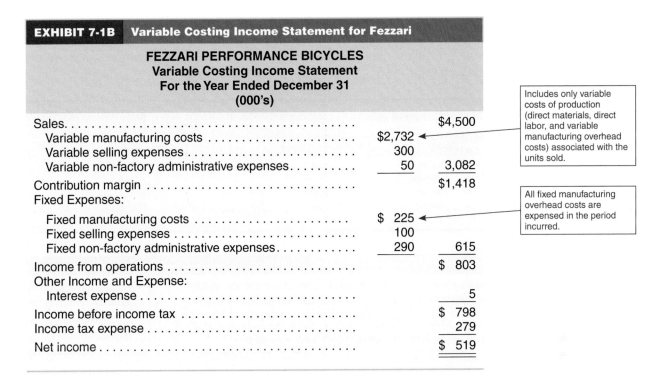

EXHIBIT 7-1B **Variable Costing Income Statement for Fezzari**

FEZZARI PERFORMANCE BICYCLES
Variable Costing Income Statement
For the Year Ended December 31
(000's)

Sales.		$4,500
Variable manufacturing costs	$2,732	
Variable selling expenses	300	
Variable non-factory administrative expenses.	50	3,082
Contribution margin		$1,418
Fixed Expenses:		
Fixed manufacturing costs	$ 225	
Fixed selling expenses	100	
Fixed non-factory administrative expenses.	290	615
Income from operations		$ 803
Other Income and Expense:		
Interest expense		5
Income before income tax		$ 798
Income tax expense		279
Net income		$ 519

> Includes only variable costs of production (direct materials, direct labor, and variable manufacturing overhead costs) associated with the units sold.

> All fixed manufacturing overhead costs are expensed in the period incurred.

The only difference between absorption and variable costing is the treatment of fixed manufacturing overhead costs. **Exhibit 7-2** illustrates this difference.

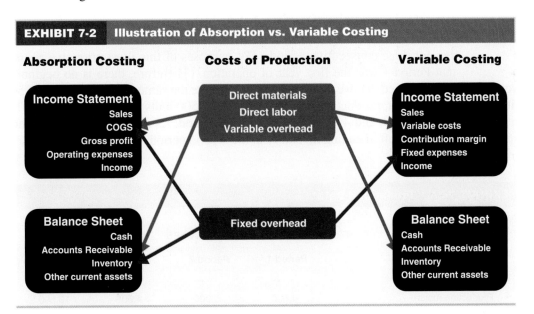

EXHIBIT 7-2 **Illustration of Absorption vs. Variable Costing**

Appropriate Use of Absorption Costing and Variable Costing

In general, variable costing (carrying only variable costs in the inventory accounts) is considered a departure from generally accepted accounting standards. These standards require that published financial reports attested to by CPAs be prepared on an absorption costing basis. In these reports, all manufacturing costs should be attributed to products, and inventories of work-in-process and finished goods should contain their allocable shares of manufacturing costs, both fixed and variable. Likewise, the Internal Revenue Service has generally insisted on the use of absorption costing in determining net income for tax purposes, with some adjustments.

Although variable costing should not be used to prepare financial statements for external use, management may use variable costing statements for internal decision-making. A principal benefit is that variable costing usually causes net income figures to move in the same direction as sales.

YOUR TURN! 7.1	How are fixed overhead production costs treated under absorption and variable costing methods?

The solution is on page 7-23.

GuidedExample

MBC

	Absorption	Variable Costing
a.	Period	Period
b.	Product	Product
c.	Period	Product
d.	Product	Period

TAKEAWAY 7.1	Concept	→	Method	→	Assessment
	How should a firm report its inventory in accordance with generally accepted accounting principles?		Firms are required to use the absorption costing method, which requires that all production costs, including fixed overhead costs, be included in the inventory valuation reported on the balance sheet.		• Absorption costing for external reporting purposes. • Variable costing for internal decision-making.

VARIABLE COSTING INCOME STATEMENT

LO2 Prepare an income statement under both variable costing and absorption costing methods.

eLecture

MBC

Income Statement Preparation

Exhibit 7-3a provides comparative production and sales information for Fezzari for three consecutive periods. For purposes of this illustration, we assume that Period 1 was the first year of operation. (Therefore, there is no beginning inventory balance.) Notice that we assume that unit sales are the same in all three years: 4,500 units each year. However, production varies over time—4,500 units in the first period, 5,000 units in the second period, and 4,000 units in the third period. As a result of this production schedule, 500 units are left in ending inventory in the second period. These units are then sold during the third period.

EXHIBIT 7-3A	Production Data				
	A	B	C	D	E
1	FEZZARI PERFORMANCE BICYCLES				
2		Period 1	Period 2	Period 3	Total
3	Beginning Inventory (units)	—	—	500	—
4	Production (units)	4,500	5,000	4,000	13,500
5	Sales (units)	4,500	4,500	4,500	13,500
6	Ending Inventory (units)	—	500	—	—

Exhibit 7-3b shows the absorption income statement that would be prepared for the three periods. Assume that Fezzari sells each bicycle for $1,000 per unit, that variable product costs are $618 per unit, and that fixed manufacturing costs are $225,000 per period. In the absorption income statement, the cost of goods manufactured includes both fixed and variable product costs. The inventory balance presented at the end of Period 2 consists of $309,000 of variable production costs (500 units × $618 per unit) and $22,500 in fixed production costs (because 10% of the units produced in Period 2 remain in inventory, 10% of the $225,000 in fixed production costs is assigned to the units in inventory).

EXHIBIT 7-3B   Partial Absorption Income Statement

	A	B	C	D	E	F
1		FEZZARI PERFORMANCE BICYCLES				
2			Period 1	Period 2	Period 3	Total
3		Beginning Inventory (units)	—	—	500	—
4		Production (units)	4,500	5,000	4,000	13,500
5		Sales (units)	4,500	4,500	4,500	13,500
6		Ending Inventory (units)	—	500	—	—
7			Absorption Costing Income Statement ($000s)			
8			Period 1	Period 2	Period 3	Total
9	(1)	Sales	$4,500	$4,500	$4,500	$13,500
10	(2)	Beginning Inventory	—	—	332	—
11	(3)	Cost of Goods Manufactured	3,006	3,315	2,697	9,018
12	(4)	Less Ending Inventory	—	332	—	—
13	(5)	Cost of Goods Sold [(2) + (3) − (4)]	$(3,006)	$(2,983)	$(3,029)	$ (9,018)
14	(6)	Gross Profit on Sales [(1) + (5)]	$ 1,494	$ 1,517	$ 1,471	$ 4,482

Period 1: (4,500 units × $618) + $225,000 = $3,006,000
Period 2: (5,000 units × $618) + $225,000 = $3,315,000
Period 3: (4,000 units × $618) + $225,000 = $2,697,000

Note that although sales were steady over the three periods, gross profit changed with production. (As production increased, so did profit; as production decreased, so did profit.)

Variable cost: 500 units × $618 =	$309,000
Fixed cost: 500 units/5,000 units × $225,000 =	22,500
Total cost:	$331,500

Exhibit 7-3c shows the variable costing income statement for the periods. The variable cost of goods sold includes only the variable costs of production at $618 per unit. The inventory balance presented at the end of Period 2 consists of only the variable costs of production (500 units × $618 per unit, or $309,000).

EXHIBIT 7-3C   Partial Variable Income Statement

	A	B	C	D	E	F
1		FEZZARI PERFORMANCE BICYCLES				
2			Period 1	Period 2	Period 3	Total
3		Beginning Inventory (units)	—	—	500	—
4		Production (units)	4,500	5,000	4,000	13,500
5		Sales (units)	4,500	4,500	4,500	13,500
6		Ending Inventory (units)	—	500	—	—
7			Variable Costing Income Statement ($000's)			
8			Period 1	Period 2	Period 3	Total
9	(1)	Sales	$4,500	$4,500	$4,500	$13,500
10	(2)	Beginning Inventory	—	—	309	—
11	(3)	Variable Cost of Goods Manufactured	2,781	3,090	2,472	8,343
12	(4)	Less Ending Inventory	—	309	—	—
13	(5)	Variable Manufacturing Costs [(2) + (3) − (4)]	$(2,781)	$(2,781)	$(2,781)	$ (8,343)
14	(6)	Contribution Margin [(1) + (5)]	$ 1,719	$ 1,719	$ 1,719	$ 5,157
15	(7)	Fixed Manufacturing Costs	(225)	(225)	(225)	(675)
16	(8)	Income from Operations [(6) + (7)]	$ 1,494	$1 ,494	$ 1,494	$ 4,482

Variable cost: 500 units × $618 =	$309,000
Fixed cost:	0
Total cost:	$309,000

Note that, unlike absorption costing, income from operations follows sales, not production.

TAKEAWAY 7.2	Concept	→	Method	→	Assessment
	How do cost of goods sold and inventory values differ between absorption and variable costing income statements?		• Absorption costing: Includes all production costs (direct materials, direct labor, variable and fixed manufacturing overhead) • Variable costing: Includes only variable production costs (direct materials, direct labor, variable manufacturing overhead)		Under variable costing, both cost of goods sold and inventory valuation will be less than under absorption costing.

A total of $4,482,000 gross profit/income from operations is reported for the three periods under both methods. However, the variable costing method indicates the same income from operations figures in each period ($1,494,000), which are correlated with the constant sales volume over the three periods. On the other hand, under the absorption costing method, gross profit moves up and down with production (from $1,494,000 to $1,517,000 to $1,471,000). The reason, of course, is that the fixed costs are added to the inventory (and therefore not included in cost of goods sold) when production exceeds sales in period 2 and are released (through cost of goods sold) when the company sells more than it produces in period 3.

ENVIRONMENTAL, SOCIAL, AND GOVERNANCE — Triple Bottom Line Reporting

This chapter has introduced an internal reporting approach called variable costing, which allows management to more easily focus on the contribution of customers, products, product lines, business segments, and other business units to the overall profitability of the company. Another type of reporting has also gained in importance. That other type of reporting, called triple-bottom-line reporting, considers not just financial results, but also environmental and social results as well. As stated on GM's website, "Through the lens of sustainability, we view industry challenges and change as new business opportunities that can drive additional value for our customers. We call this Customer-Driven Sustainability. From designing more fuel-efficient vehicles and deploying advanced-safety technologies to being the workplace of choice for employees and the neighbor of choice for communities, we make strategic decisions based on how the outcome of those decisions ultimately translates into value for our customers." An example of this behavior is illustrated by GM's greening of the General Motors Baltimore Operations complex. The LEED Silver building exceeds the voluntary U.S. Environmental Protection Agency's ENERGY STAR® Challenge for Industry, which requires a 10% reduction in energy intensity within 5 years. "We believe reducing our environmental footprint is good for the climate and good for our business," said Greg Martin, executive director of Global Public Policy. "Wherever we can, we are reducing our energy use, powering our plants with renewable energy and conserving resources."

YOUR TURN! 7.2

The solution is on page 7-23.

MBC

Tilley Manufacturing Company produces one product, which sells for $100. Product costs at the normal level of manufacturing operations (100,000 units) are the following:

Direct materials	$25 per unit
Direct labor	$20 per unit
Variable overhead	$10 per unit
Fixed overhead	$495,000

During its first year of operations, Tilley produced 100,000 units and sold 90,000 units. Determine:
1. Gross profit using absorption costing.
2. Income from operations using variable costing.

LO3
Explain why net income differs between absorption costing and variable costing. Reconcile the two different income amounts.

MBC

Income Reconciliation

Once the relationship between variable costing and absorption costing is understood, it is possible to determine the differences between variable income and absorption income using a "short-cut" calculation without having to prepare separate financial statements. Remember that the only difference between variable income and absorption income is the treatment of the fixed costs of production—under absorption costing, some of these fixed production costs are included in inventory on the balance sheet, whereas they are all expensed under variable costing. So, if inventory increases by 500 units from one period to the next (as illustrated previously in **Exhibit 7-3b**), each unit in inventory will have $45.00 ($225,000/5,000 units) of fixed manufacturing costs. Because all fixed manufacturing costs have been expensed under the variable costing approach, absorption income should be $22,500 more than variable income, as shown:

$$\begin{array}{ccc} \textbf{\$45.00 fixed manufacturing} & & \textbf{500 units added to} & & \textbf{\$22,500 (or \$23,000 as} \\ \textbf{cost per unit} & \times & \textbf{inventory} & = & \textbf{rounded in the Excel exhibit)} \end{array}$$

$$\begin{array}{ccc} \textbf{\$1,517,000} & & \textbf{\$23,000} & & \textbf{\$1,494,000} \\ \textbf{(absorption} & - & \textbf{(fixed manufacturing} & = & \textbf{(variable} \\ \textbf{income)} & & \textbf{cost added to inventory)} & & \textbf{income)} \end{array}$$

With absorption costing, net income may increase in periods when production volume exceeds sales (increasing inventory on the balance sheet) and decrease when sales volume exceeds production (decreasing inventory on the balance sheet). Why is this important to understand? This is important knowledge because it may be possible for managers to increase reported net income to meet analysts' expectations by increasing production of product during the last few weeks of a reporting period. Of course, this short-term "fix" could result in excess inventory levels that lead to obsolescence and inventory write-offs in subsequent periods. The impact of differences between production and sales under both absorption and variable costing is summarized in **Exhibit 7-4**.

EXHIBIT 7-4	Impact of Varying Levels of Production		
	Income Statement	**Balance Sheet**	**Explanation**
Production = Sales	No difference in reported income	No change in inventory values	Current period fixed costs expensed under both absorption and variable costing methods
Production > Sales	Absorption net income is greater than variable net income	Absorption balance sheet inventory increases by more than variable balance sheet inventory	Some current period fixed costs are added to inventory under absorption costing method, but all are expensed under variable costing method
Production < Sales	Absorption net income is less than variable net income	Absorption balance sheet inventory decreases by more than variable balance sheet inventory	Some prior period fixed costs that are in the beginning inventory balance along with current period fixed costs under absorption costing method are expensed in the current period as cost of goods sold, but only current period fixed costs are expensed under variable costing method

To highlight the effect of variable costing on inventories and income in the foregoing illustration, we consider only manufacturing costs. When detailed income statements are prepared under the variable costing method, fixed and variable costs of all types—including selling and administrative expenses—must be properly segregated. **Exhibit 7-5** presents an example of a complete and detailed income statement prepared in accordance with the variable costing concept. As illustrated in **Exhibit 7-5**, absorption net income changes with the level of production and variable net income changes with the level of sales. Because unit sales does not change over the three periods, reported variable net income does not change. The reason is that, as noted previously, fixed costs are not included in the inventory account on the balance sheet but are expensed in the period that they are incurred under variable costing.

EXHIBIT 7-5	Absorption vs. Variable Costing Income Statements				
	FEZZARI PERFORMANCE BICYCLES				
		Period 1	Period 2	Period 3	Total
	Beginning Inventory (units)	—	—	500	—
	Production (units)	4,500	5,000	4,000	13,500
	Sales (units)	4,500	4,500	4,500	13,500
	Ending Inventory (units)	—	500	—	—
	Absorption Costing Income Statement ($000s)				
		Period 1	Period 2	Period 3	Total
(1)	Sales	$ 4,500	$ 4,500	$ 4,500	$13,500
(2)	Beginning Inventory	—	—	332	—
(3)	Cost of Goods Manufactured	3,006	3,315	2,697	9,018
(4)	Less Ending Inventory	—	332	—	—
(5)	Cost of Goods Sold [(2) + (3) − (4)]	$(3,006)	$(2,983)	$(3,029)	$ (9,018)
(6)	Gross Profit on Sales [(1) + (5)]	$ 1,494	$ 1,517	$ 1,471	$ 4,482
	Operating Expenses:				
(7)	Selling Expenses	(400)	(400)	(400)	(1,200)
(8)	Administrative Expenses	(340)	(340)	(340)	(1,020)
(9)	Income from Operations [(6) + (7) + (8)]	$ 754	$ 777	$ 731	$ 2,262
	Variable Costing Income Statement ($000s)				
		Period 1	Period 2	Period 3	Total
(1)	Sales	$ 4,500	$ 4,500	$ 4,500	$13,500
(2)	Beginning Inventory	—	—	309	—
(3)	Variable Cost of Goods Manufactured	2,781	3,090	2,472	8,343
(4)	Less Ending Inventory	—	309	—	—
(5)	Variable Manufacturing Costs [(2) + (3) − (4)]	$(2,781)	$(2,781)	$(2,781)	$ (8,343)
(6)	Variable Selling Expenses	(300)	(300)	(300)	(900)
(7)	Variable Administrative Expenses	(50)	(50)	(50)	(150)
(8)	Contribution Margin [(1) + (5) + (6) + (7)]	$ 1,369	$ 1,369	$ 1,369	$ 4,107
	Fixed Expenses:				
(9)	Fixed Manufacturing Costs	(225)	(225)	(225)	(675)
(10)	Fixed Selling Expenses	(100)	(100)	(100)	(300)
(11)	Fixed Administrative Expenses	(290)	(290)	(290)	(870)
(12)	Income from Operations [(8) + (9) + (10) + (11)]	$ 754	$ 754	$ 754	$ 2,262

All production costs, including fixed overhead, are included in cost of goods sold under absorption costing.

Only variable production costs are included in cost of goods sold under variable costing.

All variable costs (including selling and administrative) are subtracted to determine contribution margin under absorption costing.

Fixed overhead costs are treated as period costs and expensed in the period incurred under variable costing.

Contribution margin can be determined by deducting all variable expenses (cost of goods sold, selling, and administrative expenses) from sales. (This concept was previously introduced in Chapter 6.) All types of fixed expenses (manufacturing, selling, and administrative) are deducted to arrive at net income.

Assume that Fezzari's reported absorption costing income was $1,600,000 in Year 1. What would variable costing income be if Fezzari's inventory increased by 100 units during Year 1 and fixed manufacturing cost was equal to $50 per unit?

YOUR TURN! 7.3

The solution is on page 7-23.

ADVANTAGES AND DISADVANTAGES OF VARIABLE COSTING

The following advantages and disadvantages of using variable costing result from the fact that under variable costing no fixed overhead costs are assigned to inventory carrying values.

LO4 Describe the advantages and disadvantages of the variable costing methods.

Advantages

1. Variable costing assigns only variable costs to inventory. Reporting inventory values in this manner helps managers avoid making "death spiral" decisions.

2. Under variable costing, because all fixed costs are reported separately, managers are able to see how much fixed cost must be covered before a profit will be generated.

3. Reported net income tends to follow sales volume, eliminating the incentive to temporarily boost income by producing more product than can be sold in the short term.

4. Cost-volume-profit (CVP) relationships are more easily discerned from variable costing income statements than from conventional absorption costing statements. The cost information needed for CVP analysis (which was discussed in **Chapter 6**) is readily available from variable cost financial statements.

5. Variable costing statements make it easier to determine the contribution of customers, products, product lines, business segments, and other business units to the overall profitability of the company. This is typically obscured by the allocation of fixed costs under absorption costing.

Disadvantages

1. Accounting measures derived under variable costing are not in conformity with generally accepted accounting principles, nor are they acceptable for reporting purposes under the Internal Revenue Code.

2. Inventories (and therefore working capital and owners' equity) tend to be understated.

3. Carrying inventories at only their variable costs may lead to long-run pricing decisions that provide for recovery of variable cost only rather than total cost, which will not produce net income in the long run.

4. Variable costing generally requires that a "second set" of accounting records be kept, increasing the cost of the required accounting systems and possible confusion among managers.

Hint: A "death spiral" decision is one in which management eliminates a product or division that has a positive contribution margin but shows a loss when other non-controllable costs are allocated to it. By eliminating the product or division, the positive contribution margin is lost so that other products or divisions now have to cover all of the fixed costs. This may cause another product or division to appear unprofitable, leading to additional decisions to eliminate products or divisions that have positive contribution margins.

Which of the following is a disadvantage of using the variable costing method to value inventory?

a. Managers are able to determine the amount of revenue needed to cover fixed costs.

b. Because net income follows production, incentives to increase profit by boosting production are eliminated.

c. Variable costing is not allowed under generally accepted accounting principles.

d. Cost-volume-profit relationships are more easily discerned.

SERVICES INDUSTRY IN FOCUS

SERVICE AND MERCHANDISING

Environmental Business Consultants (EBC) compensates all of its employees as salaried workers. Thus, EBC considers its labor cost as fixed—that is, EBC consultants are paid their full salary and benefits regardless of the number of consulting projects that they perform during a year. The only other fixed cost is the office lease expense. A partial trial balance for the year ended December 31 is provided next.

Description	Trial Balance		Variable or Fixed	Direct Service or SGA
	Debit	**Credit**		
Sales.		3,715,000		
Executive salaries.	844,500		F	D
Clerical salaries	217,500		F	D
Consultant salaries.	1,050,000		F	D
Employee benefits	145,500		F	D
Payroll taxes	123,000		F	D
Employee bonuses.	126,000		V	SGA
Marketing expenses	48,000		V	SGA
Employee continuing education expenses	27,000		V	SGA
Office lease expense	202,500		F	D
Office supplies expense	64,500		V	D
Other general administrative expense	355,500		V	SGA

EBC's typical project takes several months to complete. Thus, at year-end, several projects may be in process. Costs incurred to date on those projects are accumulated in Work-in-Process Inventory until completed. Assume that EBC's beginning absorption Work-in-Process Inventory is $223,000 and its ending absorption Work-in-Process (WIP) Inventory is $247,000. Further, assume that EBC's beginning variable WIP inventory is $5,400 and its ending variable WIP inventory is $6,000.

Required

a. Determine income from operations using

   1. Absorption costing.

   2. Variable costing.

b. Compare the income from operations derived under the two methods.

Solution

a. 1.

ENVIRONMENTAL BUSINESS CONSULTANTS, LLC Absorption Income Statement For the Year Ended December 31		
Sales		$3,715,000
Direct labor		$2,380,500
General overhead:		
Office lease expense	$202,500	
Office supplies expense	64,500	
Total general overhead		267,000
Total service costs for the year		$2,647,500
Add: beginning work-in-process inventory		223,000
Total cost of work-in-process during the year		$2,870,500
Less: ending work-in-process inventory		(247,000)
Cost of services		2,623,500
Gross profit on sales		$1,091,500
Operating expenses:		
Employee bonuses	$126,000	
Marketing expenses	48,000	
Employee continuing education expenses	27,000	
Other general administrative expenses	355,500	
Total operating expenses		556,500
Income from operations		$ 535,000

2.

ENVIRONMENTAL BUSINESS CONSULTANTS, LLC Variable Income Statement For the Year Ended December 31		
Sales		$3,715,000
Beginning variable WIP		$ 5,400
Variable costs		
Office supplies expense		64,500
Less ending variable WIP		(6,000)
Variable cost of service		$ 63,900
Other variable expenses		
Employee bonuses	$ 126,000	
Marketing expenses	48,000	
Employee continuing education expenses	27,000	
Other general administrative expenses	355,500	
Total other variable cost		556,500
Total variable costs		$ 620,400
Contribution margin		$3,094,600
Fixed costs		
Direct labor	$2,380,500	
Office lease expense	202,500	
Total fixed costs		2,583,000
Income from operations		$ 511,600

b.

Absorption income from operations		$535,000
Less:		
Increase in fixed costs in WIP inventory:		
Ending (247,000 – 6,000).	241,000	
Beginning (223,000 – 5,400)	217,600	
		(23,400)
Variable income from operations		$511,600

Data Analytics

DATA ANALYTICS   Drowning in Data

When one thinks of the companies that have amassed the greatest amount of customer data, Amazon, Google, and Facebook probably come to mind. It might come as a surprise, but **General Motors** has also collected an enormous amount of data on its customers. Thanks to OnStar, the platform that controls a vehicle's telematics, GM has collected data from 20 million drivers in 47 countries. This treasure trove of data makes GM one of the top ten largest data collectors in the United States. A big challenge with collecting all this data is the tension between collecting useful data and protecting customer privacy. GM attempts to satisfy both requirements by anonymizing the data so that the driver's identity is not linked with the vehicular data.

COMPREHENSIVE PROBLEM

Tuttle Manufacturing Company produces only one product, which sells for $50. Product costs at the normal level of manufacturing operations (10,000 units) are the following:

Direct materials.	$14 per unit
Direct labor.	$12 per unit
Variable overhead.	$ 4 per unit
Fixed overhead.	$49,500

Selling expenses (100% variable) are $3 per unit; administrative expenses (100% fixed) are $30,000. During the year, Tuttle produced 11,000 units and sold 9,000 units. Tuttle had no beginning inventory of product.

Required

a. Determine net income (ignoring income taxes) using

  1. Absorption costing.   2. Variable costing.

b. Compare the total net income derived under the two methods.

Solution

a.

Absorption Costing		
Sales (9,000 units × $50)		$450,000
Cost of goods sold:		
Direct materials (11,000 × $14)	$154,000	
Direct labor (11,000 × $12).	132,000	
Variable overhead (11,000 × $4).	44,000	
Fixed overhead	49,500	
	379,500	
Less: Ending inventory [($379,500/11,000) × 2,000] . . .	69,000	
Cost of goods sold		310,500
Gross profit.		$139,500
Selling expense (9,000 units × $3)	27,000	
Administrative expense.	30,000	57,000
Net income		$ 82,500

continued

continued from previous page

Variable Costing		
Sales (9,000 units × $50)		$450,000
Variable expenses:		
Direct materials (11,000 × $14)	$154,000	
Direct labor (11,000 × $12).	132,000	
Variable overhead (11,000 × $4).	44,000	
	330,000	
Less: Ending inventory [($330,000/11,000) × 2,000] . . .	60,000	
Variable manufacturing costs		270,000
Variable selling expense (9,000 × $3)		27,000
Contribution margin		153,000
Fixed expenses:		
Fixed overhead	49,500	
Administrative expense.	30,000	79,500
Net income		$ 73,500

b.

Comparison	
Absorption costing net income	$82,500
Variable costing net income	73,500
Difference (explained below)	$ 9,000

The amount of fixed overhead contained in the absorption costing ending inventory is $9,000 [($49,500/11,000) × 2,000].

The amount of fixed overhead contained in the variable costing ending inventory is 0. The different treatment of fixed overhead fully explains the difference.

SUMMARY OF LEARNING OBJECTIVES

Describe the difference in the treatment of product costs between variable costing and absorption costing. (p. 7-3)   **LO1**

- Absorption costing capitalizes all manufacturing costs as inventory during the production period and recognizes them as expense (cost of goods sold) only when the related merchandise is sold.
- Variable costing does not assign fixed manufacturing overhead as a product cost but expenses it in the period incurred.
- Accounting measures derived under variable costing are not in accord with generally accepted accounting principles, nor are they acceptable for tax reporting.

Prepare an income statement under both variable costing and absorption costing methods. (p. 7-5)   **LO2**

- For absorption costing, include the fixed costs and variable costs of manufacturing in the computation of cost of goods sold.
- For variable costing, only include the variable costs of manufacturing in the computation of variable manufacturing cost. Expense all fixed costs, including fixed manufacturing costs, in the period.

Explain why net income differs between absorption costing and variable costing. Reconcile the two different income amounts. (p. 7-7)   **LO3**

- The difference between absorption income and variable income will be the amount of fixed manufacturing costs either added to or subtracted from work-in-process inventory during the period.
- When production volume exceeds sales volume, absorption income will be greater than variable income.
- When production volume is less than sales volume, absorption income will be less than variable income.

LO4   **Describe the advantages and disadvantages of the variable costing methods. (p. 7-10)**

- The primary advantage of variable costing is that reported income follows changes in production volume, reducing the risk of "death spiral" decisions.
- Variable costing provides all of the information required for CVP analysis.
- The primary disadvantage of variable costing is that it is not acceptable for financial statement reporting or tax reporting.
- Because variable costing requires the maintenance of a "second set" of books, it is more costly.

SUMMARY	Concept ➜	Method ➜	Assessment
TAKEAWAY 7.1	How should a firm report its inventory in accordance with generally accepted accounting principles?	Firms are required to use the absorption costing method, which requires that all production costs, including fixed overhead costs, be included in the inventory valuation reported on the balance sheet.	• Absorption costing for external reporting purposes. • Variable costing for internal decision-making.
TAKEAWAY 7.2	How do cost of goods sold and inventory values differ between absorption and variable costing income statements?	• Absorption costing: Includes all production costs (direct materials, direct labor, variable and fixed manufacturing overhead) • Variable costing: Includes only variable production costs (direct materials, direct labor, variable manufacturing overhead)	Under variable costing, both cost of goods sold and inventory valuation will be less than under absorption costing.

KEY TERMS

Absorption costing (p. 7-3)   Full costing (p. 7-3)
Contribution margin (p. 7-10)   Variable costing (p. 7-3)
Direct costing (p. 7-3)

Assignments with the ⬤ logo in the margin are available in ᵐʸBusinessCourse.
See the Preface of the book for details.

SELF-STUDY QUESTIONS

(Answers to Self-Study Questions are at the end of this chapter.)

LO1   1. In determining inventory costs, which of the following cost elements is included when using absorption costing but excluded when using variable costing?

    a. Selling costs   *c.* Non-factory administrative costs
    b. Direct labor cost   *d.* Fixed overhead

LO2   2. Under which costing method are fixed overhead production costs excluded from cost of goods sold and inventory?

    a. Full costing   *c.* Variable costing
    b. Absorption costing   *d.* Normal costing

LO2, 3 3. If unit production exceeds unit sales during the period, absorption income will be

    a. less than variable income.   *c.* equal to variable income.
    b. more than variable income.

LO3   4. If unit production is less than unit sales during the period, absorption income will be

    a. less than variable income.   *c.* equal to variable income.
    b. more than variable income.

LO3   5. If unit production is equal to unit sales during the period, absorption income will be

    a. less than variable income.   *c.* equal to variable income.
    b. more than variable income.

6. **True or false: Variable costing may be used by management in preparing audited financial statements.**

    a.   True   *b.*   False

LO1, 4

QUESTIONS

1. Which method, absorption or variable costing, is used for external reporting purposes in accordance with generally accepted accounting principles?   **LO1**
2. Which method, absorption or variable costing, is used for internal management reporting purposes?   **LO1**
3. When inventories are increasing, will absorption income be higher or lower than variable income?   **LO3**
4. What generalizations can be made about the difference in income reported under variable and absorption costing?   **LO3**
5. What is variable costing? List its advantages and disadvantages.   **LO4**

SHORT EXERCISES

SE7-1. If a manufacturing company uses variable costing to cost inventories, which of the following costs are considered inventoriable costs?   **LO1**

    a.   Only raw materials, direct labor, and variable manufacturing overhead costs
    b.   Only raw materials, direct labor, and variable and fixed manufacturing overhead costs
    c.   Only raw materials, direct labor, variable manufacturing overhead, and variable selling and administrative costs
    d.   Only raw materials and direct labor costs

SE7-2. Which one of the following is true with respect to variable and absorption costing systems?   **LO1**

    a.   Variable costing systems include fixed manufacturing overhead as period costs.
    b.   Absorption costing systems include fixed manufacturing overhead as period costs.
    c.   Variable costing systems include variable manufacturing overhead as period costs.
    d.   Absorption costing systems include variable manufacturing overhead as period costs.

SE7-3. Operating income under variable costing is contribution margin minus   **LO2**

    a.   cost of goods sold and administrative expenses.
    b.   fixed manufacturing overhead and fixed selling and administrative expenses.
    c.   fixed manufacturing overhead and variable manufacturing overhead.
    d.   variable selling and administrative expenses and fixed selling and administrative expenses.

SE7-4. The following data relate to Smurf Corporation for the year just ended: **LO2**

Sales revenue	$550,000
Cost of goods sold:	
Variable portion	170,000
Fixed portion	110,000
Variable selling and administrative cost	50,000
Fixed selling and administrative cost	125,000

Which of the following statements is correct?

    a.   Smurf's variable costing income statement would reveal a gross margin of $270,000.
    b.   Smurf's variable costing income statement would reveal a contribution margin of $330,000.
    c.   Smurf's absorption costing income statement would reveal a contribution margin of $220,000.
    d.   Smurf's absorption costing income statement would reveal a gross margin of $330,000.

SE7-5. When comparing absorption costing with variable costing, the difference in operating income can be explained by the difference between the   **LO3**

    a.   units sold and the units produced, multiplied by the unit sales price.
    b.   ending inventory in units and the beginning inventory in units, multiplied by the budgeted fixed manufacturing cost per unit.

    c.   ending inventory in units and the beginning inventory in units, multiplied by the unit sales price.

    d.   units sold and the units produced, multiplied by the budgeted variable manufacturing cost per unit.

LO3

SE7-6. Mill Corporation had the following unit costs for the recently concluded calendar year:

	Variable	Fixed
Manufacturing.	$8.00	$3.00
Non-manufacturing.	$2.00	$5.50

Inventory for Mill's sole product totaled 6,000 units on January 1 and 5,200 units on December 31. When compared to variable costing income, Mill's absorption costing income is

    a. $2,400 lower.   *c.* $6,800 lower.

    b. $2,400 higher.   *d.* $6,800 higher.

LO3

SE7-7. During the month of May, Robinson Corporation sold 1,000 units. The cost per unit for May was as follows:

	Cost Per Unit
Direct materials.	$ 5.50
Direct labor	3.00
Variable manufacturing overhead	1.00
Fixed manufacturing overhead	1.50
Variable administrative costs	.50
Fixed administrative costs	3.50
Total	$15.00

May's income using absorption costing was $9,500. The income for May, if variable costing had been used, would have been $9,125. The number of units Robinson produced during May was

    a.   750 units.   *c.*   1,075 units.

    b.   925 units.   *d.*   1,250 units.

LO3

SE7-8. Jorgensen Company has 10,000 units in its ending inventory. During the year, the company's variable production costs were $10 per unit and its fixed manufacturing overhead application rate was $5 per unit. The company's net income for the year was $15,000 lower under absorption costing than it was under variable costing. Given these facts, what was the number of units in the beginning inventory? (Assume the company uses normal costing and closes over- and under-applied overhead directly to COGS, and that the fixed manufacturing overhead application rate is constant from year to year.)

    a.   7,000 units   *c.*   11,500 units

    b.   8,500 units   *d.*   13,000 units

LO3

SE7-9. Drake Company has the following information:

Variable production costs	$10 per unit
Fixed OH production costs	$100,000 per year
Variable selling & admin.	$5 per unit
Fixed selling & admin..	$80,000 per year
Normal annual production	20,000 units
Budgeted annual production.	19,000 units
Actual annual production	15,000 units
Actual annual sales	19,000 units
Beginning inventory	5,000 units

The company uses the FIFO inventory method. Over- and under-applied overhead is closed directly to cost of goods sold.

       If income under absorption costing for the year is $100,000, what was the net income under the variable costing method assuming that overhead was applied to production using a rate based on normal production?

    a. $80,000   *c.* $120,000

    b. $100,000   *d.* $125,000

SE7-10. Which one of the following is the **best** reason for using variable costing?

    a. Fixed factory overhead is more closely related to the capacity to produce than to the production of specific units.

    b. All costs are variable in the long term.

    c. Variable costing is acceptable for income tax reporting purposes.

    d. Variable costing usually results in higher operating income than if a company uses absorption costing.

LO4

DATA ANALYTICS, DATA VISUALIZATION, AND EXCEL ACTIVITIES

Data Analytics, Data Visualization, and Excel Activities are available in myBusinessCourse. These assignments develop Excel, Tableau, and Data Analytics skills, which will enhance students' career readiness. These exercises are assignable and auto graded by MBC. For an overview of data analytics, see the appendix at the end of this book.

EXERCISES—SET A

E7-1A. Variable and Absorption Costing Chandler Company sells its product for $100 per unit. Variable manufacturing costs per unit are $40, and fixed manufacturing costs at the normal operating level of 10,000 units are $240,000. Variable selling expenses are $16 per unit sold. Fixed administrative expenses total $104,000. Chandler had no beginning inventory in Year 1. During the year, the company produced 10,000 units and sold 8,000. Would net income for Chandler Company in Year 1 be higher if calculated using variable costing or using absorption costing? Calculate reported income using each method.

LO2

E7-2A. Variable and Absorption Costing—Service Company Lawn RX, Inc. prepares a variable costing income statement for internal management and an absorption costing income statement for its bank. Lawn RX provides a quarterly lawn care service that is sold for $140. The variable and fixed cost data are as follows:

LO2, 3

Direct labor	$ 80.00
Overhead:	
Variable cost per unit	$ 5.00
Fixed cost	$100,000
Marketing, general, and administrative:	
Variable cost (per contract completed)	$ 6.00
Administrative expense (fixed) (per month)	$ 42,000

During the year, 10,000 service contracts were signed and 9,800 service contracts were completed. Lawn RX had no service contracts at the beginning of the year.

Required

    a. Calculate reported income for management.

    b. Calculate reported income for the bank.

    c. Reconcile the two income amounts.

E7-3A. Variable and Absorption Costing During its first year, Walnut, Inc., showed a $14 per-unit profit under absorption costing but would have reported a total profit $16,000 less under variable costing. If production exceeded sales by 1,000 units and an average contribution margin of 62.5% was maintained, what is the apparent:

LO3

    a. Fixed cost per unit?

    b. Sales price per unit?

    c. Variable cost per unit?

    d. Unit sales volume if total profit under absorption costing was $168,000?

E7-4A. Variable and Absorption Costing Pyne Company produces a single product. The company has 50,000 units in its ending inventory. Pyne's variable production costs during the year were $10 per unit and fixed manufacturing overhead costs were applied at $25 per unit (which was the same as last

LO3

year). The company's net operating income is $120,000 higher under variable costing than it is under absorption costing; and the company uses FIFO and closes any over- or under-applied overhead directly to cost of goods sold. Given these facts, what was the number of units of product in beginning inventory?

EXERCISES—SET B

LO2 **E7-1B.** **Variable and Absorption Costing** Grant Company sells its product for $50 per unit. Variable manufacturing costs per unit are $30, and fixed manufacturing costs at the normal operating level of 15,000 units are $90,000. Variable selling expenses are $4 per unit sold. Fixed administrative expenses total $155,000. Grant had 7,000 units at a per-unit cost of $35 in beginning inventory. During the year, the company produced 15,000 units and sold 20,000. Would net income for Grant Company be higher if calculated using variable costing or using absorption costing? Calculate reported income using each method.

LO2, 3 **E7-2B.** **Variable and Absorption Costing—Service Company** Tech Helpers Company prepares a variable costing income statement for internal management and an absorption costing income statement for its bank. Tech Helpers provides a personal computer maintenance service that is sold for $100. The variable and fixed cost data are as follows:

Direct labor	$ 25.00
Overhead:	
Variable cost per unit	$ 5.00
Fixed cost	$240,000
Marketing, general, and administrative:	
Variable cost (per service contract completed)	$ 5.00
Fixed cost (per month)	$ 20,000

During the year, 4,500 service contracts were started and 5,000 service contracts were completed. At the beginning of the year, Tech Helpers had 500 service contracts in process at a per-unit cost of $90 in beginning work-in-process inventory.

Required
a. Calculate reported income for management.
b. Calculate reported income for the bank.
c. Reconcile the two income amounts.

LO3 **E7-3B.** **Variable and Absorption Costing** During its first year, Concord, Inc., showed a $20 per-unit profit under absorption costing but would have reported a total profit $16,800 less under variable costing. If production exceeded sales by 600 units and an average contribution margin of 60% was maintained, what is the apparent:

a. Fixed cost per unit?
b. Sales price per unit?
c. Variable cost per unit?
d. Unit sales volume if total profit under absorption costing was $189,000?

LO3 **E7-4B.** **Variable and Absorption Costing** Beech Company produces a single product. The company has 50,000 units in its beginning inventory. Beech's variable production costs during the year were $10 per unit and fixed manufacturing overhead costs were applied at $30 per unit (which was the same as last year). The company's net operating income is $120,000 lower under variable costing than it is under absorption costing; and the company uses FIFO and closes any over- or under-applied overhead directly to cost of goods sold. Given these facts, what was the number of units of product in beginning inventory?

PROBLEMS—SET A

LO2 **P7-1A.** **Variable and Absorption Costing** Summarized data for the first year of operations for Gorman Products, Inc., are as follows:

Sales (70,000 units)	$2,800,000
Production costs (80,000 units):	
Direct materials.	880,000
Direct labor	720,000
Manufacturing overhead:	
Variable.	544,000
Fixed	320,000
Operating expenses:	
Variable.	175,000
Fixed	240,000
Depreciation on equipment.	60,000
Real estate taxes	18,000
Personal property taxes (on inventory and equipment)	28,800
Personnel department expenses	30,000

Required

a.   Prepare an income statement based on full absorption costing.

b.   Prepare an income statement based on variable costing.

c.   If the ending inventory is destroyed by fire, which costing approach would you use as a basis for filing an insurance claim for the fire loss? Why?

P7-2A.   Variable and Absorption Costing—Service Company   Jensen's Tailoring provides custom tailoring services. After the company's first year of operations, its owner prepared the following summarized data report:

LO2

SERVICE AND
MERCHANDISING

Sales (500 completed jobs)	$100,000
Tailoring costs (550 jobs):	
Direct labor	47,000
Manufacturing overhead:	
Variable.	12,000
Fixed	9,000
Operating expenses:	
Variable.	5,600
Fixed	5,800

Required

a.   Prepare an income statement based on full absorption costing. (Round ending inventory to the nearest $.)

b.   Prepare an income statement based on variable costing. (Round ending inventory to the nearest $.)

P7-3A.   Variable and Absorption Costing   Scott Manufacturing makes only one product with total unit manufacturing costs of $54, of which $40 is variable. No units were on hand at the beginning of Year 1. During Year 1 and Year 2, the only product manufactured was sold for $65 per unit, and the cost structure did not change. Scott uses the first-in, first-out inventory method and has the following production and sales for Year 1 and Year 2:

LO2, 3

	Units Manufactured	Units Sold
Year 1	110,000	90,000
Year 2	110,000	120,000

Required

a.   Prepare gross profit computations for Year 1 and Year 2 using absorption costing.

b.   Prepare contribution margin computations for Year 1 and Year 2 using variable costing.

c.   Explain how your answers illustrate the impact of differences between production and sales volumes on the net incomes reported each year under absorption and variable costing.

LO3   **P7-4A.** **Variable and Absorption Costing** The following information shows the expected client invoice work-in-process levels for the staff group at Smith & Smith, LLP, a local CPA firm. Fixed overhead is applied based on labor hours.

Units in WIP	Percent Complete	Fixed Overhead Rate
Beginning Inventory: 10 units..........	40%	$200 per unit
Ending Inventory: 20 units..........	30%	

How is absorption costing income expected to compare to variable costing income?

PROBLEMS—SET B

LO2   **P7-1B.** **Variable and Absorption Costing** Summarized data for the first year of operations for Trenton Products, Inc., are as follows:

Sales (100,000 units)	$8,000,000
Production costs (105,000 units):	
Direct materials......................................	2,100,000
Direct labor	1,680,000
Manufacturing overhead:	
Variable...	1,260,000
Fixed...	1,050,000
Operating expenses:	
Variable...	560,000
Fixed...	640,000

Required

a.   Prepare an income statement based on full absorption costing.

b.   Prepare an income statement based on variable costing.

c.   If the ending inventory is destroyed by fire, which costing approach would you use as a basis for filing an insurance claim for the fire loss? Why?

LO2   **P7-2B.** **Variable and Absorption Costing—Service Company** Rocky's Automotive specializes in performing automobile safety checks. After the company's first year of operations, its accountant prepared the following summarized data report for the year's safety checks:

Sales (7,000 safety checks)	$700,000
Production costs (7,010 safety checks):	
Direct labor	490,700
Shop overhead:	
Variable...	112,160
Fixed...	70,100
Operating expenses:	
Variable...	21,030
Fixed...	16,000

Required

a.   Prepare an income statement based on full absorption costing.

b.   Prepare an income statement based on variable costing.

LO2, 3   **P7-3B.** **Variable and Absorption Costing** Frances Manufacturing makes a product with total unit manufacturing cost of $64, of which $36 is variable. No units were on hand at the beginning of Year 1. During Year 1 and Year 2, the only product manufactured was sold for $96 per unit, and the cost structure did not change. Frances uses the first-in, first-out inventory method and has the following production and sales for Year 1 and Year 2:

	Units Manufactured	Units Sold
Year 1	90,000	70,000
Year 2	90,000	100,000

Required

a. Prepare gross profit computations for Year 1 and Year 2 using absorption costing.

b. Prepare contribution margin computations for Year 1 and Year 2 using variable costing.

c. Explain how your answers illustrate the impact of differences between production and sales volumes on the net incomes reported each year under absorption and variable costing.

P7-4B. Variable and Absorption Costing The following information shows the expected client invoice work-in-process levels for the staff group at Tayler & Swain, LLP, a local CPA firm. Fixed overhead is applied based on labor hours. **LO3**

Units in WIP	Percent Complete	Fixed Overhead Rate
Beginning Inventory: 30 units.	20%	$150 per unit
Ending Inventory: 10 units.	60%	

How is absorption costing income expected to compare to variable costing income?

EXTENDING YOUR KNOWLEDGE

EYK7-1. Business Decision Case Ben and Chris have been lifelong friends. They are engineer-minded and have always dreamed of starting a manufacturing company. They want to manufacture tires but realize that this industry is heavily regulated and that achieving profitable operations will require skillful management. Despite the odds, they form Smooth Ride, Inc., and resolve to only stay in business if they report a positive net income after the company's first year of operations. At the end of its first year of operations, Smooth Ride reported the following summarized data:

Sales (105,000 tires)	$13,125,000
Production costs (120,000 tires):	
Direct materials.	4,750,000
Direct labor	3,675,000
Manufacturing overhead:	
Variable.	2,300,000
Fixed	950,000
Operating expenses:	
Variable.	1,050,000
Fixed	800,000
Depreciation on machinery.	455,000
Property taxes	330,000
Personnel department expenses	140,000

Required

a. Prepare income statements based on full absorption costing and based on variable costing. Based on the reported incomes using these methods, did Smooth Ride exceed the expectations of Ben and Chris?

b. Smooth Ride follows generally accepted accounting standards. Which method, full absorption or variable costing, will the company use to report its net income?

ANSWERS TO SELF-STUDY QUESTIONS:

1. d   2. c   3. b   4. a   5. c   6. b

YOUR TURN! SOLUTIONS

Solution 7.1

d.

Solution 7.2

	Absorption Costing	Variable Costing
Sales.	$9,000,000	$9,000,000
Cost of goods sold		
Cost of goods manufactured		
100,000 units × ($25 + $20 + $10 + $495,000/100,000).	5,995,000	
100,000 units × ($25 + $20 + $10)		5,500,000
Less ending inventory		
10,000 units × ($25 + $20 + $10 + $495,000/100,000).	599,500	
10,000 units × ($25 + $20 + $10)		550,000
Cost of goods sold	$5,395,500	$4,950,000
Gross profit.	$3,604,500	
Contribution margin		$4,050,000
Less fixed overhead costs		495,000
Income from operations		$3,555,000

Solution 7.3

$1,600,000 − (100 × $50) = $1,595,000

Solution 7.4

c.

Chapter **8**

Relevant Costs and Short-Term Decision-Making

Road Map

LO	Learning Objective	Page	eLecture	Guided Example	Assignments
LO1	**Describe management's use of accounting information in the decision-making process. Define relevant costs and describe the use of differential analysis.**	8-3	E8-1	YT8.1	SS1, Q1, Q2, Q3, Q4, Q5, Q6, SE1, E1A, E2A, E3A, E1B, E2B, E3B, PA1, P1B
LO2	**Demonstrate when to accept a special order.**	8-9	E8-2	YT8.2	SS2, Q7, SE2, SE3, E4A, E5A, E6A, E4B, E5B, E6B, P2A, P2B
LO3	**Demonstrate when to make or buy needed parts.**	8-10	E8-3	YT8.3	SS3, Q7, SE4, SE5, SE6, E7A, E8A, E9A, E7B, E8B, E9B, P3A, P3B
LO4	**Demonstrate when to drop an unprofitable product or segment.**	8-12	E8-4	YT8.4	SS4, Q7, SE7, E10A, E10B, P4A, P4B
LO5	**Demonstrate when to sell a product or process it further.**	8-13	E8-5	YT8.5	SS5, Q7, Q8, SE8, E11A, E12A, E11B, P5A
LO6	**Demonstrate how to determine which product to produce when a resource is constrained.**	8-17	E8-6	YT8.6	SS6, Q7, Q9, SE9, SE10, E13A, E12B, P6A, P5B

What did you have for dinner last night? If it included fresh produce, grains, dairy, or meat from U.S. farms, there is a 60% chance that it was planted, fertilized, irrigated, harvested, or fed with a **John Deere** product. John Deere didn't start out with the intent of becoming the world's largest manufacturer of agriculture and construction equipment. In 1837, John Deere, a blacksmith in Illinois, was simply looking for a way to help the local farmers plow their fields without frequently stopping to clean sticky prairie soil off their wooden or cast-iron plows. Today, the company he founded has become the world's largest producer and seller of farm and industrial tractors and equipment.

Along the way, the company's management faced many challenges and questions, including

- Whether to introduce new products and product lines;
- Whether to produce or purchase new technology (e.g., steam tractors);
- Whether to drop products and product lines (e.g., bicycles and snowmobiles); and,
- How to deal with restricted production capacity during World War II.

In this chapter, we examine some of the decision tools and techniques that managers may use in answering these strategic questions.

PAST

Chapter 7 discussed the preparation of a variable income statement.

PRESENT

Chapter 8 describes some of the tools and techniques that management can use in making short-term business decisions.

FUTURE

Chapter 9 discusses the budgeting process, the components of the master budget, and the interrelationships of the individual budgets, and presents an illustration of a budget for a manufacturer and a service company.

```
┌─────────────────────────────────────────────────────────────┐
│        RELEVANT COSTS AND SHORT-TERM DECISION-MAKING          │
└─────────────────────────────────────────────────────────────┘
```

Management and the Decision-Making Process	Relevant Costs and Differential Analysis	Illustrations of Differential Analysis
• Who Makes Decisions? • Phases of Decision-Making	• Relevant Costs • Differential Analysis	• The Special Order • Make or Buy? • Dropping Unprofitable Segments • Sell or Process Further? • Constrained Resources

The traditional measurement is not the right measurement; if it were, there would be no need for decisions.

PETER DRUCKER

A well-developed accounting system is a continuing source of operational information for management. The quality of information available to management will influence the success of the operating decisions based on that information. In this chapter, we consider the management decision-making process and some cost concepts that are used in managerial analyses.

There are many definitions of **management**. In the broad sense, anyone who directs the activities of others is a manager. For a manufacturing firm like John Deere, this includes shop supervisors, department heads, plant supervisors, division managers, and the company president. A large, complex firm may have many management levels.

MANAGEMENT AND THE DECISION-MAKING PROCESS

LO1 Describe management's use of accounting information in the decision-making process. **Define** relevant costs and **describe** the use of differential analysis.

eLecture

MBC

Who Makes Decisions?

As **Exhibit 8-1** illustrates, upper-level management is responsible for establishing long-range goals and policies, including major financing, expansion into new markets (foreign and domestic), and acquisitions of or mergers with other firms. Middle-level management may deal with the strategies and tactics related to the automation of a department, the establishment of new product lines, and the direction of the marketing plan. Such matters as daily production quotas, compliance with planned costs, and other detailed operating concerns are the responsibility of lower-level management. To varying degrees, therefore, all levels of management are involved in decision-making.

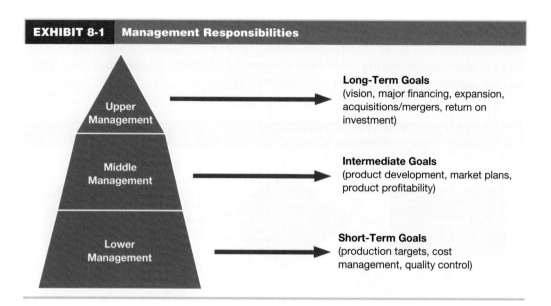

EXHIBIT 8-1   **Management Responsibilities**

Long-Term Goals
(vision, major financing, expansion, acquisitions/mergers, return on investment)

Intermediate Goals
(product development, market plans, product profitability)

Short-Term Goals
(production targets, cost management, quality control)

Upper Management

Middle Management

Lower Management

Decision-making requires that a choice be made among alternatives. The business decision process is analogous to the play of a well-organized football team. Virtually all elements of decision-making are present in football: the establishment of the objectives and goals that lead to winning; the development of organization, strategy, and tactics in a competitive environment; the creation of plays with the hope of achieving particular results; the period of execution; and, finally, the informal evaluation of performance on the field followed by a formal evaluation when game films are analyzed.

ENVIRONMENTAL, SOCIAL, AND GOVERNANCE	Triple Bottom Line Reporting

This chapter discusses the concept of decision-making. One of the decisions a company like John Deere must make is how many resources it should invest in items benefiting non-shareholder stakeholders, and whether these investments will benefit shareholders in the long run. John Deere has been making these types of decisions for well over a century. Some of the early decisions, noted on its website, include

- 1901—Deere implements voluntary workers' compensation program. This is 10 years before the first U.S. workers' compensation statutes.
- 1920—Deere designs and builds its own cloth-screen filtering system to clean exhaust from plow-grinding operations.
- 1936—First foundry equipped with air-pollution-controlled molding equipment.
- 1938—Product safety committee formed; warning decals placed on corn pickers; shielding for power take-offs introduced.
- 1940—Power take-off shields installed on tractors and made available in retrofit programs for tractors produced after 1932.
- 1947—Corporate industrial safety department established.
- 1949—First boiler equipped with a device to control fly-ash emission at Waterloo Tractor Works. Planter Works, Moline, Illinois, installs a wetcap to control cupola emissions.

These investments in its employees' welfare and in the environment appear to have been wise ones, as John Deere is still around more than a hundred years later, delivering billions of dollars of annual net income to its shareholders.

Phases of Decision-Making

Decision-making may be divided roughly into a planning phase, an execution phase, and an evaluation phase incorporating some form of remedial feedback. **Exhibit 8-2** illustrates the sequential nature of the elements of most decision processes.

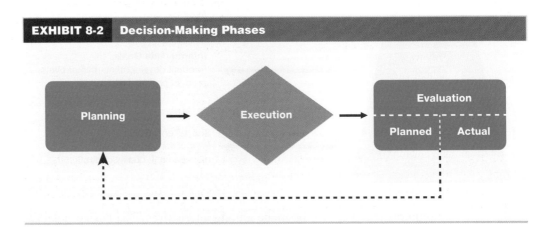

EXHIBIT 8-2   Decision-Making Phases

The **planning phase** begins with *goal identification,* the specification of objectives to be sought or accomplished. One of the most common business goals is the long-run optimization of net income, often expressed in terms of return on assets. Other goals include target growth rates in sales revenue or total assets, target market shares in various markets, or leadership in product research, innovation, and quality.

The next steps in planning are identifying feasible alternative courses of action for achieving desired goals and estimating their qualitative and quantitative effects on the specified goals. Because planning involves the future, data related to the alternative courses of action must be estimated and projected in an environment of uncertainty.

The **execution phase** begins with the actual moment of decision: management commits to a specific plan of action. Because of the complexity of modern business, some elaborate plans may need lead times of several years. Poor planning, or the absence of planning, may lead to operating crises that carry significant penalties for the firm in terms of extra costs, lost opportunities, and—in extreme cases—bankruptcy.

Once a decision has been made, the plan is implemented, which usually involves the acquisition and commitment of materials, labor, and long-lived assets such as machinery and buildings. Management is kept informed through periodic accounting reports on the acquisition and use of these facilities during the execution phase.

In the **evaluation phase**, steps are taken to control the outcome of a specific plan of action. Virtually every important aspect of business—costs, product quality, inventory levels, and sales revenue—must be reasonably well controlled if a firm is to operate successfully. Measuring performance is an essential element of control. Performance measurement must compare actual operations with planned operations to allow management to take remedial action when significant unfavorable variations exist. Managerial accounting data and reports play a key role in informing management about performance in various areas during the evaluation phase of decision-making.

Decision processes do not, however, fall into three neatly divided phases. Changes in competition, technology, and customer demand must be considered. Furthermore, most management teams are engaged in all three decision-making phases at any given time. They may be planning decisions in one area, executing them in a second, and evaluating them in a third.

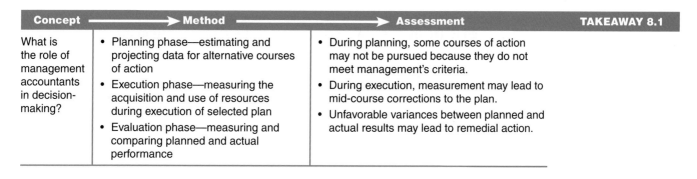

RELEVANT COSTS AND DIFFERENTIAL ANALYSIS

Relevant Costs

Decision-making involves choosing among different alternatives. In business, managers make decisions by evaluating the costs and benefits associated with each alternative. However, not all costs and benefits should be considered. Sound decision-making is based on the widely accepted decision rule that only the aspects of a choice that differ among alternatives are relevant to a decision.

For example, imagine that you want to see an action movie in the theater. There are two theaters in your local community that are showing the movie. As a college student on a limited budget, you are careful with your money and want to choose the least-cost alternative, so you assemble the following information:

Cost/Benefit	Theater #1	Theater #2
Ticket price	$ 9.25	$ 9.25
Parking	$ 3.00	$ 4.00
Popcorn and drink	$10.00	$10.00
Concessions coupon	N/A	50% off
Gas for car	$0.10/mile	$0.10/mile
Car insurance (based on 10,000 miles per year)	$0.06/mile	$0.06/mile
Depreciation on car (based on 10,000 miles per year).	$0.30/mile	$0.30/mile
Distance to theater	5 miles	10 miles

When you are deciding which theater to attend, the admission price is irrelevant if both theaters charge the same price. However, if the cost to park is $4 at one and $3 at the other, then the $1 differential parking cost is relevant to the choice. Likewise, if the popcorn and drink are $10 at both theaters, but you have a coupon for half off at one theater, the $5 savings is also relevant to the choice. If you plan to drive to the theater, the cost of the gas that would be consumed would be relevant if the theaters are different distances away, but the cost that you paid for your car (reflected in the annual depreciation cost) would not be because it was incurred in the past and is considered a **sunk cost**. Finally, the cost of insurance will be incurred regardless of which theater you choose, so it is not relevant to the decision. The decision process is simplified by concentrating only on the factors that are different between the alternatives the manager is evaluating. Thus, **relevant costs** in making a decision are defined as those that differ between alternatives.

In choosing between alternatives, managers must exercise care to avoid including irrelevant data that could lead to a poor decision. In the theater example, two categories of irrelevant costs were identified: costs that do not differ among the alternatives and sunk costs. Sunk costs are costs that have been incurred in the past and cannot be avoided regardless of the decision made.

Finally, managers should consider **opportunity costs**. Opportunity cost is the future benefit that is given up when a choice is made. In our theater example, assume that a third alternative is to stay home and study for an upcoming exam. A potential opportunity cost of choosing to go to the theater is the higher score that might result from the additional three hours of study.

Differential Analysis

Suppose that by 1860 John Deere had determined that he could use his blacksmith shop to produce and sell either plows or hayforks. His decision would have been in favor of the product promising the higher net income based on the estimated operating data shown in **Exhibit 8-3**.

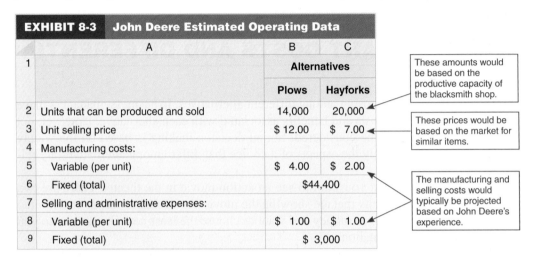

EXHIBIT 8-3	John Deere Estimated Operating Data		
	A	B	C
1		Alternatives	
		Plows	Hayforks
2	Units that can be produced and sold	14,000	20,000
3	Unit selling price	$ 12.00	$ 7.00
4	Manufacturing costs:		
5	Variable (per unit)	$ 4.00	$ 2.00
6	Fixed (total)	$44,400	
7	Selling and administrative expenses:		
8	Variable (per unit)	$ 1.00	$ 1.00
9	Fixed (total)	$ 3,000	

These amounts would be based on the productive capacity of the blacksmith shop.

These prices would be based on the market for similar items.

The manufacturing and selling costs would typically be projected based on John Deere's experience.

We may compare the alternatives by preparing comparative income statements, as shown in **Exhibit 8-4**, from these data.

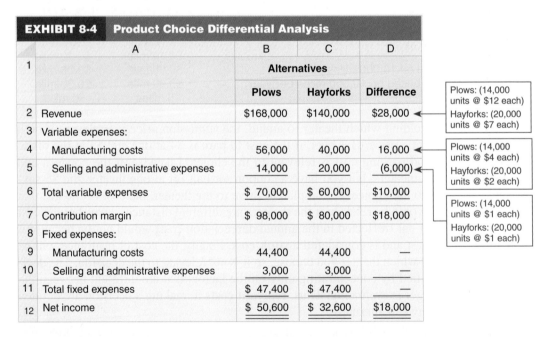

EXHIBIT 8-4	Product Choice Differential Analysis			
	A	B	C	D
1		Alternatives		
		Plows	Hayforks	Difference
2	Revenue	$168,000	$140,000	$28,000
3	Variable expenses:			
4	Manufacturing costs	56,000	40,000	16,000
5	Selling and administrative expenses	14,000	20,000	(6,000)
6	Total variable expenses	$ 70,000	$ 60,000	$10,000
7	Contribution margin	$ 98,000	$ 80,000	$18,000
8	Fixed expenses:			
9	Manufacturing costs	44,400	44,400	—
10	Selling and administrative expenses	3,000	3,000	—
11	Total fixed expenses	$ 47,400	$ 47,400	—
12	Net income	$ 50,600	$ 32,600	$18,000

Plows: (14,000 units @ $12 each) Hayforks: (20,000 units @ $7 each)

Plows: (14,000 units @ $4 each) Hayforks: (20,000 units @ $2 each)

Plows: (14,000 units @ $1 each) Hayforks: (20,000 units @ $1 each)

ACCOUNTING IN PRACTICE Quantitative vs. Qualitative Factors in Decision-Making

Differential analysis considers revenues and expenses that differ among alternatives. However, it does not include qualitative factors, such as impact on labor force or customer base. Thus, the results of differential analysis are only one input into the decision-making process—successful managers must also consider qualitative factors.

This analysis shows an $18,000 increase in net income associated with plows as a result of a $28,000 increase in total revenue that is partially offset by a $10,000 net increase in cost of goods sold and variable selling and administrative expenses.

A simple differential analysis of the same situation is as follows, where consideration is limited to the revenue and expense factors that differ if plows are produced rather than hayforks:

Differential analysis if plows are produced rather than hayforks		
Differential revenue:		
Revenue forgone on 6,000 hayforks..........	[$7 × 6,000 units]	$(42,000)
Additional revenue from increased sales price over hayforks.....................	[($12 – $7) × 14,000 units]	70,000
Net additional revenue		$ 28,000
Differential costs:		
Additional cost of goods sold	[($4 – $2) × 14,000 units]	$(28,000)
Savings on last 6,000 hayforks...........	[$2 × 6,000 units]	12,000
Savings on variable selling and administrative expenses..........................	[$1 × 6,000 units]	6,000
Net differential income in favor of plows.......		$ 18,000

> If plows are sold, 6,000 fewer hayforks will be produced and sold.

> If plows are sold, each unit sold will generate $12, or $5 more than hayforks.

> Each plow costs $2 more to produce than a hayfork.

> The variable production and selling costs will not be incurred on 6,000 hayforks.

Note that the cost of John Deere's blacksmith shop would be considered a sunk cost, and not relevant to the choice between producing plows or hayforks.

Clearly, the differential approach indicates the same net advantage for plows as the income statements, but it does so more concisely. In reality, a company's income statement is much more complex than that presented in Exhibit 8-4. In addition, analyzing the incremental differences among alternatives allows management to focus on the critical elements of the decision and is less prone to making errors than creating a complete set of income statements. Therefore, management uses the more efficient differential analysis in decision-making.

A.K.A. A *differential cost*, also called an *incremental cost*, is any cost present in one alternative but absent in whole or part in another alternative.

YOUR TURN! 8.1

The solution is on page 8-40.

MBC

A yard tool manufacturer can produce either metal shovels or rakes. Given the following estimated operating data, use differential analysis to determine which product would result in the highest net income?

	Shovels	Rakes
Units produced and sold..................	200,000	250,000
Unit selling price........................	$ 30.00	$ 20.00
Manufacturing costs:		
Variable (per unit)	$ 18.00	$ 9.00
Fixed (total)........................	$600,000	
Selling and administrative expenses:		
Variable (per unit)	$ 2.00	$ 2.00
Fixed (total)........................	$140,000	

ILLUSTRATIONS OF DIFFERENTIAL ANALYSIS

This section presents six scenarios where differential analysis is commonly used. Note that for each scenario, the differential analysis results in a measurable financial outcome: a net increase or decrease in the company's profit or loss. However, management would be mistaken to base their decision solely on this projected financial outcome. There are many other potential factors that should be considered in making these decisions. For each scenario, some of these factors are discussed in the paragraph titled "Additional Decision Factors." As with most business decisions, the "number" is just one factor to be considered, albeit an important one.

The Special Order

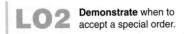

Demonstrate when to accept a special order.

eLecture

MBC

Businesses occasionally receive special orders from purchasers who request a price concession. The prospective buyer may suggest a price or ask for a bid. Sometimes the buyer may request that the firm produce a special version of a product to be identified with the buyer's private brand. As long as no overriding qualitative considerations exist, management should evaluate such propositions and accept the special order if incremental revenues exceed incremental costs.

Business Situation

Assume that Fezzari Bicycles makes an entry-level mountain bike, the Lone Peak, which it sells to retail customers for $549. A bike share company has proposed that Fezzari supply 300 bikes for $400 per bike for a new bike share program in Salt Lake City, Utah. The bikes would carry the brand name of the bike share company. If Fezzari were to accept the order, a special machine attachment would be needed in production to differentiate the bike and affix the private brand logo. This attachment, which costs $1,500, would be discarded after the completion of this order. Also assume that Fezzari has unused production capacity, and thus anticipates no change in fixed capacity costs. The following unit cost data are available for the regular production of the Lone Peak bike:

Direct materials.	$233
Direct labor.	100
Variable manufacturing overhead.	20
Fixed manufacturing overhead (allocated)	47
Total cost per unit.	$400

Analysis and Recommendation

At first glance, the proposal seems unprofitable because the unit cost figure is $400, which is exactly equal to the buyer's offered price, and an additional one-time cost of $1,500 must be incurred to process the order. However, the fixed overhead of $47 included in the $400 total unit cost is not relevant to the decision and should not be considered because Fezzari's total fixed costs will be incurred whether or not the special order is accepted. The differential cost and revenue analysis in **Exhibit 8-5** demonstrates that the special order should be accepted.

EXHIBIT 8-5	**Special Order Differential Analysis**			
	A	B	C	D
1	Increase in sales revenue (300 units × $400)			$120,000
2	Increase in variable production costs:			
3	Direct materials (300 units × $233)	$(69,900)		
4	Direct labor (300 units × $100)	(30,000)		
5	Variable manufacturing overhead (300 units × $20)	(6,000)		
6	Total increase in production costs (300 units × $353)		$(105,900)	
7	Cost of special attachment		(1,500)	
8	Total differential cost			(107,400)
9	Net advantage in accepting special order			$ 12,600

The differential costs of accepting the order consist of the variable production costs and the additional cost of the attachment needed to affix the private brand. Actually, with any price higher than $358 ($107,400 total differential costs ÷ 300 units), Fezzari would earn a profit on the order.

Note that excess production capacity is significant to the special order decision. Without sufficient excess capacity, the additional production would probably cause additional amounts of fixed costs to be incurred or the loss of productive capacity for Fezzari's normal bike production. In addition, Fezzari management would want to consider the opportunity cost of utilizing the available production capacity for this special order, because accepting the order would limit Fezzari's ability to meet increased demand for a higher-margin bike. Also note that although the $1,500 special attachment in this example is a fixed cost, it is relevant to this decision because it differs between alternatives.

Concept ➝	Method ➝	Assessment	TAKEAWAY 8.2
Should a company accept a special order at a reduced price?	Compare incremental revenues to incremental costs for the order.	Accept the order if incremental revenues exceed incremental costs (assuming there are no qualitative factors deemed to outweigh the quantitative analysis).	

Additional Decision Factors

Specific qualitative factors that should be considered here include ascertaining that (1) the special price does not constitute unfair price discrimination; (2) the special order does not negatively impact the actual or perceived quality of the retail bikes; and (3) the long-term price structure for the product is not adversely affected by the special order. Significant concern in any of these, or other areas, might be a basis for rejecting the special order despite the potential $12,600 profit.

Current sales are 50,000 units at $25 per unit. Production capacity is 80,000 units. Variable costs are $14 per unit. Fixed costs are $400,000. A special order for 10,000 units at $20 each is received. It will require the purchase of new equipment for $40,000. The equipment will have a salvage value of $5,000 at the end of the contract. Should the offer be accepted?

YOUR TURN! 8.2

The solution is on page 8-40.

GuidedExample

MBC

Make or Buy?

Many manufacturing situations require the assembly of large numbers of specially designed components and subassemblies. Usually, the manufacturer must choose between making these components and subassemblies and buying them from outside suppliers. In each situation, management should evaluate the relative costs of the two choices and buy from outside if the differential cost of buying is less than the differential cost of making the components or subassemblies. Because making a component uses some portion of the firm's manufacturing capacity, we assume that if the manufacturer decides to buy the component or subassembly from an outside supplier, the space previously utilized to make it could not be used to manufacture a different component or subassembly.

LO3

Demonstrate when to make or buy needed parts.

eLecture

MBC

Business Situation

To illustrate the make-or-buy decision, we assume that John Deere manufactures a loader-backhoe with the following costs:

Manufactured Cab:	
Direct materials..	$3,000
Direct labor..	1,190
Variable manufacturing overhead...........................	750
Fixed manufacturing overhead..............................	650
Total cost..	$5,590

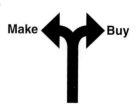

Investigations by John Deere's purchasing department indicate that the loader-backhoe cab assembly can be purchased in sufficient quantities at a unit price of $5,031, an indicated savings of 10% per unit. At first glance, the opportunity to purchase seems attractive.

Analysis and Recommendation

A review of operations indicates that by purchasing the component, John Deere can reduce its variable costs of production, but the fixed overhead costs will remain. The fixed overhead costs related to equipment used to manufacture the cabs are an example of a sunk cost. The differential analysis in **Exhibit 8-6** indicates that by purchasing the cab, John Deere's overall costs would increase by $91 per unit. Thus, John Deere should continue to manufacture the cab.

EXHIBIT 8-6	Make or Buy Differential Analysis		
	A	B	C	D
1		Manufacture Cab	Purchase Cab	Incr/(Decr) in Cost if Cab Is Purchased
2	Cost per unit:			
3	Direct materials	$3,000		$(3,000)
4	Direct labor	1,190		(1,190)
5	Variable manufacturing overhead	750		(750)
6	Fixed manufacturing overhead	650	$ 650	—
7	Purchase price of components		5,031	5,031
8		$5,590	$5,681	$ 91
9				
10	The following differential analysis confirms the more comprehensive one above:			
11	Cost to purchase cab			$ 5,031
12	Less costs avoided by purchasing:			
13	Direct materials		$3,000	
14	Direct labor		1,190	
15	Variable manufacturing overhead		750	$ 4,940
16	Increase in acquisition cost by purchasing			$ 91

The fixed manufacturing cost is irrelevant to the decision because it does not differ between the alternatives. (note pointing to row 6)

Represents incremental cost to purchase the cab assembly. (note pointing to row 11)

Represents the incremental cost avoided by purchasing the cab assembly. (note pointing to row 15)

Additional Decision Factors

These analyses assume that the manufacturing capacity released by the decision to purchase would not be used. However, should an opportunity arise to use this capacity to generate another product with more than $91 of contribution margin per unit, then the opportunity to purchase the components would be more attractive. However, qualitative factors, such as the effects on employee morale, product quality, and dependability of the supply chain, are also very important. Once a decision is reached based on the quantitative analyses, it should be weighed against these and other qualitative factors that may be important to management.

TAKEAWAY 8.3	Concept ➡	Method ➡	Assessment
	Should a company continue to make a component of a product or buy from an outside supplier?	Compare incremental costs to make the component to incremental costs to buy the product from outside.	Buy from the outside supplier if the differential cost of buying is less than the differential cost of making (assuming there are no qualitative factors deemed to outweigh the quantitative analysis).

Scott Corporation produces a part for use in the production of one of its products. The per-unit costs associated with the annual production of 1,000 units of this part are as follows:

Direct materials.	$10.50
Direct labor	24.00
Variable factory overhead.	5.50
Fixed factory overhead	12.00
Total costs.	$52.00

Larson Company has offered to sell 1,000 units of the same part to Scott Corporation for $42 per unit. Should Scott accept Larson's offer?

Dropping Unprofitable Segments

Occasionally, a company's financial reporting system provides its management with segment information that suggests that a particular division, department, office, product, or product line is losing money. As discussed in Chapter 11, segments usually are based on organizational units (divisions or departments) or areas of economic activity (geographic regions or product lines). In these situations, management should compare the direct segment cost saved to the revenue lost if the segment were to be dropped. The company should drop the segment if the cost saved is greater than the revenue lost.

LO4 **Demonstrate** when to drop an unprofitable product or segment.

eLecture

MBC

Business Situation

Assume that EBC's segment financial statements show that the Water/Wastewater segment lost $5,298 for 2022. It would appear that dropping the segment would increase EBC's profit by $5,298, or almost 1% (see **Exhibit 8-7**).

SERVICE AND MERCHANDISING

EXHIBIT 8-7	Segment Income Statement

ENVIRONMENTAL BUSINESS CONSULTANTS, LLC
Line of Business Statement
For the Year Ended December 31, 2022

	Solid Waste	Water/ Wastewater	Firm Total
Gross sales.	$3,676,000	$470,000	$ 4,146,000
Less reimbursable costs	(366,350)	(64,650)	(431,000)
Net sales.	$3,309,650	$405,350	$ 3,715,000
Cost of services	(2,238,787)	(384,713)	(2,623,500)
Gross profit on sales.	$1,070,863	$ 20,637	$ 1,091,500
Direct operating expenses	(166,065)	(25,935)	(192,000)
Line of business contribution	$ 904,798	$ (5,298)	$ 899,500
Common operating expenses.			(364,500)
Interest revenue			7,500
Income before tax.			$ 542,500

Assume that the Water/Wastewater cost of services includes an office lease expense of $38,625 that would continue even if the business line were discontinued. The rest of the Water/Wastewater cost of services and direct operating expenses are variable in nature and would be eliminated with the dropping of the segment.

Analysis and Recommendation

The differential analysis in **Exhibit 8-8** indicates that EBC's overall income would decrease, rather than increase, by discontinuing the Water/Wastewater.

EXHIBIT 8-8	Dropping Unprofitable Segment Differential Analysis		
	A	B	C
1	Decrease in net revenue		$(405,350)
2	Decrease in expenses:		
3	Variable cost of goods sold*	$346,088	
4	Variable direct operating expenses	25,935	$ 372,023
5	Decrease in total contribution margin (and net income) from discontinuing Water/Wastewater		$ (33,327)
6	*$384,713 – $38,625		

Even though Water/Wastewater reports a $5,298 annual loss, it does generate a contribution margin of $33,327 toward the absorption of fixed costs and expenses. If Water/Wastewater is discontinued, there would be no contribution margin, although $38,625 of fixed cost would remain. This would result in a loss of $38,625, which is $33,327 worse than the current $5,298 loss. Thus, EBC should maintain its Water/Wastewater segment and look for ways to either increase revenue or decrease costs.

Additional Decision Factors

Management must often consider other factors in decisions of this type. Among these are (1) the potential termination of employees and subsequent effects on non-terminated employee morale, and (2) the possible effects on customer patronage (for example, customers of the Solid Waste line of business may go to other firms for all of their consulting services if Water/Wastewater's services are no longer available from the same source). On the other hand, EBC management might also begin to explore other potential services that might generate greater profits than the Water/Wastewater segment.

TAKEAWAY 8.4	Concept ➝	Method ➝	Assessment
	Should a company drop an unprofitable segment?	Compare the direct cost savings to the lost revenue from dropping the segment.	Drop the segment if the direct cost savings is greater than the revenue lost from dropping the segment (assuming there are no qualitative factors deemed to outweigh the quantitative analysis).

YOUR TURN! 8.4

The solution is on page 8-41.

GuidedExample

MBC

GPS Corporation, a manufacturer of global positioning system devices, is considering eliminating the Oceania Model from its line of devices because of losses over the past year. The past year's information on the Oceania Model is provided below:

Sales (10,000 units)	$1,000,000
Manufacturing costs:	
Direct materials	450,000
Direct labor	250,000
Overhead	400,000
Gross Margin	$ (100,000)

Overhead costs are 80% variable, and the remaining 20% is an allocation of the general manager's salary. (The general manager is over multiple product lines.) If the Oceania Model is dropped, what will be the most likely impact on gross margin for the firm in the next year?

L05 Demonstrate when to sell a product or process it further.

eLecture

MBC

Sell or Process Further?

Firms sometimes face the decision of either selling products at one point in the production sequence or processing them further and selling them at a higher price. Examples are finished versus unfinished furniture, crude oil versus gasoline, and unassembled kits versus assembled units of product. In these process-further decision situations, management should compare the incremental revenue to the additional processing costs and process the products further if the incremental revenue exceeds the incremental processing costs.

Business Situation

Assume that Sunrise Landscape sells screened topsoil with the following values per yard:

Current sales price (per cubic yard)		$20.00
Costs:		
Direct materials	$5.00	
Direct labor	5.00	
Variable overhead	1.00	
Fixed overhead*	2.50	13.50
Gross margin per unit		$ 6.50

*Applied at 50% of direct labor costs.

Sunrise has excess productive capacity, which should remain available in the foreseeable future. Consequently, management believes that part of this excess capacity could be used to create a garden mix blended soil (topsoil that has been amended with compost and peat) and sell it at $30.00 per cubic yard to homeowners for their vegetable gardens and planting beds. A study carried out by the company's management indicates that the additional processing will add $5.00 to the direct materials cost and $2.00 to the direct labor cost of each unit and that variable overhead will continue to be incurred at 20% of direct labor cost. See **Exhibit 8-9** for the specific steps involved.

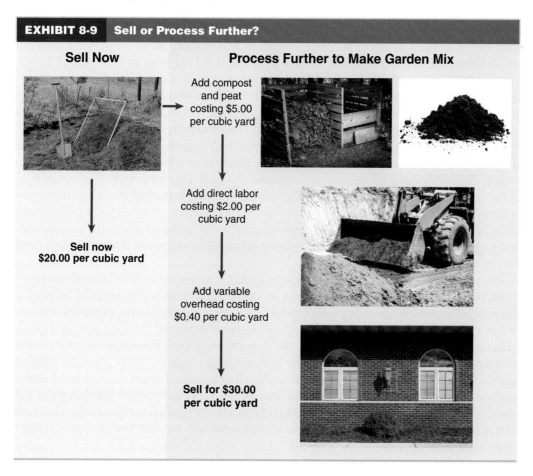

EXHIBIT 8-9   Sell or Process Further?

Sell Now

Sell now
$20.00 per cubic yard

Process Further to Make Garden Mix

Add compost and peat costing $5.00 per cubic yard

Add direct labor costing $2.00 per cubic yard

Add variable overhead costing $0.40 per cubic yard

Sell for $30.00 per cubic yard

Analysis and Recommendation

The differential analysis in **Exhibit 8-10** supports the proposal to process further:

	A	B	C
EXHIBIT 8-10	**Sell or Process Further Differential Analysis**		
1			**Per Cubic Yard**
2	Differential revenue ($30.00 – $20.00)		$10.00
3	Differential cost:		
4	Direct materials	$5.00	
5	Direct labor	2.00	
6	Variable manufacturing overhead (20% of direct labor)	0.40	
7	Fixed manufacturing overhead	—	
8	Total differential cost		7.40
9	Excess of differential revenue over differential cost		$ 2.60

The per-unit differential analyses indicate that Sunrise will earn an additional $2.60 per cubic yard for every yard of garden mix processed and sold.

TAKEAWAY 8.5	Concept ⟶	Method ⟶	Assessment
	Should a company sell a product or process it further to sell at a higher price?	Compare the differential revenues after processing to the differential costs of processing.	Process further if the differential revenues are greater than the differential costs after processing (assuming there are no qualitative factors deemed to outweigh the quantitative analysis).

Joint Products

A.K.A. *Joint product costs* are manufacturing costs incurred in producing joint products up to the split-off point.

Often, the processing of direct materials results in two or more products of significant commercial value. Such products derived from a common input are **joint products,** and the related cost of the direct materials is a joint product cost. An obvious example of a direct materials whose processing results in joint products is crude oil, from which a variety of fuels, solvents, lubricants, and residual petrochemical pitches are derived. Cattle, from which the meat packer obtains many cuts and grades of meat, hides, and other products, are another example.

It is impossible to allocate a joint product cost among joint products in such a way that management can decide whether to continue production or what price to charge for a joint product. To decide to produce one joint product is to decide to produce all related joint products, even if some are discarded. Therefore, to make informed decisions about joint products, management must compare the total revenue generated by all joint products with their total production costs. The joint costs incurred to the point at which the joint products are separately identified are irrelevant with regard to decisions about whether to sell or process any of the joint products further.

The primary reason for allocating a joint product cost among two or more products is to assign cost to the ending inventories of joint products when determining periodic income. The most popular method of allocating joint product costs for inventory costing purposes is the relative sales value method. This approach uses arithmetic proportions. The total joint product cost is allocated to the various joint products in the proportions of their individual sales values to the total sales value of all joint products at the split-off point—that is, where physical separation takes place. For example, assume that 50,000 55-gallon barrels of crude oil costing $5,000,000 are processed into 800,000 gallons of fuel selling for $3.00 per gallon, 400,000 gallons of lubricants selling for $5.00 per gallon, and 1,000,000 gallons of petrochemical residues selling for $1.50 per gallon. The following calculations illustrate the joint product cost allocation using the relative sales value approach:

Joint Product	Quantity Produced (gallons)	Unit Sales Value	Product Sales Value	Proportion of Total Product Sales Value	Allocated Cost	Quantity Produced (gallons)	Cost per Unit
Fuel.	800,000	$3.00	$2,400,000	40.68%	$2,034,000	800,000	$2.54
Lubricants. . .	400,000	$5.00	2,000,000	33.90%	1,695,000	400,000	$4.24
Residues. . . .	1,000,000	$1.50	1,500,000	25.42%	1,271,000	1,000,000	$1.27
			$5,900,000	100.00%	$5,000,000		

Note that the relative sales value approach results in assigned unit costs that are the same percentage of the selling price for each product. In our illustration, the cost per unit equals approximately 85% of the sales value per unit.

Exhibit 8-11 illustrates the allocation of the $5,000,000 joint product cost to the three joint products. Note also that each product may then incur additional manufacturing costs before it is completed and ready for sale. For example, in **Exhibit 8-11**, an additional $206,000 of costs are incurred after the split-off point to finish the production of the fuel. When added to the allocated joint costs, the total cost of the fuel is $2,240,000, or $2.80 per gallon.

EXHIBIT 8-11	Joint Product Costs

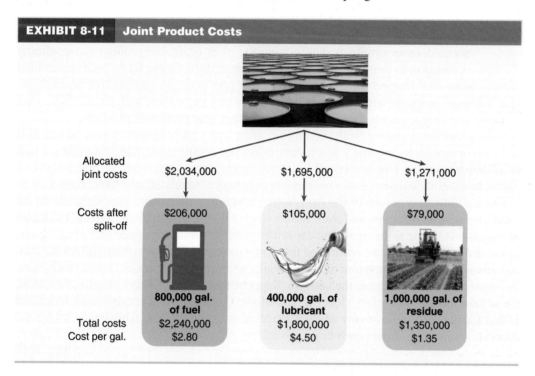

By-Products

By-products have relatively little sales value compared with the other products derived from a particular process. By-products are considered incidental to the manufacture of the more important products. For example, the sawdust and shavings generated in a lumber mill or in a furniture manufacturer's cutting department are by-products.

We may account for by-products by assigning them a cost equal to their sales value less any disposal costs. This net amount is charged to an inventory account for the by-product and credited to the work-in-process account that was charged with the original materials. For example, consider a furniture factory in which walnut boards are processed through a cutting and shaping department. In processing $40,000 worth of lumber, 800 bushels of sawdust and shavings are generated, which, after treatment costing $80, can be sold for $1 per bushel. The amount to be charged to the Sawdust and Shavings Inventory account would be $720 [(800 bushels × $1) – $80].

This procedure reduces the costs of the main products by the net amount recovered from by-products.

YOUR TURN! 8.5

The solution is on page 8-41.

GuidedExample

MBC

Wright Company produces two products from a joint batch process. Both products are processed further before they are sold. Joint costs per batch are $350,000. Information for each product includes:

	Product X	Product Y
Units produced per batch	10,000	20,000
Further processing and marketing cost per unit	$2.50	$1.75
Final sales value per unit	5.00	3.00

If Wright uses the net realizable value method of allocating joint costs, how much of the joint costs should be allocated to Product Y?

Constrained Resources

LO6 **Demonstrate** how to determine which product to produce when a resource is constrained.

eLecture

MBC

A.K.A. Constrained resources are commonly referred to as *bottlenecks*.

Because most firms produce several products, management must continually examine operating data and decide which combination of products offers the greatest total long-term profit potential. The decisions related to product emphasis are seldom as simple as determining the most profitable product and confining production to that one product. For example, John Deere faces such operational constraints as limited demand for the most profitable products, the competitive necessity of offering a line of products with a variety of qualities and capacities, and, in seeking better utilization of existing capacity, the need to produce other, less profitable products.

In a **constrained resource** analysis, an important and widely accepted generalization is that the firm optimizes its income when it maximizes the contribution margin earned per unit of constraining resource. The concept of constraining resource stems from the realization that as a firm increases its volume, some resource is eventually exhausted and thus constrains, or limits, the continued expansion of the firm. Which resources are constraining depends on the firm, the operating conditions, and even the products under consideration. Typical examples are key materials, labor skills, machine capacities, and factory floor space or storage space. Simply stated, management has optimized the firm's product mix when it maximizes the contribution margin earned on each unit of the particular resource that limits increased production.

An example will help explain the concept. Suppose that Larry's Brakes manufactures three different brake models: Model A, Model B, and Model C. Assume that enough market demand exists that Larry could sell as many of each model as it can build. The table below shows the prices and costs associated with each brake model.

	Model A	Model B	Model C
Selling price	$150	$200	$300
Direct materials cost	40	50	100
Direct labor cost ($30 per hour)	60	60	90
Variable support cost ($10 per machine hour)	10	20	40
Fixed support cost	10	10	10

Also assume that the number of machine hours is limited (i.e., machine hours represent a constrained resource). Which brake model should Larry produce? Larry would want to produce the model that generates the largest contribution margin per machine hour. **Exhibit 8-12** shows the calculation of the contribution margin per machine hour for each brake model. As shown in the exhibit, Model A generates the largest contribution margin per machine hour at $40 per hour. With unlimited demand for Model A, Larry should devote all of its production capacity to producing Model A.

EXHIBIT 8-12	Constrained Resource Example			
	A	B	C	D
1		Model A	Model B	Model C
2	Selling price	$150.00	$200.00	$300.00
3	Less variable costs			
4	Direct materials	40.00	50.00	100.00
5	Direct labor	60.00	60.00	90.00
6	Variable support	10.00	20.00	40.00
7	Total variable costs	$110.00	$130.00	$230.00
8	Contribution margin per unit	$ 40.00	$ 70.00	$ 70.00
9	Machine hours per unit	1	2	4
10	Contribution margin per machine hour	$ 40.00	$ 35.00	$ 17.50

Variable support cost/Cost per machine hour = # of machine hours
A: $10/$10 = 1 hour
B: $20/$10 = 2 hours
C: $40/$10 = 4 hours

How can we be sure that this is the correct solution? Assume that the maximum number of hours that Larry can run his machine is 2,000 hours. **Exhibit 8-13** shows the contribution margin for each brake model, assuming that Larry produces only that model. Model A generates the largest contribution margin at $80,000, which could also be calculated as the product of the number of machine hours available (2,000 hours) and the contribution margin per machine hour ($40; see **Exhibit 8-12**).

EXHIBIT 8-13	Contribution Margin by Model Under Constraint			
	A	B	C	D
1		Model A	Model B	Model C
2	Constrained resource:			
3	Machine hours available	2,000	2,000	2,000
4	Machine hours per unit	1	2	4
5	Total units of production	2,000	1,000	500
6				
7	Sales revenue	$300,000	$200,000	$150,000
8	Less variable costs			
9	Direct materials	80,000	50,000	50,000
10	Direct labor	120,000	60,000	45,000
11	Variable support	20,000	20,000	20,000
12	Total variable costs	220,000	130,000	115,000
13	Contribution margin	$ 80,000	$ 70,000	$ 35,000

Most companies do not enjoy unlimited demand for their products. How does this analysis change if there is limited demand for one or more products? Assume that Larry can sell 1,000 units of Model A, 400 units of Model B, and 300 units of Model C. In this case, Larry should make

- all 1,000 units of Model A, which would use 1,000 of the available machine hours;
- all 400 units of Model B, which would use 800 of the remaining available machine hours; and,
- the remaining 200 machine hours to produce 50 units of Model C. **Exhibit 8-14** shows the calculation of the resulting contribution margin.

EXHIBIT 8-14	Contribution Margin by Model Under Constraint with Limited Demand				
A	B	C	D	E	F
1		Model A	Model B	Model C	Total
2	(1) Market demand	1,000	400	300	
3	(2) Machine hours per unit	1	2	4	
4	(3) Total machine hours required to meet demand [(1) × (2)]	1,000	800	1,200	3,000
5	(4) Total machine hours available	1,000	800	200	2,000
6	(5) Total units produced and sold [(4)/(2)]	1,000	400	50	1,450
7					
8	Sales revenue	$150,000	$80,000	$15,000	$245,000
9	Less variable costs				
10	Direct materials	40,000	20,000	5,000	65,000
11	Direct labor	60,000	24,000	4,500	88,500
12	Variable support	10,000	8,000	2,000	20,000
13	Total variable costs	$110,000	$52,000	$11,500	$173,500
14	Contribution margin	$40,000	$28,000	$3,500	$71,500

Hours are assigned to produce as many of each model as possible beginning with the largest contribution margin per machine hour (see Exhibit 8-12) until the total of 2,000 machine hours is reached.

Business Situation

To illustrate constrained resource decisions, assume that John Deere's Waterloo Works Tractor, Cab, and Assembly Operations in Waterloo, Illinois, produces three 6R Series row-crop tractors: the 6140R, the 6150R, and the 6170R. Also assume the operation's constraining resource is its factory machine capacity. John Deere operates at 90% capacity, and management wants to devote the unused capacity to one of the three products. The following data represent John Deere's current operations:

	Products		
	6140R	6150R	6170R
Per-unit data:			
Sales price	$130,000	$143,000	$150,000
Variable costs	99,450	109,000	117,000
Contribution margin	$30,550	$34,000	$33,000
Fixed costs*	16,150	18,700	17,850
Net income	$14,400	$15,300	$15,150
Machine hours required	38	44	42

*Allocated on basis of machine hours at $425 per hour.

Analysis and Recommendation

Intuition suggests that the extra capacity should be devoted either to the 6170R, which has the highest sales price, or to the 6150R, which has the highest per-unit contribution margin and net income. However, an analysis of the contribution margin of each product per unit of constraining resource (machine hour) reveals that the 6140R should receive the added capacity.

Note that fixed costs are allocated among products on the basis of machine hours—the constraining resource in our example. Furthermore, the unit allocations of fixed costs, noted previously, indicate that the 6170R requires fewer machine hours than the 6150R and more than the 6140R. The contribution per unit of machine capacity for each product is shown in **Exhibit 8-15**.

EXHIBIT 8-15	Constrained Resource Differential Analysis		
		Products	
	6140R	**6150R**	**6170R**
Contribution margin per unit.	$30,550	$34,000	$33,000
Divided by machine hours required	38	44	42
Contribution margin per machine hour (the constraining resource) . . .	$ 804	$ 773	$ 786

Use of the remaining capacity generates a greater contribution margin if devoted to the 6140R. As this example illustrates, in deciding how to utilize the constraining resource, management should use contribution margin per unit of constraining resource, rather than the relative sales prices, unit contribution margins, or even unit profit of various products.

Concept ⟶	Method ⟶	Assessment	TAKEAWAY 8.6
When resource constraints exist, which product(s) should a company manufacture and sell to maximize profits?	Calculate the contribution margin per constrained resource for each product.	Produce as much of the product with the highest contribution margin per constrained resource as possible, then the next highest, and so forth (assuming there are no qualitative factors deemed to outweigh the quantitative analysis).	

YOUR TURN! 8.6

The solution is on page 8-41.

Product A requires 2 machine hours per unit, has a unit contribution margin of $15, and a contribution margin ratio of 60%. Product B requires 1 machine hour per unit, has a unit contribution margin of $12, and a contribution margin ratio of 40%. Which product should be emphasized if machine hours are limited?

GuidedExample

MBC

SERVICE INDUSTRY IN FOCUS

Environmental Business Consultants, LLC (EBC) has been approached by Terrabean Coffee, a large retail coffee company with 5,000 shops across North America, to manage Terrabean Coffee's waste disposal and recycling services under a 3-year contract. It is unlikely that the contract would be extended beyond the initial 3-year term. Terrabean has asked EBC to provide these services at a discounted average hourly billing rate of $60 per hour.

In order to take on this major new contract, EBC would need to establish a call center to receive calls from the 5,000 shops and coordinate the appropriate response. The call center would be in a leased office space at a cost of $3,000 per month, including utilities. Additional capital, including office furniture, computers, and phones, would be purchased at a total cost of $35,000. The office furniture, computers, and phones are expected to have a value of $5,000 at the end of the contract and would not be of use to EBC in its regular business. The call center would be managed by a current EBC consultant that normally bills 1,800 hours per year at a rate of $125 per hour. An additional ten call center employees would be hired at an average hourly wage of $25, plus benefits equal to 50% of the hourly wage. Each employee would be expected to work 2,000 hours per year. EBC expects to bill Terrabean 20,000 hours per year for the call center under the contract.

SERVICE AND MERCHANDISING

Required

1. Determine whether EBC should accept this new contract offer from Terrabean. Calculate the differential net revenue or cost associated with the contract. (Hint: Don't forget that the call center manager is a current EBC employee and would not be available for any other work.)

2. What other factors should EBC management consider in making the decision?

Solution

1.

SOLUTION	Service Industry in Focus	
Increase in annual revenue (20,000 hours × $60)		$1,200,000
Lost revenue from call center manager (1,800 × $125)		(225,000)
Total differential billing revenue.		$ 975,000
Increase in costs:		
Direct labor (10 employees × 2,000 hours × $37.50)	$750,000	
Office lease ($3,000 × 12 months)	36,000	
Other capital costs [($35,000 – 5,000)/3 years)].	10,000	
Total differential cost.		$ 796,000
Net advantage in accepting contract offer		$ 179,000

2. EBC management should consider the impact on the ten employees who will need to be hired for the call center. At the end of the contract term, these employees will need to be terminated unless other work can be found.

Data Analytics

DATA ANALYTICS   **From farm to data table**

Self-driving cars are not the only vehicles using sensors. Those big green John Deere farm machines can be equipped with sensors to help farmers manage their fleet and reduce their tractors downtime and fuel use. Data from the sensors is combined with historical and current weather data, soil conditions, crop data, and other data sets to enhance yields and reduce costs. All this information can be viewed on the MyJohnDeere. com website as well as on the iPad or iPhone app, Mobile Farm Manager. While not a total substitute for the Farmer's Almanac, these apps help the farmer determine what crops to plant, where and when to plant them, and even the optimal path to follow when plowing.

SUMMARY OF LEARNING OBJECTIVES

LO1   Describe management's use of accounting information in the decision-making process. Define relevant costs and describe the use of differential analysis. (p. 8-3)

- Top management establishes long-range goals, middle management deals with intermediate goals, and lower management focuses on short-range goals.
- Decision-making, which is essentially choosing among alternatives, usually comprises three phases: planning, execution, and evaluation.
- Relevant costs are those that differ between alternatives.
- Differential analysis is the study of those amounts that are expected to differ among alternatives.

LO2   Demonstrate when to accept a special order. (p. 8-9)

- Management should evaluate special order propositions and accept the special order if incremental revenues exceed incremental costs.
- Management should also consider qualitative factors that could be the basis of rejecting a special order despite a net increase in revenues, such as unfair pricing, impact on quality, and long-term pricing impact.

LO3   Demonstrate when to make or buy needed parts. (p. 8-10)

- Management should evaluate the relative costs of the two choices and buy from outside if the differential cost of buying is less than the differential cost of making the components or subassemblies.
- Management should also consider qualitative factors such as the effects on employee morale, product quality, and dependability of the supply chain.

LO4   Demonstrate when to drop an unprofitable product or segment. (p. 8-12)

- Management should compare the direct segment cost saved to the revenue lost if the segment were to be dropped. The company should drop the segment if the cost saved is greater than the revenue lost.

- Management should also consider the potential termination of employees and subsequent effects on non-terminated employee morale, and the possible effects on customer patronage.

Demonstrate when to sell a product or process it further. (p. 8-13) **LO5**

- Management should compare the incremental revenue to the additional processing costs and process the products further if the incremental revenue exceeds the incremental processing costs.
- The joint costs incurred to the point at which the joint products are separately identified are irrelevant with regard to decisions about whether to sell or process any of the joint products further.

Demonstrate how to determine which product to produce when a resource is constrained. (p. 8-17) **LO6**

- Management should maximize the contribution margin earned on each unit of the particular resource that limits increased production.

Concept	Method	Assessment	SUMMARY
What is the role of management accountants in decision-making?	• Planning phase—estimating and projecting data for alternative courses of action • Execution phase—measuring the acquisition and use of resources during execution of selected plan • Evaluation phase—measuring and comparing planned and actual performance	• During planning, some courses of action may not be pursued because they do not meet management's criteria. • During execution, measurement may lead to mid-course corrections to the plan. • Unfavorable variances between planned and actual results may lead to remedial action.	TAKEAWAY 8.1
Should a company accept a special order at a reduced price?	Compare incremental revenues to incremental costs for the order.	Accept the order if incremental revenues exceed incremental costs (assuming there are no qualitative factors deemed to outweigh the quantitative analysis).	TAKEAWAY 8.2
Should a company continue to make a component of a product or buy from an outside supplier?	Compare incremental costs to make the component to incremental costs to buy the product from outside.	Buy from the outside supplier if the differential cost of buying is less than the differential cost of making (assuming there are no qualitative factors deemed to outweigh the quantitative analysis).	TAKEAWAY 8.3
Should a company drop an unprofitable segment?	Compare the direct cost savings to the lost revenue from dropping the segment.	Drop the segment if the direct cost savings is greater than the revenue lost from dropping the segment (assuming there are no qualitative factors deemed to outweigh the quantitative analysis).	TAKEAWAY 8.4
Should a company sell a product or process it further to sell at a higher price?	Compare the differential revenues after processing to the differential costs of processing.	Process further if the differential revenues are greater than the differential costs after processing (assuming there are no qualitative factors deemed to outweigh the quantitative analysis).	TAKEAWAY 8.5
When resource constraints exist, which product(s) should a company manufacture and sell to maximize profits?	Calculate the contribution margin per constrained resource for each product.	Produce as much of the product with the highest contribution margin per constrained resource as possible, then the next highest, and so forth (assuming there are no qualitative factors deemed to outweigh the quantitative analysis).	TAKEAWAY 8.6

KEY TERMS

Bottlenecks (p. 8-17)	Evaluation phase (p. 8-5)	Management (p. 8-3)
Constrained resource (p. 8-17)	Execution phase (p. 8-5)	Opportunity costs (p. 8-6)
Decision-making (p. 8-4)	Incremental cost (p. 8-8)	Planning phase (p. 8-5)
Differential analysis (p. 8-7)	Joint product costs (p. 8-15)	Relevant costs (p. 8-6)
Differential cost (p. 8-8)	Joint products (p. 8-15)	Sunk cost (p. 8-6)

Assignments with the ⓂBC logo in the margin are available in BusinessCourse.
See the Preface of the book for details.

SELF-STUDY QUESTIONS

(Answers to Self-Study Questions are at the end of this chapter.)

LO1 1. **When using differential analysis to analyze two alternatives to the current operation, what factors should *not* be considered?**

    a. Direct materials costs that are different

    b. Direct labor costs that exist for only one alternative

    c. Overhead costs that are the same for both alternatives

    d. Sales commissions that apply to only one alternative

LO2 2. **When considering a special order, management should accept the order if which of the following conditions is met?**

    a. Incremental costs are greater than incremental revenues.

    b. There is excess production capacity.

    c. Incremental costs are less than incremental revenues.

    d. Employees are willing to work overtime.

LO3 3. **When considering whether to continue to manufacture a part or buy it from an outside supplier, management should buy the part if the**

    a. incremental cost to buy is less than the incremental cost to manufacture the part.

    b. equipment used for making the part is fully depreciated.

    c. equipment used for making the part could be sold.

    d. incremental cost to buy is less than the total cost to manufacture the part.

LO4 4. **A business segment reports segment revenues of $1.2 million, segment costs of $1.0 million, and allocated corporate overhead costs of $300,000. If management were to drop the segment, overall corporate profits would**

    a. increase by $100,000.   *c.* increase by $200,000.

    b. decrease by $100,000.   *d.* decrease by $200,000.

LO5 5. **True or false: Costs incurred to the split-off point in the manufacture of joint products are always relevant to the decision of whether to sell the joint products or process them further.**

    a. True   *b.* False

LO6 6. **Smith Construction typically struggles to complete the plumbing work on schedule and within budget on new residential homes that it constructs because of a shortage of local plumbing subcontractors. In selecting among several floorplans for new homes that it plans to construct, which measurement tool should Smith select?**

    a. Contribution margin   *c.* Contribution margin ratio

    b. Gross profit   *d.* Contribution margin per plumbing hour

QUESTIONS

LO1 1. Identify three phases of decision-making and briefly discuss the role of each phase in the decision process.

LO1 2. Although separate phases of decision-making are identifiable, management is usually involved in all phases at the same time. Explain.

LO1 3. In the chapter we discuss quantitative methods to assist management in making business decisions. Discuss other common aspects of decision-making that are not often subject to quantification.

LO1 4. Explain what is meant by the term *differential analysis*.

LO1 5. "In differential analysis, we can generally count on variable cost being relevant and fixed cost being irrelevant." Comment.

LO1 6. If both approaches to a decision lead to the same conclusion, why might differential analysis be considered superior to a comprehensive analysis that reflects all revenue and costs?

LO2, 3, 4, 5, 6 7. Explain how differential analysis can be applied to the following types of decisions:

    a. Accepting special orders   *d.* Selling or processing further

    b. Making or buying product components   *e.* Product emphasis

    c. Dropping unprofitable segments of the firm

8. Delton Company produces unassembled picture frames at the following average per-unit costs: direct materials, $X; direct labor, $Y; and manufacturing overhead, $Z. Delton can assemble the frames at a unit cost of $2.50 and raise the selling price from $11 to $15. What is the apparent advantage or disadvantage of assembling the frames?   **LO5**

9. Explain the concept of *constraining resource*, and present a general rule for optimizing product mixes.   **LO6**

SHORT EXERCISES

SE8-1. With respect to relevant information for decision-making, which of the following is TRUE?   **LO1**
    a.   Fixed costs are never relevant costs.
    b.   Managers should pay little attention to bottleneck operations since they have limited capacity for producing output.
    c.   Customer satisfaction and quality concerns are not relevant for management accounting decision-making.
    d.   Relevant costs will include opportunity costs if current production is at capacity.

SE8-2. Johnson Company manufactures a variety of shoes and has received a special one-time-only order directly from a wholesaler. Johnson has sufficient idle capacity to accept the special order to manufacture 15,000 pairs of sneakers at a price of $7.50 per pair. Johnson's normal selling price is $11.50 per pair of sneakers. Variable manufacturing costs are $5.00 per pair, and fixed manufacturing costs are $3.00 a pair. Johnson's variable selling expense for its normal line of sneakers is $1.00 per pair. What would the effect on Johnson's operating income be if the company accepted the special order?   **LO2**

    a.   Decrease by $60,000   *c.*   Increase by $37,500
    b.   Increase by $22,500   *d.*   Increase by $52,500

SE8-3. The loss of a key customer has temporarily caused Bedford Machining to have some excess manufacturing capacity. Bedford is considering the acceptance of a special order that involves Bedford's most popular product. Consider the following types of costs: **LO2**

    I.   Variable costs of the product
    II.   Fixed costs of the product
    III.   Direct fixed costs associated with the order
    IV.   Opportunity cost of the temporarily idle capacity

Which one of the following combinations of cost types should be considered in the special order acceptance decision?

    a.   I and II   *c.*   II and III
    b.   I and IV   *d.*   I, III, and IV

SE8-4. Refrigerator Company manufactures ice-makers for installation in refrigerators. The costs per unit, for 20,000 units of ice-makers, are as follows: **LO3**

Direct materials.	$ 7
Direct labor.	12
Variable overhead.	5
Fixed overhead.	10
Total costs.	$34

Cool Compartments Inc. has offered to sell 20,000 ice-makers to Refrigerator Company for $28 per unit. If Refrigerator accepts Cool Compartments's offer, the facilities used to manufacture ice-makers could be used to produce water filtration units. Revenues from the sale of water filtration units are estimated at $80,000, with variable costs amounting to 60% of sales. In addition, $6 per unit of the fixed overhead associated with the manufacture of ice-makers could be eliminated.

    For Refrigerator Company to determine the **most** appropriate action to take in this situation, the total relevant costs of make vs. buy, respectively, are

    a. $600,000 vs. $560,000.   *c.* $600,000 vs. $528,000.
    b. $648,000 vs. $528,000.   *d.* $680,000 vs. $440,000.

LO3   **SE8-5.** Scott Corporation produces a part for use in the production of one of its products. The per-unit costs associated with the annual production of 1,000 units of this part are as follows:

Direct materials.	$10.50
Direct labor	$24.00
Variable factory overhead	$ 5.50
Fixed factory overhead	$12.00
Total costs	$52.00

$5,000 of the fixed factory overhead costs associated with the production of this product are common fixed costs.

Larson Company has offered to sell 1,000 units of the same part to Scott Corporation for $42 per unit. Scott should:

a. buy the part, because this would save $10.00 per unit.
b. buy the part, because this would save the company $5,000 annually.
c. make the part, because this would save $2.00 per unit.
d. make the part, because this would save the company $5,000 annually.

LO3   **SE8-6.** A company currently sells 6,000 units per month and has received a special order from an international customer. The international customer would like to purchase 1,500 units for a price of $80 per unit. The company currently sells the product to regular customers for $95 per unit. The company has excess capacity to produce the special order. The product unit cost is shown below.

Direct materials.	$49.50
Direct labor	16.50
Variable overhead.	9.50
Fixed overhead.	3.50

Fixed manufacturing overhead totals $35,000 per month. Management has determined that the additional shipping costs for the international delivery would be $4 per unit. Should the company accept the special order?

a. Yes, because operating income will increase by $750.
b. Yes, because operating income will increase by $6,750.
c. No, because operating income will decrease by $4,500.
d. No, because operating income will decrease by $21,000.

LO4   **SE8-7.** Current business segment operations for Whitman, a mass retailer, are presented below.

	Merchandise	Automotive	Restaurant	Total
Sales.	$500,000	$400,000	$100,000	$1,000,000
Variable costs	300,000	200,000	70,000	570,000
Fixed costs	100,000	100,000	50,000	250,000
Operating income (loss) . . .	$100,000	$100,000	$ (20,000)	$ 180,000

Management is contemplating the discontinuance of the Restaurant segment because "it is losing money." If this segment is discontinued, $30,000 of its fixed costs will be eliminated. In addition, Merchandise and Automotive sales will decrease 5% from their current levels. What will Whitman's total contribution margin be if the Restaurant segment is discontinued?

a. $160,000
b. $220,000
c. $367,650
d. $380,000

LO5   **SE8-8.** Tucariz Company processes Duo into two joint products: Big and Mini. Duo is purchased in 1,000-gallon drums for $2,000. Processing costs are $3,000 to process the 1,000 gallons of Duo into 800 gallons of Big and 200 gallons of Mini. The selling price is $9 per gallon for Big and $4 per gallon for Mini. If the sales value at split-off method is used to allocate joint costs to the final products, the per-gallon cost (rounded to the nearest cent) of producing Big is

a. $5.63 per gallon.
b. $5.00 per gallon.
c. $4.50 per gallon.
d. $3.38 per gallon.

SE8-9. Cervine Corporation makes two types of motors for use in various products. Operating data and unit cost information for its products are presented below.

	Product A	Product B
Annual unit capacity	10,000	20,000
Annual unit demand	10,000	20,000
Selling price	$100	$80
Variable manufacturing cost	53	45
Fixed manufacturing cost	10	10
Variable selling & administrative	10	11
Fixed selling & administrative	5	4
Fixed other administrative	2	0
Unit operating profit	$ 20	$10
Machine hours per unit	2.0	1.5

Cervine has 40,000 productive machine hours available. The relevant contribution margins, per machine hour for each product, to be utilized in making a decision on product priorities for the coming year, are

	Product A	Product B
a.	$17.00	$14.00.
b.	$18.50	$16.00.
c.	$20.00	$10.00.
d.	$37.00	$24.00.

SE8-10. Paul's Pumps manufactures three different product lines: Model A, Model B, and Model C. Plenty of market demand exists for all models. The table below reports the prices and costs per unit of each product.

	Model A	Model B	Model C
Selling price	$50	$60	$70
Direct materials costs	$ 6	$ 6	$ 6
Direct labor costs ($12 per labor hour)	$12	$12	$24
Variable support costs ($4 per machine hour)	$ 4	$ 8	$ 8
Fixed support costs	$10	$10	$10

Assuming that machine hours are limited (i.e., this is the constrained resource), which model is the most profitable to produce?

a. Model A   *c.* Model C

b. Model B   *d.* Model A and B would be equally profitable.

DATA ANALYTICS, DATA VISUALIZATION, AND EXCEL ACTIVITIES

Data Analytics, Data Visualization, and Excel Activities are available in myBusinessCourse. These assignments develop Excel, Tableau, and Data Analytics skills, which will enhance students' career readiness. These exercises are assignable and auto graded by MBC. For an overview of data analytics, see the appendix at the end of this book.

EXERCISES—SET A

E8-1A. Analyzing Operational Changes Annual operating results for department B of Delta Company are as follows:

Sales.	$540,000
Cost of goods sold	378,000
Gross profit.	$162,000
Direct expenses	$120,000
Common expenses.	66,000
Total expenses	$186,000
Net loss.	$ (24,000)

If department B could maintain the same physical volume of product sold while raising selling prices an average of 5% and making an additional advertising expenditure of $30,000, what would be the effect on the department's net income or net loss? (Ignore income tax in your calculations.)

LO1 **E8-2A. Analyzing Operational Changes** Suppose that department B in Exercise E8-1A could increase physical volume of product sold by 10% if it spent an additional $40,000 on advertising while leaving selling prices unchanged. What effect would this have on the department's net income or net loss? (Ignore income tax in your calculations.)

LO1 **E8-3A. Differential Analysis** In each of four independent cases, the amount of differential revenue or differential cost is as follows (parentheses indicate decreases):

	1	2	3	4
Increases (decreases) in:				
Revenue	$18,000	$-0-	?	?
Costs.	?	?	($12,000)	$-0-

For each case, determine the missing amount that would be necessary for the net differential amount to be

a. $8,000   *b.* ($4,000)

Indicate whether your answers reflect increases or decreases.

LO2 **E8-4A. Special Order** Carson Manufacturing, Inc., sells a single product for $36 per unit. At an operating level of 8,000 units, variable costs are $18 per unit and fixed costs $10 per unit.

Carson has been offered a price of $20 per unit on a special order of 2,000 units by Big Mart Discount Stores, which would use its own brand name on the item. If Carson accepts the order, materials cost will be $3 less per unit than for regular production. However, special stamping equipment costing $4,000 would be needed to process the order; the equipment would then be discarded.

Assuming that volume remains within the relevant range, prepare an analysis of differential revenue and costs to determine whether Carson should accept the special order.

LO2 **E8-5A. Special Order** Pope Company manufactures a variety of hiking boots and has received a special one-time-only order from a new customer. Pope has sufficient idle capacity to accept the special order to manufacture 1,000 pairs of boots at a price of $50.00 per pair. Pope's normal selling price is $65.00 per pair of boots. Variable manufacturing costs are $35.00 per pair, and fixed manufacturing costs are $12.00 a pair. Pope's variable selling expense for its normal line of boots is $1.00 per pair. What would be the effect on Pope's operating income be if the company accepted the special order?

LO2 **E8-6A. Special Order** Roy & Roy, CPAs currently provides tax return preparation services to individuals in the local community. Roy has received a one-time only request to prepare 100 tax returns for clients of another CPA firm in the community while the owner recovers from major surgery. Roy has the capacity to prepare 700 returns. Roy has an effective income tax rate of 40%. Roy's income statement, before consideration of the one-time-only request, is as follows:

Sales (500 returns at $300 per return)	$150,000
Variable preparation costs	20,000
Contribution margin	130,000
Fixed preparation costs	80,000
Operating income.	50,000
Income taxes	20,000
Net income	$ 30,000

In negotiating a price for the special request, at what amount should Roy & Roy set the minimum per-return price?

E8-7A. Make or Buy Eastside Company incurs a total cost of $120,000 in producing 10,000 units of a component needed in the assembly of its major product. The component can be purchased from an outside supplier for $11 per unit. A related cost study indicates that the total cost of the component includes fixed costs equal to 25% of the variable costs involved.

  LO3

  a. Should Eastside buy the component if it cannot otherwise use the released capacity? Present your answer in the form of differential analysis.
  b. What would be your answer to requirement (a) if the released capacity could be used in a project that would generate $20,000 of contribution margin?

E8-8A. Make or Buy Filtration, Inc., manufactures filters for use in secondary water irrigation systems. The costs per unit, for 20,000 filters, are as follows.

  LO3

Direct materials.	$5.00
Direct labor.	6.00
Variable overhead.	1.00
Fixed overhead.	2.00
Total costs.	$14.00

Irrigation Products has offered to sell 20,000 filters to Filtration for $14 per filter. If Filtration accepts Irrigation Products's offer, the facilities used to manufacture filters could be used to produce refrigerator filtration units. Revenues from the sale of refrigerator filtration units are estimated at $50,000, with variable costs amounting to 50% of sales. In addition, $1 per unit of the fixed overhead associated with the manufacture of secondary water irrigation filters could be eliminated.

Should Filtration, Inc., accept Irrigation Product's offer?

E8-9A. Make or Buy Desert Industries manufactures 5,000 units of Part X300 each month for use in production. The facilities now being used to produce Part X300 have fixed monthly overhead costs of $40,000, and a theoretical capacity to produce 7,000 units per month. If Desert were to buy Part X300 from an outside supplier, the facilities would be idle, and 80% of the fixed costs would continue to be incurred. There are no alternative uses for the production facilities. The variable production costs of Part X300 are $24 per unit. Fixed overhead is allocated based on planned production levels.

  LO3

If Desert Industries continues to use 5,000 units of Part X300 each month, it would realize a net benefit by purchasing Part X300 from an outside supplier only if the supplier's unit price is less than what amount?

E8-10A. Dropping Unprofitable Department Thomas Corporation has four departments, all of which appear to be profitable except department 4. Annual operating data are as follows:

  LO4

	Total	Departments 1–3	Department 4
Sales.	$950,000	$800,000	$150,000
Cost of sales.	626,000	512,000	114,000
Gross profit.	$324,000	$288,000	$ 36,000
Direct expenses	$144,000	$120,000	$ 24,000
Department contribution.	$180,000	$168,000	$ 12,000
Common expenses.	125,000		
Net income (Loss)	$ 55,000		

Required
  a. Calculate the gross profit percentage for departments 1–3 combined and for department 4.
  b. What effect would elimination of department 4 have had on total firm net income? (Ignore the effect of income tax.)

LO5   **E8-11A. Sell or Process Further** Jensen Manufacturing Company makes a partially completed assembly unit that it sells for $36 per unit. Normally, 42,000 units are sold each year. Variable unit cost data on the assembly are as follows:

Direct materials.	$10
Direct labor	8
Variable manufacturing overhead	4

The company is now using only 70% of its normal capacity; it could fully use its normal capacity by processing the assembly further and selling it for $41 per unit. If the company does this, materials and labor costs will each increase by $2 per unit and variable overhead will go up by $1 per unit. Fixed costs will increase from the current level of $160,000 to $180,000.

Prepare an analysis showing whether Jensen should process the assemblies further.

LO5   **E8-12A. Joint Cost** Cheyenne, Inc., produces three products from a common input. The joint costs for a typical quarter follow:

Direct materials.	$45,000
Direct labor	55,000
Overhead	60,000

The revenues from each product are as follows:

Product A	$75,000
Product B	80,000
Product C	30,000

Management is considering processing Product A beyond the split-off point, which would increase the sales value of Product A to $116,000. However, to process Product A further means that the company must rent some special equipment costing $17,500 per quarter. Additional materials and labor also needed would cost $12,650 per quarter.

Required

a.   What is the gross profit currently being earned by the three products for one quarter?

b.   What is the effect on quarterly profits if the company decides to process Product A further?

LO6   **E8-13A. Constrained Resource** The following analysis of selected data is for each of the two services Gates Corporation provides.

SERVICE AND
MERCHANDISING

	Service A	Service B
Per-service data at 10,000 services		
Sales price	$26	$22
Service costs:		
Variable	9	9
Fixed	6	4
Selling and administrative expenses:		
Variable	5	3
Fixed	3	1

In the Gates operation, labor capacity is the company's constraining resource. Each unit of A requires 3 hours of labor, and each unit of B requires 2 hours of labor. Assuming that all services can be sold at a normal price, prepare an analysis showing which of the two services should be provided with any unused productive capacity that Gates might have.

EXERCISES—SET B

E8-1B. Analyzing Operational Changes Annual operating results for department B of Shaw Company are as follows: **LO1**

Sales.	$800,000
Cost of goods sold	480,000
Gross profit.	$320,000
Direct expenses	$200,000
Common expenses.	123,000
Total expenses	$323,000
Net loss.	$ (3,000)

If department B could maintain the same physical volume of product sold while raising selling prices an average of 6% and making an additional advertising expenditure of $40,000, what would be the effect on the department's net income or net loss? (Ignore income tax in your calculations.)

E8-2B. Analyzing Operational Changes Suppose that department B in Exercise E8-1B could increase physical volume of product sold by 10% if it spent an additional $50,000 on advertising while leaving selling prices unchanged. What effect would this have on the department's net income or net loss? (Ignore income tax in your calculations.)   **LO1**

E8-3B. Differential Analysis In each of four independent cases, the amount of differential revenue or differential cost is as follows (parentheses indicate decreases):   **LO1**

	1	2	3	4
Increases (decreases) in:				
Revenue	$36,000	$-0-	?	?
Costs.	?	?	$(20,000)	$-0-

For each case, determine the missing amount that would be necessary for the net differential amount to be

a. $22,000
b.   ($9,000)

Indicate whether your answers reflect increases or decreases.

E8-4B. Special Order Northern Company regularly sells its only product for $34 per unit and has a 25% profit on each sale. The company has accepted a special order for a number of units, the production of which would use part of its unused capacity. The special order sales price is 50% of the normal price, and the profit margin is only 60% of the regular dollar profit. What, apparently, is   **LO2**

a.   Northern's profit per unit on the special order?
b.   Northern's variable cost per unit?
c.   Northern's average fixed cost per unit on regular sales?

E8-5B. Special Order Plastic Pipe Company manufactures a variety of pipes, and has received a special one-time-only order from a new customer. Plastic Pipe has sufficient idle capacity to accept the special order to manufacture 2,000 16-foot lengths of pipe at a price of $8.00 per pipe. Plastic Pipe's normal selling price is $12.00 per 16-foot length. Variable manufacturing costs are $7.00 per pipe and fixed manufacturing costs are $1.00 per pipe. Plastic Pipe's variable selling expense for its normal line of pipes is $0.50 per pipe. What would the effect on Plastic Pipe's operating income be if the company accepted the special order?   **LO2**

E8-6B. Special Order William A. Smith Pest Control, Inc. (WASP) currently provides pest control services to households in the local community. WASP has an opportunity to service 250 customers of another pest control firm that has also been selling in the community. WASP has the capacity to service 1,000 homes. WASP has an effective income tax rate of 30%. WASP's income statement, before consideration of the new opportunity, is as follows.   **LO2**

SERVICE AND MERCHANDISING

Sales (750 homes at $250 per home)	$187,500
Variable service costs.	135,000
Contribution margin	52,500
Fixed service costs.	30,000
Operating income	22,500
Income taxes	6,750
Net income	$ 15,750

In negotiating a price for the special opportunity, at what amount should WASP set the minimum per-home price?

LO3

E8-7B.   Make or Buy Harper Company incurs a total cost of $252,000 in producing 20,000 units of a component needed in the assembly of its major product. The component can be purchased from an outside supplier for $7 per unit. A related cost study indicates that the total cost of the component includes fixed costs equal to 75% of the variable costs involved.

a.   Should Harper buy the component if it cannot otherwise use the released capacity? Present your answer in the form of differential analysis.

b.   What would be your answer to requirement (a) if the released capacity could be used in a project that would generate $5,000 of contribution margin?

LO3

E8-8B.   Make or Buy Specialty Metal Products, Inc., manufactures filters for use in custom over-the-range hoods. The costs per unit, for a batch of 10,000 filters, are as follows.

Direct materials.	$ 5.00
Direct labor	3.00
Variable overhead.	1.00
Fixed overhead	4.00
Total costs.	$13.00

Custom Kitchens has offered to sell 10,000 filters to Specialty Metal Products for $14 per filter. If Specialty Metal Products accepts Custom Kitchens's offer, the facilities used to manufacture filters could be used to produce BBQ grates. Revenues from the sale of BBQ grates are estimated at $20,000, with variable costs amounting to 80% of sales. In addition, $1 per unit of the fixed overhead associated with the manufacture of filters could be eliminated.

Should Specialty Metal Products accept Custom Kitchens' offer?

LO3

E8-9B.   Make or Buy RKR Consultants produces a monthly report on the semiconductor chip manufacturing industry for use by its consultants in serving RKR clients. The research office now being used to produce the report has fixed monthly overhead costs of $2,000. The research staff have a theoretical capacity to prepare another report on a second industry each month.

RKR has learned that a semiconductor industry trade group produces a similar industry report that is available on a subscription basis. If RKR were to subscribe to the report from the industry trade group, the research office would be idle and 90% of the fixed costs would continue to be incurred. There are no alternative uses for the research office. The variable costs associated with preparing the monthly research report are $500 per report. Fixed overhead is allocated based on planned production levels.

If RKR Consultants continues to use the monthly research report, it would realize a net benefit by purchasing the report from the semiconductor industry trade group only if the monthly subscription price is less than what amount?

LO4

E8-10B.   Dropping Unprofitable Department Penn Corporation has four departments, all of which appear to be profitable except department 4. Annual operating data are as follows:

	Total	Departments 1-3	Department 4
Sales.	$1,052,000	$900,000	$152,000
Cost of sales.	654,000	540,000	114,000
Gross profit.	$ 398,000	$360,000	$ 38,000
Direct expenses	$ 177,000	$150,000	$ 27,000
Department contribution.	$ 221,000	$210,000	$ 11,000
Common expenses.	140,000		
Net income (loss)	$ 81,000		

a. Calculate the gross profit percentage for departments 1–3 combined and for department 4.

b. What effect would elimination of department 4 have had on total firm net income? (Ignore the effect of income tax.)

E8-11B. Sell or Process Further Turner Manufacturing Company makes a partially completed assembly unit that it sells for $50 per unit. Normally, 35,000 units are sold each year. Variable unit cost data on the assembly are as follows:

LO5

Direct materials.	$12
Direct labor	7
Variable manufacturing overhead	9

The company is now using only 75% of its normal capacity; it could fully use its normal capacity by processing the assembly further and selling it for $58 per unit. If the company does this, materials and labor costs will each increase by $2 per unit and variable overhead will go up by $1 per unit. Fixed costs will increase from the current level of $125,000 to $165,000.

Prepare an analysis showing whether Turner should process the assemblies further.

E8-12B. Constrained Resource The following analysis of selected data is for each of the two services Rockville Corporation provides.

LO6

	Service G	Service H
Per-unit data @ 10,000 services		
Sales price	$29	$16
Service costs:		
Variable	9	7
Fixed	6	4
Selling and administrative expenses:		
Variable	5	2
Fixed	3	1

In Rockville's operation, labor capacity is the company's constraining resource. Each unit of G requires 3 hours of labor, and each unit of H requires 1 hour of labor. Assuming that all services can be sold at a normal price, prepare an analysis showing which of the two services should be provided with any unused productive capacity that Rockville might have.

PROBLEMS—SET A

P8-1A. Analyze Operational Changes Richmond's is a retail store with eight departments, including a garden department that has been operating at a loss. The following condensed income statement gives the latest year's operating results:

LO1

	Garden Department	All Other Departments
Sales.	$336,000	$2,400,000
Cost of sales.	201,600	1,560,000
Gross profit.	$134,400	$ 840,000
Direct expenses	$108,000	$ 273,000
Common expenses.	48,000	312,000
Total expenses	$156,000	$ 585,000
Net income (Loss)	$ (21,600)	$ 255,000

Required

a. Calculate the gross profit percentage for the garden department and for the other departments as a group.

b. Suppose that if the garden department were discontinued, the space occupied could be rented to an outside firm for $18,000 per year, and the common expenses of the firm would be reduced by $4,500. What effect would this action have on Richmond's net income? (Ignore income tax in your calculations.)

c. It is estimated that if an additional $6,000 were spent on advertising, prices in the garden center could be raised an average of 5% without a change in physical volume of products sold. What effect would this have on the operating results of the garden department? (Again, ignore income tax in your calculations.)

LO2   P8-2A.   Special Order Total cost data follow for Glendale Manufacturing Company, which has a normal capacity per period of 8,000 units of product that sell for $60 each. For the foreseeable future, regular sales volume should continue to equal normal capacity.

Direct materials.	$100,800
Direct labor.	62,400
Variable manufacturing overhead.	46,800
Fixed manufacturing overhead (Note 1)	38,400
Selling expense (Note 2)	35,200
Administrative expense (fixed)	15,000
	$298,600

Notes:

1. Beyond normal capacity, fixed overhead costs increase $1,800 for each 500 units *or fraction thereof* until a maximum capacity of 10,000 units is reached.

2. Selling expenses consist of a 6% sales commission and shipping costs of 80 cents per unit. Glendale pays only three-fourths of the regular sales commission on sales totaling 501 to 1,000 units and only two-thirds the regular commission on sales totaling 1,000 units or more.

Glendale's sales manager has received a special order for 1,200 units from a large discount chain at a price of $36 each, F.O.B. factory. The controller's office has furnished the following additional cost data related to the special order:

1. Changes in the product's design will reduce direct materials costs $1.50 per unit.
2. Special processing will add 20% to the per-unit direct labor costs.
3. Variable overhead will continue at the same proportion of direct labor costs.
4. Other costs should not be affected.

Required

a. Present an analysis supporting a decision to accept or reject the special order. (Round computations to the nearest cent.)

b. What is the lowest price Glendale could receive and still make a $3,600 profit before income taxes on the special order?

c. What general qualitative factors should Glendale consider?

P8-3A. Make or Buy Allen Corporation currently makes the nylon convertible top for its main product, a fiberglass boat designed especially for water skiing. The costs of producing the 1,500 tops needed each year follow:

LO3

Nylon fabric.	$270,000
Aluminum tubing.	96,000
Frame fittings	24,000
Direct labor.	162,000
Variable manufacturing overhead.	30,000
Fixed manufacturing overhead	180,000

Dustin Company, a specialty fabricator of synthetic materials, can make the needed tops of comparable quality for $390 each, F.O.B. shipping point. Allen would furnish its own trademark insignia at a unit cost of $12. Transportation would be $18 per unit, paid by Allen Corporation.

    Allen's chief accountant has prepared a cost analysis that shows that only 20% of fixed overhead could be avoided if the tops are purchased. The tops have been made in a remote section of Allen's factory building, using equipment for which no alternate use is apparent in the foreseeable future.

Required

a. Prepare a differential analysis showing whether or not you would recommend that the convertible tops be purchased from Dustin Company.

b. Assuming that the production capacity released by purchasing the tops could be devoted to a subcontracting job for another company that netted a contribution margin of $42,000, what maximum purchase price could Allen Corporation pay for the tops?

c. Identify two important qualitative factors that Allen Corporation should consider in deciding whether to purchase the needed tops.

P8-4A. Dropping Unprofitable Division Based on the following analysis of last year's operations of Bingham, Inc., a financial vice president of the company believes that the firm's total net income could be increased by $400,000 if its engineering division were discontinued. (Amounts are given in thousands of dollars.)

LO4

	Totals	All Other Divisions	Engineering Division
Sales.	$11,000	$8,000	$ 3,000
Cost of services:			
Variable	(3,880)	(2,600)	(1,280)
Fixed	(2,120)	(1,400)	(720)
Gross profit.	$ 5,000	$4,000	$ 1,000
Operating expenses:			
Variable	(3,000)	(2,000)	(1,000)
Fixed	(1,600)	(1,200)	(400)
Net income (loss)	$ 400	$ 800	$ (400)

Required

Provide answers for each of the following independent situations:

a. Assuming that total fixed costs and expenses would not be affected by discontinuing the engineering division, prepare an analysis showing why you agree or disagree with the vice president.

b. Assume that discontinuance of the engineering division will enable the company to avoid 40% of the fixed portion of cost of services and 25% of the fixed operating expenses allocated to the engineering division. Calculate the resulting effect on net income.

c. Assume that in addition to the cost avoidance in requirement (b), the capacity released by discontinuance of the engineering division can be used to provide 6,000 new services that would have a variable cost per service of $36 and would require additional fixed costs totaling $72,000. At what unit price must the new service be sold if Bingham is to increase its total net income by $120,000?

P8-5A. Joint Cost The Sun-Kissed Company manufactures two skin-care lotions, Soft Skin and Silken Skin, out of a joint process. The joint (common) costs incurred are $420,000 for a standard production run that generates 180,000 gallons of Soft Skin and 120,000 gallons of Silken Skin. Additional processing costs beyond the split-off point are $1.40 per gallon for Soft Skin and $0.90 per gallon for Silken Skin. Soft Skin sells for $2.40 per gallon, while Silken Skin sells for $3.90 per gallon.

LO5

The Best Eastern Hotel chain has asked the Sun-Kissed Company to supply it with 240,000 gallons of Silken Skin at a price of $3.65 per gallon. Best Eastern plans to have the Silken Skin bottled in 1.5-ounce personal-use containers that are supplied in each of its hotel rooms as part of the complimentary personal products for guest use.

If Sun-Kissed accepts the order, it will save $0.05 per gallon in packaging of Silken Skin. There is sufficient excess capacity in Sun-Kissed's production system to handle just one more production run in order to have sufficient Silken Skin for this special order. However, the nature of the joint process always results in 180,000 gallons of Soft Skin and 120,000 gallons of Silken Skin. Also, the market for Soft Skin is saturated; hence, any additional sales of Soft Skin would take place at a price of $1.60 per gallon.

Required

a. What is the profit normally earned on one production run of Soft Skin and Silken Skin?

b. What is the incremental effect on overall income if the Sun-Kissed Company accepts the special order for Silken Skin?

LO6

P8-6A. Constrained Resource Lowell Corporation manufactures both a deluxe and a standard model of a household food blender. Because of limited demand, for several years production has been at 80% of estimated capacity, which is thought to be limited by the number of machine hours available. At current operation levels, a profit analysis for each product line shows the following data:

	Per-Unit Data			
	Deluxe		Standard	
Sales price		$216		$84
Production costs:				
Direct materials	$89		$12	
Direct labor	36		23	
Variable manufacturing overhead	15		11	
Fixed manufacturing overhead*	25	$165	10	$56
Variable operating expenses		18		10
Fixed operating expenses		8		5
Total cost		$191		$71
Operating income		$ 25		$13

* Assigned on the basis of machine hours at normal capacity.

Management wants to utilize the company's current excess capacity by increasing production.

Required

a. What general decision guideline applies in this situation?

b. Assuming that sufficient units of either product can be sold at current prices to use existing capacity fully and that total fixed cost will not be affected, prepare an analysis showing which product line should be emphasized if net income for the firm is the decision basis.

PROBLEMS—SET B

LO1

P8-1B. Analyze Operational Changes The management of Manchester's Department Store is concerned about the operation of its sporting goods department, which has not been very successful. The following condensed income statement gives the latest year's results:

	Sporting Goods Department	All Other Departments
Sales	$480,000	$2,400,000
Cost of goods sold	360,000	1,560,000
Gross profit	$120,000	$ 840,000
Direct expenses	$ 67,500	$ 336,000
Indirect expenses	48,000	240,000
Total expenses	$115,500	$ 576,000
Net income	$ 4,500	$ 264,000

Required

a. Calculate the gross profit percentage for the sporting goods department and for the other departments as a group.

b. It is estimated that if an additional $10,500 were spent on promotion of sporting goods, average prices can be raised 5% without affecting physical volume of goods sold. What effect would this have on the operating results of the sporting goods department? (Ignore the effect of income tax.)

c. Alternatively, it is estimated that physical volume of goods sold could be increased 8% if an additional $15,000 were spent on promotion of sporting goods and prices were not increased. Assuming that operating expenses remain the same, what effect would this have on the operating results of the sporting goods department? (Ignore the effect of income tax.)

P8-2B. Special Order Total cost data follow for Greenfield Manufacturing Company, which has a normal capacity per period of 20,000 units of product that sell for $54 each. For the foreseeable future, regular sales volume should continue to equal normal capacity.

Direct materials.	$266,800
Direct labor.	200,000
Variable manufacturing overhead.	152,000
Fixed manufacturing overhead (Note 1)	118,800
Selling expense (Note 2)	129,600
Administrative expense (fixed)	50,000
	$917,200

Notes:

1. Beyond normal capacity, fixed overhead costs increase $4,500 for each 1,000 units *or fraction thereof* until a maximum capacity of 24,000 units is reached.

2. Selling expenses consist of a 10% sales commission and shipping costs of $1 per unit. Greenfield pays only one-half of the regular sales commission rates on sales amounting to $3,000 or more.

Greenfield's sales manager has received a special order for 2,500 units from a large discount chain at a price of $44 each, F.O.B. factory. The controller's office has furnished the following additional cost data related to the special order:

1. Changes in the product's design will reduce direct materials costs by $4 per unit.
2. Special processing will add 10% to the per-unit direct labor costs.
3. Variable overhead will continue at the same proportion of direct labor costs.
4. Other costs should not be affected.

Required

a. Present an analysis supporting a decision to accept or reject the special order.

b. What is the lowest price Greenfield could receive and still make a profit of $5,000 before income taxes on the special order?

c. What general qualitative factors should Greenfield consider?

P8-3B. Make or Buy Walsh Corporation currently makes the nylon mooring cover for its main product: a fiberglass boat designed for tournament bass fishing. The costs of producing the 2,000 covers needed each year follow:

Nylon fabric.	$320,000
Wood battens	64,000
Brass fittings.	32,000
Direct labor.	128,000
Variable manufacturing overhead.	96,000
Fixed manufacturing overhead.	170,000

Calvin Company, a specialty fabricator of synthetic materials, can make the needed covers of comparable quality for $290 each, F.O.B. shipping point. Walsh would furnish its own trademark insignia at a unit cost of $20. Transportation would be $15 per unit, paid by Walsh Corporation.

Walsh's chief accountant has prepared a cost analysis that shows that only 30% of fixed overhead could be avoided if the covers are purchased. The covers have been made in a remote section of Walsh's factory building, using equipment for which no alternate use is apparent in the foreseeable future.

Required

a. Prepare a differential analysis showing whether or not you would recommend that the mooring covers be purchased from Calvin Company.

b. Assuming that the production capacity released by purchasing the covers could be devoted to a subcontracting job for another company that netted a contribution margin of $64,000, what maximum purchase price could Walsh pay for the covers?

c. Identify two important qualitative factors that Walsh Corporation should consider in deciding whether to purchase the needed covers.

LO4

SERVICE AND MERCHANDISING

MBC

P8-4B. Dropping Unprofitable Division Based on the following analysis of last year's operations of Groves, Inc., a financial vice president of the company believes that the firm's total net income could be increased by $(560,000) if its design division were discontinued. (Amounts are given in thousands of dollars.)

	Totals	All Other Divisions	Design Division
Sales.	$18,400	$14,400	$4,000
Cost of services:			
Variable	(7,600)	(5,600)	(2,000)
Fixed	(4,800)	(4,000)	(800)
Gross profit	$ 6,000	$ 4,800	$1,200
Operating expenses:			
Variable	(3,360)	(2,000)	(1,360)
Fixed	(1,600)	(1,200)	(400)
Net income (loss)	$ 1,040	$ 1,600	$ (560)

Required

Provide answers for each of the following independent situations:

a. Assuming that total fixed costs and expenses would not be affected by discontinuing the design division, prepare an analysis showing why you agree or disagree with the vice president.

b. Assume that discontinuance of the design division will enable the company to avoid 30% of the fixed portion of cost of services and 40% of the fixed operating expenses allocated to the design division. Calculate the resulting effect on net income.

c. Assume that in addition to the cost avoidance in requirement (b), the capacity released by discontinuance of the design division can be used to provide 6,000 new services that would have a variable cost per service of $60 and would require additional fixed costs totaling $80,000. At what unit price must the new service be sold if Groves is to increase its total net income by $180,000?

LO6

X

P8-5B. Constrained Resource McDermott Corporation manufactures both automatic and manual residential water treatment units. Because of limited demand, for several years production has been at 90% of estimated capacity, which is thought to be limited by the number of machine hours available. At current operation levels, a profit analysis for each product line shows the following:

	Per-Unit Data			
	Automatic		Manual	
Sales price		$800		$416
Production costs:				
Direct materials.	$144		$80	
Direct labor	128		64	
Variable manufacturing overhead	64		32	
Fixed manufacturing overhead*	144	$480	72	$248
Variable operating expenses		80		16
Fixed operating expenses.		144		96
Total cost		$704		$360
Operating income.		$ 96		$ 56

*Assigned on the basis of machine hours at normal capacity.

Management wants to utilize the company's current excess capacity by increasing production.

Required

a. What general decision guideline applies in this situation?

b. Assuming that sufficient units of either product can be sold at current prices to use existing capacity fully and that total fixed cost will not be affected, prepare an analysis showing which product line should be emphasized if net income for the firm is the decision basis.

EXTENDING YOUR KNOWLEDGE

EKY8-1. **Business Decision Case** Marvin Corporation manufactures both an automatic and a manual household dehumidifier. Because of limited demand, for several years production has been at 80% of estimated capacity, which is thought to be limited by the number of machine hours available. At current operation levels, a profit analysis for each product line shows the following:

	Per-Unit Data			
	Automatic		Manual	
Sales price		$350		$150
Production costs:				
Direct materials.	$65		$32	
Direct labor	35		25	
Variable manufacturing overhead	68		16	
Fixed manufacturing overhead	50	$218	18	$ 91
Variable operating expenses		52		21
Fixed operating expenses.		30		13
Total cost		$300		$125
Operating income.		$ 50		$ 25

Management wants to make use of the company's current excess capacity by increasing production. Each unit of the automatic model requires 2.5 machine hours; the manual model requires 1 machine hour per unit.

Required
Present answers for the following questions in each independent situation:

a. Assume that sufficient units of either product can be sold at current prices to utilize existing capacity fully and that fixed costs will not be affected.
  1. To which product should the excess capacity be devoted if the decision basis is maximization of contribution margin per unit of product?
  2. Prepare an analysis showing which product line should be emphasized if the firm's net income is the decision basis.
  3. What general decision guideline applies in this situation?

b. Suppose the excess capacity represents 10,000 machine hours, which can be used to make 4,000 automatic units or 10,000 manual units or any proportionate combination. The only market available for these extra units is a foreign market in which the sales prices must be reduced by 20% and in which no more than 6,000 units of either model can be sold. All costs will remain the same except that the sales commission of 10% (included in the variable operating expenses) will be avoided. Prepare an analysis showing which product should be emphasized and the effect on the firm's net income.

c. Assume that the excess capacity can be used as indicated in requirement (b) and that the firm's market research department believes that the production available from using the excess capacity exclusively on either model can be sold in the domestic market at regular prices if a promotion campaign costing $225,000 is undertaken for the automatic model or $235,000 for the manual model. Prepare an analysis indicating for which product the campaign should be undertaken.

EKY8-2. **Business Decision Case** Hall Manufacturing Corporation makes a new high-tech adhesive in a single process that blends and bottles die product, which currently sells for $20 per gallon. Market demand for the product seems good, but management is not satisfied with the product's seemingly low profit margin and has sought your advice.

Because of its concern, management has allocated a $60,000 fund for a program of product promotion or cost reduction, or both. Members of the firm's controller's office and marketing staff have identified the following three possible plans:

1. Plan A: Devote all funds to product promotion, which allows all costs and the sales volume to remain the same but permits a sales price increase of $3.50 per gallon.
2. Plan B: Spend $32,000 on product promotion and $28,000 on cost reduction techniques, which maintains sales volume, permits a price increase of $2 per gallon, and reduces conversion costs by 10% per gallon.
3. Plan C: Devote all funds to cost reduction efforts. Sales volume and price do not change. For each gallon produced, however, direct materials cost decreases 10%, and conversion cost decreases 20%.

The controller's office also provides you with the following operating data for a typical period. (All materials are added initially; conversion costs occur evenly throughout the process. The weighted average method is used for process costing.)

Beginning work in process (2,500 gallons, 60% processed)	$ 32,250
Units started in process (34,000 gallons)	
Ending work in process (3,500 gallons, 60% processed)	
Costs charged to the department:	
Direct materials.	275,400
Direct labor	186,390
Manufacturing overhead	156,330
	$650,370

Required

Using the data from this representative production period, analyze the apparent relative benefits derived from each plan and make a recommendation supported by relevant calculations. Assume that sales for each period will equal units completed in that period. *Hint:* You will need to prepare a Production Report, Cost per Equivalent Unit Report, and Production Cost Report to analyze the three plans. These reports were discussed in Chapter 4.

EKY8-3.   **Ethics Case** Swan Sports manufactures golfing equipment. Traditionally, the company has been busy all year but has noticed that over the past few years business has fallen off in October and November. If new business does not come in this year, the company will have to lay off some long-time employees for those 2 months. Rob Patell, a sales representative, received an order from Better Equipment Co., a competitor. Better Equipment cannot meet a customer's rush order on time and is willing to subcontract the work to Swan Sports on the condition that the Better Equipment Co. name—not Swan Sports' name—appear on all products. The order is at a price substantially below Swan Sports' usual selling price. The only way this order can be produced is to use lower-quality materials than Swan Sports normally uses in its own products.

Rob Patell has recommended to his supervisor that this order be accepted and that lower-quality materials be used. Patell's reasoning includes the following points:

a.   It is clearly a one-time order.
b.   Swan Sports' name will not appear on it.
c.   Workers will not have to be laid off during October and November.

A differential analysis shows that Swan Sports will lose $1,000 on the order.

Required

What should the sales supervisor consider before making a decision?

EKY8-4.   **Environmental, Social, and Governance** The ESG box in this chapter highlights some early citizenship milestones of John Deere. Go to John Deere's website (https://www.deere.com) and search under "Company Information" at the bottom of the page for "Sustainability." Under the Sustainability page, review one of John Deere's Citizenship initiatives. Read about one of the reported initiatives and briefly summarize your findings. Can you think of a good business purpose for these initiatives, or are they simply things that make John Deere a good corporate citizen?

ANSWERS TO SELF-STUDY QUESTIONS:

1. c   2. c   3. a   4. d   5. b   6. d

YOUR TURN! SOLUTIONS

Solution 8.1

Assume that rakes are produced. What are the incremental revenues and costs if shovels are produced instead?

Incremental revenue:		
Revenue forgone on 50,000 rakes	[$20 × 50,000 units]	$(1,000,000)
Additional revenue from shovels price	[($30 – $20) × 200,000 units]	2,000,000
Incremental revenue		$ 1,000,000
Incremental costs:		
Additional cost of goods sold	[($18 – $9) × 200,000 units]	$(1,800,000)
Savings on 50,000 rakes not produced	[$9 × 50,000]	450,000
Savings on selling and administrative	[$2 × 50,000]	100,000
Incremental costs		$(1,250,000)
Net differential cost of producing shovels		$ (250,000)

So, the manufacturer should produce rakes.

Solution 8.2

Yes.

Differential revenue	$200,000
Differential cost (10,000 × $14) + ($40,000 – $5,000)	175,000
Net increase in profit	$ 25,000

Solution 8.3

Relevant per-unit costs to manufacture:	
Direct materials	$10.50
Direct labor	24.00
Variable factory overhead	5.50
Total	$40.00
Relevant per-unit cost to purchase	42.00
Net cost to purchase	($ 2.00)

Scott should continue to manufacture the part.

Solution 8.4

Differential analysis:	
Lost revenue..................................	$1,000,000
Expenses eliminated:	
Direct materials...............................	$ 450,000
Direct labor....................................	250,000
Variable overhead [80% × 400,000]...............	320,000
Decreased expenses	1,020,000
Incremental increase in gross profit	$ 20,000

Solution 8.5

Product X	[10,000 units × ($5.00 − $2.50)] ...	$ 25,000
Product Y	[20,000 units × ($3.00 − $1.75)] ...	25,000
Total		$ 50,000
Product Y allocation	[$25,000/$50,000].............	50%
	[$350,000 × 50%].............	$175,000

Solution 8.6
Product B. ($12/1 hour is greater than $15/2 hours)

Chapter 9
Planning and Budgeting

Road Map

LO	Learning Objective	Page	eLecture	Guided Example	Assignments
LO1	Describe the planning process, including strategic planning and operational planning.	9-3	E9-1	YT9.1	SS1, Q1, Q2, Q3
LO2	Discuss the budgeting process and summarize its advantages. Define the key elements of effective budgeting.	9-6	E9-2	YT9.2	SS2, Q4, Q5, Q6, Q7, Q8, SE1, SE2, SE3, SE4
LO3	Define the components of a master budget and illustrate the interrelationships of the individual budgets that comprise the master budget.	9-10	E9-3	YT9.3	SS3, Q9, Q10, SE5
LO4	Prepare individual budgets for a manufacturing and a service company, including the cash budget.	9-11	E9-4	YT9.4	SS4, SS5, SS6, Q11, Q12, Q13, Q14, Q15, SE6, SE7, SE8, SE9, SE10, E1A, E2A, E3A, E4A, E5A, E6A, E7A, E8A, E9A, E1B, E2B, E3B, E4B, E5B, E6B, E7B, E8B, E9B, P1A, P2A, P4A, P1B, P2B, P4B
LO5	Prepare budgeted financial statements.	9-20	E9-5	YT9.5	SS7, Q16, P3A, P4A, P5A, P3B, P4B, P5B

Adecoagro LP S.C.S. is a leading agro-industrial company in South America with a broad range of businesses, including farming crops, dairy operations, sugar, ethanol and energy production, and land transformation. Adecoagro's business is inherently seasonal, with a significant "off-season" between January and April. Forecasting or budgeting its sales revenues is complicated by the need to estimate crop yields, sucrose content, harvesting costs, transportation costs, and market prices well in advance.

Adecoagro attempts to mitigate the uncertainties of its business by pursuing geographical diversification of its farms, diversifying its products, vertically integrating its rice, dairy, sugar, ethanol, and energy businesses, and developing a hedge risk management strategy for each product. Despite these steps, uncertainty will always make the budgeting process a challenge to manage.

This chapter discusses the planning and budgeting process and describes the major components of a master budget.

PAST

Chapter 8 described some of the tools and techniques that management can use in making short-term business decisions.

PRESENT

Chapter 9 discusses the budgeting process, the components of the master budget, and the interrelationships of the individual budgets and presents an illustration of a budget for a manufacturer and a service company.

FUTURE

Chapter 10 provides an overview of standard costing and variance analysis. Moreover, it describes how standard costs influence financial statements.

PLANNING AND BUDGETING

The Planning Process	The Budgeting Process	The Framework of the Master Budget	Illustration of a Master Budget and Its Components
• Strategic Planning • Operational Planning • Progress Measurement and Reporting	• Advantages of Budgeting • Elements of Effective Budgeting • Zero-Based Budgeting	• Master Budget Components • Budget Interrelationships	• Sales Budget • Production Budget • Direct Materials Budget • Direct Labor Budget • Manufacturing Overhead Budget • Selling and Administrative Expense Budget • Capital Expenditures Budget • Cash Budget • Illustration of a Service Firm's Budgets • Budgeted Financial Statements

Prediction is very difficult, especially about the future.

NIELS BOHR

Your ability to live within your means over the long term and meet your financial obligations from paycheck to paycheck depends in large part on your ability to accurately identify your income and manage your expenses. If you consistently overestimate your income or underestimate your expenses, you may find yourself getting deeper and deeper into debt. Without a financial plan, or budget, you run the risk of financial hardship or ruin.

Likewise, to be successful, every business needs to produce products or provide services at competitive costs for a growing customer base to ensure that reasonable profits are made to continue to grow the business. Management has a basic responsibility to plan, control, and measure performance and to make decisions. To carry out these responsibilities, management must develop plans and budgets, determine actual operating results, compare actual results to planned results, evaluate differences, and take corrective action to improve operations. This chapter focuses on managerial planning and budgeting.

THE PLANNING PROCESS

LO1 Describe the planning process, including strategic planning and operational planning.

eLecture

MBC

All types of organizations—service organizations, merchandising firms, manufacturing companies, government agencies, and not-for-profit entities—can benefit from formalized planning. A formal planning process usually includes strategic planning and operational planning.

A **planning horizon** is the future time span, usually expressed in years, for which a particular plan is developed. Different types of plans have different planning horizons. Typically, longer planning horizons are associated with higher-level planning (e.g., strategic planning), whereas shorter planning horizons are associated with lower-level planning (e.g., annual operational planning.) **Exhibit 9-1** is an example of a formal planning process. As illustrated, the planning process begins with the definition of a vision or mission statement. This statement defines what the company is and provides a focus for its strategy and operational planning. The best vision statements are succinct and clear. Adecoagro states that it is an agro industrial company that produces and manufactures food and renewable energy.

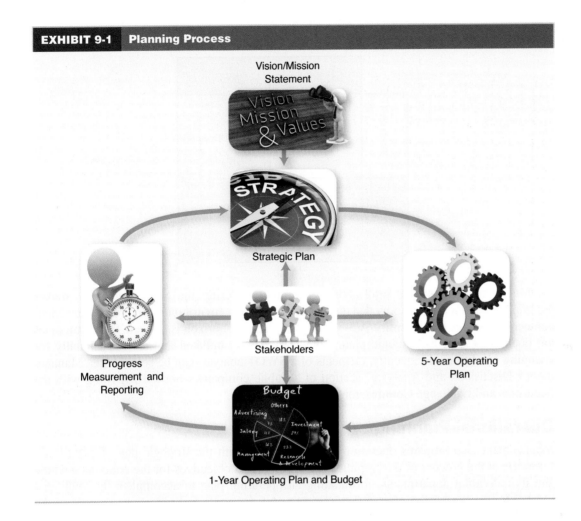

Strategic Planning

Strategic planning is a formal process that addresses and documents the overall mission and long-term goals of the organization based on the vision statement. Management must evaluate and decide in what directions the organization should go in the future. Issues to be decided include what basic lines of business to pursue, which geographic markets to establish, what organizational structure to develop, where to locate facilities, which means of sales and distribution to use, and how aggressively the organization should grow. For example, Adecoagro's strategic plan is focused on producing agricultural products in regions where they believe they have competitive advantages, reducing volatility through product and geographic diversification and advanced technology, acquiring and transforming land to improve its productivity, and implementing sustainable production practices and technologies.

Management must accumulate and analyze a great deal of information to create an appropriate strategic plan incorporating these decisions. Many companies use a technique such as a **strengths, weaknesses, opportunities, and threats (SWOT) analysis** to begin this accumulation and analysis process. **Exhibit 9-2** illustrates this process in the form of a 2 × 2 matrix.

Management uses SWOT analysis to analyze and document those internal and external factors that both help and harm the company's ability to achieve its strategy. The SWOT analysis will specifically address management, employees, products, services, physical facilities, customers, competitors, distribution channels, and systems. It is very important to recognize and document the current strengths and weaknesses of the firm as well as the future opportunities and threats facing it when formulating the firm's future strategic directions.

EXHIBIT 9-2	SWOT Matrix

	Helpful	Harmful
Internal	Strengths	Weaknesses
External	Opportunities	Threats

Management takes the information accumulated during the SWOT analysis, makes assumptions about the economy and the future competitive environment, and formulates management strategies for the entity. A 5- or 10-year planning horizon is typical. These strategies are documented in the strategic plan, which is typically updated and revised annually for changing conditions. Frequently, elements of a SWOT analysis can be seen in the "Management's Discussion and Analysis" section of a public company's Form 10-K filing with the Securities and Exchange Commission.

Operational Planning

Management also prepares operating plans consistent with the strategic plan. **Operational planning** is the process of developing specific goals and objectives for the entity as a whole and its individual departments, formulating an operating plan to accomplish the goals and objectives, and preparing written documentation of the goals and objectives as well as the operating plan. Firms frequently develop a long-term operating plan that covers a 3- to 5-year planning horizon as well as an annual operating plan that covers a 1-year planning horizon. The annual operating plan is typically more detailed than the long-term operating plan.

The annual operating plan projects some of the current operations as they exist and provides for changes in others to reflect management's desires for improvements in the operations. The annual operating plan reflects the strategies, goals, objectives, and action plan documented in the strategic plan and the long-term operating plan. Further, the annual operating plan is usually not in a format that enables management to determine whether the plans are economically feasible. Management tests the economic feasibility of the annual operating plan through the development of the annual operating budget.

For example, Adecoagro's 2021 Annual Report[1] noted its use of a silo bag storage method in its crop production operation, utilizing large polyethylene bags with a capacity of 180–200 tons, resulting in low-cost, scalable, and flexible storage on the field during harvest that allows the company to generate freight savings by moving product in the off-season when freight fares are lower.

Progress Measurement and Reporting

No planning process is complete without an accounting of the progress achieved in pursuing the plans made. A periodic accounting is helpful in measuring progress, holding individuals accountable for aspects of the plan that are within their area of responsibility, and evaluating whether changes need to be made to future plans based on changes in the internal or external environment in which the company operates. This accounting takes many forms, including

---

[1] https://www.sec.gov/ix?doc=/Archives/edgar/data/1499505/000162828021007998/agro-20201231.htm

internal management reports and external reports to owners, creditors, and other stakeholders. For example, Adecoagro's external reports include quarterly earnings releases, Securities and Exchange Commission reports, and a corporate sustainability report. Each of these reports highlights different results of Adecoagro's operations.

ENVIRONMENTAL, SOCIAL, AND GOVERNANCE   Adecoagro's Local Social Investment Activities

This chapter discusses the importance of budgeting to a company's financial performance. A 2012 *Forbes* article discusses the importance of budgeting for corporate social responsibility success.* The article discusses how doing good through employee volunteering programs leads to the company doing well through increased employee engagement, employee retention, and employee recruitment.

Adecoagro appears to agree with the article's author. As noted in Adecoagro's 2020 Sustainability Report, its employees are helping fight local hunger by donating 844,000 kilos of food to local food banks in the communities where they are located. They contributed 25,000 liters of milk and 50,000 kilos of rice to the SEAMOS UNO campaign. In addition, in response to the COVID-19 pandemic, employees distributed over 90,000 liters of sanitizer and tens of thousands of gloves, masks, head covers, and disposable gowns to local institutions and municipalities.

*Ryan Scott, "'Tis the Season to Budget for CSR Success," *Forbes*, November 19, 2012.

YOUR TURN! 9.1

The solution is on page 9-44.

Assume that you are performing a SWOT analysis for the retail company Target. List at least two strengths, weaknesses, opportunities, and threats that might apply to the company in the coming years.

GuidedExample
MBC

THE BUDGETING PROCESS

A **budget** is a detailed plan for the acquisition and use of financial resources during a specific period of time. A budget serves as a plan for how a firm will achieve its quantifiable goals and a basis for measuring performance against those goals.

Budgeting is the process of developing a formal, written operating plan that presents management's planned actions in financial terms. Budgeting should reflect the conclusions reached in the strategic plan and the operating plan. Two budgets usually result from the budgeting process: the annual operating budget and the capital expenditures budget. We present and discuss the annual operating budget in this chapter and the capital expenditures budget in Chapter 12. **Exhibit 9-1** presents the sequence for preparing the various types of plans and budgets.

All types of entities can derive benefits from the budgeting process. Although the basic concepts of budgeting apply to all types of entities, the precise budget form will vary among those entities. Budgeting typically incorporates many accounting concepts discussed in previous chapters. In fact, some components of the annual operating budget have familiar accounting formats.

LO2 Discuss the budgeting process and **summarize** its advantages. **Define** the key elements of effective budgeting.

eLecture
MBC

A.K.A. The **annual operating budget** is also called the **master budget**.

Concept	Method	Assessment	TAKEAWAY 9.1
How can management best ensure that the efforts of all employees are congruent with the company's strategy?	Develop multi-year operating plans and budgets (both operating and capital) linked to the company's strategy.	Compare actual results with operating plans and budgets to evaluate company performance.	

Advantages of Budgeting

The use of budgets to manage and control a firm's activities is known as **budgetary control**. Budgetary control involves the steps taken by management to ensure that the goals and objectives established during the planning stage are attained and to ensure that all segments of the firm operate in a manner consistent with organizational policies. Used properly, a budget can sharpen management's focus, ensure that operating activities will help achieve management's overall strategy, and be useful in evaluating performance.

The annual planning and budgeting process forces management to step back from the daily operations of the entity, examine current operations, decide what improvements are necessary, and formulate plans and budgets that implement the established goals and objectives for the entity. The annual operating budget represents a specific plan for accomplishing these goals and objectives.

A budget can be used to control operations. When a business is large enough to be divided into departments, management needs to ensure that the operation of each department is consistent with the overall plans for the entity as a whole. The budget provides guidance for the departmental managers so their decisions will be consistent with decisions in other departments. For example, the budget provides guidance so the purchasing department buys quantities of material consistent with the factory's budget of units to be manufactured; that budget, in turn, is consistent with the sales department's budget of units to be sold.

Budgets serve as guides and targets to managers when they make decisions and as one basis for performance evaluation. Performance evaluations could be based on comparison of actual results to prior-period results. However, comparison to prior-period results fails to take into account the changes and improvements that have been incorporated into the budget. As a result, the budget is frequently the basis for evaluating performance. Because the budget is used as a basis for evaluating performance, it can also be a motivating factor for individual managers. Assuming that the budget is realistic, it provides a target that each manager will try to attain.

Elements of Effective Budgeting

Even though specific budgeting procedures vary widely among business firms, all entities engaged in comprehensive budgeting should consider the following elements of effective budgeting.

Identifying a **budget director** is vital to effective budgeting. Budget director may be a full-time or part-time position, depending on the size and complexity of the business. The budget director must be well organized and good at communicating, since he or she is responsible for organizing the budgeting process, communicating with the people involved in budgeting, and monitoring the process to ensure that it proceeds on a timely basis.

The **budget committee** generally consists of representatives from all major areas of the firm, such as sales, manufacturing, purchasing, and accounting, and is usually headed by the budget director. The primary functions of the budget committee are to provide central guidance to the budget preparation process, ensure that all departments participate in the process, and evaluate the proposed budget segments for reasonableness.

The task of developing the detailed amounts for the budget is usually not done by the budget director or the budget committee. **Participative budgeting** requires that detailed budget amounts be formulated "from the bottom up." That is, all departments should participate in the development and refinement of the budget amounts so they will be accepted by the departments as reasonable standards of performance. The participants in this process are illustrated in **Exhibit 9-3**.

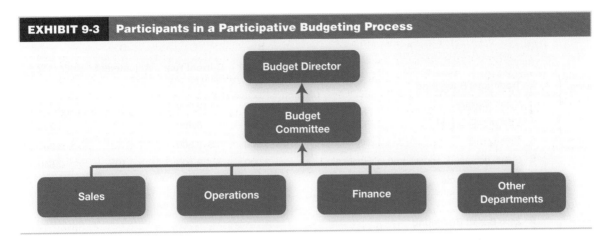

EXHIBIT 9-3 **Participants in a Participative Budgeting Process**

There are advantages to participative budgeting:

1. Individuals at all levels are part of a team.

2. The person in direct contact with the activity is in the best position to make the estimates.

3. A person has ownership of and is therefore more motivated to work at fulfilling a budget that he or she has helped establish.

The **budget period**, the future time span for which the budget is prepared, varies according to the nature of the specific activity involved. Most companies, however, prepare annual operating budgets, which are segmented into quarterly or monthly budgets. Short-term operating budgets covering a month or a quarter may be useful benchmarks as one element of performance evaluations, enabling management to compare budgeted amounts to actual results and initiate corrective action as required.

The capital expenditures budget usually covers a multiyear period, often 3 to 5 years. This longer budget period is necessary because of the long time period required to construct or acquire long-term assets of a unique nature.

Many businesses use **continuous budgeting** techniques for the operating budget. As each monthly or quarterly budget period passes, the oldest month or quarter is removed from the budget and another month or quarter is added to extend the budget to a full year in the future. With this approach, regardless of the time of the year, the budget always covers 12 months or four quarters.

A.K.A. Continuous **budgets** are also known as **perpetual** and **rolling budgets**.

Zero-Based Budgeting

Traditional budgeting procedures typically use an incremental approach to the development of the annual operating budget. For example, the level of each expense for the prior year is used as the starting point for determining the budgeted level for the next year. The person preparing the budget then either adds to or subtracts from the amount in the previous budget. During the budget process, only the increase or decrease is justified to the managers reviewing the proposed budget drafts. The prior year base amount is assumed to be reasonable. For example, the simple traditional budget example in **Exhibit 9-4** shows a budget based on a 10% increase from the current year.

Many organizations—manufacturing companies, merchandising firms, service organizations, governmental agencies, and not-for-profit entities—have experienced increases in their annual operating budgets that they deem to be unacceptable. Some of these organizations have decided to use zero-based budgeting techniques to address this problem. **Zero-based budgeting** requires budget preparers to start at a zero level for every item in the budget and justify every dollar, not just the increases or decreases. In effect, the budget is prepared "from the ground up" as if the entity had just been formed. The simple zero-base budget example in **Exhibit 9-4** shows that the budget is created without reference to the previous year's budgets.

EXHIBIT 9-4   Traditional Budgeting versus Zero-Based Budgeting

	A	B	C	D	E
1		Prior Year	Current Year	Adjustment	Budget Year
2	**Traditional Budgeting**				
3	Sales revenue	$10,000	$12,000	10%	$13,200
4	Cost of goods sold	7,000	8,400	10%	9,240
5	Gross profit	$ 3,000	$ 3,600		$ 3,960
6	Sales, general, & administrative expenses	2,000	2,400	10%	2,640
7	Operating income	$ 1,000	$ 1,200		$ 1,320
8					
9	**Zero-Based Budgeting**				
10	Sales revenue	$ —	$ —	$13,200	$13,200
11	Cost of goods sold	—	—	9,240	9,240
12	Gross profit	—	—	$ 3,960	$ 3,960
13	Sales, general, & administrative expenses	—	—	2,640	2,640
14	Operating income	$ —	$ —	$ 1,320	$ 1,320

With traditional budgeting, the budget is typically based on the prior year's budget, adjusted for inflation or other incremental changes.

With zero-based budgeting, each budget is created from scratch, without reference to prior year amounts.

Organizations that have adopted zero-based budgeting use a variety of specific procedures. A common approach is to segment the budget into "decision packages" in which the preparer ranks all of the activities according to their relative importance for each activity. The preparer might note the consequences of not performing the activity, possible alternative activities, and whether there is an external mandate to perform the activity. This approach enables various levels of management to eliminate low-ranking activities until a desired budget level is reached.

Note that zero-based budgeting is a time-consuming and costly process. As a result, many entities that employ the technique usually do not apply it to all portions of the operating budget each year. Some use zero-based budgeting every year but apply the technique to only selected segments of the budget so that all segments will be subjected to the technique once during each 5-year period. Others apply the technique to all segments periodically (e.g., every third year). As a result, traditional budgeting techniques might be used to prepare budgets for years 1 and 2, with zero-based budgeting used to prepare the budget for year 3.

TAKEAWAY 9.2	Concept ⟶	Method ⟶	Assessment
	How should a company implement a zero-based budgeting approach?	1. Determine goals, operations, and costs for all activities. 2. Determine alternative means of conducting each activity. 3. Evaluate the implications of changes in the level of each activity. 4. Establish workload. 5. Rank activities in order of importance. 6. Select activities necessary to accomplish goals at the minimum cost.	Although costly and time-consuming, zero-based budgeting results in a careful examination and justification of all critical activities, rooting out inefficient and ineffective activities.

YOUR TURN! 9.2

The solution is on page 9-44.

All of the following are advantages of budgeting except:
a. Helps management ensure that operating activities will help achieve the overall corporate strategy.
b. Provides guidance to mid-level department managers so that their decisions are consistent with other departments.
c. Allows individual managers to act independently of other managers within the organization.
d. Provides a basis for evaluating performance.

MBC

THE FRAMEWORK OF THE MASTER BUDGET

Master Budget Components

Master budget is the name given to the comprehensive annual operating budget. The master budget combines and integrates all of the individual, detailed operating budgets for all of the firm's various activities for the year. All amounts in the master budget are usually based on the expected level of operations. The exact structure of the master budget varies according to whether the firm's operations are manufacturing, merchandising, service, or government oriented. In this chapter, we illustrate budgeting and a master budget for Fezzari, the small bicycle manufacturer introduced in Chapter 1. The following budgets constitute Fezzari's master budget:

LO3 Define the components of a master budget and **illustrate** the interrelationships of the individual budgets that comprise the master budget.

MBC

1. Sales budget
2. Production budget
3. Direct materials budget
4. Direct labor budget
5. Manufacturing overhead budget
6. Selling and administrative expense budget
7. Capital expenditures budget
8. Cash budget
9. Budgeted income statement
10. Budgeted balance sheet
11. Budgeted statement of cash flows

Budget Interrelationships

Fezzari's master budget includes budgets that are interdependent and must be prepared in a specific sequence. **Exhibit 9-5** presents Fezzari's master budget and the data flows that are necessary between the individual budgets during their preparation.

The sales budget is prepared first. It is based on the sales forecast and typically includes both sales dollars and quantities. As the sales budget feeds into each of the succeeding budgets, the quality of the sales forecast determines the success of the remaining process. Then the production budget is prepared to identify the number of units of each product to be manufactured. Then the direct materials budget, the direct labor budget, and the manufacturing overhead budget determine the levels of product cost to be incurred based on the units to be manufactured. The selling and administrative expense budget determines the level of selling and general administrative expense necessary to support the sales budget.

The cash budget receives input from the budgets established previously as well as the capital expenditures budget and the budgeted income statement. In turn, the cash budget provides inputs to the budgeted balance sheet and the budgeted statement of cash flows. The budgeted balance sheet also receives input from the budgeted income statement and the capital expenditures budget and supplies input to the budgeted income statement. We illustrate these interrelationships in the following example.

A.K.A. Budgets may be called **pro forma statements**. They are forecasted financial statements instead of actual financial statements.

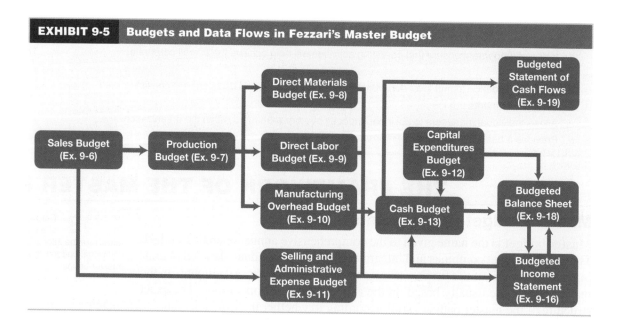

EXHIBIT 9-5   Budgets and Data Flows in Fezzari's Master Budget

---

YOUR TURN! 9.3

The solution is on page 9-44.

GuidedExample

MBC

Place the following budgets in the order that they would normally be prepared:

1. Direct materials budget
2. Production budget
3. Manufacturing overhead budget
4. Capital expenditures budget
5. Cash budget
6. Direct labor budget
7. Sales budget

ILLUSTRATION OF A MASTER BUDGET AND ITS COMPONENTS

Sales Budget

LO4 **Prepare** individual budgets for a manufacturing and a service company, including the cash budget.

eLecture

MBC

The **sales budget** provides the basis for all subsequent budgets. Anticipated unit sales volume is based on the **sales forecast**. The sales forecast is the sales department's best estimate of what sales will be for the company and the industry in which it operates. Factors that are evaluated in preparing the sales forecast include prior company sales levels, future pricing policies, market research studies, general economic conditions, specific economic indicators, advertising and promotion plans, and anticipated activities of the competition. Overestimating sales volume can lead to large unwanted inventories, which in turn result in extra storage costs and possibly sales price reductions when liquidating the excess inventory. Underestimating sales can lead to loss of sales revenue and customer ill will stemming from unfilled orders.

Assume that Fezzari managers are preparing their budget for the upcoming fiscal year. As we have discussed in earlier chapters, Fezzari sells two types of bikes—road and mountain—with several different models of each type. For purposes of this illustration, we will assume that the budget is prepared at the bike-type level, although in reality the budget would be prepared at the model level. Further, assume that Fezzari's management anticipates a 20% growth in sales in the next year.

The estimated unit sales volume of each product is multiplied by planned average unit sales prices to estimate total sales revenue. We present an example of a sales budget in **Exhibit 9-6**. To simplify the presentation of the cash budget, assume all Fezzari's sales are on a cash basis; therefore, Fezzari carries no accounts receivable balances. This assumption is consistent with a bike manufacturer selling customized bikes to customers via e-commerce. We will demonstrate a sales budget for a service firm with credit sales later in the chapter.

EXHIBIT 9-6 *Sales Budget Illustration*

FEZZARI PERFORMANCE BICYCLES
Sales Budget
For the Year Ended December 31

> The sales budget forms the basis of all other budgets, so it is usually created first.

	Forecast Unit Sales Volume	Average Unit Sales Price	Budgeted Total Sales
Road bicycles.	2,160	$1,250	$2,700,000
Mountain bicycles.	3,240	$1,000	3,240,000
Total bicycles	5,400		$5,940,000
Other bicycle accessories.			297,000
Total sales revenue.			$6,237,000

Production Budget

The **production budget** reflects the quantity of each product to be produced during the budget period. Scheduled production should specifically provide for anticipated sales and desired ending inventories and, of course, consider the beginning inventories of each product. Assume that Fezzari wants to increase its inventory of road bikes from 8 to 12 units and its inventory of mountain bikes from 14 to 18 units. Fezzari's production budget appears in **Exhibit 9-7**. Note that the desired change in inventory of each product is accomplished by scheduling the appropriate production volumes. Because bicycle accessories are not manufactured by Fezzari, but simply purchased from vendors for resale, they are not included in the production budget.

Hint: Companies that do not use the just-in-time inventory method often determine required inventory levels based on a percentage of unit sales.

Like Fezzari, many manufacturing companies use the just-in-time approach for finished goods inventory to reduce their inventory carrying costs. When the **just-in-time inventory** approach is used, finished goods are not produced until they are needed for shipment to customers. As a result, the planned ending inventory of finished goods is zero or nearly zero.

EXHIBIT 9-7 *Production Budget Illustration*

FEZZARI PERFORMANCE BICYCLES
Production Budget
For the Year Ended December 31

> The production budget reflects the quantity of each product to be produced during the budget period.

	Units of Finished Product	
	Road Bikes	Mountain Bikes
Forecast unit sales	2,160	3,240
Desired ending finished goods inventories.	12	18
Quantities to be available	2,172	3,258
Less: Beginning finished goods inventories	8	14
Total production to be scheduled	2,164	3,244

> The forecasted unit sales numbers come from the sales budget (Exhibit 9-6).

This approach is practical only for companies that can forecast their sales very accurately, that do not have highly seasonal demand, and that have highly reliable suppliers of the materials and components needed to manufacture the finished goods. Many companies prefer to maintain a **safety stock** of finished goods inventory, so they minimize the risk of running out of stock. Safety stock is defined as a quantity of inventory maintained to supply unexpected demand or to provide stock when manufacturing is slowed through delays in receipt of materials and components from suppliers.

Hint: Running out of an item of inventory not only results in the loss of a current sale but could also cause the loss of future sales due to negative publicity.

Direct Materials Budget

The quantities of materials to be purchased to meet scheduled production and desired ending materials inventory requirements are presented in the **direct materials budget**. Any beginning materials inventory must be considered in estimating purchases for the budget period. Because Fezzari assembles its bikes only after receiving a customer order, it does not maintain a large inventory of direct materials. The quantities to be acquired are multiplied by the anticipated unit prices to calculate the total dollar amounts of materials purchases. In the direct materials budget illustrated in **Exhibit 9-8**, we assume that Fezzari uses only two direct materials—a frame and a build kit containing all of the other components—in producing road and mountain bikes. Further, Fezzari targets to have sufficient frames and build kits in ending inventory for 6 road bikes and 10 mountain bikes.

The direct materials budget presents the quantities of materials to be purchased to meet scheduled production and desired ending materials inventory requirements.

The forecasted unit production numbers come from the production budget (Exhibit 9-7).

EXHIBIT 9-8   Direct Materials Budget Illustration

FEZZARI PERFORMANCE BICYCLES
Direct Materials Budget
For the Year Ended December 31

	Frame	Build Kit	Total
Road bicycles:			
Units to be produced	2,164	2,164	
Desired ending materials inventory	6	6	
Total units of materials to be available	2,170	2,170	
Less: Beginning materials inventory	8	8	
Total units of materials to be purchased	2,162	2,162	
Average unit purchase price	$ 325	$ 275	
Total road bike materials purchases	$ 702,650	$ 594,550	$1,297,200
Mountain bicycles:			
Units to be produced	3,244	3,244	
Desired ending materials inventory	10	10	
Total units of materials to be available	3,254	3,254	
Less: Beginning materials inventory	14	14	
Total units of materials to be purchased	3,240	3,240	
Average unit purchase price	$ 350	$ 290	
Total mountain bike materials purchases	$1,134,000	$ 939,600	$2,073,600
Total materials purchases	$1,836,650	$1,534,150	$3,370,800
Add: Beginning accounts payable balance			50,000
Less: Ending accounts payable balance			(75,000)
Cash budgeted for materials purchases			$3,345,800

The just-in-time inventory philosophy may also apply to the materials inventory of manufacturing firms. Under this philosophy, materials and components needed to manufacture finished products would not be received from the suppliers until immediately before they are needed for manufacturing. As a result, the materials inventory would be zero or nearly zero. Many firms prefer to carry safety stocks of materials and components to ensure that the manufacturing facility is not slowed or stopped by a supplier missing a scheduled delivery.

The direct materials budget in **Exhibit 9-8** shows the total purchases that are budgeted for the year. However, because Fezzari purchases these materials on credit from its suppliers, the dollar amount of purchases may not equal the cash that will be expended for materials during the year. Thus, in preparing the cash budget, an adjustment must be made for the change in the accounts payable balance during the year. **Exhibit 9-8** illustrates how the cash expended for direct materials might be calculated assuming that the balance in accounts payable was expected to increase from $50,000 to $75,000.

The increase in the accounts payable balance of $25,000 over the year means that Fezzari will spend $25,000 less than the total materials purchases in cash.

Direct Labor Budget

The **direct labor budget** presents the number of direct labor hours necessary for the production volume planned for the budget period. These hours are multiplied by the applicable hourly labor rates to determine the total dollar amounts of direct labor costs to be budgeted. In the direct labor budget for Fezzari in **Exhibit 9-9**, we have assumed that both road and mountain bikes require the following average hours in the assembly and quality control and packaging departments:

	Assembly Hours	Quality Control and Packaging Hours
Road bikes	5.5	2.0
Mountain bikes	7.0	2.0

EXHIBIT 9-9   **Direct Labor Budget Illustration**

FEZZARI PERFORMANCE BICYCLES
Direct Labor Budget ◄
For the Year Ended December 31

> The direct labor budget presents the number of direct labor hours necessary for the planned production volume.

	Assembly Department	Quality Control and Packaging Department	Total
Road bicycles			
Total units to be produced (from Exhibit 9-7) . .	2,164	2,164	
Average hours per unit	5.5	2.0	
Total road bike direct labor hours	11,902	4,328	
Mountain bicycles			
Total units to be produced (from Exhibit 9-7) . .	3,244	3,244	
Average hours per unit	7.0	7.0	
Total mountain bike direct labor hours	22,708	6,488	
Total direct labor hours	34,610	10,816	45,426
Hourly rate for direct labor	$ 25	$ 20	
Total direct labor cost	$865,250	$216,320	$1,081,570

Manufacturing Overhead Budget

Recall from earlier chapters that manufacturing overhead comprises all manufacturing costs that are not direct materials or direct labor. Examples of manufacturing overhead are indirect materials, indirect labor, supervisory salaries, utilities, depreciation, maintenance, property taxes, and insurance. Because of the variety of cost factors, manufacturing overhead includes both variable and fixed cost elements.

The **manufacturing overhead budget** for Fezzari's Assembly and Packaging departments is shown in **Exhibit 9-10**. Note that the format separates variable and fixed overhead cost elements and presents budgeted overhead costs for the 45,426 direct labor hours expected to be incurred.

Management would determine the budgeted variable costs based on purchase agreements with its vendors (indirect materials), labor agreements with its employees (indirect

Hint: Manufacturing overhead is any cost incurred within the factory that is not direct in nature. Hence, factory costs – direct costs = indirect costs.

labor), and contracted rates for other services (utilities). Management would determine the budgeted fixed costs based on lease agreements, insurance contracts, local government tax notices, and current levels of equipment. These amounts would not be expected to vary from year to year. Usually, lease agreements are multiyear agreements with fixed rates for each year of the agreement and insurance coverage is adjusted only as manufacturing facilities are expanded. To simplify the presentation of the cash budget, assume that all overhead expenses, except depreciation, are paid in the month they are incurred.

As we discussed in **Chapter 3**, the predetermined overhead rate is determined by dividing the total budgeted manufacturing overhead by the budgeted activity level, or direct labor hours in this example. For the year ended December 31, the total cost formula for overhead at the planned operating volume of 45,426 direct labor hours (DLH) would be as follows:

$$\text{Total manufacturing overhead cost} = \$1.66 \times \text{DLH} + \$225,000$$

EXHIBIT 9-10   Manufacturing Overhead Budget Illustration

FEZZARI PERFORMANCE BICYCLES
Overhead Budget
For the Year Ended December 31

	Variable Cost per Direct Labor Hour	Total Costs at 45,426 Direct Labor Hours
Variable manufacturing costs		
Indirect materials	$0.07	$ 3,180
Indirect labor	0.62	28,164
Factory utilities	0.68	30,890
Other	0.29	13,174
Total variable manufacturing overhead	$1.66	$ 75,408
Fixed manufacturing costs		
Lease expense		$100,000
Insurance		68,000
Property taxes		12,000
Depreciation		45,000
Total fixed manufacturing overhead		$225,000
Total manufacturing overhead		$300,408
Less: Depreciation		(45,000)
Cash budgeted for manufacturing overhead		$255,408
Direct labor hours		45,426
Budgeted predetermined manufacturing overhead rate (rounded)		$ 6.61

The manufacturing overhead budget includes all production costs that are not direct materials and direct labor.

Note that variable and fixed overhead elements are presented separately.

Noncash expenses are deducted to determine cash expenditures for the cash budget.

The direct labor hours come from the direct labor budget, Exhibit 9-9.

Selling and Administrative Expense Budget

The **selling and administrative expense budget** will consist of variable and fixed expenses. The variable selling expenses will typically vary with dollars of sales. To simplify the presentation of the cash budget, assume that selling and administrative expenses, except depreciation, are paid in the month incurred. **Exhibit 9-11** presents Fezzari's selling and administrative expense budget.

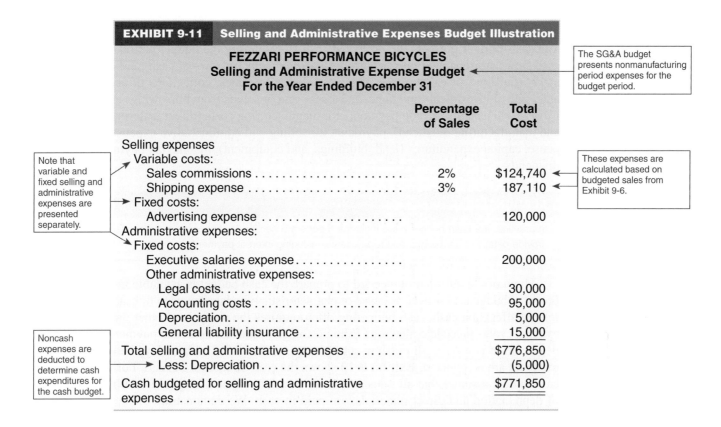

EXHIBIT 9-11 Selling and Administrative Expenses Budget Illustration

FEZZARI PERFORMANCE BICYCLES
Selling and Administrative Expense Budget
For the Year Ended December 31

The SG&A budget presents nonmanufacturing period expenses for the budget period.

	Percentage of Sales	Total Cost
Selling expenses		
Variable costs:		
Sales commissions	2%	$124,740
Shipping expense	3%	187,110
Fixed costs:		
Advertising expense		120,000
Administrative expenses:		
Fixed costs:		
Executive salaries expense.		200,000
Other administrative expenses:		
Legal costs.		30,000
Accounting costs		95,000
Depreciation.		5,000
General liability insurance		15,000
Total selling and administrative expenses		$776,850
Less: Depreciation		(5,000)
Cash budgeted for selling and administrative expenses		$771,850

Note that variable and fixed selling and administrative expenses are presented separately.

These expenses are calculated based on budgeted sales from Exhibit 9-6.

Noncash expenses are deducted to determine cash expenditures for the cash budget.

Capital Expenditures Budget

Expenditures for property, plant, and equipment are among a firm's most important transactions. The type of analysis that is undertaken to determine whether a particular item should be acquired is known as capital budgeting and is discussed in detail in Chapter 12. The **capital expenditures budget** lists long-term assets that are planned to be acquired over a multiyear period. **Exhibit 9-12** presents an illustration for Fezzari. We will assume that it is abstracted from the complete capital expenditures budget.

EXHIBIT 9-12 Capital Expenditures Budget Illustration

FEZZARI PERFORMANCE BICYCLES
Capital Expenditures Budget
For the Year Ended December 31

The capital expenditures budget lists investments in assets that are expected to be used over a multiyear period.

	1st Quarter	2nd Quarter	3rd Quarter	4th Quarter	Total
Assembly equipment	$25,000		$25,000		$50,000
Packaging equipment		$10,000			$10,000
Administrative computers				$5,000	$ 5,000
Total	$25,000	$10,000	$25,000	$5,000	$65,000

The capital expenditures budget has an impact on many other budgets. The plant and equipment available at any point in time determine the productive capacity of the firm. Further, depreciation expense in both the overhead budgets and the selling and administrative expense budget is affected by the capital expenditures budget, as are the cash expenditures in the cash budget and the property, plant, and equipment assets on the balance sheet.

Cash Budget

The **cash budget** presents the projected cash flows during the budget period. The budgeted cash flows are separated into two groups: *cash receipts* (inflows of cash) and *cash disbursements* (outflows of cash). *Cash receipts* include cash sales, collections of accounts receivable, sale of investments and unneeded assets, and proceeds from borrowings and stock sales. *Cash disbursements* include payments for manufacturing costs (direct materials, direct labor, and manufacturing overhead), payments for selling and administrative expenses, interest expense, capital expenditures (land, buildings, and equipment), income tax payments, and cash dividends.

ACCOUNTING IN PRACTICE   **Financing Cash Flows**

In practice, the cash budget often includes a separate section for financing activities. This section would provide details of borrowings and repayments, including interest payments.

Much of the information needed to prepare the cash budget is available in the previously prepared budgets. However, because of characteristic time lags between transactions and their related effects on cash, cash budgeting often requires the analysis of other data as well. For example, sales precede collections from customers, purchases precede payments on account, depreciation is not a cash outflow, and prepayments call for cash outlays before the related expenses are recognized. **Exhibit 9-13** shows the cash budget for Fezzari. For simplicity, the cash budget assumes that all sales are made in cash and that all expenses, with the exception of depreciation and direct materials, are paid in cash. We demonstrate the determination of cash from sales when sales are made on account in the following section.

EXHIBIT 9-13	Cash Budget Illustration	
	FEZZARI PERFORMANCE BICYCLES **Cash Budget** ◄ **For the Year Ended December 31**	The cash budget presents the projected cash inflows and outflows for the budget period.
	Amount	**Source**
Cash receipts:		
Sales	$6,237,000	Exhibit 9-6
Cash disbursements:		
Direct materials.	(3,345,800)	Exhibit 9-8
Direct labor	(1,081,570)	Exhibit 9-9
Manufacturing overhead	(255,408)	Exhibit 9-10 (excluding depreciation)
Selling and administrative costs	(771,850)	Exhibit 9-11
Capital expenditures	(65,000)	Exhibit 9-12
Interest	(5,000)	Financing budget (not shown)
Income taxes.	(176,395)	Exhibit 9-16
Net change in cash.	$ 535,977	
Beginning cash.	550,905	
Ending cash	$1,086,882	

Illustration of a Service Firm's Budgets

SERVICE AND MERCHANDISING

Assume that Environmental Business Consultants (EBC) has collected the following actual data for February and March and developed the following forecasted data for the quarter ended June 30:

1. Actual sales for February and March were the following:

	Actual Credit Sales
February.........................	$310,000
March	290,000

2. Forecast sales for the quarter ended June 30 are as follows:

	Forecast Credit Sales
April	$400,000
May.............................	350,000
June	380,000

3. The collection of cash from credit sales during the quarter ended June 30 will follow the same pattern as the previous quarter:

   a. In the month of sale, 10% is collected.

   b. In the month following sale, 50% is collected.

   c. In the second month following sale, 38% is collected. The remaining 2% of accounts receivable are written off as uncollectible.

   Based on the information in items 1–3, the cash collections can be computed as follows:

	A	B	C	D	E
1		Cash Collections from Customers			
	Month of Credit Sale	April	May	June	Quarter Total
2	February	$117,800			
3	March	145,000	$110,200		
4	April	40,000	200,000	$152,000	
5	May		35,000	175,000	
6	June			38,000	
7	Month total	$302,800	$345,200	$365,000	$1,013,000

4. Forecast cash disbursements for the quarter ended June 30 are as follows:

	A	B	C	D
1		Forecast Cash Disbursements		
		April	May	June
2	Labor	$195,000	$195,000	$195,000
3	Office lease	16,875	16,875	16,875
4	Office supplies	2,000	5,000	3,000
5	Selling and administrative expenses	31,000	32,000	62,000
6	Interest expense (on existing debt)	417	417	417
7	Cash distributions to owners	—	—	100,000

The increase in the selling and administrative expense in June is due to the anticipated payment of employee midyear bonuses.

5. EBC has a policy of maintaining a cash balance of $500,000. All borrowings and repayments are made at the end of the month, and the short-term loan carries an annual interest rate of 6%.

The cash budget for EBC is shown in **Exhibit 9-14**. A three-column format is used so the cash flow of each month of the quarter can be analyzed separately. The starting point in preparing this cash budget is a beginning cash balance for April of $400,000. The cash receipts and cash disbursements for April are then added to the budget. Note that interest is assumed to be paid in the period in which it is incurred. The preliminary ending cash balance of $457,508 is then calculated.

Remember that EBC has a policy of maintaining a cash balance of $500,000. As shown in **Exhibit 9-14**, EBC starts and ends the month of April with a cash balance below this target. To meet its target by the end of April, EBC could budget to borrow $42,492 ($500,000 – $457,508) on a short-term basis. In May, EBC would have sufficient cash to repay this short-term borrowing.

The budgeted ending cash balance for April becomes the budgeted beginning cash balance for May. The procedure described earlier is then repeated for May.

EXHIBIT 9-14	Service Firm Cash Budget Illustration		
ENVIRONMENTAL BUSINESS CONSULTANTS			
Cash Budget			
For the Quarter Ended June 30			
	April	**May**	**June**
Beginning cash balance	$400,000	$500,000	$553,204
Cash receipts:			
Collections from customers	302,800	345,200	365,000
Cash available	$702,800	$845,200	$918,204
Cash disbursements:			
Labor	$195,000	$195,000	$195,000
Office lease	16,875	16,875	16,875
Office supplies	2,000	5,000	3,000
Selling and administrative costs	31,000	32,000	62,000
Interest (on existing debt)	417	629	417
Cash distributions to owners	—	—	100,000
Total disbursements	$245,292	$249,504	$377,292
Preliminary ending cash balance	$457,508	$595,696	$540,912
Target cash balance	$500,000	$500,000	$500,000
Required short-term borrowing (repayment)	42,492	(42,492)	—
Final ending cash balance	$500,000	$553,204	$540,912

Interest on existing debt	$417
Interest on short-term borrowing	212 [$42,492 × (6.0%/12)]
Total interest	$629

The budgeted ending cash balance for May then becomes the budgeted beginning cash balance for June, and the process is repeated again. One additional cash disbursement appears in June: the $100,000 quarterly cash distribution to the owners.

Zinc Company's management team is preparing a cash budget for the coming quarter. They have prepared the following budgeted information for the first quarter:

	January	February	March
Revenue	$500,000	$600,000	$700,000
Inventory purchases	400,000	500,000	550,000
Other expenses	200,000	225,000	225,000

The company expects to collect 60% of its monthly sales in the month of sale and 40% in the following month. Seventy percent of inventory purchases are paid in the month of purchase and the other 30% in the following month. All payments for other expenses are made in the month incurred.
Zinc forecasts the following account balances at the beginning of the quarter:

Cash	$200,000
Accounts receivable	200,000
Accounts payable (Inventory)	150,000

Given the above information, what is the projected change in cash during the coming quarter?

Budgeted Financial Statements

Budgeted Income Statement

The development of the master budget is completed with the preparation of the budgeted financial statements: the budgeted income statement, the budgeted balance sheet, and the budgeted statement of cash flows. The **budgeted income statement** is usually prepared first. In addition to the budgets that were previously prepared, supplemental schedules and worksheets may be needed to prepare the budgeted income statement. Returning to the Fezzari example, one of these supplementary schedules is the schedule of estimated product cost per unit, which is presented in **Exhibit 9-15**. We then use the estimated cost per unit to calculate our budgeted cost of goods sold, which is included in our budgeted income statement (**Exhibit 9-16**).

LO5   Prepare budgeted financial statements.

eLecture

MBC

EXHIBIT 9-15	Estimated Product Cost per Unit Illustration

FEZZARI PERFORMANCE BICYCLES
Estimated Product Cost per Unit
For the Year Ended December 31

			Cost			
	Quantity		Road Bicycle	Mountain Bicycle	Road Bicycle	Mountain Bicycle
Direct materials:						
Frame	1.0	×	$325.00	$350.00 =	$325.00	$350.00
Build kit	1.0	×	275.00	290.00 =	275.00	290.00

See Exhibit 9-8

	Cost per unit		Quantity			
Direct labor:						
Assembly	$ 25.00	×	5.5	7.0 =	137.50	175.00
QC and packaging	$ 20.00	×	2.0	2.0 =	40.00	40.00
Manufacturing overhead:						
Combined	$ 6.61	×	7.5	9.0 =	49.58	59.49
Product cost per unit.					$827.08	$914.49

See Exhibit 9-10

See Exhibit 9-9

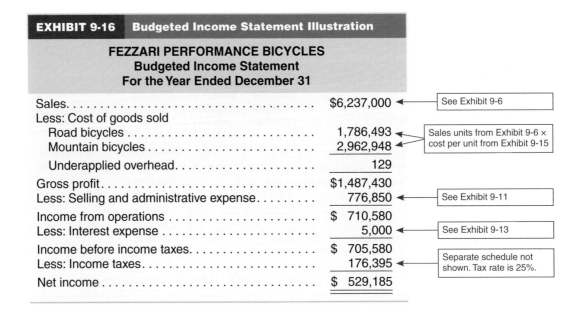

EXHIBIT 9-16 **Budgeted Income Statement Illustration**

FEZZARI PERFORMANCE BICYCLES
Budgeted Income Statement
For the Year Ended December 31

Sales.	$6,237,000	← See Exhibit 9-6
Less: Cost of goods sold		
Road bicycles	1,786,493	← Sales units from Exhibit 9-6 × cost per unit from Exhibit 9-15
Mountain bicycles	2,962,948	
Underapplied overhead.	129	
Gross profit.	$1,487,430	
Less: Selling and administrative expense.	776,850	← See Exhibit 9-11
Income from operations	$ 710,580	
Less: Interest expense	5,000	← See Exhibit 9-13
Income before income taxes.	$ 705,580	
Less: Income taxes.	176,395	← Separate schedule not shown. Tax rate is 25%.
Net income	$ 529,185	

Budgeted Balance Sheet

The preparation of the **budgeted balance sheet** usually follows the preparation of the budgeted income statement. It is important to note that the budgeted balance sheet is based on the ending balance sheet from the prior year adjusted for budgeted changes. **Exhibit 9-17** presents Fezzari's beginning balance sheet as of December 31.

EXHIBIT 9-17 **Actual Prior Year Balance Sheet**

FEZZARI PERFORMANCE BICYCLES
Balance Sheet
As of December 31

Assets

Current assets:		
Cash.		$550,905
Inventories		33,178
Total current assets		$584,083
Plant assets:		
Equipment	$135,000	
Less: Accumulated depreciation.	(45,000)	90,000
Total assets		$674,083

Liabilities

Current liabilities:		
Accounts payable		50,000
Long-term liabilities:		
Long-term borrowing.		83,333
Total liabilities		$133,333

Stockholders' Equity

Common stock ($1 par value; 10,000 shares authorized and issued)	$10,000	
Paid-in capital—excess of par—common stock	90,000	
Total paid-in capital		$100,000
Retained earnings		440,750
Total stockholders' equity		$540,750
Total liabilities and stockholders' equity		$674,083

Exhibit 9-18 presents the budgeted balance sheet for the year ended December 31. This balance sheet reflects the changes in the asset, liability, and equity accounts that result from the budgeted activity for the year. For the year, Fezzari management has assumed that there will be no additional borrowings or stock sales.

EXHIBIT 9-18	Budgeted Balance Sheet Illustration

FEZZARI PERFORMANCE BICYCLES
Budgeted Balance Sheet
As of December 31

Assets

Current assets:			
Cash...		$1,086,882	a
Inventories			
Direct materials..	$ 10,000		b
Finished goods	26,387	36,387	c
Total current assets		$1,123,269	
Plant assets:			
Equipment..	$200,000		d
Less: Accumulated depreciation...........................	(95,000)	105,000	e
Total assets...		$1,228,269	

Liabilities

Current liabilities:		
Accounts payable	75,000	
Long-term liabilities:		
Long-term borrowing.....................................	83,333	f
Total liabilities	$ 158,333	

Stockholders' Equity

Common stock ($1 par value; 10,000 shares authorized and issued) ...	$ 10,000		f
Paid-in capital—excess of par—common stock	90,000		f
Total paid-in capital...		$ 100,000	
Retained earnings		969,936	g
Total stockholders' equity		$1,069,936	
Total liabilities and stockholders' equity		$1,228,269	

[a] Beginning cash balance from Exhibit 9-17 plus net cash increase from Exhibit 9-13.

[b] (6 road bike units × [$325 + $275]) + (10 mountain bike units × [$350 + $290]) = $10,000

[c] (12 road bike units × $827.08) + (18 mountain bike units × $914.49) = $26,387. Difference due to rounding.

[d] Beginning equipment ($135,000) plus budgeted capital purchases from Exhibit 9-12 ($65,000).

[e] Beginning accumulated depreciation ($45,000) plus current year depreciation from Exhibit 9-10 ($45,000) and Exhibit 9-11($5,000).

[f] No change.

[g] Beginning retained earnings ($440,750) plus net income from Exhibit 9-16 ($529,185). Difference due to rounding.

Budgeted Statement of Cash Flows

The **budgeted statement of cash flows** follows directly from the cash budget. The dollar amounts will be the same, but the grouping and sequence will usually be different. **Exhibit 9-19** presents Fezzari's budgeted statement of cash flows. Note that this statement groups the cash flows into three sections: cash flows from operating activities, cash flows from investing activities, and cash flows from financing activities.

EXHIBIT 9-19	**Budgeted Statement of Cash Flows Illustration**

FEZZARI PERFORMANCE BICYCLES
Budgeted Statement of Cash Flows—Direct Method
For the Period Ended December 31

Cash flows from operating activities		
Cash receipts from customers	$6,237,000	
Cash payments for inventory	(4,682,778)	
Cash paid for selling and administrative expenses	(771,850)	
Cash paid for interest	(5,000)	
Income tax payment	(176,395)	
Net cash provided by operating activities		$ 600,977
Cash flows from investing activities		
Capital expenditures	(65,000)	
Net cash used by investing activities		(65,000)
Cash flows from financing activities		
Net cash provided by financing activities		—
Net increase (decrease) in cash		$ 535,977
Beginning cash balance		550,905
Ending cash balance		$1,086,882

YOUR TURN! 9.5	What is the proper order for the preparation of the budgeted financial statements?

The solution is on page 9-45.

MBC

a. Budgeted income statement, budgeted balance sheet, budgeted statement of cash flows

b. Budgeted statement of cash flows, budgeted balance sheet, budgeted income statement

c. Budgeted balance sheet, budgeted income statement, budgeted statement of cash flows

d. Budgeted cost of goods sold statement, budgeted income statement, budgeted statement of cash flows

SERVICES INDUSTRY IN FOCUS

SERVICE AND MERCHANDISING

Refer to the Environmental Business Consultants (EBC) illustration on page 9-19 in the chapter. Assume that local governments (EBC's target market) are experiencing a sharp reduction in the collection of tax revenues due to a recession in the general economy. EBC anticipates that this will impact the timeliness of payments made by its clients *beginning in April* as shown below:

a. In the month of sale, 10% is collected.

b. In the month following sale, 30% is collected.

c. In the second month following sale, 30% is collected.

d. In the third month following sale, 20% is collected. The remaining 10% of accounts receivable will be written off as uncollectible.

Note that payments related to the February and March sales that have yet to be collected will be impacted by the recession also. For example, 10% of the February sales were collected in February, 50% were collected in March, but only 30% will be collected in April (not 38%), and the remaining 10% will be written off. Further, 10% of the March sales were collected in March, but only 30% will be collected in April (not 50%), 30% will be collected in May, and 20% will be collected in June. Assume that all other forecasted data remain the same.

Assume that because of the recession, EBC has temporarily eliminated its policy of maintaining a cash balance of $500,000.

Required

1. Recompute the forecasted cash collections for the quarter ended June 30.
2. Prepare a new cash budget reflecting these new cash collections.

Solution

1.

Month of Credit Sale	Cash Collections from Customers			
	April	May	June	Quarter Total
February.	$ 93,000			
March	87,000	$ 87,000	$ 58,000	
April	40,000	120,000	120,000	
May.		35,000	105,000	
June			38,000	
Month total	$220,000	$242,000	$321,000	$783,000

2.

ENVIRONMENTAL BUSINESS CONSULTANTS
Cash Budget
For the Quarter Ended June 30

	April	May	June
Beginning cash balance	$400,000	$374,708	$367,416
Cash receipts			
Collections from customers.	220,000	242,000	321,000
Cash available	$620,000	$616,708	$688,416
Cash disbursements			
Labor.	$195,000	$195,000	$195,000
Office lease.	16,875	16,875	16,875
Office supplies	2,000	5,000	3,000
Selling and administrative expenses.	31,000	32,000	62,000
Interest expense (on existing debt).	417	417	417
Cash distributions to owners.	—	—	100,000
Total disbursements	$245,292	$249,292	$377,292
Ending cash balance	$374,708	$367,416	$311,124

DATA ANALYTICS   **Soybean seeds with a side of precision planting sensors**

Data Analytics

Monsanto (now part of Bayer) was once known primarily as an industrial chemical company. That was before it transformed into a biotech company and then a seeds company. It appears Bayer is in the process of transforming again. This time, it's becoming a data analytics company. The company is aiming to shift its emphasis to data science with products including soil analysis, planting forecasts, and precision planting sensors. The overall goal is to diversify its business offerings to include more data-based services, with the software and hardware to support those services. Ultimately, the company wants to help its farmer customers boost their crop yields from the seeds and chemicals that it also sells.

COMPREHENSIVE PROBLEM

The sales department of Jackson Manufacturing, Inc., has completed the following sales forecast for the months of January through March 20X5 for its only two products: 40,000 units of P1 to be sold at $110 each and 20,000 units of P2 to be sold at $85 each. The desired unit inventories at March 31, 20X5, are 10% of the next quarter's unit sales forecast, which are 50,000 units of P1 and 25,000 units of P2. The January 1, 20X5, unit inventories were 7,000 units of P1 and 1,500 units of P2.

Guided Example

MBC

Each unit of P1 requires 4 pounds of material R and 2 pounds of material S for its manufacture; P2 requires 2 pounds of R and 3 pounds of S. The purchase cost of R is $10 per pound and of S is $5 per pound. Materials on hand at January 1, 20X5, were 20,000 pounds of R and 8,000 pounds of S. Desired inventories at March 31, 20X5, are 15,000 pounds of R and 6,000 pounds of S.

Each unit of P1 requires 0.5 hours of direct labor in the factory; each unit of P2 requires 1.0 hour of direct labor. The average hourly rate for direct labor is $12 per hour. Estimated manufacturing overhead cost is $8 per direct labor hour plus $100,000 per month. Selling and administrative expenses are estimated to be 10% of sales revenue plus $200,000 per month.

Cash sales in December 20X4 were $250,000, and credit sales were $2,000,000. Cash sales for the first quarter are estimated to be $200,000 per month. It is forecast that 40% of the credit sales for the quarter ended March 31, 20X5, will occur in January, 30% in February, and 30% in March. Of credit sales (December through March), 40% will be collected as cash in the month of sale, and 50% will be collected in the following month. The remainder will be uncollectible.

The January 1, 20X5, cash balance was $60,000. The minimum acceptable cash balance at the end of each month is $50,000. Short-term borrowings are made in multiples of $10,000, with interest charged at the rate of 1% per month. The first interest payment is made the month following the borrowing. Cash disbursements (excluding interest on short-term borrowings) are estimated as follows:

	January	February	March
Manufacturing costs	$1,200,000	$1,100,000	$1,000,000
Selling and administrative expenses	$ 380,000	$ 400,000	$ 340,000
Interest expense.	$ 100,000	$ 100,000	$ 100,000
Income tax payment.	—	—	200,000
Capital expenditures.	100,000	340,000	60,000
Cash dividends.	400,000	—	—

Required

a. Prepare the sales budget for the quarter ended March 31, 20X5.
b. Prepare the production budget for the quarter ended March 31, 20X5.
c. Prepare the direct materials budget for the quarter ended March 31, 20X5.
d. Prepare the direct labor budget for the quarter ended March 31, 20X5.
e. Prepare the overhead budget for the quarter ended March 31, 20X5.
f. Prepare a schedule of estimated product cost per unit for the quarter ended March 31, 20X5.
g. Prepare a schedule of cash collected from customers for the quarter ended March 31, 20X5.
h. Prepare the cash budget for the quarter ended March 31, 20X5.

Solution to Comprehensive Problem

a.

JACKSON MANUFACTURING, INC.
Sales Budget
For the Quarter Ended March 31, 20X5

Product	Forecasted Unit Sales Volume	Planned Unit Sales Price	Budgeted Total Sales
P1.	40,000	$110.00	$4,400,000
P2.	20,000	$ 85.00	1,700,000
Total sales revenue.			$6,100,000

b.

JACKSON MANUFACTURING, INC.
Production Budget
For the Quarter Ended March 31, 20X5

	Units of Finished Product	
	P1	**P2**
Forecast unit sales	40,000	20,000
Desired ending inventories:		
10% × 50,000	5,000	
10% × 25,000		2,500
Quantities to be available	45,000	22,500
Less: Beginning inventories	7,000	1,500
Total production to be scheduled	38,000	21,000

c.

JACKSON MANUFACTURING, INC.
Direct Material Budget
For the Quarter Ended March 31, 20X5

	Material R	Material S
Direct materials required:		
Product P1: 38,000 × 4	152,000	
38,000 × 2		76,000
Product P2: 21,000 × 2	42,000	
21,000 × 3		63,000
Desired ending materials inventories	15,000	6,000
Total pounds of materials to be available	209,000	145,000
Less: Beginning materials inventories	20,000	8,000
Total pounds of materials to be purchased.	189,000	137,000
Unit purchase price.	$ 10.00	$ 5.00
Total materials purchases.	$1,890,000	$685,000

d.

JACKSON MANUFACTURING, INC.
Direct Labor Budget
For the Quarter Ended March 31, 20X5

Direct labor hours required for production:	
Product P1: 38,000 × 0.5 hours	19,000
Product P2: 21,000 × 1.0 hours	21,000
Total direct labor hours required	40,000
Hourly rate for direct labor	$ 12.00
Total direct labor cost	$480,000

e.

JACKSON MANUFACTURING, INC.
Overhead Budget
For the Quarter Ended March 31, 20X5

Total direct labor hours.	40,000
Variable manufacturing overhead rate	$ 8.00
Variable manufacturing overhead cost	$320,000
Fixed manufacturing overhead cost ($100,000 × 3 months)	$300,000
Total manufacturing overhead cost.	$620,000

f.

JACKSON MANUFACTURING, INC.
Schedule of Estimated Product Cost Per Unit
For the Quarter Ended March 31, 20X5

| | Quantity | | | | |
	Product P1	Product P2	Cost	Product P1	Product P2
Direct materials:					
Material R	4	2	$10.00	$40.00	$20.00
Material S	2	3	$ 5.00	$10.00	$15.00
Direct labor	0.5	1	$12.00	$ 6.00	$12.00
Manufacturing overhead	0.5	1	$15.50*	$ 7.75	$15.50
Product cost per unit				$63.75	$62.50

*$620,000/40,000 = $15.50 per direct labor hour

g.

JACKSON MANUFACTURING, INC.
Schedule of Cash Collected From Customers
For the Quarter Ended March 31, 20X5

	January	February	March
Cash sales	$ 200,000	$ 200,000	$ 200,000
Credit sales			
December: $2,000,000 × 50%	1,000,000		
January: $2,200,000* × 40%	880,000		
$2,200,000* × 50%		1,100,000	
February: $1,650,000** × 40%		660,000	
$1,650,000** × 50%			825,000
March: $1,650,000** × 40%			660,000
	$1,880,000	$1,760,000	$1,485,000
Total cash collected	$2,080,000	$1,960,000	$1,685,000

*($6,100,000 total sales – $600,000 cash sales) × 40% = $2,200,000

**($6,100,000 total sales – $600,000 cash sales) × 30% = $1,650,000

h.

JACKSON MANUFACTURING, INC.
Cash Budget
For the Quarter Ended March 31, 20X5

	January	February	March
Beginning cash balance	$ 60,000	$ 50,000	$ 69,100
Cash receipts:			
Cash sales	200,000	200,000	200,000
Collections from credit customers	1,880,000	1,760,000	1,485,000
Short-term borrowing	90,000	—	—
Cash available	$2,230,000	$2,010,000	$1,754,100
Cash disbursements:			
Manufacturing costs	$1,200,000	$1,100,000	$1,000,000
Selling and administrative expenses	380,000	400,000	340,000
Interest expense*	100,000	100,900	100,900
Income tax payments	—	—	200,000
Capital expenditures	100,000	340,000	60,000
Cash dividends	400,000	—	—
Total disbursements	$2,180,000	$1,940,900	$1,700,900
Ending cash balance	$ 50,000	$ 69,100	$ 53,200

* For February and March: $100,000 + ($90,000 × 1%) = $100,900

SUMMARY OF LEARNING OBJECTIVES

Describe the planning process, including strategic planning and operational planning. (p. 9-3)   **LO1**

- Strategic planning is a formal process that addresses and documents the mission and long-term goals of the organization. SWOT analysis is used to develop and analyze the data needed for this type of planning.

- Operational planning is the development of specific goals and objectives for the entity as a whole and its individual departments, the formulation of a plan of attack to accomplish the goals and objectives, and the written documentation of the goals and objectives and the plan of attack.

Discuss the budgeting process and summarize its advantages. Define the key elements of effective budgeting. (p. 9-6)   **LO2**

- Budgeting is the process of developing a formal, written operational plan that presents management's planned actions in financial terms.

- Two budgets result from the budgeting process: the annual operating budget that covers a 1-year budget period and the capital expenditures budget that covers a multiple-year budget period.

- Budgets represent a plan for accomplishing goals and objectives. They provide operational guidance to the department managers, so they make decisions that are consistent with decisions made in other departments.

- Because the budget is used as a basis for evaluating performance, it serves as a target for individual managers.

- A budget director should be identified to organize the budgeting process, communicate with people involved in budgeting, and monitor the budgeting process.

- A budget committee, consisting of representatives from all major areas of the company, should provide general guidance to the budgeting process and evaluate proposed budget segments for reasonableness.

- Participative budgeting requires that all departments participate in the development and refinement of the budget amounts so that departmental managers will accept the budget as a reasonable standard of performance.

- The future time span, for which the budget is prepared, known as the budget period, varies according to the activity involved.

- The use of budgets to manage and control a firm's activities is known as budgetary control.

- Zero-based budgeting requires budget preparers to start at a zero level for every item in the budget and justify every dollar, not just the increases or decreases.

Define the components of the master budget and illustrate the interrelationships of the individual budgets that comprise the master budget. (p. 9-10)   **LO3**

- The master budget for a manufacturing firm consists of at least the following individual budgets:
  - Sales budget
  - Production budget
  - Direct materials budget
  - Direct labor budget
  - Manufacturing overhead budget
  - Selling and administrative expense budget
  - Capital expenditures budget
  - Cash budget
  - Budgeted income statement
  - Budgeted balance sheet
  - Budgeted statement of cash flows

- The individual budgets must be prepared in a specific sequence, beginning with the sales budget, to properly reflect the interrelationships among the individual budgets.

Prepare individual budgets for a manufacturing and a service company, including the cash budget. (p. 9-11)   **LO4**

- The sales budget is based on the sales forecast.

- The production budget determines the number of units of each product that should be manufactured during the budget period.

- The direct materials budget displays the amount of each direct materials item that should be purchased to supply the budgeted production.

- The direct labor budget presents the amount of direct labor, by department, that is required to accomplish the budgeted production.

- The manufacturing overhead budget determines, for each factory department, the amount of variable overhead and the amount of fixed overhead needed to complete the budgeted production.

- The selling and administrative expense budget accumulates the variable and fixed selling and administrative expenses for the entity. Some of the expenses may vary with sales; others may vary with production.
- The capital expenditures budget presents the planned expenditures for property, plant, and equipment over an extended budget period, possibly 5 years.
- The cash budget, usually segmented by month, presents all of the cash receipts and cash disbursements planned for the budget period.
- Much of the information needed to prepare the cash budget comes from previously prepared budgets. However, additional schedules and worksheets are usually needed to place required information in proper form.
- Cash collected from customers from prior credit sales needs careful analysis to take into account timing, cash discounts, and uncollectible accounts.

LO5 **Prepare budgeted financial statements. (p. 9-20)**

- The budgeted income statement is prepared for the budget period.
- The budgeted balance sheet is prepared as of the ending date of the budget period.
- The budgeted statement of cash flows is prepared for the budget period, based primarily on data from the cash budget.

SUMMARY	Concept ⟶	Method ⟶	Assessment
TAKEAWAY 9.1	How can management best ensure that the efforts of all employees are congruent with the company's strategy?	Develop multiyear operating plans and budgets (both operating and capital) linked to the company's strategy.	Compare actual results with operating plans and budgets to evaluate company performance.
TAKEAWAY 9.2	How should a company implement a zero-based budgeting approach?	1. Determine goals, operations, and costs for all activities. 2. Determine alternative means of conducting each activity. 3. Evaluate the implications of changes in the level of each activity. 4. Establish workload. 5. Rank activities in order of importance. 6. Select activities necessary to accomplish goals at the minimum cost.	Although costly and time-consuming, zero-based budgeting results in a careful examination and justification of all critical activities, rooting out inefficient and ineffective activities.

KEY TERMS

Annual operating
  budget (p. 9-6)

Budget (p. 9-6)

Budgetary control (p. 9-7)

Budget committee (p. 9-7)

Budget director (p. 9-7)

Budgeted balance
  sheet (p. 9-21)

Budgeted income
  statement (p. 9-20)

Budgeted statement of cash
  flows (p. 9-22)

Budgeting (p. 9-6)

Budget period (p. 9-8)

Capital expenditures
  budget (p. 9-16)

Cash budget (p. 9-17)

Continuous budgeting (p. 9-8)

Continuous budgets (p. 9-8)

Direct labor budget (p. 9-14)

Direct materials
  budget (p. 9-13)

Just-in-time inventory (p. 9-12)

Manufacturing overhead
  budget (p. 9-14)

Master budget (p. 9-6, 9-10)

Operational planning (p. 9-5)

Participative budgeting (p. 9-7)

Perpetual budgets (p. 9-8)

Planning horizon (p. 9-3)

Production budget (p. 9-12)

Pro forma statements (p. 9-10)

Rolling budgets (p. 9-8)

Safety stock (p. 9-12)

Sales budget (p. 9-11)

Sales forecast (p. 9-11)

Selling and administrative
  expense budget (p. 9-15)

Strategic planning (p. 9-4)

Strengths, weaknesses,
  opportunities, and threats
  (SWOT) analysis (p. 9-4)

Zero-based budgeting (p. 9-8)

Assignments with the (MBC) logo in the margin are available in BusinessCourse.
See the Preface of the book for details.

SELF-STUDY QUESTIONS

(Answers to Self-Study Questions are at the end of this chapter.)

1. **Analyzing a company's technological capabilities, employee skills, and sales team performance will provide** **LO1**
   a. external factors that identify the company's strengths and threats.
   b. internal factors that identify the company's strengths and opportunities.
   c. external factors that identify the company's strengths and weaknesses.
   d. internal factors that identify the company's strengths and weaknesses.

2. **If a company uses participative budgeting, which group should prepare the initial set of budget dollar amounts?** **LO2**
   a. Budget committee
   b. Operating department managers
   c. Top management
   d. Accounting department

3. **Which of the following budgets should be prepared before all of the others listed below?** **LO3**
   a. Cash budget
   b. Direct materials budget
   c. Manufacturing overhead budget
   d. Production budget

4. **Which of the following budgets will typically have the longest budget period?** **LO4**
   a. Capital expenditures budget
   b. Cash budget
   c. Sales budget
   d. Budgeted income statement

5. **If the beginning inventory of a company that manufactures only one product is 5,000 units, the sales forecast is 34,000 units sold, and the desired ending inventory is 6,000 units, how many units should be produced?** **LO4**
   a. 35,000
   b. 33,000
   c. 40,000
   d. 39,000

6. **Smith Company started business on September 1. Smith had credit sales of $200,000 in September and $300,000 in October. The pattern for collection of cash from customers is expected to be 40% in the month of sale (subject to a 2% cash discount), 50% in the month following the month of sale, and 7% in the second month following the month of sale, with 3% uncollectible. How much cash did Smith Company receive from customers on account during October?** **LO4**
   a. $120,000
   b. $117,600
   c. $217,600
   d. $220,000

7. **The budgeted statement of cash flows is most closely related to** **LO5**
   a. the sales budget
   b. the capital expenditures budget
   c. the cash budget
   d. the budgeted balance sheet

QUESTIONS

1. What is a planning horizon? How will it differ between strategic planning and operational planning? **LO1**
2. Describe strategic planning. **LO1**
3. Describe operational planning. **LO1**
4. Define budgeting. **LO2**
5. List and briefly explain four advantages of budgeting. **LO2**
6. Describe the budget committee. **LO2**
7. Why is participative budgeting important to the success of the budgeting process? **LO2**
8. What is meant by continuous budgeting? **LO2**
9. What is the master budget? List, in the order of preparation, the various budgets that the master budget for a small manufacturing company might comprise. **LO3**
10. Why do most firms prepare the sales budget first? **LO3**

LO4 11. Beginning finished goods inventory is 10,000 units, anticipated sales volume is 60,000 units, and the desired ending finished goods inventory is 12,000 units. What number of units should be produced?

LO4 12. Three pounds of material R (costing $5 per pound) and 4 pounds of material S (costing $7 per pound) are required to make one unit of product T. If management plans to increase the inventory of material R by 500 pounds and reduce the inventory of material S by 800 pounds during a period when 3,000 units of product T are to be produced, what are the budgeted purchase costs of material R and material S?

LO4 13. Carroll Manufacturing Company has two labor operations in its factory: machining and assembly. Workers in the machining department are paid $14 per hour; workers in the assembly department are paid $12 per hour. During January, 10,000 units of product A and 20,000 units of product B are to be manufactured. Each unit of A requires 1 hour of machining and 2 hours of assembly; each unit of B requires 3 hours of machining and 1 hour of assembly. What is the total direct labor budget for January?

LO4 14. Johnson Manufacturing Company has budgeted 30,000 direct labor hours for March. The budgeted cost formula for monthly manufacturing overhead is $4 per direct labor hour plus $65,000. What is the manufacturing overhead budget for March?

LO4 15. A company collects cash from its credit sales in the following pattern: 30% in the month of sale, 50% in the month following the month of sale, and 20% in the second month following the month of sale. What percentage of which months' credit sales will be collected during October?

LO5 16. What are the three major groupings of cash flows in the budgeted statement of cash flows?

SHORT EXERCISES

LO2 **SE9-1.** All of the following are advantages of the use of budgets in a management control system, *except* that budgets

    a. force management planning.
    b. provide performance criteria.
    c. promote communication and coordination within the organization.
    d. limit unauthorized expenditures.

LO2 **SE9-2.** Which one of the following items would most likely cause the planning and budgeting system to fail?

    a. Lack of historical financial data
    b. Lack of input from several levels of management
    c. Lack of top management support
    d. Lack of adherence to rigid budgets during the year

LO2 **SE9-3.** Which one of the following statements concerning approaches for the budget development process is **correct**?

    a. The authoritative approach to budgeting discourages strict adherence to strategic organizational goals.
    b. To prevent ambiguity, once departmental budgeted goals have been developed, they should remain fixed even if the sales forecast upon which they are based proves to be wrong in the middle of the fiscal year.
    c. With the information technology available, the role of budgets as an organizational communication device has declined.
    d. Because department managers have the most detailed knowledge about organizational operations, they should use this information as the building blocks of the operating budget.

LO2 **SE9-4.** Cerawell Products Company is a ceramics manufacturer that is facing several challenges in its operations due to economic and industry conditions. The company is currently preparing its annual plan and budget. Which one of the following is subject to the **least** control by the management of Cerawell in the current fiscal year?

    a. A new machine that was purchased this year has not helped reduce Cerawell's unfavorable labor efficiency variances.
    b. A competitor has achieved an unexpected technological breakthrough that has given them a significant quality advantage and has caused Cerawell to lose market share.

c.   Vendors have asked that the contract price for the goods they supply to Cerawell be renegotiated and adjusted for inflation.

d.   Experienced employees have decided to terminate their employment with Cerawell and go to work for the competition.

SE9-5.   What would be the correct chronological order of preparation for the following budgets?

I.   Cost of goods sold budget   III.   Purchases budget
II.   Production budget   IV.   Administrative budget

a.   I, II, III, IV.   c.   IV, II, III, I.
b.   III, II, IV, I.   d.   II, III, I, IV.

SE9-6.   Hannon Retailing Company prices its products by adding 30% to its cost. Hannon anticipates sales of $715,000 in July, $728,000 in August, and $624,000 in September. Hannon's policy is to have on hand enough inventory at the end of the month to cover 25% of the next month's sales. What will be the cost of the inventory that Hannon should budget for purchase in August?

a. $509,600   c. $560,000
b. $540,000   d. $680,000

SE9-7.   Netco's sales budget for the coming year is as follows.

Item	Volume in Units	Sales Price	Sales Revenue
1	200,000	$50	$10,000,000
2	150,000	10	1,500,000
3	300,000	30	9,000,000
Total sales revenue			$20,500,000

Items 1 and 3 are different models of the same product. Item 2 is a complement to Item 1. Past experience indicates that the sales volume of Item 2 relative to the sales volume of Item 1 is fairly constant. Netco is considering a 10% price increase for the coming year for Item 1, which will cause sales of Item 1 to decline by 20% while simultaneously causing sales of Item 3 to increase by 5%. If Netco institutes the price increase for Item 1, total sales revenue will decrease by

a. $1,050,000.   c. $750,000.
b. $850,000.   d. $550,000.

SE9-8.   Streeter Company produces plastic microwave turntables. Sales for the next year are expected to be 65,000 units in the first quarter, 72,000 units in the second quarter, 84,000 units in the third quarter, and 66,000 units in the fourth quarter. Streeter maintains a finished goods inventory at the end of each quarter equal to one-half of the units expected to be sold in the next quarter. How many units should Streeter produce in the second quarter?

a.   72,000 units.   c.   78,000 units.
b.   75,000 units.   d.   84,000 units.

SE9-9.   Stevens Company manufactures electronic components used in automobile manufacturing. Each component uses two raw materials: Geo and Clio. Standard usage of the two materials required to produce one finished electronic component, as well as the current inventory, are shown below.

Material	Standard Per Unit	Price	Current Inventory
Geo.	2.0 pounds	$15/lb.	5,000 pounds
Clio	1.5 pounds	$10/lb.	7,500 pounds

Stevens forecasts sales of 20,000 components for each of the next two production periods. Company policy dictates that 25% of the raw materials needed to produce the next period's projected sales be maintained in ending direct materials inventory.

Based on this information, what would the budgeted direct materials purchases for the coming period be?

	Geo	Clio
a.	$450,000	$450,000
b.	$675,000	$300,000
c.	$675,000	$400,000
d.	$825,000	$450,000

LO4   **SE9-10.** Petersons Planters Inc. budgeted the following amounts for the coming year:

Beginning inventory, finished goods	$ 10,000
Cost of goods sold	400,000
Direct materials used in production	100,000
Ending inventory, finished goods	25,000
Beginning and ending work-in-process inventory	0

Overhead is estimated to be two times the amount of direct labor dollars. What amount should be budgeted for direct labor for the coming year?

- a. $315,000
- b. $210,000
- c. $157,500
- d. $105,000

DATA ANALYTICS, DATA VISUALIZATION, AND EXCEL ACTIVITIES

Data Analytics, Data Visualization, and Excel Activities are available in myBusinessCourse. These assignments develop Excel, Tableau, and Data Analytics skills, which will enhance students' career readiness. These exercises are assignable and auto graded by MBC. For an overview of data analytics, see the appendix at the end of this book.

EXERCISES—SET A

LO4   **E9-1A.** **Budgeting Inventories** For each independent situation below, determine the amounts indicated by the question marks:

	A	B	C	D
Beginning inventory	12,000	?	7,000	?
Produced	40,000	27,000	?	56,000
Available	?	?	32,000	64,000
Sold	45,000	28,000	?	?
Ending inventory	?	12,000	6,000	2,000

LO4   **E9-2A.** **Budget Preparation** Collins Company is preparing its master budget for April. Use the given estimates to determine the amounts necessary for each of the following requirements. (Estimates may be related to more than one requirement.)

- a.   What should total sales revenue be if territories A and B estimate sales of 10,000 and 12,000 units, respectively, and the unit selling price is $46?
- b.   If the beginning finished goods inventory is an estimated 3,000 units and the desired ending inventory is 2,000 units, how many units should be produced?
- c.   What dollar amount of materials should be purchased at $4 per pound if each unit of product requires 3 pounds and beginning and ending materials inventories should be 4,000 and 5,000 pounds, respectively?
- d.   How much direct labor cost should be incurred if each unit produced requires 1.5 hours at an hourly rate of $20?
- e.   How much manufacturing overhead should be incurred if fixed manufacturing overhead is $50,000 and variable manufacturing overhead is $3 per direct labor hour?

LO4   **E9-3A.** **Budget Preparation** Westport Company is preparing its master budget for May. Use the estimates provided to determine the amounts necessary for each of the following requirements. (Estimates may be related to more than one requirement.)

- a.   What should total sales revenue be if territories E and W estimate sales of 50,000 and 100,000 units, respectively, and the unit selling price is $30?

b. If the beginning finished goods inventory is an estimated 6,000 units and the desired ending inventory is 7,000 units, how many units should be produced?

c. What dollar amount of materials should be purchased at $2 per pound if each unit of product requires 2.5 pounds and beginning and ending materials inventories should be 12,000 and 13,500 pounds, respectively?

d. How much direct labor cost should be incurred if each unit produced requires 0.5 hours at an hourly rate of $15?

e. How much manufacturing overhead should be incurred if fixed manufacturing overhead is $45,000 and variable manufacturing overhead is $1.50 per direct labor hour?

E9-4A. Budgeting Cash Collections Spencer Consulting, which invoices its clients on terms 2/10, n/30, had credit sales for May and June of $150,000 and $170,000, respectively. Analysis of Spencer's operations indicates that the pattern of customers' payments on account is as follows. (Percentages are of total monthly credit sales.)

	Receiving Discount	Beyond Discount Period	Totals
In month of sale	50%	25%	75%
In month following sale	10%	10%	20%
Uncollectible accounts, returns, and allowances			5%
			100%

Determine the estimated cash collected on customers' accounts in June.

E9-5A. Budgeting Cash Flow The following various elements relate to Whitfield, Inc.'s cash budget for April of the current year. For each item, determine the amount of cash that Whitfield should receive or pay in April.

a. At $28 each, unit sales are 5,000 and 6,000 for March and April, respectively. Total sales are typically 40% for cash and 60% on credit; 30% of credit sales are collected in the month of sale, with the balance collected in the following month. Uncollectible accounts are negligible.

b. Merchandise purchases were $45,000 and $78,000 for March and April, respectively. Typically, 20% of total purchases are paid for in the month of purchase with a 5% cash discount. The balance of purchases is paid for (without discount) in the following month.

c. Fixed administrative expenses, which total $11,000 per month, are paid in the month incurred. Variable administrative expenses amount to 20% of total monthly sales revenue, one-half of which is paid in the month incurred, with the balance paid in the following month.

d. A store asset originally costing $8,000, on which $6,000 depreciation has been taken, is sold for cash at a loss of $400.

E9-6A. Prepare Cash Budget for 3 Months Brewster Corporation expects the following cash receipts and disbursements during the first quarter of the year. (Receipts exclude new borrowings and disbursements exclude interest payments on borrowings since January 1.)

	January	February	March
Cash receipts	$260,000	$280,000	$250,000
Cash disbursements	240,000	320,000	260,000

The expected cash balance at January 1 is $42,000. Brewster wants to maintain a cash balance at the end of each month of at least $40,000. Short-term borrowings at 1% interest per month will be used to accomplish this, if necessary. Borrowings (in multiples of $1,000) will be made at the beginning of the month in which they are needed, with interest for that month paid at the end of the month. Prepare a cash budget for the quarter ended March 31.

E9-7A. Prepare Cash Budget from Budgeted Transactions Prepare a cash budget for the month ended May 31. Campton Company anticipates a cash balance of $84,000 on May 1. The following budgeted transactions for May present data related to anticipated cash receipts and cash disbursements:

1. For May, budgeted cash sales are $60,000 and budgeted credit sales are $500,000. (Credit sales for April were $450,000.) In the month of sale, 40% of credit sales are collected, with the balance collected in the month following sale.

2. Budgeted merchandise purchases for May are $280,000. (Merchandise purchases in April were $240,000.) In the month of purchase, 70% of merchandise purchases are paid for, and the balance is paid for in the following month.

3. Budgeted cash disbursements for salaries and operating expenses for May total $165,000.

4. During May, $25,000 of principal repayment and $4,000 of interest payment are due to the bank.

5. A $20,000 income tax deposit is due to the federal government during May.

6. A new delivery truck will be purchased during May for $6,000 cash and an $8,000 note payable. Depreciation for May will be $500.

Prepare a cash budget for Campton Company for the month of May.

LO4

SERVICE AND
MERCHANDISING

MBC

E9-8A. Budgeted Cash Collection In an effort to improve cash collection, Suburban Medical Clinic offers terms of 2/10, n/30, with a 5% discount on patient payments made with cash. Suburban estimates its total billings for the second calendar quarter of the year as follows: April, $200,000; May, $240,000; and June, $290,000. Historically, Suburban has had the following patient collection patterns:

	Portions of Total Sales
In month of sale:	
Cash at time of sale	25%
On account during the discount period	20%
On account after the discount period	10%
In month following sale:	
On account after the discount period	25%
In second month following sale:	
On account after discount period	15%
Average portion uncollectible	5%
	100%

What would be Suburban's budgeted total cash collection for June?

LO4

SERVICE AND
MERCHANDISING

MBC

E9-9A. Purchases Budget Rest Inn provides four-star accommodations for the vacation traveler. It is located just off a major interstate freeway. There are three other competing motels at the same exit. Hotel management is preparing its budget for the busiest three-month period of the year, June through August. To differentiate themselves from the competition, Rest Inn provides a complimentary spa package for each guest stay that includes specialty shampoo, conditioner, soap, lotion, toothpaste, lavender essential oil, slippers, earplugs, and a sleep mask. Rest Inn purchases the spa package from a local vendor that puts the Rest Inn private label on the products. The hotel follows a policy of purchasing enough spa packages to ensure that 40% of next month's bookings are in the current month's ending inventory. Rest Inn's sales budget for guest stays for the next quarter is as follows:

June	2,300 guest stays
July	2,500 guest stays
August	2,100 guest stays

How many spa packages should Rest Inn budget for purchase in July?

EXERCISES—SET B

LO4

MBC

E9-1B. Budgeting Inventories For each independent situation below, determine the amounts indicated by the question marks.

Number of Units	A	B	C	D
Beginning inventory	7,500	?	6,000	?
Produced	15,000	27,000	?	70,000
Available	?	?	46,000	85,000
Sold	18,000	31,000	?	?
Ending inventory	?	3,000	5,000	11,000

LO4

MBC

E9-2B. Budget Preparation Reeves Company is preparing its master budget for July. Use the given estimates to determine the amounts necessary for each of the following requirements. (Estimates may be related to more than one requirement.)

a. What should total sales revenue be if territories A and B estimate sales of 8,000 and 20,000 units, respectively, and the unit selling price is $55?

b. If the beginning finished goods inventory is an estimated 2,500 units and the desired ending inventory is 1,000 units, how many units should be produced?

c. What dollar amount of materials should be purchased at $3 per pound if each unit of product requires 2 pounds and beginning and ending materials inventories should be 3,000 and 4,000 pounds, respectively?

d. How much direct labor cost should be incurred if each unit produced requires 1.5 hours at an hourly rate of $16?

e. How much manufacturing overhead should be incurred if fixed manufacturing overhead is $60,000 and variable manufacturing overhead is $2 per direct labor hour?

E9-3B. Budget Preparation Tuttle Company is preparing its master budget for November. Use the estimates provided to determine the necessary amounts for each of the following requirements. (Estimates may be related to more than one requirement.)

LO4

a. What should total sales revenue be if territories N and S estimate sales of 40,000 and 80,000 units, respectively, and the unit selling price is $20?

b. If the beginning finished goods inventory is an estimated 5,000 units and the desired ending inventory is 6,000 units, how many units should be produced?

c. What dollar amount of materials should be purchased at $2 per pound if each unit of product requires 3 pounds and beginning and ending materials inventories should be 10,000 and 12,000 pounds, respectively?

d. How much direct labor cost should be incurred if each unit produced requires 0.5 hours at an hourly rate of $14?

e. How much manufacturing overhead should be incurred if fixed manufacturing overhead is $32,000 and variable manufacturing overhead is $2 per direct labor hour?

E9-4B. Budgeting Cash Collections Lowell Consulting, which sells on terms 2/10, n/30, had credit sales for March and April of $200,000 and $180,000, respectively. Analysis of Lowell's operations indicates that the pattern of customers' payments on account is as follows. (Percentages are of total monthly credit sales.)

LO4

SERVICE AND
MERCHANDISING

	Receiving Discount	Beyond Discount Period	Totals
In month of sale	40%	25%	65%
In month following sale	20%	10%	30%
Uncollectible accounts, returns, and allowances			5%
			100%

Determine the estimated cash collected on customers' accounts in April.

E9-5B. Budgeting Cash Flow The following various elements relate to Murphy, Inc.'s cash budget for October of the current year. For each item, determine the amount of cash that Murphy should receive or pay in October.

LO4

SERVICE AND
MERCHANDISING

a. At $24 each, unit sales are 10,000 and 12,000 for September and October, respectively. Total sales are typically 30% for cash and 70% on credit; 40% of credit sales are collected in the month of sale, with the balance collected in the following month. Uncollectible accounts are negligible.

b. Merchandise purchases were $43,000 and $76,000 for September and October, respectively. Typically, 20% of total purchases are paid for in the month of purchase with a 5% cash discount. The balance of purchases is paid for (without discount) in the following month.

c. Fixed administrative expenses, which total $15,000 per month, are paid in the month incurred. Variable administrative expenses amount to 20% of total monthly sales revenue, 65% of which is paid in the month incurred, with the balance paid in the following month.

d. Fixed selling expenses, which total $4,200 per month, are paid in the month incurred. Variable selling expenses, which are 5% of total sales revenue, are paid in the month following their incurrence.

LO4   **E9-6B. Prepare Cash Budget for 3 Months** Windsor Corporation expects the following cash receipts and disbursements during the first quarter. (Receipts exclude new borrowings and disbursements exclude interest payments on borrowings since January 1.)

	January	February	March
Cash receipts	$430,000	$440,000	$400,000
Cash disbursements	390,000	520,000	420,000

The expected cash balance at January 1 is $75,000. Windsor wants to maintain a cash balance at the end of each month of at least $60,000. Short-term borrowings at 1% interest per month will be used to accomplish this, if necessary. Borrowings (in multiples of $1,000) will be made at the beginning of the month in which they are needed, with interest for that month paid at the end of the month.

Prepare a cash budget for the quarter ended March 31.

LO4

SERVICE AND
MERCHANDISING

E9-7B. Prepare Cash Budget from Budgeted Transactions McCall Company anticipates a cash balance of $100,000 on July 1. The following budgeted transactions for July present data related to anticipated cash receipts and cash disbursements:

1. For July, budgeted cash sales are $72,000 and budgeted credit sales are $600,000. (Credit sales for June were $550,000.) In the month of sale, 40% of credit sales are collected, with the balance collected in the month following sale.
2. Budgeted merchandise purchases for July are $340,000. (Merchandise purchases in June were $290,000.) In the month of purchase, 70% of merchandise purchases are paid for, and the balance is paid for in the following month.
3. Budgeted cash disbursements for salaries and operating expenses for July total $200,000.
4. During July, $30,000 of principal repayment and $5,000 of interest payment are due to the bank.
5. A $25,000 income tax deposit is due to the federal government during July.
6. A new delivery truck will be purchased during July for $7,000 cash and a $10,000 note payable. Depreciation for July will be $600.

Prepare a cash budget for McCall Company for the month of July.

LO4

SERVICE AND
MERCHANDISING

E9-8B. Budgeted Cash Collection The Smile Doctor offers terms of 3/10, n/30, with a 10% discount on patient payments made with cash. The Smile Doctor estimates its total billings for the first calendar quarter of the year as follows: January, $125,000; February, $110,000; and March, $130,000. Historically, the Smile Doctor has had the following patient collection patterns:

	Portions of Total Sales
In month of sale:	
Cash at time of sale	25%
On account during the discount period	15%
On account after the discount period	10%
In month following sale:	
On account after the discount period	30%
In second month following sale:	
On account after discount period	15%
Average portion uncollectible	5%
	100%

What would the Smile Doctor's budgeted total cash collection be for March?

LO4

SERVICE AND
MERCHANDISING

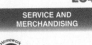

E9-9B. Sales Budget Hawaiian Style supplies island-inspired clothing to hotel gift shops, golf shops, and specialty boutiques throughout the Hawaiian islands. The clothing distributor purchases its inventory from a Chinese clothing manufacturer that uses the latest designs provided by Hawaiian Style.

Due to manufacturing lead times, Hawaiian Style must provide the final designs no later than 90 days before it receives the completed clothing. Due to the costs of retooling and the risks associated with consumers' changing tastes for clothing styles and colors, the Chinese clothing manufacturer requires Hawaiian Style to order its clothing in large batches, effectively resulting in Hawaiian Style ordering its entire annual inventory at the beginning of each year.

Hawaiian Style attempts to balance its concerns about stockouts of popular styles with its concerns about excess inventory from season to season by carefully budgeting its purchases for the next fashion year. Based on its analysis, Hawaiian Style has developed the following probabilities for sales for the coming year:

Sales Level	Probability
$ 750,000	20%
900,000	30%
1,100,000	30%
1,250,000	15%
1,300,000	5%

What amount should Hawaiian Style budget for sales for the coming year?

PROBLEMS—SET A

P9-1A. Budgeting Cash Whitney's, Inc., sells on terms of 5% discount for "cash and carry" or 2/10, n/30 and estimates its total sales for the second calendar quarter of next year as follows: April, $300,000; May, $240,000; and June, $360,000. An analysis of operations indicates the following customer collection patterns:

LO4

	Portions of Total Sales
In month of sale:	
Cash at time of sale	30%
On account during discount period.	15%
On account after discount period	10%
In month following sale:	
On account during discount period.	15%
On account after discount period	10%
In second month following sale:	
On account after discount period	15%
Average portion uncollectible	5%
	100%

Prepare an estimate of the cash to be collected from customers during June.

P9-2A. Monthly Cash Budget Grove, Inc., is a wholesaler for its only product, deluxe wireless electric drills, which sell for $90 each and cost Grove $54 each. On December 1, Grove's management requested a cash budget for December. The following selected account balances at November 30 were gathered by the accounting department:

LO4

Cash.	$ 135,000
Marketable securities (at cost)	210,000
Accounts receivable (all trade)	1,710,000
Inventories (15,000 units)	810,000
Operating expenses payable	140,400
Accounts payable (all merchandise).	583,200
Note payable (due 12/31/2019)	393,000

Actual sales for the months of October and November were 20,000 and 30,000 units, respectively. Projected unit sales for December and January are 50,000 and 40,000, respectively. Experience indicates that 50% of sales should be collected in the month of sale, 30% in the month following sale, and the balance in the second month following sale. Uncollectible accounts, returns, and allowances are negligible.

Planned purchases should provide ending inventories equal to 30% of next month's unit sales volume. Approximately 70% of the purchases are paid for in the month of purchase and the balance in the following month.

Monthly operating expenses are budgeted at $8.10 per unit sold plus a fixed amount of $189,000, including depreciation of $81,000. Except for depreciation, 60% of operating expenses are paid in the month incurred and the balance in the following month. Interest expense is included in operating expenses.

Special anticipated year-end transactions include the following:

1. Declaration of a $22,500 cash dividend to be paid 2 weeks after the December 20 date of record.

2. Sale of one-half of the marketable securities held on November 30; a gain of $21,000 is anticipated.

3. Pay off the note payable due December 31.

4. Trade-in of an old computer originally costing $675,000 and now having accumulated depreciation of $540,000 at a gain of $157,500 on a new computer costing $1,350,000. Sufficient cash will be paid at the time of trade-in so that only 50% of the total price will have to be financed.

5. Grove's treasurer has a policy of maintaining a minimum month-end cash balance of $135,000 but wants to raise this to $225,000 at December 31. She has a standing arrangement with the bank to borrow any amount up to a limit of $450,000.

Required

Prepare a cash budget for Grove, Inc., for December.

LO5   P9-3A. Budgeting Production and Purchases and Just-in-Time Materials Inventory Hancock Manufacturing, Inc., is preparing budgets for the third quarter of the year. Hancock produces only one product in its factory. This product requires 5 pounds of material B, 2 pounds of material G, and a component, K, that is purchased from another manufacturer. Hancock operates on a just-in-time basis for material B. As a result, Hancock maintains no inventory of material B. On July 1, the inventory of material G is expected to be 2,000 pounds and the inventory of component K is expected to be 500 units. Hancock wants the inventories of G and K at September 30 to be 20% less than the inventories at July 1. The inventory of finished products at June 30 is expected to be 1,000 units; the desired inventory at September 30 is 3,000 units to allow a buildup for heavy sales in the fourth quarter. The sales forecast for the third quarter is 12,000 units at $300 each. Budgeted purchase costs are $10 per pound for B, $7 per pound for G, and $40 per component for K.

Required

a. Prepare the production budget for Hancock Manufacturing, Inc., for the third quarter.

b. Prepare the direct materials budget for Hancock Manufacturing, Inc., for the third quarter.

LO4, 5   P9-4A. Preparation of Individual Budgets During the first calendar quarter of the year, Clinton Corporation is planning to manufacture a new product and introduce it in two regions. Market research indicates that sales will be 6,000 units in the urban region at a unit price of $53 and 5,000 units in the rural region at $48 each. Because the sales manager expects the product to catch on, he has asked for production sufficient to generate a 4,000-unit ending inventory. The production manager has furnished the following estimates related to manufacturing costs and operating expenses:

	Variable (per unit)	Fixed (total)
Manufacturing costs:		
Direct materials:		
A (4 lbs. @ $3.15/lb.)	$12.60	—
B (2 lbs. @ $4.65/lb.)	9.30	—
Direct labor (0.5 hrs./unit)	7.50	—
Manufacturing overhead:		
Depreciation	—	$ 7,650
Factory supplies	0.90	4,500
Supervisory salaries	—	28,800
Other	0.75	22,950
Operating expenses:		
Selling:		
Advertising	—	22,500
Sales salaries and commissions*	1.50	15,000
Other*	0.90	3,000
Administrative:		
Office salaries	—	2,700
Supplies	0.15	1,050
Other	0.08	1,950

*Varies per unit sold, not per unit produced.

Required

a. Assuming that the desired ending inventories of materials A and B are 4,000 and 6,000 pounds, respectively, and that work-in-process inventories are immaterial, prepare budgets for the calendar quarter in which the new product will be introduced for each of the following operating factors:

1. Total sales
2. Production
3. Material purchases cost
4. Direct labor costs
5. Manufacturing overhead costs
6. Selling and administrative expenses

b. Using data generated in requirement (a), prepare a budgeted income statement for the calendar quarter. Assume an overall effective income tax rate of 30%.

P9-5A. Prepare and Evaluate Budgeted Income Statement Fairfield Stores, a retailer in a shopping mall, prepared the following income statement for its operations for the month just ended:

LO5

SERVICE AND MERCHANDISING

MBC

FAIRFIELD STORES Income Statement For the Month Ended April 30		
Sales.		$500,000
Cost of goods sold		240,000
Gross profit.		$260,000
Operating expenses:		
Sales commissions expense.	$25,000	
Advertising expense	60,000	
Lease expense	20,000	
Depreciation expense.	10,000	
Salaries expense	30,000	
Other operating expenses.	15,000	160,000
Income before income taxes.		$100,000
Income tax expense		30,000
Net income.		$ 70,000

Sales commissions were 5% of sales. Income taxes were 30% of income before income taxes. Both should continue at the same rate for the remainder of the year.

Fairfield Stores is preparing the budget for the month of May. If no basic changes are made, Fairfield's management expects that the income statement would be virtually identical to the one for April. However, Fairfield's management has decided to make some changes in the operations. The plans include the following:

1. Increase advertising expense by 40%.
2. Decrease all selling prices by 10%.
3. Increase the number of units sold by 25% as a result of the first two changes.

Required
a. Prepare a budgeted income statement for the month of May. (Round all amounts on the income statement to the nearest dollar.)
b. Should Fairfield's management make the planned changes?

PROBLEMS—SET B

P9-1B. Budgeting Cash Judson, Inc., sells on terms of 5% discount for "cash and carry" or 2/10, n/30 and estimates its total sales for the second calendar quarter of next year as follows: July, $225,000; August, $150,000; and September, $180,000. An analysis of operations indicates the following customer collection patterns:

LO4

MBC

	Portions of Total Sales
In month of sale:	
Cash at time of sale	30%
On account during discount period.	20%
On account after discount period	5%
In month following sale:	
On account during discount period.	20%
On account after discount period	15%
In second month following sale:	
On account after discount period	7%
Average portion uncollectible	3%
	100%

Required

Prepare an estimate of the cash to be collected from customers during September.

LO4   P9-2B.   Monthly Cash Budget Sutter, Inc., is a wholesaler for its only product, deluxe wireless rechargeable electric shavers, which sell for $70 each and cost Sutter $48 each. On June 1, Sutter's management requested a cash budget for June. The following selected account balances at May 31 were gathered by the accounting department:

Cash.	$ 56,000
Marketable securities (at cost)	160,000
Accounts receivable (all trade)	2,170,000
Inventories (12,000 units)	576,000
Operating expenses payable	196,800
Accounts payable (all merchandise)	902,400
Note payable	600,000

Actual sales for April and May were 30,000 and 50,000 units, respectively. Projected unit sales for June and July are 40,000 and 20,000, respectively. Experience indicates that 50% of sales should be collected in the month of sale, 30% in the month following sale, and the balance in the second month following sale. Uncollectible accounts, returns, and allowances are negligible.

Planned purchases should provide ending inventories equal to 30% of next month's unit sales volume. Approximately 60% of the purchases are paid for in the month of purchase and the balance in the following month.

Monthly operating expenses are budgeted at $9.60 per unit sold plus a fixed amount of $288,000, including depreciation of $112,000. Except for depreciation, 70% of operating expenses are paid in the month incurred and the balance in the following month. Interest expense is included in operating expenses.

Special anticipated June transactions include the following:

1. Declaration of a $60,000 cash dividend to be paid 2 weeks after the June 20 date of record.
2. Sale of all but $40,000 of the marketable securities held on May 31; a gain of $18,000 is anticipated.
3. Payment of $50,000 installment on the note payable.
4. Trade-in of an old company plane originally costing $300,000 and now having accumulated depreciation of $200,000 at a gain of $160,000 on a new plane costing $2,000,000. Sufficient cash will be paid at the time of trade-in so that only 50% of the total price will have to be financed.
5. Sutter's treasurer has a policy of maintaining a minimum month-end cash balance of $40,000 and has a standing arrangement with the bank to borrow any amount up to a limit of $400,000.

Required

Prepare a cash budget for Sutter, Inc., for June.

LO5   P9-3B.   Budgeting Production and Purchases and Just-in-Time Materials Inventory Central Manufacturing, Inc., is preparing budgets for the second quarter. Central produces only one product in its factory. This product requires 4 pounds of material C, 3 pounds of material H, and a component, M, that is purchased from another manufacturer. Central operates on a just-in-time basis for material C. As a result, Central maintains no inventory of material C. On April 1, the inventory of material H is expected to be 3,000 pounds and the inventory of component M is expected to be 600 units. Central wants the inventories of H and M at June 30 to be 20% less than the inventories at April 1. The inventory of finished products at March 31 is expected to be 2,000 units; the desired inventory at June 30 is 4,000 units to allow a buildup for heavy sales in the third quarter. The sales forecast for the second quarter is 14,000 units at $200 each. Budgeted purchase costs are $5 per pound for C, $6 per pound for H, and $50 per component for M.

Required

a.   Prepare the production budget for the second quarter.
b.   Prepare the direct materials budget for the second quarter.

LO4, 5   P9-4B.   Preparation of Individual Budgets During the first calendar quarter, Williams Corporation is planning to manufacture a new product and introduce it in two regions. Market research indicates that sales will be 8,000 units in the urban region at a unit price of $65 and 6,000 units in the rural region at $55 each. Because the sales manager expects the product to catch on, she has asked for production sufficient to generate a 4,000-unit ending inventory. The production manager has furnished the following estimates related to manufacturing costs and operating expenses:

	Variable (per Unit)	Fixed (Total)
Manufacturing costs:		
Direct materials:		
A (2 lbs. @ $2.50/lb.)	$ 5.00	—
B (5 lbs. @ $1.40/lb.)	7.00	—
Direct labor (2 hrs./unit)	10.00	—
Manufacturing overhead:		
Depreciation	—	$22,500
Factory supplies	0.55	2,500
Supervisory salaries	—	16,250
Other	0.65	9,200
Operating expenses:		
Selling:		
Advertising	—	12,500
Sales salaries and commissions*	1.25	20,000
Other*	0.50	4,200
Administrative:		
Office salaries	—	15,000
Supplies	0.40	1,200
Other	0.25	5,000

*Varies per unit sold, not per unit produced.

Required

a. Assuming that the desired ending inventories of materials A and B are 4,000 and 20,000 pounds, respectively, and that work-in-process inventories are immaterial, prepare budgets for the calendar quarter in which the new product will be introduced for each of the following operating factors:
1. Total sales
2. Production
3. Material purchases cost
4. Direct labor costs
5. Manufacturing overhead costs
6. Selling and administrative expenses

b. Using data generated in requirement (a), prepare a budgeted income statement for the calendar quarter. Assume an overall effective income tax rate of 35%. (Round income statement amounts to the nearest dollar.)

P9-5B. Prepare and Evaluate Budgeted Income Statement Medford Stores, a retailer in a shopping mall, prepared the following income statement for its operations for the month just ended:

LO5

MEDFORD STORES Income Statement for the Month Ended April 30		
Sales		$700,000
Cost of goods sold		330,000
Gross profit		$370,000
Operating expenses:		
Sales commissions expense	$35,000	
Advertising expense	90,000	
Lease expense	50,000	
Depreciation expense	20,000	
Salaries expense	40,000	
Other operating expenses	25,000	260,000
Income before income taxes		$110,000
Income tax expense		33,000
Net income		$ 77,000

Sales commissions were 5% of sales. Income taxes were 30% of income before income taxes. Both should continue at the same rate for the remainder of the year.

Medford Stores is preparing the budget for the month of May. If no basic changes are made, Medford's management expects that the income statement would be virtually identical to the one for April. However, Medford's management has decided to make some changes in the operations. The plans include the following:

1. Increase advertising expense by 20%.
2. Decrease all selling prices by 10%.
3. Increase the number of units sold by 25% as a result of the first two changes.

Required

a. Prepare a budgeted income statement for the month of May. (Round all amounts on the income statement to the nearest dollar.)
b. Should Medford's management make the planned changes?

EXTENDING YOUR KNOWLEDGE

EYK9-1. Business Decision Case The sales department of Donovan Manufacturing, Inc., has completed the following sales forecast for the months of January through March 20X1 for its only two products: 50,000 units of J to be sold at $90 each and 30,000 units of K to be sold at $70 each. The desired unit inventories at March 31, 20X1, are 10% of the next quarter's unit sales forecast, which are 60,000 units of J and 30,000 units of K. The January 1, 20X1, unit inventories were 5,000 units of J and 2,000 units of K.

Each unit of J requires 3 pounds of material A and 2 pounds of material B for its manufacture; K requires 2 pounds of A and 4 pounds of B. The purchase cost of A is $9 per pound and the purchase cost of B is $5 per pound. Materials A and B on hand at January 1, 20X1, were 19,000 pounds of A and 7,000 pounds of B. Desired inventories at March 31, 20X1, are 14,000 pounds of A and 8,000 pounds of B.

Each unit of J requires 0.5 hours of direct labor in the factory; each unit of K requires 1.0 hour of direct labor. The average hourly rate for direct labor is $12 per hour. Estimated manufacturing overhead cost is $6 per direct labor hour plus $90,000 per month. Selling and administrative expenses are estimated to be 10% of sales revenue plus $180,000 per month.

Cash sales for the first quarter are estimated to be $300,000 per month. It is forecast that 30% of the credit sales for the quarter ended March 31, 20X1, will occur in January, 30% in February, and 40% in March. Of credit sales (December through March), 40% will be collected as cash in the month of sale and 55% will be collected in the following month. The remainder will be uncollectible. Cash collected in January 20X1 from December 20X0 sales will be $1,050,000.

The January 1, 20X1, cash balance was $70,000. The minimum acceptable cash balance at the end of each month is $60,000. Short-term borrowings (6-month term) are made in multiples of $10,000. Interest is charged at the rate of 1% per month on short-term borrowings. The first interest payment is made the month following the borrowing. Cash disbursements (excluding interest on short-term borrowings) are estimated as follows:

	January	February	March
Manufacturing costs	$1,500,000	$1,300,000	$1,400,000
Selling and administrative expenses	390,000	410,000	400,000
Interest expense	90,000	90,000	90,000
Income tax payment	0	0	210,000
Capital expenditures	124,000	110,000	50,000
Cash dividends	300,000	0	0

Required

a. Prepare the sales budget for the quarter ended March 31, 20X1.
b. Prepare the production budget for the quarter ended March 31, 20X1.
c. Prepare the direct materials budget for the quarter ended March 31, 20X1.
d. Prepare the direct labor budget for the quarter ended March 31, 20X1.
e. Prepare the manufacturing overhead budget for the quarter ended March 31, 20X1.
f. Prepare the selling and administrative expense budget for the quarter ended March 31, 20X1.
g. Prepare a schedule of cash collected from customers for the quarter ended March 31, 20X1.
h. Prepare the cash budget for the quarter ended March 31, 20X1.

EYK9-2. **Ethics Case** Steve Waller is the corporate accounting manager for Giant Video Stores. As part of the budgeting process for the entire corporation, he has asked the manager of each video store to prepare a store master budget.

SERVICE AND MERCHANDISING

The manager of one of the largest stores, Jeff Miller, decides to understate the sales budget and overstate all the budgets related to expenses. Jeff believes this is a more conservative approach than using the estimated numbers he honestly believes will be achieved for the year. He also thinks that the corporate office will look more favorably on his store's actual achievements when they are subsequently compared to this budget.

Jeff has asked Lisa Dorton, his assistant manager, to review the budget before it is submitted. Lisa is aware of the real estimates that Jeff made.

Required

What is the impact of Jeff Miller's budget for the corporation? What ethical issues face Lisa Dorton?

ANSWERS TO SELF-STUDY QUESTIONS:

1. d 2. b 3. d 4. a 5. a 6. c 7. c

YOUR TURN! SOLUTIONS

Solution 9.1

Items might include but not be limited to the following:

Strengths: Perception of quality products, strong brand loyalty, appeal to younger customers, move to online retail sales, diversification beyond fashion and housewares

Weaknesses: Dependence on U.S. consumers (virtually no international sales), in store online pick-up

Opportunities: Smaller neighborhood stores, capitalize on urban brand expertise among increasingly urbanized country, continued modernization of stores

Threats: Amazon.com's e-commerce shopping experience, intense competition from Walmart and other similar retailers, and an economic slowdown in the United States

Solution 9.2

c. Budgeting requires coordination among departments to ensure that all are working toward a common goal.

Solution 9.3

7, 2, 1, 6, 3, 4, 5

Solution 9.4

Change in cash:

Collection of beginning A/R . . .	$ 200,000	Given
January sales	300,000	$500,000 × 60%
February sales	560,000	($500,000 × 40%) + ($600,000 × 60%)
March sales	660,000	($600,000 × 40%) + ($700,000 × 60%)
Payment of beginning A/P	(150,000)	Given
January purchases	(280,000)	$400,000 × 70%
February purchases	(470,000)	($400,000 × 30%) + ($500,000 × 70%)
March purchases	(535,000)	($500,000 × 30%) + ($550,000 × 70%)
January other	(200,000)	$200,000 × 100%
February other	(225,000)	$225,000 × 100%
March other	(225,000)	$225,000 × 100%
Change in cash.	$(365,000)	

Solution 9.5

a.

Chapter **10**

Flexible Budgets, Segment Reporting, and Performance Analysis

Road Map

LO	Learning Objective	Page	eLecture	Guided Example	Assignments
LO1	Describe a static budget, illustrate its use, and present an example of a static budget performance report.	10-3	E10-1	YT10.1	SS1, Q1, Q2, SE1, E1A
LO2	Introduce the flexible budget and present an example of a flexible budget performance report. Explain how flexible budgeting helps in variance analysis.	10-4	E10-2	YT10.2	SS2, Q1, Q2, Q3, SE2, SE3, SE4, E1A, E2A, E1B, P1A, P1B
LO3	Present an overview of reporting operations for segments of a business.	10-10	E10-3	YT10.3	SS3, Q4, Q5, SE5
LO4	Construct a segmented contribution margin income statement. Identify the difference between traceable and common fixed costs.	10-13	E10-4	YT10.4	SS4, SS5, Q6, Q7, Q8, Q9, Q10, Q11, E3A, E2B, P2A, P3A, P4A, P2B, P3B, P4B
LO5	Compute return on investment, return on sales, return on assets, and residual income for business segments. Discuss the importance of each indicator in assessing a company's performance.	10-20	E10-5	YT10.5, YT10.6	SS6, SS7, Q12, Q13, Q14, SE6, SE7, SE8, SE9, E4A, E3B, E4B, P5A, P6A, P5B, P6B
LO6	Appendix 10A: Determine the proper transfer price to maximize company profit with and without excess productive capacity.	10-27	E10-6	YT10.7	SS8, Q15, SE10, P7A, P7B

Microsoft 365 Business Standard

Chances are the software you use on your computer was produced by **Microsoft Corporation**. Microsoft commands a dominating presence in the software industry. As the global leader in software production, Microsoft is one of the world's most valuable companies.

Microsoft has maintained an edge in the software industry through the careful application of managerial accounting concepts. In budgeting sales and production needs for future periods, Microsoft is never 100% accurate in its forecasts. To accommodate the fluctuation in sales, the company uses a budgeting approach called "flexible budgeting."

In this chapter, we will introduce flexible budgeting, segment reporting, and performance analysis and explain performance measures that are helpful in assessing the health of a company. Segment reporting allows managers to compare and assess the performance of individual segments of the company by evaluating key performance indicators, such as return on investment, profit margin, asset turnover, and residual income. Another tool used to assess performance is the balanced scorecard, which includes both financial and nonfinancial measures of performance.

PAST

Chapter 9 discussed the budgeting process, the components of the master budget, and interrelationships of the individual budgets. It also presented an illustration of a budget for a manufacturer and a service company.

PRESENT

Chapter 10 introduces flexible budgets and performance evaluation of business segments. In addition, it explores both performance and variance analysis.

FUTURE

Chapter 11 introduces standard costs and standard cost variances: direct material, direct labor, and variable overhead variances.

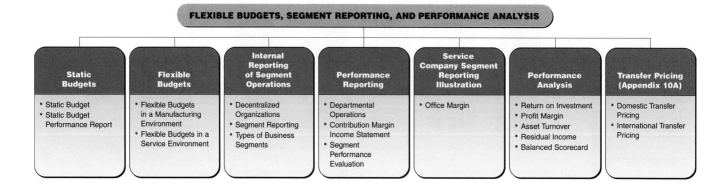

It is critically important that management have a means of measuring and evaluating the performance of employees, departments, segments, and the overall company to ensure that all are working toward the achievement of the company's strategic vision. In this chapter, we discuss several tools available to assist managers in evaluating performance: flexible budgets, segment reporting, and performance analysis and reporting.

STATIC BUDGETS

LO1 **Describe** a static budget, **illustrate** its use, and **present** an example of a static budget performance report.

eLecture

MBC

A.K.A. Static budgets are also called nonmoving or stationary budgets.

The master budget is made up of budgets known as static budgets. A **static budget** is a financial plan developed for a fixed level of operating activity, typically the expected or most likely level. If actual results are compared to a static budget, the calculated differences that result are of little use to management because the budget is often based on a different level of activity than the actual operations. The following example illustrates this point.

Exhibit 10-1 presents a simple static budget for Fezzari's Foré CR1 product line. Although Fezzari's management has a target production of 500 Foré CR1 road bikes during the year, it anticipates that this may be an aggressive projection.

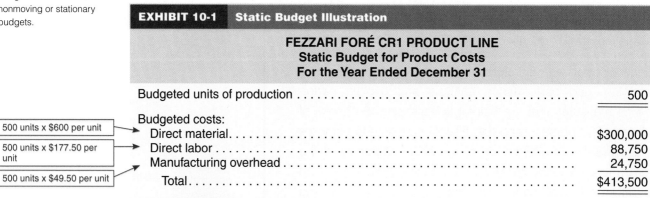

EXHIBIT 10-1	Static Budget Illustration

FEZZARI FORÉ CR1 PRODUCT LINE
Static Budget for Product Costs
For the Year Ended December 31

Budgeted units of production	500
Budgeted costs:	
Direct material.	$300,000
Direct labor	88,750
Manufacturing overhead	24,750
Total.	$413,500

500 units x $600 per unit
500 units x $177.50 per unit
500 units x $49.50 per unit

Static Budget Performance Report

Exhibit 10-2 presents a static budget performance report for the CR1 product line. The static budget performance report compares the *actual* costs to produce 480 units with the *budgeted* costs to produce 500 units. The performance report accurately reveals that actual units of CR1 production were 20 less than management had budgeted. In a performance report comparing actual costs to budgeted costs, "F" indicates a favorable difference, or **variance**, and "U" identifies an unfavorable difference.

EXHIBIT 10-2	Static Budget Performance Report Illustration

FEZZARI FORÉ CR1 PRODUCT LINE
Static Budget Performance Report
For the Year Ended December 31

Budgeted units of production	500	
Actual units of production	480	
Units of production variance	20	U

> These are the actual costs of producing 480 units.

> This is the static budget from Exhibit 10-1.

	Actual Cost Incurred for 480 Units	Budget Based on 500 Units	Cost Variances	
Direct material	$292,800	$300,000	($7,200)	F
Direct labor	91,200	88,750	2,450	U
Manufacturing overhead	21,600	24,750	(3,150)	F
Total	$405,600	$413,500	$(7,900)	F

> Cost variances are unfavorable if actual costs exceed budgeted costs, and favorable if actual costs are less than budgeted costs.

U = Unfavorable
F = Favorable

The static budget performance report, however, provides misleading cost variances. For example, the direct material variance is $7,200 favorable. (The actual cost is less than budgeted cost.) This comparison is misleading because the actual cost to produce 480 units is being compared to the budgeted cost to produce 500 units, not 480 units. Moreover, although the total variance is $7,900 favorable, the actual cost per unit is about $845 per unit ($405,600/480 CR1s), and the budgeted cost per CR1 is only $827($413,500/500 CR1s). Hence, although the cost per unit is actually higher than the budgeted cost per unit, the total static budget variance appears to be favorable simply because the company produced 20 fewer CR1s than it anticipated.

Carson CPAs specializes in preparing 1040EZ returns for low-income clients. The firm charged $100 per return this year and budgeted $100 per return. Additional information for the firm includes:

	Actual	Budgeted
Returns processed	800	750
Variable costs	$36,000	$37,500
Fixed costs	12,500	12,000

Prepare Carson's static budget and the static budget performance report.

The solution is on page 10-51.

GuidedExample

MBC

FLEXIBLE BUDGETS

A **flexible budget** is a financial plan in the form of a cost formula or a multiple-column presentation that makes cost projections for various activity levels within a relevant range.

LO2 Introduce the flexible budget and **present** an example of a flexible budget performance report. **Explain** how flexible budgeting helps in variance analysis.

Flexible Budgets in a Manufacturing Environment

Exhibit 10-3 presents a flexible budget for Fezzari's Foré CR1 product line. The first two columns show the CR1 budgeted per-unit variable costs and budgeted total fixed costs of production. The last three columns present the budget for different levels of production. The middle column is the budget for 500 units of production that would be comparable

eLecture

MBC

to the static budget in **Exhibit 10-1**. Knowing the per-unit variable costs and the fixed costs of production allows Fezzari management to prepare a budget for any level of production within the relevant range.

| EXHIBIT 10-3 | Flexible Budget for Fezzari Foré CR1 |

FEZZARI FORÉ CR1 PRODUCT LINE
Flexible Budget for Product Costs
For the Year Ended December 31

This is the static budget from Exhibit 10-1.

	1			2	
	Variable Cost per Unit	Total Fixed Cost	480 Units	500 Units	520 Units
Variable costs					
Direct material	$600.00		$288,000	$300,000	$312,000
Direct labor	177.50		85,200	88,750	92,300
Variable overhead	12.45		5,976	6,225	6,474
	$789.95		$379,176	$394,975	$410,774
Fixed costs					
Fixed overhead		18,525	$ 18,525	$ 18,525	$ 18,525
Total			$397,701	$413,500	$429,299

The manufacturing overhead has been split into variable and fixed components.

Exhibit 10-3 demonstrates a number of the characteristics about flexible budgets. First, the flexible budget usually divides costs and expenses into two groups: variable and fixed. Second, the flexible budget typically presents the variable costs and expenses on a per-unit basis and the fixed costs and expenses in total. Third, in using a columnar format, all of the columns are based on levels of activity within the relevant range. It is important to remember that the flexible budget formula is valid only for the range of activity for which it is formulated.

| ACCOUNTING IN PRACTICE | Relevant Range |

To illustrate the concept of relevant range, assume that XYZ Company has one manufacturing building in which it manufactures toys. As long as no more than 10,000 toys are produced, the fixed costs associated with this building belong to one relevant range: 0–10,000 toys. If more than 10,000 toys are produced, XYZ will need an additional building, thus incurring additional fixed costs. The costs will be in a new relevant range.

A flexible budget, prepared with columns representing different projected levels of activity, provides managers with targets for various activity levels. Hence, during the period, a flexible budget can help managers assess the reasonableness of the firm's performance as the period progresses. However, one of the most important uses of the flexible budget comes not during, but *after* the end of the period. The flexible budget formula also allows managers to compare actual costs to budgeted costs based on the actual production level achieved. Specifically, the flexible budget performance report compares actual costs at the actual level of activity to the budgeted costs at the actual level of activity.

Exhibit 10-4 presents Fezzari's flexible budget performance report for the Foré CR1 product line. This performance report allows managers to evaluate how the company's actual performance compares to budgeted performance (based on the actual level of production) for different products. Specifically, the flexible budget performance report compares actual performance in column A to budgeted performance in column B with a flexible budget (rate or price) variance for each component of product cost (direct materials, direct labor, variable overhead, and fixed overhead). Further, it compares the flexible budget in column A (based on 480 actual units) to the static budget in column C (based on 500 budgeted units). These differences are called efficiency variances, as discussed in more detail in Chapter 11.

EXHIBIT 10-4	Flexible Budget Performance Report Illustration

FEZZARI FORÉ CR1 PRODUCT LINE
Flexible Budget Performance Report
For the Year Ended December 31

Budgeted units of production	500
Actual units of production	480
Units of production variance	20 U

	A Actual Costs Incurred for 480 Units	B Flexible Budget Based on 480 Units	(A-B) Flexible Budget Variance	C Static Budget Based on 500 Units	(A-C) Static Budget Variance
Variable costs:					
Direct material.	$292,800	$288,000	$ 4,800 U	$300,000	$(7,200) F
Direct labor	91,200	85,200	6,000 U	88,750	2,450 U
Variable overhead	5,400	5,976	(576) F	6,225	(825) F
	$389,400	$379,176	$10,224 U	$394,975	$(5,575) F
Fixed costs:					
Fixed overhead	$ 16,200	$ 18,525	$(2,325) F	$ 18,525	$(2,325) F
Total	$405,600	$397,701	$ 7,899 U	$413,500	$(7,900) F

U = Unfavorable

F = Favorable

In essence, the flexible budget performance report compares "what we actually spent" to "what we should have spent" for the final production level. The flexible performance report is prepared by simply using the flexible budget formula to budget what the company "should have spent" based on the actual level of production (i.e., inserting the actual number of CR1 units produced, 480, into the flexible product costs budget).

A comparison of cost variances in the static budget performance report (**Exhibit 10-2**) and the flexible budget performance report (**Exhibit 10-4**) reveals a very different result. The static budget performance report indicates a total favorable cost variance of $7,900, whereas the flexible budget performance report reveals a total unfavorable flexible budget variance of $7,899. As explained previously, one reason the budget projections in **Exhibit 10-2** do not provide an accurate depiction of budgeted costs is that the static budget is based on the projected production level (500 CR1s) when actual production fell short (480 CR1s). Thus, part of the difference in the two comparisons is related to the volume differential (i.e., actual production came up 20 units short of the static budget production level). Clearly, the variances from the flexible budget performance report provide a more complete explanation because they are based on a comparison of what the costs actually were to what the costs should have been at the actual level of activity.

ACCOUNTING IN PRACTICE	Management by Exception

Performance reports should incorporate the management-by-exception concept. Variances outside acceptable ranges should be identified so management attention can be directed to those exceptional items.

Flexible Budgets in a Service Environment

SERVICE AND MERCHANDISING

Flexible budgets can be used in a service company just like in a manufacturing firm. For example, Old Rosebud is a 400-acre farm on the outskirts of the Kentucky Bluegrass region that specializes in boarding broodmares and their foals. An economic downturn in the thoroughbred industry has led to a decline in breeding activities. As a consequence, the demand for thoroughbred boarding has decreased, making the boarding business extremely competitive. To meet the competition, Old Rosebud planned to entertain clients, advertise, and absorb expenses formerly borne by clients (for example, the company would pay for both veterinary and blacksmith's fees).

Exhibit 10-5 presents the variances between Old Rosebud's actual operating results and amounts budgeted for the year. Its budget—like those of most service organizations—was a static one (i.e., it forecast an expected level of activity). Old Rosebud expected to log 21,900 boarding days, and it budgeted boarding rates at $25 per day per mare.

The variable expenses per mare per day were budgeted as follows:

Feed	$5.00
Veterinary fees	$3.00
Blacksmith fees.	$0.30
Supplies	$0.40

All other budgeted expenses were either semi-fixed or fixed.

The static budget in **Exhibit 10-5** can be used to explain only two factors: sales and fixed expenses. As sales volume problems arose during the year, Old Rosebud decided not to replace a farm worker who quit in March. It also developed a new farm brochure and entertained more potential clients. These strategies generated the fixed-expense variances—that is, the differences between the budgeted and actual line item amounts in the income statement.

No sound conclusions can be drawn about either the effect of price changes on the decrease in net income or the expense variances. When sales volume declines, sales revenue and variable expenses may be expected to decrease proportionately. However, the rate of Old Rosebud's decline in the number of boarding days (13%) differs from the rate of decrease in sales revenue (31%) and the rate of decrease in variable expenses (7%).

A plausible interpretation of the variances in **Exhibit 10-5** is that the large variance in net income is caused by a decrease in sales volume. This interpretation follows from the large unfavorable sales revenue variance and the generally favorable expense variances.

Indeed, at first glance, it appears as though expenses are well under control. All variable-expense variances are favorable, and the total of the two unfavorable fixed-expense variances is insignificant in relation to the total sales-revenue variance. The unfavorable advertising and entertainment variances may be interpreted as having prevented the unfavorable net income variance from being even greater. More business might have been lost had Old Rosebud not overspent its budgeted amounts for those items.

Because sales are down and expenses are well under control, this analysis suggests an obvious but faulty remedy: Do more advertising and entertaining.

EXHIBIT 10-5	Static Budget Illustration—Service

OLD ROSEBUD
Static Budget Income Statement
Year Ended December 31

	Actual	Static Budget	Variance
Number of mares	52	60	(8) U
Number of boarding days	18,980	21,900	(2,920) U
Sales.	$379,600	$547,500	$(167,900) U
Less variable expenses:			
Feed	104,390	109,500	(5,110) F
Veterinary fees	58,838	65,700	(6,862) F
Blacksmith fees.	6,074	6,570	(496) F
Supplies	7,402	8,760	(1,358) F
Total variable expenses	$176,704	$190,530	(13,826) F
Contribution margin	$202,896	$356,970	$(154,074) U
Less fixed expenses:			
Depreciation	$ 45,000	$ 45,000	$ —
Insurance	11,000	11,000	—
Utilities	12,000	14,000	(2,000) F
Repairs and maintenance.	10,000	11,000	(1,000) F
Labor.	88,000	96,000	(8,000) F
Advertisement.	11,000	8,000	3,000 U
Entertainment	8,000	5,000	3,000 U
Total fixed expenses	$185,000	$190,000	$ (5,000) F
Net income	$ 17,896	$166,970	$(149,074) U

U = Unfavorable
F = Favorable

Exhibit 10-6 compares Old Rosebud's actual operating results with those in a flexible budget. The flexible budget takes the same budgeted per-unit amounts for sales and variable expenses and applies them to the actual number of boarding days achieved. Because, by definition, fixed expenses don't vary with volume, they're the same as in the static budget. A budget constructed in this way removes the distortion in the sales-revenue and variable-expense variances of a static budget.

Two surprises are immediately apparent. First, when the unfavorable sales-revenue variance of $167,900 is separated into the unfavorable sales-price ($94,900) and unfavorable sales-volume ($73,000) variances, it becomes clear that the sales-price variance is larger. Further investigation of the sales-price variance revealed that Old Rosebud lost a major client during the year. Moreover, because of fierce competition, the farm reduced its boarding charges well below $25 per day per mare as the year progressed. As a result, the average boarding rate declined for the year.

The second surprise in **Exhibit 10-6** is that expense control was far worse than analysis of the static budget variance had indicated. All variable-expense variances, except supplies, were unfavorable. The unfavorable feed variance of $9,490 alone accounted for nearly 82% of the net unfavorable variable-expense variances of $11,578. The large feed variance was explained by the drought that hit Kentucky and most of the rest of the nation. In addition, several recent studies had indicated that copper feed supplements may be necessary to minimize skeletal bone disease in young horses. Old Rosebud incorporated the supplement at an increased cost and continued to feed first-class hay despite the drought.

EXHIBIT 10-6	Flexible Budget Illustration—Service

OLD ROSEBUD
Flexible Budget Income Statement
Year Ended December 31

Budgeted number of boarding days . . .   21,900
Actual number of boarding days   18,980

	Budget (per mare per day)	Actual	Flexible Budget	Variance
Number of mares		52	52	0
Number of boarding days		18,980	18,980	0
Sales.	$25.00	$379,600	$474,500	$ (94,900) U
Less variable expenses:				
Feed	5.00	104,390	94,900	9,490 U
Veterinary fees	3.00	58,838	56,940	1,898 U
Blacksmith fees.	0.30	6,074	5,694	380 U
Supplies	0.40	7,402	7,592	(190) F
Total variable expenses	$ 8.70	$176,704	$165,126	$ 11,578 U
Contribution margin	$16.30	$202,896	$309,374	$(106,478) U
Less fixed expenses:				
Depreciation		$ 45,000	$ 45,000	$ —
Insurance		11,000	11,000	—
Utilities		12,000	14,000	(2,000) F
Repairs and maintenance.		10,000	11,000	(1,000) F
Labor.		88,000	96,000	(8,000) F
Advertisement.		11,000	8,000	3,000 U
Entertainment		8,000	5,000	3,000 U
Total fixed expenses		$185,000	$190,000	(5,000) F
Net income		$ 17,896	$119,374	$(101,478) U

U = Unfavorable
F = Favorable

Accurate information about what causes the differences between actual and expected results is a precondition for corrective action. Variance analysis can lead to an accurate analysis. In contrast, a static budget can focus only on sales and fixed expenses that differ from budgeted figures, and not realizing this may lead to faulty analysis of the results. Flexible budget variances aren't misleading because they incorporate actual levels of activity if different from those expected.

For Old Rosebud, the main problem is price—not volume. Had the farm been able to maintain its boarding rates but not the number of boarding days, its actual net income would have been:

Sales revenue.	$474,500
Less total variable expenses	(176,704)
Less total fixed expenses	(185,000)
Net income	$112,796

This amount is six times greater than the net income of $17,896 actually achieved. The farm needs to develop a strategy that restores boarding rates more than it needs to replace the eight horses it lost.[1]

Concept ➡	Method ➡	Assessment	TAKEAWAY 10.1
How can management evaluate the company's performance relative to the budget?	• Prepare a flexible budget based on actual output achieved. • Compare the actual results to the flexible budget.	• Actual costs for materials, labor, or variable overhead that are less than the flexible budget amounts result in favorable variances. • Actual costs that are greater than the flexible budget amounts result in unfavorable variances.	

YOUR TURN! 10.2

The solution is on page 10-51.

MBC

The following static budget performance report was prepared for Chip Manufacturing for July.

	Actual Results	Static Budget	Variance
Sales units	100,000	90,000	10,000 F
Sales dollars	$190,000	$180,000	$10,000 F
Variable costs	125,000	108,000	17,000 U
Fixed costs	50,000	45,000	5,000 U
Operating income	$ 15,000	$ 27,000	$12,000 U

Using a flexible budget, calculate Chip's total flexible budget variance for variable costs.

ENVIRONMENTAL, SOCIAL, AND GOVERNANCE   **Microsoft's Corporate Citizenship "Budget"**

The opening vignette discussed the importance of budgeting to Microsoft's operations, in particular financial measures such as sales. The process of budgeting as discussed in this chapter is applicable to far more than just financial results. Microsoft uses budgets to track revenues and expenses that are eventually communicated to interested parties in its annual financial report. In addition, Microsoft sets goals and tracks these goals with budgeting techniques outlined in this chapter for its annual Citizenship Report. In this report Microsoft highlights its performance in such areas as Ethical Business Conduct and Governance, People, Serving Communities, Human Rights, Responsible Sourcing, and Environmental Sustainability. The report can be found at and downloaded from Microsoft's website under the Corporate Social Responsibility section at the following link: https://www.microsoft.com/about/

INTERNAL REPORTING OF SEGMENT OPERATIONS

Decentralized Organizations

As businesses grow, management of the organization becomes more and more difficult. Most large businesses are decentralized, meaning that the authority to make decisions is spread throughout the business.

Although decentralization occurs almost out of necessity as businesses grow, there are significant advantages to involving lower-level management in the decision-making process of the business:

LO3   Present an overview of reporting operations for segments of a business.

eLecture

MBC

---

[1] SOURCE: Adapted from Hans Sprohge and John Talbott, "New Applications for Variance Analysis," *Journal of Accountancy*, April 1989, pp. 137, 138, 140, 141. Reprinted with permission from the *Journal of Public Accountancy*, copyright © 1989 by the American Institute of Certified Public Accountants, Inc. Opinions of the authors are their own and do not necessarily reflect the policies of the AICPA.

1. Delegation of day-to-day operational decisions frees up upper management to focus on strategy and business development.

2. Involvement of lower-level management in running the business provides excellent on-the-job training for those who will eventually become the upper management of the business.

3. Empowering lower-level managers may increase their job satisfaction and motivation to work hard.

4. Because lower-level managers are more familiar with the day-to-day operation of the business, they are more likely to identify and react more quickly to trends in the marketplace.

On the other hand, decentralization can lead to less desirable consequences:

1. Lower-level managers may not be privy to the larger business strategy.

2. Decisions made by lower-level managers may not be consistent with and supportive of goals and objectives of other departments or divisions within the business.

3. Largely autonomous departments or divisions may lead to "silos" within the business, resulting in important operating information or innovative ideas not being shared with other departments or divisions, to the detriment of the business overall.

Segment Reporting

Many business entities are very complex, with diverse divisions and departments in multiple locations. Managers of this type of entity often find it useful to divide the entity into segments to enhance managerial planning and control. Segments usually are based on organizational units (divisions or departments) or areas of economic activity (geographic regions or product lines). Many large companies have found that segmentation by organizational unit is the approach that proves most useful. It is important that the managerial accounting systems and procedures that develop information for planning and control decisions be structured to reflect the segmentation.

Internal reporting of segment operations deals primarily with the measurement of operating performance. As a result, segmented reports usually take the format of a contribution margin income statement. These statements may provide information to answer the following types of questions:

1. What amount does each segment contribute to the sales and operating income of the entity as a whole?

2. How do revenues and expenses for each segment compare to planned or budgeted amounts?

3. What is the rate of profitability of each segment? Should any segment be expanded, reduced, or eliminated?

4. Which areas need corrective action, and what should be done?

5. Where should promotional efforts be directed?

Types of Business Segments

With delegated authority comes accountability. In a decentralized organization, segment managers must demonstrate that the results of their decisions support and are congruent with the overall business strategy of the organization. Portions of a business for which a manager has been given a measure of authority and accountability are often referred to as **responsibility centers**. Depending on the authority delegated, these responsibility centers may be described as cost centers, profit centers, and investment centers. An example of these responsibility centers may be seen in PACCAR, a heavy-duty truck manufacturer.

PACCAR is a Fortune 200 company that designs, manufactures, and distributes trucks and related aftermarket parts that are sold worldwide under the Kenworth, Peterbilt, and DAF name-plates. It ranked as the fourth-largest manufacturer of medium- and heavy-duty trucks in the world in 2020.

The company has its headquarters in Bellevue, Washington. It began in 1905 as Seattle Car Manufacturing Company, at which time it produced railway and logging equipment. Over time, it expanded through acquisitions of commercial truck manufacturers and parts suppliers. As it grew and became more complex, management organized various business segments or responsibility centers. As described in the following discussion, some of PACCAR's responsibility centers might be considered cost centers, profit centers, or investment centers.

The manager of a **cost center** is responsible for the costs and expenses of only that segment of the business. He or she has no responsibility for revenue generation. An example of a PACCAR cost center is its Technical Centers, which provide research, development, and testing for new products. The output of these Technical Centers is a service to other PACCAR divisions or segments that is not sold to consumers outside the company. As a result, no revenue is generated directly by these centers.

The manager of a **profit center** is responsible for revenue generation as well as for cost and expense control. An example of a PACCAR profit center is its PACCAR Parts business, which operates a network of parts distribution centers that offer aftermarket support to its truck dealerships and customers throughout the world. PACCAR evaluates the performance of PACCAR Parts on its operating profit or segment contribution margin.

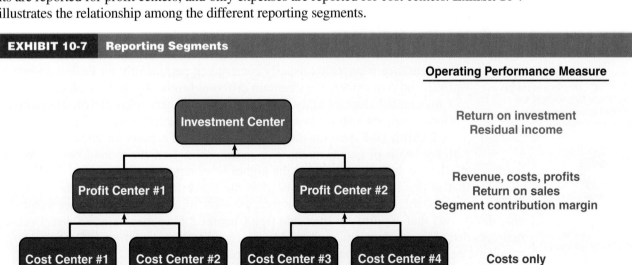

The manager of an **investment center** is responsible for the use of capital (productive assets), along with revenues and costs. The manager is typically evaluated on a measure of return on assets or return on investment. An example of a PACCAR investment center is its PACCAR Mexico (KENMEX) division, which manufactures trucks for Mexico and exports to other countries in a 590,000-square-foot facility.

Managerial reports that measure the operating performance of a business entity and its segments reflect whether the segments are investment, profit, or cost centers. Return on investment, revenue, expenses, and profits are reported for investment centers; revenue, expenses, and profits are reported for profit centers; and only expenses are reported for cost centers. **Exhibit 10-7** illustrates the relationship among the different reporting segments.

EXHIBIT 10-7   Reporting Segments

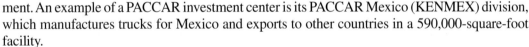

Operating Performance Measure

Investment Center — Return on investment / Residual income

Profit Center #1   Profit Center #2 — Revenue, costs, profits / Return on sales / Segment contribution margin

Cost Center #1   Cost Center #2   Cost Center #3   Cost Center #4 — Costs only

ACCOUNTING IN PRACTICE	Segment Reporting

In June 2013, the Securities and Exchange Commission (SEC) charged PACCAR for various account-ing deficiencies that obscured the company's financial reporting to investors and regulators from 2008 through 2012. Among the charges was that PACCAR failed to report the operating results of its aftermar-ket parts business separately from its truck sales business as required under segment reporting require-ments. These requirements are intended to allow investors to gain the same insight into the company's operations as its executives.

How significant was this violation of generally accepted accounting principles (GAAP)? In its 2009 annual report, PACCAR reported $68 million in income before taxes for its truck segment. However, had it followed GAAP, it would have reported a $474 million loss in the truck segment and a $542 million profit in its parts segment.

The SEC and PACCAR agreed to a settlement under which, without admitting or denying the charges, PACCAR agreed to the entry of a permanent injunction and the payment of a $225,000 pen-alty. Michael S. Dicke, associate regional director of the SEC's San Francisco Regional Office said, "Companies must continually and diligently monitor their internal accounting systems to ensure that the information they are providing investors is accurate and consistent with relevant accounting guid-ance. The deficient controls and procedures at PACCAR caused inconsistencies in its financial report-ing and kept investors and regulators from seeing the company through the eyes of management." http://www.sec.gov/News/PressRelease/Detail/PressRelease/1365171575142#.VATK9_IdV8E

TAKEAWAY 10.2	Concept ⟶	Method ⟶	Assessment
	How might firm management measure and evaluate the performance of its responsibility centers?	• Cost center: cost variances, measuring differences between actual and budgeted costs • Profit center: revenue and cost variances, return on sales, and segment contribution margin • Investment center: return on investment and residual income	• Variances help managers identify explanations for differences between actual and expected performance. • Financial ratios are compared to targets and benchmarks to determine whether the firm met its goals and evaluate its performance relative to its competitors' performance.

YOUR TURN! 10.3	Access the most recent 10-K filing of PACCAR at sec.gov/edgar/searchedgar/companysearch.html. What operating segments does PACCAR report (search for the term "segment" under Item 1 of the 10-K filing)?
The solution is on page 10-51.	

MBC

PERFORMANCE REPORTING

MBC

LO4 Construct a segmented contribution margin income statement. **Identify** the difference between traceable and common fixed costs.

Hint: Direct expenses do not need to be allocated.

Performance reports are usually constructed periodically for each investment, profit, and cost center. They contain different levels of detail for different levels of managerial responsibility. Whereas top managers need highly summarized information, lower-level managers require more detailed, specialized reports.

Exhibit 10-8 presents multilevel performance reports for three successively higher levels of management. The arrows show how the totals from the lower-level reports flow to and are included in the higher-level reports.

Note that in this illustration, all costs from the lower level are included in the upper level. In practice, this may not always be the case—for proper decision-making purposes, only those costs that are directly traceable (see Chapter 2 for a discussion of direct versus indirect costs) to each department should be assigned to that department. Common costs would not be assigned for purposes of performance evaluation.

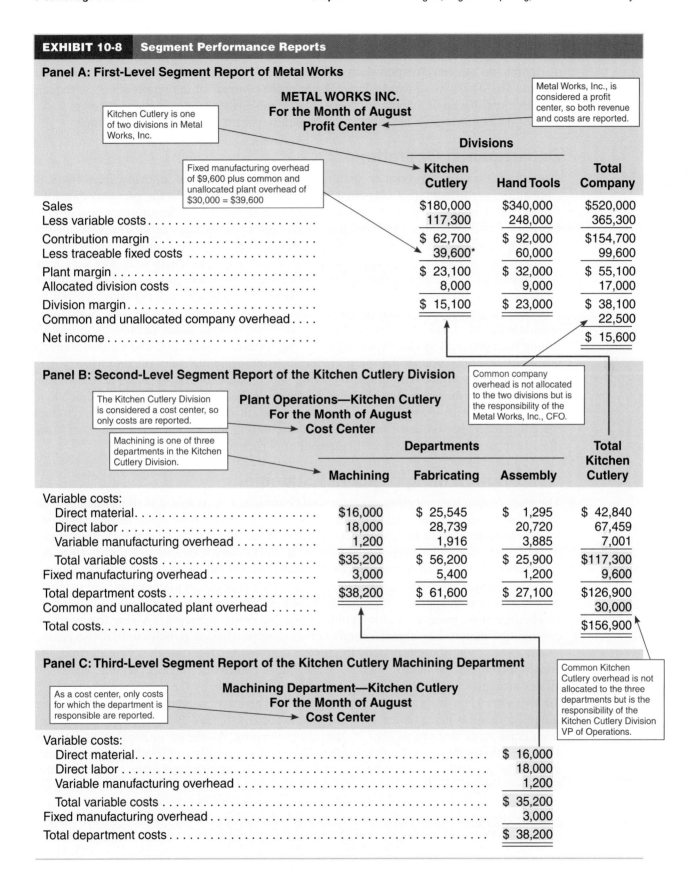

Also note that the reports in Panels B and C are for cost centers, so these reports only contain cost information. The manager of machining operations and the vice president of operations do not have responsibility for revenue, so revenues are not allocated to their reports. The divisions shown in Panel A are profit centers, so the report shows revenues, traceable variable costs, contribution margin, traceable fixed costs, allocated segment costs, and segment contribution margin in a contribution margin income statement format.

Departmental Operations

Departmentalization is a common and logical type of segmentation for many firms. In many companies, departments are classified by processes performed. In the previous example, the Kitchen Cutlery division is composed of three segments, or departments: machining, fabricating, and assembly. These departments represent the primary processes performed in making the knives, forks, and spoons that comprise a set of kitchen cutlery.

In other companies, departments might be classified by products sold. The very term *department store* signifies a type of merchandising by product (men's clothing, women's clothing, home furnishings, etc.). Grocery stores are also commonly departmentalized by product groups such as meat, produce, groceries, bakery, and delicatessen. Sometimes departments are classified by type of customer. For example, home improvement centers selling such products as floor coverings, lighting fixtures, and heating and air-conditioning units may separate commercial sales operations from residential sales operations.

The methods of accounting and reporting departmental operating activities depend on the performance measures used and the degree of analysis desired by management. Some firms may desire to identify only contribution margin by department. Others may adopt a more detailed performance measure, such as contribution margin less those fixed costs directly incurred by the department (segment or department income).

Contribution Margin Income Statement

The main reason for analyzing segment contribution margin is that it permits management to review pricing policies and supplier costs. Comparisons can be made among segments to determine areas with high segment contribution margin and areas that may need major promotional efforts. For example, in the Metal Works, Inc., example in **Exhibit 10-8**, the segment report permits a comparison of the Cutlery and Hand Tools divisions (or segments) of the company. Comparisons can also be made with contribution margin achieved in previous periods or with statistics for other firms selling similar products. (These statistics may be obtained from trade association publications and credit agencies.[2]) A very low segment contribution margin may signal a need to investigate purchasing policies or to revise prices.

To obtain contribution margin figures by segment or department, a firm customarily creates a contribution margin income statement. A contribution margin income statement allows managers to identify those costs that are controllable by the segment and for which the segment manager should be held accountable. The use of a contribution margin income statement requires management to segregate those costs that are attributable to the segment from those costs that are attributable to other segments. As shown in Panel A of **Exhibit 10-8**, the attributable costs must be further classified as variable and fixed costs (both traceable to the department and common). Recall that in a contribution margin income statement, cost of goods sold consists of only variable manufacturing costs, all variable costs (both production and selling and administrative) are deducted from sales revenue to compute the contribution margin, and all fixed costs are deducted from the contribution margin to compute the division margin. Note that in creating a segment contribution margin income

---

[2] For example, the Risk Management Association publishes the RMA Annual Statement Studies, which is a source of comparative data drawn from the financial statements of the small- and medium-sized business customers of RMA's member institutions.

statement, only fixed costs that are traceable to the segment are deducted to arrive at the segment contribution margin.

Segment Performance Evaluation

Department managers should be held responsible only for costs and expenses that they control. Therefore, in segment reporting, costs are commonly classified and reported as traceable (controlled by the segment) or common (not controlled by the segment). **Traceable expenses** are those operating expenses or costs traceable to and incurred for the benefit of a single department and thus ordinarily controllable by the department. **Common expenses** are those operating expenses or costs incurred for the benefit of multiple departments and thus neither traceable to nor controllable by a specific department. In Panel A of **Exhibit 10-8**, $22,500 of company expenses is determined to be common and unallocated to the Kitchen Cutlery and Hand Tools divisions.

Frequently, costs are considered controllable at one level of management but not at other levels. For example, the vice president of marketing for Metal Works, Inc., may be responsible for decisions related to advertising. Even though the cost of advertising is incurred at the division level (Kitchen Cutlery and Hand Tools), the manager of these divisions should not be held responsible for that expense if the vice president of marketing makes all the decisions relative to that cost or expense. These costs would be included in the common and unallocated company overhead costs shown in Panel A of **Exhibit 10-8**.

Concept ⟶	Method ⟶	Assessment	TAKEAWAY 10.3
How can a firm hold segment managers responsible for revenues and costs?	Prepare periodic performance reports for each segment.	• Cost center managers are responsible for directly traceable variable and fixed costs. • Profit center managers are responsible for directly traceable revenues and variable and fixed costs. • Investment center managers are responsible for invested capital, revenues, and variable and fixed costs.	

SERVICE COMPANY SEGMENT REPORTING ILLUSTRATION

Let's review an example of segment reporting with Environmental Business Consultants (EBC). EBC, which has two offices in northern and southern California, was introduced to you in earlier chapters. Within EBC, each office is considered a department—the word *department* is used interchangeably with *office* in the following discussion.

SERVICE AND MERCHANDISING

Office Margin

EBC maintains its accounting records to produce absorption income statements in accordance with GAAP as required by its bank. However, assume that EBC's management desires a better measure of operating performance. It is then faced with the problem of assigning or *allocating* operating expenses to the offices. If managers desire a measure of office margin, it is necessary to trace the operating expenses to the offices.

Some expenses may be readily identified with the operation of particular offices, but others cannot be. To identify expenses with offices, it is helpful to classify them into traceable and common expenses. For example, payroll expense related to personnel who work exclusively in one office is a traceable expense of that office. Payroll expense related to administrative personnel whose work benefits all offices is a common expense of the offices. EBC also has several common expenses, incurred for the benefit of both offices. Some examples are marketing expenses, some administrative salaries, and a variety of other administrative expenses. These expenses must be fairly assigned, where traceable, to the offices if the measure of office net income is to be meaningful. Note that some general administrative costs such as executive salaries, general accounting expenses, and general legal expenses should not be allocated for purposes of evaluating an office's performance because the office manager has no control over those items.

Assume that EBC management classifies its operating costs as variable or fixed as follows:

Variable Expenses	Amount
Employee bonuses...	$126,000
Marketing expenses...	48,000
Office supplies expense..	64,500
Other general administrative expenses	70,000
Total variable operating expenses	$308,500

Fixed Expenses	Amount
Executive salaries...	$ 844,500
Clerical salaries	217,500
Consultant salaries..	1,050,000
Employee benefits	145,500
Payroll taxes...	123,000
Employee continuing education expenses	27,000
Office lease expense	202,500
Other general administrative expenses	285,500
Total fixed operating expenses................................	$2,895,500

In preparing an office income statement, EBC might analyze and assign these expenses as described in the following subsections.

Employee Bonuses

All EBC employees are eligible for bonuses based on the profits earned during the year. Because each employee is assigned to an office, the bonuses for each office can be directly determined from payroll records, which show $96,178 for northern California and $29,822 for southern California.

Marketing Expenses

Of EBC's $48,000 marketing expenses, $28,000 was spent on proposal preparation in northern California, $11,000 on proposal preparation in southern California, $4,000 on attendance at industry trade shows that benefit both markets, and $5,000 on general professional journal advertisements directed at both markets. The latter two amounts are not assigned to the offices because they are considered common expenses, as shown in **Exhibit 10-9**.

EXHIBIT 10-9	Marketing Expenses Allocation		
	Northern California	Southern California	Firm Total
Proposal preparation	$28,000*	$11,000*	$39,000
Trade shows....................................			4,000
Advertising			5,000
			$48,000

* Directly identified

Office Supplies Expenses

Office supplies are purchased by each office as needed, so they are easily traceable to each office. EBC records show that $51,600 and $12,900 of office supplies were purchased by the northern and southern California offices, respectively, during the year.

Other General Administrative Expenses

Other general administrative expenses include the salaries and benefits for the office manager and bookkeeper and other costs associated with billings, collections, and customer inquiries. These costs—both the variable and fixed portions—are considered common costs and are not assigned to the individual offices.

Salaries and Related Benefits

Executive, clerical, and consultant salaries and related employee benefits and taxes are traceable to the office in which the employee works. EBC payroll records show that the total salaries, benefits, and taxes for each office are $1,876,200 and $504,300 for the northern and southern California offices, respectively.

Employee Continuing Education Expenses

All professional consultants are required to complete 40 hours of continuing education (CE) credits each year. As with salaries and related benefits, these costs can be determined directly for each office. The firm's time records show CE expenses of $20,828 for northern California consultants and $6,172 for southern California consultants.

Office Lease Expense

Each of the EBC offices negotiates and pays for its own office space. EBC records show that $154,500 in lease expense was paid by the northern California office and $48,000 was paid by the southern California office.

Exhibit 10-10 presents a summary of the operating expenses, showing the traceable variable and traceable fixed expenses of each department and common expenses for the firm.

EXHIBIT 10-10	Operating Expense Assignment			
	A	B	C	D	E
1		Northern California	Southern California	Common	Firm Total
2	Variable costs				
3	Employee bonuses	$ 96,178	$ 29,822		$ 126,000
4	Marketing expenses	28,000	11,000	9,000	48,000
5	Office supplies expense	51,600	12,900		64,500
6	Other general administrative expenses			70,000	70,000
7	Total variable costs	$ 175,778	$ 53,722	$ 79,000	$ 308,500
8	Fixed costs				
9	Salaries and benefits	$1,876,200	$504,300		$2,380,500
10	Employee continuing education expenses	20,828	6,172		27,000
11	Office lease expense	154,500	48,000		202,500
12	Other general administrative expenses			$285,500	285,500
13	Total fixed costs	$2,051,528	$558,472	$285,500	$2,895,500
14	Total costs	$2,227,306	$612,194	$364,500	$3,204,000

The traceable variable and fixed costs are used to prepare the office margin statement in Exhibit 10-11.

The common costs are NOT allocated to the offices in the office margin statement in Exhibit 10-11.

This departmental expense distribution is used to prepare the variable income statement for EBC shown in **Exhibit 10-11**, which extends the departmental operating results through office margin. Note that in this presentation, traceable variable costs are deducted to compute office contribution margin, from which traceable fixed costs are subtracted to compute office margin. Common expenses are not allocated to the individual offices.

Operating statements that extend departmental results to operating or net income measures are often criticized on the grounds that the indirect or common expenses are not controllable at the departmental level and therefore should not be assigned to departments when measuring performance. An additional criticism is that the bases for assignment of common expenses are frequently arbitrary.

In the EBC example, the other general administrative costs, although necessary expenses for the firm overall, are not controllable by the individual office managers. Thus, they should not be allocated to the offices at all. Allocating these costs on some arbitrary basis could lead management to draw incorrect conclusions and make poor business decisions.

EXHIBIT 10-11	**Office Margin Statement**		
	A	B	C	D
1	ENVIRONMENTAL BUSINESS CONSULTANTS, LLC Office Margin Statement For the Year Ended December 31			
2		Northern California	Southern California	Firm Total
3	Gross sales	$2,900,000	$1,246,000	$4,146,000
4	Less reimbursable costs	(344,800)	(86,200)	(431,000)
5	Net sales	2,555,200	1,159,800	3,715,000
6	Traceable variable costs	(175,778)	(53,722)	(229,500)
7	Office contribution margin	2,379,422	1,106,078	3,485,500
8	Traceable fixed costs	(2,051,528)	(558,472)	(2,610,000)
9	**Office margin**	**$ 327,894**	**$ 547,606**	875,500
10	Common expenses			(364,500)
11	Operating income			511,000
12	Interest revenue			7,500
13	Income before tax			$ 518,500

The traceable variable and fixed costs were assigned to each office in Exhibit 10-10.

The common costs are not allocated to the offices because they are not controllable by the office managers.

YOUR TURN! 10.4

The solution is on page 10-51.

MBC

Departmental revenue is $600,000 for Department X, and departmental operating income is $350,000. Traceable expenses for this department are as follows:

Direct labor.	$25,000
Other traceable costs	$40,000
Direct materials.	$30,000

Compute common expenses for this department.

PERFORMANCE ANALYSIS

The contribution margin income statement that was discussed in the previous section may be used to evaluate the performance of a profit center. This section addresses evaluation of investment centers.

Managers use a number of methods for evaluating the performance of investment centers. We explore several performance evaluation methods and discuss their relative strengths and weaknesses. To illustrate these different performance methods, we compare hypothetical data for Fezzari's mountain bike and road bike divisions. **Exhibit 10-12** indicates that the mountain bike division earned $2.5 million, and the road bike division earned $1.7 million. It also shows that the mountain bike division's investment in operating assets is $18.3 million, and the road bike division's investment is $11 million. We use this information to demonstrate the relative pros and cons of the various performance methods.

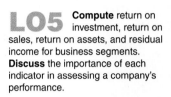

MBC

Compute return on investment, return on sales, return on assets, and residual income for business segments. **Discuss** the importance of each indicator in assessing a company's performance.

We note that one might be tempted to simply compare the operating income numbers of the two divisions and conclude that the mountain bike division is outperforming the road bike division because it has a higher operating income for the period. However, some of the other performance metrics we discuss here may provide different insights.

EXHIBIT 10-12	Performance Analysis		

FEZZARI PERFORMANCE BICYCLES
Division Performance
For the Year Ended December 31

(in thousands)	Divisions	
	Mountain	**Road**
Sales.	$14,400	$ 7,900
Expenses	(11,900)	(6,200)
Operating income	$ 2,500	$ 1,700
Asset investment	$18,300	$11,000

Return on Investment

One of the problems with simply comparing the net income figures of the two divisions is that they differ in size. One way to "level the playing field" of two divisions of different sizes is to compare the divisions on a relative basis based on a ratio.

One ratio that is useful in comparing the profitability of two divisions is the **return on investment** (ROI) ratio, which is calculated as the operating income number divided by the investment in operating assets:

$$ROI = \frac{\text{Operating income}}{\text{Operating asset investment}}$$

ROI examines the division's operating income as a percentage of the asset base used to generate that income.

Given the information in **Exhibit 10-12**, Fezzari's mountain bike division has an ROI of 13.7% ($2,500/$18,300), and the road bike division has an ROI of 15.5% ($1,700/$11,000). Therefore, the ROI ratio indicates that the road bike division earns a higher rate of return on its investment in assets than the mountain bike division earns on its investment. Thus, Fezzari's division ROI measures indicate that the mountain bike division generates 13.7 cents of profit for every dollar invested in assets, and the road bike division earns 15.5 cents of profit on every dollar invested in its asset base. Therefore, the ROI ratio provides evidence that the road bike division is more profitable on a relative basis, given its investment in assets.

In the 1920s, the DuPont brothers recognized that ROI could be further divided into two ratios, profit margin and asset turnover, which provided managers additional levers to improve the overall ROI. This has come to be referred to as the **DuPont formula**. The formula for ROI can be expressed as:

$$\text{ROI} = \text{Profit margin} \times \text{Asset turnover} = \frac{\text{Operating income}}{\text{Sales}} \times \frac{\text{Sales}}{\text{Investment}}$$

Exhibit 10-13 summarizes the calculation of ROI based on the DuPont formula for Fezzari's mountain and road bike divisions. The calculations of Fezzari's return on sales and asset utilization are discussed in the following sections.

EXHIBIT 10-13	ROI Analysis			

FEZZARI PERFORMANCE BICYCLES
DuPont ROI Analysis
For the Year Ended December 31

	ROI	=	Profit Margin	×	Asset Utilization
Mountain	13.7%	=	17.4%	×	78.7%
Road	15.5%	=	21.5%	×	71.8%*

* Difference due to rounding

Profit Margin

AKA Profit margin is also known as return on sales.

The **profit margin** ratio (the first component of the DuPont ROI formula) is useful in comparing the profitability of two divisions, which is simply calculated as the operating income number divided by sales:

$$\text{Profit margin} = \frac{\text{Operating income}}{\text{Sales}}$$

As shown in **Exhibit 10-13**, Fezzari's mountain bike division has a profit margin of 17.4% ($2,500/$14,400), whereas the road bike division has a profit margin of 21.5% ($1,700/$7,900). Thus, even though the road bike division has a lower net income than the mountain bike division, it is higher as a percentage of sales. One way of interpreting the profit margin ratio is the number of pennies left over from each dollar of sales after covering all costs. Thus, Fezzari's division profit margin measures indicate that although the mountain bike division may have a greater operating income number, it does not manage expenses as efficiently as the road bike division, because only 17.4 cents of every sales dollar is left over after covering operating costs, whereas the road bike division generates 21.5 cents of operating income for every sales dollar generated. At least based on this profitability measure, the road bike division is actually relatively more profitable.

Asset Turnover

The **asset turnover** ratio (the second component of the DuPont ROI formula) is used to compare the efficiency with which the divisions are using their operating assets to generate sales. It is calculated as sales divided by the investment in operating assets:

$$\text{Asset turnover} = \frac{\text{Sales}}{\text{Investment}}$$

As shown in **Exhibit 10-13**, Fezzari's mountain bike division has an asset turnover ratio of 78.7% ($14,400/$18,300), and the road bike division has an asset turnover ratio of 71.8%

($7,900/$11,000). This means that the mountain bike division generates 78.7 cents in sales for every dollar of operating assets, whereas the road bike division generates only 71.8 cents in sales for every dollar of operating assets. The mountain bike division uses its operating assets more efficiently.

Interestingly, the DuPont analysis indicates that the road bike division has higher core profitability, but the mountain bike division uses its assets more efficiently. Nevertheless, the result of multiplying the profit margin ratio by the asset turnover ratio is that the road bike division has a higher ROI.

Residual Income

Another method for comparing two subsidiary companies or operating divisions is based on **residual income**. Similar to ROI, residual income takes the size of the division into account. However, unlike ROI, residual income is not a ratio; it is defined as the income that is left over after the company or division earns some minimum return on investment. Residual income is based on the idea that owners or investors expect a company to provide a reasonable rate of return on their investment. Investors could invest their money in other types of investments, so they likely have some minimum rate of return (called a hurdle rate) they would like to earn on their investment in the company. Another way of looking at residual income is to calculate the amount of extra income after a division earns a minimum ROI. The formula for residual income is:

Residual income = Net operating income − (Average operating assets × Minimum ROI)

Exhibit 10-14 first assumes that managers or owners expect each division to earn a hurdle rate of 5%. Given the mountain bike division's investment in assets of $18.3 million and the company's desired ROI of $915,000 ($18.3 million × 0.05), it has residual income of $1.59 million. Similarly, the road bike division has a desired ROI of $550,000 ($11.0 million × 0.05) and residual income of $1.15 million. Thus, we would conclude that the mountain bike division generates more residual income than the road bike division.

EXHIBIT 10-14	Residual Income Analysis		
	A	B	C
1	FEZZARI PERFORMANCE BICYCLES Residual Income Analysis For the Year Ended December 31		
2		Divisions	
3	(in thousands)	Mountain	Road
4	Net income	$2,500	$1,700
5	Required return (5% rate)	(915)	(550)
6	Residual income	$1,585	$1,150
7			
8	Net income	$2,500	$1,700
9	Required return (12% rate)	(2,196)	(1,320)
10	Residual income	$ 304	$ 380

On the other hand, what if managers or owners expect each division to earn a hurdle rate of 12%? Given the mountain bike division's investment in assets of $18.3 million and the company's desired ROI of $2.20 million ($18.3 million × 0.12), it has residual income of $304,000. Similarly, the road bike division has a desired ROI of $1.32 million ($11.0 million × 0.12) and residual income of $380,000. Thus, we would conclude that the road bike division's $380,000 of residual income exceeds the mountain bike division's $304,000 of residual income.

How is it possible that the mountain bike division has higher residual income if the required ROI is 5% and the road bike division has a higher residual income when the desired ROI is 12%? The answer is in the size of the asset base. When interest rates are low, it is relatively inexpensive to borrow money to buy assets. However, when interest rates are high, it becomes more costly to borrow money to buy assets. Hence, when the required ROI is low, larger divisions are favored, but when the desired ROI is high, smaller divisions have an advantage.

Balanced Scorecard

One drawback to the performance measures discussed so far is that they focus solely on financial measures. Over time, managers have become more aware of the fact that there are also many *nonfinancial* measures that influence both performance and other major corporate decisions. Thus, in recent years, many companies have begun evaluating performance using the balanced scorecard.[3] The **balanced scorecard** seeks to provide a "balanced view" of company performance by evaluating a company's subunits based on both financial and nonfinancial measures in each of the following areas:

1. Financial performance
2. Customer satisfaction
3. Internal business processes
4. Learning and growth

Obviously, financial performance remains perhaps the most important area of focus for most managers, because if a business isn't profitable and if it doesn't generate positive cash flows, it won't survive for long. Examples of financial measures include ratios and other financial statement measures. However, the long-term health of a company depends largely on its ability to attract and retain customers. Hence, the second focus area relates to customer satisfaction. Customer-related performance measures include such factors as the number of customer complaints. A well-run company seeks to achieve the highest level of efficiency. In their quest to maximize financial goals and maintain customer satisfaction, companies constantly seek to improve internal operations to achieve highly efficient processes. Evaluation of internal processes can measure factors such as throughput time and the number of quality inspection failures. Finally, effective organizations recognize that their greatest asset doesn't appear on the balance sheet. A company's employees bring perhaps the greatest value in determining the organization's continued success. Attracting and developing the best people is a constant struggle for any organization and is directly associated with an organization's capacity to grow and improve. Thus, the learning and growth aspect of a business can measure factors such as training and employee development efforts.

Exhibit 10-15 illustrates how Fezzari might evaluate itself based on the objectives it has defined in each of the four areas of focus.

YOUR TURN! 10.5 The solution is on page 10-52. MBC	Company X has a profit margin of 8% and a return on investment of 10%, with a net profit for the year of $50,000. The required return for the company investments has been set at 8%. The company plans to purchase a new machine worth $100,000 and expects sales and net profit to rise by an additional $150,000 and $15,000, respectively. The new purchase decision will increase profit margin, asset turnover, return on investment, and residual income to what amounts?
YOUR TURN! 10.6 The solution is on page 10-52. MBC	Assume that you are the managing partner of a small CPA firm. You have decided to evaluate the firm's performance using a balanced scorecard. Identify at least one measure that you might use in each of the four areas of the balanced scorecard: financial performance, customer satisfaction, internal business processes, and learning and growth.

---

[3] The balanced scorecard originated in the 1990s with Robert Kaplan and David Norton at the Harvard Business School ("Using the Balanced Scorecard as a Strategic Management System," *Harvard Business Review,* January–February 1996, p. 76).

Concept ⟶	Method ⟶	Assessment	TAKEAWAY 10.4
How might an investment center's performance be evaluated?	$\text{Profit margin} = \dfrac{\text{Operating income}}{\text{Sales}}$ $\text{Asset turnover} = \dfrac{\text{Sales}}{\text{Investment in operating assets}}$ $\dfrac{\text{Return on}}{\text{investment}} = \dfrac{\text{Operating income}}{\text{Investment in operating assets}}$ $\dfrac{\text{Residual}}{\text{income}} = \dfrac{\text{Net}}{\text{operating}} - \left(\begin{array}{ccc} \text{Average} & & \text{Required} \\ \text{operating} & \times & \text{minimum} \\ \text{assets} & & \text{return} \end{array} \right)$ Balanced scorecard (financial performance, customer satisfaction, internal business practices, learning and growth)	• Calculated ratios can be compared to similar ratios determined over time or to ratios for similar companies in the same industry. • Balanced scorecards include nonfinancial measures that impact a company's performance and provide a more balanced view of performance.	

EXHIBIT 10-15   **Balanced Scorecard Illustration**

FEZZARI PERFORMANCE BICYCLES
Balanced Scorecard
For the Year Ended December 31

	Objectives	Measures	Targets	Initiatives
Financial	Maximize returns	ROI	14%	
	Profitable growth	Revenue growth	6%	
	Manage operating costs	Operating costs/customer	$1,000	
Customer	Industry-leading customer loyalty	Customer satisfaction survey	90%	Customer loyalty program
Internal Processes	Business growth -Use alliances and joint ventures	% of customers serviced through alliances	10%	
	Customer service excellence -Educate customers	% education plans executed	90%	
	-Effective customer service	Problem resolution cycle time	6 hrs.	Customer service software integration
Learning & Growth	Leading employee satisfaction	Employee satisfaction rating	3 on 5-point scale	Performance compensation link

---

SERVICE INDUSTRY IN FOCUS

In addition to evaluating its operations by office as shown earlier, EBC wishes to evaluate the performance of its two lines of business: Solid Waste and Water/Wastewater (Water/WW). EBC management has prepared the following line of business income statement:

SERVICE AND MERCHANDISING

ENVIRONMENTAL BUSINESS CONSULTANTS, LLC
Line of Business Statement
For the Year Ended December 31

	Solid Waste	Water/WW	Firm Total
Gross sales.	$3,676,000	$470,000	$ 4,146,000
Less reimbursable costs.	(366,350)	(64,650)	(431,000)
Net sales.	$3,309,650	$405,350	$ 3,715,000
Cost of services	(2,256,787)	(390,713)	(2,647,500)
Gross profit on sales.	$1,052,863	$ 14,637	$ 1,067,500
Operating expenses			(556,500)
Operating income.			$ 511,000
Interest revenue			7,500
Income before tax.			$ 518,500

EBC accountants have provided the following analysis of the cost of services, all of which are considered traceable:

Cost of Services

Solid Waste			Water/WW			
Variable	**Fixed**	**Total**	**Variable**	**Fixed**	**Total**	**Firm Total**
$51,600	$2,205,187	$2,256,787	$12,900	$377,813	$390,713	$2,647,500

In addition, EBC has accumulated the following information regarding the operating expenses. Variable costs are shown in red; fixed costs are shown in black.

	A	B	C	D	E	F	G	H	I
1					Operating Expenses Allocation				
2			Solid Waste				Water/WW		
3		Traceable	Common	Total		Traceable	Common	Total	Firm Total
4	**Employee bonuses**	$109,722	$ —	$109,722		$16,278	$ —	$16,278	$126,000
5	**Proposal preparation**	31,400	—	31,400		7,600	—	7,600	39,000
6	Trade shows	—	3,000	3,000		—	1,000	1,000	4,000
7	Advertising	—	4,000	4,000		—	1,000	1,000	5,000
8	Employee CE expenses	24,943	—	24,943		2,057	—	2,057	27,000
9	Other general admin. expenses	—	306,849	306,849		—	48,651	48,651	355,500
10		$166,065	$313,849	$479,914		$25,935	$50,651	$76,586	$556,500

Required

1. Prepare a line of business contribution margin statement for EBC (similar to **Exhibit 10-11**) that extends the line of business operating results through line of business contribution to common expenses.

2. Comment on the operating results for each line of business. What should EBC management do with regard to the Water/WW business based on these results?

Solution

1.

SOLUTION 1	Service Industry in Focus		

ENVIRONMENTAL BUSINESS CONSULTANTS, LLC
Line of Business Statement
For the Year Ended December 31

	Solid Waste	Water/WW	Firm Total
Gross sales.	$3,676,000	$470,000	$4,146,000
Less reimbursable costs.	(366,350)	(64,650)	(431,000)
Net sales.	$3,309,650	$405,350	$3,715,000
Traceable variable costs	(192,722)*	(36,778)*	(229,500)
Contribution margin.	$3,116,928	$368,572	$3,485,500
Traceable fixed costs	(2,230,130)**	(379,870)**	(2,610,000)
Line of business contribution	$ 886,798	$ (11,298)	$ 875,500
Common operating expenses.			(364,500)***
Interest revenue			7,500
Income before tax.			$ 518,500

*Solid Waste: $51,600 + $109,722 + $31,400 = $192,722
Water/WW: $12,900 + $16,278 + $7,600 = $36,778

**Solid Waste: $2,205,187 + $24,943 = $2,230,130
Water/WW: $377,813 + $2,057 = $379,870

*** $313,849 + $50,651 = $364,500

2. The Water/WW line of business has a net loss at the line of business contribution level. It is not covering its own traceable operating costs, let alone contributing to the firm's common operating expenses. EBC management has several possible courses of action to consider:

   a.   Determine whether revenues can be increased through higher fees for the service provided. An increase of just over 2.4% (11,298/470,000) would eliminate the loss.

   b.   Carefully review the classification of expenses as cost of service and traceable operating expenses. Even a minor misclassification of an expense could make a difference in the reported results.

   c.   Consider whether some of the Water/WW traceable expenses could be reduced or eliminated. For example, given these results, perhaps Water/WW employees should not be receiving bonuses.

   d.   Consider whether the Water/WW line of business should be spun off or eliminated. This is a major decision with significant implications for EBC and its owners and employees. It may be that the Water/WW line of business provides cross-selling opportunities for the Solid Waste line of business that would have a greater impact on income before tax if eliminated.

DATA ANALYTICS   Humana uses Microsoft Power BI to gain insights into customer health

Data Analytics

Microsoft is probably best known for its Windows operating system and its Office suite of products; however, Microsoft also produces a leading business intelligence program named Power BI. **Humana** health insurance uses Power BI to learn how social determinants, such as the environments in which people live, work, and play, and health-related social needs affect its customers. Humana combines data from multiple sources to develop a more complete picture of its customers. The resulting data visualizations are easy to access and provide insights during a rapidly changing environment. The ability to understand large amounts of data in a short period of time proved invaluable as Covid-19 presented new challenges. As Dr. Andrew Renda, Associate Vice President of Population Health Strategy at Humana stated, "Humana needed to understand new data and make some key decisions about how to respond. Having access to Power BI tools to very quickly build dashboards to visualize all that information and update it in real time was absolutely critical to both forming our strategy and executing on it."

APPENDIX 10A: Transfer Pricing

LO6 **Determine** the proper transfer price to maximize company profit with and without excess productive capacity.

eLecture

MBC

DOMESTIC TRANSFER PRICING

Management of a large, complex company usually divides the business into a number of segments. A segment is a logical portion of a business, such as a division or department. When a segment is established as a profit center, the segment's manager is responsible for revenue generation as well as cost and expense control. If the profit center receives products or services from another profit center within the same business or provides products or services to another profit center within the same business, the two profit center managers must agree on a transfer price for the product or service. The **transfer price** is the price that the selling profit center will charge the buying profit center for the product or service provided.

Objectives for Transfer Pricing

Two objectives should be met when establishing transfer prices. First, the transfer price of the product or service transferred should allow both the selling and the buying divisions to make a reasonable gross profit. Second, the contribution margin of the entire business should be maximized.

Reasonable Gross Profit

Assume that John Deere Waterloo Works has two operating divisions: the Drivetrain Operations division and the Tractor, Cab, and Assembly Operations division. Top management has decided that the Drivetrain Operations division should sell a particular component to the Tractor, Cab, and Assembly Operations division, which will incorporate the component into the 6170R tractor that it manufactures and sells for $150,000 per unit. The per-unit product costs incurred in this process are the following:

	Drivetrain Operations Division	Tractor, Cab, and Assembly Operations Division
Direct material	$6,250	$62,250
Direct labor	1,500	27,750
Variable overhead	1,000	17,000
Fixed overhead	1,250	17,850
Transfer price of component	?	

A negotiated transfer price below market price can be justified. Expenses may be less when intercompany sales are made, or volume may be large enough to justify quantity discounts.

BUSINESS SITUATION 1:   Assume that the transfer price is established as $10,000, the total absorption product cost of the component in the Drivetrain Operations division ($6,250 + $1,500 + $1,000 + $1,250 = $10,000). The resulting gross profit per unit for the two divisions would be calculated as follows:

	Drivetrain Operations Division	Tractor, Cab, and Assembly Operations Division
Revenue:		
Transfer price	$10,000	
Sales price		$150,000
Cost:		
Transfer price		$10,000
Direct material	$6,250	62,250
Direct labor	1,500	27,750
Variable overhead	1,000	17,000
Fixed overhead	1,250	17,850
	10,000	$134,850
Gross profit per unit	$ —	$ 15,150

BUSINESS SITUATION 2:   Assume that the transfer price is established as $12,000, the price that the Drivetrain Operations division would receive from an outside customer and the cost that the Tractor, Cab, and Assembly Operations division would incur from an outside supplier. The resulting gross profit per unit for the two divisions would be calculated as follows:

	Drivetrain Operations Division	Tractor, Cab, and Assembly Operations Division
Revenue:		
Transfer price	$12,000	
Sales price		$150,000
Cost:		
Transfer price		$12,000
Direct material.	$6,250	62,250
Direct labor	1,500	27,750
Variable overhead	1,000	17,000
Fixed overhead	1,250	17,850
	10,000	$136,850
Gross profit per unit	$ 2,000	$ 13,150

In situation 1, the Tractor, Cab, and Assembly Operations division generates a 10.1% gross profit ($15,150/$150,000 = 0.101), and the Drivetrain Operations division generates no gross profit. In situation 2, the Drivetrain Operations division generates a gross profit of $2,000 and the Tractor, Cab, and Assembly division generates a gross profit of $13,150. Situation 1 illustrates a full absorption product cost transfer price, and situation 2 illustrates a market price transfer price. In both situations, total John Deere gross profit per 6170R is $15,150.

Situation 2 meets the first objective—the transfer price of the product or service transferred should allow both the selling and buying divisions to make a reasonable gross profit. In general, a transfer price based on market price, not absorption product cost, will satisfy the objective of reasonable gross profits for both the selling and the buying profit centers or divisions.

Maximize Contribution Margin

The second objective—that the contribution margin of the entire business should be maximized—can be met by identifying a proper minimum transfer price and allowing the manager of the buying profit center to decide whether to buy from the selling profit center or from an outside supplier. As shown in **Exhibit 10A-1**, assume the Drivetrain Operations division of John Deere is currently manufacturing and selling only component A to outside customers for $7,500 per unit.

EXHIBIT 10A-1   **Transfer Pricing Decisions**

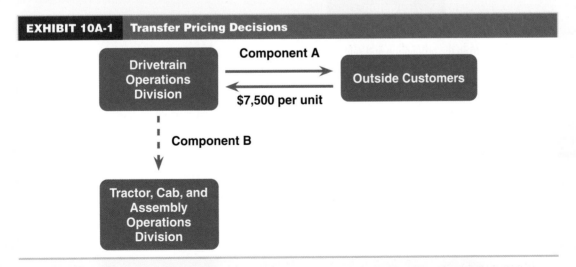

The Tractor, Cab, and Assembly Operations division has proposed that the Drivetrain Operations division begin manufacturing and selling 2,000 units of component B per year to the Tractor, Cab, and Assembly Operations division. The formula for the minimum transfer price for component B is the following:

Product B minimum transfer price	=	Variable cost of product B, per unit	+	Contribution margin lost from not selling product A, per unit of product B

Next we will apply these objectives of transfer pricing to two situations: one in which the supplier does not have any excess capacity and one in which the supplier does have excess capacity.

No Excess Capacity

Assume the Drivetrain Operations division has no excess manufacturing capacity. Therefore, if the Drivetrain Operations division produces component B for the Tractor, Cab, and Assembly Operations division, the Drivetrain Operations division will have to reduce its production and sale of component A to outside customers. Assume that 5,000 fewer units of component A will have to be produced and sold to allow the manufacture of 2,000 units of component B.

The minimum transfer price that the Drivetrain Operations division is willing to accept is one that maintains the contribution margin of the Drivetrain Operations division at its current level. The formula given earlier will generate a transfer price that would allow this to happen. Assume that the variable cost per unit of component A is $5,000, and its selling price is $7,500. The variable cost per unit of component B is $8,750. The total contribution margin that would be given up on 5,000 units of component A is $12,500,000 (5,000 units × [$7,500 2 $5,000]). Using the formula, the minimum transfer price for component B is $15,000 ($8,750 + [$12,500,000/2,000 units of B]) (see **Exhibit 10A-2**).

EXHIBIT 10A-2   Transfer Pricing Decisions, No Excess Capacity

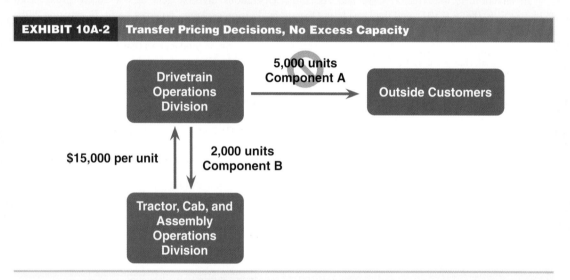

The switch from the production and sale of 5,000 units of component A to 2,000 units of component B would not affect total fixed costs, would create new variable costs of $8,750 per unit, and would eliminate $12,500,000 of contribution margin. The $15,000 transfer price would reimburse the Drivetrain Operations division for the additional variable costs and the lost contribution margin. As a result, the Drivetrain Operations division would generate exactly the same contribution margin whether it produced and sold component A or component B.

TAKEAWAY 10.5	Concept ➡	Method ➡	Assessment
	How do transfer prices between domestic divisions of a company affect the company's overall profit?	Division managers negotiate the transfer price to be paid and received for transactions between the two divisions.	Because the transfer price represents a cost to the buying division and a revenue to the selling division in the same amount, total company profits are unaffected by the transfer price.

With the transfer price set at $15,000, the Tractor, Cab, and Assembly Operations division is in a position to make a decision that will maximize its contribution margin and the contribution margin of the entire business. Assume that the Tractor, Cab, and Assembly Operations division adds $107,000 of variable cost in addition to the costs of the Drivetrain Operations division and then sells the end product for $150,000. If the Tractor, Cab, and Assembly Operations division can only buy component B from an outside supplier for a price greater than $15,000, then it will choose to buy component B from the Drivetrain Operations division. However, if the product division can buy component B from an outside supplier for a price less than $15,000, then it will choose to buy the component from the outside supplier (see **Exhibit 10A-3**). In either case, the contribution margin of the company as a whole has been maximized.

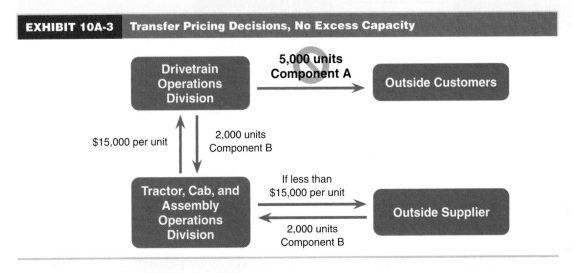

To illustrate, let us assume two situations:
(1) the outside supplier's price is $16,000; and,
(2) the outside supplier's price is $14,000.

BUSINESS SITUATION 1:   **Exhibit 10A-4** shows the calculation of the contribution margin for the first situation. If the Tractor, Cab, and Assembly Operations division purchases component B from the Drivetrain Operations division at a per-unit transfer price of $15,000, the Drivetrain Operations division would earn a contribution margin of $12,500,000 and the Tractor, Cab, and Assembly Operations division would earn a contribution margin of $56,000,000 on the sale of the 6170R to its customers, for a total contribution margin of $68,500,000.

Situation 1: Alternative 1: Buy from Drivetrain Operations Division

5,000 units
Component A

Drivetrain Operations Division → Outside Customers

$15,000 per unit   2,000 units Component B

Drivetrain Operations Division Contribution Margin

(Unit Price	–	Unit VC)	×	# of Units	=	$CM
$15,000		$8,750		2,000		$12,500,000

Total Contribution Margin = $68,500,000

Tractor, Cab, and Assembly Operations Division

Tractor, Cab, and Assembly Operations Division Contribution Margin

(Unit Price	–	Comp. B	–	Other VC)	×	# of Units	=	$CM
$150,000		$15,000		$107,000		2,000		$56,000,000

However, **Exhibit 10A-5** shows the calculation of the contribution margin if the Tractor, Cab, and Assembly Operations division purchases component B from outside suppliers at a price of $16,000 per unit. This would allow the Drivetrain Operations division to continue to sell component A to its outside customers at a contribution margin of $12,500,000. The Tractor, Cab, and Assembly Operations division would earn a contribution margin of $54,000,000 on the sale of the 6170R, for a total contribution margin of $66,500,000.

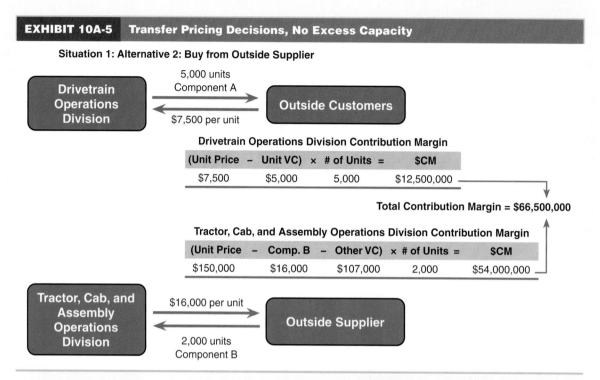

EXHIBIT 10A-5   Transfer Pricing Decisions, No Excess Capacity

Situation 1: Alternative 2: Buy from Outside Supplier

Drivetrain Operations Division Contribution Margin

(Unit Price	–	Unit VC)	×	# of Units	=	$CM
$7,500		$5,000		5,000		$12,500,000

Total Contribution Margin = $66,500,000

Tractor, Cab, and Assembly Operations Division Contribution Margin

(Unit Price	–	Comp. B	–	Other VC)	×	# of Units	=	$CM
$150,000		$16,000		$107,000		2,000		$54,000,000

A careful study of **Exhibits 10A-4** and **10A-5** shows that John Deere will earn $2,000,000 more in contribution margin by purchasing component B from the Drivetrain Operations division.

BUSINESS SITUATION 2: **Exhibit 10A-6** shows the calculation of the contribution margin for the second situation. If the Tractor, Cab, and Assembly Operations division purchases component B from the Drivetrain Operations division at a per-unit transfer price of $15,000, the Drivetrain Operations division would earn a contribution margin of $12,500,000, and the Tractor, Cab, and Assembly Operations division would earn a contribution margin of $56,000,000 on the sale of the 6170R to its customers, for a total contribution margin of $68,500,000. This is exactly the same as the first situation.

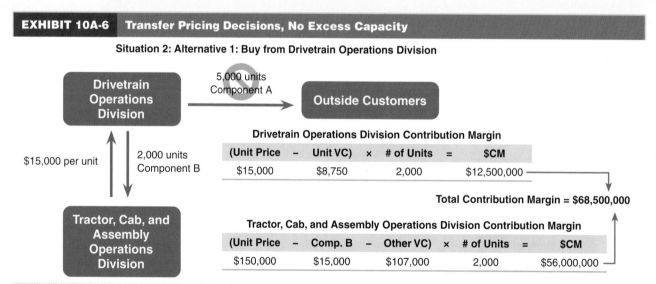

EXHIBIT 10A-6   Transfer Pricing Decisions, No Excess Capacity

Situation 2: Alternative 1: Buy from Drivetrain Operations Division

Drivetrain Operations Division Contribution Margin

(Unit Price	–	Unit VC)	×	# of Units	=	$CM
$15,000		$8,750		2,000		$12,500,000

Total Contribution Margin = $68,500,000

Tractor, Cab, and Assembly Operations Division Contribution Margin

(Unit Price	–	Comp. B	–	Other VC)	×	# of Units	=	$CM
$150,000		$15,000		$107,000		2,000		$56,000,000

However, **Exhibit 10A-7** shows the calculation of the contribution margin if the Tractor, Cab, and Assembly Operations division purchases component B from outside suppliers at a price of $14,000 per unit. This would allow the Drivetrain Operations division to continue to sell component A to its outside customers at a contribution margin of $12,500,000. The Tractor, Cab, and Assembly Operations division would earn a contribution margin of $58,000,000 on the sale of the 6170R, for a total contribution margin of $70,500,000.

EXHIBIT 10A-7   **Transfer Pricing Decisions, No Excess Capacity**

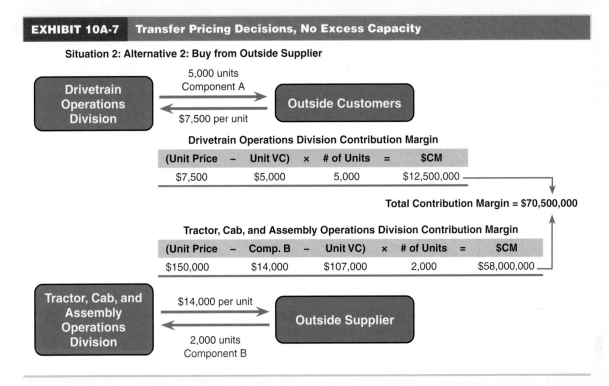

Situation 2: Alternative 2: Buy from Outside Supplier

Drivetrain Operations Division Contribution Margin

(Unit Price	–	Unit VC)	×	# of Units	=	$CM
$7,500		$5,000		5,000		$12,500,000

Total Contribution Margin = $70,500,000

Tractor, Cab, and Assembly Operations Division Contribution Margin

(Unit Price	–	Comp. B	–	Unit VC)	×	# of Units	=	$CM
$150,000		$14,000		$107,000		2,000		$58,000,000

A comparison of **Exhibits 10A-6** and **10A-7** shows that John Deere will earn $2,000,000 more in contribution margin by purchasing component B from the outside supplier.

Excess Capacity

In the John Deere example, we assumed that the Drivetrain Operations division had no excess manufacturing capacity. If we now assume that the Drivetrain Operations division has sufficient capacity to produce and sell the 2,000 units of component B without reducing the production and sale of component A, we will determine a different minimum transfer price. Applying the previous formula for the minimum transfer price, we determine that the minimum transfer price is $8,750 ($8,750 + [$0/2,000]) (see **Exhibit 10A-8**).

EXHIBIT 10A-8   **Transfer Pricing Decisions, Excess Capacity**

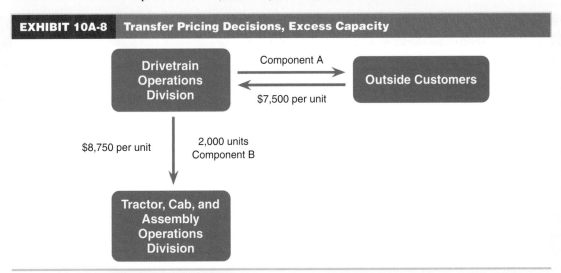

In this case, the production and sale of 2,000 units of component B would not affect total fixed costs, would create new variable costs of $8,750 per unit, and would eliminate no contribution margin from the production and sale of component A. The $8,750 transfer price would reimburse the Drivetrain Operations division for the additional variable costs. As a result, the Drivetrain Operations division would generate exactly the same contribution margin whether or not it produced and sold product B.

Negotiated Transfer Prices

The formula that determines minimum transfer price results in a transfer price that is frequently different from the market value of the product or service being transferred. If the minimum transfer price is greater than the market price, then the buying profit center will buy the product or service from an outside supplier and there will be no need for a transfer price.

If the minimum transfer price is less than the market price, however, then the buying profit center will buy the product or service from the other profit center in the same company. The exact transfer price will be negotiated by the two profit centers. The resulting amount will be greater than or equal to the minimum transfer price and less than or equal to the market price. Any negotiated transfer price within this range will result in the same total contribution margin for the firm. In the John Deere example, with a minimum transfer price of $8,750 and a market price of $15,000, any transfer price from $8,750 to $15,000 results in a contribution margin of $12,500,000 for John Deere.

INTERNATIONAL TRANSFER PRICING

Transfer pricing becomes more complex if one of the segments is in a different country than the other. When products or services are being transferred between segments in different countries, the two objectives stated earlier still apply. However, there also are additional objectives that may conflict with the two previously mentioned. The additional objectives include minimization of international income taxes and tariffs and conformance with international trade agreements. These topics are beyond the scope of this introduction to transfer pricing. Intermediate cost accounting textbooks generally provide a more in-depth coverage of these topics related to international transfer pricing.

YOUR TURN! 10.7

The solution is on page 10-52.

Able Corporation has a manufacturing division that manufactures valves and an assembly division that produces final products. Currently, the manufacturing division has sufficient capacity to manufacture an additional 400 valves. An external market exists for the valves. The market price for one valve is $100, and the cost to sell is $10. The fixed manufacturing cost per valve is $25, and the unit variable cost is $60. The assembly division plans to purchase 400 valves. Management of the assembly division thinks that it should be able to purchase from the manufacturing division at a lower price since both divisions are under common control of the corporation. What is the minimum transfer price between the manufacturing division and the assembly division?

COMPREHENSIVE PROBLEM

LT Roofing Company sells roofing products through two departments: composite and steel. Operating information for the year is as follows:

	Composite Department	Steel Department
Inventory, January 1	$ 90,000	$ 39,000
Inventory, December 31	75,000	45,000
Net sales	1,170,000	720,000
Purchases	726,000	543,000
Purchases returns	42,000	12,000
Purchases discounts	24,000	6,000
Transportation in	27,000	21,000
Traceable department expenses	162,000	84,000

Common operating expenses of the firm were $180,000.

Required

a. Prepare a department income statement showing department contribution to common expenses and net income of the firm. Assume an overall effective income tax rate of 30%. LT uses a periodic inventory system.

b. Calculate the gross profit percentage for each department.

c. If the common expenses were allocated 55% to the composite department and 45% to the steel department, what would the net income be for each department?

Solution

a.

LT ROOFING COMPANY Department Income Statement For the Year Ended December 31			
	Composite Department	**Steel Department**	**Total**
Net sales.	$1,170,000	$720,000	$1,890,000
Cost of goods sold:			
Inventory, January 1	90,000	39,000	129,000
Purchases.	726,000	543,000	1,269,000
Less: Purchases returns	(42,000)	(12,000)	(54,000)
Purchases discounts.	(24,000)	(6,000)	(30,000)
Transportation in	27,000	21,000	48,000
Cost of goods available for sale	$ 777,000	$585,000	$1,362,000
Inventory, December 31	75,000	45,000	120,000
Cost of goods sold	$ 702,000	$540,000	$1,242,000
Gross profit.	$ 468,000	$180,000	$ 648,000
Traceable department expenses	162,000	84,000	246,000
Department margin.	$ 306,000	$ 96,000	$ 402,000
Common expenses.			180,000
Income before tax.			$ 222,000
Income tax expense (30% × $222,000)			66,600
Net income			$ 155,400

b.   Gross profit percentages:
   Composite dept.: $468,000/$1,170,000 = 40%
   Steel dept.: $180,000/$720,000 = 25%

c.

	Composite	Steel	Total
Department margin.	$ 306,000	$ 96,000	$ 402,000
Common expenses*	99,000	81,000	180,000
Income before tax	$ 207,000	$ 15,000	$ 222,000
Income tax expense (30% × $207,000 and 30% × $15,000)	62,100	4,500	66,600
Net income	$ 144,900	$ 10,500	$ 155,400

* 55% × $180,000 = $99,000
  45% × $180,000 = $81,000

SUMMARY OF LEARNING OBJECTIVES

Describe a static budget, illustrate its use, and present an example of a static budget performance report. (p. 10-3)   LO1

■   A static budget is a financial plan developed for a fixed level of operating activity—typically the expected or most likely level.
■   If actual results are compared to a static budget, the variances that result are of little use to management because the budget is often based on a different level of activity than the actual operations.

Introduce the flexible budget and present an example of a flexible budget performance report. Explain how flexible budgeting helps in variance analysis. (p. 10-4)   LO2

■   A flexible budget is a financial plan that makes cost projections for various activity levels within a relevant range.
■   A flexible budget usually divides costs and expenses into variable and fixed costs.
■   A flexible budget performance report compares actual costs to budgeted costs based on the actual production level achieved.

LO3   Present an overview of reporting operations for segments of a business. (p. 10-10)

- Business segments may consist of organizational units (departments or divisions) or areas of economic activity (product lines or markets).
- A business segment may be an investment center (where management is responsible for the efficient use of capital as well as revenues and expenses), a profit center (where management is responsible for both revenues and expenses), or a cost center (where management is responsible for expenses only).
- Internal reporting of segment operations deals primarily with the measurement of operating performance.
- Accounting and reporting by business segment are indispensable to management and very important to external groups such as investors and creditors.

LO4   Construct a segmented contribution margin income statement. Identify the difference between traceable and common fixed costs. (p. 10-13)

- Total amounts from lower-level reports flow to and are included in higher-level reports.
- A performance report is usually prepared for each accounting period for each profit center and each cost center.
- Expenses incurred by, or for the benefit of, one business segment are called traceable expenses. Expenses incurred for more than one business segment are called common expenses.
- Reporting for segments of a firm is typically extended to contribution to common expenses. Only traceable expenses are deducted.

LO5   Compute return on investment, return on sales, return on assets, and residual income for business segments. Discuss the importance of each indicator in assessing a company's performance. (p. 10-20)

- Return on investment is operating income as a percentage of the asset base used to generate that income. It illustrates the amount of profit generated for every dollar invested in the company's asset base.
- The DuPont formula recognizes that ROI can be further divided into two ratios: return on sales and asset utilization.
- Return on sales is operating income as a percentage of sales revenue. It may be interpreted as the number of pennies left over from each dollar of sales after covering all costs.
- Asset utilization is sales divided by the investment in operating assets. It is a measure of a company's efficiency in utilizing its operating assets. It represents the amount of sales per dollar of operating asset.
- Residual income is the income that is left over after the company or division earns some minimum return on investment.
- The balanced scorecard seeks to provide a "balanced view" of company performance by evaluating a company's subunits based on both financial and nonfinancial measures, including financial performance, customer satisfaction, internal business processes, and learning and growth.

LO6   Appendix 10A: Determine the proper transfer price to maximize company profit with and without excess productive capacity. (p. 10-27)

- The transfer price of the product or service transferred should allow both the selling and the buying divisions to make a reasonable gross profit.
- The negotiated transfer price should maximize the contribution margin of the entire business.
- A transfer price based on market price will satisfy the objective of reasonable gross profits for both the selling and the buying profit centers or divisions.

SUMMARY	Concept	Method	Assessment
TAKEAWAY 10.1	How can management evaluate the company's performance relative to the budget?	• Prepare a flexible budget based on actual output achieved. • Compare the actual results to the flexible budget.	• Actual costs for materials, labor, or variable overhead that are less than the flexible budget amounts result in favorable variances. • Actual costs that are greater than the flexible budget amounts result in unfavorable variances.

Concept ⟶	Method ⟶	Assessment	SUMMARY
How might firm management measure and evaluate the performance of its responsibility centers?	• Cost center: cost variances, measuring differences between actual and budgeted costs • Profit center: revenue and cost variances, return on sales, and segment contribution margin • Investment center: return on investment and residual income	• Variances help managers identify explanations for differences between actual and expected performance. • Financial ratios are compared to targets and benchmarks to determine whether the firm met its goals and evaluate its performance relative to its competitors.	TAKEAWAY 10.2
How can a firm hold segment managers responsible for revenues and costs?	Prepare periodic performance reports for each segment.	• Cost center managers are responsible for directly traceable variable and fixed costs. • Profit center managers are responsible for directly traceable revenues and variable and fixed costs. • Investment center managers are responsible for invested capital, revenues, and variable and fixed costs.	TAKEAWAY 10.3
How might an investment center's performance be evaluated?	$\text{Profit margin} = \dfrac{\text{Operating income}}{\text{Sales}}$ $\text{Asset turnover} = \dfrac{\text{Sales}}{\text{Investment in operating assets}}$ $\text{Return on investment} = \dfrac{\text{Operating income}}{\text{Investment in operating assets}}$ $\text{Residual income} = \text{Net operating income} - \left(\text{Average operating assets} \times \text{Required minimum return}\right)$ Balanced scorecard (financial performance, customer satisfaction, internal business practices, learning and growth)	• Calculated ratios can be compared to similar ratios determined over time or to ratios for similar companies in the same industry. • Balanced scorecards include nonfinancial measures that impact a company's performance and provide a more balanced view of performance.	TAKEAWAY 10.4
How do transfer prices between domestic divisions of a company affect the company's overall profit?	Division managers negotiate the transfer price to be paid and received for transactions between the two divisions.	Because the transfer price represents a cost to the buying division and a revenue to the selling division in the same amount, total company profits are unaffected by the transfer price.	TAKEAWAY 10.5

KEY TERMS

Asset turnover (p. 10-21)	Investment center (p. 10-12)	Return on investment (p. 10-20)
Balanced scorecard (p. 10-23)	Performance reports (p. 10-13)	Static budget (p. 10-3)
Common expenses (p. 10-16)	Profit center (p. 10-12)	Traceable expenses (p. 10-16)
Cost center (p. 10-12)	Profit margin (p. 10-21)	Transfer price (p. 10-27)
DuPont formula (p. 10-21)	Residual income (p. 10-22)	Variance (p. 10-4)
Flexible budget (p. 10-4)	Responsibility centers (p. 10-11)	

Assignments with the (MBC) logo in the margin are available in *BusinessCourse*.
See the Preface of the book for details.

SELF-STUDY QUESTIONS

(Answers to Self-Study Questions are at the end of this chapter.)

LO1   1. Mabel's Mobile Pet Grooming Service specializes in providing outrageous dog grooming services, turning the average household pet into a lion, tiger, dinosaur, or other non-canine-looking animal. The average grooming session takes several hours and is done in the back of a specially outfitted van at the client's home. Mabel budgeted $200 per grooming session for the coming year. Additional information for the company includes:

	Budgeted
Sessions.	250
Variable costs.	$31,250
Fixed costs	$20,000

Mabel's static budget income for the year is

a. a profit of $18,750.   *c.* a loss of $1,250.
b. a profit of $1,250.   *d.* a loss $32,500.

LO2   2. The following static budget performance report was prepared for Chip Manufacturing for July.

	Actual Results	Static Budget	Variance
Sales units	100,000	90,000	10,000 F
Sales dollars.	$190,000	$180,000	$10,000 F
Variable costs.	125,000	108,000	17,000 U
Fixed costs	50,000	45,000	5,000 U
Operating income.	$ 15,000	$ 27,000	[$12,000 U]

What is Chip's total flexible budget variance for operating income?

a. $10,000 favorable   *c.* $12,000 unfavorable
b. $10,000 unfavorable   *d.* $20,000 unfavorable

LO3   3. The manager of which of the following segments of a business is responsible for revenue generation as well as for cost and expense control?

a. Cost center   *c.* Profit center
b. Accounting department   *d.* Assembly line

LO4   4. Which of the following is not considered in determining contribution to common expenses?

a. Income taxes   *c.* Traceable expenses
b. Cost of goods sold   *d.* Net sales

LO4   5. In performance reporting (budgeted cost compared to actual cost), which performance report must be prepared first?

a. Division, consisting of five departments   *c.* Department, consisting of four cost centers
b. Region, consisting of three divisions   *d.* Company, consisting of two regions

LO5   6. Which of the following is the correct formula for return on sales (or profit margin)?

a. Income/Investment   *c.* Income/Revenue
b. Investment/Income   *d.* Revenue/Investment

LO5   7. During the past twelve months, the Aaron Corporation had an operating income of $50,000. What is the amount of the investment if the return on investment is 20%?

a. $100,000   *c.* $250,000
b. $200,000   *d.* $500,000

8. Morrison's Plastics Division, a profit center, sells its products to external customers as well as to other internal profit centers. Which one of the following circumstances would justify the Plastics Division selling a product internally to another profit center at a price that is below the market-based transfer price?

LO6
(Appendix 10A)

   a. The buying unit has excess capacity.
   b. The selling unit is operating at full capacity.
   c. Routine sales commissions and collection costs would be avoided.
   d. The profit centers' managers are evaluated on the basis of unit operating income.

QUESTIONS

1. Explain the difference between a static budget and a flexible budget. **LO1, 2**
2. Explain what is meant by a static budget variance and a flexible budget variance. **LO1, 2**
3. "The higher the management level receiving reports, the more detailed the reports should be." Comment. **LO2**
4. Give examples of segments of business firms segmented by (a) organizational unit and (b) economic activity. **LO3**
5. Distinguish between a profit center and a cost center. **LO3**
6. Distinguish between traceable expenses and common expenses. Which are more likely to be controllable at the department level? **LO4**
7. Suggest an allocation basis for each of the following traceable expenses of a departmentalized firm that uses a net income measure to determine the profitability of departments: **LO4**

   a. Janitorial expense
   b. Plant manager's salary
   c. Utilities (heat, light, and air conditioning)
   d. Property taxes

8. What is meant by departmental contribution to common expenses? What advantages does this measure have over net income in measuring departmental performance? **LO4**
9. Department B of the local Top Value Store shows a contribution to common expenses of $22,000 and a net loss of $9,000 (before taxes). The firm believes that discontinuing department B will not affect sales, gross profit, or traceable expenses of other departments. If total common expenses remain unchanged, what effect will discontinuing department B have on the income before taxes of the Top Value Store? **LO4**
10. Department 2 of Kapp Company has a gross profit of $100,000, representing 40% of net departmental sales. Traceable departmental expenses are $75,000. Management believes that an increase of $6,500 in advertising, coupled with a 5% average increase in sales prices, will permit the physical volume of products sold to remain the same next period but will improve the department's contribution to common expenses. If management's expectations are correct, what will be the effect on this contribution? **LO4**
11. Department A of Racine Company has a gross profit of $140,000, representing 35% of net departmental sales. Management believes that an increase of $36,000 in advertising will increase volume of product sold by 20%. Other traceable departmental expenses are $64,000. What effect will this decision have on department A's contribution to common expenses? **LO4**
12. If a firm wishes to compare the performance of two divisions, why might divisional operating income be a poor basis for comparison? **LO5**
13. What is the primary purpose of the balanced scorecard? **LO5**
14. What are the four key performance measures in the balanced scorecard? **LO5**
15. What is the maximum amount that one division should pay to another division of the same company for a component needed in manufacturing its product? **LO6**
(Appendix 10A)

SHORT EXERCISES

SE10-1. Rainbow Inc. recently appointed Margaret Joyce as vice president of finance and asked her to design a new budgeting system. Joyce has changed to a monthly budgeting system by dividing the company's annual budget by twelve. Joyce then prepared monthly budgets for each department and asked the managers to submit monthly reports comparing actual to budget. A sample monthly report for Department A is shown next.

LO1

RAINBOW INC. Monthly Report for Department A			
	Actual	**Budget**	**Variance**
Units	1,000	900	100F
Variable production costs			
Direct material.	$ 2,800	$ 2,700	$ 100U
Direct labor	4,800	4,500	300U
Variable factory overhead	4,250	4,050	200U
Fixed costs			
Depreciation	3,000	2,700	300U
Taxes.	1,000	900	100U
Insurance	1,500	1,350	150U
Administration.	1,100	990	110U
Marketing	1,000	900	100U
Total costs.	$19,450	$18,090	$1,360U

This monthly budget has been imposed from the top and will create behavior problems. All of the following are causes of such problems **except**

a. the use of a flexible budget rather than a fixed budget.
b. top management authoritarian attitude toward the budget process.
c. the inclusion of non-controllable costs such as depreciation.
d. the lack of consideration for factors such as seasonality.

LO2   **SE10-2.**   When compared to static budgets, flexible budgets

a. offer managers a more realistic comparison of budget and actual fixed cost items under their control.
b. provide a better understanding of the capacity variances during the period being evaluated.
c. encourage managers to use less fixed cost items and more variable cost items that are under their control.
d. offer managers a more realistic comparison of budget and actual revenue and cost items under their control.

LO2   **SE10-3.**   Arkin Co.'s controller has prepared a flexible budget for the year just ended, adjusting the original static budget for the unexpected large increase in the volume of sales. Arkin's costs are mostly variable. The controller is pleased to note that both actual revenues and actual costs approximated amounts shown on the flexible budget. If actual revenues and actual costs are compared with amounts shown on the original (static) budget, what variances would arise?

a. Both revenue variances and cost variances would be favorable.
b. Revenue variances would be favorable and cost variances would be unfavorable.
c. Revenue variances would be unfavorable and cost variances would be favorable.
d. Both revenue variances and cost variances would be unfavorable.

LO2   **SE10-4.**   Of the following pairs of variances found in a flexible budget report, which pair is **most likely** to be related?

a. Material price variance and variable overhead efficiency variance.
b. Labor rate variance and variable overhead efficiency variance.
c. Material usage variance and labor efficiency variance.
d. Labor efficiency variance and fixed overhead volume variance.

LO3   **SE10-5.**   Sara Bellows, manager of the telecommunication sales team, has the following department budget.

Billings—long distance	$350,000
Billings—phone card.	75,000
Billings—toll free.	265,000

Her responsibility center is **best** described as a

a. cost center.
b. revenue center.
c. profit center.
d. investment center.

SE10-6. A company's year-end selected financial data is shown below.

	Year 2	Year 1
Current assets	$250,000	$175,000
Total assets	600,000	500,000
Total liabilities	300,000	225,000
Net sales	200,000	150,000
Net income	75,000	60,000

The company's rate of return on average assets and rate of return on average equity for Year 2 are:

a. 12% and 22%, respectively.   *c.* 14% and 26%, respectively.

b. 13% and 25%, respectively.   *d.* 36% and 25%, respectively.

SE10-7. Snug-fit, a maker of bowling gloves, is investigating the possibility of liberalizing its credit policy. Currently, payment is made on a cash-on-delivery basis. Under a new program, sales would increase by $80,000. The company has a gross profit margin of 40%. The estimated bad debt loss rate on the incremental sales would be 6%. Ignoring the cost of money, what would be the return on sales before taxes for the new sales?

a. 34.0%.   *b.* 36.2%.   *c.* 40.0%.   *d.* 42.5%.

SE10-8. A company had $5 million in sales, $3 million in cost of goods sold, and $1 million in selling and administrative expenses during the last fiscal year. If the company's income tax rate was 25%, what was the company's gross profit margin percentage?

a. 20%.   *b.* 30%.   *c.* 40%.   *d.* 50%.

SE10-9. The assets of Moreland Corporation are presented below.

	January 1	December 31
Cash	$ 48,000	$ 62,000
Marketable securities	42,000	35,000
Accounts receivable	68,000	47,000
Inventory	125,000	138,000
Plant & equipment (net of accumulated depreciation)	325,000	424,000

For the year just ended, Moreland had net income of $96,000 on $900,000 of sales. Moreland's total asset turnover ratio is: (Hint: Use average total assets.)

a. 1.27.   *b.* 1.37.   *c.* 1.48.   *d.* 1.50.

SE10-10. The Robo Division, a decentralized division of GMT Industries, has been approached to submit a bid for a potential project for the RSP Company. Robo Division has been informed by RSP that they will not consider bids over $8,000,000. Robo Division purchases its materials from the Cross Division of GMT Industries. There would be no additional fixed costs for either the Robo or the Cross Divisions. Information regarding this project is as follows.

	Cross Division	Robo Division
Variable Costs	$1,500,000	$4,800,000
Transfer Price	3,700,000	—

If Robo Division submits a bid for $8,000,000, the amount of contribution margin recognized by the Robo Division and GMT Industries, respectively, is:

a. $(500,000) and $(2,000,000).   *c.* $(500,000) and $1,700,000.

b. $3,200,000 and $(500,000).   *d.* $3,200,000 and $1,700.000.

DATA ANALYTICS, DATA VISUALIZATION, AND EXCEL ACTIVITIES

Data Analytics, Data Visualization, and Excel Activities are available in myBusinessCourse. These assignments develop Excel, Tableau, and Data Analytics skills, which will enhance students' career readiness. These exercises are assignable and auto graded by MBC. For an overview of data analytics, see the appendix at the end of this book.

EXERCISES—SET A

LO1, 2

E10-1A. **Static and Flexible Budgets** Graham Corporation used the following data to evaluate its current operating system. The company sells items for $10 each and used a budgeted selling price of $10 per unit.

	Actual	Budgeted
Units sold	400,000 units	430,000 units
Variable costs	$1,250,000	$1,500,000
Fixed costs	$1,500,000	$1,290,000

a. Prepare the actual income statement, flexible budget, and static budget.
b. What is the static-budget variance of revenues?
c. What is the flexible budget variance for variable costs?
d. What is the flexible budget variance for fixed costs?

LO2

E10-2A. **Using Flexible Budgets** The following summary data are from a performance report for Sterling Company for May, during which 9,600 units were produced. The budget reflects the company's normal capacity of 10,000 units.

	Actual Costs (9,600 Units)	Budget (10,000 Units)	Variances
Direct material	$136,800	$140,000	[$3,200 F]
Direct labor	277,200	280,000	[2,800 F]
Variable overhead	98,400	96,000	2,400 U
Fixed overhead	72,400	72,000	400 U
Total	$584,800	$588,000	[$3,200 F]

a. What is the general implication of the performance report? Why might Sterling question the significance of the report?
b. Revise the performance report using flexible budgeting, and comment on the general implication of the revised report.

LO4

E10-3A. **Assigning Traceable Fixed Expenses** Selected data for Miller Company, which operates three departments, follow:

	Department A	Department B	Department C
Inventory	$ 80,000	$288,000	$112,000
Equipment (average cost)	$720,000	$432,000	$288,000
Payroll	$405,000	$360,000	$135,000
Square feet of floor space	18,000	9,000	3,000

During the year, the company's fixed expenses included the following:

Depreciation on equipment	$140,000
Real estate taxes	48,000
Personal property taxes (on inventory and equipment)	28,800
Personnel department expenses	225,000

Assume that the property tax rate is the same for both inventory and equipment. Using the most causally related bases, prepare a schedule assigning the fixed expenses to the three departments. *Hint:* Not all fixed expenses are traceable to the three departments. One of these fixed costs should be considered a common cost and not traceable to the departments.

LO5

E10-4A. **Return on Investment and Residual Income** Johnson Company has two sources of funds: long-term debt and equity capital. Johnson Company has profit centers in the following locations with the following net incomes and total assets:

	Net Income	Assets
Las Vegas..	$ 960,000	$ 4,000,000
Dallas	$1,200,000	$ 9,600,000
Tampa...	$2,280,000	$12,000,000

a. Calculate ROI for each profit center and rank them from highest to lowest based on ROI.

b. Calculate residual income for each profit center based on a desired ROI of 12% and rank them from highest to lowest based on residual income.

EXERCISES—SET B

E10-1B. **Using Flexible Budgets** The following summary data are from a performance report for Hyland Company for June, during which 9,600 units were produced. The budget reflects the company's normal capacity of 10,000 units.

LO2

	Actual Costs (9,600 Units)	Budget (10,000 Units)	Variances
Direct material	$102,600	$105,000	[$2,400 F]
Direct labor...............................	207,900	210,000	[2,100 F]
Variable overhead........................	73,800	72,000	1,800 U
Fixed overhead...........................	54,300	54,000	300 U
Total	$438,600	$441,000	[$2,400 F]

a. What is the general implication of the performance report? Why might Hyland question the significance of the report?

b. Revise the performance report using flexible budgeting and comment on the general implication of the revised report.

E10-2B. **Assigning Traceable Fixed Expenses** Selected data for Colony Company, which operates three departments, follow:

LO4

	Department A	Department B	Department C
Inventory................................	$ 40,000	$144,000	$ 56,000
Equipment (average cost).................	$360,000	$216,000	$144,000
Payroll..................................	$607,500	$540,000	$202,500
Square feet of floor space	27,000	13,500	4,500

During the year, the company's fixed expenses included the following:

Depreciation on equipment...	$ 90,000
Real estate taxes	112,500
Personal property taxes (on inventory and equipment)	14,400
Personnel department expenses	337,500

Assume that the property tax rate is the same for both inventory and equipment. Using the most causally related bases, prepare a schedule assigning the fixed expenses to the three departments. *Hint:* Not all fixed expenses are traceable to the three departments. One of these fixed costs should be considered a common cost and not traceable to the departments.

E10-3B. **Return on Investment and Residual Income** The Emergency Medical Services Company has two divisions that operate independently of one another. The financial data for the year 20X5 reported the following results:

LO5

SERVICE AND MERCHANDISING

	North	South
Sales...	$3,000,000	$2,500,000
Operating income...	750,000	550,000
Taxable income...	650,000	375,000
Investment	5,000,000	4,400,000

The company's desired rate of return is 15%. Income is defined as operating income.

a.   What are the respective return-on-investment ratios for the North and South divisions?

b.   What are the respective residual incomes for the North and South divisions?

c.   Which division has the better return on investment and which division has the better residual income figure?

LO5   E10-4B.   Evaluating Investment Centers Terry Enterprises, Inc., has two divisions: the Foods division and the Clothes division. Historically, Terry has used the division's ROI as the performance measure for the bonus determinations. Terry Foods division has gross total assets of $1,000,000, accumulated depreciation of $350,000, current liabilities of $250,000, and sales of $2,000,000. The operating income for Foods is $200,000. Clothes division has gross total assets of $5,000,000, accumulated depreciation of $2,100,000, current liabilities of $1,500,000, and sales of $8,000,000. The operating income for Clothes is $750,000.

Required

Use the DuPont formula to compute ROI for each division and for Terry Enterprises as a whole. Use operating income and gross total assets as the measures of income and investment. *Hint:* Calculate each of the ROIs for Terry Enterprises to three decimal places.

PROBLEMS—SET A

LO2   P10-1A.   Flexible Budget Application The polishing department of Taylor Manufacturing Company operated during April with the following manufacturing overhead cost budget based on 4,000 hours of monthly productive capacity:

TAYLOR MANUFACTURING COMPANY Polishing Department Overhead Budget (4,000 Hours) for the Month of April		
Variable costs:		
Factory supplies	$100,000	
Indirect labor	152,000	
Utilities (usage charge)	68,000	
Patent royalties on secret process	296,000	
Total variable overhead		$ 616,000
Fixed costs:		
Supervisory salaries	$160,000	
Depreciation on factory equipment	144,000	
Factory taxes	48,000	
Factory insurance	32,000	
Utilities (base charge)	80,000	
Total fixed overhead		$ 464,000
Total manufacturing overhead		$1,080,000

The polishing department was operated for 4,600 hours during April and incurred the following manufacturing overhead costs:

Factory supplies	$ 97,520
Indirect labor	136,160
Utilities (usage factor)	82,800
Utilities (base factor)	96,000
Patent royalties	280,416
Supervisory salaries	168,000
Depreciation on factory equipment	144,000
Factory taxes	56,000
Factory insurance	32,000
Total manufacturing overhead incurred	$1,092,896

Required

Using a flexible budgeting approach, prepare a performance report for the polishing department for April, comparing actual overhead costs with budgeted overhead costs for 4,600 hours. Separate overhead costs into variable and fixed components and show the amounts of any variances between actual and budgeted amounts.

P10-2A. **Departmental Income Statement** Elgin Flooring Company sells floor coverings through two departments: carpeting and hard covering (tile and linoleum). Operating information for the year appears below.

LO4

	Carpeting Department	Hard Covering Department
Inventory, January 1	$ 60,000	$ 26,000
Inventory, December 31	50,000	30,000
Net sales	500,000	800,000
Purchases	300,000	560,000
Purchases returns	28,000	8,000
Purchases discounts	16,000	4,000
Transportation in	18,000	14,000
Traceable departmental expenses	108,000	56,000

Common operating expenses of the firm were $225,000.

Required

a. Prepare a departmental income statement showing departmental contribution to common expenses and net income of the firm. Assume an overall effective income tax rate of 20%. Elgin uses a periodic inventory system.

b. Calculate the gross profit percentage for each department.

c. If the common expenses were allocated 40% to the carpeting department and 60% to the hard covering department, what would the net income be for each department?

P10-3A. **Departmental Income Statement** The following information was obtained from the ledger of Woodfield Candies, Inc.:

LO4

WOODFIELD CANDIES, INC, Trial Balance December 31		
	Debit	Credit
Cash	$ 42,000	
Accounts receivable (net)	156,000	
Inventory, December 31	180,000	
Equipment and fixtures (net)	540,000	
Accounts payable		$ 108,000
Common stock		450,000
Retained earnings		180,000
Revenue—department X		840,000
Revenue—department Y		360,000
Cost of goods sold—department X	420,000	
Cost of goods sold—department Y	216,000	
Sales salaries expense	192,000	
Advertising expense	42,000	
Insurance expense	24,000	
Uncollectible accounts expense	9,000	
Occupancy expense	36,000	
Office and other administrative expense	81,000	
	$1,938,000	$1,938,000

Woodfield analyzes its operating expenses at the end of each period in order to prepare an income statement that will exhibit departmental contribution to common expenses. From payroll records, advertising copy, and other records, the following tabulation was obtained:

| | Traceable Expense | | Common Expense |
	Dept. X	Dept. Y	
Sales salaries expense.	$147,000	$45,000	
Advertising expense	18,000	6,000	$18,000
Insurance expense	15,000	9,000	
Uncollectible accounts expense	6,000	3,000	
Occupancy expense			36,000
Office and other administrative expense	12,000	9,000	60,000

Required

Prepare a departmental income statement for Woodfield Candies, Inc., showing departmental contribution to common expenses, assuming an overall income tax rate of 35%.

LO4

SERVICE AND
MERCHANDISING

MBC

P10-4A.   Departmental Contribution to Common Expenses Certain operating information is shown below for Palmer Department Store:

	Department A	Department B	All Other Departments
Sales.	$600,000	$900,000	$2,100,000
Traceable expenses	105,000	165,000	600,000
Common expenses.	90,000	120,000	300,000
Gross profit percentage	30%	40%	50%

The managers are disappointed with the operating results of department A. They do not believe that competition will permit raising prices; however, they believe that spending $21,000 more for promoting this department's products will increase the physical volume of products sold by 20%.

An alternative is to discontinue department A and use the space to expand department B. It is believed that department B's physical volume of products sold can thus be increased 37.5%. Special sales personnel are needed, however, and department B's traceable expenses would increase by $90,000. Neither alternative would appreciably affect the total common departmental expense.

Required

a. Calculate the contribution now being made to common expenses by department A, by department B, and by the combination of other departments.

b. Which of the two alternatives should management choose: increase promotional outlays for department A or discontinue department A and expand department B? Support your answer with calculations.

LO5

MBC

P10-5A.   Return on Investment and Residual Income For many years, Miner Industries has manufactured prefabricated garden sheds where the sheds are constructed in sections to be assembled on customers' property. The company expanded into the pre-fabricated shed market when it acquired V-Shed Company. V-Shed pre-cuts various types of lumber into the appropriate lengths, packages them, and ships the product to customers' for assembly. Miner decided to maintain V-Shed's separate identity and, thus, established the V-Shed Division as an investment center of Miner.

Miner uses return on *average* investment (ROI) as a performance measure, with the investment defined as "operating assets employed." All investments in operating assets are expected to earn a minimum return of 12% before income taxes. V-Shed's ROI has ranged from 15% to 18% since it was acquired.

V-Shed's operating statement for the year just ended is presented below. The division's "operating assets employed" were $5,250,000 at the end of the year, a 5% increase over the balance at the end of the previous year.

V-Shed Division Operating Statement For the Year Ended December 31 ($000 omitted)		
Sales revenue.		$10,000
Cost of goods sold		6,500
Gross profit		$ 3,500
Operating expenses		
Administrative	$1,200	
Selling.	1,500	2,700
Income from operations before income taxes.		$ 800

Required

Calculate the following performance measures for the year just ended for the V-Shed Division of Miner Industries:

a.   Return on *average* investment in operating assets employed (ROI).

b.   Residual income calculated on the basis of *average* operating assets employed.

P10-6A.   **Return on Investment and Residual Income**   Skyview Company has two divisions: Residential Skylights and Automotive Sunroofs. The manager of the Residential Skylights Division is evaluated based on return on investment (ROI). The manager of the Automotive Sunroofs Division is evaluated based on residual income. The required return is 12% and the return on investment has been 16% for the two divisions. Each manager is currently considering a project with the following projections (in $000s):   **LO5**

	Residential Skylights	Automotive Sunroofs
Projected operating income	$350	$560
Investment in operating assets.	$2,500	$4,000

Required

a.   What is the Residential Skylights' ROI?

b.   What is Automotive Sunroofs' residual income?

c.   According to the current evaluation system for managers, which manager(s) would have incentive to undertake the project?

P10-7A.   **Transfer Price**   Sell Division makes part JS13 with the following characteristics: **LO6** (Appendix 10A)

Production capacity	15,000 units
Selling price of JS13 to outside customers.	$40 per unit
Variable cost per unit	$21
Fixed cost per unit	$5
Total fixed costs	$75,000

Buy Division, another division of the same company, wants to purchase 5,000 units of part OC53 each period from Sell Division. Parts JS13 and OC53 have the same variable cost per unit for Sell Division. Producing Part OC53 will not change Sell Division's total fixed costs. Buy Division is now purchasing Part OC53 from an outside supplier at a price of $29 each. Hence, Buy Division won't pay more than $29 to Sell Division for the same product.

     Suppose that Sell Division has ample idle capacity to handle all of Buy Division's needs for Part OC53 without any increase in fixed costs and without cutting into current sales to outside customers for Part JS13.

Required

If Sell Division refuses to accept the $29 price to produce and sell Part OC53 to Buy Division, what will be the impact on the company as a whole?

PROBLEMS—SET B

LO2 **P10-1B.** **Flexible Budget Application** The cutting department of Liberty Manufacturing Company operated

during September with the following manufacturing overhead cost budget based on 5,000 hours of monthly productive capacity:

LIBERTY MANUFACTURING COMPANY Cutting Department Overhead Budget (5,000 Hours) for the Month of September		
Variable costs:		
Factory supplies	$ 48,000	
Indirect labor	72,000	
Utilities (usage charge)	36,000	
Patent royalties on secret process	144,000	
Total variable overhead		$300,000
Fixed costs:		
Supervisory salaries	$ 96,000	
Depreciation on factory equipment	140,000	
Factory taxes	40,000	
Factory insurance	24,000	
Utilities (base charge)	32,000	
Total fixed overhead		$332,000
Total manufacturing overhead		$632,000

The cutting department was operated for 4,500 hours during September and incurred the following manufacturing overhead costs:

Factory supplies	$ 40,400
Indirect labor	67,200
Utilities (usage factor)	38,100
Utilities (base factor)	32,000
Patent royalties	134,000
Supervisory salaries	96,000
Depreciation on factory equipment	140,000
Factory taxes	43,400
Factory insurance	27,000
Total manufacturing overhead incurred	$618,100

Required
Using a flexible budgeting approach, prepare a performance report for the cutting department for September, comparing actual overhead costs with budgeted overhead costs for 4,500 hours. Separate overhead costs into variable and fixed components and show the amounts of any variances between actual and budgeted amounts.

LO4 **P10-2B.** **Departmental Income Statement** Perkins Appliance & Furniture Company has two departments: appliances and furniture. Operating information for the year appears below.

	Appliance Department	Furniture Department
Inventory, January 1	$ 120,000	$ 90,000
Inventory, December 31	75,000	50,000
Net sales	1,120,000	760,000
Purchases	600,000	500,000
Purchases discounts	8,000	6,000
Transportation in	18,000	16,000
Traceable departmental expenses	199,600	82,000

Common operating expenses of the firm were $180,000.

Required

a. Prepare a departmental income statement showing departmental contribution to common expenses and net income of the firm. Assume an overall effective income tax rate of 25%. Perkins uses a periodic inventory system.

b. Calculate the gross profit percentage for each department.

c. If the common expenses were allocated 60% to the appliance department and 40% to the furniture department, what would the net income be for each department?

P10-3B. Departmental Income Statement The following information was obtained from the ledger of Stillwell Emporium, Inc.:   **LO4**

STILLWELL EMPORIUM, INC. Trial Balance December 31		
	Debit	**Credit**
Cash.	$ 18,000	
Accounts receivable (net).	70,000	
Inventory, December 31	45,000	
Equipment and fixtures (net)	97,000	
Accounts payable.		$ 34,000
Common stock		120,000
Retained earnings		30,000
Sales—department a		360,000
Sales—department b		140,000
Cost of goods sold—department a.	216,000	
Cost of goods sold—department b.	70,000	
Sales salaries expense.	74,000	
Advertising expense.	31,000	
Insurance expense (on merchandise)	10,000	
Uncollectible accounts expense.	3,000	
Occupancy expense.	16,000	
Office and other administrative expense	34,000	
	$684,000	$684,000

Stillwell analyzes its operating expenses at the end of each period in order to prepare an income statement that will exhibit departmental contribution to common expenses. From payroll records, advertising copy, and other records, the following tabulation was obtained:

	Traceable Expense		Common
	Dept. A	**Dept. B**	**Expense**
Sales salaries expense.	$48,000	$20,000	$ 6,000
Advertising expense.	15,000	6,000	10,000
Insurance expense.	8,000	2,000	
Occupancy expense.			16,000
Uncollectible accounts expense	2,000	1,000	
Office and other administrative expense	17,000	9,000	8,000

Required

Prepare a departmental income statement for Stillwell Emporium, Inc., showing departmental contribution to common expenses, assuming an overall income tax rate of 30%.

LO4   **P10-4B.**   **Departmental Contribution to Common Expenses** Certain operating information is shown next for Harris Department Store:

	Department R	Department S	All Other Departments
Sales.	$320,000	$480,000	$1,120,000
Traceable expenses	56,000	88,000	320,000
Common expenses.	48,000	64,000	160,000
Gross profit percentage	30%	40%	50%

The managers are disappointed with the operating results of department R. They do not believe that competition will permit raising prices; however, they believe that spending $10,000 more for promoting this department's products will increase the physical volume of products sold by 20%.

An alternative is to discontinue department R and use the space to expand department S. It is believed that department S's physical volume of products sold can thus be increased 35%. Special sales personnel are needed, however, and department S's traceable expenses would increase by $48,000. Neither alternative would appreciably affect the total common departmental expense.

Required

a.   Calculate the contribution now being made to common expenses by department R, by department S, and by the combination of other departments.

b.   Which of the two alternatives should management choose: increase promotional outlays for department R, or discontinue department R and expand department S? Support your answer with calculations.

LO5   **P10-5B.**   **Return on Investment and Residual Income** Simonsen Structural Engineers provides engineering consulting services to clients engaged in major commercial construction projects. The company expanded into the wastewater treatment market when it acquired Scott Industries. Scott Industries fabricates equipment used in wastewater treatment plants. Simonsen decided to maintain Scott's separate identity and, thus, established the Scott Division as an investment center of Simonsen.

Simonsen uses return on *average* investment (ROI) as a performance measure, with the investment defined as "operating assets employed." All investments in operating assets are expected to earn a minimum return of 18% before income taxes. Scott's ROI has ranged from 18% to 21% since it was acquired.

Scott's operating statement for the year just ended is presented below. The division's "operating assets employed" were $21,000,000 at the end of the year, a 5% increase over the balance at the end of the previous year.

Scott Division Operating Statement For the Year Ended December 31 ($000 omitted)		
Sales revenue.		$25,000
Cost of goods sold		14,000
Gross profit.		$11,000
Operating expenses		
Administrative	$4,000	
Selling.	3,000	7,000
Income from operations before income taxes.		$ 4,000

Required

Calculate the following performance measures for the year just ended for the Scott Division of Simonsen Structural Engineers:

a.   Return on *average* investment in operating assets employed (ROI).

b.   Residual income calculated on the basis of *average* operating assets employed.

P10-6B.   Return on Investment and Residual Income A company has a 10% required rate of return. It is   **LO5**
evaluating the following four mutually exclusive projects as possible investments.

	Estimated Operating Income	Assets
Project A.	$1,750,000	$ 7,000,000
Project B.	1,900,000	9,500,000
Project C.	2,275,000	6,500,000
Project D.	825,000	11,000,000

Required
a.   Calculate each project's ROI.
b.   Calculate each project's residual income.
c.   Using the residual income method, which one of the four projects should the company accept?

P10-7B.   Transfer Price Sell Division makes part JS13 with the following characteristics:

LO6
(Appendix 10A)

Production capacity	15,000 units
Selling price of JS13 to outside customers.	$40 per unit
Variable cost per unit	$21
Fixed cost per unit	$5
Total fixed costs	$75,000

Buy Division, another division of the same company, wants to purchase 5,000 units of part OC53
each period from Sell Division. Parts JS13 and OC53 have the same variable cost per unit for Sell
Division. Producing Part OC53 will not change Sell Division's total fixed costs. Buy Division is now
purchasing Part OC53 from an outside supplier at a price of $29 each. Hence, Buy Division won't
pay more than $29 to Sell Division for the same product.

Suppose that Sell Division is producing at capacity and would have to forego some of its current
sales to outside customers to handle all of Buy Division's needs for Part OC53.

Required
If Sell Division accepts the $29 price to produce and sell Part OC53 to Buy Division, what will be the
impact on the company as a whole?

EXTENDING YOUR KNOWLEDGE

EYK10-1. Business Decision Case The monthly sales volume of Shugart Corporation varies from 7,000 units
to 9,800 units over the course of a year. Management is currently studying anticipated selling expenses along with the related cash resources that will be needed. Which type of budget (flexible or
static) (1) should be used by Shugart in planning, and (2) will provide Shugart the best feedback
in performance reports for comparing planned expenditures with actual amounts? When Shugart's
CEO asks you why it is advantageous to use a flexible budget instead of a static budget, what is one
example you could give him?

EYK10-2. Ethics Case CJ Corporation manufactures steel rebar for use in construction. The accounting staff
is currently preparing next year's budget. Bob Johnson is new to the firm and is interested in learning
how this process occurs. He has lunch with the sales manager and the production manager to discuss
further the planning process. Over the course of lunch, Bob discovers that the sales manager adjusts
sales projections between a flexible amount and a static amount based on which will reflect the
lowest variance from actual results. The production manager does the same for cost estimates. Both
managers' year-end bonus is determined based on how low of a variance is achieved. When Bob asks
about why they adjust their projections between flexible and static budgets, the response is simply
that everyone around here does it.

Required
a.   What do the sales and production managers hope to accomplish by their methods?
b.   How might this backfire and work against them?
c.   Are the actions of the sales and production managers unethical?

ANSWERS TO SELF-STUDY QUESTIONS:

1. c   2. a   3. c   4. a   5. c   6. c   7. c   8. c

YOUR TURN! SOLUTIONS

Solution 10.1

Budgeted returns	750
Actual returns	800
Returns processed variance	[(50) F]

	Actual Results for 800 Returns Processed	Budget Based on 750 Returns	Variances
Revenue	$80,000	$75,000	$ 5,000 F
Variable costs	36,000	37,500	[1,500 F]
Fixed costs	12,500	12,000	500 U
Net income	$31,500	$25,500	[$ 6,000 F]

Solution 10.2

	Actual Results	Flexible Budget	Variance
Sales units	100,000	100,000	
Sales dollars	$190,000	$200,000	[$10,000 U]
Variable costs	125,000	120,000	5,000 U
Fixed costs	50,000	45,000	5,000 U
Operating income	$ 15,000	$ 35,000	[$20,000 U]

Solution 10.3

PACCAR Trucks segment, Parts segment, and Financial Services segment.

Solution 10.4

Revenue	$600,000
Traceable departmental expenses:	
Direct materials	$30,000
Direct labor	25,000
Other traceable expenses	40,000
Department contribution	$505,000
Common expenses	**155,000**
Departmental operating income	$350,000

Solution 10.5
Profit margin:
Current sales = $50,000/0.08 = $625,000 + $150,000 = $775,000 new total sales
New profit margin = ($50,000 + $15,000)/$775,000 = .084 or 8.4%

Asset turnover:
Current investment in assets = $50,000/0.10 = $500,000 + $100,000 = $600,000 new total assets
Current asset turnover = $625,000/$500,000 = 1.25 or 125%
New asset turnover ratio = $775,000/$600,000 = 1.29 or 129%

Return on investment:
New return on investment = ($50,000 + $15,000)/($500,000 + $100,000) = 0.108 or 10.8%

Residual income:
New residual income = ($50,000 + $15,000) − (0.08 × $600,000) = $17,000

Solution 10.6
A CPA firm's balanced scorecard might include some of the following measures:

Financial Performance
Segment margin by practice area (tax, audit, consulting)
Average collection period by practice area
Revenue by partner

Customer Satisfaction
Summary of customer satisfaction survey results
Percentage of repeat customers
Average number of years completing customer tax returns

Internal Business Processes
Ratio of new sales to billings for the period
Ratio of chargeable hours to total available hours by staff level
Ratio of billable hours to hours (actually) charged

Learning and Growth
Average number of annual continuing education hours
Partner-to-staff ratio
Average number of community service hours per staff

Solution 10.7
Because the manufacturing division has adequate capacity to fill the assembly division's needs, it should be willing to establish a transfer price that will cover its variable cost per unit. Because it would not incur any selling cost for the internal transfer, the minimum transfer price would be $60, equal to the variable cost per unit.

Chapter 11

Standard Costing and Variance Analysis

Road Map

LO	Learning Objective	Page	eLecture	Guided Example	Assignments
LO1	Define standard costs and describe their use in standard cost accounting.	11-3	E11-1	YT11.1	SS1, Q1, Q2, Q3, Q4
LO2	Develop an overall understanding of the determination of standard costs for direct materials, direct labor, and variable overhead.	11-5	E11-2	YT11.2	SS2, Q5, Q6, Q7, Q8, Q9, SE1, SE2, E1A, E1B
LO3	Understand and calculate direct materials variances.	11-9	E11-3	YT11.3	SS3, Q10, Q11, SE3, SE4, SE5, E2A, E4A, E5A, E2B, E4B, E5B, P1A, P2A, P3A, P4A, P1B, P2B, P3B, P4B
LO4	Understand and calculate direct labor variances.	11-13	E11-4	YT11.4	Q12, Q13, SE5, SE6, SE7, SE8, E2A, E4A, E5A, E2B, E4B, E5B, P1A, P2A, P3A, P4A, P1B, P2B, P3B, P4B
LO5	Understand and calculate variable overhead variances.	11-16	E11-5	YT11.5	SS4, Q14, SE9, SE10, E3A, E4A, E5A, E3B, E4B, E5B, P1A, P2A, P3A, P4A, P1B, P2B, P3B, P4B
LO6	Present and illustrate the use of standard costs in financial statements.	11-18	E11-6	YT11.6	SS5, Q15, P2A, P2B
LO7	Appendix 11A: Present journal entries associated with standard costs.	11-20	E11-7	YT11.7	Q16, P2A, P3A, P2B, P3B

Boeing is the world's largest aerospace company and a leading manufacturer of commercial jetliners and defense, space, and security systems. Its products include commercial and military aircraft, satellites, weapons, electronic and defense systems, launch systems, and advanced information and communication systems. As the largest American manufacturing exporter, Boeing employs more than 140,000 employees in the U.S. and in more than 65 other countries. Nearly half of the world's fleet of commercial jetliners currently in service (more than 10,000 jets) were made by Boeing. The main commercial jetliner products include the familiar 737, 747, 767, 777, and 787 families of airplanes. New jetliner products include the 787-10 Dreamliner, 737 MAX, and the 777X.

In an industry where safety is a critical concern, the company is under constant scrutiny. Balancing intense regulatory constraints and increasing competition requires a delicate balance in maintaining extremely high quality standards and monitoring costs. This chapter introduces standard costing and variance analysis, tools that are critical for companies like Boeing.

PAST

Chapter 10 discussed methods used to analyze companies' overall performance, including static and flexible budgets, variances between actual activity and budgeted activity, segment reporting, and performance analysis.

PRESENT

Chapter 11 defines standard costs and standard cost variances: direct materials, direct labor, and variable overhead variances.

FUTURE

Chapter 12 introduces capital budgeting and illustrates how capital budgeting is used to make capital budgeting decisions.

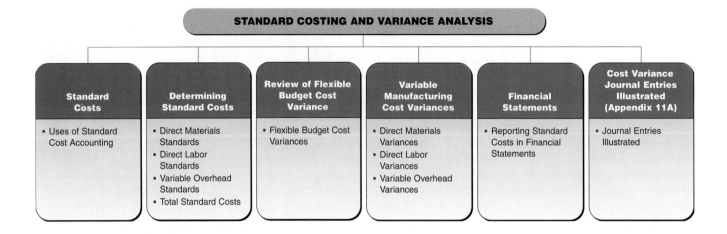

STANDARD COSTS

LO1 **Define** standard costs and **describe** their use in standard cost accounting.

eLecture

MBC

Managers follow a cycle of planning (budgeting) before each accounting period and then following up with performance evaluation after the period ends. An important tool that managers use in both the pre-planning phase and the post-evaluation phase is standard costing. Standard costing consists of setting targets, benchmarks, or goals for performance. In other words, managers define standards or expectations of what they consider to be efficient quantities, costs, and rates they expect to achieve in the production process. After setting these objectives at the beginning of the period (during the budgeting phase), they use them to evaluate performance after the period ends. Specifically, in order to budget expected costs for a period, managers determine how much they "should" spend to produce products or services. Thus, **standard costs** are the costs that should be incurred under normal, efficient operating conditions to produce specific products or to perform specific services. Standards should be attainable through efficient efforts by the typical worker at a task. A complex process, involving engineering specifications, time and motion studies, estimates of supply and demand, and analyses of historical trends, is used to develop standard costs. Standard costs are usually stated per unit of product or service and are useful for a number of purposes, including preparing flexible budgets and master budgets, establishing selling prices, and preparing performance reports.

Standard costs are budgeted costs, the costs that should be incurred during the upcoming year. Obviously, managers use past performance to set standards, but these standards are not intended to simply be a description of past performance, but are intended to be their best projection of *future* performance. In other words, managers want to spend their time looking through the windshield to see where they are going rather than looking at the rearview mirror. Nevertheless, the past is often the best way to project the firm's trajectory for the future. Reasonably attainable levels of efficiency and productivity are used to establish standard costs, so they can serve as a motivating factor and a standard of performance. Typically, standard costs are revised no more frequently than once each year.

Standard costs are usually established prior to the beginning of each year as part of the budgeting process. They should not be updated during the year unless there are major, unexpected changes in vendor costs, wage rates, technology, or product design. One of the important uses of standard costs is to compare them to actual costs to identify significant differences. This comparison process will be most meaningful when the standards used represent the level of efficiency and productivity that was planned during the budgeting process.

Uses of Standard Cost Accounting

Many companies, especially manufacturing firms, adopt **standard cost accounting** for product costs. Although we focus on manufacturing firms in this chapter, it is important to note that standard costing concepts also apply in service companies. The concepts discussed in this chapter relative to labor and overhead apply equally in service and manufacturing environments. When this approach is taken in a manufacturing setting, all inventory accounts—materials, work-in-process, and finished goods—and the cost of goods sold account are stated in terms of standard or predetermined costs rather than actual costs incurred. Specifically, standard costs are used for direct materials, direct labor, variable overhead, and fixed overhead. (Fixed overhead standard costs and variances are beyond the scope of this textbook. We will limit our discussion to variable production costs and assume that in each example, actual fixed overhead costs are equal to standard fixed overhead costs for the period.)

Standard cost accounting can be used with either job order costing or process costing. When standard cost accounting is used, standard costs are carried in the inventory accounts and the cost of goods sold account, and the differences between the standard costs and actual costs are recorded as **variances**. Essentially, variances are the deviations from the company's predetermined standards. Thus, variances serve as an important evaluation tool to help managers assess how realistic their budgeted costs determined at the beginning of the period were. Moreover, they allow managers to pinpoint areas for improvement in future periods. **Exhibit 11-1** illustrates how standard costs are set at the beginning of the period. Managers rely on many sources to determine the costs they "should" incur under efficient operating conditions by consulting with engineers regarding historical and projected production rates, past purchase contracts for materials, historical labor rates, and so forth. These standard costs become the basis for the current-period budget. At the end of the period, managers compare the actual costs to the previously defined standard costs to evaluate performance and to help them identify areas for improvement.

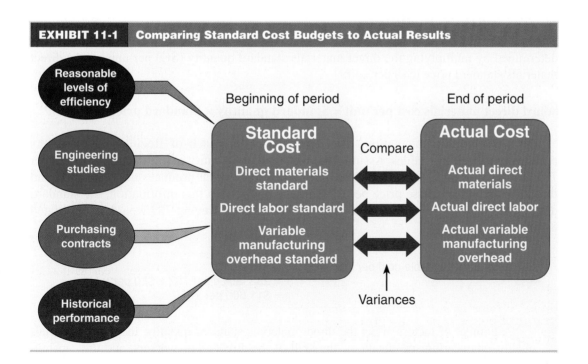

EXHIBIT 11-1 Comparing Standard Cost Budgets to Actual Results

Nelson Electronics Inc. began a new standard cost accounting system after monitoring costs over the past several years. Based on expected production of 8,000 units, Nelson's new standard costing system would have predicted the following costs for the month of January for its main product line:

Direct materials.	$32,000
Direct labor	11,500
Variable overhead.	2,900

Assume that the company achieved the expected output of 8,000 units, but the actual costs for the month were as follows:

Direct materials.	$34,600
Direct labor	11,200
Variable overhead.	2,400

How would you evaluate the company's performance during January?

DETERMINING STANDARD COSTS

LO2 **Develop** an overall understanding of the determination of standard costs for direct materials, direct labor, and variable overhead.

MBC

Hint: The product of direct materials standard price and direct materials standard quantity is part of a static budget.

The development of standard costs per unit of product for all variable inputs requires the use of six components: (1) direct materials standard price, (2) direct materials standard quantity, (3) direct labor standard rate, (4) direct labor standard time allowed, (5) standard variable overhead rate, and (6) variable overhead standard capacity. The cost-related components are developed and updated as part of the budgeting process, and quantity and capacity standards are usually developed as part of the product design and engineering process. We describe the six standard costing components in the following sections.

Direct Materials Standards

The standard direct materials cost to produce one unit of a particular finished product is determined by multiplying the direct materials standard quantity (SQ) per unit by the direct materials standard price (SP) per unit:

Standard direct materials cost per unit = Standard quantity × Standard price = SQ × SP

To illustrate this calculation, consider the fact that each of Boeing's 787 jetliners requires seat-back tray tables. Assume that the standard quantity of seat-back tray tables per 787 is 232. Moreover, assume that Boeing has a supplier that produces the tray tables and that the standard purchase price per tray table is $50. Given this information, the standard direct materials cost to provide seat-back tray tables for a Boeing 787 would be calculated as follows:

Standard tray table cost per 787 airplane = SQ × SP
= 232 tables per 787 × $50 per table
= $11,600 per 787

A number of factors affect the direct materials standard quantity, including materials quality, engineering specifications, the skill of the direct labor workers, and the capabilities of the equipment used to process the materials. Factors affecting the direct materials standard price include the quality of the materials, its availability, and discounts for volume purchases.

Direct Labor Standards

The standard cost of direct labor required to produce one unit of a particular product is determined by multiplying the direct labor standard time allowed, usually specified in hours (SH), by the direct labor standard wage rate (SR):

Standard direct labor cost per unit = Standard hours × Standard wage rate = SH × SR

Continuing the Boeing illustration, assume that the standard amount of direct labor needed to install the seat-back tray tables is 8 hours per 787 and that the standard wage rate for direct labor is \$30 per direct labor hour. The resulting standard direct labor cost per 787 is \$240:

Standard direct labor cost per 787 = SH × SR
= 8 direct labor hours per 787 × \$30 per direct labor hour
= \$240 per 787

The direct labor standard wage rate represents the expected weighted average of labor rates for all levels of workers who undertake direct labor tasks on the product. The rates for the various levels of workers are set by the company or prescribed by labor contract. Direct labor standard times are based primarily on prior employee performance and current time and motion studies. Moreover, these wage rates include all compensation components guaranteed to employees (such as health insurance, payroll taxes, retirement plans, etc.).

Variable Overhead Standards

The standard cost of variable overhead needed to manufacture one unit of a particular product is determined by multiplying the variable overhead standard capacity (SC) by the standard (or predetermined) variable overhead application rate (SR):

$$\text{Standard variable overhead cost per unit} = \text{Variable overhead standard capacity} \times \text{Variable overhead application rate} = \text{SC} \times \text{SR}$$

Traditionally we separate overhead costs into fixed and variable components. This is necessary because fixed costs hold constant within all production levels within our relevant range. Only the variable component fluctuates in response to changes in volume. Therefore, our variable overhead application rate (SR) is the variable portion of the predetermined overhead application rate that was explained in the discussion of job order costing in **Chapter 3**. Recall that the basis for determining the rate can be direct labor hours, direct labor dollars, machine hours, or some other overhead application base. The basis selected should be the best common measure of variable overhead capacity utilized during production.

The variable overhead standard capacity (SC) should be stated in the same terms as the rate (SR). For instance, if the basis for the variable overhead application rate is direct labor hours, then the variable overhead standard capacity allowed will be the number of direct labor hours expected to produce one unit. This will also typically be the same application base used to apply the overhead application rate to production.

In the Boeing illustration, assume that Boeing allocates variable overhead based on direct labor hours and that the standard variable overhead application rate (SR) is calculated to be $50 per direct labor hour and that the variable overhead standard capacity (SC) for installing the seat-back tray tables is 8 direct labor hours per 787 (i.e., the same as the direct labor standard time or SH allowed). The resulting standard variable overhead cost per 787 associated with the tray installation is calculated as follows:

$$\begin{aligned} \text{Standard variable overhead cost per 787} &= \text{SC} \times \text{SR} \\ &= 8 \text{ Direct labor hours per 787} \times \$50 \text{ per direct labor hour} \\ &= \$400 \text{ per 787} \end{aligned}$$

A.K.A. The standard variable overhead rate is also known as the predetermined variable overhead rate.

The standard variable overhead rate is based on the expected level of operations. Because a wide variety of cost items is included in variable overhead, many different factors affect the rate. The variable overhead standard capacity is influenced by such factors as prior employee performance, prior machine performance, and current time and motion studies.

TAKEAWAY 11.1	Concept ➤	Method ➤	Assessment
	Management needs to understand and utilize standard costs and variances.	Establishing standards helps managers track actual results and compare them to standards.	The process of comparing actual to budgeted results guides management to better understand factors that cause cost fluctuations.

Total Standard Costs

Exhibit 11-2 summarizes the relationships described so far. Most firms that use standard costs prepare a summary of the standard product costs for each product they produce.

EXHIBIT 11-2	Standard Cost Summary

Standard direct materials cost per unit...	=	SQ × SP
Standard direct labor cost per unit	=	SH × SR
Standard variable overhead cost per unit.	=	SC × SR

Where: SQ = Standard Quantity
SP = Standard Price
SH = Standard Hours
SR = Standard Rate
SC = Standard Capacity

Based on the preceding concepts, Boeing's standard cost summary for seat-back tray tables in a 787 would appear as in **Exhibit 11-3**.

EXHIBIT 11-3	Standard Cost Summary

BOEING 787
Seat-Back Tray Tables

Direct materials............................	(232 tables × $50 per table) =	$11,600
Direct labor...............................	(8 DLH × $30 per DLH) =	240
Variable overhead..........................	(8 DLH × $50 per DLH) =	400
Total standard product cost per 787..		$12,240

Where: DLH = Direct Labor Hours

Standard costs can also used in determining product cost variances. The remaining sections of this chapter deal with the calculation and use of product cost variances.

ACCOUNTING IN PRACTICE   **Use of Standard Costs in Setting Selling Prices**

Standard costs of products are an important consideration in setting selling prices but are certainly not the only, or even the most important, consideration. Prices of competitors' products and prices of substitute products must also be considered when determining product selling prices.

REVIEW OF FLEXIBLE BUDGET COST VARIANCE

Standard costs are extremely helpful in budgeting prior to the start of a fiscal period. Moreover, when standards are used to determine a flexible budget, they can also be very useful in evaluating performance at the end of a period. Even in well-managed companies with carefully established and currently maintained cost standards, actual costs will differ from standard costs. The differences, often called *variances*, should be analyzed for indications of their cause so that appropriate action may be taken to prevent them in future periods.

We first review the concept of flexible budget variances introduced in Chapter 10 and then illustrate the calculation of these variances based on the production data for an important Fezzari product. Suppose that during June of the current year, Fezzari Bicycles produced 100 Fore CR2 road bikes for which it incurred the following actual costs. (Assume no beginning or ending work-in-process inventories.)

Direct materials:	
Frame	$33,600
Build kit	31,500
Direct labor:	
Assembly	15,000
Quality control and packaging	5,000
Variable overhead	1,525
Total actual variable production costs	$86,625

Exhibit 11-4 compares the actual costs with the flexible budget (using standard unit costs) to produce 100 bikes and calculates the differences, or variances, for each cost category. We multiply the standard costs by the actual quantity of 100 bikes produced in June. Note that both favorable and unfavorable variances exist and that the overall net variance of $7,315 is unfavorable. While calculating the direct materials, direct labor, and variable overhead flexible budget variances is an important first step, the individual total variances do not provide very much actionable direction for managers. In order to initiate corrective action, management must analyze the variance for each cost element further to determine the underlying causal factors. For example, **Exhibit 11-4** depicts an unfavorable total direct labor variance of $2,250. The current level of variance analysis does not provide an indication of what is actually causing the variance. Did Fezzari pay its workers a higher wage rate than the standard or did the workers exceed the number of standard direct labor hours allowed to manufacture the 100 bikes? Either circumstance individually or a combination of both circumstances would have resulted in an unfavorable direct labor flexible budget variance. The good news is that we have a very simple tool that allows us to further analyze the total flexible budget variances of each of the cost elements to determine the underlying causal factors.

EXHIBIT 11-4	Comparison of Standard and Actual Costs		

FEZZARI PERFORMANCE BICYCLES
Variance Analysis
June 30

	Actual Costs to Produce 100 Bikes	Flexible Budget to Produce 100 Bikes	Total Flexible Budget Variances	
Direct materials.	$65,100	$60,000	$5,100	Unfavorable*
Direct labor	20,000	17,750	2,250	Unfavorable
Variable overhead. . .	1,525	1,560	(35)	Favorable
Total	$86,625	$79,310	$7,315	Unfavorable

*The total materials variance calculated in the next section is not equal to the difference between the total standard costs and total actual costs because the amount purchased is different from the amount used in production. See the chapter discussion for a detailed explanation.

YOUR TURN! 11.2

The solution is on page 11-36.

MBC

Feagin Company planned to produce 22,000 units of product during the current month. In order to produce this level of output, the standard costing system predicts the use of 88,000 feet of material at a standard rate of $3.00 per foot. The standard costing system would anticipate 33,000 direct labor hours at a standard rate is $7.00 per hour. Finally, the standard (predetermined) variable overhead rate is $2.00 per direct labor hour based on the standard number of direct labor hours for this production level. Assume Feagin achieved the projected output of 22,000 units by incurring the following actual costs for the month:

Direct materials.	$261,000
Direct labor	262,500
Variable overhead.	63,000

Determine Feagin Company's total flexible budget variance for the month.

VARIABLE MANUFACTURING COST VARIANCES

We begin our discussion for analyzing each of the variable manufacturing cost variances by introducing the "fork diagram." The fork diagram helps with (i) understanding how variances work, (ii) remembering how variances are calculated, and (iii) visualizing each type of variance. The great thing about the fork diagram is that even though the names of the inputs may change slightly (e.g., "standard price" for the direct material variance and "standard rate" for the direct labor variance), it can be applied to EACH of the variable manufacturing costs identically. So even though it may appear as though we need to memorize several different "forks," we really only need to memorize the fork one time and then apply it to each of the variable manufacturing cost elements. Analyzing each of the cost elements, direct materials, direct labor, and variable overhead will always involve calculating three items:

1. an actual cost (actual × actual),
2. a split cost (actual × standard), and
3. a standard cost (standard × standard).

Direct Materials Variances

LO3 Understand and calculate direct materials variances.

MBC

Let's start with direct materials as our example. Direct materials variances are often slightly more complicated than the other variable manufacturing cost variances simply because the quantity of materials purchased often differs from the quantity used in production during the period. **Exhibit 11-5** provides our first look at a fork diagram, using the cost element direct materials (assuming the quantity purchased is equal to the quantity used in production).

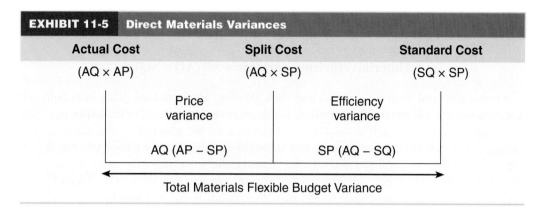

EXHIBIT 11-5 **Direct Materials Variances**

Actual Cost	Split Cost	Standard Cost
(AQ × AP)	(AQ × SP)	(SQ × SP)
	Price variance	Efficiency variance
	AQ (AP – SP)	SP (AQ – SQ)

Total Materials Flexible Budget Variance

Total materials flexible budget variance analysis simply compares actual costs with standard costs. We place the actual materials cost on the left. How much did we actually spend to purchase materials? Actual materials purchased equals the actual quantity (AQ) purchased times the actual price per unit (AP). We place the standard cost of materials allowed for this level of production on the far right of the diagram. How much should we have spent on raw materials at this level of production? As explained previously, standard materials cost equals the standard quantity allowed (SQ) for this level of output times the standard price per unit (SP). The total difference between actual and standard costs (as explained in more detail in **Chapter 10**) is called the total materials flexible budget variance. However, there are two reasons we may spend more or less than our standards would indicate. First, we may pay too much or too little when we purchase the materials. Second, we may not use the materials efficiently in the production process. Hence, it is useful to split the total materials flexible budget variance into its two main components: (1) the **materials price variance** and (2) the **materials efficiency variance**. In order to facilitate this analysis, we place a new number in the middle of the diagram (the split cost), which takes the actual quantity purchased (AQ) from the far left of the diagram and multiplies it by the standard price (SP) from the far right of the diagram. This number represents the standard price we should have spent to buy the actual quantity purchased (AQ × SP).

We calculate the materials price variance by subtracting the standard price we should have paid for the actual quantity purchased from our actual purchase price:

$$\text{Materials price variance} = (AQ \times AP) - (AQ \times SP)$$

Using simple algebra, we can factor out the common element in each number (AQ) and rewrite the materials price variance as follows:

$$\text{Materials price variance} = AQ \, (AP - SP)$$

Written this way, we see that the *cause* of this variance is the difference between the actual price paid to purchase materials compared to the standard price management had budgeted at the beginning of the period. If the actual price exceeds the standard price (i.e., we paid too much), the materials price variance will appear as a positive number. Thus, a positive price variance is "unfavorable" because it would indicate that we paid too much per unit when we purchased the materials. On the other hand, if the materials price variance is a negative number (i.e., we paid less than our standards had predicted), the variance is "favorable."

We calculate the materials efficiency variance by subtracting the standard materials cost (SQ × SP) from what we should have paid for the actual quantity purchased according to our standards (AQ × SP):

$$\text{Materials efficiency variance} = (AQ \times SP) - (SQ \times SP)$$

Again, we can use basic algebra to factor out the common element (SP) to rewrite the materials efficiency variance to better illustrate what causes the variance:

Materials efficiency variance = SP (AQ − SQ)

When expressed this way, it is clear that, holding the standard price constant, what *causes* the variance is the quantity used. If we do not use the materials efficiently in production, we may spend too much or too little. Similar to what we observe for the materials price variance, if the actual quantity exceeds the standard quantity (i.e., we used too much of the material in producing products during this period), the materials efficiency variance will appear as a positive number, suggesting that we did not use our materials efficiently (thus the variance will be "unfavorable"). On the other hand, if we use less than our budgeted standards would dictate (i.e., the materials efficiency variance is negative), we conclude that we used less than we expected (and we would label this negative number as a "favorable" materials efficiency variance).

When the quantity of materials purchased is exactly equal to the quantity used in production, this simple diagram indicates that the total materials flexible budget variance is equal to the sum of the materials price variance and the materials efficiency variance. However, it is common in practice that companies purchase more or less than they actually use in production. To account for these common differences, **Exhibit 11-6** illustrates how we modify the "fork diagram" for materials to better differentiate between these two quantities because the materials price variance is based on the quantity of materials *purchased*, whereas the materials efficiency variance depends on the amount of materials *used* in the production process. In other words, the split cost number (AQ × SP), the actual quantity at the standard price, must actually be shown twice because the price variance is based on the quantity *purchased*, whereas the efficiency variance is calculated using the actual quantity *used* in the production process. It is easy to make mistakes in calculating variances if you don't pay close attention to which quantity you are referring to. The version of the materials "fork diagram" in **Exhibit 11-6** can help you avoid these careless errors. We illustrate these calculations next.

ACCOUNTING IN PRACTICE   **Managing Variances**

Managers may trade off one variance for another. For example, a manager may decide to use a pre-cut material rather than a bulk material. This usually will result in higher cost (unfavorable price variance) and lower quantities (favorable quantity variance) than budgeted.

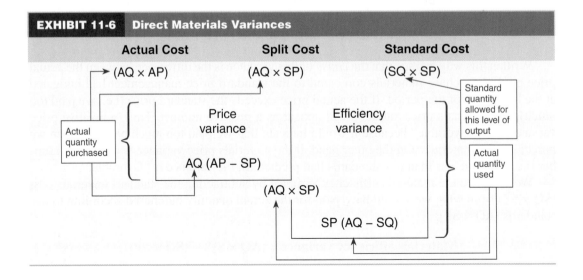

EXHIBIT 11-6   Direct Materials Variances

Fezzari's Direct Materials Variances

We first calculate the materials price variance for frames. Fezzari actually ***purchased*** 105 frames at a price of $320 per frame and ***used*** 101 in production during the month. Assume that the standard price is $325 per frame.

The calculations in **Exhibit 11-7** indicate a favorable price variance for frames of $525. This is calculated as the difference between the actual and budgeted price for frames ($320 − $325) multiplied by the number of frames purchased (105). The variance is favorable because Fezzari spent $5 less per frame than anticipated in the budget. However, these calculations also indicate an unfavorable efficiency variance of $325. This is calculated as the budgeted price per frame ($325) multiplied by the difference between the actual number of frames used and the budgeted number of frames used (101 − 100). Fezzari used one more frame than anticipated for this level of production because one bike was damaged beyond repair during production.

EXHIBIT 11-7 **Direct Materials Variances—Frames**

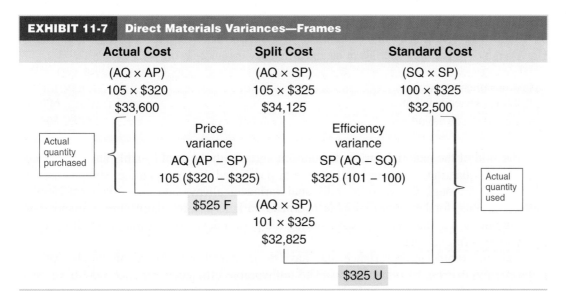

Next, we use the same process to calculate the materials price variance for build kits. Fezzari actually ***purchased*** 105 build kits at a price of $300 per build kit and ***used*** 101 in production during the month. Assume that the standard price is $275 per build kit.

EXHIBIT 11-8 **Direct Materials Variances—Build Kits**

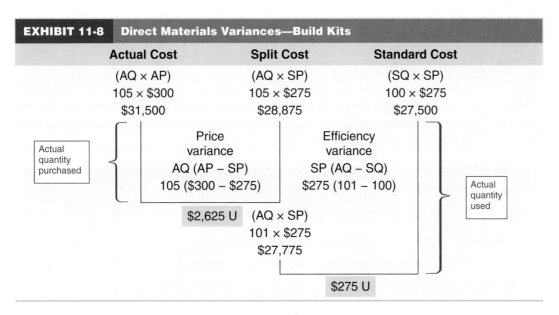

The calculations in **Exhibit 11-8** indicate an unfavorable price variance for build kits of $2,625 (105 build kits × $25 per build kit) because Fezzari spent $25 more per build kit than anticipated in the budget. These calculations also indicate an unfavorable efficiency variance of $275 ($275 × 1 extra build kit). Fezzari used one more build kit than would normally be anticipated for this level of production because one bike was damaged beyond repair during production.

The net materials price variance of $2,100 ($2,625 U – $525 F) is unfavorable because the actual price for build kits was $25 per unit greater than the standard price (even though the price of frames was actually $5 per unit lower than anticipated). Note that for the materials price variance, the quantity represents the number of units purchased, not the number of units manufactured.

The net materials efficiency variance of $600 ($325 U + $275 U) is unfavorable because the actual quantity is greater than the standard quantity. (Because one frame and one build kit were damaged beyond repair, Fezzari used materials for 101 bikes to only produce 100 usable bikes.) Note that for the materials efficiency variance, the quantity represents the number of units issued into production, not the number of units purchased.

Exhibit 11-4 indicates that the total flexible budget variance for direct materials is $5,100 U. However, the sum of the materials price and efficiency variances is only $2,700 U:

Materials price variance	$2,100 U
Materials efficiency variance	600 U
Sum of materials variances	$2,700 U

The sum of the material variances does not agree with the total flexible budget variance because the quantities of frames and build kits purchased do not equal the amounts used in production. Although the sums of individual variances always add up to the total flexible budget variance for labor and variable overhead variances, this relationship does not hold for materials if the quantity purchased during the period does not equal the quantity used in production during the period.

The unfavorable price variance may have been caused by increases in supplier prices, improper purchasing, or other factors. The unfavorable efficiency variance may have been caused by inefficient workers, inferior-quality materials, or other factors.

YOUR TURN! 11.3

The solution is on page 11-36.

GuidedExample

MBC

Feagin Company purchased and used 90,000 feet of material at $2.90 per foot to make 22,000 units of a finished product. The per-unit standard for material is 4 feet @ $3.00 = $12.00. What were the materials price variance and the materials efficiency variance?

Direct Labor Variances

LO4 Understand and **calculate** direct labor variances.

eLecture

MBC

After gaining experience with materials variances, most students find labor variances to be much easier. In order to visualize direct labor variances, we use the same "fork diagram" to calculate an actual cost, a split cost, and a standard cost, as illustrated in **Exhibit 11-9**.

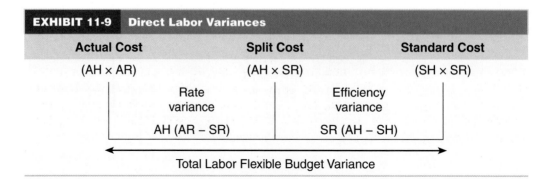

EXHIBIT 11-9 **Direct Labor Variances**

Actual Cost	**Split Cost**	**Standard Cost**
(AH × AR)	(AH × SR)	(SH × SR)
	Rate variance	Efficiency variance
	AH (AR – SR)	SR (AH – SH)

Total Labor Flexible Budget Variance

Similar to materials variances, we place the actual direct labor cost on the left. How much did we pay our labor force? Actual labor costs equal the actual number of hours worked (AH) times the actual wage rate (AR). We place the standard direct labor cost on the far right of the diagram. How much should we have paid our employees to produce this level of output? As explained previously, standard labor costs equal the standard number of hours to produce this many units (SH) times the standard hourly wage rate (SR). The total difference between actual and standard costs (as explained in more detail in Chapter 10) is called the total labor flexible budget variance. However, there are two reasons we may spend more or less than our standards would indicate. First, we may pay our employees too much or too little relative to what we expected when we prepared our budget at the beginning of the period. Second, we may not use our workforce efficiently in producing inventory. Similar to what we observed for materials, it is useful to split the total labor flexible budget variance into its two main components: (1) the **labor rate variance** and (2) the **labor efficiency variance**. In order to facilitate this analysis, we place a split cost number in the middle of the diagram, which takes the actual hours worked (AH) from the far left of the diagram and multiplies it by the standard wage rate (SR) from the far right of the diagram. This number represents the standard amount we should have spent to pay our workforce (AH × SR) to produce this level of output.

We calculate the labor rate variance by subtracting the standard price we should have paid our employees for the actual level of production from our actual labor costs:

$$\textbf{Labor rate variance} = \textbf{(AH} \times \textbf{AR)} - \textbf{(AH} \times \textbf{SR)}$$

Using simple algebra, we can factor out the common element in each number (AH) and rewrite the labor rate variance as follows:

$$\textbf{Labor rate variance} = \textbf{AH (AR} - \textbf{SR)}$$

When the equation is written this way, we see that the *cause* of this variance is the difference between the actual wage rate as compared with the standard wage rate management had forecasted at the beginning of the period. If the actual rate exceeds the standard rate (i.e., we paid employees more than expected), the labor rate variance will appear as a positive number. Thus, a positive price variance is "unfavorable" because we paid more than we had budgeted. On the other hand, if the labor rate variance is a negative number (i.e., we paid less than our standards had predicted), the variance is "favorable."

We calculate the labor efficiency variance by subtracting the standard labor cost (SH × SR) from what we should have paid for the actual hours worked according to our standards (AH × SR):

$$\textbf{Labor efficiency variance} = \textbf{(AH} \times \textbf{SR)} - \textbf{(SH} \times \textbf{SR)}$$

Again, we can use basic algebra to factor out the common element (SR) to rewrite the labor efficiency variance to better illustrate what causes the variance:

$$\textbf{Labor efficiency variance} = \textbf{SR (AH} - \textbf{SH)}$$

When expressed this way, it is clear that when the labor rate is held constant, what causes the variance is the quantity of hours used. If we do not use our employees efficiently in production, we may spend too much or too little. If the actual number of hours worked exceeds the standard number of hours (i.e., we used too many employee hours), the labor efficiency variance will appear as a positive number, suggesting that we did not use our labor force efficiently (thus, the variance will be "unfavorable"). On the other hand, if we use fewer hours than our standards would have predicted (i.e., the labor efficiency variance is negative), we conclude that we were able to use our workers less than we expected (and we would label this negative number as a "favorable" labor efficiency variance).

Fezzari's Direct Labor Variances

We illustrate the calculation of direct labor variances using the Fezzari data presented previously. Specifically, we use the data for the assembly department. Assembly personnel actually worked 750 hours during June at an average rate of $20 per hour. However, the standard number of hours to produce 100 CR2 bikes is 550 hours and the standard wage rate in this department is $25 per hour. Using this information, we can calculate assembly labor variances as illustrated in **Exhibit 11-10**. These calculations indicate a favorable rate variance in the assembly department of $3,750, calculated as 750 hours multiplied by the $5-per-hour difference between the actual and standard rate. The variance is favorable because Fezzari paid an average of $5 less per hour than anticipated in the budget. However, these calculations also indicate an unfavorable efficiency variance of $5,000 ($25 standard rate × 200 extra hours) because Fezzari's assembly crew worked 200 hours more than anticipated for this level of production.

EXHIBIT 11-10	**Assembly Labor Variances**	
Actual Cost	**Split Cost**	**Standard Cost**
(AH × AR)	(AH × SR)	(SH × SR)
750 × $20	750 × $25	550 × $25
$15,000	$18,750	$13,750

Rate variance
AH (AR − SR)
750 ($20 − $25)
$3,750 F

Efficiency variance
SR (AH − SH)
$25 (750 − 550)
$5,000 U

Total Labor Flexible Budget Variance = $1,250 U

Next, **Exhibit 11-11** calculates the labor variances for the quality control (QC) and packaging department. Employees in this department actually worked 250 hours during June at an average rate of $20 per hour. Assume that the standard number of hours at this production level is 200 and the standard wage rate is exactly $20 per hour.

EXHIBIT 11-11	**QC and Packaging Labor Variances**	
Actual Cost	**Split Cost**	**Standard Cost**
(AH × AR)	(AH × SR)	(SH × SR)
250 × $20	250 × $20	200 × $20
$5,000	$5,000	$4,000

Rate variance
AH (AR − SR)
250 ($20 − $20)
$0

Efficiency variance
SR (AH − SH)
$20 (250 − 200)
$1,000 U

Total Labor Flexible Budget Variance = $1,000 U

Because the actual wage rate coincides perfectly with the standard wage rate, there is no labor rate variance. However, these calculations indicate an unfavorable efficiency variance of $1,000 ($20 standard rate × 50 extra hours) because Fezzari's QC and packaging employees worked 50 hours more than anticipated for this level of production.

Combining the results for the assembly and the QC and packaging departments, we calculate the following total variances:

Labor rate variance.	$3,750 F
Labor efficiency variance	6,000 U
Total flexible budget variance for labor	$2,250 U

Notice that the sum of the labor rate and efficiency variances equals the total flexible budget variance for labor in **Exhibit 11-4**.

YOUR TURN! 11.4

The solution is on page 11-36.

> Feagin Company's actual hours worked were 35,000 at a rate of $7.50 per hour to make 22,000 units of a finished product. The per-unit standard for labor is 1.5 hours @ $7.00 = $10.50. What were the labor rate variance and the labor efficiency variance?

Variable Overhead Variances

Variable overhead variances are virtually identical to labor variances. Therefore, we can visualize variable overhead variances using the **Exhibit 11-12** "fork diagram" that is very similar to the direct labor diagram. As explained previously, overhead may be applied to product cost based on any application base that represents the "cost driver." Therefore, the standard cost of variable overhead needed to manufacture one unit of a particular product, shown on the far right of the diagram, is determined by multiplying the variable overhead standard capacity (SC) of that "cost driver" by the standard (or predetermined) variable overhead application rate (SR). Note that variable overhead items are recorded as "actual" debits to the manufacturing overhead account as they occur. There is no "rate" applied to these actual amounts. The "actual" amount spent, shown on the far left of the diagram, is simply the sum of all indirect variable items (such as indirect materials, indirect labor, etc.). For simplicity, assume that a company uses direct labor hours as that cost driver in developing a predetermined variable overhead application rate.

LO5   **Understand** and **calculate** variable overhead variances.

EXHIBIT 11-12	**Variable Overhead Variances**	
Actual Cost	**Split Cost**	**Standard Cost**
	(AH × SR)	(SH × SR)
	Spending variance	Efficiency variance
	(Actual – Split)	SR (AH – SH)

Total Variable Overhead Flexible Budget Variance

In this diagram, the predetermined variable overhead application rate (i.e., the standard rate, SR) is based on direct labor hours. The variable overhead spending variance (i.e., the rate variance) determines whether that predetermined overhead application rate is higher or lower than the standard rate determined by managers in the budgeting process. Similarly, variable overhead efficiency variance is attributable to the use of that overhead application base or "driver." In this diagram, we list the number of direct labor hours as the "cause" of the efficiency variance. Obviously, if some other application base were used to calculate the predetermined overhead application rate, such as machine hours, direct labor dollars, or quality inspections, the efficiency variance would be based on that factor. For example, if we had used the number of inspections as our variable overhead application base, the formula for the variable overhead efficiency variance would be SR (AI – SI), where "AI" would represent the actual number of quality inspections and "SI" would represent the standard number of quality inspections for that production run.

> ### ENVIRONMENTAL, SOCIAL, AND GOVERNANCE   Boeing sets measurable ESG goals
>
> Variance analysis can prove very useful for understanding why actual results deviate from budgeted expectations. Before variance analysis can be performed, the entity must determine its goals. Goal setting is just as important for ESG as it is for financial performance. **Boeing** received the 2020 Sustainability Leadership Award from the National Association of Manufacturers for its innovative efforts to recycle aerospace carbon fiber. Scrap carbon fiber material is treated in a furnace to remove the binding agents yielding a clean material that can then be sold to third parties. Carbon fiber recycling is only one area where Boeing has set environmental goals to be obtained by 2025. Other goals include reducing greenhouse gas emissions by 25%, reducing water use and solid waste to landfills by 20%, reducing energy use by 10%, and reducing hazardous waste at worksites by 5%.

Fezzari's Variable Overhead Variances

Fezzari's variable overhead variances result from paying more or less than planned for items that comprise variable overhead (the **variable overhead spending variance**) and from using more or less than the standard amount of capacity (the **variable overhead efficiency variance**).

> ### ACCOUNTING IN PRACTICE   Standard Capacity
>
> The standard capacity allowed for variable overhead and fixed overhead will be stated in terms of a common measure of plant capacity, such as direct labor hours or machine hours. A different measure may be used for variable overhead and fixed overhead.

Assume that Fezzari incurs actual variable overhead during the month of June of $1,525, comprised of the following items:

Indirect materials	$ 55
Indirect labor	550
Factory utilities	645
Other	275
Total	$1,525

These items would be recorded as debits to the manufacturing overhead account as incurred:

Manufacturing overhead	1,525	
Raw materials inventory		55
Wages payable		550
Utilities payable		645
Other payables (or cash)		275

Also assume that during its budgeting process for the year, Fezzari decided to allocate variable overhead based on estimated labor hours in the QC and packaging department and that the predetermined overhead application rate is $7.80 per hour. Therefore, the variable overhead variances for Fezzari are computed and recorded as shown in **Exhibit 11-13**. The calculations are similar to those for materials and labor, which, like variable overhead, are variable product cost components.

The actual variable overhead costs are less than would be projected, based on the actual number of hours worked in this department multiplied by the predetermined (standard) variable overhead application rate. Therefore, the variable overhead spending variance is $425 favorable. The variable overhead efficiency variance is $390 unfavorable simply because employees in the QC and packaging department worked 50 hours more than was anticipated for this level of projection.

EXHIBIT 11-13	Variable Overhead Variances

Actual Cost	Split Cost	Standard Cost
	(AH × SR)	(SH × SR)
	250 × $7.80	200 × $7.80
$1,525	$1,950	$1,560

Spending variance	Efficiency variance
(Actual – Split)	SR (AH – SH)
$1,525 – $1,950	$7.80 (250 – 200)
$425 F	$390 U

Total Variable Overhead Flexible Budget Variance = $35 F

The total variable overhead variance would be as follows:

Variable overhead spending variance.	$425 F
Variable overhead efficiency variance	390 U
Total variable overhead variance	$ 35 F

Notice that the total variable overhead variance agrees with the amount in **Exhibit 11-4**.

Feagin Company's actual variable overhead was $63,000. Actual hours were 35,000 to make 22,000 finished products. The per-unit standard for variable overhead is 1.5 hours @ $2.00, or $3.00. What were the variable overhead spending variance and the variable overhead efficiency variance?	**YOUR TURN! 11.5** The solution is on page 11-36.

MBC

STANDARD COSTS IN FINANCIAL STATEMENTS

When the standard costs and related variances for direct materials, direct labor, and variable overhead are recorded as previously illustrated, the work-in-process account is debited for each in amounts representing standard quantities and standard prices. All variances—favorable and unfavorable—are carried in separate accounts with appropriate titles. Fezzari records completed production for June in the following entry. (Assume no beginning or ending work-in-process inventories.)

LO6   Present and Illustrate the use of standard costs in financial statements.

MBC

Finished goods inventory (at standard cost)	79,310	
Work-in-process inventory (at standard cost)		79,310
To record completion of June's production of 100 units at a standard variable unit cost of		
$793.10 ($60,000 materials, $17,750 labor, and $1,560 variable overhead).		

As each month's production is sold, the related amounts of standard costs are transferred from Finished Goods Inventory to Cost of Goods Sold.

Standard costs and related variances are usually reported in financial reports intended only for management's use. **Exhibit 11-14** contains a partial income statement that illustrates how variances might appear on interim financial statements for Fezzari's internal use. (Amounts are assumed.)

EXHIBIT 11-14	Summary

FEZZARI PERFORMANCE BICYCLES
Partial Income Statement
For the Month Ended June 30

Sales.	$375,000
Cost of goods sold at standard cost	250,000
Gross profit at standard cost	$125,000
Less: Net unfavorable cost variance.	6,500
Gross profit.	$118,500

> The "net" cost variance is simply the net of all individual materials, labor, and overhead variances.

The total net variance could be broken down into sub-variances or detailed in a schedule of variances accompanying the financial statements.

At year-end, firms commonly close the variance accounts by transferring their balances to Cost of Goods Sold. In effect, this transfer converts Cost of Goods Sold from standard costs to be accurate costs. If large variances exist at year-end and there is evidence that the standards may not be accurate, a firm may be justified in allocating all or part of the variances to Work-in-Process Inventory, Finished Goods Inventory, and Cost of Goods Sold.

YOUR TURN! 11.6	Assume that Paterson Company reports sales of $500,000 and cost of goods sold (based on standard costs) of $460,000 for the year just ended. However, during the year the company also reports the following variances:

The solution is on page 11-36.

MBC

Materials price variance	6,000
Materials efficiency variance	(2,000)
Labor rate variance.	(9,000)
Labor efficiency variance	(1,500)
Variable overhead spending variance.	11,000
Variable overhead efficiency variance	(2,000)

Note that positive numbers denote unfavorable variances. How would Paterson incorporate these variances in the income statement?

SERVICES INDUSTRY IN FOCUS

> SERVICE AND MERCHANDISING

Environmental Business Consultants, Inc. (EBC) has hired several new staff members in the last year and has invested considerable effort in training these new employees in the EBC approach to conducting rate review projects. Due to the unique market in which EBC operates, there are not commercial training conferences or online training materials available to provide the necessary training. Therefore, the training is done primarily on the job by EBC managers, resulting in extra hours over what is typically incurred in completing this type of project. EBC management is interested in estimating the cost of this on-the-job training in terms of "lost billings"—that is, the billing value of the extra hours incurred by both managers and staff as compared with normal budgeted hours. This is equivalent to the labor efficiency variance.

Assume that for the year just ended, EBC completed 25 rate review projects. The following table shows the normal hourly budget for managers and staff on a rate review project. EBC managers billed a total of 1,200 hours and staff billed a total of 3,500 hours on rate review projects during the year. For the year, managers were billed at a standard rate of $200 per hour and staff were billed at a standard rate of $120 per hour.

	Managers	Staff
Budgeted hours per rate review project	40	120

Required:
Determine the total labor efficiency variance for both managers and staff for the year.

Solution

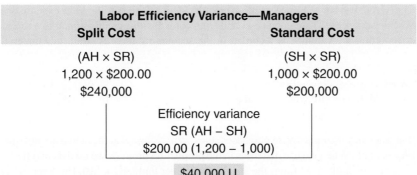

Labor Efficiency Variance—Managers	
Split Cost	**Standard Cost**
(AH × SR)	(SH × SR)
1,200 × $200.00	1,000 × $200.00
$240,000	$200,000

Efficiency variance
SR (AH − SH)
$200.00 (1,200 − 1,000)

$40,000 U

Labor Efficiency Variance—Staff	
Split Cost	**Standard Cost**
(AH × SR)	(SH × SR)
3,500 × $120.00	3,000 × $120.00
$420,000	$360,000

Efficiency variance
SR (AH − SH)
$120.00 (3,500 − 3,000)

$60,000 U

Total Efficiency Variance = $40,000 U + $60,000 U = $100,000 U

DATA ANALYTICS   **Data Analytics helps optimize airplane maintenance**

Data Analytics

Emirates airlines has the largest fleet of Boeing 777 airplanes in the world and decided to sign up for Boeing's specialized maintenance program that combines advanced data analytics with Boeing's engineering expertise. According to the Emirates, "The success from the Optimized Maintenance Program has been immediate." Boeing analyzes the airline's in-service maintenance, business model, retirement plans, and other key items. Boeing combines this research with its data analytics and engineering abilities to recommend proposed changes in the Emirates's maintenance program. Further, Boeing is able to provide projected benefits once the program is completed.

APPENDIX 11A: Cost Variance Journal Entries Illustrated

This appendix illustrates the journal entries used in a standard costing system to record materials, labor, and variable overhead variances based on the Fezzari example used throughout the chapter.

LO7   **Present** journal entries associated with standard costs.

JOURNAL ENTRIES ILLUSTRATED

MBC

The materials price variance is recorded in the accounting system at the time materials are purchased. Although the amount paid to suppliers is always the "actual" invoice price, we enter materials into the raw materials inventory account at the standard price:

Raw materials inventory	(AQ × SP)	
Materials price variance	U	or F
Accounts payable (or cash)		(AQ × AP)

Thus, the credit to Accounts Payable (or Cash) is for the actual amount (AQ × AP), whereas the debit to Raw Materials Inventory is for the standard price to purchase the actual quantity acquired (AQ × SP). We record the difference as the raw materials price variance to allow the manager of the purchasing department to explain the variance at the end of the fiscal period. Note that the materials price variance can either be a debit or a credit. Unfavorable variances (U) are bad news. Hence, they are recorded with a debit (similar to an expense or a loss). On the other hand, favorable variances (F) are good news and are recorded with a credit (similar to a revenue or a gain).

The materials efficiency variance is recorded in the accounting records when raw materials are used in production:

Work-in-process inventory	(SQ × SP)	
Materials efficiency variance	U	or F
Raw materials inventory		(AQ × SP)

We note that when raw materials were purchased, they were recorded at the actual quantity purchased times the standard price per unit. When we use materials in the production process, we take them out of Raw Materials Inventory as the actual quantity used times the standard price per unit (AQ × SP). However, we enter materials into Work-in-Process Inventory completely at standard (SQ × SP). We record the difference as the materials efficiency variance to allow the production manager to explain the variance at the end of the fiscal period. We again note that the materials efficiency variance can either be a debit or a credit. Unfavorable variances (U) are bad news. Hence, they are recorded with a debit (similar to an expense or a loss). On the other hand, favorable variances (F) are good news and are recorded with a credit (similar to a revenue or a gain).

Fezzari's journal entry to record material purchases and the price variance for CR2 road bikes would be as follows (see **Exhibits 11-7** and **11-8**):

Raw materials inventory	63,000	
Materials price variance	2,100	
Accounts payable (or cash)		65,100

Moreover, Fezzari's journal entry to record the materials that are used in production for CR2s would be as follows:

Work-in-process inventory	60,000	
Materials efficiency variance	600	
Raw materials inventory		60,600

The purchasing department's manager can best explain the higher-than-expected prices paid for materials and the production manager would be responsible for explaining the unfavorable materials efficiency variance.

We only record one entry in the accounting records relative to direct labor. As employees work directly on our products (or in providing services), we increase Work-in-Process Inventory and show either a decrease to cash or an increased liability, as follows:

Work-in-process inventory	(SH × SR)	
Labor rate variance	U	or F
Labor efficiency variance	U	or F
Wages payable (or cash)		(AH × AR)

Obviously, our employees won't continue working for us if we don't pay them for their services. Moreover, they are not likely to be happy if we tell them, "We're sorry, but your wage rates are higher than our budget anticipated, so we're only going to pay you the standard wage rate." We have to pay our employees whatever wage rate we contracted with them when we hired them (or when they received their last raise). Hence, the credit to Wages Payable (or Cash) must be for the amount the employees actually earned (AH × AR). However, as explained previously, under a standard costing approach, we record manufacturing costs in Work-in-Process Inventory completely at standard (SH × SR). Thus, the difference between actual and standard costs can be explained by both the labor rate variance and the labor efficiency variance. As explained previously, positive variances are deemed to be "unfavorable" (U) and are recorded with debits, whereas negative variances are deemed to be "favorable" (F) and are recorded with a credit.

The following journal entry records these costs and variances (see **Exhibits 11-11** and **11-11**):

Work-in-process inventory	17,750	
Labor efficiency variance	6,000	
Labor rate variance		3,750
Wages payable (or cash)		20,000

The journal entry charges Work-in-Process Inventory with standard direct labor costs, records the unfavorable labor efficiency variance as a debit and the favorable labor rate variance as a credit, and records the liability for direct labor (or cash) at the amount owed, which is determined using actual hours worked and actual rates paid.

The unfavorable labor efficiency variance might be charged to the production supervisor, who presumably oversees the production teams. The favorable labor rate variance resulted from assigning lower-paid employees to perform the assembly. Other reasons for a favorable labor rate variance include using less overtime or paying decreased labor rates.

Similar to direct labor, we only record one entry in the accounting records relative to the application of variable overhead to units produced. In this example, because we use direct labor hours as the application base in our predetermined variable overhead rate, it would be driven by the actual number of direct labor hours. As employees work directly on our products (or in providing services), we apply more variable overhead to Work-in-Process Inventory and a corresponding decrease to Manufacturing Overhead, as follows:

Work-in-process inventory	(SC × SR)	
Variable overhead spending variance	U	or F
Variable overhead efficiency variance	U	or F
Manufacturing overhead		(AC × AR)

The interpretations of the variable overhead variances are identical to those for the labor variances.

For Fezzari, the general journal entry to record variable overhead costs and variances is as follows (see **Exhibit 11-13**):

Work-in-process inventory	1,560	
Variable overhead efficiency variance	390	
Variable overhead spending variance		425
Manufacturing overhead		1,525

This journal entry assumes that no overhead is applied to Work-in-Process Inventory until the end of the accounting period. When this entry is recorded at period end, all of the efficiency and spending variances are recorded simultaneously. In this example, the "applied overhead" for the entire period is actually $1,950 (250 actual hours worked × 7.80 predetermined overhead rate). If overhead were applied to Work-in-Process during the period as jobs were completed, the applied overhead for each job would be analogous to smaller pieces of the middle number in the fork diagram (i.e., the credit to Manufacturing Overhead), and a portion of the variable overhead efficiency variance would be recorded with each portion of the overhead applied. The entire variable overhead spending variance would be recorded at the end of the period as the over- or under-applied overhead amount written off to Cost of Goods sold.

This journal entry charges Work-in-Process Inventory with standard variable overhead costs. It records the unfavorable variable overhead efficiency variance as a debit and the favorable variable overhead spending variance as a credit.

YOUR TURN! 11.7

The solution is on page 11-37.

D'Adduzio Company planned to produce 11,000 units of finished product during the current month. The company was able to achieve this desired level of production. During the month, D'Adduzio purchased and used 55,000 pounds of material at $5.30 per pound. The per-unit standard for material established by management was 4 pounds @ $5.10 = $20.40. D'Adduzio used 23,000 actual direct labor hours at a rate of $3.00 per hour to make the 11,000 units of a finished product. The company's per-unit labor standard for each unit is 2 hours @ 3.50 = $7.00. Finally, D'Adduzio actually incurred $32,500 in variable overhead costs in producing the 11,000 completed units. D'Adduzio's standard (predetermined) variable overhead rate is $1.50 per direct labor hour based on the standard number of direct labor hours for a particular production level.

1. What were the materials price and efficiency variances, and what journal entries would management make to record these variances?
2. What were the labor rate and efficiency variances, and what journal entry would management make to record these variances?
3. What were the variable overhead spending and efficiency variances, and what journal entry would management make to record these variances?

COMPREHENSIVE PROBLEM

GuidedExample
MBC

Crenshaw Manufacturing, Inc., planned to produce 25,000 units of its only product during the year. The standard cost data for this product are as follows:

	Per Unit
Direct materials (3 lb. @ $2 per lb.)	$ 6
Direct labor (0.5 hr. @ $8 per hr.)	4
Variable overhead (0.5 hr. @ $4 per hr.)	2
Total standard cost per unit	$12

The actual level of production was 24,000 units, with the following actual total costs incurred:

	Total Cost
Direct materials (74,000 lb. @ $1.80)	$133,200
Direct labor (13,000 hr. @ $8.10)	105,300
Variable overhead	50,200
Total actual cost	$288,700

Required

a. Calculate the variances for materials, labor, and variable overhead.
b. Is the difference between total actual cost and total standard cost equal to the sum of all the variances? Why?

Solution to Comprehensive Problem

a.

Materials Variances		
Actual Cost	**Split Cost**	**Standard Cost**
(AQ × AP)	(AQ × SP)	(SQ × SP)
74,000 × $1.80	74,000 × $2.00	72,000 × $2.00
$133,200	$148,000	$144,000

	Price variance		Efficiency variance	
	AQ (AP − SP)		SP (AQ − SQ)	
	74,000 ($1.80 − $2.00)		$2.00 (74,000 − 72,000)	
	$14,800 F		$4,000 U	

Labor Variances		
Actual Cost	**Split Cost**	**Standard Cost**
(AH × AR)	(AH × SR)	(SH × SR)
13,000 × $8.10	13,000 × $8.00	12,000 × $8.00
$105,300	$104,000	$96,000

	Rate variance		Efficiency variance	
	AH (AR − SR)		SR (AH − SH)	
	13,000 ($8.10 − $8.00)		$8.00 (13,000 − 12,000)	
	$1,300 U		$8,000 U	

	Variable Overhead Variances		
Actual Cost	**Split Cost**	**Standard Cost**	
	(AH × SR)	(SH × SR)	
(AH × AR)	(13,000 × $4.00)	(12,000 × $4.00)	
$50,200	$52,000	$48,000	

Spending variance	Efficiency variance
(Actual – Split)	SR (AH – SH)
($50,200 – $52,000)	$4.00 (13,000 –12,000)
$1,800 F	$4,000 U

b.

Total actual cost	$288,700
Total standard cost ($12 X 24,000).	288,000
Total variance	$ 700 U
Materials price variance	$ 14,800 F
Materials quantity variance.	4,000 U
Labor rate variance.	1,300 U
Labor efficiency variance	8,000 U
Variable overhead spending variance.	1,800 F
Variable overhead efficiency variance	4,000 U
Sum of all variances	$ 700 U

In this example, the difference between total actual cost and total standard cost is equal to the sum of all variances. However, this is only true because, in this example, the amount of direct materials *purchased* is equal to the direct materials *used* in production. If this were not the case, the materials price variance plus the materials efficiency variance would not be equal to the total flexible budget variance for materials. Hence, in a broader sense, it is also true that if the amount of direct materials *purchased* had not been equal to the direct materials *used* in production, the difference between total actual costs and total standard costs would not have been equal to the sum of all of the variances. This is a key concept to remember.

SUMMARY OF LEARNING OBJECTIVES

Define standard costs and describe their use in standard cost accounting. (p. 11-3)   **LO1**

- Standard costs represent the costs per unit that should be incurred during the upcoming year. They are established as part of the budgeting process.
- When standard cost accounting is used, all inventory accounts—materials, work-in-process, and finished goods—and the cost of goods sold account are stated in terms of standard costs. Actual costs are accumulated separately.

Develop an overall understanding of the determination of standard costs for direct materials, direct labor, and variable overhead. (p. 11-5)   **LO2**

- Six components are required to develop standard variable product costs:

Direct materials standard price	Direct labor standard time allowed
Direct materials standard quantity	Standard variable overhead rate
Direct labor standard rate	Variable overhead standard capacity

- The standard direct materials cost to produce a unit of a particular finished product is determined by multiplying the direct materials standard quantity per unit by the direct materials standard price per unit.
- The standard cost of direct labor required to produce one unit of a particular product is determined by multiplying the direct labor standard time allowed, usually specified in hours, by the direct labor standard wage rate.
- The standard cost of variable overhead needed to manufacture one unit of a particular product is determined by multiplying the variable overhead standard capacity by the standard (or predetermined) variable overhead application rate.

- A standard cost summary is usually prepared for each product that is manufactured. Standard costs are extremely helpful in budgeting prior to the start of a fiscal period. Moreover, they can also be very useful in evaluating performance at the end of a period.

LO3   Understand and calculate direct materials variances. (p. 11-9)

- We calculate the materials price variance by subtracting the standard price we should have paid for the actual quantity purchased from our actual purchase price.
- We calculate the materials efficiency variance by subtracting the standard materials cost from what we should have paid according to our standards for the actual quantity purchased.
- Each variance can be either favorable or unfavorable.

LO4   Understand and calculate direct labor variances. (p. 11-13)

- We calculate the labor rate variance by subtracting the standard price we should have paid our employees for the actual level of production from our actual labor costs.
- We calculate the labor efficiency variance by subtracting the standard labor cost from what we should have paid according to our standards for the actual hours worked.
- Each variance can be either favorable or unfavorable.

LO5   Understand and calculate variable overhead variances. (p. 11-16)

- The variable overhead "rate" variance (i.e., the spending variance) determines whether the predetermined overhead application rate is higher or lower than the standard rate determined by managers in the budgeting process.
- Similarly, variable overhead efficiency variance is attributable to the use of that overhead application base or "driver."
- Each variance can be either favorable or unfavorable.

LO6   Present and illustrate the use of standard costs in financial statements. (p. 11-18)

- When the standard costs and related variances for direct materials, direct labor, and variable overhead are recorded, the work-in-process account is debited for each in amounts representing standard quantities and standard prices.
- All variances—favorable and unfavorable—are carried in separate accounts with appropriate titles.
- Standard costs are typically used in financial statements for internal use only by management.
- At year-end, firms commonly close the variance accounts by transferring their balances to Cost of Goods Sold.
- If large variances exist at year-end and there is evidence that the standards may not apply, a firm may be justified in allocating all or part of the variances to Work-in-Process Inventory, Finished Goods Inventory, and Cost of Goods Sold.

LO7   Appendix 11A: Present journal entries associated with standard costs. (p. 11-20)

- Illustration of journal entries related to raw materials
- Illustration of journal entries related to direct labor
- Illustration of journal entries related to variable overhead

SUMMARY	Concept ⟶	Method ⟶	Assessment
TAKEAWAY 11.1	Management needs to understand and utilize standard costs and variances.	Establishing standards helps managers track actual results and compare them to standards.	The process of comparing actual to budgeted results guides management to better understand factors that cause cost fluctuations.

KEY TERMS

Labor efficiency variance (p. 11-14)	Materials price variance (p. 11-10)	Variable overhead efficiency variance (p. 11-17)
Labor rate variance (p. 11-14)	Standard cost accounting (p. 11-4)	Variable overhead spending variance (p. 11-17)
Materials efficiency variance (p. 11-10)	Standard costs (p. 11-3)	Variances (p. 11-4)

Assignments with the (MBC) logo in the margin are available in BusinessCourse.
See the Preface of the book for details.

SELF-STUDY QUESTIONS

(Answers to Self-Study Questions are at the end of this chapter.)

1. **When a standard costing system is used, which of the following accounts will be reported at standard costs?**   **LO1**
   a. Accounts payable
   b. Wages payable
   c. Work-in-process inventory
   d. Accounts receivable

2. **In what terms are standard variable overhead application rates (SR) usually stated?**   **LO2**
   a. Per dollar
   b. Per direct labor hour
   c. Per unit of product
   d. Per month

3. **The formula [(Actual Price − Standard Price) × Actual Quantity] can be used to calculate which cost variance?**   **LO3**
   a. Variable overhead volume
   b. Labor efficiency
   c. Materials efficiency
   d. Materials price

4. **Which variance considers production capacity not used?**   **LO5**
   a. Variable overhead efficiency
   b. Labor efficiency
   c. Variable overhead spending
   d. Materials efficiency

5. **The gross profit on the interim income statement of a firm using standard costs is computed as:**   **LO6**
   a. Sales less cost of goods sold at standard
   b. Sales less cost of goods sold at standard plus net unfavorable variances
   c. Sales less cost of goods sold at standard less net unfavorable variances
   d. Sales less cost of goods sold at actual

QUESTIONS

1. What is the difference between budgeted costs and standard costs?   **LO1**

2. When should standard costs be established, and how often should such standards be changed?   **LO1**

3. "Standard costs can be set too high or too low for motivational purposes." Comment.   **LO1**

4. "Total actual cost exactly equals total standard cost, so everything must be okay." Comment.   **LO1**

5. What is standard cost accounting?   **LO2**

6. Define standard costs and describe how they are developed.   **LO2**

7. A finished product requires 2 pounds of materials costing $6 per pound. What is the standard cost of direct materials per unit of product?   **LO2**

8. A finished product requires 20 minutes of direct labor to complete each unit. Factory workers are paid $12 per hour. What is the standard cost of direct labor per unit of product?   **LO2**

9. Assume that the variable overhead rate for the product described in Question 8 is $9 per hour. What is the standard cost of variable overhead per unit of product?   **LO2**

10. Name and briefly describe the two direct materials variances.   **LO3**

11. Garcia Company used 6,300 pounds of direct materials costing $7.80 per pound for a batch of products that should have consumed 6,000 pounds costing $8 per pound. What are the materials variances?   **LO3**

12. Name and briefly describe the two direct labor variances.   **LO4**

13. Wong Lee used 1,200 direct labor hours at an average wage rate of $8.70 to manufacture products that should have used 1,300 direct labor hours at an average wage rate of $8.50 per hour. What are the labor variances?   **LO4**

14. The variable overhead rate is $5 per direct labor hour; 31,000 direct labor hours were used to produce 7,500 units of product. The standard is 4 direct labor hours per unit. Actual, variable overhead cost was $153,000. Determine the variable overhead variances.   **LO5**

15. Briefly explain how standard cost variances are reported on financial statements.   **LO6**

LO7
(Appendix 11A)

16. Who in the firm might be responsible for each of the following variances?
   a. Materials price and efficiency variances
   b. Labor rate and efficiency variances
   c. Variable overhead spending and efficiency variances

SHORT EXERCISES

LO2

SE11-1. Which one of the following statements is correct concerning a flexible budget cost formula? Variable costs are stated

   a. per unit and fixed costs are stated in total.
   b. in total and fixed costs are stated per unit.
   c. in total and fixed costs are stated in total.
   d. per unit and fixed costs are stated per unit.

LO2

SE11-2. Marten Company has a cost-benefit policy to investigate any variance that is greater than $1,000 or 10% of budget, whichever is larger. Actual results for the previous month indicate the following.

	Budget	Actual
Raw materials.	$100,000	$89,000
Direct labor.	50,000	54,000

The company should investigate

   a. neither the materials variance nor the labor variance.
   b. the materials variance only.
   c. the labor variance only.
   d. both the materials variance and the labor variance.

LO3

SE11-3. Frisco Company recently purchased 108,000 units of raw materials for $583,200. Three units of raw materials are budgeted for use in each finished good manufactured, with the raw materials standard set at $16.50 for each completed product. Frisco manufactured 32,700 finished units during the period just ended and used 99,200 units of raw materials. If management is concerned about the timely reporting of variances in an effort to improve cost control and bottom-line performance, the materials purchase price variance should be reported as

   a. $6,050 unfavorable.   *c.* $10,800 unfavorable.
   b. $9,920 favorable.   *d.* $10,800 favorable.

LO3

SE11-4. Micah Corporation purchased 3,800 pounds of raw materials on March 1 at a price of $5.20 per pound to use in production during March. Micah produced 2,000 units during March though the production budget anticipated production of 2,200 units. The company's standards recommend 2 pounds of materials per unit and dictate a standard price of $5.05 per pound. Which of the following is correct with respect to Micah's materials variances for the month of March?

   a. The materials price variance is $570 favorable.
   b. The materials efficiency variance is $1,010 unfavorable.
   c. The materials price variance is $570 unfavorable.
   d. The materials efficiency variance is $3,030 favorable.

LO3, 4

SE11-5. Of the following pairs of variances found in a flexible budget report, which pair is most likely to be related?

   a. Materials price variance and variable overhead efficiency variance.
   b. Labor rate variance and variable overhead efficiency variance.
   c. Materials usage variance and labor efficiency variance.
   d. Labor efficiency variance and fixed overhead volume variance.

LO4

SE11-6. A company budgets to sell 4,000 units of its product. Actual sales are 4,200 units. The product has a standard price of $43. When analyzing its direct labor flexible-budget variance for the period, the company determined that its direct labor efficiency variance was an unfavorable variance of $8,600.

Which one of the following is closest to the actual price for direct labor if the total direct labor flexible-budget variance was an unfavorable variance of $4,000?

a. $39   c. $41
b. $40   d. $42

SE11-7. Randall Company uses standard costing and flexible budgeting and is evaluating its direct labor. The total budget variance can usually be broken down into two other variances identified as the

a. direct labor rate variance and direct labor efficiency variance.
b. direct labor cost variance and direct labor volume variance.
c. direct labor rate variance and direct labor volume variance.
d. direct labor cost variance and direct labor labor efficiency variance.

SE11-8. Caleb manufacturing produced 3,000 units during June even though the company had anticipated producing 2,800 units. The company's employees actually logged 3,200 hours during the month and were paid $8.40 per hour. The company's standard costing system indicates 1 direct labor hour per unit at a standard wage rate of $8.70. Which of the following is incorrect?

a. The labor rate variance is $960 favorable.
b. The labor efficiency variance is $3,480 unfavorable.
c. The labor efficiency variance is $1,740 unfavorable.
d. The actual amount paid to employees for their labor during the month is $26,880.

SE11-9. Lee manufacturing uses a standard cost system with overhead applied based on direct labor hours. The manufacturing budget for the production of 5,000 units for the month of June included 10,000 hours of direct labor at $15 per hour, $150,000. During June, 4,500 units were produced, using 9,600 direct labor hours, incurring $39,360 of variable overhead, and showing a variable overhead efficiency variance of $2,400 unfavorable. The standard variable overhead rate per direct labor hour was

a. $3.85.   c. $4.10.
b. $4.00.   d. $6.00.

SE11-10. James manufacturing produced 3,000 units during June even though the company had anticipated producing 2,800 units. The company's employees actually logged 3,200 hours during the month. The company's standard costing system allocates variable overhead at a rate of $6.00 per direct labor hour. Standards also dictate 1 direct labor hour per unit produced. Assume that James actually incurred $19,500 of variable overhead costs. Which of the following is true?

a. The variable overhead rate variance is $300 favorable.
b. The variable overhead efficiency variance is is $1,400 unfavorable.
c. The variable overhead efficiency variance is $1,000 unfavorable.
d. The variable overhead rate variance is $300 unfavorable.

DATA ANALYTICS, DATA VISUALIZATION, AND EXCEL ACTIVITIES

Data Analytics, Data Visualization, and Excel Activities are available in myBusinessCourse. These assignments develop Excel, Tableau, and Data Analytics skills, which will enhance students' career readiness. These exercises are assignable and auto graded by MBC. For an overview of data analytics, see the appendix at the end of this book.

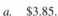

EXERCISES—SET A

E11-1A. Standard Product Costs Deerfield Company manufactures product M in its factory. Production of M requires 2 pounds of material P, costing $4 per pound and 0.5 hour of direct labor costing $10 per hour. The variable overhead rate is $8 per direct labor hour, and the fixed overhead rate is $12 per direct labor hour. What is the standard product cost for product M?

E11-2A. Materials and Labor Variances The following actual and standard cost data for direct materials and direct labor relate to Hadley Company's production of 2,000 units of a product:

	Actual Costs	Standard Costs
Direct materials.	3,900 lb. @ $5.20	4,000 lb. @ $5.10
Direct labor.	6,200 hr. @ $8.40	6,000 hr. @ $8.60

Determine the following variances:

a. Materials price   c. Labor rate
b. Materials efficiency   d. Labor efficiency

LO5   E11-3A. Variable Overhead Variances Smith Tax Company considers 6,000 direct labor hours or 300 tax returns its normal monthly capacity. Its standard variable overhead rate is $50 per direct labor hour. During the current month, $250,400 of variable overhead cost was incurred in working 5,500 direct labor hours to prepare 270 tax returns. Determine the following variances, and indicate whether each is favorable or unfavorable:

a. Variable overhead spending   b. Variable overhead efficiency

LO3, 4, 5   E11-4A. Materials, Labor, and Variable Overhead Variances The following summarized manufacturing data relate to Steffan Corporation's April operations, during which 2,000 finished units of product were produced. Normal monthly capacity is 1,100 direct labor hours.

	Standard Unit Costs	Total Actual Costs
Direct materials:		
Standard (2 lb. @ $9.50/lb).	$19	
Actual (4,200 lb. @ $10.20/lb.)		$42,840
Direct labor:		
Standard (0.5 hr. @ $24/hr.)	12	
Actual (970 hr. @ $23.40/hr.)		22,698
Variable overhead:		
Standard (0.5 hr. @ $6/hr.)	3	
Actual		6,200
Total.	$34	$71,738

Assume that the 4,200 lb. of materials purchased were all used in producing the 2,000 completed units. Determine the materials price and efficiency variances, labor rate and efficiency variances, and variable overhead spending and efficiency variances.

LO3, 4, 5   E11-5A. Working with Variances From the following data, determine the total actual costs incurred for direct materials, direct labor, and variable overhead.

	Standard Costs	Variances
Direct materials.	$120,000	
Price variance.		$3,000 U
Quantity variance		4,000 F
Direct labor.	100,000	
Rate variance		1,400 U
Efficiency variance		1,800 U
Variable overhead.	44,000	
Spending variance		1,000 F
Efficiency variance		600 U

EXERCISES—SET B

LO2   E11-1B. Standard Product Costs Harrison Company manufactures product Q in its factory. Production of Q requires 3 pounds of material T, costing $7 per pound and 2 hours of direct labor, costing $10 per hour. The variable overhead rate is $6 per direct labor hour, and the fixed overhead rate is $9 per direct labor hour. What is the standard product cost for product Q?

E11-2B. Materials and Labor Variances The following actual and standard cost data for direct materials and direct labor relate to Jones Company's production of 2,000 units of a product:

LO3, 4

	Actual Costs	Standard Costs
Direct materials.	4,200 lb. @ $4.90	4,000 lb. @ $5.10
Direct labor	5,800 hr. @ $9.30	6,000 hr. @ $9.50

Determine the following variances:

a. Materials price
b. Materials efficiency
c. Labor rate
d. Labor efficiency

E11-3B. Variable Overhead Variances Dallin Tax Company considers 8,000 direct labor hours or 400 tax returns its normal monthly capacity. Its standard variable overhead rate is $40 per direct labor hour. During the current month, $308,500 of variable overhead cost was incurred in working 7,400 direct labor hours to produce 360 units of product. Determine the following variances, and indicate whether each is favorable or unfavorable:

LO5

a. Variable overhead spending
b. Variable overhead efficiency

E11-4B. Materials, Labor, and Variable Overhead Variances The following summarized manufacturing data relate to Kiosse Corporation's May operations, during which 2,000 finished units of product were produced. Normal monthly capacity is 1,100 direct labor hours.

LO3, 4, 5

	Standard Unit Costs	Total Actual Costs
Direct materials:		
Standard (3 lb. @ $2.00/lb.)	$ 6	
Actual (6,200 lb. @ $2.20/lb.)		$13,640
Direct labor:		
Standard (0.5 hr. @ $14/hr.)	7	
Actual (980 hr. @ $13.70/hr.)		13,426
Variable overhead:		
Standard (0.5 hr. @ $4/hr.)	2	
Actual		4,200
Total.	$15	$31,266

Assume that the 6,200 lb. of materials purchased were all used in producing the 2,000 completed units. Determine the materials price and efficiency variances, labor rate and efficiency variances, and variable overhead spending and efficiency variances.

E11-5B. Working with Variances From the following data, determine the total actual costs incurred for direct materials, direct labor, and variable overhead.

LO3, 4, 5

	Standard Costs	Variances
Direct materials.	$55,000	
Price variance		$1,200 U
Quantity variance		2,200 F
Direct labor	46,000	
Rate variance		500 U
Efficiency variance		800 U
Variable overhead.	18,000	
Spending variance		400 F
Efficiency variance		700 U

PROBLEMS—SET A

P11-1A. Calculate Variances The following summary data relate to the operations of Dobson Company for April, during which 9,000 finished units were produced. Normal monthly capacity was 20,000 direct labor hours.

LO3, 4, 5

	Standard Unit Costs	Total Actual Costs
Direct materials:		
Standard (4 lb. @ $2.20/lb.)	$ 8.80	
Actual (38,000 lb. @ $2.00/lb.)		$ 76,000
Direct labor:		
Standard (2 hr. @ $11.00/hr.)	22.00	
Actual (18,500 hr. @ $11.30/hr.)		209,050
Variable overhead:		
Standard (2 hr. @ $3.00/hr.)	6.00	
Actual		54,900
Total...	$36.80	$339,950

Required

Determine the following variances and indicate whether each is favorable or unfavorable:

a. Materials price and efficiency variances
b. Labor rate and efficiency variances
c. Variable overhead spending and efficiency variances

LO3, 4, 5, 6, 7

P11-2A. Variances, Entries, and Income Statement A summary of Martindale Company's manufacturing variance report for May follows:

	Total Standard Costs (9,200 units)	Total Actual Costs (9,200 units)	Variances
Direct materials.....................	$ 38,640	$ 41,760	$3,120 U
Direct labor........................	193,200	191,760	1,440 F
Variable overhead...................	22,080	23,230	1,150 U
Fixed overhead.....................	9,660	9,660	
Total	$263,580	$266,410	$2,830 U

Standard materials cost per unit of product is 0.5 pounds at $8.40 per pound, and standard direct labor cost is 1.5 hours at $14.00 per hour. The total actual materials cost represents 4,800 pounds purchased at $8.70 per pound. Total actual labor cost represents 14,100 hours at $13.60 per hour. According to standards, variable overhead rate is applied at $1.60 per direct labor hour (based on a normal capacity of 15,000 direct labor hours or 10,000 units of product). Assume that all fixed overhead is applied to work-in-progress inventory.

Required

a. Calculate variances for materials price and efficiency, labor rate and efficiency, and variable overhead spending and efficiency.
b. Prepare general journal entries to record standard costs, actual costs, and related variances for materials, labor, and overhead.
c. Prepare journal entries to record the transfer of all completed units to Finished Goods Inventory and the subsequent sale of 8,400 units on account at $54 each. (Assume no beginning finished goods inventory.)
d. Prepare a partial income statement (through gross profit on sales) showing gross profit based on standard costs, the incorporation of variances, and gross profit based on actual costs.

LO3, 4, 5, 7

P11-3A. Variances and Journal Entries Jacobs Company manufactures a single product and uses a standard costing system. The nature of its product dictates that it be sold in the period it is produced. Thus, no ending work-in-process or finished goods inventories remain at the end of the period. However, raw materials can be stored and are purchased in bulk when prices are favorable. Per-unit standard product costs are materials, $8 (4 pounds); labor, $6 (0.5 hour); and variable overhead, $4 (based on direct labor hours). Budgeted fixed overhead is $54,000.

Jacobs accounts for all inventories and cost of goods sold at standard cost and records each variance in a separate account. The following data relate to May when 17,700 finished units were produced.

Required

a. Assume Jacobs purchased 69,000 pounds of raw materials on account at $2.20 per pound and used 67,000 pounds in May's production, prepare a journal entry to record the purchase of raw materials and a separate journal entry to record the use of raw materials in production. Record these entries using standard costs and include the appropriate materials variances.

b. Assuming employees worked 8,900 direct labor hours at an average hourly rate of $11.70, prepare a journal entry to record actual costs, standard costs, and any labor variances.

c. Assuming Jacobs' actual and applied variable overhead was $74,200 and that budgeted and actual fixed overhead incurred was $54,000, prepare a journal entry to record actual and standard overhead costs and any overhead variances.

P11-4A. Variances, Total Overhead Variances, and Variance Reconciliation Milton Company planned to produce 21,000 units of its only product during the year. Milton established the following standard cost data for this product prior to the beginning of the year:

LO3, 4, 5

	Per Unit
Direct materials (3 lb. @ $5.00 per lb.)	$15.00
Direct labor (2 hr. @ $17.50 per hr.)	35.00
Variable overhead (2 hr. @ $6 per hr.)	12.00
Total standard cost per unit	$62.00

Total budgeted fixed overhead is $400,000.

Assume that Milton (1) actually produced 22,000 units, (2) used 68,000 pounds of direct materials in production, (3) and incurred the following actual total costs:

	Total Cost
Direct materials purchased (70,000 lb. @ 4.80)	$ 336,000
Direct labor (43,000 hr. @ $18.00)	774,000
Variable overhead	262,320
Fixed overhead	400,000
Total actual costs	$1,772,320

Required

a. Calculate the variances for materials, labor, and variable overhead.

b. Does the difference between total actual costs and total standard costs equal the sum of all of the variances? Explain.

PROBLEMS—SET B

P11-1B. Calculate Variances The following summary data relate to the operations of Randolph Company for July, during which 4,500 finished units were produced:

LO3, 4, 5

	Standard Total Unit Costs	Total Actual Costs
Direct materials:		
Standard (0.6 lb. @ $9.00/lb.)	$ 5.40	
Actual (3,000 lb. @ $9.40/lb.)		$ 28,200
Direct labor:		
Standard (0.8 hr. @ $12.80/hr.)	10.24	
Actual (3,800 hr. @ $12.50/hr.)		47,500
Variable overhead:		
Standard (0.8 hr. @ $7.50/hr.)	6.00	
Actual		30,100
Total	$21.64	$105,800

Required

Determine the following variances and indicate whether each is favorable or unfavorable:

a.   Materials price variance and efficiency variance
b.   Labor rate variance and efficiency variance
c.   Variable overhead spending variance and efficiency variance

LO3, 4, 5, 6, 7   **P11-2B. Variances, Entries, and Income Statement** A summary of Flaker Company's manufacturing variance report for June follows.

	Total Standard Costs (7,600 units)	Total Actual Costs (7,600 units)	Variances
Direct materials.	$ 66,880	$ 66,150	$ 730 F
Direct labor.	77,520	81,420	3,900 U
Variable overhead.	33,060	33,000	60 F
Fixed overhead.	102,600	102,600	
Total	$280,060	$283,170	$3,110 U

Standard materials cost per unit of product is 4 pounds at $2.20 per pound, and standard direct labor cost is 0.75 hour at $13.60 per hour. Total actual materials cost represents 31,500 pounds purchased at $2.10 per pound. Total actual labor cost represents 5,900 hours at $13.80 per hour. According to standards, variable overhead rate is applied at $5.80 per direct labor hour (based on a normal capacity of 6,000 direct labor hours or 8,000 units of product). Assume that all fixed overhead is applied to work-in-progress inventory.

Required

a.   Calculate variances for materials price and efficiency, labor rate and efficiency, and variable overhead spending and efficiency.
b.   Prepare general journal entries to record standard costs, actual costs, and related variances for materials, labor, and overhead.
c.   Prepare journal entries to record the transfer of all completed units to Finished Goods Inventory and the subsequent sale of 6,400 units on account at $60 each. (Assume no beginning finished goods inventory.)
d.   Prepare a partial income statement (through gross profit on sales) showing gross profit based on standard costs, the incorporation of variances, and gross profit based on actual costs.

LO3, 4, 5, 7   **P11-3B. Variances and Journal Entries** Kent Company manufactures a single product and uses a standard costing system. The nature of its product dictates that it be sold in the period it is produced. Thus, no ending work-in-process or finished goods inventories remain at the end of the period. However, raw materials can be stored and are purchased in bulk when prices are favorable. Per-unit, standard product costs are materials, $6 (0.5 pound); labor, $15 (1.5 hours); and variable overhead, $3 (based on direct labor hours). Budgeted fixed overhead is $96,000.

Kent Company accounts for all inventories and cost of goods sold at standard cost and records each variance in a separate account. The following data relate to June when 7,800 finished units were produced.

Required

a.   Assuming Kent purchased 4,500 pounds of raw materials on account at $11.60 per pound and used 4,200 pounds in June's production, prepare a journal entry to record the purchase of raw materials and a separate journal entry to record the use of raw materials in production. Record these entries using standard costs and include the appropriate materials variances.
b.   Assuming Kent's employees worked 12,000 direct labor hours at an average hourly rate of $10.50, prepare a journal entry to record actual costs, standard costs, and any labor variances.
c.   Assuming Kent's actual and applied variable overhead was $23,100 and that budgeted and actual fixed overhead incurred was $96,000, prepare a journal entry to record actual and standard overhead costs and any overhead variances.

LO3, 4, 5   **P11-4B. Variances, Total Overhead Variances, and Variance Reconciliation** Sanchez Company planned to produce 10,000 units of its only product during the year. Sanchez established the following standard cost data for this product prior to the beginning of the year:

	Per Unit
Direct materials (2 lb. @ $7.50 per lb.).	$15.00
Direct labor (1.5 hr. @ $13.50 per hr.)	20.25
Variable overhead (1.5 hr. @ $6 per hr.).	9.00
Total standard cost per unit	$44.25

Total budgeted fixed overhead is $144,000.

Assume that Sanchez (1) actually produced 9,000 units, (2) used 17,000 pounds of direct materials in production, (3) and incurred the following actual total costs:

	Total Cost
Direct materials purchased (19,000 lb. @ 7.80).	$148,200
Direct labor (14,000 hr. @ $13.35).	186,900
Variable overhead.	80,250
Fixed overhead.	144,000
Total actual costs.	$559,350

Required

a. Calculate the variances for materials, labor, and variable overhead.

b. Does the difference between total actual costs and total standard costs equal the sum of all of the variances? Explain.

EXTENDING YOUR KNOWLEDGE

EYK11-1. **Business Decision Case** Porter Corporation has just hired Bill Harlow as its new controller. Although Harlow has had little formal accounting training, he professes to be highly experienced, having learned accounting "the hard way" in the field. At the end of his first month's work, Harlow prepared the following performance report:

PORTER CORPORATION Performance Report for the Month of June			
	Total Actual Costs	Total Budgeted Costs	Variances
Direct materials.	$216,630	$237,600	$20,970 F
Direct labor.	119,340	132,000	12,660 F
Variable overhead.	63,000	66,000	3,000 F
Fixed overhead.	184,000	184,000	
	$582,970	$619,600	$36,630 F

In his presentation at Porter's month-end management meeting, Harlow indicated that things were going "fantastically." "The figures indicate," he said, "that the firm is beating its budget in all cost categories." This good news made everyone at the meeting happy and furthered Harlow's acceptance as a member of the management team.

After the management meeting, Susan Jones, Porter's general manager, asked you, as an independent consultant, to review Harlow's report. Jones's concern stemmed from the fact that Porter has never operated as favorably as Harlow's report seems to imply, and she cannot explain the apparent significant improvement.

While reviewing Harlow's report, you are provided the following cost and operating data for June: Porter has a monthly normal capacity of 11,000 direct labor hours or 8,800 units of product. Standard costs per unit for its only product are direct materials 3 pounds at $9 per pound; direct labor, 1.25 hours at $12 per hour; and variable overhead rate per direct labor hour of $6. During June, Porter produced 8,000 units of product, using 24,900 pounds of materials costing $8.70 each, 10,200 direct labor hours at an average rate of $11.70 each, and incurred variable overhead costs of $63,000 and fixed overhead costs of $184,000.

After reviewing Porter's June cost data, you tell Harlow that his cost report contains a classic budgeting error, and you explain how he can remedy it. In response to your suggestion, Harlow revises his report as follows:

	Total Actual Costs	Total Budgeted Costs	Variances
Direct materials.	$216,630	$216,000	$ 630 U
Direct labor	119,340	120,000	660 F
Variable overhead.	63,000	60,000	3,000 U
Fixed overhead.	184,000	184,000	
	$582,970	$580,000	$2,970 U

Harlow's revised report is accompanied by remarks expressing regret at the oversight in the original report.

Required
In your role as consultant,

a. Verify that Harlow's actual cost figures are correct.
b. Identify and explain the classic budgeting error that Harlow apparently incorporated into his original cost report.
c. Explain why Harlow's revised figures could be considered deficient.
d. Further analyze Harlow's revised variances, isolating underlying potential causal factors. How do your analyses indicate bases for concern to management?

EYK11-2. **Ethics Case** Custom Furniture, manufacturer of handmade furniture, uses standard cost accounting for the company. Standards are developed annually based on input from production workers and supervisors.

The supervisor of the table department has approached several employees that work for him and suggested that the employees overestimate the amount of materials (by 20%) and labor (by 30%) involved in producing certain new tables. He states that it is better to overestimate than underestimate costs as the product has never been manufactured in quantity before and it is uncertain what the actual materials and labor will be. In addition, he states that this would result in any variances being favorable to the department.

The employees are not sure what estimates they should discuss with the accounting department. The accounting department wants accurate input that it will adjust for uncertainty.

Required
How would you advise the employees? What ethical issues are involved?

ANSWERS TO SELF-STUDY QUESTIONS:

1. c   2. b   3. d   4. a   5. c

YOUR TURN! SOLUTIONS

Solution 11.1

Nelson spent $2,600 more than expected for materials. The company would have to investigate the extent to which this unfavorable variance is attributable to higher materials prices or inefficient operations. Nelson actually spent $300 less on labor than would be expected based on the new standard costing system. The company would need to explore the extent to which this favorable variance relates to a difference in the expected wage rates of employees or their efficiency. Finally, Nelson also spent $500 less than expected for variable overhead. The company would need to determine the extent to which this favorable variance resulted from actual spending being less than standard rates would predict or whether efficiencies in the process resulted in the use of lower quantities of overhead drivers.

Solution 11.2

	Actual Costs	Standard Costs	Total Flexible Budget Variances
Direct materials.	$261,000	$264,000	($ 3,000)
Direct labor.	262,500	231,000	31,500
Variable overhead.	63,000	66,000	(3,000)
Total	$586,500	$561,000	$25,500

Solution 11.3

Materials price variance: AQ (AP − SP) = 90,000 ($2.90 − $3.00) = $9,000 F

Materials efficiency variance: SP (AQ − SQ) = $3.00 [90,000 − (4 × 22,000)] = $6,000 U

Solution 11.4

Labor rate variance: AH (AR − SR) = 35,000 × ($7.50 − $7.00) = $17,500 U

Labor efficiency variance: SR (AH − SH) = $7.00 [35,000 − (1.5 × 22,000)] = $14,000 U

Solution 11.5

Variable overhead spending variance: Actual VOH − (AQ × SR) = $63,000 − (35,000 × $2.00) = $7,000 F

Variable overhead efficiency variance: SR (AH − SH) = $2.00 [35,000 − (1.5 × 22,000)] = $4,000 U

Solution 11.6

Sales.	$500,000
Cost of goods sold at standard cost	460,000
Gross profit at standard cost	40,000
Less: Net unfavorable cost variance	(2,500)
Gross profit.	$ 37,500

Solution 11.7

1. What were the materials price and efficiency variances, and what journal entries would management make to record these variances?

   Materials price variance: AQ (AP − SP) = 55,000 ($5.30 − $5.10) = $11,000 U

Raw Materials Inventory	280,500	
Materials Price Variance	11,000	
Accounts Payable (or Cash)		291,500

   Materials efficiency variance: SP (AQ − SQ) = $5.10 [55,000 − (4 × 11,000)] = $56,100 U

Work-in-Process Inventory	224,400	
Materials Efficiency Variance	56,100	
Raw Materials Inventory		280,500

2. What were the labor rate and efficiency variances, and what journal entry would management make to record these variances?

   Labor rate variance: AH (AR − SR) = 23,000 ($3.00 − $3.50) = $11,500 F

   Labor efficiency variance: SR (AH − SH) = $3.50 [23,000 − (2 × 11,000)] = $3,500 U

Work-in-Process Inventory	77,000	
Labor Efficiency Variance	3,500	
Labor Rate Variance		11,500
Wages Payable		69,000

3. What were the variable overhead spending and efficiency variances, and what journal entry would management make to record these variances?

   VOH spending variance: Actual spending − (AH × SR) = $32,500 − (23,000 × $1.50) = $2,000 F

   VOH efficiency variance: SR (AH − SH) = $1.50 [23,000 − (2 × 11,000)] = $1,500 U

Work-in-Process Inventory	33,000	
VOH Efficiency Variance	1,500	
VOH Spending Variance		2,000
Manufacturing Overhead		32,500

Chapter 12
Capital Budgeting

Road Map

LO	Learning Objective	Page	eLecture	Guided Example	Assignments
LO1	**Introduce and illustrate the elements of capital budgeting.**	12-3	E12-1	YT12.1	Q1, Q2, Q3
LO2	**Discuss required rates of return and the time value of money.**	12-5	E12-2	YT12.2	SS1, SS2, Q4, Q5, Q6, Q7, SE2, SE3, E1A, E1B, P6A, P6B
LO3	**Demonstrate the use of present value factors to perform time value of money calculations.**	12-8	E12-3	YT12.3	Q8, Q9, Q10, Q13, SE4, SE5, E2A, E2B
LO4	**Explain and illustrate the determination of after-tax cash flows.**	12-10	E12-4	YT12.4	SS3, Q11, Q12, SE1, SE4, SE10, E3A, E4A, E5A, E3B, E4B, E5B, P1A, P3A, P5A, P1B, P3B, P5B
LO5	**Describe the net present value method of capital expenditure analysis.**	12-14	E12-5	YT12.5	SS4, Q13, Q14, SE6, SE10, E6A, E6B, P2A, P3A, P4A, P5A, P6A, P2B, P3B, P4B, P5B, P6B
LO6	**Demonstrate the internal rate of return method of capital expenditure analysis.**	12-20	E12-6	YT12.6	SS5, Q15, SE7, SE8, SE10, E7A, E7B, E8B, P3A, P4A, P5A, P3B, P4B, P5B
LO7	**Present the cash payback and average rate of return methods of capital expenditure analysis.**	12-21	E12-7	YT12.7	SS6, Q16, Q17, SE9, E8A, E9A, E9B, E10B, P3A, P4A, P5A, P3B, P4B, P5B
LO8	**Appendix 12A: Demonstrate the use of a financial calculator and an electronic spreadsheet to perform time value of money calculations.**	12-26	E12-8		

Waste Management (WM) is the largest environmental solutions provider in North America.[1] At the end of 2019, the company employed approximately 44,900 people, had approximately 20 million customers, owned or operated 249 landfills and 103 material recovery facilities, managed 302 waste transfer stations, and had 124 landfill gas beneficial use projects. WM has the permitted capacity to handle approximately 4.9 billion cubic yards of solid waste and projects that it will manage over 100 million tons of waste annually for the foreseeable future.

The current facilities that WM operates require significant capital outlays to upgrade or replace old equipment and buildings and close and maintain landfills. In addition, expenditures are needed for new equipment and buildings to accommodate the company's growth opportunities. WM has a team dedicated to evaluating these seemingly continuous capital expenditure opportunities designed to maintain, supplement, or expand its current operations.

This chapter introduces the process of and analysis techniques for capital budgeting decision-making.

PAST

Chapter 11 discussed methods used to analyze companies' performance, including flexible budgets, segment reporting, and performance analysis.

PRESENT

Chapter 12 introduces capital budgeting and illustrates how capital budgeting is used to make capital investment decisions.

FUTURE

In Chapter 13, we shift our focus to the statement of cash flows.

---

[1] https://investors.wm.com/static-files/1d9c9790-1e40-40c4-8887-05b68361ef1d

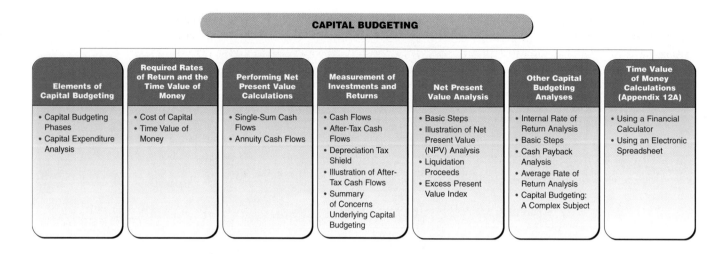

Planning long-term investments in productive assets is known as **capital budgeting**. The term reflects the fact that for most firms the total cost of all attractive investment opportunities exceeds the available investment capital. Thus, management must ration, or budget, investment capital among competing investment proposals. In deciding which new long-term assets to acquire, management must seek investments that promise to optimize return on the funds employed.

Capital budgeting is most valuable for organizations in which managers are responsible for the long-term profitability of their area of concern and are therefore encouraged to develop new products and more efficient production processes. Firms often make their most capable employees responsible for capital budgeting decisions because such decisions determine how large sums of money are invested and commit the firm for extended future periods. Furthermore, investment decision errors are often difficult and costly to remedy or abandon.

Managers as well as accountants should be familiar with the special analytical techniques that evaluate the relative attractiveness of alternative uses of available capital. In this chapter, we first discuss the nature and procedures of capital budgeting, how required investment earning rates are determined, the time value of money, and the effect of income taxes on capital expenditure decisions. We conclude by illustrating four approaches to capital expenditure analysis: the net present value method, the internal rate of return method, the cash payback method, and the average rate of return method.

ELEMENTS OF CAPITAL BUDGETING

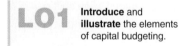

Introduce and **illustrate** the elements of capital budgeting.

MBC

Hint: Inventory and other current asset purchases are not capital expenditures, even though they are commonly referred to as working "capital."

Capital Budgeting Phases

Capital budgeting has three phases:

1. Identify potential investments,
2. Select investments to be undertaken, and
3. Monitor the selected investments.

Many firms have a capital budgeting calendar calling for consideration of capital expenditure proposals at regular intervals, such as every 6 months or every year. Proposals are usually examined with respect to (1) compliance with capital budget policies and procedures; (2) aspects of operational urgency, such as the need to replace critical equipment; (3) established criteria for minimum return on capital investments; and, (4) consistency with the firm's operating policies and long-term goals. Proposals for relatively small cash outlays may require the approval of low-level management only, whereas major proposals with more long-term impact are subject to approval at high management levels, perhaps including the board of directors. These major proposals and the decisions based on them profoundly affect a firm's long-term success.

Once approved, capital expenditures should be monitored to ensure that amounts and purposes are consistent with the original proposal. At appropriate intervals, the actual rates of return earned on important expenditures should be compared with projected rates. These periodic reviews encourage those responsible to formulate thorough and realistic proposals and often provide an incentive for improving overall capital budgeting procedures.

Capital Expenditure Analysis

The scope of capital expenditures varies widely, ranging from the routine replacement of production equipment to the construction of entire manufacturing complexes. Whatever their size, most capital expenditure projects have the three stages shown in **Exhibit 12-1**.

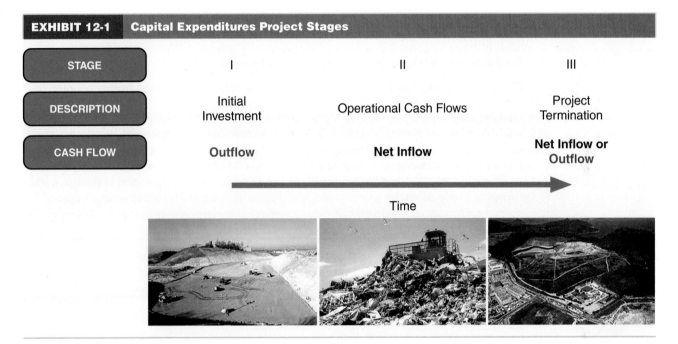

EXHIBIT 12-1	Capital Expenditures Project Stages		
STAGE	I	II	III
DESCRIPTION	Initial Investment	Operational Cash Flows	Project Termination
CASH FLOW	Outflow	**Net Inflow**	**Net Inflow or** Outflow

Time

Initial investment (stage I) consists of a net cash outlay for a project or an asset. Net operational cash flows during the life of the project (stage II) may result from either an excess of periodic cash revenues over related cash expenditures or a periodic saving in some cash expenditure. Finally, the termination of a project (stage III) often results in some amount of liquidation proceeds from the sale of the project capital or could result in some cash outlay for the removal of the project or restoration of the property to its former condition.

For example, the development of a new WM municipal waste landfill (stage I) requires millions of dollars for the purchase of the property, performance of the necessary environmental studies, obtainment of land use approvals and permits, and the development of appropriate access roads, gatehouse and vehicle scales, administrative buildings, security fencing, and environmental protection systems.

Over the life of the landfill (stage II), WM will collect cash fees from users of the landfill and expend cash for the compacting and covering of the trash and the monitoring, collection, and treatment of liquids and methane gas created by the decomposing waste.

Finally, once the landfill reaches its permitted capacity, WM must close the landfill (stage III), applying a final cap on the waste, and then monitor, collect, and treat the liquids and methane gas created by the decomposing waste for a period of 30 to 40 years.

The attractiveness of a particular investment is determined in large part by the quantitative relationship between the cash investment in stage I and the net cash receipts expected in stages II and III. In its simplest form, this relationship is usually expressed as a ratio known as the **rate of return**:

$$\text{Rate of return} = \frac{\text{Returns}}{\text{Investment}}$$

All other things being equal, the higher the expected rate of return, the more attractive the investment opportunity. Proposed investments can be ranked according to their expected rates of return, and capital outlays can be allocated among the most attractive investments. Capital expenditure analysis consists of judging the attractiveness of income-producing or cost-saving opportunities in relation to required investments. The results of this analysis are among the most important input data in capital budgeting decisions.

Three questions are of considerable concern in capital budgeting:

1. How do we determine an acceptable rate of return for a given project?
2. How can we meaningfully compare investments made now with returns to be received in the future?
3. In what terms should investments and returns be measured?

These challenging problems are considered in the following sections of this chapter.

ACCOUNTING IN PRACTICE   **Capital Budgeting in Growing a Company**

Waste Management's 2021 annual report includes the following on page 59 of the management discussion and analysis (MD&A) section: "We used $1,904 million, $1,632 million, and $1,818 million for capital expenditures in 2021, 2020, and 2019, respectively. The increase in 2021 is due in part to intentional steps the company took to accelerate growth capital spending on recycling and renewable energy projects."

YOUR TURN! 12.1   Provide an explanation of the capital budgeting process and the importance of capital investments.

The solution is on
page 12-45.

REQUIRED RATES OF RETURN AND THE TIME VALUE OF MONEY

LO2 **Discuss** required rates of return and the time value of money.

The mix of capital sources (i.e., available cash or proceeds from new debt or equity) that a company uses will depend on market conditions as well as the philosophies of the members of the board of directors and the management team.

Cost of Capital

In determining an acceptable rate of return for a given project, we must consider not only the initial capital outlay, but also all of the costs associated with the acquisition of that capital. The parties providing the funds expect to be reasonably compensated for their use. When the money is borrowed from a bank or through a bond issuance, the interest paid by the firm is a cost of using the funds. When stockholder funds are used, we assume that some combination of dividend payments and increase in the value of the capital stock compensates stockholders for furnishing the investment capital. The cost to the firm of acquiring the funds used in capital investment projects—typically expressed as an annual percentage rate—is called the **cost of capital**.

A firm may acquire capital by issuing preferred or common stock, using retained earnings, borrowing, or some combination of these. Consequently, the overall cost of capital for a given project should reflect the cost rates of the several sources of funds in proportion to the amounts obtained from each source. This is called the **weighted average cost of capital**, or **WACC**.

Hint: Because the earnings retained by the firm might otherwise have been distributed to the common shareholders in the form of dividends, firms often use the same cost of capital for retained earnings as is used for common stock.

Assume that a particular company had acquired capital through all four sources and in the proportions and with the cost of capital rates as shown here:

	A	B	C	D	E	F
1	**Source of Capital**	**Percentage of Total**	**×**	**Cost of Capital Rate**	**=**	**Weighted Average Cost of Capital Component**
2	Debt	40%	×	8%	=	3.2%
3	Preferred stock	10%	×	9%	=	0.9%
4	Common stock	20%	×	12%	=	2.4%
5	Retained earnings	30%	×	12%	=	3.6%
6	Weighted average cost of capital					10.1%

Multiplying the percentage of each capital source by its cost of capital rate provides weighted cost factors whose sum is the weighted average cost of capital. This percentage (in this case, 10.1%) can then be used to compare the attractiveness of proposed investments.

Concept ⟶	Method ⟶	Assessment	**TAKEAWAY 12.1**
Can a firm determine the cost of acquiring resources to fund capital investment decisions?	Use the weighted average cost of capital to determine the cost of aquiring capital by issuing stock, using retained earnings, borrowing, or a combination thereof.	At a minimum, capital investments should provide a rate of return at least as high as a firm's weighted average cost of capital.	

Logically, for a capital investment to be considered favorably by a firm, its expected rate of return must be at least as high as the cost of capital. Therefore, the cost of capital represents a minimum required rate of return, or **hurdle rate**. In other words, a firm whose cost of capital is 10% will ordinarily want to invest only in an asset or project whose expected rate of return is more than 10%. An investment whose return is less than the cost of capital would be economically detrimental, although firms sometimes disregard their cost of capital if qualitative considerations override the quantitative aspects of the decision. Qualitative considerations might include the desire to achieve environmental goals, the desire to maintain research leadership in the industry, the need to maintain full employment of the workforce during a business slowdown, or the desire to maintain a percentage of market share or to penetrate a specific market.

Some firms consider only investments whose rates of return are at least a certain number of percentage points higher than the cost of capital. This **buffer margin** acts as a safety factor because proposals that project estimated cash inflows and outflows years into the future have a significant amount of uncertainty regarding the amount and timing of those cash flows. Of course, in an environment of limited resources, even proposals whose expected rate of return is higher than the hurdle rate may be rejected if other investment opportunities offer still higher returns.

Time Value of Money

We have seen that in determining the desirability of a proposed capital investment, management compares the amount of investment required at the beginning of a project with its expected returns—typically a series of returns extending several years into the future. This comparison, which is so important in capital budgeting decisions, cannot be made properly using the absolute amounts of the future returns because money has a time value. The **time value of money** means that the right to receive an amount of money today is worth more than the right to receive the same amount at some future date because a current receipt can be invested to earn interest over the intervening period. Thus, if 10% annual interest can be obtained on investments, $100 received today is equal in value to $110 received one year from now. Assuming a 10% rate of return, $100 today will have a future value of $110 in one year's time. Conversely, assuming the same 10% rate of return, a $110 cash receipt expected in one year's time has a present value of $100 today.

A.K.A. The minimum rate of return is also known as the hurdle rate or target rate.

The difference between present and future values is a function of interest rates and time periods. The higher the interest rate or longer the time period involved, the higher the amount by which a future value is reduced, or discounted, in deriving its present value. For example, **Exhibit 12-2** shows just how significant the time value of money can be at various interest rates and time periods. As the table indicates, five years from now $100 has a present value of $78, $62, or $50 if the applicable interest rates are 5%, 10%, and 15%, respectively. Note also that the longer the time period or higher the interest rate, the larger the difference between the future value of $100 and its present value. Comparing a current investment with its future returns without discounting the returns to their present value would substantially overstate the economic significance of the returns. We must therefore recognize the time value of money in capital budgeting procedures.

The longer the time period, the larger the difference between the future value of $100 and its present value.

The higher the interest rate, the larger the difference between the future value of $100 and its present value.

EXHIBIT 12-2	Time Value of Money		
	A	B	C	D
1	Present Value of $100 (Rounded to Nearest Dollar)			
2			Rate	
3	Years	5%	10%	15%
4	1	$95	$91	$87
5	2	91	83	76
6	3	86	75	66
7	4	82	68	57
8	5	78	62	50
9	10	61	39	25
10	20	38	15	6
11	30	23	6	2
12	40	14	2	0
13	50	9	1	0

Hint: Discounted cash flows (DCFs) are also known as the present value of future cash flows. The cash flows can either be inflows (receipts) or outflows (payments).

Techniques for discounting future cash flows to their present values apply to both cash receipts and cash outlays. In other words, the current value of the right to receive—or the current value of the obligation to pay—a sum in the future is its present value computed at an appropriate interest rate. We maximize our economic position by arranging to receive amounts as early as possible and postponing amounts to be paid as long as possible. These generalizations will be apparent in the capital budgeting illustrations later in the chapter.

TAKEAWAY 12.2	Concept	Method	Assessment
	What is the time value of money?	Money available at the present time is worth more than the identical sum in the future due to its potential earning capacity. That is, the provided money can earn interest.	The time value of money explains why interest is paid or earned. Interest, whether it is on a deposit or debt, compensates the depositor or lender for the time value of money.

YOUR TURN! 12.2

The solution is on page 12-45.

MBC

The following sources of financing, their proportions, and their cost of capital rates are for a merchandising company. Calculate and interpret the WACC for this company.

	Percentage of Total	Cost of Capital Rate
Bank loan	45%	12%
Equity capital	55%	9%

PERFORMING NET PRESENT VALUE CALCULATIONS

Present value tables simplify our work considerably in computing present values. These tables provide factors for combinations of time periods and interest rates that may be multiplied by a stream of cash flows or a one-time future cash flow to determine its present value. In this chapter we demonstrate how to do these calculations using factors from present value tables. These tables can be found in Appendix A of the text, along with a more detailed discussion of time value of money concepts. In Appendix 12A we demonstrate how to use a financial calculator and an Excel spreadsheet to perform those same calculations.

LO3 Demonstrate the use of present value factors to perform time value of money calculations.

eLecture

MBC

Throughout the chapter, the following abbreviations, related to time value of money calculations, are used:

> PV = **present value at time 0**
> FV = **future value at time N**
> *i* = **interest at which the amount compounds each period**
> N = **number of periods (time)**
> PMT = **periodic cash flow (payment)**

Single-Sum Cash Flows

Let us first consider how to compute the present value of a single-sum cash flow. This calculation will be used to determine the present value of sporadic cash flows when the returns expected on an investment, or the expenditures it requires, are unequal amounts or are expected at irregular intervals during or at the end of the life of the investment.

To illustrate, we assume that an investment project promises a return of $2,000 at the end of two years and another $1,000 at the end of five years. The desired rate of return is 10% per year. **Exhibit 12-3** illustrates the cash flows on a timeline.

Hint: Present values should always be less than future values; otherwise, the calculation was performed incorrectly.

EXHIBIT 12-3	**Calculating the Present Value of a Lump Sum**

Periodic rate of return   *i* = 10%   *i* = 10%   *i* = 10%   *i* = 10%   *i* = 10%

Time period   Now   N = 1   N = 2   N = 3   N = 4   N = 5

Payments
PV = ? ← – – – – FV = $2,000
PV = ? ← – FV = $1,000
Total   PV = ?

Using factors from Table III, Present Value of $1, from Appendix A, we calculate the present value of each cash flow separately using the following process.

First, calculate the present value of the $2,000 cash flow. The formula for calculating the present value of a future sum is as follows:

Present value (PV) = Future value (FV) × PV table factor*

$$PV = \$2,000 \times 0.82645$$
$$PV = \$1,652.90$$

*Because the $2,000 cash flow occurs at the end of Year 2, we use the factor associated with a 10% rate of return and 2 years (0.82645; see Table III in Appendix A).

Calculator
N = 2
I/Yr = 10
PMT = 0
FV = $2,000
Compute PV

PV = –1,652.89

	A	B
1	Discount rate (rate)	10%
2	Number of periods (nper)	2
3	Annuity (pmt)	0
4	Future value (fv)	2,000.00
5	Present value(pv)	
6	= PV(B1,B2,B3,B4)	(1,652.89)
7	= (1,652.89)	

This value may be interpreted as the amount that, if invested today in an account paying 10% interest, would allow for the withdrawal of $2,000 at the end of two years. This can be proved as follows: $1,652.90 invested today would earn $165.29 in interest in the first year, for a total value of $1,818.19 ($1,652.90 + $165.29). This balance would earn $181.82 in interest in the second year, for a total value of $2,000.01 ($1,818.19 + $181.82).

Next, calculate the present value of the $1,000 cash flow:

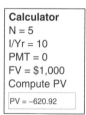

	A	B
1	Discount rate (rate)	10%
2	Number of periods (nper)	5
3	Annuity (pmt)	0
4	Future value (fv)	1,000
5	Present value(pv)	(620.92)
6	= PV(B1,B2,B3,B4)	
7	= (620.92)	

PV = FV × PV table factor*

PV = $1,000 × 0.62092

PV = $620.92

*Because the $1,000 cash flow occurs at the end of Year 5, we use the factor from a present value table for a single amount associated with a 10% rate of return and 5 years (0.62092; see Table III in Appendix A).

This value may be interpreted as the amount that, if invested today in an account paying 10% interest, would allow for the withdrawal of $1,000 at the end of five years.

The total present value of the combined flows is $2,273.82 ($1,652.90 + $620.92). That is, $2,273.82 invested today in an account paying 10% interest would allow withdrawal of $2,000 at the end of two years and $1,000 at the end of five years.

Annuity Cash Flows

Let us next consider how to compute the present value of an annuity. An **annuity** is cash flows that are the same each period over two or more equal periods.

To illustrate, we assume that a project has expected cash inflows of $1,000 at the end of each of the next three periods, and 8% is the appropriate cost of capital. **Exhibit 12-4** illustrates the cash flows on a timeline.

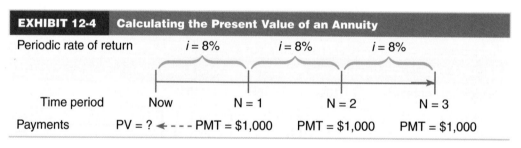

Using factors from Table IV, Present Value of an Ordinary Annuity of $1 per Period, from Appendix A, we calculate the present value of these cash flows using the following formula:

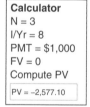

	A	B
1	Discount rate (rate)	8%
2	Number of periods (nper)	3
3	Annuity (pmt)	1,000
4	Future value (fv)	0
5	Present value(pv)	(2,577.10)
6	= PV(B1,B2,B3,B4)	
7	= (2,577.10)	

PV = PMT × PV table factor*

PV = $1,000 × 2.57710

PV = $2,577.10

*Because the $1,000 cash flow occurs at the end of each year for 3 years, we use the factor associated with an 8% rate of return and 3 years (2.57710; see Table IV in Appendix A).

This value may be interpreted as the amount that, if invested today in an account paying 8% interest annually, would allow for the withdrawal of $1,000 at the end of each year for the next three years. This can be proved as follows: $2,577.10 invested today would earn $206.17 ($2,577.10 × 0.08) in interest in the first year, for a total value of $2,783.27 ($2,577.10 + $206.17). A withdrawal of $1,000 would leave a balance of $1,783.27. This balance would earn $142.66 ($1,783.27 × 0.08) in interest in the second year, for a total value of $1,925.93 ($1,783.27 + $142.66). A second withdrawal of $1,000 would leave a balance of $925.93. This balance would earn $74.07 ($925.93 × 0.08) in interest in the third year, for a total value of $1,000 ($925.93 + $74.07), allowing for a third and final withdrawal of $1,000.

Both illustrations assume that all cash flows occur at the end of the periods. This assumption is somewhat simplistic because cash receipts or cost savings from most industrial investments occur in a steady stream throughout the operating periods. Nevertheless, businesses assume end-of-period cash flows for ease of use. These calculations will understate the present values of flows that are gradual throughout the period because the present values of cash flows early in the period are higher than similar inflows or outlays at the end of the period. The difference, however, is normally not material.

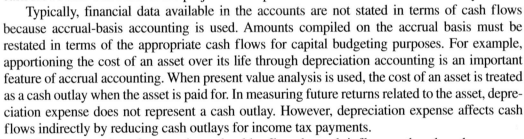

JB Enterprises has a cost of capital of 12%. Calculate the present value of the following investment opportunities:

a.   An investment project promises a return of $3,000 at the end of year 3 and $5,000 at the end year 4.

b.   An investment project promises a return of $2,000 at the end of each of the next four years.

YOUR TURN! 12.3

The solution is on page 12-45.

GuidedExample

MBC

MEASUREMENT OF INVESTMENTS AND RETURNS

Cash Flows

LO4

Explain and illustrate the determination of after-tax cash flows.

When present value analysis is used to make investment decisions, investments and returns must be stated in the form of cash flows. Present value determinations are basically interest calculations, and therefore only money amounts—cash flows—are properly used in interest calculations. Furthermore, only the *incremental* cash flows that will occur if the project is accepted should be considered in the analysis.

Typically, financial data available in the accounts are not stated in terms of cash flows because accrual-basis accounting is used. Amounts compiled on the accrual basis must be restated in terms of the appropriate cash flows for capital budgeting purposes. For example, apportioning the cost of an asset over its life through depreciation accounting is an important feature of accrual accounting. When present value analysis is used, the cost of an asset is treated as a cash outlay when the asset is paid for. In measuring future returns related to the asset, depreciation expense does not represent a cash outlay. However, depreciation expense affects cash flows indirectly by reducing cash outlays for income tax payments.

eLecture

MBC

Likewise, earnings from projects should reflect the cash inflows rather than the revenue amounts computed using accrual accounting. The timing of the cash collections is important, too, because the essence of present value analysis is that cash received can be reinvested.

After-Tax Cash Flows

Both federal and state income taxes are important to investment decisions; for some companies, the combined federal and state income tax rate may approach 30%. Generally, income taxes reduce the economic significance of taxable receipts and deductible expenditures.

EXHIBIT 12-5	Tax Impact on Cash Flows		
A		B	C
1		**Inflow**	**Outflow**
2	Pre-tax amount	$40,000	$(15,000)
3	Income tax rate	30%	30%
4	Tax benefit/(expense)	(12,000)	4,500
5	After-tax amount	28,000	(10,500)

As illustrated in **Exhibit 12-5**, assuming a 30% tax rate, a $40,000 before-tax gain (cash inflow) would increase taxable income by $40,000 and income taxes by $12,000 (30% × $40,000), resulting in a $28,000 after-tax cash inflow. A $15,000 before-tax expense would reduce taxable income by $15,000 and income taxes by $4,500 (30% × $15,000), resulting in a $10,500 after-tax cash outflow. In general terms, the formulas for determining after-tax cash flows are as follows:

After-tax cash inflow = Pre-tax cash inflow × (1 – tax rate)

After-tax cash outflow = Pre-tax cash outflow × (1 – tax rate)

After-tax cash flows are more relevant than before-tax cash flows because they represent the amounts available to retire debt, finance expansions, or pay dividends. For this reason, investment decision analyses must be formulated in terms of after-tax cash flows.

Depreciation Tax Shield

Depreciation deductions *shield* revenues from taxation and thus reduce the taxes a company must pay. Depreciation creates a tax savings. **Exhibit 12-6** illustrates how to compute the amount of tax savings created by depreciation.

EXHIBIT 12-6	Tax Impact of Depreciation	
	A	B
1		**Inflow**
2	Pre-tax amount	$30,000
3	Income tax rate	30%
4	Tax benefit/(expense)	9,000

To understand this effect, assume that a company had taxable revenues of $30,000 and no expenses. Assuming a 30% tax rate, this company would owe $9,000 in tax ($30,000 × 30%). Now, assume that the company had one deductible expense: depreciation in the amount of $30,000. In this case, the company would owe no taxes because it can deduct the depreciation expense from its taxable revenue ($30,000 – $30,000 = $0 taxable income). Thus, the depreciation saved the company from having to pay $9,000 in tax. The formula for determining the **tax shield** is as follows:

After-tax depreciation tax shield = Depreciation expense × Tax rate

Illustration of After-Tax Cash Flows

Thinking in terms of after-tax cash flows represents a significant departure from the accrual-based accounting for revenue and expenses. However, remember that the pre-tax cash flows are available to us in the cash flow statement. We can use our understanding of the cash flow statement to determine the after-tax cash flows needed for capital budgeting and other time value of money analyses.

To explore the relationship between the traditional income statement and the related after-tax cash flows, let's revisit Fezzari's income statement from Chapter 9. **Exhibit 12-7** shows Fezzari's income statement in column A. Column B identifies the related cash flows from Fezzari's cash flow statement. An understanding of **Exhibit 12-7** will provide a basis for understanding the comprehensive illustration of capital budgeting later in the chapter.

Column A in **Exhibit 12-7** is the traditional income statement, showing that revenue minus operating expenses and income taxes results in a net income of $529,185. For simplicity, we assume that revenue and cash expenses involve no significant accruals and that depreciation is the same on both the books and the tax return. Ordinarily, net income does not represent after-tax cash flows because depreciation expense—a noncash expense—is deducted to derive net income. As indicated in column A of **Exhibit 12-7**, to convert the $529,185 net income to after-tax cash flow, we must add back the depreciation of $45,000, resulting in $574,185 of after-tax cash flow.

Column B of **Exhibit 12-7** confirms the $574,185 amount of after-tax cash flow determined in column A. This is accomplished by simply listing the amounts in column A that constitute cash inflows (revenue of $6,237,000) and cash outflows (cash expenses of $4,704,570, $776,850, and $5,000 and income tax payments of $176,395). Depreciation is excluded because it does not represent a cash payment.

Column C in **Exhibit 12-7** illustrates the determination of the individual amounts of after-tax cash flows for each item on the income statement. We use this approach in the comprehensive illustration of capital budgeting appearing later in the chapter. Amounts in column C are determined as follows. (Again, a 25% income tax rate is assumed.)

EXHIBIT 12-7	Illustration of Determining After-Tax Cash Flows			
	A	B	C	D
1	Fezzari Performance Bicycles For the Period Ended December 31			
2		A	B	C
3		Traditional Income Statement	Income Statement Cash Inflows (Outflows)	Individual After-Tax Cash Inflow (Outflow) Effects	
4	Sales	$6,237,000	$6,237,000	$ 4,677,750	
5	Less: Cost of goods sold (excluding depreciation)	4,704,570	(4,704,570)	$(3,528,427)	
6	Less: Depreciation expense	45,000		11,250	
7	Gross profit	$1,487,430			
8	Less: Selling and administrative expense	776,850	(776,850)	$ (582,638)	
9	Income from operations	$ 710,580			
10	Less: Interest expense	5,000	(5,000)	$ (3,750)	
11	Income before income taxes	$ 705,580			
12	Less: Income taxes	176,395	(176,395)		
13	Net income	$ 529,185			
14	Add back depreciation expense	45,000			
15	After-tax cash flow	$ 574,185	$ 574,185	$ 574,185	

Receipt of $6,237,000 cash revenue

Receipt of $6,237,000 cash revenue would, by itself, increase taxable income by $6,237,000, adding $1,559,250 ($6,237,000 × 25%) to income taxes. The $4,677,750 after-tax cash inflow is the difference between the $6,237,000 cash revenue received and the related $1,559,250 increase in income taxes (a cash outflow). Applying the previous formula for an after-tax inflow results in the same amount:

$$\text{After-tax cash inflow} = \text{Pre-tax cash inflow} \times (1 - \text{Tax rate})$$

OR

$$\$4,677,750 = \$6,237,000 \times (1 - 0.25)$$

Payment of $4,704,570 in cash operating expenses

Payment of $4,704,570 in cash operating expenses represents a deductible cash outflow that reduces taxable income by $4,704,570 and thus reduces income taxes by $1,176,143 ($4,704,570 × 25%). The $3,528,427 net cash outflow is the difference between the $4,704,570 actually paid out for expenses and the $1,176,143 of income tax payments avoided by virtue of the tax deductibility of the expenses. Applying the previous formula for an after-tax outflow results in the same amount:

$$\text{After-tax cash outflow} = \text{Pre-tax cash outflow} \times (1 - \text{Tax rate})$$

OR

$$\$3,528,427 = \$4,704,570 \times (1 - 0.25)$$

Hint: The depreciation amount that provides a tax shield is the depreciation deduction on the tax return. Tax depreciation deductions are governed by tax regulations, not by generally accepted accounting principles. Often the periodic tax depreciation will differ from depreciation expense on the income statement. (In Exhibit 12-7 we assume that the amounts are equal.) When identifying the depreciation tax shield in capital budgeting analysis, then, it is important to use the depreciation amount from the tax return.

Notice that *avoiding a cash outflow* has the same effect on net cash flows as a cash inflow. In other words, total net cash inflows can be increased by adding to cash inflows or by avoiding cash outflows.

Recording $45,000 of depreciation expense

Although depreciation expense is tax deductible, no related cash expenditure occurs during the period. The $45,000 deduction reduces taxable income by $45,000 and income taxes by $11,250 ($45,000 × 25%). Depreciation expense and similar noncash expense deductions are often referred to as *tax shields* because they shield an equal amount of income from whatever income tax rate is applicable.

Payment of $776,850 in cash selling and administrative expenses

Payment of $776,850 in cash selling and administrative expenses represents a deductible cash outflow that reduces taxable income by $776,850 and thus reduces income taxes by $194,212 ($776,850 × 25%). The $582,638 net cash outflow is the difference between the $776,850 actually paid out for expenses and the $194,212 of income tax payments avoided by virtue of the tax deductibility of the expenses. Applying the previous formula for an after-tax outflow results in the same amount:

$$\textbf{After-tax cash outflow = Pre-tax cash outflow} \times \textbf{(1 − Tax rate)}$$

OR

$$\mathbf{\$582,638 = \$776,850 \times (1 − 0.25)}$$

Payment of $5,000 in cash interest expense

Payment of $5,000 in cash interest expense represents a deductible cash outflow that reduces taxable income by $5,000 and thus reduces income taxes by $1,250 ($5,000 × 25%). The $3,750 net cash outflow is the difference between the $5,000 actually paid out for interest expense and the $1,250 of income tax payments avoided by virtue of the tax deductibility of the expense. Applying the previous formula for an after-tax outflow results in the same amount:

$$\textbf{After-tax cash outflow = Pre-tax cash outflow} \times \textbf{(1 − Tax rate)}$$

OR

$$\mathbf{\$3,750 = \$5,000 \times (1 − 0.25)}$$

Combining the after-tax cash flow effect of each amount in column C again confirms that net cash inflows total $574,185.

Summary of Concerns Underlying Capital Budgeting

1. The typical investment pattern involves a present investment of funds resulting in anticipated returns, often extending years into the future.
2. The basic question in capital budgeting is whether present investments are justified by related future returns.
3. Because money has a time value, returns that occur in the future must be discounted to their present values for a proper comparison with present investments.
4. To use discounting (interest) calculations properly, we must state amounts in capital budgeting analyses in terms of cash flows.
5. Because income tax rates are substantial, capital budgeting analyses should be formulated in terms of after-tax cash flows.

Thus far in the chapter, we have presented a number of important aspects of capital budgeting as background for the review of several approaches to capital expenditure analysis. These background materials have focused on the analytical concept known as net present value. Accountants generally concede that the net present value approach is conceptually and analytically superior to the other two approaches that we will also illustrate: cash payback and average rate of return.

Calculate the individual after-tax cash flow effect of each of the following relevant items, assuming the income tax rate is 30%:

a. Cash revenue received of $90,000   c. Depreciation expense on tax return of $10,000

b. Cash operating expenses paid of $45,000   d. Interest expense paid of $5,000

NET PRESENT VALUE ANALYSIS

Basic Steps

The basic approach to the **net present value method** is shown in **Exhibit 12-8**. Each step described here and used in the example that follows is color coded to correspond to the exhibit. Referring to the items in the exhibit, the steps in the net present value approach are to:

LO5 **Describe** the net present value method of capital expenditure analysis.

eLecture

MBC

Step 1: Determine the amount of the **investment outlay** required in terms of incremental after-tax cash flows.

Step 2: Estimate the amounts and timing of **future operating receipts or cost savings** in terms of incremental after-tax cash flows.

Step 3: Estimate any **incremental after-tax liquidation proceeds** to be received on termination of the project.

Step 4: Discount all future cash flows to their **present value** at an appropriate interest rate, usually the minimum desired rate of return on capital.

A.K.A. The present value of cash flows is also known as discounted cash flows.

Step 5: Subtract the investment outlay from the total present value of future cash flows to determine **net present value**. If net present value is zero or positive (returns equal or exceed investment), then the project's rate of return equals or exceeds the minimum desired rate and should be accepted. Negative net present values indicate that the project's return is less than desired, and the project should be rejected.

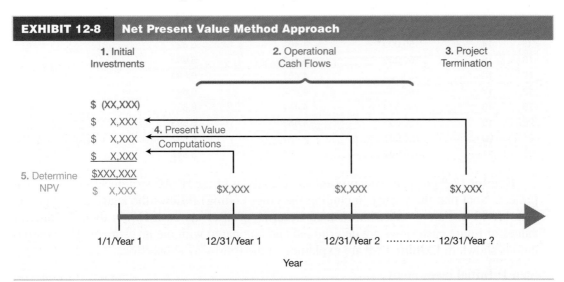

EXHIBIT 12-8   Net Present Value Method Approach

Illustration of Net Present Value (NPV) Analysis

To illustrate net present value analysis, assume that Fezzari owns its bicycle assembly facility. The building is 30 years old, and its heating, ventilating, and air-conditioning (HVAC) systems are functioning, but significantly out of date. A local HVAC contractor has told Fezzari management that new HVAC technology could significantly reduce Fezzari's monthly utility bill. The HVAC contractor has offered to replace the current HVAC system with a new, state-of-the-art system for an installed price of $150,000. The new system has an expected useful life of 20 years, at which point it will be worthless, but it will save an estimated $22,500 per year in cash utilities expenses during its useful life. Fezzari management has a minimum desired return of 10% on any capital project. Fezzari's tax rate is 25%.

To evaluate the local contractor's proposal, management decides to use a net present value analysis.

Recall that depreciation is based on the depreciation deduction from the tax return. Based on a half-year convention (one-half of the first year's depreciation is recognized in the year of acquisition and disposition), the annual depreciation (rounded to the nearest dollar) would be computed as follows:

	A	B	C	D
1	Year	Capitalized Cost	Depreciation Rate	Annual Depreciation
2	1	$150,000	3.750%	$ 5,625
3	2	150,000	7.219	10,829
4	3	150,000	6.677	10,016
5	4	150,000	6.177	9,266
6	5	150,000	5.713	8,570
7	6	150,000	5.285	7,928
8	7	150,000	4.888	7,332
9	8	150,000	4.522	6,783
10	9	150,000	4.462	6,693
11	10	150,000	4.461	6,692
12	11	150,000	4.462	6,693
13	12	150,000	4.461	6,692
14	13	150,000	4.462	6,693
15	14	150,000	4.461	6,692
16	15	150,000	4.462	6,693
17	16	150,000	4.461	6,692
18	17	150,000	4.462	6,693
19	18	150,000	4.461	6,692
20	19	150,000	4.462	6,693
21	20	150,000	4.461	6,692
22	21	150,000	2.231	3,347

Tax return depreciation, 150% declining balance, half-year convention.

Exhibit 12-9 presents a net present value analysis of the HVAC system as an investment project. Note that the format (including the color coding) follows the analysis outlined in **Exhibit 12-8**: Future returns are stated in terms of after-tax cash flows; then the present values of future cash flows are determined and compared with the investment. The computations shown in **Exhibit 12-9** are explained in the following subsections.

Step 1: Initial investment
The initial investment of $150,000 occurs at the beginning of Year 1, which we identify as Year 0. It is shown in **Exhibit 12-9** as a negative number, signifying that it represents an outflow of cash.

Step 2: Annual cash flows (expense savings)
Cash savings or expense reductions have the same effects as cash revenue, income, or gains. Thus, these amounts are shown as positive amounts, signifying that they represent an inflow

EXHIBIT 12-9 Illustration of Net Present Value Analysis: After-Tax Cash Flows (Rounded to Nearest Dollar)

	A	B Present Value	C Year 0	D Year 1	E Year 2	F Year 3	G Year 4	H Year 5	I Year 6	J Year 7	K Year 8	L Year 9	M	N Year 19	O Year 20	P Year 21
2								Projected After-Tax Cash Flows								
3	Initial investment	$(150,000)	$(150,000)													
4																
5	Annual cash expenses savings			$22,500	$22,500	$22,500	$22,500	$22,500	$22,500	$22,500	$22,500	$22,500		$22,500	$22,500	
6	Less income tax @ 25%			5,625	5,625	5,625	5,625	5,625	5,625	5,625	5,625	5,625		5,625	5,625	—
7	After-tax expenses savings	$ 143,666		$16,875	$16,875	$16,875	$16,875	$16,875	$16,875	$16,875	$16,875	$16,875		$16,875	$16,875	$ —
8																
9	Tax savings from depreciation tax shield:															
10	Year 1	$ 1,278		$ 1,406												
11	Year 2	2,237			$ 2,707											
12	Year 3	1,881				$ 2,504										
13	Year 4	1,583					$ 2,317									
14	Year 5	1,331						$ 2,143								
15	Year 6	1,119							$ 1,982							
16	Year 7	941								$ 1,833						
17	Year 8	791									$ 1,696					
18	Year 9	710										$ 1,673				
19	Year 10	645														
20	Year 11	586														
21	Year 12	533														
22	Year 13	485														
23	Year 14	440														
24	Year 15	400														
25	Year 16	364														
26	Year 17	331														
27	Year 18	301														
28	Year 19	274												$ 1,673		
29	Year 20	249													$ 1,673	
30	Year 21	113														$ 837
31	Total PV of future cash flows	$ 160,258		$18,281	$19,582	$19,379	$19,192	$19,018	$18,857	$18,708	$18,571	$18,548		$18,548	$18,548	$ 837
32	Net present value	$ 10,258														

of cash. They also have the same consequence of increasing income taxes. In our example, saving $22,500 in cash expenses each year raises taxable income by $22,500, which leads to an increase in taxes of $5,625 ($22,500 × 25%). Thus, the annual after-tax cash flow is $16,875—the $22,500 savings less the $5,625 tax increase.

Annual depreciation tax shield: The depreciation deduction on the tax return shields an equal amount of income from taxes. The avoided taxes are equal to the depreciation deduction multiplied by the applicable tax rate. In our illustration, the annual tax savings from the depreciation tax shield are as follows:

Tax return depreciation, 150% declining balance, half-year convention.

	A	B	C	D
1	Year	Annual Depreciation	Tax Rate	Tax Shield
2	1	$ 5,625	25%	$1,406
3	2	10,829	25	2,707
4	3	10,016	25	2,504
5	4	9,266	25	2,317
6	5	8,570	25	2,143
7	6	7,928	25	1,982
8	7	7,332	25	1,833
9	8	6,783	25	1,696
10	9	6,693	25	1,673
11	10	6,692	25	1,673
12	11	6,693	25	1,673
13	12	6,692	25	1,673
14	13	6,693	25	1,673
15	14	6,692	25	1,673
16	15	6,693	25	1,673
17	16	6,692	25	1,673
18	17	6,693	25	1,673
19	18	6,692	25	1,673
20	19	6,693	25	1,673
21	20	6,692	25	1,673
22	21	3,347	25	837

Step 3: Project termination
For purposes of this illustration, we have assumed that the HVAC system will be worthless at the end of its 20-year life. Thus, there will be no additional incremental cash flow at the end of the project. When the system is replaced, any cost of removing the old system will be added to the cost of the installation of a new HVAC system as part of the initial investment in the new system.

Step 4: Present value calculations
The present value column in **Exhibit 12-9** shows the results of the calculations of the present values of the cash flows discussed earlier. Proper consideration of the required investment involves neither an income tax nor a present value calculation. Fezzari's $150,000 investment itself is not tax deductible; the related depreciation deductions are tax deductible and are, of course, incorporated into our previous analysis. Because the investment expenditure is immediate, no discounting for present value is required. Thus, $150,000 represents the after-tax present value of the required investment outflow.

The $16,875 saved each year for 20 years can be treated as an annuity. The present value of an annuity of $16,875 for 20 years at 10% is $143,666 (PV = $16,875 × 8.51356).

Because the tax shield amounts differ from year to year based on the tax depreciation deduction, the present value of each year's amount must be computed separately. These amounts are computed using the PV factors as shown next:

	A	B	C	D
1	**Year**	**Depreciation**	**PV Factor**	**PV**
2	1	$1,406	0.90909	$1,278
3	2	2,707	0.82645	2,237
4	3	2,504	0.75131	1,881
5	4	2,317	0.68301	1,583
6	5	2,143	0.62092	1,331
7	6	1,982	0.56447	1,119
8	7	1,833	0.51316	941
9	8	1,696	0.46651	791
10	9	1,673	0.42410	710
11	10	1,673	0.38554	645
12	11	1,673	0.35049	586
13	12	1,673	0.31863	533
14	13	1,673	0.28966	485
15	14	1,673	0.26333	440
16	15	1,673	0.23939	400
17	16	1,673	0.21763	364
18	17	1,673	0.19784	331
19	18	1,673	0.17986	301
20	19	1,673	0.16351	274
21	20	1,673	0.14864	249
22	21	837	0.13501*	113
23	* Manually computed.			

> Present value of a single sum payment, over 20 periods, at a 10% discount factor. See Table III in Appendix A.

These amounts are summed to arrive at the total present value of the future cash flows, or $160,258.

Step 5: Net present value calculation

The net present value is calculated by subtracting the initial investment from the total present value of the future cash flows. With its annual savings of cash expense and tax savings from the depreciation tax shield, the $150,000 investment results in future cash flows with a total present value of $160,258 and therefore a net present value of $10,258. This positive return on the capital invested, adjusted for the time value of money, means that the project will return more than the 10% return sought by Fezzari management.

On the basis of the net present value analysis alone, it would appear that Fezzari management should accept the proposal. However, rather than accept the project outright, this analysis may provide a basis to review the underlying assumptions of the analysis that resulted in acceptance of the project. For example, management may wish to evaluate the estimate of $22,500 in annual utility savings. If the anticipated savings are expected to decrease, then the project becomes more risky.

Hint: Note that net present value calculations do not provide an exact rate of return provided by the capital investment decision. The net present value method only tells management whether the investment exceeds the minimum required rate of return.

Liquidation Proceeds

The amount realized when an asset is liquidated contributes to the relative attractiveness of an investment in capital equipment. Liquidation proceeds on long-lived assets are sometimes disregarded because their occurrence is so far in the future that the amounts are difficult to predict, and their present values tend to be small. When useful lives are short, however, liquidation proceeds may be a deciding factor in the analysis. In our illustration, the HVAC system has a 20-year life with no salvage value. However, assume that as a sales promotion, the manufacturer of the HVAC system guaranteed to buy back the system for $20,000 after 20 years. For tax purposes, salvage value may be ignored in computing depreciation, so the machine is fully depreciated over the 20 years to a zero book value. The HVAC's sale for $20,000, then, creates a $20,000 gain on the tax return ($20,000 sales price − $0 tax book value). The $20,000 gain increases income taxes by $5,000, which is deducted from the sales price of $20,000 to produce a net after-tax cash flow of $15,000 in Year 20. The present value of $15,000 for 20 years at 10% is $2,229.60 ($15,000 × 0.14864; see Table III in Appendix A).

Note that if an asset is sold before the end of its tax depreciation period, a loss may be generated for tax purposes. The loss operates as a tax shield because it shields an equal amount of income from taxes. The tax savings is added to the cash proceeds to determine the net after-tax cash flow.

TAKEAWAY 12.3	Concept ➝	Method ➝	Assessment
	You have been asked to calculate the NPV of a potential investment in a new piece of machinery used in your company's manufacturing process.	Perform NPV Analysis: • Step 1: Identify the initial investment. • Step 2: Calculate the annual cash flows. • Step 3: Project any termination values. • Step 4: Perform present value calculations. • Step 5: Calculate the net present value.	The calculated NPV is then compared to the company's minimum required rate of return. However, rather than accept or reject the project outright, this may provide a basis to review the underlying assumptions of the analysis.

Excess Present Value Index

Alternative capital expenditure proposals may be compared in terms of their **excess present value index**, defined as follows:

$$\text{Excess present value index} = \frac{\textbf{Total present value of future cash flows}}{\textbf{Initial investment}}$$

For the investment presented in **Exhibit 12-9**, the excess present value index would be

$$\frac{\$160,258}{\$150,000} = 1.068$$

The higher the ratio of return on investment, the more attractive is the proposal. A ratio below 1.00 means that the project returns less than the target rate of return, and a ratio above 1.00 means that the project return exceeds the target rate of return. Although the excess present value index may be a convenient measure for ranking various proposals, it does not reflect the amount of the investment. Two proposals, requiring initial cash investments of $5,000 and $5,000,000, respectively, could have identical excess present value indexes but could hardly be considered equal investment opportunities.

YOUR TURN! 12.5

The solution is on page 12-46.

MBC

Mining Equipment Manufacturer is considering the purchase of a new building. The building would require an initial outlay of $350,000. It would be depreciated using the straight-line method over 20 years, with a $15,000 salvage value. The building would generate cash inflows of $47,200/year; the company's income tax rate is 30% and WACC is 8%. Calculate the NPV of this project and decide whether the investment should be undertaken.

ENVIRONMENTAL, SOCIAL, AND GOVERNANCE   Sustainability in capital budget decisions

There is a strong business case for considering sustainability issues as central rather than tangential to the capital budgeting analysis. For example, more energy and water efficient designs can result in lower costs over the project's lifetime. In addition, considering sustainability issues upfront can help protect the project from future sustainability risks, such as climate change and resource scarcity. Furthermore, intangible benefits of demonstrating a commitment to sustainability can build trust among stakeholders, including regulators and local communities. Finally, there is growing evidence that firms with better sustainability performance enjoy lower costs of capital because of a lower risk profile.*

*CAPEX. A practical guide to embedding sustainability into capital investment appraisal. A4S Chief Financial Officer Leadership Network

OTHER CAPITAL BUDGETING ANALYSES

Internal Rate of Return Analysis

The net present value (NPV) method only tells management whether an investment exceeds (a positive NPV) or fails to exceed (a negative NPV) the minimum required rate of return used in the NPV calculation. Managers may prefer to know the exact rate of return of the capital investment.

LO6 **Demonstrate** the internal rate of return method of capital expenditure analysis.

eLecture

MBC

The **internal rate of return (IRR)** method provides the rate of return, based on the present value of all future cash flows, that a company can expect to earn on a capital investment decision. More specifically, the IRR method calculates the interest rate that makes the NPV of the capital investment exactly equal to zero. Another way of thinking about IRR is that the calculation provides the exact interest rate that makes the initial cost of the investment equal to the present value of the investment's net cash flows. The higher the IRR, the more advantageous the project.

IRR calculations are quite burdensome when done manually, as it often requires trial-and-error NPV calculations before a discount rate that yields an NPV value equal to zero can be discovered. However, IRR calculations are very simple to perform using Excel or business calculators.

Basic Steps

Exhibit 12-10 illustrates the IRR method using Excel. For simplicity and comparison purposes, we will use the same after-tax cash flows presented in **Exhibit 12-9**.

In **Exhibit 12-9** the net present value calculations indicate a positive NPV of $10,258. Again, the positive return on capital invested, adjusted for the time value of money, simply indicates that the project will return more than the 10% return sought by Fezzari management. As illustrated in **Exhibit 12-10**, the IRR method provides the actual rate of return of the project: 11.0%. Again, note that the IRR analysis returns a rate greater than the minimum required rate of return of 10%.

	IRR Method Using Excel
Step 1	Enter the initial investment as a negative number [Cell D2]. In our example, the new HVAC system has an installed price of $150,000.
Step 2	In [Cell D3], immediately under the initial investment [Cell D2], enter the sum of net cash after-tax cash flows for Year 1. In our example, Year 1 provides after-tax expense savings of $16,875 and after-tax savings from the depreciation tax shield of $1,406, for a total of $18,281 in after-tax savings.
Step 3	Continue to enter the sum of net after-tax cash flows for Years 2 through 21. Each year's cash flows should be entered in its own cell immediately under the prior year's value of cash flows.
Step 4	Click on **Formulas**.
Step 5	Choose **IRR** from the **Financial** drop-down list.
Step 6	The Formula Builder diolog box will appear. With the cursor in the Value dialog box, highlight the entire array of cells containing the sum of net after-tax cash flows. In **Exhibit 12-10**, this array would be (D2:D23).
Step 7	Press **Enter**, and the result will appear in the cell. The result is in the Internal Rate of Return (IRR) and is 11%.

| EXHIBIT 12-10 | Internal Rate of Return (IRR) Example | | |
A	B	C	D
1 Year	After-Tax Expense Savings	Tax-Savings from Depr. Tax Shield	Sum of Net After-Tax Cash Flows
2 0			$(150,000)
3 1	$16,875	$1,406	18,281
4 2	16,875	2,707	19,582
5 3	16,875	2,504	19,379
6 4	16,875	2,317	19,192
7 5	16,875	2,143	19,018
8 6	16,875	1,982	18,857
9 7	16,875	1,833	18,708
10 8	16,875	1,696	18,571
11 9	16,875	1,673	18,548
12 10	16,875	1,673	18,548
13 11	16,875	1,673	18,548
14 12	16,875	1,673	18,548
15 13	16,875	1,673	18,548
16 14	16,875	1,673	18,548
17 15	16,875	1,673	18,548
18 16	16,875	1,673	18,548
19 17	16,875	1,673	18,548
20 18	16,875	1,673	18,548
21 19	16,875	1,673	18,548
22 20	16,875	1,673	18,548
23 21	—	837	837
24			
25 IRR			11.00%
26 Minimum required rate of return			10.00%

11% is the interest rate that makes the initial investment of $150,000 equal to the present value of the investment's net cash flows.

The IRR of 11% indicates that the project will provide a greater return than the minimum required rate of return of 10%.

YOUR TURN! 12.6

The solution is on page 12-46.

MBC

The Farm Company is considering investing in solar panels to generate enough power to run its irrigation system. The local utility company has agreed to purchase any unused power generated by the Farm Company's new solar panels. Between the new source of revenue and the cost savings provided by the solar panels, the company expects to generate $225,000 per year in net after-tax cash inflows. The solar panels will cost $1,750,000 to purchase and install and have an expected useful life of 15 years with no residual value. Calculate the internal rate of return (IRR) of the capital investment.

Cash Payback Analysis

LO7 Present the cash payback and average rate of return methods of capital expenditure analysis.

MBC

The **cash payback method** is a form of capital expenditure analysis that evaluates investment proposals in terms of the **cash payback period**. The cash payback period is the time in years that it takes net future after-tax cash inflows to equal the original investment.

Assume that Fezzari received a competing proposal for its new HVAC system. Management is considering purchasing either system A or system B, for which the following data are given:

System	Investment Required	Annual Net After-Tax Cash Inflows	Useful Life
A................................	$150,000	$17,250	20 years
B................................	115,000	15,000	15 years

For this illustration, we have assumed that the systems will be depreciated on a straight-line basis for tax purposes, making the annual net cash inflows equal over time. The cash payback period is computed as follows:

$$\frac{\text{Original investment}}{\text{Annual net cash inflows}} = \text{Cash payback in years}$$

Thus, for the two systems, we obtain:

$$\text{System A: } \frac{\$150,000}{\$17,250} = \textbf{8.70-year cash payback}$$

$$\text{System B: } \frac{\$115,000}{\$15,000} = \textbf{7.67-year cash payback}$$

This analysis shows that system A will pay back its required investment in 8.7 years, and system B will take 7.67 years. Because the decision rule in cash payback analysis states that the shorter the payback period, the better, system B would be considered the better investment.

If annual net cash inflows are not equal, the cash payback period is computed by summing the annual cash inflows until the cumulative amount equals the initial investment. For example, refer back to **Exhibit 12-9**. The investment is expected to generate annual net after-tax cash inflows for nine years, as follows:

Year	Annual After-Tax Cash Inflows	Cumulative Cash Payback	Amount Required to Reach $150,000
1	$18,281	$ 18,281	$131,719
2	19,582	37,863	112,137
3	19,379	57,242	92,758
4	19,192	76,434	73,566
5	19,018	95,452	54,548
6	18,857	114,309	35,691
7	18,708	133,017	16,983
8	18,571	151,588	
9	18,548	170,136	

As shown in the amount required to reach $150,000 column, the original investment in the HVAC system will be recovered in cash partway through Year 8. The portion of the year required may be computed by dividing the remaining amount needed by the next year's inflow ($16,983/$18,571 = 0.914). The cash payback period, then, is 7.914 years.

Concern for the payback of investments is quite natural because the shorter a project's payback period, the more quickly the funds invested in that project are recovered and available for other investments. In high-risk investments, the payback period indicates how soon a firm is "bailed out" of an investment should projected cash inflows prove inaccurate.

Concept ➝	Method ➝	Assessment	TAKEAWAY 12.4
You work for a startup that needs to make quick cash recovery on its capital investments. You are asked to analyze a capital investment project.	The cash payback in years is computed as the original investment divided by the annual net cash flows. If annual net cash inflows are not equal, the cash payback period is determined by summing the annual cash inflows until the cumulative amount equals the initial investment.	The cash payback period is the time in years that it takes net future after-tax cash inflows to equal the original investment. The cash payback is particularly important to new companies or companies that may need a fast recovery of cash.	

The cash payback method is considered less sophisticated than net present value analysis. A primary limitation of cash payback analysis is that the relative profitability of various investments is not specifically considered. Note, for example, that in the previous illustration, system B has the better (shorter) cash payback period. However, its useful life, which is ignored in cash payback analysis, indicates that system B will stop generating cash inflows about seven years beyond payback. In contrast, although system A has a longer payback period, it will generate future cash inflows for over 11 years beyond payback and therefore promises to be more profitable.

Regardless of its failure to consider profitability, cash payback analysis is widely used, probably because of its relative simplicity. It can be useful in conjunction with other analyses or as a preliminary screening device for investment projects under consideration.

Average Rate of Return Analysis

The **average rate of return method** uses accrual accounting information in its calculation, not cash flows. This approach addresses the future impact on the income statement.

This measure is calculated as follows:

$$\text{Average rate of return} = \frac{\text{Average annual net income from investment}}{\text{Average investment}}$$

Note that the focus here is not on after-tax cash flows but on traditional accounting net income.

Assume that system A described earlier requires an initial investment of $150,000, provides $17,250 annual cash inflows from operations, and has a useful life of 20 years. Assuming no salvage value, the accounting annual straight-line depreciation on system A would be ($150,000/20), or $7,500. With an income tax rate of 25%, the average annual net income from the investment would be $7,312, computed as follows:

Cash inflow from operations.	$17,250
Depreciation expense.	7,500
Pre-tax income from investment.	$ 9,750
Income tax expense	2,438
Net income from investment.	$ 7,312

If the annual net incomes from investment are unequal, we would compute the average annual net income from investment by (1) summing the annual net incomes and (2) dividing by the number of years.

We may calculate average investment simply by adding the beginning and ending investments and dividing by 2. The ending investment is the expected salvage value. In our illustration, system A has no salvage value, so the ending investment is zero. Average investment is therefore $75,000 [($150,000 + $0)/2].

The average rate of return on system A is

$$\frac{\$7,312}{\$75,000} = 9.75\%$$

The decision rule for average rate of return analyses states that the higher the return, the more attractive the investment.

ACCOUNTING IN PRACTICE   **According to the U.S. Annual Capital**

According to the U.S. Census Bureau's 2019 Capital Spending Report, capital spending by U.S. nonfarm businesses increased 73.6% over the ten-year period from 2010 to 2019[1] and 6.4% (or $108.7 billion) from 2018 to 2019[2]. Capital spending between 2018 and 2019 in the U.S. manufacturing sector was up 5.7% (or $14.8 billion), construction was up 29.6% (or $11.5 billion), educational services were down 3.7% (or $3.7 billion), and healthcare and social assistance were up 7.5% (or $8.1 billion).

[1] https://www.census.gov/library/publications/2020/econ/2021-csr.html
[2] https://www.census.gov/content/dam/Census/library/publications/2019/econ/e19-aces.pdf

As an approach to capital expenditure analysis, the average rate of return method is often defended as being most easily understood by management personnel who are accustomed to thinking in accounting terms and concepts. It has two major limitations, however. First, the calculations rely heavily on accounting computations of net income and depreciation and are thus subject to arbitrary choices, such as the selection of a depreciation method. Second, average rate of return calculations do not consider the time value of money. Future cash flows are treated the same as current cash flows. Our discussion of net present value analysis illustrates the often substantial differences between future values and related present values discounted by even moderate interest rates.

As an example of how deceptive the average annual income figures used in average rate of return computations can be, consider three investment proposals, each of which requires a $40,000 initial investment (with a zero salvage value) and promises the annual cash inflows shown in **Exhibit 12-11**. Note that cash flows are concentrated in Year 1 in proposal A, are uniform in proposal B, and are concentrated in Year 5 in proposal C. Because average rate of return calculations fail to consider the timing of cash flows from operations, these three proposals would have identical 10% average rates of return and therefore would be considered equally attractive. Such an implication is hardly defensible in view of the substantial differences in the relative net present values of the operating cash flows. In our illustration, the difference between the present values of A and C is $12,968, an amount equal to 41% of the present value of C.

ACCOUNTING IN PRACTICE   **Sensitivity Analysis**

In practice, NPV projects often involve the use of sensitivity analysis. Sensitivity analysis provides a method of assessing the amount of risk involved in a proposed project. Sensitivity analysis also involves calculating the impact of variations on different quantifiable components of a project, helping management identify potential pitfalls. Management may also use sensitivity analysis to identify components (such as the discount rate or yearly cash inflows) of a plan that, when changed even slightly, will most impact the outcome of a project.

EXHIBIT 12-11 **Present Value Comparison of Equal Annual Average Incomes**			
A	B	C	D
1		**Proposals**	
	A	**B**	**C**
2 Annual net cash inflows:			
3 Year 1	$46,000	$10,000	$ 1,000
4 Year 2	1,000	10,000	1,000
5 Year 3	1,000	10,000	1,000
6 Year 4	1,000	10,000	1,000
7 Year 5	1,000	10,000	46,000
8 Aggregate net cash inflows	$50,000	$50,000	$50,000
9 Average annual net cash inflows ($50,000/5)	$10,000	$10,000	$10,000
10 Less depreciation ($40,000/5)	8,000	8,000	8,000
11 Average annual net income	$ 2,000	$ 2,000	$ 2,000
12 Average rate of return on investment			
13 $2,000/[($40,000 + $0)/2]	10%	10%	10%
14 Present value of net cash inflows at 10%	$44,700	$37,908	$31,732

Capital Budgeting: A Complex Subject

Because it incorporates aspects of such fields as economics, finance, business management, and accounting, the subject of capital budgeting is too complex to treat comprehensively in an introductory accounting book. In this chapter, we have simply provided some insight into problem-solving techniques in capital budgeting by stating decision rules in their simplest form, showing the relevance of present value concepts and after-tax cash flows, and creating an awareness of the potentials and limitations of several widely used approaches to capital expenditure analysis. The illustrations have highlighted key relationships. The rudiments presented here should serve as a basis for further study in finance and economics courses.

YOUR TURN! 12.7 The solution is on page 12-46. **MBC**	The Farm Company is considering investing in solar panels to generate enough power to run its irrigation system. The local utility company has agreed to purchase any unused power generated by the Farm Company's new solar panels. Between the new source of revenue and the cost savings provided by the solar panels, the company expects to generate $225,000 per year in net after-tax cash inflows. The solar panels will cost $1,750,000 to purchase and install and have an expected useful life of 15 years with no residual value. Calculate the cash payback period.

SERVICE INDUSTRY IN FOCUS

SERVICE AND MERCHANDISING

Environmental Business Consultants (EBC) is deciding whether to purchase an office building. EBC has found a three-story Class A office building in San Jose, California, with a purchase price of $2,000,000. Only two stories are needed to operate, and as such EBC can lease out the lower story, which consists of 3,000 square feet of floor space. The average full-service market lease rate for Class A office buildings in San Jose is $40 per square foot per year. In order to prepare the lower floor for lease, EBC will need to spend $250,000 on leasehold improvements. The building will be useful for 30 years and will be depreciated on a straight-line basis. EBC's income tax rate is 25% and its cost of capital is 10%.

The following table summarizes the cash flows from purchasing the building and leasing out the lower floor:

Initial outflows:	
Building purchase	$(2,000,000)
Leasehold improvements	(250,000)
Total initial outflows.	$(2,250,000)
Annual cash flows:	
Lease revenue*	$ 120,000
Total annual inflows	$ 120,000
Annual depreciation expense**	$ 75,000
Building useful life (years).	30
Income tax rate.	25%
Cost of capital	10%

* 3,000 sq. ft. × $40/sq. ft. per year

** $2,250,000/30 years

Required

Perform a capital expenditure analysis to decide whether EBC should purchase the building, analyzing the net present value as well as payback period and average rate of return.

Solution

Net present value analysis:

Annual after-tax revenues	$120,000 × (1 – 25%)	$	90,000
Tax shield from depreciation	$75,000 × 25%		18,750
Annual net cash inflows		$	108,750
Present value of the annual cash inflows	($108,750 × 9.42691)	$	1,025,176
Net present value			
Initial outflows		$(2,250,000)	
PV of future cash flows		1,025,176	
NPV		$(1,224,824)	

Cash payback analysis:

Initial cash outflow	$2,250,000
Divided by the annual net cash inflows. . . .	$108,750
Payback period	20.69 years

Average rate of return analysis:

Annual revenues.	$	120,000
Annual expenses		(75,000)
Average annual net income		45,000
Income tax @ 25%.		(11,250)
Average after-tax net income		33,750
Initial investment.		2,250,000
Ending investment		0
Average investment	($2,250,000 + $0)/2	$ 1,125,000
Average rate of return	$33,750/$1,125,000	3.0%

Based on the negative NPV, the long cash payback period and the small average rate of return, EBC should *not* purchase the building for $2,000,000.

DATA ANALYTICS   **Garbage In, Garbage Out**

Operating in a sustainable manner has become a major focus of businesses as we have all grown more aware of the devasting potential of climate change on our lives. The trouble is that knowing how to achieve the desired results can prove overwhelming. That is why **Waste Management** created Waste Management Sustainability Services to partner with businesses to help them achieve their sustainability goals. But as the old axiom goes, garbage in, garbage out. If you want to achieve meaningful results, you need good data for your decision-making process. To help, Waste Management offers their ENSPIRE® business intelligence data platform. The platform helps customers view all their sustainability-related data on web-based dashboards, thus simplifying the task of reporting and analysis.

Data Analytics

APPENDIX 12A: Time Value of Money Calculations

Using a Financial Calculator

Although present value tables can provide a handy method to solve some time value of money problems, they are not suitable for many real-world situations. For example, many real-world interest rates are not "even integers" like those appearing in Table I through Table IV of Appendix A, nor are many problems limited to the number of time periods appearing in the tables. Although it is still possible to solve these problems with the provided formulas, a financial calculator provides a quicker solution. Financial calculators can be distinguished from other calculators by the presence of dedicated keys for present and future values, along with keys for the number of periods, interest rates, and annuity payments.

L08 **Demonstrate** the use of a financial calculator and an electronic spreadsheet to perform time value of money calculations.

eLecture

MBC

There exist many brands of financial calculators; however, all of them work in much the same way. We demonstrate the calculation of time value of money problems using a Hewlett-Packard 10BII financial calculator, as illustrated in **Exhibit 12A-1**. (It is usually necessary to do some preliminary setup on a financial calculator before performing time value of money calculations. For example, the HP 10BII calculator has a default setting of monthly compounding; this may need to be changed if the problem calls for a different number of compounding periods, such as annual. In addition, the calculator assumes interest payments occur at the end of each period; this will need to be changed if the problem requires beginning-of-period payments. See your calculator manual to determine how to make these setting changes.)

EXHIBIT 12A-1   Hewlett-Packard 10BII Financial Calculator

The dedicated time value of money keys appear on the top row and are reproduced here:

Where

N = number of periods
i/YR = interest rate per period
PV = present value
PMT = annuity payment
FV = future value

To solve a time value of money problem using a financial calculator, input the known values and then press the key of the unknown value. **Exhibit 12A-2** illustrates the time value of money calculations from the NPV analysis example related to Fezzari's proposed new HVAC system presented earlier in the chapter in **Exhibit 12-9**. Panel 1 of **Exhibit 12A-2** demonstrates the present value of the project's expense savings of $16,875 (PMT = $16,875). Panels 2 and 3 present the present values of the depreciation tax shield amounts for Years 1 and 2 (FV Year 1 = $1,406; FV Year 2 = $2,707). These numbers are shown as positive numbers, indicating cash inflows or cash savings. Solving for the present value of these cash flows yields the present value in today's dollars. Financial calculators require cash outflows and inflows to be of opposite signs. If we were to enter PMT and FV as negative numbers, PV would be displayed as a positive number. Calculator solutions can be slightly different from the solutions using either the tables or the formulas due to rounding of the future value and present value multipliers.

EXHIBIT 12A-2   Time Value of Money Calculations Using a Financial Calculator

(1) Present value of after-tax expense savings of $16,875, over 20 years, discounted at 10%.*

Enter		Display		
20	N	N	=	20
10	i/YR	i/YR	=	10
16,875	PMT	PMT	=	16,875
0	FV	FV	=	0
Press	PV	PV	=	(143,666)

(2) Present value of Year 1 depreciation tax shield, discounted at 10%.*

Enter		Display		
1	N	N	=	1
10	i/YR	i/YR	=	10
0	PMT	PMT	=	0
1,406	FV	FV	=	1,406
Press	PV	PV	=	(1,278)

(3) Present value of Year 2 depreciation tax shield, discounted at 10%.*

Enter		Display		
2	N	N	=	2
10	i/YR	i/YR	=	10
0	PMT	PMT	=	0
2,707	FV	FV	=	2,707
Press	PV	PV	=	(2,237)

---

* Be sure to "clear all" and preset your compounding to annual.

Using an Electronic Spreadsheet

In addition to present value tables and financial calculators, another way to solve time value of money problems is with an electronic spreadsheet such as Excel. Excel has several built-in functions that allow calculation of time value of money problems. Depending on the version of Excel, these functions are accessed differently. Within Excel 2016, select Financial within the Formulas tab and then select PV from the drop-down menu. The following examples show how to use Excel to solve the same problems we previously solved using a financial calculator.

Example 1

Find the present value of 20 cash inflows of $16,875 at a 10% discount rate. Use the PV function and enter the values as follows:

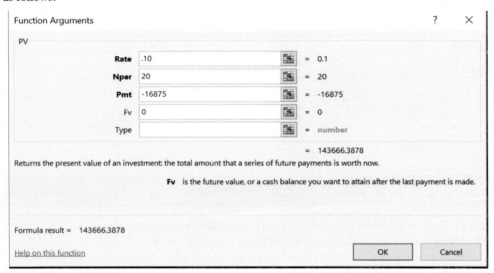

Example 2

Find the present value of a $1,406 depreciation tax shield for 1 year at a 10% discount rate. Use the PV function and enter the values as follows:

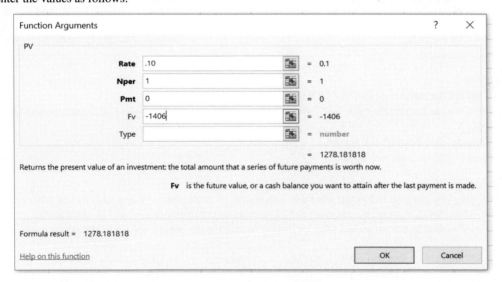

Example 3

Find the present value of a $2,707 depreciation tax shield for two years at a 10% discount rate. Use the PV function and enter the values as follows:

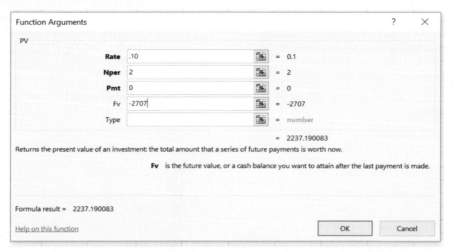

COMPREHENSIVE PROBLEM

MBC

Carolina Company is evaluating a possible $150,000 investment in equipment that would increase cash flows from operations for four years. The equipment will have no salvage value.

The income tax rate is 30%. Carolina uses a 15% hurdle rate when using net present value analysis. Other information regarding the proposal is as follows:

	Year 1	Year 2	Year 3	Year 4
Cash inflow from operations (pre-tax)	$60,000	$87,000	$42,000	$40,000
Depreciation on tax return	50,000	67,000	22,000	11,000
Depreciation in financial statements	37,500	37,500	37,500	37,500
Net income from investment	15,750	34,650	3,150	1,750
PV Factor @ 15%	0.86957	0.75614	0.65752	0.57175

Required

a. What are the annual net after-tax cash inflows from this proposal?
b. Compute the net present value and indicate whether it is positive or negative. (Round amounts to nearest dollar.)
c. Compute the cash payback period.
d. Compute the average rate of return.

Solution

a. We may compute the individual after-tax cash effects by multiplying (1) the cash inflow from operations by 70% (that is, 1 – Income tax rate) and (2) the tax return depreciation by 30% (that is, the income tax rate). Combining the individual after-tax cash effects gives the annual net after-tax cash inflows:

Year 1:	$60,000 × 70% = $42,000		Year 3:	$42,000 × 70% = $29,400
	50,000 × 30% = 15,000			22,000 × 30% = 6,600
	After-tax cash flow $57,000			After-tax cash flow $36,000

Year 2:	$87,000 × 70% = $60,900		Year 4:	$40,000 × 70% = $28,000
	67,000 × 30% = 20,100			11,000 × 30% = 3,300
	After-tax cash flow $81,000			After-tax cash flow $31,300

Alternatively, we may compute the net after-tax cash inflows by subtracting the cash income tax payments from the cash inflows from operations. The annual cash income tax payments are 30% of the cash inflow from operations less the tax return depreciation.

	Year 1	Year 2	Year 3	Year 4
Cash inflow from operations............................	$60,000	$87,000	$42,000	$40,000
Cash payment for income taxes......................	3,000	6,000	6,000	8,700
After-tax cash flows	$57,000	$81,000	$36,000	$31,300

b.

Year	Annual Net After-Tax Cash Inflows	PV Factor	Present Value
1	$57,000	0.86957	$ 49,565
2	81,000	0.75614	61,247
3	36,000	0.65752	23,671
4	31,300	0.57175	17,896
Total present value			152,379
Investment required in equipment			150,000
Net positive present value			$ 2,379

c. The cash payback period is 2 1/3 years, computed as follows:

Year	Annual Net After-Tax Cash Inflows	Cumulative Cash Payback	
1	$57,000	$ 57,000	
2	81,000	138,000	
3	36,000	150,000	(requires 1/3 of $36,000 to reach $150,000)
4	31,300		

d.

Annual net income from investment:	Year 1...........	$15,750
	Year 2...........	34,650
	Year 3...........	3,150
	Year 4...........	1,750
	Total	$55,300

Average annual net income from investment: $55,300/4 = $13,825
Average investment: ($150,000 + $0)/2 = $75,000
Average rate of return: $13,825/$75,000 = 18.4%

SUMMARY OF LEARNING OBJECTIVES

Introduce and illustrate the elements of capital budgeting. (p. 12-3)   **LO1**

- Capital budgeting is the planning of long-lived asset investments. Capital expenditure analysis basically examines how well prospective future returns justify related current investments.
- Most capital expenditures have three stages: (1) initial investment, (2) operational cash flows, and (3) project termination.

Discuss required rates of return and the time value of money. (p. 12-5)   **LO2**

- Cost of capital is a measure of the firm's cost for investment capital; it usually represents the minimum acceptable return for investment opportunities.
- The time value of money concept recognizes that the further into the future cash flows occur, the less current economic worth they have.
- The difference between present and future values is a function of interest rates and time periods.

LO3   **Demonstrate the use of present value factors to perform time value of money calculations. (p. 12-8)**

- Present value factor tables enable us to compute the present values of future cash flows at appropriate interest rates.
- The present value calculations used most frequently in capital budgeting are those for future single-sum flows and end-of-period annuity flows.
- The present value of a single sum calculation is used to determine the present value of sporadic cash flows when the returns expected on an investment, or the expenditures it requires, are unequal amounts or are expected at irregular intervals during or at the end of the life of the investment. The formula for the present value of a single sum is PV = FV × PV table factor.
- The present value of an annuity is used to determine the present value of cash flows that are the same each period over two or more equal periods. The formula for the present value of an annuity is PV = PMT × PV table factor.

LO4   **Explain and illustrate the determination of after-tax cash flows. (p. 12-10)**

- After-tax cash flows probably represent the most relevant measure of the prospective returns of proposed investments.
- We convert cash flows from revenues and expenses into after-tax amounts by multiplying them by (1 – Income tax rate).
- Depreciation deductions shield revenues from taxation, referred to as a tax shield. We convert depreciation deductions into their after-tax cash flow effect by multiplying the deduction by the applicable income tax rate.

LO5   **Describe the net present value method of capital expenditure analysis. (p. 12-14)**

- Net present value analysis compares the present value of net future cash flow returns with the investment. Projects having zero or positive net present value are acceptable.
- Alternative investment proposals may be compared in terms of their excess present value index; the higher the index, the more attractive is the proposal.

LO6   **Demonstrate the internal rate of return method of capital expenditure analysis. (p. 12-19)**

- Internal rate of return (IRR) is the interest rate that makes the net present value (NPV) of all cash flows (both positive and negative) from an investment equal to zero.
- The IRR represents the expected rate of return that will be earned on a capital investment.

LO7   **Present the cash payback and average rate of return methods of capital expenditure analysis. (p. 12-21)**

- Cash payback analysis measures the time in years necessary for the net future after-tax cash flows to equal the original investment. In this type of analysis, the shorter the payback period, the more attractive is the investment.
- Average rate of return analysis compares the annual average net income with the average investment. The higher this ratio is, the more attractive is the investment.
- Cash payback analysis fails to consider the relative profitability of alternative projects. Average rate of return analysis fails to consider the time value of money.

LO8   **Demonstrate the use of a financial calculator and an electronic spreadsheet to perform time value of money calculations. (p. 12-26)**

- Financial calculators and spreadsheet programs also enable us to compute the present values of future cash flows at appropriate interest rates.

SUMMARY	Concept ⟶	Method ⟶	Assessment
TAKEAWAY 12.1	Can a firm determine the cost of acquiring resources to fund capital investment decisions?	Use the weighted average cost of capital to determine the cost of aquiring capital by issuing stock, using retained earnings, borrowing, or a combination therof.	At a minimum, capital investments should provide a rate of return at least as high as a firm's weighted average cost of capital.

Concept ➡	Method ➡	Assessment	SUMMARY
What is the time value of money?	Money available at the present time is worth more than the identical sum in the future due to its potential earning capacity. That is, the provided money can earn interest.	The time value of money explains why interest is paid or earned. Interest, whether it is on a deposit or debt, compensates the depositor or lender for the time value of money.	**TAKEAWAY 12.2**
You have been asked to calculate the NPV of a potential investment in a new piece of machinery used in your company's manufacturing process.	Perform NPV Analysis: • Step 1: Identify the initial investment. • Step 2: Calculate the annual cash flows. • Step 3: Project any termination values. • Step 4: Perform present value calculations. • Step 5: Calculate the net present value.	The calculated NPV is then compared to the company's minimum required rate of return. However, rather than accept or reject the project outright, this may provide a basis to review the underlying assumptions of the analysis.	**TAKEAWAY 12.3**
You work for a startup that needs to make quick cash recovery on its capital investments. You are asked to analyze a capital investment project.	The cash payback in years is computed as the original investment divided by the annual net cash flows. If annual net cash inflows are not equal, the cash payback period is determined by summing the annual cash inflows until the cumulative amount equals the initial investment.	The cash payback period is the time in years that it takes net future after-tax cash inflows to equal the original investment. The cash payback is particularly important to new companies or companies that may need a fast recovery of cash.	**TAKEAWAY 12.4**

KEY TERMS

Annuity (p. 12-9)

Average rate of return method (p. 12-23)

Buffer margin (p. 12-6)

Capital budgeting (p. 12-3)

Cash payback method (p. 12-21)

Cash payback period (p. 12-21)

Cost of capital (p. 12-5)

Excess present value index (p. 12-19)

Hurdle rate (p. 12-6)

Internal rate of return (IRR) (p. 12-19)

Net present value method (p. 12-14)

Rate of return (p. 12-4)

Tax shield (p. 12-11)

Time value of money (p. 12-6)

Weighted average cost of capital, or WACC (p. 12-5)

Assignments with the 🔵MBC logo in the margin are available in my BusinessCourse.
See the Preface of the book for details.

SELF-STUDY QUESTIONS

(Answers to Self-Study Questions are at the end of this chapter.)

1. **A firm's cost of acquiring the funds for capital investment projects is known as the**
   a. Payback period.
   b. Rate of return.
   c. Cost of capital.
   d. Time value of money.

   LO2

2. **All other things remaining the same, when the interest rate used to discount future values increases, present values**
   a. Decrease.
   b. Increase in proportion to the interest rate increase.
   c. Remain the same.
   d. Increase but not in proportion to the interest rate increase.

   LO2

LO4   3. **Although depreciation is a noncash expense, it does have an indirect effect on cash flows because it shelters an equal amount of income from income taxes. This feature is known as a**

    a. Buffer margin.   *c.* Depreciation flow.

    b. Cash payback.   *d.* Tax shield.

LO5   4. **Blaine Company is considering four investment proposals, each requiring the same amount of initial cash investment. The excess present value index for each proposal is listed below. Using the index as a selection criterion, identify the index of the most attractive proposal.**

    a. 90   *c.* 110

    b. 100   *d.* 115

LO6   5. **Using internal rate of return, a project is rejected if the IRR**

    a. Is less than the required rate of return.   *d.* Is greater than the required rate of return.

    b. Is equal to the required rate of return.   *e.* Produces an NPV equal to zero.

    c. Is greater than the cost of capital.

LO7   6. **The primary limitation of the cash payback method is that it**

    a. Uses before-tax cash flows.

    b. Identifies the length of time it will take to recover the investment outlay in cash.

    c. Ignores the profitability of one investment project as compared to another.

    d. Involves a more sophisticated analysis than the net present value method.

QUESTIONS

LO1   1. What is capital budgeting?

LO1   2. List three reasons why capital budgeting decisions are often important.

LO1   3. What are the three stages typical of most investments in plant and equipment?

LO2   4. Briefly describe the concept of weighted average cost of capital.

LO2   5. In what sense does the cost of capital limit a firm's investment considerations?

LO2   6. A company plans to accumulate 75% of its needed investment capital by issuing bonds having a capital cost percentage of 12%; the balance will be raised by issuing stock having a capital cost percentage of 16%. What would be the weighted average cost of capital for the total amount of capital?

LO2   7. Briefly describe the concept of the time value of money.

LO3   8. You have the right to receive $30,000 at the end of each of the next four years, and money is worth 8%. Using the PV tables, your financial calculator, or Excel, compute the present value of this annuity.

LO3   9. A rich uncle allows you to stipulate which of two ways you receive your inheritance:

    a. $850,000 one year after his death or

    b. $250,000 on his death and $200,000 each year at the end of the first, second, and third years following his death. If money is worth 10%, what is the relative advantage of the more attractive alternative?

LO3   10. You can settle a debt with either a single payment now of $30,000 or with payments of $8,000 at the end of each of the next five years. If money is worth 10%, what is the relative advantage of the most attractive alternative? If money is worth 12%, would your answer change? Why?

LO4   11. Explain how to convert before-tax cash operating expenses and depreciation deductions into after-tax amounts.

LO4   12. What is meant by the term *depreciation tax shield*?

LO3, 5   13. What amounts are compared in net present value analysis? State the related decision rule.

LO5   14. What is an excess present value index?

LO6   15. Briefly describe the concept of internal rate of return.

LO7   16. Define cash payback period, state the related decision rule, and specify an important limitation of this analysis.

LO7   17. Define average rate of return, state the related decision rule, and specify an important limitation of this analysis.

SHORT EXERCISES

SE12-1. The following schedule reflects the incremental costs and revenues for a capital project. The company uses straight-line depreciation. The interest expense reflects an allocation of interest on the amount of this investment, based on the company's weighted average cost of capital.

Revenues		$650,000
Direct costs	$270,000	
Variable overhead	50,000	
Fixed overhead	20,000	
Depreciation	70,000	
General & administrative	40,000	
Interest expense	8,000	
Total costs		458,000
Net profit before taxes		$192,000

The annual cash flow from this investment, before tax considerations, would be

a. $192,000. c. $262,000.
b. $200,000. d. $270,000.

SE12-2. An accountant for Stability Inc. must calculate the weighted average cost of capital of the corporation using the following information.

		Interest Rate
Accounts payable	$35,000,000	0
Long-term debt	10,000,000	8%
Common stock	10,000,000	15%
Retained earnings	5,000,000	18%

What is the weighted average cost of capital of Stability?

a. 6.88% c. 10.25%
b. 8.00% d. 12.80%

SE12-3. Kielly Machines Inc. is planning an expansion program estimated to cost $100 million. Kielly is going to raise funds according to its target capital structure shown below.

Debt	0.30
Preferred stock	0.24
Equity	0.46

Kielly had net income available to common shareholders of $184 million last year of which 75% was paid out in dividends. The company has a marginal tax rate of 40%.

Additional data:

- The before-tax cost of debt is estimated to be 11%.
- The market yield of preferred stock is estimated to be 12%.
- The after-tax cost of common stock is estimated to be 16%.

What is Kielly's weighted average cost of capital?

a. 12.22% c. 13.54%
b. 13.00% d. 14.00%

SE12-4. Which one of the following items is **least** likely to directly impact an equipment replacement capital expenditure decision?

a. The net present value of the equipment that is being replaced.
b. The depreciation rate that will be used for tax purposes on the new asset.
c. The amount of additional accounts receivable that will be generated from increased production and sales.
d. The sales value of the asset that is being replaced.

LO3   **SE12-5.**   Wilcox Corporation won a settlement in a lawsuit and was offered four different payment alternatives by the defendant's insurance company. A review of interest rates indicates that 8% is appropriate for analyzing this situation. Ignoring any tax considerations, which one of the following four alternatives should the controller recommend to Wilcox management?

    a. $135,000 now

    b. $40,000 per year at the end of each of the next four years

    c. $5,000 now and $20,000 per year at the end of each of the next ten years

    d. $5,000 now and $5,000 per year at the end of each of the next nine years, plus a lump-sum payment of $200,000 at the end of the tenth year

LO5   **SE12-6.**   Allstar Company invests in a project with expected cash inflows of $9,000 per year for four years. All cash flows occur at year-end. The required return on investment is 9%. If the project generates a net present value (NPV) of $3,000, what is the amount of the initial investment in the project?

    a. $11,253.   c. $26,157.

    b. $13,236.   d. $29,160.

LO6   **SE12-7.**   Diane Harper, Vice President of Finance for BGN Industries, is reviewing material prepared by her staff prior to the board of directors meeting at which she must recommend one of four mutually exclusive options for a new product line. The summary information below indicates the initial investment required, the present value of cash inflows (excluding the initial investment) at BGN's hurdle rate of 16%, and the internal rate of return (IRR) for each of the four options.

Option	Investment	Present Value of Cash Inflows at 16%	IRR
X..	$3,950,000	$3,800,000	15.5%
Y..	3,000,000	3,750,000	19.0%
Z..	2,000,000	2,825,000	17.5%
W	800,000	1,100,000	18.0%

If there are no capital rationing constraints, which option should Harper recommend?

    a.   Option X.   c.   Option Z.

    b.   Option Y.   d.   Option W.

LO6   **SE12-8.**   For a given investment project, the interest rate at which the present value of the cash inflows equals the present value of the cash outflows is called the

    a.   hurdle rate.   c.   internal rate of return.

    b.   payback rate.   d.   cost of capital.

LO7   **SE12-9.**   Quint Company uses the payback method as part of its analysis of capital investments. One of its projects requires a $140,000 investment and has the following projected before-tax cash flows.

Year 1	$60,000
Year 2	$60,000
Year 3	$60,000
Year 4	$80,000
Year 5	$80,000

Quint has an effective 40% tax rate. Based on these data, the after-tax payback period is

    a.   1.5.   c.   3.4.

    b.   2.3.   d.   3.7.

LO4, 5   **SE12-10.**   A company is considering the purchase of a new production machine and is not sure whether the project fulfills its investment objective. The company requires that all investments must have a positive net present value (NPV). The machine costs $100,000 and will be depreciated for tax purposes on a straight-line basis over its useful life of five years. The machine has a $0 salvage value. The project will generate $30,000 of pretax operating cash inflow annually. The company has a 25% effective income tax rate and uses a 10% discount rate for investment projects. Which of the following represents the NPV of the project?

    a. $13,724   c. $(14,707)

    b. $4,246   d. $(33,661)

DATA ANALYTICS, DATA VISUALIZATION, AND EXCEL ACTIVITIES

Data Analytics, Data Visualization, and Excel Activities are available in myBusinessCourse. These assignments develop Excel, Tableau, and Data Analytics skills, which will enhance students' career readiness. These exercises are assignable and auto graded by MBC. For an overview of data analytics, see the appendix at the end of this book.

EXERCISES—SET A

E12-1A. Weighted Average Cost of Capital Gardner, Inc., plans to finance its expansion by raising the needed investment capital from the following sources in the indicated proportions and respective capital cost rates.

LO2

	Capital Cost	
Source	Proportion	Rate
Bonds	30%	13%
Preferred stock	10	9
Common stock	50	12
Retained earnings.	10	9
	100%	

Calculate the weighted average cost of capital.

E12-2A. Present Value Computations Assuming that money is worth 8%, compute the present value of

LO3

1. $7,000 received 15 years from today.
2. The right to inherit $1,000,000 14 years from now.
3. The right to receive $1,000 at the end of each of the next six years.
4. The obligation to pay $3,000 at the end of each of the next 10 years.
5. The right to receive $5,000 at the end of seven, eight, nine, and ten years from today.

E12-3A. After-Tax Cash Flows For each of the following independent situations, compute the net after-tax cash flow amount by subtracting cash outlays for operating expenses and income taxes from cash revenue. The cash outlay for income taxes is determined by applying the income tax rate to the cash revenue received less the cash and noncash (depreciation) expenses.

LO4

	A	B	C
Cash revenue received.	$110,000	$525,000	$275,000
Cash operating expenses paid	64,000	385,000	165,000
Depreciation on tax return	14,000	32,000	25,000
Income tax rate.	30%	25%	20%

E12-4A. After-Tax Cash Flows Using the data in E12-3A, (a) calculate the individual after-tax cash flow effect of each relevant item in each independent situation, and (b) sum the individual after-tax cash flows in each situation to determine the overall net after-tax cash flow.

LO4

E12-5A. Depreciation Tax Shields Lee & Company has purchased equipment for $200,000. After it is fully depreciated, the equipment will have no salvage value. Lincoln may select either of the following depreciation schedules for tax purposes:

LO4

Year	Option 1 Depreciation	Option 2 Depreciation
1	$40,000	$20,000
2	64,000	40,000
3	38,400	40,000
4	23,040	40,000
5	23,040	40,000
6	11,520	20,000

Assuming a 40% tax rate and a 12% desired annual return, compute the total present value of the tax savings provided by these alternative depreciation tax shields. Which depreciation schedule would be more attractive to Lincoln?

LO5   E12-6A. Net Present Value Analysis Cooper Corporation must evaluate two capital expenditure proposals. Cooper's hurdle rate is 10%. Data for the two proposals follow.

	Proposal X	Proposal Y
Required investment.	$120,000	$120,000
Annual after-tax cash inflows	24,000	
After-tax cash inflows at the end of years 3, 6, 9, and 12.		72,000
Life of project	12 years	12 years

Using net present value analysis, which proposal is the more attractive? If Cooper has sufficient funds available, should both proposals be accepted?

LO6   E12-7A. Internal Rate of Return Analysis Refer to data in E12-6A. What is the internal rate of return for Proposal X? For Proposal Y?

LO7   E12-8A. Cash Payback Refer to the data in E12-6A. What is the cash payback period for Proposal X? For Proposal Y?

LO7   E12-9A. Average Rate of Return Lakeland Company is considering the purchase of equipment for $175,000. The equipment will expand the company's production and increase revenue by $40,000 per year. Annual cash operating expenses will increase by $12,000. The equipment's useful life is 10 years with no salvage value. Lakeland uses straight-line depreciation. The income tax rate is 25%. What is the average rate of return on the investment?

EXERCISES—SET B

LO2   E12-1B. Weighted Average Cost of Capital Athens Manufacturing plans to finance its expansion by raising the needed investment capital from the following sources in the indicated proportions and respective capital cost rates.

Source	Proportion	Capital Cost Rate
Bonds	45%	12%
Preferred stock	10	14
Common stock	25	8
Retained earnings	20	10
	100%	

Calculate the weighted average cost of capital.

LO3   E12-2B. Present Value Computations Assuming that money is worth 12%, compute the present value of
1. $6,000 received 15 years from today.
2. The right to inherit $2,000,000 14 years from now.
3. The right to receive $2,000 at the end of each of the next six years.
4. The obligation to pay $1,000 at the end of each of the next 10 years.
5. The right to receive $10,000 at the end of seven, eight, nine, and ten years from today.

LO4   E12-3B. After-Tax Cash Flows For each of the following independent situations, compute the net after-tax cash flow amount by subtracting cash outlays for operating expenses and income taxes from cash revenue. The cash outlay for income taxes is determined by applying the income tax rate to the cash revenue received less the cash and noncash (depreciation) expenses.

	A	B	C
Cash revenue received.	$74,000	$430,000	$210,000
Cash operating expenses paid.	48,000	240,000	130,000
Depreciation on tax return	11,000	28,000	18,000
Income tax rate.	25%	35%	30%

E12-4B. After-Tax Cash Flows Using the data in E12-3B, (a) calculate the individual after-tax cash flow effect of each relevant item in each independent situation, and (b) sum the individual after-tax cash flows in each situation to determine the overall net after-tax cash flow.

LO4

SERVICE AND MERCHANDISING

E12-5B. Depreciation Tax Shields Mendota Company has purchased equipment for $100,000. After it is fully depreciated, the equipment will have no salvage value. Mendota may select either of the following depreciation schedules for tax purposes:

LO4

Year	Option 1 Depreciation	Option 2 Depreciation
1	$20,000	$10,000
2	32,000	20,000
3	19,200	20,000
4	11,520	20,000
5	11,520	20,000
6	5,760	10,000

Assuming a 40% tax rate and a 12% desired annual return, compute the total present value of the tax savings provided by these alternative depreciation tax shields. Which depreciation schedule would be more attractive to Mendota?

E12-6B. Net Present Value Analysis Hermson Company must evaluate two capital expenditure proposals. Hermson's hurdle rate is 12%. Data for the two proposals follow.

LO5

	Proposal X	Proposal Y
Required investment	$190,000	$190,000
Annual after-tax cash inflows	42,000	—
After-tax cash inflows at the end of years 3, 6, 9, and 12	—	126,000
Life of project	12 years	12 years

Using net present value analysis, which proposal do you find to be the more attractive? If Hermson has sufficient funds available, should both proposals be accepted?

E12-7B. Internal Rate of Return Analysis Refer to the data in E12-6B. What is the internal rate of return of Proposal X? For Proposal Y?

LO6

E12-8B. Internal Rate of Return Analysis White Mountain Mining, LLC, is considering the purchase of a new piece of machinery. The initial cost of the machine will be $6,250,000, and the machine will have a useful life of five years. The company's hurdle rate is 8%. The following cash flow projections have been made:

LO6

Year 1	$1,200,000
Year 2	$1,850,000
Year 3	$2,500,000
Year 4	$1,950,000
Year 5	$1,500,000

Calculate the internal rate of return for the machinery. Should White Mountain purchase the machinery?

E12-9B. Cash Payback Refer to the data in E12-6B. What is the cash payback period for proposal X? for proposal Y?

LO7

E12-10B. Average Rate of Return Thompson Furniture is considering the purchase of equipment for $120,000. The equipment will expand the company's production and increase revenue by $30,000 per year. Annual cash operating expenses will increase by $7,000. The equipment's useful life is 10 years with no salvage value. Thompson uses straight-line depreciation. The income tax rate is 35%. What is the average rate of return on the investment?

LO7

PROBLEMS—SET A

P12-1A. After-Tax Cash Flows Below is a list of aspects of various capital expenditure proposals that the capital budgeting team of Anchor, Inc., has incorporated into its net present value analyses during the

LO4

past year. Unless otherwise noted, the items listed are unrelated to each other. All situations assume a 40% income tax rate and an 11% minimum desired rate of return.

1. Pre-tax savings of $4,000 in cash expenses will occur in each of the next three years.
2. A machine is purchased now for $37,000 cash.
3. A long-haul tractor costing $27,000 will be depreciated $9,000, $12,000, $4,050, and $1,950, respectively, on the tax return over four years.
4. Equipment costing $200,000 will be depreciated over five years on the tax return in the following amounts: $25,000; $50,000; $50,000; $50,000; and $25,000.
5. Pre-tax savings of $8,800 in cash expenses will occur in each of the next six years.
6. Pre-tax savings of $7,000 in cash expenses will occur in one, three, and five years from now.
7. The tractor described in aspect 3 will be sold after four years for $5,000 cash.
8. The equipment described in aspect 4 will be sold after four years for $20,000 cash.

Required
Set up an answer form with the two column headings as shown below. Answer each investment aspect separately. Prepare your calculations on a separate paper and key them to each item. The answer to investment aspect 1 is presented as an example.

Investment Aspect 1	A After-Tax Cash Flow Effect(s) Inflows (Outflows)	B Year(s) of Cash Flow
	$2,400	1, 2, 3

Calculations:
1. Pre-tax cash savings.	$4,000
Less income tax at 40%	1,600
After-tax cash inflow	$2,400

a. Calculate and record in column A the related after-tax cash flow effect(s). Place parentheses around outflows.
b. Indicate in column B the timing of each cash flow shown in column A. Use 0 to indicate immediately and 1, 2, 3, 4, and so on for each year involved.

LO5   P12-2A. Net Present Value Analysis Champion Company is considering a contract that would require an expansion of its food processing capabilities. The contract covers five years. To provide the required products, Champion would have to purchase additional equipment for $58,000. Champion estimates the contract will provide annual net cash inflows (before taxes) of $21,000. For tax purposes, the equipment will be depreciated as follows:

Year 1	$ 8,000
Year 2	16,000
Year 3	16,000
Year 4	10,000
Year 5	8,000

Although salvage value is ignored in the tax depreciation calculations, Champion estimates the equipment will be sold for $5,000 after five years.

Required
Assuming a 35% income tax rate and a 10% hurdle rate, compute the net present value of this contract proposal. Using net present value analysis, should Champion accept the contract? (Round amounts to the nearest dollar.)

LO4, 5, 6, 7   P12-3A. Net Present Value, Cash Payback, and Average Rate of Return Methods Eastern Incorporated is evaluating a possible $64,000 investment in special tools that would increase cash flows from operations for four years. The tools will have no salvage value. The income tax rate is 40%. Western uses a 12% hurdle rate when using present value analysis. Other information regarding the proposal is as follows:

	Year 1	Year 2	Year 3	Year 4
Cash inflow from operations (pre-tax)	$25,000	$45,000	$22,500	$18,000
Depreciation on tax return	21,500	28,100	9,800	4,600
Depreciation in financial statements.	16,000	16,000	16,000	16,000
Net income from investment.	5,400	17,400	3,900	1,200

Required

a. What are the annual net after-tax cash inflows from this proposal?

b. Compute the net present value and indicate whether it is positive or negative. (Round amounts to nearest dollar.)

c. Compute the excess present value index.

d. Compute the cash payback period.

e. Compute the average rate of return.

f. Compute the internal rate of return.

P12-4A. Excess Present Value Index and Average Rate of Return Highpoint Company is evaluating five different capital expenditure proposals. The company's hurdle rate for net present value analyses is 12%. A 10% salvage value is expected from each of the investments. Information on the five proposals is as follows:

LO5, 6, 7

Proposal	Required Investment	Present Value at 12% of After-Tax Cash Flows	Average Annual Net Income from Investment
A.	$270,000	$310,030	$37,400
B.	200,000	236,780	26,000
C.	160,000	173,040	19,200
D.	180,000	216,300	27,600
E.	128,000	136,990	14,960

Required

a. Compute the excess present value index for each of the five proposals.

b. Compute the average rate of return for each of the five proposals.

c. Assume that Highpoint will commit no more than $500,000 to new capital expenditure proposals. Using the excess present value index, which proposals would be accepted? Using the average rate of return, which proposals would be accepted?

P12-5A. Cash Payback, Average Rate of Return, and Net Present Value Methods Landover Amusement Park is considering the construction of a new facility to house a curved, multistory movie screen. The facility will cost $400,000 and be useful for 10 years, with no salvage value. The facility will be depreciated on a straight-line basis over 10 years on both the books and the tax return. The following annual results are expected if the facility is constructed:

LO4, 5, 6, 7

SERVICE AND MERCHANDISING

Increase in annual cash revenue		$200,000
Increase in expenses:		
Cash operating expenses	$80,000	
Depreciation	40,000	120,000
Pretax income.		$ 80,000
Income tax expense (40%).		32,000
Net income		$ 48,000

Landover uses a 12% hurdle rate when analyzing capital expenditure proposals using net present value.

Required

a. What are the annual net cash flows (net inflows) from this project?

b. Compute the cash payback period.

c. Compute the average rate of return.

d. Compute the net present value and indicate whether it is positive or negative.

e. Compute the internal rate of return.

f. Assume that Landover decides to use a 10% hurdle rate when using net present value analysis. Compute the net present value using a 10% hurdle rate and indicate whether it is positive or negative.

LO2, 5 **P12-6A. Weighted Average Cost of Capital and Net Present Value Analysis** Reed Incorporated is considering a proposal to acquire new equipment for its manufacturing division. The equipment will cost $192,000, be useful for four years, and have a $12,000 salvage value. Reed expects annual savings in cash operating expenses (before taxes) of $68,000. For tax purposes, the annual depreciation deduction will be $64,000, $86,000, $28,000, and $14,000, respectively, for the four years. (The salvage value is ignored on the tax return.) The income tax rate is 40%.

Reed establishes a hurdle rate for a net present value analysis at the company's weighted average cost of capital plus 1 percentage point. Reed's capital is provided in the following proportions: debt, 50%; common stock, 35%; and retained earnings, 15%. The cost rates for these capital sources are debt, 8%; common stock, 10%; and retained earnings, 12%.

Required
a. Compute Reed's (1) weighted average cost of capital and (2) hurdle rate.
b. Using Reed's hurdle rate, compute the net present value of this capital expenditure proposal. Under net present value analysis, should Reed accept the proposal? (Round amounts to the nearest dollar.)

PROBLEMS—SET B

LO4 **P12-1B. After-Tax Cash Flows** Below is a list of aspects of various capital expenditure proposals that the capital budgeting team of Modern Systems, Inc., has incorporated into its net present value analyses during the past year. Unless otherwise noted, the items listed are unrelated to each other. All situations assume a 30% income tax rate and a 10% minimum desired rate of return.

1. Pre-tax savings of $5,000 in cash expenses will occur in each of the next three years.
2. A machine is purchased now for $82,000.
3. Special tools costing $45,000 will be depreciated $9,000, $18,000, and $18,000, respectively, on the tax return over a three-year life.
4. A patent purchased for $330,000 will be amortized on a straight-line basis over 15 years on the tax return. No salvage value is expected.
5. Pre-tax savings of $8,000 in cash expenses will occur in each of the next seven years.
6. Pre-tax savings of $5,500 in cash expenses will occur in one, four, and seven years from now.
7. The special tools described in aspect 3 will be sold after three years for $10,000 cash.
8. A truck with a tax book value of $7,200 after two years will be sold at that time for $4,600.

Required
Set up an answer form with the four column headings as shown below. Answer each investment aspect separately. Prepare your calculations on a separate paper and key them to each item. The answer to investment aspect 1 is presented as an example.

Investment Aspect 1	A After-Tax Cash Flow Effect(s) Inflows (Outflows)	B Year(s) of Cash Flow
	$3,500	1, 2, 3

Calculations:
1. Pre-tax cash savings..........................	$5,000
Less income tax at 30%	1,500
After-tax cash inflow	$3,500

a. Calculate and record in column A the related after-tax cash flow effect(s). Place parentheses around outflows.
b. Indicate in column B the timing of each cash flow shown in column A. Use 0 to indicate immediately and 1, 2, 3, 4, and so on for each year involved.

P12-2B. **Net Present Value Analysis** You have an opportunity to invest in a concession at a world exposition. To use the building and exhibits more fully, the venture is expected to cover a six-year period consisting of a preliminary year, the two years of formal exposition, and a three-year period of reduced operation as a regional exposition.

LO5

The terms of the concession agreement specify the following:

1. At inception, a $60,000 deposit is paid to Global Expo, Inc., the promoting organization. This amount is returned in full at the end of the six years if the operator maintains the concession in order and keeps it open during scheduled hours. The deposit is not tax deductible, nor is its return subject to income taxes.
2. The operator must install certain fixtures that will cost $240,000. The fixtures become the property of Global Expo, Inc., at the end of the six years.

After careful investigation and consultation with local experts, you conclude that the following schedule reflects the estimated pre-tax income of the concession. (Amounts are in thousands of dollars.)

	Year 1	Year 2	Year 3	Year 4	Year 5	Year 6
Sales (all cash).	$150	$435	$488	$300	$240	$180
Operating expenses:						
Cash	$ 75	$228	$279	$170	$140	$106
Tax depreciation	48	77	46	28	28	13
Total expenses.	$123	$305	$325	$198	$168	$119
Pre-tax income	$ 27	$130	$163	$102	$ 72	$ 61

Required
Assuming an income tax rate of 35% and a desired annual return of 12%, what is the net present value of this investment opportunity? What is the maximum amount that could be invested and still earning a 12% annual return? (Round amounts to the nearest dollar.)

P12-3B. **Cash Payback, Average Rate of Return, and Net Present Value Methods** At a cash cost of $330,000, Monona, Inc., can acquire equipment that will save $100,000 in annual cash operating expenses. No salvage value is expected at the end of its five-year useful life. Assume the machine will be depreciated over five years on a straight-line basis on both the books and the tax return. The income tax rate is 30% and Monona has a 10% hurdle rate when using a net present value analysis.

LO4, 5, 6, 7

Required
a. What are the annual after-tax cash savings in operating expenses?
b. What are the annual tax savings from the depreciation tax shield?
c. Compute the cash payback period.
d. Compute the average rate of return.
e. Compute the net present value and indicate whether it is positive or negative. (Round amounts to the nearest dollar.)
f. Compute the excess present value index.
g. Compute the internal rate of return.

P12-4B. **Excess Present Value Index and Average Rate of Return** Swanson Corporation is evaluating five different capital expenditure proposals. The company's hurdle rate for net present value analysis is 12%. A 15% salvage value is expected from each of the investments. Information on the five proposals is as follows:

LO5, 6, 7

SERVICE AND MERCHANDISING

Proposal	Required Investment	Net Present Value	Average Annual Net Income from Investment
A.	$ 50,000	$ 8,996	$ 9,100
B.	80,000	5,812	12,000
C.	110,000	27,034	18,300
D.	150,000	7,544	21,500
E.	72,000	15,822	13,960

Required

a.   Compute the excess present value index for each of the five proposals.

b.   Compute the average rate of return for each of the five proposals.

c.   Assume that Swanson will commit no more than $200,000 to new capital expenditure proposals. Using the excess present value index, which proposals would be accepted? Using the average rate of return, which proposals would be accepted?

 **LO4, 5, 6, 7**   **P12-5B.   Cash Payback, Average Rate of Return, and Net Present Value Methods** Lyle Company is considering whether to enter into a franchise agreement that would give the company exclusive distribution rights in a three-state region to a quality line of leisure spas. The franchise agreement will extend eight years and cost $600,000. There is no salvage value. The franchise cost will be amortized on a straight-line basis over eight years on both the books and the tax return. The following annual results are expected if the franchise is acquired:

Increase in annual cash revenue		$230,000
Increase in expenses:		
Cash operating expenses	$95,000	
Amortization	75,000	170,000
Pretax income		$ 60,000
Income tax expense (35%)		21,000
Net income		$ 39,000

Lyle uses a 12% hurdle rate when analyzing capital expenditure proposals using net present value.

Required

a.   What are the annual net cash flows (net inflows) from this proposal?

b.   Compute the cash payback period.

c.   Compute the average rate of return.

d.   Compute the net present value and indicate whether it is positive or negative.

e.   Assume that Lyle decides to use a 10% hurdle rate when using net present value analysis. Compute the net present value using a 10% hurdle rate and indicate whether it is positive or negative.

f.   Compute the internal rate of return.

 LO2, 5   **P12-6B.   Weighted Average Cost of Capital and Net Present Value Analysis** Manchester Company is considering a proposal to purchase special equipment at a cost of $740,000. The equipment will be useful for five years and has an expected $60,000 salvage value. Manchester expects annual savings in cash operating expenses (before taxes) of $255,000. For tax purposes, the annual depreciation deduction will be as follows. (Salvage value is ignored on the tax return.)

Year 1	$100,000
Year 2	180,000
Year 3	180,000
Year 4	180,000
Year 5	100,000

The income tax rate is 40%.

Manchester establishes a hurdle rate for a net present value analysis at the company's weighted average cost of capital plus 2 percentage points. Manchester's capital is provided in the following proportions: debt, 70%; common stock, 20%; and retained earnings, 10%. The cost rates for these capital sources are debt, 8%; common stock, 12%; and retained earnings, 10%.

Required

a.   Compute Manchester's (1) weighted average cost of capital and (2) hurdle rate.

b.   Using Manchester's hurdle rate, compute the net present value of this capital expenditure proposal. Under net present value analysis, should Manchester accept the proposal?

EYK12-1. **Business Decision Case** New Haven Corporation recently identified an investment opportunity involving the purchase of a patent that will permit the company to modify its line of CD recorders. The patent's purchase price is $720,000, and the legal protection it provides will last for five more years; there is no salvage value. However, after preparing the capital expenditure analysis below, New Haven's treasurer has recommended to the company's capital budgeting committee that the investment be rejected. Brad Decker, chairperson of the capital budgeting committee, finds it difficult to accept the treasurer's analysis because he "feels intuitively" that the investment is attractive. For this reason, he has retained you to review the treasurer's analysis and recommendation. You are provided with the following data and summary of the treasurer's analysis:

1. Required investment: $720,000 cash for the patent to be amortized on a straight-line basis, five-year useful life, with a zero salvage value.
2. Projected cash revenue and operating expenses:

Year	Cash Revenue	Cash Expenses
1	$ 620,000	$240,000
2	560,000	200,000
3	400,000	170,000
4	250,000	80,000
5	200,000	50,000
	$2,030,000	$740,000

3. Source of capital: New Haven plans to raise 10% of the needed capital by issuing bonds, 30% by issuing stock, and the balance from retained earnings. For these sources, the capital cost rates are 8%, 9%, and 10%, respectively. New Haven has a policy of seeking a return equal to the weighted average cost of capital plus 2.5 percentage points as a "buffer margin" for the uncertainties involved.
4. Income taxes: New Haven has an overall income tax rate of 30%.
5. Treasurer's analysis:

Average cost of capital		
(8% + 9% + 10%)/3 = 9%		
Total cash revenue		$2,030,000
Total cash expenses	$740,000	
Total amortization	720,000	
Total operating expenses		1,460,000
Projected net income over five years		$ 570,000
Average annual income		$ 114,000
Present value of future returns		$ 443,420
Required investment		720,000
Negative net present value		$ (276,580)

Recommendation: Reject investment because of insufficient net present value.

Required

a. Review the treasurer's analysis, identifying any questionable aspects, and briefly comment on the apparent effect of each such item on the treasurer's analysis.
b. Prepare your own analysis of the investment, including a calculation of the proper cost of capital and hurdle rates, a net present value analysis of the project, and a brief recommendation to Decker regarding the investment. (Round amounts to the nearest dollar.)
c. Because of his concern for the uncertainties of the CD recorder business, Decker also has asked you to provide analyses supporting whether or not your recommendation would change
   1. If estimates of projected cash revenue were reduced by 10%.
   2. If the "buffer margin" were tripled from 2.5% to 7.5%.

EYK12-2. **Ethics Case** Sandy Williams is the manager of General Company's cutting department, which employs 70 people. The cutting department desperately needs new equipment to increase productivity and thus avoid the layoff of 25 people. This department is one of four departments being considered for new equipment. The budget committee has announced that only one department's capital request will be approved this year.

Williams works up the cost savings from the new machinery and contacts suppliers to learn the equipment's estimated cost. Williams knows that General Company uses the payback method to evaluate capital projects. The estimated costs for the equipment are extremely high, particularly with all the safety shields recommended by the manufacturer. If one of these recommended safety features, electronic safety sensors not on the current equipment, were left off, the cost would be $200,000 less and the payback period would decrease by three years. If only minimum electronic safety sensors required by the union contract were included, the cost would be $70,000 less and the payback period would decrease by one year.

Required
What are the ethical considerations Sandy Williams faces as she prepares the equipment proposal?

ANSWERS TO SELF-STUDY QUESTIONS:

1. c   2. a   3. d   4. d   5. a   6. c

YOUR TURN! SOLUTIONS

Solution 12.1
Capital budgeting is the planning of major plant and equipment investments. These investments are important because they involve *long-term commitments of significant amounts of capital* and the decisions cannot be easily reversed.

Solution 12.2

Bank loan	45% × 12% =	5.40%
Equity capital	55% × 9% =	4.95%
Weighted average cost of capital		10.35%

Solution 12.3
a. PV = [$3,000 × 0.71178] + [$5,000 × 0.63552] = $2,135.34 + $3,177.60 = $5,312.94
b. PV = [$2,000 × 3.03735] = $6,074.70

Solution 12.4
a. [$90,000 × (1 – 30%)] = $63,000
b. [$45,000 × (1 – 30%)] = $(31,500)
c. ($10,000 × 30%) = $3,000
d. [$5,000 × (1 – 30%)] = $3,500

Solution 12.5

Depreciation tax shield:
[($350,000 – $15,000)/20 years] × 0.30 = $5,025

After-tax cash inflow:
[$47,200 × (1 – 0.30)] = $33,040

Total cash inflow:
($5,025 + $33,040) = $38,065

Present value of cash flows:
N = 20; i/YR = 8; PMT = 38,065; PV = $38,065 × 9.81815, so PV = $373,727.88.

NPV:
($350,000) + $373,727.88 = $23,727.88

Because the NPV is positive, the company should purchase the building.

Solution 12.6

Year 0	$(1,750,000)
Year 1	$225,000
Year 2	$225,000
Year 3	$225,000
Year 4	$225,000
Year 5	$225,000
Year 6	$225,000
Year 7	$225,000
Year 8	$225,000
Year 9	$225,000
Year 10	$225,000
Year 11	$225,000
Year 12	$225,000
Year 13	$225,000
Year 14	$225,000
Year 15	$225,000
IRR	*9.61%*
Formula in Cell B18 . . .	*=IRR (B1:B16)*

Solution 12.7

Cash Payback Period = $1,750,000/$225,000 = 7.78 years

Chapter 13
Statement of Cash Flows

Road Map

LO	Learning Objective	Page	eLecture	Guided Example	Assignments
LO1	Discuss the content and format of the statement of cash flows.	13-3	E13-1	YT13.1	SS1, SS2, SS3, SS6, SS8, SE1, SE2, SE3, E1A, E2A, E1B, E2B
LO2	Explain the preparation of a statement of cash flows using the indirect method.	13-9	E13-2	YT13.2	SS4, SS9, SE1, SE2, SE3, E3A, E4A, E5A, E6A, E11A, E3B, E4B, E5B, E6B, E11B, P1A, P2A, P3A, P4A, P1B, P2B, P3B, P4B
LO3	Define ratios used to analyze the statement of cash flows and explain their use.	13-18	E13-3	YT13.3	SS5, SS7, SE4, SE5, SE6, E4A, E7A, E3B, E7B, P1A, P5A, P6A, P1B, P5B, P6B
LO4	Appendix 13A: Explain the preparation of a statement of cash flows using the direct method.	13-22	E13-4	YT13.4	SS10, SS11, SS12, SE7, SE8, SE9, SE10, E8A, E9A, E10A, E11A, E8B, E9B, E10B, E11B, P6A, P7A, P8A, P9A, P6B, P7B, P8B, P9B

Home Depot is the largest home improvement retailer in the United States. Founded in 1978 in Atlanta, Georgia, the company now operates nearly 2,000 stores in the United States, Canada, and Mexico.

It takes a lot of cash to build and operate a business as big as Home Depot, especially when the average size of each store is over 105,000 square feet. In fiscal year 2019 alone Home Depot spent over $2.6 billion on capital expenditures.

How can a financial statement user determine where a company obtained the cash to fund its growth? This chapter introduces the statement of cash flows and explores how a company discloses both the sources and uses of its cash. Understanding the content, format, and construction of the statement of cash flows enables a financial statement user to assess how a company like Home Depot was able to finance its capital expenditures for new store growth.

PAST

Chapter 12 introduced capital budgeting and illustrated how capital budgeting is used to make capital investment decisions.

PRESENT

In this chapter we turn our attention to the statement of cash flows.

FUTURE

Chapter 14 completes our study of managerial accounting by looking at the analysis and interpretation of financial statements.

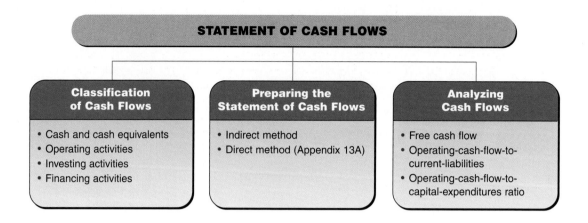

CASH AND CASH EQUIVALENTS

LO1 **Discuss** the content and format of the statement of cash flows.

In the eyes of most creditors, investors, and managers, cash is a business's most important asset. Without cash, a business would be unable to pay employees, lenders, suppliers, service providers, or shareholders. In short, cash is the only asset that a business can't operate without.

The dilemma for most managers, however, is knowing exactly how much cash to keep on hand. Although managers know that they need to keep some cash on hand in a checking account and/or petty cash fund to pay their immediate bills, they also know that cash is the lowest return generating asset that a business has. Keeping too much cash on hand means that a business is not maximizing the value of its assets. For this reason, most managers spend considerable time assessing their cash needs—an activity called **cash management**. Because the science of cash management is inexact, managers have derived ways to help them minimize the amount of cash that they need to keep on hand while also maximizing the return on a business's assets. One method is to invest any excess cash in alternative investments that are readily convertible back into cash and earn a higher rate of return than cash, but which do not place the invested cash at risk of loss. These alternative investments are known as cash equivalents.

Cash equivalents are short-term, highly liquid investments that are (1) easily convertible into cash and (2) close enough to maturity so that their market value is relatively insensitive to interest rate changes (generally, investments with maturities of three months or less). U.S. Treasury bills, certificates of deposit (CDs), commercial paper (short-term notes issued by corporations), and money market funds are examples of cash equivalents. Because firms may differ with respect to which investments they consider to be cash equivalents, GAAP requires that each firm disclose in the notes to the financial statements the company's policy regarding which investments are treated as cash equivalents.

When preparing a statement of cash flows, the cash and cash equivalents are added together and treated as a single amount because the purchase and sale of investments in cash equivalents are considered to be part of a firm's overall cash management strategy rather than a source or use of cash. As financial statement users evaluate a firm's cash flows, it should not matter whether the cash is on hand, deposited in a bank account, or invested in cash equivalents. Transfers back and forth between a firm's Cash account and its investments in cash equivalents, consequently, are not treated as cash inflows or outflows in the statement of cash flows.

When discussing the statement of cash flows, accountants often just use the word *cash* rather than the term *cash and cash equivalents.* We follow that practice in this chapter.

ACCOUNTING IN PRACTICE   **Definition of Cash Equivalents**

There are some differences between firms regarding which investments of cash are considered to be cash equivalents. For example, **PepsiCo, Inc.**, the beverage and snack food company, states in the notes to its financial statements that "Cash equivalents are investments with original maturities of three months or less." **International Game Technology**, a manufacturer of gaming machines and proprietary gaming software systems, on the other hand, notes that "In addition to cash deposits at major banks, cash and equivalents include other marketable securities with original maturities of 90 days or less, primarily in U.S. Treasury-backed money market funds." The commonality among all firms, however, is that cash equivalents represent a temporary investment of excess cash in risk-free investments until such time as the cash is needed to support a business's operations.

ACTIVITY CLASSIFICATIONS IN THE STATEMENT OF CASH FLOWS

A statement of cash flows classifies a company's cash receipts and cash payments into three major business activity categories: operating activities, investing activities, and financing activities. Grouping cash flows into these categories identifies the effect on cash of each of the major business activities of a firm. The combined effects on cash from all three categories explain the net change in cash for the period. The net change in cash is then reconciled with the beginning and ending balances of cash from the balance sheet. **Exhibit 13-1** illustrates the basic format for a statement of cash flows.

EXHIBIT 13-1 **Format for the Statement of Cash Flows**		
SAMPLE COMPANY **Statement of Cash Flows** **For Year Ended December 31, Year 2**		
Cash Flow from Operating Activities		
(Details of cash flow from operating activities)	$###	
Cash provided (used) by operating activities		$###
Cash Flow from Investing Activities		
(Details of investing cash inflows and outflows)	###	
Cash provided (used) by investing activities		###
Cash Flow from Financing Activities		
(Details of financing cash inflows and outflows)	###	
Cash provided (used) by financing activities		###
Net increase (decrease) in cash		###
Cash at beginning of year		###
Cash at end of year		$###

Exhibit 13-2 illustrates the purpose of the statement of cash flows. In this illustration, the water level in the bucket represents the cash balance. The water level changes from the beginning of the period to the end of the period. Why does the water level change? Water is flowing into the bucket through three spigots, representing the three sources of cash inflows (operating, investing, and financing activities). However, the bucket also has three holes near the bottom, representing the three categories of cash outflows (operating, investing, and financing activities). Thus, water flows in and out of the bucket through all three types of activities and the cash flow statement explains the change in the water level (the cash balance) from the beginning to the end of the period.

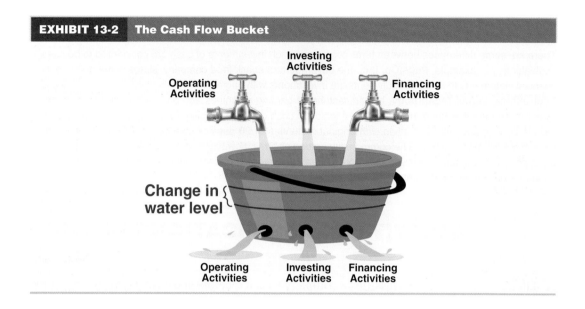

EXHIBIT 13-2 **The Cash Flow Bucket**

Operating Activities

A company's income statement reflects the transactions and events that constitute its operating activities. The focus of a firm's operating activities involves selling goods or rendering services. The cash flow from **operating activities** is defined broadly enough, however, to include any cash receipts or payments that are not classified as investing activities or financing activities. For example, cash received from a lawsuit settlement and cash payments to charity are treated as cash flow from operating activities. The following are examples of cash inflows and outflows relating to a firm's operating activities:

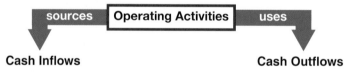

Cash Inflows

1. Receipts from customers for sales of goods or services.
2. Receipts of interest and dividends.
3. Other receipts that are not related to investing or financing activities, such as lawsuit settlements and refunds received from suppliers.

Cash Outflows

1. Payments to suppliers.
2. Payments to employees.
3. Payments of interest to creditors.
4. Payments of taxes to governmental agencies.
5. Other payments that are not related to investing or financing activities, such as contributions to charity.

Investing Activities

A firm's **investing activities** include transactions involving (1) the acquisition or disposal of plant assets and intangible assets, (2) the purchase or sale of stocks, bonds, and other securities (that are not cash equivalents), and (3) the lending and subsequent collection of money.[1] The related cash receipts and cash payments appear in the investing activities section of the statement of cash flows. Examples of these cash flows include:

---

[1] There are exceptions to the classification of these events as investing activities. For example, the purchase or sale of mortgage loans by a mortgage banker, like Bank of America, and the purchase or sale of securities in the trading account of a broker/dealer in financial securities, like Merrill Lynch, represent operating activities for these businesses.

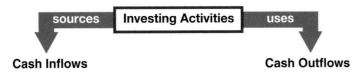

Cash Inflows

1. Receipts from the sale of plant assets and intangible assets.
2. Receipts from sales of investments in stocks, bonds, and other securities (other than cash equivalents).
3. Receipts from repayments of loans by borrowers.

Cash Outflows

1. Payments to purchase plant assets and intangible assets.
2. Payments to purchase stocks, bonds, and other securities (other than cash equivalents).
3. Payments made to lend money to borrowers.

Financing Activities

A firm engages in **financing activities** when it obtains cash from shareholders, returns cash to shareholders, borrows from creditors, and repays amounts borrowed from creditors. Cash flows related to these events are reported in the financing activities section of the statement of cash flows. Examples of these cash flows include:

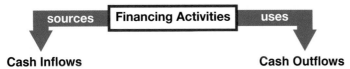

Cash Inflows

1. Receipts from the issuance of common stock and preferred stock and from sales of treasury stock.
2. Receipts from the issuance of bonds payable, mortgage notes payable, and other notes payable.

Cash Outflows

1. Payments to acquire treasury stock.
2. Payments of dividends.
3. Payments to settle outstanding bonds payable, mortgage notes payable, and other notes payable.

Note that paying cash to settle obligations such as accounts payable, wages payable, interest payable, and income tax payable is an operating activity, not a financing activity. Also observe that cash received as interest and dividends and cash paid as interest are classified as cash flows from operating activities, although cash paid as dividends to a company's stockholders is classified as a financing activity.

THINKING GLOBALLY

Although the statement of cash flows under U.S. GAAP has three activity categories—operating, investing, and financing—this is not the case under International Financial Reporting Standards (IFRS). Under IFRS, the statement of cash flows may have either four or five activity categories: Operations, Investing, Debt Financing, Equity Financing, and sometimes a category called the Effect of Foreign Currency Translation. In essence, IFRS segments the financing activities category into two separate categories relating to financing with debt and financing with equity. The sum of these two categories is equivalent to the single category of financing activities under U.S. GAAP.

Usefulness of Activity Classification

The classification of cash flows into the three business activity categories helps financial statement users analyze and interpret a company's cash flow data. To illustrate, assume that companies D, E, and F operate in the same industry and that each company reported a $100,000 increase in cash during the period. Information from each company's statement of cash flows is summarized below:

	Company		
	D	**E**	**F**
Cash flow from operating activities................	$100,000	$ 0	$ 0
Cash flow from investing activities:			
Sale of plant assets.........................	0	100,000	0
Cash flow from financing activities:			
Issuance of notes payable	0	0	100,000
Net increase in cash.........................	$100,000	$100,000	$100,000

Although each company's increase in cash is exactly $100,000, the source of the cash increase varied by company. This variation affects the analysis of the cash flow data, particularly for potential creditors who must evaluate the likelihood of the repayment of funds loaned to a company. Based only on this cash flow data, a potential creditor would feel more comfortable lending money to Company D than to either Company E or F. D's cash increase comes from its operating activities, whereas E's cash increase comes from the sale of plant assets, a source that is unlikely to recur, and F's cash increase comes from borrowed funds. Company F faces additional future uncertainty when the interest and principal payments on the existing notes become due, and for this reason, a potential creditor would be less inclined to extend additional loans to Company F.

NONCASH INVESTING AND FINANCING ACTIVITIES

Although many investing and financing activities affect cash and therefore are included in the investing and financing sections of the statement of cash flows, some significant investing and financing events do not affect current cash flow. An example of **noncash investing and financing activities** is the issuance of stock or bonds (a financing activity) in exchange for plant assets or intangible assets (an investing activity). Other examples include the exchange of long-term assets for other long-term assets, and the conversion of long-term debt into common stock. The key feature of each of these transactions is that no cash is exchanged between the parties involved in the transaction.

Noncash investing and financing transactions generally do, however, affect future cash flows. Issuing bonds in exchange for equipment, for example, requires future cash payments for interest and principal on the bonds. On the other hand, converting bonds into common stock eliminates the future cash payments related to the bonds' interest and principal, but may result in future cash dividend payments. Knowledge of these types of events, therefore, is helpful to financial statement users who wish to evaluate a firm's future cash flows.

Companies are required to disclose information regarding material noncash investing and financing transactions in a separate accounting schedule. The separate schedule may be placed immediately below the statement of cash flows, or it may be placed among the notes to the financial statements.

PRINCIPLE ALERT   **Objectivity Principle**

The *objectivity principle* asserts that the usefulness of financial statements is enhanced when the underlying data are objective and verifiable. Measuring cash and the changes in cash are among the most objective measurements that accountants make. The statement of cash flows, therefore, is the most objective financial statement required under generally accepted accounting principles. This characteristic of the statement of cash flows is welcomed by investors and creditors interested in evaluating the quality of a firm's net income and assets. Financial statement users often feel more confident about the quality of a company's net income and assets when there is a high correlation between, or relationship with, a company's cash flow from operating activities and its net income.

USING THE STATEMENT OF CASH FLOWS

The Financial Accounting Standards Board believes that one of the principal objectives of financial reporting is to help financial statement users assess the amount, timing, and uncertainty of a business's future cash flows. These assessments, in turn, help users evaluate prospective future cash receipts from their investments in, or loans to, a business. Although the statement of cash flows describes a company's past cash flows, the statement is also useful for assessing future cash flows since the recent past is often a very good predictor of the future.

The statement of cash flows shows the cash effects of a firm's operating, investing, and financing activities. Distinguishing among these different categories of cash flow helps financial statement users compare, evaluate, and predict a business's future cash flows. With cash flow information, creditors and investors are better able to assess a company's ability to repay its liabilities and pay dividends. A firm's need for outside financing can also be evaluated using the statement of cash flows. Further, the statement enables users to observe and analyze management's investing and financing policies, plans, and strategies.

The statement of cash flows also provides information useful in evaluating a firm's financial flexibility. **Financial flexibility** is a company's ability to generate sufficient amounts of cash to respond to unanticipated needs and opportunities. Information about past cash flows, particularly cash flow from operations, helps in assessing financial flexibility. An evaluation of a firm's ability to survive an unexpected drop in demand for its goods and services, for example, may include a review of its past cash flow from operations. The larger these past cash flows, the greater a firm's ability to withstand adverse changes in future economic conditions.

Some investors and creditors find the statement of cash flows useful in evaluating the "quality" of a firm's net income. Determining net income under the accrual basis of accounting requires many accruals, deferrals, allocations, and valuations. These adjustment and measurement procedures introduce greater subjectivity into a company's income determination than some financial statement users are comfortable with. Consequently, these users can relate a more objective performance measure—a firm's cash flow from operations—to net income. To these users, the closer the relation between a company's net income and their cash flow from operations, the higher the quality of the firm's net income.

CASH FLOW FROM OPERATING ACTIVITIES

The first section of the statement of cash flows presents a firm's cash flow from operating activities. Two alternative formats are available to present cash flow from operating activities: the indirect method and the direct method. Both methods report the same amount of cash flow from operating activities and differ only in how the cash flow from operating activities is derived. The indirect method and direct method refer only to how the cash flow from operating activities section is prepared. The cash flow from investing activities and cash flow from financing activities sections do not change.

The **indirect method** starts with net income using the accrual basis of accounting and applies a series of adjustments to convert it to net income under the cash basis of accounting, which is equivalent to the cash flow from operating activities. The adjustments to net income do not represent specific cash flows; consequently, the indirect method does not report any detail concerning individual operating cash inflows and outflows.

The **direct method** shows individual amounts of cash inflows and cash outflows for the major operating activities. The net difference between these inflows and outflows is the cash flow from operating activities.

While the presentation of the operating section is different under the two methods, the adjustments in the indirect method to convert net income to operating cash flows are the same adjustments that are made to individual income statement line items to convert revenues and expenses under the accrual basis of accounting to cash inflows and outflows under the cash basis of accounting presented in the direct method. Thus, the two methods for presenting the operating section are really just "two sides of the same coin." We present the indirect method in this chapter, but we explain the direct method (and how the two methods integrate with one another) in Appendix 13A.

The Financial Accounting Standards Board encourages companies to use the direct method but permits the use of the indirect method. Despite the FASB's preference for the direct method, almost all companies use the indirect method. The indirect method is popular because (1) it is easier and less expensive to prepare than the direct method and (2) the direct method requires a supplemental disclosure showing cash flow from operating activities prepared under the indirect method.

ACCOUNTING IN PRACTICE   **Popularity of Direct and Indirect Method**

Do you think a direct approach in communicating with financial statement users is best, or should your approach be more indirect? When it comes to reporting the cash flow from operations, companies appear to favor the indirect approach by a wide margin, as evidenced by the responses to a survey of 600 large U.S. companies.

Source: Accounting Trends and Techniques

YOUR TURN! 13.1

The solution is on page 13-48.

MBC

Classify each of the cash flow events listed below as either an (1) operating activity, (2) investing activity, or (3) financing activity:

1. Cash received from customers
2. Cash sale of land
3. Cash paid to suppliers
4. Cash purchase of equipment
5. Payment on note payable
6. Cash dividend payment
7. Cash wages paid
8. Purchase of treasury stock
9. Cash sale of investments

The following section on preparing the statement of cash flows uses the indirect method. Appendix 13A uses the direct method. Your instructor can choose to cover either one or both methods. If the indirect method is skipped, then read Appendix 13A and return to the section (9 pages ahead) titled "Analyzing Cash Flows."

PREPARING THE STATEMENT OF CASH FLOWS USING THE INDIRECT METHOD

LO2 **Explain** the preparation of a statement of cash flows using the indirect method.

eLecture
MBC

To prepare the operating section of the statement of cash flows, the following information is needed: a company's income statement, balance sheets for the current and prior year, and possibly additional data taken from the company's financial statements. **Exhibit 13-3** presents this information for the Bennett Company. We will use these data to prepare Bennett's Year 2 statement of cash flows using the indirect method. As will be seen shortly, Bennett's statement of cash flows will explain the $25,000 increase in the company's cash account that occurred during Year 2 (from $10,000 at the beginning of the year to $35,000 at the end of the year) by classifying the firm's cash inflows and outflows into the three business activity categories of operating, investing, and financing.

EXHIBIT 13-3	Financial Data of Bennett Company

BENNETT COMPANY Income Statement For Year Ended December 31, Year 2		
Sales revenue.		$250,000
Cost of goods sold	$148,000	
Wages expense	52,000	
Insurance expense	5,000	
Depreciation expense	10,000	
Income tax expense	11,000	
Gain on sale of plant assets.	(8,000)	218,000
Net income		$ 32,000

Additional Data Year 2
1. Sold a plant asset (land) costing $20,000 for $28,000 cash.
2. Declared and paid cash dividends of $13,000.

BENNETT COMPANY Balance Sheets		
As of December 31	Year 2	Year 1
Assets		
Cash.	$ 35,000	$ 10,000
Accounts receivable	39,000	34,000
Inventory.	54,000	60,000
Prepaid insurance.	17,000	4,000
Long-term investments	15,000	—
Plant assets	180,000	200,000
Accumulated depreciation	(50,000)	(40,000)
Patent	60,000	—
Total assets.	$350,000	$268,000
Liabilities and Equity		
Accounts payable	$ 10,000	$ 19,000
Income tax payable.	5,000	3,000
Common stock	260,000	190,000
Retained earnings	75,000	56,000
Total liabilities and equity	$350,000	$268,000

To see that the statement of cash flows can be prepared using a company's income statement and the changes in its balance sheet accounts, consider again the balance sheet equation:

$$\text{Assets (A)} = \text{Liabilities (L)} + \text{Stockholders' equity (SE)} \qquad (1)$$

Separating a firm's assets into its cash and noncash assets (NCA) gives:

$$\text{Cash} + \text{NCA} = \text{L} + \text{SE} \qquad (2)$$

And, rewriting the balance sheet equation in changes form yields:

$$\Delta\text{Cash} + \Delta\text{NCA} = \Delta\text{L} + \Delta\text{SE} \qquad (3)$$

Finally, rearranging the components of the equation shows that the change in cash (which is the end result of the statement of cash flows) can be computed from the change in all of the other balance sheet accounts:

$$\Delta\text{Cash} = \Delta\text{L} - \Delta\text{NCA} + \Delta\text{SE} \qquad (4)$$

Breaking non-current assets and liabilities into short- and long-term components allows us to better explain cash flows in terms of the three types of business activities (operating, investing, and financing).

Finally, separating assets and liabilities into short-and long-term categories allows us to specify a general set of rules for identifying changes in balance sheet accounts associated with operating, investing, and financing activities:

$$\Delta\text{Cash} = \underbrace{[\Delta\text{STL} - \Delta\text{STA}]}_{\substack{\text{Operating} \\ \text{Activities}}} - \underbrace{\Delta\text{LTA}}_{\substack{\text{Investing} \\ \text{Activities}}} + \underbrace{[\Delta\text{LTL} + \Delta\text{SE}]}_{\substack{\text{Financing} \\ \text{Activities}}} \qquad (5)$$

As shown in equation (5), operating activities are generally associated with changes in short-term assets and liabilities, investing activities are generally associated with changes in long-term assets, and financing activities are usually associated with changes in long-term liabilities and equity accounts. We explain these concepts in more detail subsequently.

Five Steps to Preparing a Statement of Cash Flows

The process to prepare a statement of cash flows using the indirect method involves five steps. The approach begins by focusing initially only on the balance sheet and then proceeds to integrate a business's income statement through a series of systematic adjustments to a preliminary statement of cash flows derived solely from balance sheet data.

Step One: Calculate the change in all balance sheet accounts.
Using the beginning and ending balance sheets (see Columns 1 and 2 in **Exhibit 13-4**), calculate the change in each balance sheet account by subtracting the beginning balance sheet amount from the ending amount. Column 3 of **Exhibit 13-4** presents the results of this step for the Bennett Company. To simplify this step, we combine the change in the Plant Assets account with the Accumulated Depreciation account—that is, the change in the Plant Assets account is calculated net of accumulated depreciation.

EXHIBIT 13-4	**Preparing a Statement of Cash Flows: The Indirect Method**			
	BENNETT COMPANY **Balance Sheet** **December 31, Year 2**			
	(1) **Beginning of Year**	**(2)** **End of Year**	**(3)** **Change for Year**	**(4)** **Cash Flow Classification**
Assets				
Cash.	$ 10,000	$ 35,000	**$25,000**	**Cash flow increase**
Accounts receivable	34,000	39,000	5,000	Operating
Inventory.	60,000	54,000	(6,000)	Operating
Prepaid insurance.	4,000	17,000	13,000	Operating
Long-term investments.	0	15,000	15,000	Investing
Plant assets (net)	160,000	130,000	(30,000)	Investing
Patent.	0	60,000	60,000	Investing
Total assets.	$268,000	$350,000	$82,000	
Liabilities and Equity				
Accounts payable	$ 19,000	$ 10,000	$ (9,000)	Operating
Income tax payable.	3,000	5,000	2,000	Operating
Common stock	190,000	260,000	70,000	Financing
Retained earnings	56,000	75,000	19,000	Operating/Financing
Total liabilities and equity	$268,000	$350,000	$82,000	

To verify the accuracy of the Step One calculations, simply compare the sum of the changes in the asset accounts ($82,000) with the sum of the changes in the liability and stockholders' equity accounts ($82,000). These totals must be equal. If the totals are not equal, it indicates the presence of a calculation error that must be identified and corrected before proceeding to Step Two.

An important figure identified during Step One is the "bottom line" of the statement of cash flows—namely, the change in the cash account. **Exhibit 13-4** reveals that the cash account of the Bennett Company increased by $25,000 from the beginning of the year to the end of the year. Hence, the sum of the operating, investing, and financing cash flows for the company must aggregate to this figure.

Step Two: Classify each of the changes in balance sheet accounts as operating, investing, or financing.

As a general rule, the following cash flow activity classifications apply, although exceptions exist:

Balance Sheet Account	Cash Flow Activity Category
Current assets	Operating
Noncurrent assets	Investing
Current liabilities.	Operating
Noncurrent liabilities	Financing
Capital stock.	Financing
Retained earnings	Operating/Financing

Examples of exceptions to these cash flow activity classifications include the following:

■ Short-term investments, a current asset, are an investing activity item.

■ Short-term (current) notes payable, a current liability, are a financing activity item.

■ Current maturities of long-term debt, a current liability, are a financing activity item.

■ Employee pension obligations, a noncurrent liability, are an operating activity item.

Column 4 of **Exhibit 13-4** presents the cash flow activity classifications. Although measuring the change in the balance sheet accounts in Step One is a straight-forward arithmetic activity, there can be some confusion over the correct activity classification for some of the balance sheet accounts in Step Two. The changes in accounts receivable, inventory, prepaid insurance, accounts payable, and income tax payable are all easily identified as operating activities because they are associated with the day-to-day operations of a business. The change in common stock, on the other hand, is clearly a financing activity because it is associated with raising capital to finance a business.

The change in net plant assets, however, is more complex. Purchases and sales of plant assets are associated with the capital investment needed to run a business, and thus are easily identified as investing activities. However, the depreciation expense associated with plant assets is deducted as an operating expense in the calculation of a company's net income. Similarly, the change in intangible assets, such as patents, results from the acquisition or sale of intangibles and is easily identified as an investing activity. However, the amortization of intangibles is an operating expense deducted in the calculation of net income. Finally, the change in retained earnings can be associated with both operating and financing activities because retained earnings is increased by net income, an operating activity, but decreased by the payment of dividends, a financing activity.

Step Three: Prepare a preliminary statement of cash flows.   Having completed Steps One and Two, you are now ready to build a preliminary statement of cash flows using the calculated increases or decreases in the various balance sheet accounts from Step One and the identified activity classifications from Step Two. The preliminary statement of cash flows for the Bennett Company is presented in **Exhibit 13-5**.

The statement of cash flows measures the inflows and outflows of cash for a business. Recall from equation (4) that the change in cash is equal to the change in liabilities *minus* the change in non-cash assets plus the change in stockholder's equity accounts. Thus, we *add* changes in liability and equity accounts but *subtract* changes in asset accounts to explain the change in cash.

For instance, **Exhibit 13-5** shows that the change in accounts receivable is an increase of $5,000, whereas the change in inventory is a decrease of $6,000. When preparing the indirect method statement of cash flows, a $5,000 increase in accounts receivable is subtracted from net income, whereas a $6,000 decrease in inventory of $6,000 is added to net income, to arrive at the cash flow from operations. In other words, by subtracting the decrease in inventory, we end up adding it in our preliminary statement of cash flows.

To illustrate why an increase in accounts receivable must be subtracted from net income to arrive at operating cash flow, consider how sales revenue is initially recorded. Assume that a $2,000 sale of goods is paid for with $1,200 in cash and the remaining amount recorded as an increase in accounts receivable. In this example, net income increases by $2,000, but cash increases by only $1,200. Therefore, net income must be reduced by the $800 increase in accounts receivable to yield the correct cash flow from operations.

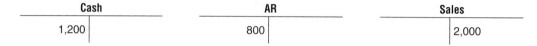

Cash		AR		Sales	
1,200		800			2,000

Hence, when preparing the preliminary statement of cash flows in Step Three, it is important to remember to *subtract* the change in asset accounts and *add* changes in the liability and stockholders' equity accounts.

EXHIBIT 13-5	An Illustration of a Preliminary Statement of Cash Flows: The Indirect Method

BENNETT COMPANY
Preliminary Statement of Cash Flows
For Year Ended December 31, Year 2

Operating Activities	
Retained earnings	$19,000
Accounts receivable	(5,000)
Inventory.	6,000
Prepaid insurance.	(13,000)
Accounts payable	(9,000)
Income tax payable.	2,000
Cash flow provided by operating activities	0
Investing Activities	
Long-term investments.	(15,000)
Plant assets (net)	30,000
Patent.	(60,000)
Cash flow used by investing activities	(45,000)
Financing Activities	
Common stock	70,000
Cash flow provided financing activities.	70,000
Change in cash (from the balance sheet).	$25,000

Exhibit 13-5 presents the preliminary statement of cash flows for the Bennett Company. This preliminary statement indicates that the firm's cash flow provided by operating activities was $0, the cash flow used by investing activities was $45,000, and the cash flow provided financing activities was $70,000. As required, the cash inflows and outflows aggregate to the change in cash from the balance sheet, an increase of $25,000.

Step Four: Integrate income statement data.   To this point we have used the balance sheet exclusively to provide the needed inputs to our statement of cash flows. In Step Four, we integrate information from the income statement (see **Exhibit 13-3**) into the preliminary statement of cash flows in **Exhibit 13-5**.

First, we replace the change in retained earnings from the balance sheet with net income from the income statement. For the Bennett Company, the change in retained earnings of $19,000 does not equal net income of $32,000. The difference of $13,000 ($32,000 – $19,000) represents a cash dividend paid to Bennett's shareholders (see the Additional Data in **Exhibit**

13-3). Thus, when we replace retained earnings of $19,000 with net income of $32,000, it is also necessary to report the $13,000 cash dividend payment as a cash outflow under the financing activities section in **Exhibit 13-6**. Increasing the cash flow from operations and decreasing the cash flow from financing activities by an equivalent amount ($13,000) keeps the statement of cash flows in balance with the net change in cash of $25,000.

Retained Earnings

	56,000 Beginning Balance
	32,000 Net Income
Dividends Paid 13,000	
	75,000 Ending Balance

Second, we adjust the Bennett Company's net income for any **noncash expenses** such as the depreciation of plant assets and the amortization of intangibles that were deducted in the process of calculating the firm's accrual basis net income. Depreciation expense and amortization expense are called noncash expenses because these expenses do not involve a current cash outflow. Depreciation expense, for example, represents the allocation of the purchase price of plant assets over the many periods that these assets produce sales revenue for a business. The matching principle requires that the cost of plant assets be matched with the sales revenue produced by these assets, and this is accomplished on the income statement by the deduction of the periodic depreciation charge. The cash flows associated with the purchase and sale of plant assets and intangible assets are appropriately classified as cash flow from investing activities (see **Exhibit 13-5**). These noncash expenses must be *added back* to net income in the operating activities section to correctly measure the firm's operating cash flow.

The Income Statement in **Exhibit 13-3** indicates that $10,000 of depreciation expense was deducted in calculating net income. Thus, we will add this amount back to net income. (Note that there was no amortization expense on the patent because it was not purchased until Year 2.) To keep the statement of cash flows in balance with an increase in cash of $25,000, it is also necessary to subtract equivalent amounts in the investing activities section. We discuss this adjustment in Step Five.

To summarize, the adjustments to the Bennett Company's preliminary statement of cash flows in **Exhibit 13-5** are:

1. Net income of $32,000 replaces the change in retained earnings of $19,000 in the operating activities section. This action adds $13,000 to the cash flow from operating activities. To keep the statement of cash flows in balance with the change in cash of $25,000, it is necessary to subtract $13,000 elsewhere on the statement. Since retained earnings is calculated as follows:

> Retained earnings (beginning)
> + Net income for the period
> − Dividends declared
> = Retained earnings (ending)

the outflow of $13,000 is shown as a cash dividend to shareholders under the financing activities section.

2. Depreciation expense of $10,000, a noncash deduction from net income, is added back to net income to avoid understating the cash flow from operations. However, to keep the statement of cash flows in balance with the change in cash of $25,000, a similar amount is subtracted from plant assets under the investing activities section.

Step Five: Remove the financial effects of any nonrecurring or nonoperating transactions from net income. A firm's operating cash flow should include only the cash flows from operating activities. Consequently, to calculate the cash flow from

operating activities, it is necessary to review a company's income statement to identify and remove the financial effects of any nonoperating transactions included in net income.[2]

To illustrate this point, note that Bennett Company sold a plant asset (land) during the year at a gain of $8,000 ($28,000 sales price less $20,000 cost). (See the Income Statement andAdditional Data in **Exhibit 13-3**.) The sale of a plant asset is an investing activity and therefore the cash received properly belongs in the investing activities section. However, the gain of $8,000 is included in net income in the operating activities section. Thus, to correctly assess Bennett's cash flows, it is necessary to subtract the gain from the operating activities section and add it to the change in plant assets in the investing activities section. (Note that if there had been a loss on the sale of plant assets, Bennett would have added it back to net income in the operating activities section because a loss reduces net income but does not represent an operating cash outflow). When combined with the adjustment for depreciation expense from Step Four, the cash flow from plant assets is $28,000 ($30,000 change in plant assets – $10,000 adjustment for depreciation expense + $8,000 adjustment for gain). The adjusted amount of $28,000 is equal to the cash received on the sale of plant assets.

Hint: The sale of a non-depreciable plant asset (like land) only affects the Plant Asset account, but if the plant asset sold had been a depreciable asset, the cost of the asset would be removed from the Plant Assets Account and the associated Accumulated Depreciation would also have to be removed.

Plant Assets				**Accumulated Depreciation**	
Beginning Balance	200,000				40,000 Beginning Balance
		20,000 Sale	Sale	0	10,000 *Depreciation Expense*
Ending Balance	180,000				50,000 Ending Balance

Cash proceeds	28,000	Investing cash flow
– Book value	(20,000)	
Gain on sale	8,000	

Exhibit 13-6 presents the final statement of cash flows for Bennett Company and includes not only the adjustments from Step Four, but also the adjustment to remove any nonoperating gains and losses from the cash flow from operating activities (Step Five). Note that the company's statement of cash flows remains in balance with the change in cash of $25,000 after the adjustments in both of these steps. This result is possible because whatever amount was added to (or subtracted from) net income under the cash flow from operating activities, an equivalent amount was subtracted from (or added to) the investing activities or the financing activities.

Bennett's statement of cash flows reveals that the cash flow provided by operating activities is $15,000, the cash flow used by investing activities is $47,000, and the cash flow provided by financing activities is $57,000. The resulting total cash flow of $25,000 exactly equals the increase in cash on the balance sheet of $25,000, as required.

---

[2] An exception is interest expense, which most investment professionals view as a financing activity. Regardless, interest payments are required to be included in the cash flow from operating activities.

EXHIBIT 13-6	Statement of Cash Flows—The Indirect Method

BENNETT COMPANY
Statement of Cash Flows
For Year Ended December 31, Year 2

Cash Flow from Operating Activities
Net income $32,000
Add (deduct) items to convert net income to cash basis
  Depreciation 10,000
  Gain on sale of plant assets . . . . (8,000)
  Accounts receivable increase . . . . (5,000)
  Inventory decrease 6,000
  Prepaid insurance increase. . . . . (13,000)
  Accounts payable decrease . . . . (9,000)
  Income tax payable increase. 2,000
    Cash provided by operating activities $15,000
Cash Flow from Investing Activities
Purchase of long-term investments . . . . (15,000)
Sale of plant assets. 28,000
Purchase of patent . . . . (60,000)
    Cash used by investing activities. . . . . (47,000)
Cash Flow from Financing Activities
Issuance of common stock 70,000
Payment of dividends . . . . (13,000)
    Cash provided by financing activities 57,000
Net increase in cash 25,000
Cash at beginning of year. 10,000
Cash at end of year $35,000

The following illustration summarizes the five-step process to prepare an indirect method statement of cash flows:

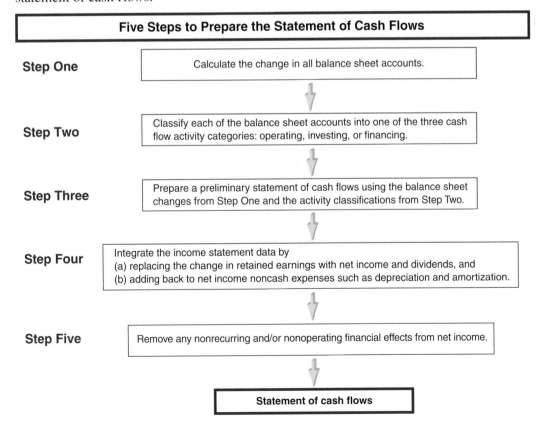

Five Steps to Prepare the Statement of Cash Flows

Step One — Calculate the change in all balance sheet accounts.

Step Two — Classify each of the balance sheet accounts into one of the three cash flow activity categories: operating, investing, or financing.

Step Three — Prepare a preliminary statement of cash flows using the balance sheet changes from Step One and the activity classifications from Step Two.

Step Four — Integrate the income statement data by
(a) replacing the change in retained earnings with net income and dividends, and
(b) adding back to net income noncash expenses such as depreciation and amortization.

Step Five — Remove any nonrecurring and/or nonoperating financial effects from net income.

Statement of cash flows

YOUR TURN! 13.2

The solution is on page 13-48.

MBC

Husky Company's current year income statement and comparative balance sheets as of December 31 of the current and previous years are shown below:

HUSKY COMPANY
Income Statement
For Year Ended December 31, Current Year

Sales revenue		$1,270,000
Cost of goods sold	$860,000	
Wages expense	172,000	
Insurance expense	16,000	
Depreciation expense	34,000	
Interest expense	18,000	
Income tax expense	58,000	1,158,000
Net income		$ 112,000

HUSKY COMPANY
Balance Sheets

	Dec. 31, Current Year	Dec. 31, Previous Year
Assets		
Cash	$ 22,000	$ 10,000
Accounts receivable	82,000	64,000
Inventory	180,000	120,000
Prepaid insurance	10,000	14,000
Plant assets	500,000	390,000
Accumulated depreciation	(136,000)	(102,000)
Total assets	$658,000	$496,000
Liabilities and Stockholders' Equity		
Accounts payable	$ 14,000	$ 20,000
Wages payable	18,000	12,000
Income tax payable	14,000	16,000
Bonds payable	260,000	150,000
Common stock	180,000	180,000
Retained earnings	172,000	118,000
Total liabilities and stockholders' equity	$658,000	$496,000

Cash dividends of $58,000 were declared and paid during the current year. Plant assets were purchased for cash, and bonds payable were issued for cash. Accounts payable relate to merchandise purchases.

Required
Prepare a statement of cash flows for the Husky Company using the indirect method.

For readers skipping the indirect method, please resume reading here.

ANALYZING CASH FLOWS

Data from the statement of cash flows are often used to calculate financial measures to evaluate a company's cash flow health. Three such measures include the company's free cash flow, the operating-cash-flow-to-current-liabilities ratio, and the operating-cash-flow-to-capital-expenditures ratio.

LO3 Define ratios used to analyze the statement of cash flows and **explain** their use.

eLecture

MBC

© Shutterstock.com

Free Cash Flow

Free cash flow (FCF) is often used by investment professionals and investors to evaluate a company's cash-flow strength. FCF is an important performance reference point for investment professionals because it indicates the amount of cash generated during the year beyond what is needed to operate the business at its current capacity. Free cash flow is calculated as follows:

FCF = Cash flow from operating activities – Capital expenditures

Capital expenditures refer to investment in a business's plant and intangible assets necessary to enable a firm to remain a going concern. Subtracting capital expenditures from the firm's cash flow from operating activities measures the amount of excess or "free" cash flow that can be used for expansion, paying dividends, reducing debt, or other purposes. A firm with strong free cash flow will generally carry a higher stock value than one with weak (or no) free cash flow.

Concept	→ Method →	Assessment	TAKEAWAY 13.1
Does a company generate cash flows in excess of its capital expenditure needs?	Statement of cash flows. Free Cash Flow = Cash flow from operating activities – Capital expenditures	The higher the free cash flow, the greater is a company's ability to generate cash for needs other than capital expenditures.	

Operating-Cash-Flow-to-Current-Liabilities Ratio

Two measures previously introduced—the current ratio and the quick ratio—emphasize the relation between a company's current or quick assets and its current liabilities to measure the ability of a firm to pay its current liabilities. The **operating-cash-flow-to-current-liabilities ratio** is another measure of a company's ability to pay its current liabilities. While the current and quick ratios focus on a firm's ability to pay liabilities using existing current or quick assets, the operating cash flow to current liabilities ratio highlights a firm's ability to pay its current liabilities using its operating cash flow. The ratio is calculated as follows:

$$\text{Operating-cash-flow-to-current-liabilities ratio} = \frac{\text{Cash flow from operating activities}}{\text{Average current liabilities}}$$

The cash flow from operating activities is obtained from the statement of cash flows. The denominator is the average of the beginning and ending current liabilities for the year.

The following amounts (in thousands of dollars) were taken from the financial statements of the **Gannett Co., Inc.**, a diversified news and information company that publishes *USA Today:*

Cash flow from operating activities.	$ 57,770
Current liabilities at beginning of the year	$718,453
Current liabilities at end of the year	$741,300

The operating cash flow to current liabilities ratio for the Gannett Co. is calculated as follows (in millions):

$$\frac{\$57,770}{\left[\frac{(\$718,453 + \$741,300)}{2}\right]} = 0.08$$

The higher this ratio, the greater is a firm's ability to pay current liabilities using its operating cash flow. A ratio of 0.5 is considered a strong ratio; consequently, Gannett's ratio of 0.08 would be interpreted as a little weak. A ratio of 0.08 indicates that Gannett generates $0.08 of operating cash flow for every dollar of current liabilities.

TAKEAWAY 13.2	**Concept** ➞	**Method** ➞	**Assessment**
	Will a company have sufficient cash to pay its current liabilities as they become due?	Statement of cash flows and balance sheet. Operating-cash-flow-to-current-liabilities ratio = $\frac{\text{Cash flow from operating activities}}{\text{Average current liabilities}}$	The higher the ratio, the higher the probability that a company will have sufficient operating cash flow to pay its current liabilities as they become due.

Operating-Cash-Flow-to-Capital-Expenditures Ratio

To remain competitive, a business must be able to replace, and expand when appropriate, its property, plant, and equipment. A ratio that evaluates a firm's ability to finance its capital investments from operating cash flow is the **operating-cash-flow-to-capital-expenditures ratio**. This ratio is calculated as follows:

$$\text{Operating-cash-flow-to-capital expenditures ratio} = \frac{\text{Cash flow from operating activities}}{\text{Annual net capital expenditures}}$$

The numerator in this ratio comes from the statement of cash flows. Information for the denominator may be found in one or more places in the financial statements. Data regarding a company's capital expenditures are presented in the investing activities section of the statement of cash flows. (When capital expenditures are reported in the statement of cash flows, the amount is often broken into two figures—(1) Proceeds from the sale of property, plant, and equipment and (2) Purchases of property, plant, and equipment. The appropriate "capital expenditures" figure for the purpose of calculating this ratio is the net of the two amounts.) Data on capital expenditures are also part of the required industry segment disclosures in the notes to the financial statements. Finally, management's discussion and analysis of the financial statements may identify the company's annual capital expenditures.

A ratio in excess of 1.0 indicates that a firm's current operating activities are providing sufficient cash to fund its desired investment in plant assets and would normally be considered a sign of financial strength. The interpretation of this ratio is influenced by the trend in recent years, the ratio being achieved by other firms in the same industry, and the stage of a firm's life cycle. A firm in the early stages of its life cycle—when periods of rapid expansion may occur—may be expected to experience a lower ratio than a firm in the later stage of its life cycle—when maintenance of plant capacity may be more likely than an expansion of plant capacity.

To illustrate the ratio's calculation, **Abbott Laboratories**, a manufacturer of pharmaceutical and health care products, reported capital expenditures (in millions of dollars) of $2,177. Abbott's cash flow from operating activities was $7,901. Thus, Abbott's operating-cash-flow-to-capital-expenditure ratio for the year was 3.63, or ($7,901/$2,177). The following are operating-cash-flow-to-capital-expenditures ratios for other well-known companies:

PepsiCo Inc. (Consumer foods and beverages) 2.50
Lockheed Martin Corporation (Aerospace). 4.63
Norfolk Southern Corporation (Freight transportation services). 2.43

DATA ANALYTICS	Using Analytics to Improve Cash Flow Management

Data Analytics

A firm's financial transactions can be complex, and with complexity comes risk. There is the risk of missing data, the risk of data duplication, and the risk that the information used for decisions is dated and doesn't reflect the current state of the firm's financial health. Business intelligence software such as Tableau can be of tremendous benefit by providing a clear understanding of a company's cash flow.

A shortcoming of using the traditional approach of reviewing month-end bank statements in a general ledger and then analyzing operating, investing, and financing activities is that this perspective is static and often not available in a timely fashion. In contrast, business intelligence software allows for real-time analysis from multiple sources. Further, the ability to display the data in easier to understand visualizations, and the ability to drill down into the data as needed provides business managers with a far better way to understand and manage cash flows.

Concept ➔	Method ➔	Assessment	TAKEAWAY 13.3
Does a company generate sufficient operating cash flows to finance its capital expenditure needs?	Statement of cash flows. Operating-cash-flow-to-capital-expenditures ratio $=\dfrac{\text{Cash flow from operating activities}}{\text{Annual net capital expenditures}}$	The higher the ratio, the higher the probability that a company will generate sufficient operating cash flow to finance its capital expenditure needs.	

YOUR TURN! 13.3

The solution is on page 13-48.

GuidedExample

MBC

The following selected data were obtained from the financial statements of Blake Enterprises:

Cash flow from operating activities.	$40,000
Annual net capital expenditures	12,500
Average current liabilities	30,000

Calculate the following financial measures for Blake Enterprises:

1. Free cash flow
2. Operating-cash-flow-to-current-liabilities ratio
3. Operating-cash-flow-to-capital-expenditures ratio

COMPREHENSIVE PROBLEM

GuidedExample

MBC

Terry Company's income statement and comparative balance sheets at December 31 of the current and previous year are as follows:

TERRY COMPANY		
Income Statement		
For Year Ended December 31, Current Year		
Sales revenue.		$385,000
Dividend income.		5,000
		390,000
Cost of goods sold	$233,000	
Wages expense	82,000	
Advertising expense	10,000	
Depreciation expense.	11,000	
Income tax expense	17,000	
Loss on sale of investments	1,000	354,000
Net income.		$ 36,000

TERRY COMPANY Balance Sheets	Dec. 31, Current Year	Dec. 31, Previous Year
Assets		
Cash	$ 8,000	$ 12,000
Accounts receivable	22,000	28,000
Inventory.	94,000	66,000
Prepaid advertising.	12,000	9,000
Long-term investments.	30,000	40,000
Plant assets	178,000	130,000
Accumulated depreciation	(72,000)	(61,000)
Total assets.	$272,000	$224,000
Liabilities and Stockholders' Equity		
Accounts payable	$ 27,000	$ 14,000
Wages payable.	6,000	2,500
Income tax payable.	3,000	4,500
Common stock	139,000	125,000
Retained earnings	97,000	78,000
Unrealized loss on investments	—	—
Total liabilities and stockholders' equity	$272,000	$224,000

Cash dividends of $17,000 were declared and paid during the year. Plant assets were purchased for cash, and, later in the year, additional common stock was issued for cash. Investments costing $10,000 were sold for cash at a $1,000 loss.

Required

a. Calculate the change in cash that occurred during the year.

b. Prepare a statement of cash flows using the indirect method.

Solution

a. $8,000 ending balance – $12,000 beginning balance = $4,000 decrease in cash

b. 1. Use the indirect method to determine the cash flow from operating activities.

- The adjustments to convert Terry Company's net income of $36,000 to the cash provided by operating activities of $38,000 are shown in the following statement of cash flows.

2. Analyze changes in remaining noncash asset (and contra asset) accounts to determine cash flows from investing activities.

- Long-term investments: $10,000 decrease resulted from sale of investments for cash at a $1,000 loss. Cash received from sale of investments = $9,000 ($10,000 cost – $1,000 loss).

- Plant assets: $48,000 increase resulted from purchase of plant assets for cash. Cash paid to purchase plant assets = $48,000.

- Accumulated depreciation: $11,000 increase resulted from the recording of 2019 depreciation. No cash flow effect.

3. Analyze changes in remaining liability and stockholders' equity accounts to determine cash flows from financing activities.

- Common stock: $14,000 increase resulted from the issuance of stock for cash. Cash received from issuance of common stock = $14,000.

- Retained earnings: $19,000 increase resulted from net income of $36,000 and dividend declaration of $17,000. Cash paid as dividends = $17,000.

The statement of cash flows (indirect method) is as follows:

TERRY COMPANY Statement of Cash Flows For the Year Ended December 31, Current Year		
Cash Flow from Operating Activities		
Net income	$36,000	
Add (deduct) items to convert net income to cash basis		
Depreciation	11,000	
Loss on sale of investments	1,000	
Accounts receivable decrease	6,000	
Inventory increase	(28,000)	
Prepaid advertising increase	(3,000)	
Accounts payable increase	13,000	
Wages payable increase	3,500	
Income tax payable decrease	(1,500)	
Cash provided by operating activities		$38,000
Cash Flow from Investing Activities		
Sale of investments	9,000	
Purchase of plant assets	(48,000)	
Cash used by investing activities		(39,000)
Cash Flow from Financing Activities		
Issuance of common stock	14,000	
Payment of dividends	(17,000)	
Cash used by financing activities		(3,000)
Net decrease in cash		(4,000)
Cash at beginning of year		12,000
Cash at end of year		$ 8,000

APPENDIX 13A: Preparing the Statement of Cash Flows Under the Direct Method

Although it is quite straightforward to create a direct method statement of cash flows given access to a company's internal accounting records, this type of access is rarely available to anyone except a company's management team. All that is necessary is to pull the numbers directly off the Cash general ledger account and place them in the appropriate section of the statement of cash flows. This is why the direct method is referred to as "direct." The cash flow from operations is taken directly from the company's general ledger, rather than being indirectly computed from net income. Unfortunately, investment professionals, lenders, and stockholders rarely have access to such proprietary internal data. Thus, it is necessary to be able to create direct method cash flow information using only publicly available data included in the indirect method statement of cash flows.

LO4 **Explain** the preparation of a statement of cash flows using the direct method.

eLecture

MBC

The adjustments in the indirect method to convert net income to operating cash flows are the same adjustments that are made to individual income statement line items to convert revenues and expenses under the accrual basis of accounting to cash inflows and outflows under the cash basis of accounting in the direct method. Thus, after learning the indirect method for preparing the operating section, it is quite simple to use the same adjustments to present the operating section using the direct method.

The process to convert an indirect method statement of cash flows to the direct method requires two steps. First, replace net income (the first line item under the operating activities section of the indirect method statement format) with the line items appearing on a firm's income statement. For instance, Bennett Company's income statement in **Exhibit 13-3** contains the following line items:

Sales revenue	$250,000
Cost of goods sold	(148,000)
Wages expense	(52,000)
Insurance expense	(5,000)
Depreciation expense	(10,000)
Income tax expense	(11,000)
Gain on sale of plant assets	8,000
Net income	$ 32,000

For the Bennett Company, we begin by replacing the net income of $32,000 under the operating activities section in **Exhibit 13-6** with the seven income statement line items, which aggregate to $32,000.

The second step involves adjusting the income statement line items by the relevant amounts from the operating activities section of the indirect method statement of cash flows. **Exhibit 13A-1** summarizes the procedures for converting individual income statement items to the corresponding cash flows from operating activities.

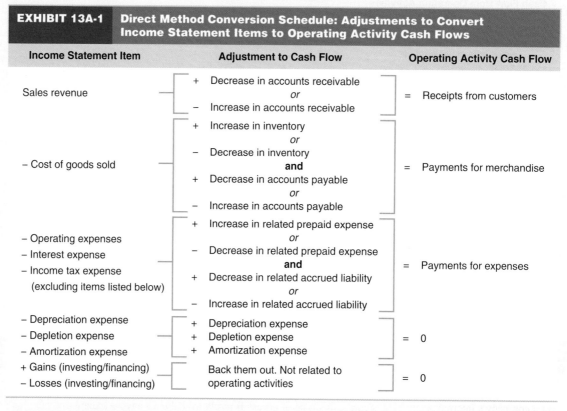

EXHIBIT 13A-1	Direct Method Conversion Schedule: Adjustments to Convert Income Statement Items to Operating Activity Cash Flows

Income Statement Item	Adjustment to Cash Flow	Operating Activity Cash Flow
Sales revenue	+ Decrease in accounts receivable *or* − Increase in accounts receivable	= Receipts from customers
– Cost of goods sold	+ Increase in inventory *or* − Decrease in inventory **and** + Decrease in accounts payable *or* − Increase in accounts payable	= Payments for merchandise
– Operating expenses – Interest expense – Income tax expense (excluding items listed below)	+ Increase in related prepaid expense *or* − Decrease in related prepaid expense **and** + Decrease in related accrued liability *or* − Increase in related accrued liability	= Payments for expenses
– Depreciation expense – Depletion expense – Amortization expense	+ Depreciation expense + Depletion expense + Amortization expense	= 0
+ Gains (investing/financing) – Losses (investing/financing)	Back them out. Not related to operating activities	= 0

In other words, rather than simply listing each adjustment to net income as in the indirect method, we align each adjustment with the associated income statement line item. For example, accounts receivable is used to record sales on credit, so we subtract the change in accounts receivable from sales revenue to calculate cash received from customers. Similarly, changes in inventory and accounts payable are used to convert cost of goods sold expense to cash payments for merchandise.

Using the Bennet Company data in **Exhibits 13-3** and **13-4**, we prepare the following schedule:

Income Statement Line Items		Operating Activities Line Items	Direct Method Operating Cash Flow	
Sales revenue	$250,000	– $5,000 ↑ accounts receivable	Cash received from customers	$245,000
Cost of goods sold	(148,000)	+ $6,000 ↓ inventory – $9,000 ↓ accounts payable	Cash paid for merchandise	(151,000)
Wage expense	(52,000)	No adjustment	Cash paid to employees	(52,000)
Insurance expense	(5,000)	– $13,000 ↑ prepaid insurance	Cash paid for insurance	(18,000)
Depreciation expense	(10,000)	+ $10,000 depreciation		0
Income tax expense	(11,000)	+ $2,000 ↑ income tax payable	Cash paid for income taxes	(9,000)
Gain on sale of plant assets	8,000	– $8,000 gain on sale of plant assets		0
Net income	$ 32,000		Cash flow from operations	$ 15,000

↑ denotes increases and ↓ denotes decreases

The first column of this schedule lists each of the income statement line items, while the middle column lists the associated adjustments. Summing across, the final column provides the amount of operating cash receipts or payments. The highlighted cells in the far right column represent the direct method operating section.

Exhibit 13A-2 presents the Bennett Company's direct method statement of cash flows. As expected, the direct method cash flow from operating activities of $15,000 is exactly equivalent to the indirect method result of $15,000 as reported in **Exhibit 13-6**. Note that the cash flow from investing activities and the cash flow from financing activities sections are exactly the same in both **Exhibit 13-6** and **Exhibit 13A-2**. The only difference between the two exhibits is the manner in which the cash flow from operating activities is presented. In **Exhibit 13-6**, the cash flow from operating activities is calculated beginning with net income and then adjusting for various noncash expenses (depreciation expense) and nonoperating transactions (gain on sale of plant assets), as well as adjusting for the changes in the various working capital accounts (accounts receivable, inventory, prepaid insurance, accounts payable, and taxes payable). In **Exhibit 13A-2**, the direct method cash flow from operating activities lists each category of cash receipts and cash payments from the highlighted column in the schedule above. But in each case, the operating cash flow is $15,000. A company using the direct method must also separately disclose the reconciliation of net income to cash flow from operating activities prepared using the indirect method.

EXHIBIT 13A-2	Statement of Cash Flows Under the Direct Method

BENNETT COMPANY
Statement of Cash Flows
For Year Ended December 31, Year 2

Cash Flow from Operating Activities		
Cash received from customers.		$245,000
Cash paid for merchandise purchased.	$(151,000)	
Cash paid to employees.	(52,000)	
Cash paid for insurance	(18,000)	
Cash paid for income taxes	(9,000)	(230,000)
Cash provided by operating activities		15,000
Cash Flow from Investing Activities		
Purchase of long-term investments	(15,000)	
Sale of plant assets	28,000	
Purchase of patent	(60,000)	
Cash used by investing activities		(47,000)
Cash Flow from Financing Activities		
Issuance of common stock.	70,000	
Payment of dividends	(13,000)	
Cash provided by financing activities		57,000
Net increase in cash.		25,000
Cash at beginning of year.		10,000
Cash at end of year		$ 35,000

Finally, note that this schedule can also be used to illustrate the connection between the direct and indirect methods. Specifically, the indirect method starts with net income and makes various adjustments to this summary number to arrive at operating cash flows, as highlighted in the schedule below. In other words, the direct and indirect methods are derived from the same data, proving that they are just "two sides of the same coin."

Income Statement Line Items		Operating Activities Line Items	Direct Method Operating Cash Flow	
Sales revenue	$250,000	– $5,000 ↑ accounts receivable	Cash received from customers	$245,000
Cost of goods sold	(148,000)	+ $6,000 ↓ inventory	Cash paid for merchandise	(151,000)
		– $9,000 ↓ accounts payable		
Wage expense	(52,000)	No adjustment	Cash paid to employees	(52,000)
Insurance expense	(5,000)	– $13,000 ↑ prepaid insurance	Cash paid for insurance	(18,000)
Depreciation expense	(10,000)	+ $10,000 depreciation		0
Income tax expense	(11,000)	+ $2,000 ↑ income tax payable	Cash paid for income taxes	(9,000)
Gain on sale of plant assets	8,000	– $8,000 gain on sale of plant assets		0
Net income	$ 32,000		Cash flow from operations	$ 15,000

↑ denotes increases and ↓ denotes decreases

YOUR TURN! 13A.1

The solution is on page 13-49.

GuidedExample

MBC

Husky Company's income statement and comparative balance sheets as of December 31 of the current and previous year are shown below:

HUSKY COMPANY		
Income Statement		
For the Year Ended December 31		
Sales revenue.		$1,270,000
Cost of goods sold	$860,000	
Wages expense	172,000	
Insurance expense	16,000	
Depreciation expense.	34,000	
Interest expense	18,000	
Income tax expense	58,000	1,158,000
Net income		$ 112,000

HUSKY COMPANY		
Balance Sheets		
	Dec. 31, Current Year	Dec. 31, Previous Year
Assets		
Cash	$ 22,000	$ 10,000
Accounts receivable	82,000	64,000
Inventory.	180,000	120,000
Prepaid insurance.	10,000	14,000
Plant assets	500,000	390,000
Accumulated depreciation	(136,000)	(102,000)
Total assets.	$658,000	$496,000
Liabilities and Stockholders' Equity		
Accounts payable	$ 14,000	$ 20,000
Wages payable	18,000	12,000
Income tax payable.	14,000	16,000
Bonds payable	260,000	150,000
Common stock	180,000	180,000
Retained earnings	172,000	118,000
Total liabilities and stockholders' equity	$658,000	$496,000

Cash dividends of $58,000 were declared and paid during the year. Plant assets were purchased for cash, and bonds payable were issued for cash. Bond interest is paid semiannually on June 30 and December 31. Accounts payable relate to merchandise purchases.

Required
Prepare a statement of cash flows using the direct method.

SUMMARY OF LEARNING OBJECTIVES

LO1   **Discuss the content and format of the statement of cash flows. (p. 13-3)**

- The statement of cash flows explains the net increase or decrease in cash and cash equivalents during the period.
- The statement of cash flows separates cash flows into operating, investing, and financing activity categories.
- The statement of cash flows also provides a required supplemental disclosure reporting noncash investing and financing activities.
- The statement of cash flows helps users compare, evaluate, and predict a firm's cash flows and also helps evaluate its financial flexibility.

LO2   **Explain the preparation of a statement of cash flows using the indirect method. (p. 13-9)**

- The indirect method of preparing the cash flow from operating activities section reconciles net income to cash flow from operating activities.

Define ratios used to analyze the statement of cash flows and explain their use. (p. 13-18)   **LO3**

- Free cash flow is defined as a company's cash flow from operations less its capital expenditures; the metric provides a measure of a firm's cash flow that can be used to fund business activities beyond the replacement of property, plant, and equipment.
- The operating-cash-flow-to-current-liabilities ratio is calculated by dividing a company's cash flow from operating activities by its average current liabilities for the year; the ratio reveals a firm's ability to repay current liabilities from operating cash flow.
- The operating-cash-flow-to-capital-expenditures ratio is calculated by dividing a firm's cash flow from operating activities by its annual net capital expenditures; the ratio evaluates a firm's ability to fund its capital investment using operating cash flow.

Appendix 13A: Explain the preparation of a statement of cash flows using the direct method. (p. 13-22)   **LO4**

- The direct method of preparing the cash flow from operating activities section shows the major categories of operating cash receipts and payments.
- The FASB encourages use of the direct method but permits use of either the direct or the indirect method.
- A firm using the direct method must separately disclose the reconciliation of net income to cash flow from operating activities.

Concept	Method	Assessment	SUMMARY
Does a company generate cash flows in excess of its capital expenditure needs?	Statement of cash flows. Free Cash Flow = Cash flow from operating activities – Capital expenditures	The higher the free cash flow, the greater is a company's ability to generate cash for needs other than capital expenditures.	**TAKEAWAY 13.1**
Will a company have sufficient cash to pay its current liabilities as they become due?	Statement of cash flows and balance sheet. $\text{Operating-cash-flow-to-current-liabilities ratio} = \dfrac{\text{Cash flow from operating activities}}{\text{Average current liabilities}}$	The higher the ratio, the higher the probability that a company will have sufficient operating cash flow to pay its current liabilities as they become due.	**TAKEAWAY 13.2**
Does a company generate sufficient operating cash flows to finance its capital expenditure needs?	Statement of cash flows. $\text{Operating-cash-flow-to-capital-expenditures ratio} = \dfrac{\text{Cash flow from operating activities}}{\text{Annual net capital expenditures}}$	The higher the ratio, the higher the probability that a company will generate sufficient operating cash flow to finance its capital expenditure needs.	**TAKEAWAY 13.3**

KEY TERMS

Cash equivalents (p. 13-3)

Cash management (p. 13-3)

Direct method (p. 13-8)

Financial flexibility (p. 13-8)

Financing activities (p. 13-6)

Free cash flow (FCF) (p. 13-18)

Indirect method (p. 13-8)

Investing activities (p. 13-5)

Noncash expenses (p. 13-14)

Noncash investing and financing activities (p. 13-7)

Operating activities (p. 13-5)

Operating-cash-flow-to-capital-expenditures ratio (p. 13-19)

Operating-cash-flow-to-current-liabilities ratio (p. 13-18)

Assignments with the 🔵 logo in the margin are available in 𝓶𝔂 BusinessCourse.
See the Preface of the book for details.

SELF-STUDY QUESTIONS

(Answers to the Self-Study Questions are at the end of the chapter.)

1. **Which of the following is not disclosed in a statement of cash flows?**   **LO1**
   a.   A transfer of cash to a cash equivalent investment
   b.   The amount of cash at year-end

    c.   Cash outflows from investing activities during the period
    d.   Cash inflows from financing activities during the period

LO1 2. **Which of the following events will appear in the cash flows from investing activities section of the statement of cash flows?**
    a.   Cash received as interest   *c.*   Cash purchase of truck
    b.   Cash received from issuance of common stock   *d.*   Cash payment of dividends

LO1 3. **Which of the following events will appear in the cash flows from financing activities section of the statement of cash flows?**
    a.   Cash purchase of equipment
    b.   Cash purchase of bonds issued by another company
    c.   Cash received as repayment for funds loaned
    d.   Cash purchase of treasury stock

LO2 4. **Tyler Company has net income of $49,000 and the following related items:**

Depreciation expense	$ 5,000
Accounts receivable increase	2,000
Inventory increase	10,000
Accounts payable decrease	4,000

    Using the indirect method, what is Tyler's cash flow from operations?
    a. $42,000   *c.* $58,000
    b. $46,000   *d.* $38,000

LO3 5. **Free cash flow is a measure of a firm's**
    a.   interest-free debt.
    b.   ability to generate net income.
    c.   ability to generate cash and invest in new capital expenditures.
    d.   ability to collect accounts receivable in a timely manner.

LO1 6. **Which of the following events will not appear in the cash flows from financing activities section of the statement of cash flow?**
    a.   Borrowing cash from a bank   *c.*   Sales of common stock
    b.   Issuance of stock in exchange for plant assets   *d.*   Payment of dividends on preferred stock

LO3 7. **Taylor Company reports free cash flow of $15,000, total cash of $18,000, net income of $50,000, current assets of $90,000, average current liabilities of $38,400, and cash flow from operating activities of $48,000. Compute the operating-cash-flow-to-current-liabilities ratio for Taylor Company.**
    a.   0.83   *c.*   0.30
    b.   0.80   *d.*   1.25

LO1 8. **Which of the following is not a cash equivalent?**
    a.   Short-term U.S. Treasury bill   *c.*   Money-market account
    b.   Short-term certificate of deposit   *d.*   IBM common stock

LO2 9. **Which of the following expenses are not added back to net income when using the indirect method to prepare a statement of cash flows?**
    a.   Amortization expense   *c.*   Interest expense
    b.   Depletion expense   *d.*   Depreciation expense

LO4 (Appendix 13A) 10. **Smith & Sons reports interest expense of $90,000 on its income statement. The beginning and ending balances for interest payable reported on its balance sheet are $15,000 and $10,000, respectively. How much cash did Smith & Sons pay for interest expense this period?**
    a. $85,000   *c.* $100,000
    b. $95,000   *d.* $105,000

LO4 (Appendix 13A) 11. **Which of the following methods will disclose the cash received from customers in the statement of cash flows?**
    a.   Indirect method   *c.*   Direct method
    b.   Reconciliation method   *d.*   Both direct and indirect methods

LO4 (Appendix 13A) 12. **Smith & Sons reports sales revenue of $1,000,000 on its income statement. Its balance sheet reveals beginning and ending accounts receivable of $92,000 and $60,000, respectively. What is the amount of cash collected from customers of the company?**

a. $1,032,000   c. $1,060,000
b. $968,000   d. $1,092,000

QUESTIONS

1. What is the definition of *cash equivalents?* Give three examples of cash equivalents.

2. Why are cash equivalents included with cash in a statement of cash flows?

3. What are the three major types of activities classified on a statement of cash flows? Give an example of a cash inflow and a cash outflow in each classification.

4. In which of the three activity categories of a statement of cash flows would each of the following items appear? Indicate for each item whether it represents a cash inflow or a cash outflow:
   a. Cash purchase of equipment
   b. Cash collection on loans
   c. Cash dividends paid
   d. Cash dividends received
   e. Cash proceeds from issuing stock
   f. Cash receipts from customers
   g. Cash interest paid
   h. Cash interest received

5. Why is a statement of cash flows a useful financial statement?

6. What is the difference between the direct method and the indirect method of presenting the cash flow from operating activities?

7. In determining the cash flow from operating activities using the indirect method, why is it necessary to add depreciation back to net income? Give an example of another item that is added back to net income under the indirect method.

8. Vista Company sold land for $98,000 cash that had originally cost $70,000. The company recorded a gain on the sale of $28,000. How is this event reported in a statement of cash flows using the indirect method?

9. A firm uses the indirect method. Using the following information, what is its cash flow from operating activities?

Net income	$88,000
Accounts receivable decrease	13,000
Inventory increase	9,000
Accounts payable decrease	3,500
Income tax payable increase	1,500
Depreciation expense.	6,000

10. If a business had a net loss for the year, under what circumstances would the statement of cash flows show a positive cash flow from operating activities?

11. A firm is converting its accrual revenues to corresponding cash amounts using the direct method. Sales revenue on the income statement are $925,000. Beginning and ending accounts receivable on the balance sheet are $58,000 and $44,000, respectively. What is the amount of cash received from customers?

12. A firm reports $86,000 wages expense in its income statement. If beginning and ending wages payable are $3,900 and $2,800, respectively, what is the amount of cash paid to employees?

13. A firm reports $43,000 advertising expense in its income statement. If beginning and ending prepaid advertising are $6,000 and $7,600, respectively, what is the amount of cash paid for advertising?

14. Rusk Company sold equipment for $5,100 cash that had cost $35,000 and had $29,000 of accumulated depreciation. How is this event reported in a statement of cash flows using the direct method?

15. What separate disclosures are required for a company that reports a statement of cash flows using the direct method?

16. How is the *operating-cash-flow-to-current-liabilities ratio* calculated? Explain its use.

17. How is the *operating-cash-flow-to-capital-expenditures ratio* calculated? Explain its use.

18. The statement of cash flows provides information that may be useful in predicting future cash flows, evaluating financial flexibility, assessing liquidity, and identifying a company's financing needs. It is not, however, the best financial statement for learning about a firm's financial performance during a period. Information about a company's financial performance is provided by the income statement. Two basic principles—the revenue recognition principle and the matching concept—work to distinguish the income statement from the statement of cash flows. (a) Define the revenue recognition principle and the matching concept. (b) Briefly explain how these two principles work to make the income statement a better report regarding a firm's periodic financial performance than the statement of cash flows.

SHORT EXERCISES

Use the following information regarding the Melville Corporation to answer Short Exercises 13-1 through 13-3:

Accounts payable increase.	$12,000
Accounts receivable increase.	4,000
Accrued liabilities decrease	5,000
Amortization expense.	7,000
Cash balance, January 1	22,000
Cash balance, December 31	23,000
Cash paid as dividends	31,000
Cash paid to purchase land	90,000
Cash paid to retire bonds payable at par	60,000
Cash received from issuance of common stock.	37,000
Cash received from sale of equipment.	19,000
Depreciation expense.	29,000
Gain on sale of equipment	4,000
Inventory decrease.	13,000
Net income.	80,000
Prepaid expenses increase	2,000

LO1, 2   **SE13-1.**   **Cash Flow from Operating Activities** Using the information for the Melville Corporation above, calculate the cash flow from operating activities.

LO1, 2   **SE13-2.**   **Cash Flow from Investing Activities** Using the information for the Melville Corporation above, calculate the cash flow from investing activities.

LO1, 2   **SE13-3.**   **Cash Flow from Financing Activities** Using the information for the Melville Corporation above, calculate the cash flow from financing activities.

The following information for Evans & Sons relates to Short Exercises 13-4 through 13-6:

Cash flow from operating activities.	$1,600,000
Capital expenditures.	850,000
Current liabilities, beginning of year	300,000
Current liabilities, end of year.	380,000

LO3   **SE13-4.**   **Free Cash Flow** Using the above data, calculate the free cash flow for Evans & Sons.

LO3   **SE13-5.**   **Operating-Cash-Flow-to-Current-Liabilities Ratio** Using the above data, calculate the operating-cash-flow-to-current-liabilities ratio for Evans & Sons.

LO3   **SE13-6.**   **Operating-Cash-Flow-to-Capital-Expenditures Ratio** Using the above data, calculate the operating-cash-flow-to-capital-expenditures ratio for Evans & Sons.

LO4
(Appendix 13A)   **SE13-7.**   **Converting Sales Revenue to Cash** Evans & Sons is converting its sales revenues to corresponding cash amounts using the direct method. Sales revenue on the income statement are $1,025,000. Beginning and ending accounts receivable on the balance sheet are $58,000 and $38,000, respectively. Calculate the amount of cash received from customers.

LO4
(Appendix 13A)   **SE13-8.**   **Direct Method** Using the following data for Evans & Sons, calculate the cash paid for rent:

Rent expense.	$80,000
Prepaid rent, January 1	10,000
Prepaid rent, December 31	8,000

LO4
(Appendix 13A)   **SE13-9.**   **Direct Method** Using the following data for Evans & Sons, calculate the cash received as interest:

Interest income.	$30,000
Interest receivable, January 1.	3,000
Interest receivable, December 31.	3,700

SE13-10. Direct Method Using the following data for Evans & Sons, calculate the cash paid for merchandise purchased:

LO4
(Appendix 13A)

Cost of goods sold	$128,000
Inventory, January 1	19,000
Inventory, December 31	22,000
Accounts payable, January 1	11,000
Accounts payable, December 31	7,000

DATA ANALYTICS, DATA VISUALIZATION, AND EXCEL ACTIVITIES

Data Analytics, Data Visualization, and Excel Activities are available in myBusinessCourse. These assignments develop Excel, Tableau, and Data Analytics skills, which will enhance students' career readiness. These exercises are assignable and auto graded by MBC. For an overview of data analytics, see the appendix at the end of this book.

EXERCISES—SET A

E13-1A. Classification of Cash Flows For each of the items below, indicate whether the cash flow item relates to an operating activity, an investing activity, or a financing activity:

LO1

    a. Cash receipts from customers for services rendered
    b. Sale of long-term investments for cash
    c. Acquisition of plant assets for cash
    d. Payment of income taxes
    e. Bonds payable issued for cash
    f. Payment of cash dividends declared in previous year
    g. Purchase of short-term investments (not cash equivalents) for cash

E13-2A. Classification of Cash Flows For each of the items below, indicate whether it is (1) a cash flow from an operating activity, (2) a cash flow from an investing activity, (3) a cash flow from a financing activity, (4) a noncash investing and financing activity, or (5) none of the above:

LO1

    a. Paid cash to retire bonds payable at a loss
    b. Received cash as settlement of a lawsuit
    c. Acquired a patent in exchange for common stock
    d. Received advance payments from customers on orders for custom-made goods
    e. Gave large cash contribution to local university
    f. Invested cash in 60-day commercial paper (a cash equivalent)

E13-3A. Cash Flow from Operating Activities (Indirect Method) The Washington Company owns no plant assets and had the following income statement for the year:

LO2

Sales revenue		$900,000
Cost of goods sold	$470,000	
Wages expense	120,000	
Rent expense	50,000	
Insurance expense	15,000	655,000
Net income		$245,000

Additional information about the company includes:

	End of Year	Beginning of Year
Accounts receivable	$54,000	$51,000
Inventory	60,000	76,000
Prepaid insurance	8,000	7,000
Accounts payable	24,000	18,000
Wages payable	7,000	11,000

Use the preceding information to calculate the cash flow from operating activities using the indirect method.

LO2, 3   E13-4A.   Statement of Cash Flows (Indirect Method) Use the following information regarding the Surpa Corporation to (a) prepare a statement of cash flows using the indirect method and (b) compute Surpa's operating-cash-flow-to-current-liabilities ratio.

Accounts payable increase.	$ 13,000
Accounts receivable increase.	4,000
Accrued liabilities decrease	6,000
Amortization expense.	7,000
Cash balance, January 1	21,000
Cash balance, December 31	17,000
Cash paid as dividends	31,000
Cash paid to purchase land	90,000
Cash paid to retire bonds payable at par	60,000
Cash received from issuance of common stock	40,000
Cash received from sale of equipment.	17,000
Depreciation expense.	29,000
Gain on sale of equipment	7,000
Inventory decrease.	13,000
Net income.	78,000
Prepaid expenses increase	3,000
Average current liabilities	140,000

LO2   E13-5A.   Cash Flow from Operating Activities (Indirect Method) The Azuza Company owns no plant assets and had the following income statement for the year:

Sales revenue.		$930,000
Cost of goods sold	$650,000	
Wages expense	210,000	
Rent expense.	42,000	
Utilities expense.	12,000	914,000
Net income.		$ 16,000

Additional information about the company includes:

	End of Year	Beginning of Year
Accounts receivable	$67,000	$59,000
Inventory.	62,000	86,000
Prepaid rent	9,000	7,000
Accounts payable	22,000	30,000
Wages payable.	9,000	7,000

Use the preceding information to calculate the cash flow from operating activities using the indirect method.

E13-6A. **Statement of Cash Flows (Indirect Method)** Use the following information regarding the Hamilton Corporation to prepare a statement of cash flows using the indirect method:

LO2

Accounts payable decrease	$ 3,000
Accounts receivable increase	10,000
Wages payable decrease	9,000
Amortization expense	19,000
Cash balance, January 1	31,000
Cash balance, December 31	2,000
Cash paid as dividends	6,000
Cash paid to purchase land	110,000
Cash paid to retire bonds payable at par	65,000
Cash received from issuance of common stock	45,000
Cash received from sale of equipment	13,000
Depreciation expense	39,000
Gain on sale of equipment	16,000
Inventory increase	11,000
Net income	94,000
Prepaid expenses increase	9,000

E13-7A. **Cash Flow Ratios** Tracy Company reports the following amounts in its annual financial statements:

LO3

Cash flow from operating activities	$90,000	Capital expenditures	$ 31,000*
Cash flow from investing activities	(70,000)	Average current assets	80,000
Cash flow from financing activities	(10,000)	Average current liabilities	60,000
Net income	44,000	Total assets	180,000

* This amount is a cash outflow.

a.   Compute Tracy's free cash flow.
b.   Compute Tracy's operating-cash-flow-to-current-liabilities ratio.
c.   Compute Tracy's operating-cash-flow-to-capital-expenditures ratio.

E13-8A. **Operating Cash Flows (Direct Method)** Calculate the cash flow in each of the following cases:

LO4
(Appendix 13A)

a.   Cash paid for advertising:

Advertising expense	$62,000
Prepaid advertising, January 1	13,000
Prepaid advertising, December 31	15,000

b.   Cash paid for income taxes:

Income tax expense	$31,000
Income tax payable, January 1	7,100
Income tax payable, December 31	5,900

c.   Cash paid for merchandise purchased:

Cost of goods sold	$180,000
Inventory, January 1	30,000
Inventory, December 31	24,000
Accounts payable, January 1	10,000
Accounts payable, December 31	11,000

LO4
(Appendix 13A)

E13-9A.   Statement of Cash Flows (Direct Method) Use the following information regarding the cash flows of Dixon Corporation to prepare a statement of cash flows using the direct method:

Cash balance, December 31	$ 9,000
Cash paid to employees and suppliers	158,000
Cash received from sale of land	42,000
Cash paid to acquire treasury stock	10,000
Cash balance, January 1	18,000
Cash received as interest	8,000
Cash paid as income taxes	9,000
Cash paid to purchase equipment	89,000
Cash received from customers	199,000
Cash received from issuing bonds payable	30,000
Cash paid as dividends	22,000

LO4
(Appendix 13A)

E13-10A. Operating Cash Flows (Direct Method) Refer to the information in Exercise E13-3A. Calculate the cash flow from operating activities using the direct method. Show a related cash flow for each revenue and expense.

LO2, 4
(Appendix 13A)

E13-11A. Investing and Financing Cash Flows During the year, Paton Corporation's Long-Term Investments account (at cost) increased $20,000, the net result of purchasing stocks costing $85,000 and selling stocks costing $65,000 at a $7,000 loss. Also, the Bonds Payable account decreased by $35,000, the net result of issuing $100,000 of bonds at 102 and retiring bonds with a face value (and book value) of $135,000 at an $8,000 gain. What items and amounts will appear in the (a) cash flows from investing activities and the (b) cash flows from financing activities sections of Paton's statement of cash flows?

EXERCISES—SET B

LO1

E13-1B.   Classification of Cash Flows For each of the items below, indicate whether the cash flow item relates to an operating activity, an investing activity, or a financing activity:

a.   Cash loaned to borrowers
b.   Cash paid as interest on bonds payable
c.   Cash received from issuance of preferred stock
d.   Cash paid as state income taxes
e.   Cash received as dividends on stock investments
f.   Cash paid to acquire treasury stock
g.   Cash paid to acquire a franchise to distribute a product line

LO1

E13-2B.   Classification of Cash Flows For each of the items below, indicate whether it is (1) a cash flow from an operating activity, (2) a cash flow from an investing activity, (3) a cash flow from a financing activity, (4) a noncash investing and financing activity, or (5) none of the above:

a.   Received cash as interest earned on bond investment
b.   Received cash as refund from supplier
c.   Borrowed cash from bank on six-month note payable
d.   Exchanged, at a gain, stock held as an investment for a parcel of land
e.   Invested cash in a money market fund (cash may be easily withdrawn from the fund)
f.   Loaned cash to help finance the start of a new biotechnology firm

E13-3B. **Cash Flow from Operating Activities (Indirect Method)** The following information was obtained   **LO2, 3** from Melville Company's comparative balance sheets:

	End of Year	Beginning of Year
Cash	$ 19,000	$ 9,000
Accounts receivable	50,000	35,000
Inventory.	55,000	49,000
Prepaid rent	6,000	8,000
Long-term investments.	21,000	32,000
Plant assets	140,000	106,000
Accumulated depreciation	(42,000)	(32,000)
Accounts payable	24,000	22,000
Income tax payable.	4,000	6,000
Common stock	127,000	92,000
Retained earnings	106,000	91,000
Capital expenditures.	15,200	

Assume that Melville Company's income statement showed depreciation expense of $10,000, a gain on sale of investments of $7,000, and a net income of $60,000. (a) Calculate the cash flow from operating activities using the indirect method and (b) compute Melville's operating-cash-flow-to-capital-expenditures ratio.

E13-4B. **Cash Flow from Operating Activities (Indirect Method)** Zaire Company had a $26,000 net loss   **LO2** from operations. Depreciation expense for the year was $9,600, and a dividend of $2,000 was declared and paid. The balances of the current asset and current liability accounts at the beginning and end of the year are as follows:

	End	Beginning
Cash.	$ 3,500	$ 7,000
Accounts receivable	16,000	27,000
Inventory.	51,000	53,000
Prepaid expenses.	5,000	9,000
Accounts payable	12,000	8,000
Accrued liabilities	6,000	7,600

Did Zaire Company's operating activities provide or use cash? Use the indirect method to determine your answer.

E13-5B. **Cash Flow from Operating Activities (Indirect Method)** The Smith Company owns no plant assets and had the following income statement for the year: **LO2**

Sales revenue.		$1,140,000
Cost of goods sold	$770,000	
Wages expense	230,000	
Rent expense	65,000	
Insurance expense	47,000	1,112,000
Net income		$ 28,000

Additional information about the company includes:

	End of Year	Beginning of Year
Accounts receivable	$74,000	$49,000
Inventory.	70,000	74,000
Prepaid insurance.	5,000	8,000
Accounts payable	26,000	28,000
Wages payable.	6,000	13,000

Use the preceding information to calculate the cash flow from operating activities using the indirect method.

LO2   **E13-6B.**   **Statement of Cash Flows (Indirect Method)** Use the following information regarding the Fremont Corporation to prepare a statement of cash flows using the indirect method:

Accounts payable increase	$ 14,000
Accounts receivable increase	7,000
Accrued liabilities decrease	5,000
Amortization expense	31,000
Cash balance, January 1	21,000
Cash balance, December 31	141,000
Cash paid as dividends	41,000
Cash paid to purchase land	81,000
Cash paid to retire bonds payable at par	70,000
Cash received from issuance of common stock	75,000
Cash received from sale of equipment	17,000
Depreciation expense	65,000
Gain on sale of equipment	12,000
Inventory decrease	11,000
Net income	126,000
Prepaid expenses increase	3,000

LO3   **E13-7B.**   **Cash Flow Ratios** Morris Company reports the following amounts in its annual financial statements:

Cash flow from operating activities	$75,000	Capital expenditures	$ 47,500*
Cash flow from investing activities	(60,000)	Average current assets	150,000
Cash flow from financing activities	(8,500)	Average current liabilities	90,000
Net income	37,500	Total assets	225,000

* This amount is a cash outflow.

a.   Compute Morris' free cash flow.

b.   Compute Morris' operating-cash-flow-to-current-liabilities ratio.

c.   Compute Morris' operating-cash-flow-to-capital-expenditures ratio.

LO4   **E13-8B.**   **Operating Cash Flows (Direct Method)** Calculate the cash flow in each of the following cases:
(Appendix 13A)

a.   Cash paid for rent:

Rent expense	$62,000
Prepaid rent, January 1	10,000
Prepaid rent, December 31	6,000

b.   Cash received as interest:

Interest income	$16,000
Interest receivable, January 1	6,000
Interest receivable, December 31	3,700

c.   Cash paid for merchandise purchased:

Cost of goods sold	$98,000
Inventory, January 1	19,000
Inventory, December 31	22,000
Accounts payable, January 1	11,000
Accounts payable, December 31	6,000

E13-9B. **Statement of Cash Flows (Direct Method)** Use the following information regarding the cash flows of Jack Corporation to prepare a statement of cash flows using the direct method:

LO4
(Appendix 13A)

Cash balance, December 31	$ 26,000
Cash paid to employees and suppliers.	151,000
Cash received from sale of equipment.	91,000
Cash paid to retire bonds payable	70,000
Cash balance, January 1	20,000
Cash paid as interest	4,000
Cash paid as income taxes	24,000
Cash paid to purchase patent.	76,000
Cash received from customers.	221,000
Cash received from issuing common stock	35,000
Cash paid as dividends	16,000

E13-10B. **Operating Cash Flows (Direct Method)** The Thurston Company's current year income statement contains the following data:

LO4
(Appendix 13A)

Sales revenue.	$790,000
Cost of goods sold	550,000
Gross profit.	$240,000

Thurston's comparative balance sheets show the following data (accounts payable relate to merchandise purchases):

	End of Year	Beginning of Year
Accounts receivable	$ 71,000	$61,000
Inventory.	120,000	96,000
Prepaid expenses.	3,000	10,000
Accounts payable	31,000	35,000

Compute Thurston's current-year cash received from customers and cash paid for merchandise purchased.

E13-11B. **Investing and Financing Cash Flows** Refer to the information in Exercise 13-3B. During the year, Melville Company purchased plant assets for cash, sold investments for cash (the entire $7,000 gain developed during the year), and issued common stock for cash. The firm also declared and paid cash dividends. What items and amounts will appear in (a) the cash flow from investing activities and (b) the cash flow from financing activities sections of a statement of cash flows?

LO2, 4
(Appendix 13A)

PROBLEMS—SET A

P13-1A. **Statement of Cash Flows (Indirect Method)** The Artic Company's income statement and comparative balance sheets at December 31 of the current and the previous year are shown next:

LO2, 3

ARTIC COMPANY Income Statement For the Year Ended December 31		
Sales revenue.		$645,000
Cost of goods sold	$430,000	
Wages expense	91,000	
Insurance expense	12,000	
Depreciation expense.	13,000	
Interest expense.	15,000	
Income tax expense	29,000	590,000
Net income		$ 55,000

ARTIC COMPANY Balance Sheets		
	Dec. 31, Current Year	Dec. 31, Previous Year
Assets		
Cash.	$ 41,000	$ 8,000
Accounts receivable	41,000	32,000
Inventory.	90,000	65,000
Prepaid insurance.	5,000	7,000
Plant assets	219,000	202,000
Accumulated depreciation	(68,000)	(55,000)
Total assets.	$328,000	$259,000
Liabilities and Stockholders' Equity		
Accounts payable	$ 7,000	$ 10,000
Wages payable.	10,000	6,000
Income tax payable.	6,000	7,000
Bonds payable	141,000	87,000
Common stock	90,000	90,000
Retained earnings	74,000	59,000
Total liabilities and stockholders' equity	$328,000	$259,000

Cash dividends of $40,000 were declared and paid during the current year. Plant assets were purchased for cash, and bonds payable were issued for cash. Bond interest is paid semi-annually on June 30 and December 31. Accounts payable relate to merchandise purchases.

Required
a. Calculate the change in cash that occurred during the current year.
b. Prepare a statement of cash flows using the indirect method.
c. Compute the free cash flow.
d. Compute the operating-cash-flow-to-current-liabilities ratio.
e. Compute the operating-cash-flow-to-capital-expenditures ratio.

LO2   P13-2A.   Statement of Cash Flows (Indirect Method) North Company's income statement and comparative balance sheets as of December 31 of the current and the previous year follow:

NORTH COMPANY Income Statement For the Year Ended December 31		
Sales revenue.		$770,000
Cost of goods sold	$550,000	
Wages expense	195,000	
Advertising expense.	31,000	
Depreciation expense.	24,000	
Interest expense.	20,000	
Gain on sale of land	(25,000)	795,000
Net loss.		$ (25,000)

NORTH COMPANY Balance Sheets		
	Dec. 31, Current Year	Dec. 31, Previous Year
Assets		
Cash.	$ 80,000	$ 32,000
Accounts receivable	42,000	49,000
Inventory.	107,000	115,000
Prepaid advertising.	10,000	14,000
Plant assets	360,000	210,000
Accumulated depreciation	(80,000)	(56,000)
Total assets.	$519,000	$364,000

continued

continued from previous page

NORTH COMPANY Balance Sheets	Dec. 31, Current Year	Dec. 31, Previous Year
Liabilities and Stockholders' Equity		
Accounts payable	$ 19,000	$ 25,000
Interest payable	6,000	—
Bonds payable	210,000	—
Common stock	245,000	245,000
Retained earnings	69,000	94,000
Treasury stock	(30,000)	—
Total liabilities and stockholders' equity	$519,000	$364,000

During the current year, North sold land for $70,000 cash that had originally cost $45,000. North also purchased equipment for cash, acquired treasury stock for cash, and issued bonds payable for cash. Accounts payable relate to merchandise purchases.

Required
a. Calculate the change in cash that occurred during the current year.
b. Prepare a statement of cash flows using the indirect method.

P13-3A. Statement of Cash Flows (Indirect Method) The Pruitt Company's income statement and comparative balance sheets as of December 31 of the current and the previous year follow:

LO2

PRUITT COMPANY Income Statement For the Year Ended December 31		
Sales revenue.		$770,000
Cost of goods sold	$450,000	
Wages and other operating expenses	195,000	
Depreciation expense.	22,000	
Goodwill amortization expense.	7,000	
Interest expense.	5,000	
Income tax expense	36,000	
Loss on bond retirement.	5,000	720,000
Net income		$ 50,000

PRUITT COMPANY Balance Sheets	Dec. 31, Current Year	Dec. 31, Previous Year
Assets		
Cash.	$ 8,000	$ 19,000
Accounts receivable	43,000	28,000
Inventory.	101,000	131,000
Prepaid expenses.	12,000	11,000
Plant assets	360,000	334,000
Accumulated depreciation	(87,000)	(84,000)
Goodwill	43,000	50,000
Total assets.	$480,000	$489,000
Liabilities and Stockholders' Equity		
Accounts payable	$ 32,000	$ 28,000
Interest payable	3,000	7,000
Income tax payable.	6,000	8,000
Bonds payable	60,000	100,000
Common stock	252,000	248,000
Retained earnings	127,000	98,000
Total liabilities and stockholders' equity	$480,000	$489,000

During the year, the company sold for $15,000 cash old equipment that had cost $34,000 and had $19,000 accumulated depreciation. New equipment worth $60,000 was acquired in exchange for $60,000 of bonds payable. Bonds payable of $100,000 were retired for cash at a loss. A $21,000 cash dividend was declared and paid. All stock issuances were for cash.

Required

a. Compute the change in cash that occurred in the current year.
b. Prepare a statement of cash flows using the indirect method.

LO2   **P13-4A.**   **Statement of Cash Flows (Indirect Method)** The Sky Company's income statement and comparative balance sheets as of December 31 of the current and the previous year follow:

SKY COMPANY Income Statement For Year Ended December 31		
Sales revenue		$800,000
Dividend income		19,000
		819,000
Cost of goods sold	$440,000	
Wages and other operating expenses	130,000	
Depreciation expense	39,000	
Patent amortization expense	7,000	
Interest expense	13,000	
Income tax expense	30,000	
Loss on sale of equipment	5,000	
Gain on sale of investments	(10,000)	654,000
Net income		$165,000

SKY COMPANY Balance Sheets	Dec. 31, Current Year	Dec. 31, Previous Year
Assets		
Cash and cash equivalents	$ 63,000	$ 29,000
Accounts receivable	45,000	35,000
Inventory	100,000	77,000
Prepaid expenses	10,000	6,000
Long-term investments—available for sale	—	50,000
Fair value adjustment to investments	—	7,000
Land	190,000	100,000
Buildings	445,000	350,000
Accumulated depreciation—Buildings	(91,000)	(75,000)
Equipment	179,000	225,000
Accumulated depreciation—Equipment	(42,000)	(46,000)
Patents	50,000	32,000
Total assets	$949,000	$790,000
Liabilities and Stockholders' Equity		
Accounts payable	$ 21,000	$ 18,000
Interest payable	6,000	5,000
Income tax payable	8,000	12,000
Bonds payable	135,000	130,000
Preferred stock ($100 par value)	100,000	75,000
Common stock ($5 par value)	379,000	364,000
Paid-in-capital in excess of par value—Common	133,000	124,000
Retained earnings	167,000	55,000
Unrealized gain on investments	—	7,000
Total liabilities and stockholders' equity	$949,000	$790,000

During the year, the following transactions occurred:

1. Sold long-term investments costing $50,000 for $60,000 cash. Unrealized gains totaling $7,000 related to these investments had been recorded in earlier years. At year-end, the fair value adjustment and unrealized gain account balances were eliminated.

2. Purchased land for cash.

3. Capitalized an expenditure made to improve the building.

4. Sold equipment for $14,000 cash that originally cost $46,000 and had $27,000 accumulated depreciation.

5. Issued bonds payable at face value for cash.

6. Acquired a patent with a fair value of $25,000 by issuing 250 shares of preferred stock at par value.

7. Declared and paid a $53,000 cash dividend.

8. Issued 3,000 shares of common stock for cash at $8 per share.

9. Recorded depreciation of $16,000 on buildings and $23,000 on equipment.

Required

a. Calculate the change in cash and cash equivalents that occurred during the current year.

b. Prepare a statement of cash flows using the indirect method.

P13-5A. **Analyzing Cash Flow Ratios** Pearce Enterprises reported the following information for the past year of operations: **LO3**

Transaction	Free Cash Flow $250,000	Operating-Cash-Flow-to-Current-Liabilities Ratio 1.0 Times	Operating-Cash-Flow-to-Capital-Expenditures Ratio 3.0 Times
a. Recorded credit sales of $9,000			
b. Collected $4,000 owed from customers			
c. Purchased $28,000 of equipment on long-term credit			
d. Purchased $16,000 of equipment for cash			
e. Paid $10,000 of wages with cash			
f. Recorded utility bill of $1,750 that has not been paid			

For each transaction, indicate whether the ratio will (I) increase, (D) decrease, or (N) have no effect.

P13-6A. **Statement of Cash Flows (Direct Method)** Refer to the data given for the Artic Company in Problem P13-1A. **LO3, 4**
(Appendix 13A)

Required

a. Calculate the change in cash that occurred during the current year.

b. Prepare a statement of cash flows using the direct method.

c. Compute free cash flow.

d. Compute the operating-cash-flow-to-current-liabilities ratio.

e. Compute the operating-cash-flow-to-capital-expenditures ratio.

P13-7A. **Statement of Cash Flows (Direct Method)** Refer to the data given for the North Company in Problem P13-2A. **LO4**
(Appendix 13A)

Required

a. Calculate the change in cash that occurred during the current year.

b. Prepare a statement of cash flows using the direct method.

P13-8A. **Statement of Cash Flows (Direct Method)** Refer to the data given for the Pruitt Company in Problem P13-3A. **LO4**
(Appendix 13A)

Required

a. Compute the change in cash that occurred in the current year.

b. Prepare a statement of cash flows using the direct method. Use one cash outflow for "cash paid for wages and other operating expenses." Accounts payable relate to inventory purchases only.

P13-9A. **Statement of Cash Flows (Direct Method)** Refer to the data given for the Sky Company in Problem P13-4A. **LO4**
(Appendix 13A)

Required

a. Calculate the change in cash that occurred in the current year.

b. Prepare a statement of cash flows using the direct method. Use one cash outflow for "cash paid for wages and other operating expenses." Accounts payable relate to inventory purchases only.

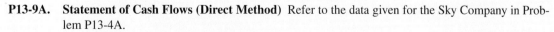

PROBLEMS—SET B

LO2, 3   **P13-1B.**   **Statement of Cash Flows (Indirect Method)** The Forrester Company's income statement and comparative balance sheets as of December 31 of the current and the previous year are shown below:

FORRESTER COMPANY Income Statement For the Year Ended December 31		
Sales revenue		$660,000
Cost of goods sold	$376,000	
Wages expense	107,000	
Depreciation expense	22,000	
Rent expense	28,000	
Income tax expense	24,000	557,000
Net income		$103,000

FORRESTER COMPANY Balance Sheets	Dec. 31, Current Year	Dec. 31, Previous Year
Assets		
Cash	$ 58,000	$ 30,000
Accounts receivable	52,000	60,000
Inventory	142,000	120,000
Prepaid rent	16,000	10,000
Plant assets	420,000	301,000
Accumulated depreciation	(127,000)	(105,000)
Total assets	$561,000	$416,000
Liabilities and Stockholders' Equity		
Accounts payable	$ 29,000	$ 17,000
Wages payable	14,000	9,000
Income tax payable	7,000	8,000
Common stock	295,000	252,000
Paid-in-capital in excess of par value	72,000	58,000
Retained earnings	144,000	72,000
Total liabilities and stockholders' equity	$561,000	$416,000

Cash dividends of $31,000 were declared and paid during the current year. Plant assets were purchased for cash, and additional common stock was issued for cash. Accounts payable relate to merchandise purchases.

Required
a.   Calculate the change in cash that occurred during the current year.
b.   Prepare a statement of cash flows using the indirect method.
c.   Compute free cash flow.
d.   Compute the operating-cash-flow-to-current-liabilities ratio.
e.   Compute the operating-cash-flows-to-capital-expenditures ratio.

LO2   **P13-2B.**   **Statement of Cash Flows (Indirect Method)** The Lowe Company's income statement and comparative balance sheets as of December 31 of the current and the previous year are presented below:

LOWE COMPANY
Income Statement
For the Year Ended December 31

Sales revenue.		$925,000
Cost of goods sold	$490,000	
Wages expense	207,000	
Depreciation expense.	62,000	
Insurance expense	17,000	
Interest expense.	12,000	
Income tax expense	57,000	
Gain on sale of equipment	(16,000)	829,000
Net income		$ 96,000

LOWE COMPANY
Balance Sheets

	Dec. 31, Current Year	Dec. 31, Previous Year
Assets		
Cash.	$ 25,000	$ 33,000
Accounts receivable	68,000	51,000
Inventory.	177,000	126,000
Prepaid insurance.	8,000	11,000
Plant assets	887,000	763,000
Accumulated depreciation	(191,000)	(175,000)
Total assets.	$974,000	$809,000
Liabilities and Stockholders' Equity		
Accounts payable	$ 37,000	$ 27,000
Interest payable	7,000	—
Income tax payable.	11,000	19,000
Bonds payable	145,000	80,000
Common stock	660,000	585,000
Retained earnings	166,000	98,000
Treasury stock	(52,000)	—
Total liabilities and stockholders' equity	$974,000	$809,000

During the year, Lowe Company sold equipment for $27,000 cash that originally cost $57,000 and had $46,000 accumulated depreciation. New equipment was purchased for cash. Bonds payable and common stock were issued for cash. Cash dividends of $28,000 were declared and paid. At the end of the year, shares of treasury stock were purchased for cash. Accounts payable relate to merchandise purchases.

Required
a. Compute the change in cash that occurred during the current year.
b. Prepare a statement of cash flows using the indirect method.

P13-3B. **Statement of Cash Flows (Indirect Method)** The Madison Company's income statement and comparative balance sheets as of December 31 of the current and the previous year follow: **LO2**

MADISON COMPANY
Income Statement
For the Year Ended December 31

Sales revenue.		$825,000
Cost of goods sold	$530,000	
Wages and other operating expenses	179,000	
Depreciation expense.	29,000	
Patent amortization expense	6,000	
Interest expense.	18,000	
Income tax expense	25,000	
Gain on exchange of land for patent.	(37,000)	750,000
Net income		$ 75,000

MADISON COMPANY Balance Sheets		
	Dec. 31, Current Year	Dec. 31, Previous Year
Assets		
Cash..	$ 67,000	$ 25,000
Accounts receivable.................................	64,000	49,000
Inventory..	85,000	66,000
Land..	117,000	160,000
Building and equipment.............................	441,000	353,000
Accumulated depreciation...........................	(122,000)	(100,000)
Patent...	74,000	—
Total assets..	$726,000	$553,000
Liabilities and Stockholders' Equity		
Accounts payable....................................	$ 36,000	$ 26,000
Interest payable.....................................	13,000	8,000
Income tax payable..................................	7,000	12,000
Bonds payable......................................	190,000	75,000
Common stock......................................	350,000	350,000
Retained earnings..................................	130,000	82,000
Total liabilities and stockholders' equity.............	$726,000	$553,000

During the current year, $27,000 of cash dividends were declared and paid. A patent valued at $80,000 was obtained in exchange for land. Equipment that originally cost $20,000 and had $7,000 accumulated depreciation was sold for $13,000 cash. Bonds payable were sold for cash, and cash was used to pay for structural improvements to the building.

Required
a.   Compute the change in cash that occurred during the current year.
b.   Prepare a statement of cash flows using the indirect method.

LO2   P13-4B.   Statement of Cash Flows (Indirect Method) The Geary Company's income statement and comparative balance sheets as of December 31 of the current and the previous year follow:

GEARY COMPANY Income Statement For the Year Ended December 31		
Service fees earned..		$320,000
Dividend and interest income.................................		16,000
		$336,000
Wages and other operating expenses............................	$288,000	
Depreciation expense...	55,000	
Franchise amortization expense................................	10,000	
Loss on sale of equipment....................................	7,000	
Gain on sale of investments..................................	(17,000)	343,000
Net loss...		$ (7,000)

GEARY COMPANY Balance Sheets		
	Dec. 31, Current Year	Dec. 31, Previous Year
Assets		
Cash..	$ 21,000	$ 33,000
Accounts receivable.................................	14,000	18,000
Interest receivable..................................	—	4,000
Prepaid expenses...................................	16,000	10,000
Long-term investments—available for sale..............	—	70,000
Fair value adjustment to investments..................	—	10,000
Plant assets..	656,000	655,000
Accumulated depreciation...........................	(237,000)	(185,000)
Franchise..	91,000	29,000
Total assets..	$561,000	$644,000

continued

continued from previous page

GEARY COMPANY Balance Sheets	Dec. 31, Current Year	Dec. 31, Previous Year
Liabilities and Stockholders' Equity		
Accrued liabilities	$ 12,000	$ 14,000
Notes payable	—	26,000
Common stock ($10 par value)	535,000	535,000
Retained earnings	34,000	59,000
Unrealized gain on investments	—	10,000
Treasury stock	(20,000)	—
Total liabilities and stockholders' equity	$561,000	$644,000

During the year, the following transactions occurred:

1. Sold equipment for $9,000 cash that originally cost $19,000 and had $3,000 accumulated depreciation.
2. Sold long-term investments that had cost $70,000 for $87,000 cash. Unrealized gains totaling $10,000 related to these investments had been recorded in earlier years. At year-end, the fair value adjustment and unrealized gain account balances were eliminated.
3. Paid cash to extend the company's exclusive franchise for another three years.
4. Paid off a note payable at the bank on January 1.
5. Declared and paid an $18,000 dividend.
6. Purchased treasury stock for cash.
7. Purchased land valued at $20,000.

Required
a. Compute the change in cash that occurred in the current year.
b. Prepare a statement of cash flows using the indirect method.

P13-5B. Analyzing Cash Flow Ratios Meagan Enterprises reported the following information for the past year of operations: **LO3**

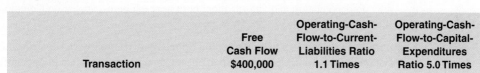

Transaction	Free Cash Flow $400,000	Operating-Cash-Flow-to-Current-Liabilities Ratio 1.1 Times	Operating-Cash-Flow-to-Capital-Expenditures Ratio 5.0 Times
a. Recorded credit sales of $17,000			
b. Collected $6,000 owed from customers			
c. Purchased $50,000 of equipment on long-term credit			
d. Purchased $70,000 of equipment for cash			
e. Paid $17,000 of wages with cash			
f. Recorded utility bill of $14,750 that has not been paid			

For each transaction, indicate whether the ratio will (I) increase, (D) decrease, or (N) have no effect.

P13-6B. Statement of Cash Flows (Direct Method) Refer to the data given for the Forrester Company in Problem P13-1B.   **LO3, 4** (Appendix 13A)

Required
a. Compute the change in cash that occurred during the current year.
b. Prepare a statement of cash flows using the direct method.
c. Compute the free cash flow.
d. Compute the operating-cash-flow-to-current-liabilities ratio.
e. Compute the operating-cash-flow-to-capital-expenditures ratio.

LO4
(Appendix 13A)

P13-7B.   Statement of Cash Flows (Direct Method) Refer to the data given for the Lowe Company in Problem P13-2B.

Required
a.   Compute the change in cash that occurred during the current year.
b.   Prepare a statement of cash flows using the direct method.

LO4
(Appendix 13A)

MBC

P13-8B.   Statement of Cash Flows (Direct Method) Refer to the data given for the Madison Company in Problem P13-3B.

Required
a.   Compute the change in cash that occurred during the current year.
b.   Prepare a statement of cash flows using the direct method. Use one cash outflow for "cash paid for wages and other operating expenses." Accounts payable relate to inventory purchases only.

LO4
(Appendix 13A)

P13-9B.   Statement of Cash Flows (Direct Method) Refer to the data given for the Geary Company in Problem P13-4B.

Required
a.   Compute the change in cash that occurred during the current year.
b.   Prepare a statement of cash flows using the direct method. Use one cash outflow for "cash paid for wages and other operating expenses."

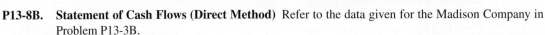

EXTENDING YOUR KNOWLEDGE

COLUMBIA
SPORTSWEAR
COMPANY

EYK13-1.   Financial Reporting Problem: Columbia Sportswear Company The financial statements for the **Columbia Sportswear Company** can be found in Appendix A at the end of this book.

Required
Answer the following questions:
a.   How much did Columbia Sportswear's cash and cash equivalents increase in 2020?
b.   What was the largest source of cash and cash equivalents in 2020?
c.   What was the single largest use of cash and cash equivalents in 2020?
d.   How much dividends were paid in 2020?
e.   Why do depreciation and amortization, both noncash items, appear on Columbia's statement of cash flows?

COLUMBIA
SPORTSWEAR
COMPANY

UNDER ARMOUR, INC.

EYK13-2.   Comparative Analysis Problem: Columbia Sportswear Company vs Under Armour, Inc. The financial statements for the Columbia Sportswear Company can be found in Appendix A at the end of this book, and the financial statements of Under Armour, Inc., can be found in Appendix B. (The complete annual report is available on this book's website.)

Required
Answer the following questions:
a.   Compute the free cash flow in 2020 for both Columbia Sportswear and Under Armour, Inc.
b.   Compute the operating cash flows to capital expenditures for both Columbia Sportswear and Under Armour, Inc.
c.   Comment on the ability of each company to finance its capital expenditures.

EYK13-3.   Business Decision Problem Recently hired as assistant controller for Finite, Inc., you are sitting next to the controller as she responds to questions at the annual stockholders' meeting. The firm's financial statements contain a statement of cash flows prepared using the indirect method. A stockholder raises his hand.
     Stockholder: "I notice that depreciation expense is shown as an addition in the calculation of the cash flow from operating activities."
     Controller: "That's correct."
     Stockholder: "What depreciation method do you use?"
     Controller: "We use the straight-line method for all plant assets."

Stockholder: "Well, why don't you switch to an accelerated depreciation method, such as double-declining balance, increase the annual depreciation amount, and thus increase the cash flow from operating activities?"

The controller pauses, turns to you, and replies, "My assistant will answer your question."

Required
Prepare an answer to the stockholder's question.

EYK13-4. **Financial Analysis Problem** Parker Hannifin Corporation, headquartered in Cleveland, Ohio, manufactures motion control and fluid system components for a variety of industrial users. The firm's financial statements contain the following data. (Year 3 is the most recent year; dollar amounts are in thousands.)

PARKER HANNIFIN
CORPORATION

	Year 3	Year 2	Year 1
Current assets at year-end.............................	$1,018,354	$1,056,443	$1,055,776
Current liabilities at year-end	504,444	468,254	358,729
Current liabilities at beginning of year	468,254	358,729	345,594
Cash provided by operating activities.................	259,204	229,382	235,186
Capital expenditures................................	99,914	91,484	84,955

    a. Calculate Parker Hannifin's current ratio (current assets/current liabilities) for Years 1, 2, and 3.

    b. Calculate Parker Hannifin's operating-cash-flow-to-current-liabilities ratio for Years 1, 2, and 3.

    c. Comment on the three-year trend in Parker Hannifin's current ratio and operating-cash-flow-to-current-liabilities ratio. Do the trends in these two ratios reinforce each other or contradict each other as indicators of Parker Hannifin's ability to pay its current liabilities?

    d. Calculate Parker Hannifin's operating-cash-flow-to-capital-expenditures ratio for Years 1, 2, and 3. Comment on the strength of this ratio over the three-year period.

EYK13-5. **Accounting Research Problem: General Mills, Inc.** The fiscal year 2020 annual report of General Mills, Inc., is available on this book's website.

GENERAL MILLS, INC.

Required
    a. Refer to Note 2. How does General Mills define its cash equivalents?

    b. What method does General Mills use to report its cash provided by operating activities?

    c. What is the change in cash and cash equivalents experienced by General Mills during fiscal 2020? What is the amount of cash and cash equivalents as of May 31, 2020?

    d. What is General Mills' operating-cash-flow-to-capital-expenditures ratio for fiscal year 2020?

    e. Calculate General Mills' 2020 operating-cash-flow-to-current-liabilities ratio.

EYK13-6. **Accounting Communication Activity** Susan Henderson, the vice president of marketing, was told by the CEO that she needs to understand the numbers because the company's existence depends on making money. It has been a long time since Susan took a class in accounting. She recalls that companies report net income and cash flows in two separate statements. She feels pretty comfortable with the income statement but is somewhat lost looking at the statement of cash flows. She asks you to help explain this statement.

Required
Write a brief memo to Susan explaining the form and content of the statement of cash flows, along with a short discussion of how to analyze the statement.

EYK13-7. **Accounting Ethics Case** Due to an economic recession, Anton Corporation faces severe cash flow problems. Management forecasts that payments to some suppliers will have to be delayed for several months. Jay Newton, controller, has asked his staff for suggestions on selecting the suppliers for which payments will be delayed.

"That's a fairly easy decision," observes Tim Haslem. "Some suppliers charge interest if our payment is late, but others do not. We should pay those suppliers that charge interest and delay payments to the ones that do not charge interest. If we do this, the savings in interest charges will be quite substantial."

"I disagree," states Tara Wirth. "That position is too 'bottom line' oriented. It's not fair to delay payments only to suppliers who don't charge interest for late payments. Most suppliers in that category are ones we have dealt with for years; selecting these suppliers would be taking dvantage of the excellent relationships we have developed over the years. The fair thing to do is to make pro-rata payments to each supplier."

"Well, making pro-rata payments to each supplier means that *all* our suppliers will be upset because no one receives full payment," comments Sue Myling. "I believe it is most important to maintain good relations with our long-term suppliers; we should pay them currently and delay payments to our newer suppliers. The interest costs we end up paying these newer suppliers are the price we must pay to keep our long-term relationships solid."

Required
Which suppliers should Jay Newton select for delayed payments? Discuss.

THE HOME DEPOT, INC.

EYK13-8.   Environmental, Social, and Governance Problem   The ESG highlighted in this chapter (see page 13-17) mentions that **Home Depot** believes in giving back. One of the ways the company has done this is through its Team Depot program of employee volunteerism. Under this program, Home Depot employees volunteer their own time to work together on projects that benefit communities in which the company does business. Each year the program provides millions of hours of employee volunteerism.

Do a computer search and report on Team Depot's activities.

EYK13-9.   Forensic Accounting Problem   Cash larceny involves the fraudulent stealing of an employer's cash. These schemes often target the company's bank deposits. The fraudster steals the money after the deposit has been prepared, but before the deposit is taken to the bank. Most often these schemes involve a deficiency in the internal control system where segregation of duties is not present. The perpetrator is often in charge of recording receipts, preparing the deposit, delivering the deposit to the bank, and verifying the receipted deposit slip. Without proper segregation of duties, the fraudster is able to cover up the theft.

In addition to segregation of duties, what internal control procedures might help deter and detect cash larceny?

EYK13-10.   Working with the Takeaways   For the fiscal year ended January 31, 2021, Home Depot reports (in millions) cash provided by operating activities of $18,839. For the same period, average current liabilities were reported to be $17,545, and annual capital expenditures were $2,463. Calculate the free cash flow, the operating-cash-flow-to-current-liabities ratio, and the operating-cash-flow-to-capital-expenditures ratio for Home Depot and comment on the results.

EYK13-11.   Analyzing IFRS Financial Statements   The 2020 financial statements of LVMH Moet Hennessey-Louis Vuitton S.A. are presented in Appendix C at the end of this book. LVMH is a Paris-based holding company and one of the world's largest and best-known luxury goods companies. As a member of the European Union, French companies are required to prepare their consolidated (group) financial statements using International Financial Reporting Standards (IFRS). After reviewing LVMH's consolidated financial statements, calculate LVMH's (a) free cash flow, (b) operating-cash-flow-to-current-liabilities ratio (use the year-end current liabilities instead of the average current liabilities), and (c) operating-cash-flow-to-capital-expenditures ratio for 2019 and 2020. What do the ratio results reveal about LVMH? *Hint:* Capital expenditures are classified as "Operating investments" on LVMH Consolidated cash flow statement.

ANSWERS TO SELF-STUDY QUESTIONS:

1. a   2. c   3. d   4. d   5. c   6. b   7. d   8. d   9. c   10. b   11. c   12. a

YOUR TURN! SOLUTIONS

Solution 13.1

1. Operating
2. Investing
3. Operating
4. Investing
5. Financing
6. Financing
7. Operating
8. Financing
9. Investing

Solution 13.2

HUSKY COMPANY Statement of Cash Flows For the Year Ended December 31		
Cash Flow from Operating Activities		
Net income.	$112,000	
Add (deduct) items to convert net income to cash basis		
Depreciation.	34,000	
Accounts receivable increase.	(18,000)	
Inventory increase.	(60,000)	
Prepaid insurance decrease.	4,000	
Accounts payable decrease.	(6,000)	
Wages payable increase.	6,000	
Income tax payable decrease.	(2,000)	
Cash provided by operating activities.		$ 70,000
Cash Flow from Investing Activities		
Purchase of plant assets.		(110,000)
Cash Flow from Financing Activities		
Issuance of bonds payable.	110,000	
Payment of dividends.	(58,000)	
Cash provided by financing activities.		52,000
Net increase in cash.		12,000
Cash at beginning of year.		10,000
Cash at end of year.		$ 22,000

Solution 13.3

Free cash flow: $40,000 – $12,500 = $27,500

Operating-cash-flow-to-current-liabilities-ratio: $40,000/$30,000 = 1.33

Operating-cash-flow-to-capital-expenditures-ratio: $40,000/$12,500 = 3.20

Solution 13A.1

Supporting Calculations:

Cash received from customers:
$1,270,000 Sales revenue – $18,000 Accounts receivable increase = $1,252,000

Cash paid for merchandise purchased:
$860,000 Cost of goods sold + $60,000 Inventory increase + $6,000 Accounts payable decrease = $926,000

Cash paid to employees:
$172,000 Wages expense – $6,000 Wages payable increase = $166,000

Cash paid for insurance:
$16,000 Insurance expense – $4,000 Prepaid insurance decrease = $12,000

Cash paid for interest:
Equal to the $18,000 balance in interest expense

Cash paid for income taxes:
$58,000 Income tax expense + $2,000 Income tax payable decrease = $60,000

Purchase of plant assets:
$500,000 Ending plant assets – $390,000 Beginning plant assets = $110,000

Issuance of bonds payable:
$260,000 Ending bonds payable – $150,000 Beginning bonds payable = $110,000

Payment of dividends
$58,000 given in problem data

Other Analysis

Accumulated depreciation increased by $34,000, which is the amount of depreciation expense.

Common stock account balance did not change.

Retained earnings increased by $54,000, which is the difference between the net income of $112,000 and the dividends declared of $58,000.

HUSKY COMPANY
Statement of Cash Flows (Direct Method)
For the Year Ended December 31

Cash Flow from Operating Activities		
Cash received from customers		$1,252,000
Cash paid for merchandise purchased	$(926,000)	
Cash paid to employees	(166,000)	
Cash paid for insurance	(12,000)	
Cash paid for interest	(18,000)	
Cash paid for income taxes	(60,000)	(1,182,000)
Cash provided by operating activities		70,000
Cash Flow from Investing Activities		
Purchase of plant assets		(110,000)
Cash Flow from Financing Activities		
Issuance of bonds payable	110,000	
Payment of dividends	(58,000)	
Cash provided by financing activities		52,000
Net increase in cash		12,000
Cash at beginning of year		10,000
Cash at end of year		$ 22,000

Chapter 14

Analysis and Interpretation of Financial Statements

Road Map

LO	Learning Objective	Page	eLecture	Guided Example	Assignments
LO1	**Identify persistent earnings and discuss the content and format of the income statement.**	14-3	E14-1	YT14.1	SS1, SE11, E1A, E1B, P1A, P3A, P1B, P3B
LO2	**Identify the sources of financial information used by investment professionals and explain horizontal financial statement analysis.**	14-6	E14-2	YT14.2	SS10, SE12, E3A, E3B, P4A, P6A, P10A, P4B, P6B, P10B
LO3	**Explain vertical financial statement analysis.**	14-12	E14-3	YT14.3	SS2, SE13, E4A, E4B, P6A, P6B
LO4	**Define and discuss financial ratios for analyzing a firm.**	14-13	E14-4	YT14.4	SS3, SS4, SS5, SS6, SS7, SS8, SS9, SE1, SE2, SE3, SE4, SE5, SE6, SE7, SE8, SE9, SE10, E2A, E5A, E6A, E7A, E8A, E9A, E2B, E5B, E6B, E7B, E8B, P2A, P3A, P5A, P6A, P7A, P8A, P9A, P2B, P3B, P5B, P6B, P7B, P8B, P9B
LO5	**Discuss the limitations of financial statement analysis.**	14-27	E14-5	YT14.5	SS11, SE14, E10A, E10B
LO6	**Appendix 14A: Describe financial statement disclosures.**	14-29	E14-6	YT14.6	SS12, SE15, E11A, E11B

The **Procter & Gamble Company (P&G)** is one of America's oldest companies, dating back to 1837 when candle maker William Procter and soap maker James Gamble combined their small businesses. Over the next few decades the company introduced such well-known products as Ivory soap and Crisco shortening that are still sold today.

P&G has continued to grow, with annual sales of over $70 billion. Not all of the company's growth, however, is the result of internally developed products like Crest toothpaste, Head & Shoulders shampoo, and Pampers diapers. A significant part of P&G's growth has come from mergers and acquisitions. P&G's largest acquisition occurred in 2005 when it acquired Gillette for $57 billion.

Acquisitions, such as the one involving Gillette, are complex transactions. Perhaps the hardest part of any merger or acquisition is determining the appropriate price to pay. Many factors go into such an analysis, but it often comes down to how much a company like Gillette will be able to add to P&G's future persistent earnings.

In this chapter we explore some of the ways that investment professionals determine how much a company is worth. The process involves analyzing a company's persistent earnings potential as well as the various risks associated with a company's day-to-day operations.

PAST

In Chapter 13, we examined the statement of cash flows.

PRESENT

In this chapter we complete our study of managerial accounting by looking at the analysis and interpretation of financial statements.

ANALYSIS AND INTERPRETATION OF FINANCIAL STATEMENTS

Income Statement and Persistent Earnings

- Persistent earnings
- Discontinued operations
- Changes in accounting principles
- Comprehensive income

Analytical Techniques

- Sources of information
- Horizontal analysis
- Trend analysis
- Vertical analysis
- Ratio analysis
- Limitations of financial analysis
- Financial statement disclosures (Appendix 14A)

PERSISTENT EARNINGS AND THE INCOME STATEMENT

LO1 **Identify** persistent earnings and **discuss** the content and format of the income statement.

eLecture

MBC

Net income is the "bottom line" measure of firm performance. It is a measure that depends on such accrual accounting procedures as the revenue recognition and expense matching policies selected by a firm's management. Generally accepted accounting principles have historically emphasized the importance of accounting earnings because past accounting earnings have been found to be a good predictor of a firm's future operating cash flow. Modern valuation theory tells us that the economic value of a company is the present value of the company's future operating cash flows. Thus, an important role for accounting numbers is their use by investment professionals when assessing the economic value of a company.

One of the determinants of the ability of historical accounting earnings to predict future cash flow is the extent to which earnings recur over time, or what is known as *earnings persistence*. Since the value of a share of common stock today is a function of a firm's ability to consistently generate earnings year in and year out, the persistence (or sustainability) of a company's operating earnings is closely linked to its economic value. **Persistent earnings** are also sometimes referred to as *sustainable earnings* or *permanent earnings*, whereas non-persistent earnings are often referred to as **transitory earnings**. In general, transitory earnings include such single-period events as special items, restructuring charges, changes in accounting principle, and discontinued operations.

Companies are required under GAAP to classify income statement accounts in a manner that aids a financial statement user in assessing persistent earnings, and hence in assessing a firm's economic value. In this chapter, we discuss a refinement of the classified income statement called the multiple-step or multi-step income statement.

Exhibit 14-1 illustrates the basic format of the multi-step income statement. While a **single-step income statement** derives the net income of a business in one step by subtracting total expenses from total revenues, a **multiple-step income statement** derives one or more intermediate performance measures before net income is reported. Examples of such intermediate performance measures are gross profit, net operating income, and net income from continuing operations before taxes.

The income statement is organized in such a way that items with greater persistence are reported higher up in the income statement, whereas items considered more transitory are reported further down in the statement. Thus, accounts representing financial events that are both usual and frequent are reported first. Usual refers to an item that is central to a firm's core operations, whereas **unusual items** are unrelated, or only incidentally related, to core operations. Frequent refers to how often an item is expected to occur, with infrequent items not reasonably expected to recur in the foreseeable future.

EXHIBIT 14-1	The Multi-Step Income Statement

KALI COMPANY
Income Statement
For Year Ended December 31

Sales revenue.		$ 500	Usual and frequent
Cost of goods sold		200	Usual and frequent
Gross profit.		300	
Operating expenses		250	Usual and frequent
Net operating income		50	
Other income and expense			
Interest income.	25		**Unusual**
Interest expense.	(35)		**Unusual**
Gain on sale of equipment	15	5	**Unusual**
Net income from continuing operations before tax		55	
Income tax expense		20	Usual and frequent
Net income from continuing operations		35	
Gain from operations of discontinued division (net of tax)	15		**Infrequent**
Loss on disposal of discontinued division (net of tax)	(5)	10	**Infrequent**
Net income		$ 45	
Earning per share (100 shares outstanding)		$0.45	

Usual and frequent items typically consist of such income statement accounts as sales revenue, cost of goods sold, and other operating expenses. Just below these usual and frequent items are items that are either unusual or infrequent, but not both. Income statement accounts such as interest expense, interest income, and gains on sales of equipment are often frequently recurring items; however, they are not considered part of a firm's central operations and therefore are considered unusual. Examples of infrequent items include such financial events as asset write-downs and restructuring charges. These items are not expected to occur regularly, but are not considered unusual in nature.

Each of the above items is reported as part of a company's continuing operations and is shown before any income tax expense. GAAP, however, requires certain single-period items, or one-time events, to be reported on an after-tax basis. For example, income from discontinued operations, or the part of a business that is being shuttered or sold, are shown net of the financial effect of any applicable income taxes. Reporting discontinued operations on a net-of-tax basis allows the income tax expense reported on the income statement to reflect only the income taxes associated with a firm's continuing operations. Segregating discontinued operations from the results of continuing operations also makes it easier for financial statement users to identify a company's persistent earnings.

Most believe that the income statement is more useful when certain types of transactions and events are reported in separate sections. The creation of sections within the income statement, however, complicates the reporting of a company's income tax expense. Items affecting the overall amount of income tax expense may appear in more than one section. If this is the case, accountants allocate a company's total income tax expense among those sections of the income statement in which the items affecting the tax expense appear.

Regardless of the format used for the income statement, companies are required to report net income on a per common share basis, called **earnings per share (EPS)**, on the income statement immediately following net income.

> **THINKING GLOBALLY**
>
> Like U.S. GAAP, IFRS encourages companies to use a multi-step income statement when presenting a company's periodic performance. Appendix C at the end of this book presents an IFRS income statement for LVMH Moet Hennessy-Louis Vuitton, a global luxury products company. Examining LVMH's income statement reveals that the retailer presents four measures of firm performance: gross margin, operating profit, net financial income, and net profit for the year. These indicators correspond closely to the four performance measures reported by the Kali Company in Exhibit 14-1: gross profit, net operating income, net income from continuing operations before tax, and net income. The income statements under U.S. GAAP and IFRS are very similar, with only minor labeling differences—like using "profit" instead of "income."

Discontinued Operations

When a company sells, abandons, or otherwise disposes of a segment of its operations, a **discontinued operations** section of the income statement reports information about the discontinued business segment. The discontinued operations section presents two categories of information:

1. The income or loss from the segment's operations for the portion of the year before its discontinuance.

Discontinued Operations

2. Any gain or loss from the disposal of the segment.

This section is reported on the income statement immediately after information regarding a firm's continuing operations.

To illustrate the reporting of discontinued operations, assume that on July 1, Kali Company, a diversified manufacturing company, sold its pet food division. **Exhibit 14-1** illustrates the income statement for Kali Company, including information regarding its pet food division in the discontinued operations section. From January 1 through June 30, Kali's pet food division operated at a profit, net of income taxes, of $15. The loss, net of income taxes, from the sale of the division's assets and liabilities was $5. Note that when there is a discontinued operations section, the difference between a firm's continuing sales revenues and expenses is labeled "net income from continuing operations."

Changes in Accounting Principles

Occasionally a company may implement a **change in accounting principle**—that is, a switch from one generally accepted method to another. For example, a company may change its inventory costing method, such as from FIFO to weighted-average cost. These changes are permitted when a business can demonstrate that the reported financial results under the new accounting method are preferable to the results reported under the replaced method.

Changing accounting principles can present a problem for financial statement users analyzing a company's performance over time because different accounting principles are likely to produce different financial statement results. Consequently, financial statements of prior years, issued in comparative form with current year financial statements, must also be presented using the new accounting principles as if the new method had been used all along.

Comprehensive Income

Most items that generate wealth changes in a business are required to be shown on the income statement. There are, however, a few items that do not appear as part of the regular content of the income statement and instead are classified under a category labeled **comprehensive income**. A business's comprehensive income includes, among other items, its net income, any changes in the market value of certain marketable securities (see Appendix D at the end of this book), and any unrealized gains and losses from translating foreign currency denominated financial statements into U.S. dollars. This latter topic is covered in more advanced accounting textbooks.

Companies are given some flexibility as to how they report their comprehensive income. They are allowed to utilize two alternative formats under GAAP: (1) appending comprehensive income to the bottom of the income statement; or (2) creating a separate statement of comprehensive income. In addition to comprehensive income for the current period, GAAP requires a company to report accumulated other comprehensive income as part of stockholders' equity on the balance sheet. Accumulated other comprehensive income serves the same role for comprehensive income as retained earnings serves for regular net income—it reports the cumulative amount of comprehensive income as of the balance sheet date.

ENVIRONMENTAL, SOCIAL, AND GOVERNANCE   **Pampers and UNICEF**

Maternal and neonatal tetanus is a disease that kills 59,000 people annually. **P&G**, through its Pampers product, has teamed up with UNICEF to fight this completely preventable disease. For every purchase of a pack of Pampers, P&G donates one dose of the tetanus vaccine. Pampers' funding has helped protect 100 million women and their babies against maternal and neonatal tetanus (MNT) and has helped eliminate this disease in Myanmar and Uganda. P&G and UNICEF are committed to the elimination of MNT from the face of the earth.

P&G and UNICEF have gone even further in their teamwork. P&G offers its employees in Europe, the Middle East, and Africa a three-month paid sabbatical to work with UNICEF. The program is aimed at employees who have always wanted to perform humanitarian work but have lacked the financial resources to do so.

Conner Company, a retail company, entered into the following transactions during the year:

1. Sold merchandise to customers
2. Settled a major lawsuit
3. Wrote down the book value of a closed warehouse
4. Paid employee wages
5. Disposed of a line of discount stores
6. Paid income taxes

Required
Classify each of the above items as either persistent earnings or transitory earnings.

YOUR TURN! 14.1

The solution is on page 14-59.

Guided Example

MBC

SOURCES OF INFORMATION

Except for closely held companies, businesses publish their financial statements at least annually. Most large companies also issue quarterly financial data. Normally, annual financial statements are attested to by a certified public accountant, and investment professionals carefully review the independent accountant's opinion to assess the reliability of the published financial data. Companies listed on stock exchanges must also submit financial statements, called a 10-K for the annual report and 10-Q for the quarterly report, to the U.S. Securities and Exchange Commission (SEC). These statements are available to any interested party and generally contain greater detail than the company's annual or quarterly reports.

Investment professionals may also want to compare the performance of a particular firm with that of the other firms in the same industry. Data on industry norms, median financial ratios by industry, and other relationships are available from such data collection services as Dun & Bradstreet, Moody's, and Standard and Poor's. In addition, some brokerage firms compile industry norms and financial ratios from their own computer databases.

LO2 **Identify** the sources of financial information used by investment professionals and **explain** horizontal financial statement analysis.

eLecture

MBC

Analytical Techniques

The dollar amounts of net income, sales revenue, total assets, and other key data are usually not meaningful when analyzed in isolation. For example, knowing that a company's annual net income is $1 million is of little informational value unless the amount of the income can be related to other factors. A $1 million profit might represent excellent performance for a company with less than $10 million in invested capital. On the other hand, $1 million in net income would be considered meager for a firm that had several hundred million dollars in invested capital. Thus, significant information can be derived by examining the relation between two or more accounting variables, such as net income and total assets, net income and sales revenue, or net income and stockholders' equity. To describe these relations clearly and to make comparisons easy, they are often expressed in terms of ratios or percentages.

For example, we might express the relation between $15,000 in net income and $150,000 in sales revenue as a ten percent ($15,000/$150,000) rate of return on sales. To describe the relation between sales revenue of $150,000 and inventory of $20,000, we might use a ratio or a percentage; ($150,000/$20,000) may be expressed as 7.5, 7.5:1, or 750 percent.

Changes in selected financial statement items compared in successive financial statements are often expressed as percentages. For example, if a firm's net income increased from $40,000 last year to $48,000 this year, the $8,000 increase relative to last year (the base year) is expressed as a 20 percent increase ($8,000/$40,000) in net income. To express a dollar increase or decrease as a percentage, however, the base year amount must be a positive figure. If, for example, a firm had a net loss of $4,000 in one year and net income of $20,000 in the next, the $24,000 increase cannot be meaningfully expressed as a percentage. Similarly, if a firm reported no debt securities in last year's balance sheet but showed $15,000 of such securities in this year's statement, the $15,000 increase cannot be expressed as a meaningful percentage.

When evaluating a firm's financial statements for two or more years, analysts often use **horizontal analysis**. Horizontal analysis is a technique that can be useful for detecting an improvement or deterioration in a firm's performance and for spotting trends regarding a firm's financial well-being. The term **vertical analysis** is used to describe the analysis of a single year of financial data.

HORIZONTAL ANALYSIS

The type of horizontal analysis most often used by investment professionals is **comparative financial statement analysis** for two or more years, showing dollar or percentage changes for important financial statement items and totals. Dollar increases and decreases are divided by data from the base year to obtain percentage changes. To illustrate, the 2020 and 2019 financial statements of Procter & Gamble (P&G) are presented in **Exhibits 14-2**, **14-3**, and **14-4**. We will use the data in these statements throughout this chapter to illustrate various analytical techniques.

EXHIBIT 14-2   **Procter & Gamble Income Statement**

THE PROCTER & GAMBLE COMPANY
Consolidated Income Statements

(in millions)	Year Ended 2020	Common-Size	Year Ended 2019	Common-Size	$ Change	% Change
Net sales.	$70,950	100.0%	$67,684	100.0%	$ 3,266	4.8 %
Cost of goods sold	35,250	49.7%	34,768	51.4%	482	1.4 %
Gross profit.	35,700	50.3%	32,916	48.6%	2,784	8.5 %
Selling, general, and administrative expense.	19,994	28.2%	27,429	40.5%	(7,435)	(27.1)%
Operating income.	15,706	22.1%	5,487	8.1%	10,219	186.2 %
Interest expense.	465	0.7%	509	0.8%	(44)	(8.6)%
Other non-operating income (expense)	593	0.8%	1,091	1.6%	(498)	(45.6)%
Earnings from continuing operations before taxes	15,834	22.3%	6,069	9.0%	9,765	160.9 %
Income taxes on continuing operations.	2,731	3.8%	2,103	3.1%	628	29.9 %
Net earnings from continuing operations.	13,103	18.5%	3,966	5.9%	9,137	230.4 %
Net earnings attributable to noncontrolling interests.	76	0.1%	69	0.1%	7	10.1 %
Net earnings.	13,027	18.4%	3,897	5.8%	9,130	234.3 %
Earnings per share.	5.13		1.45			
Dividends per share	3.03		2.90			

When analyzing financial statements, the investment professional is likely to focus his or her immediate attention on those financial statement items or percentages that are significant in amount. Although percentage changes are helpful in identifying significant items, they can sometimes be misleading. An unusually large percentage change may occur simply because the dollar amount of the base year is small. For example, P&G had a decrease in other non-operating income of $498, from $1,091 in 2019 to $593 in 2020 (**Exhibit 14-2**). This represents a decrease of 45.6 percent, yet the dollar amount of this line item is quite small and insignificant relative to the other reported dollar amounts on P&G's income statement. The financial statement user's attention should be directed first to changes in key financial statement totals: sales revenue, operating income, net income, total assets, total liabilities, and so on. Next, the changes in significant individual items, such as accounts receivable, inventory, and property, plant, and equipment should be examined.

P&G's total assets increased by 4.9 percent from 2019 to 2020 (**Exhibit 14-3**), consistent with an increase in net sales of 4.8 percent over the same time period (**Exhibit 14-2**). (Net sales equals gross sales revenue less any sales returns and allowances and sales discounts.) P&G did report a very favorable 234.3 percent increase in net earnings from 2019 to 2020. This change appears to be mostly the result of cost control reflected in a large decrease of $7,435 million in selling, general, and administrative expense.

EXHIBIT 14-3   Procter & Gamble Balance Sheet

THE PROCTER & GAMBLE COMPANY
Consolidated Balance Sheets

(in millions)	2020	Common-Size	2019	Common-Size	$ Change	% Change
Assets						
Current assets						
Cash and cash equivalents...............	$ 16,181	13.4 %	$ 4,239	3.7 %	$11,942	281.7 %
Short-term investments..................			6,048	5.3 %	(6,048)	(100.0)%
Accounts receivable	4,178	3.5 %	4,951	4.3 %	(773)	(15.6)%
Inventories	5,498	4.6 %	5,017	4.4 %	481	9.6 %
Other current assets...................	2,130	1.8 %	2,218	1.9 %	(88)	(4.0)%
Total current assets	27,987	23.2 %	22,473	19.5 %	5,514	24.5 %
Property, plant, and equipment, net..........	20,692	17.1 %	21,271	18.5 %	(579)	(2.7)%
Intangible assets.......................	63,693	52.8 %	64,488	56.0 %	(795)	(1.2)%
Other noncurrent assets..................	8,328	6.9 %	6,863	6.0 %	1,465	21.3 %
Total assets	$120,700	100.0 %	$115,095	100.0 %	$ 5,605	4.9 %
Liabilities and Stockholders' Equity						
Current liabilities						
Accounts payable	$ 12,071	10.0 %	$ 11,260	9.8 %	$ 811	7.2 %
Other current liabilities	20,905	17.3 %	18,751	16.3 %	2,154	11.5 %
Total current liabilities	32,976	27.3 %	30,011	26.1 %	2,965	9.9 %
Long-term debt........................	23,537	19.5 %	20,395	17.7 %	3,142	15.4 %
Other noncurrent liabilities	17,309	14.3 %	17,110	14.9 %	199	1.2 %
Total liabilities	73,822	61.2 %	67,516	58.7 %	6,306	9.3 %
Preferred stock.......................	897	0.7 %	928	0.8 %	(31)	(3.3)%
Common stock	4,009	3.3 %	4,009	3.5 %	—	0.0 %
Additional paid-in capital..................	64,194	53.2 %	63,827	55.5 %	367	0.6 %
Treasury stock	(105,573)	(87.5)%	(100,406)	(87.2)%	(5,167)	5.1 %
Retained earnings	100,239	83.0 %	94,918	82.5 %	5,321	5.6 %
Other stockholders' equity	(16,888)	(14.0)%	(15,697)	(13.6)%	(1,191)	7.6 %
Total stockholders' equity..............	46,878	38.8 %	47,579	41.3 %	(701)	(1.5)%
Total liabilities and stockholders' equity....	$120,700	100.0 %	$115,095	100.0 %	$ 5,605	4.9 %

We can see from P&G's statement of cash flows (**Exhibit 14-4**) that an increase in cash flow from operating activities from 2019 to 2020 and an increase in cash flow from investing activities during the same period resulted in a large increase in ending cash in 2020. Also, **Exhibit 14-4** reveals that P&G repurchased more of its common stock (treasury stock) and paid more cash dividends in 2020 than in 2019, both of which increased the amount of the cash it returned to shareholders during this period. Offsetting these financing cash outflows in 2020 was a large increase in funds borrowed.

From this limited analysis of comparative financial statements, an investment professional might conclude that P&G's operating performance for 2020 was an improvement when compared with that of 2019, mostly the result of cost controls in 2020. Further analysis using some of the techniques summarized later in the chapter, however, may cause that opinion to be either affirmed or modified.

EXHIBIT 14-4	Procter & Gamble Statement of Cash Flows

THE PROCTER & GAMBLE COMPANY
Consolidated Statements of Cash Flows

(in millions)	Year Ended 2020	Year Ended 2019	$ Change	% Change
Operating activities				
Net earnings.	$13,103	$ 3,966		
Depreciation and amortization	3,013	2,824		
Other adjustments to net income	(31)	7,771		
Changes in accounts receivable.	634	(276)		
Changes in inventories.	(637)	(239)		
Changes in liabilities.	1,923	1,856		
Changes in other operating activities	(602)	(660)		
Net cash flow provided by operating activities	17,403	15,242	$2,161	14.18%
Investing activities				
Capital expenditures.	(3,073)	(3,347)		
Investments	6,146	3,408		
Other cash flows from investing activities.	(28)	(3,551)		
Net cash flow used by investing activities.	3,045	(3,490)	6,535	(187.25)%
Financing activities				
Dividends	(7,789)	(7,498)		
Net stock purchases.	(7,405)	(5,003)		
Net borrowings	4,849	817		
Other cash flow from financing activities	1,978	3,324		
Net cash flow used by financing activities	(8,367)	(9,994)	$1,627	(16.28)%
Effect of exchange rate changes	(139)	(88)		
Change in cash and cash equivalents	11,942	1,670		
Beginning cash and cash equivalents	4,239	2,569		
Ending cash and cash equivalents.	$16,181	$ 4,239		

PRINCIPLE ALERT	Consistency Principle

Horizontal analysis is a technique for analyzing a firm's financial data across two or more years by examining dollar changes, percentage changes, or trend percentages. The utility of horizontal analysis, however, is dependent upon the effective implementation of the *consistency principle*. This accounting principle requires that a firm use the same accounting methods from one period to the next or, if a firm finds it necessary (or required) to change an accounting method, that the financial effects of any change be fully disclosed in the financial statements. The consistency principle assures financial analysts that, unless otherwise noted, changes in the accounts over time represent underlying economic changes in a business, and not the result of an accounting method change.

TREND ANALYSIS

To observe percentage changes over time in selected financial data, investment professionals often calculate **trend percentages**. Most companies provide summaries of their key financial data for the past five or ten years in their annual reports. With such information, the financial statement user can examine changes over periods longer than just the past two years. For example, suppose an analyst is interested in the trend in sales and net income for P&G for the past five years. The following are P&G's sales revenue and net income figures for 2016 through 2020:

PROCTER & GAMBLE COMPANY
Annual Performance

	2016		2017		2018		2019		2020	
	Millions of Dollars	Percentage of Base Year	Millions of Dollars	Percentage of Base Year	Millions of Dollars	Percentage of Base Year	Millions of Dollars	Percentage of Base Year	Millions of Dollars	Percentage of Base Year
Net sales................	$65,299	100%	$65,058	100%	$66,832	102%	$67,684	104%	$70,950	109%
Net earnings from continuing operations...............	10,027	100%	10,194	102%	9,861	98%	3,966	40%	13,103	131%

The pattern of changes from year to year can be determined more precisely by calculating trend percentages. To do this, we select a base year and then divide the data for each of the remaining years by the base-year data. The result is an index of the changes occurring throughout the period. If, for example, 2016 is selected as the base year, all data for 2017 through 2020 will be related to 2016, which is represented as 100 percent.

To create the table of data displayed above, we divide each year's net sales—from 2016 through 2020, by $65,299, P&G's 2016 net sales (in millions of dollars). Similarly, P&G's net earnings from continuing operations for 2016 through 2020 is divided by $10,027, the company's 2016 net earnings from continuing operations (in millions of dollars).

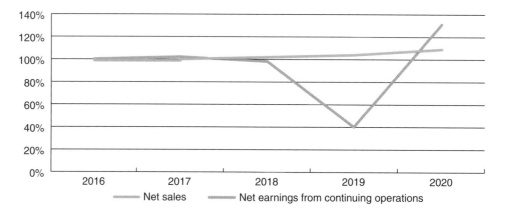

P&G's trend percentages above reveal that the company's growth in net earnings from continuing operations decreased in 2019 before recovering in 2020. In contrast, the company's net sales showed an increasing trend throughout the five-year period.

It is important to exercise care when interpreting trend percentages. Since all index percentages are related to a base year, it is important to select a good representative base year. For example, if 2016 was an unusual year for the firm, perhaps because of some large transitory items, its use in the trend analysis would be of limited value.

Other data items that an investment professional may relate to sales revenue and net income over multiple years include total assets, a company's investment in plant assets and its cash flow from operations, among others.

YOUR TURN! 14.2

The solution is on page 14-59.

MBC

The following data pertain to the Farrow Company:

	Current Year	Previous Year
Sales revenue.......................................	$800,000	$750,000
Net income...	120,000	100,000
Total assets..	300,000	290,000

Calculate both the amount in dollars and the percentage change in the current year using horizontal analysis and the previous year as the base year.

Concept ⟶	Method ⟶	Assessment	TAKEAWAY 14.1
How does a company's current performance compare with the prior year?	Income statement, balance sheet, and statement of cash flows for current and prior year. The financial statements should be compared using the prior year as the base. Percentage changes in financial statement amounts can be computed as the change between years divided by the base year amount.	Significant changes should be analyzed to determine the reason for any change.	

VERTICAL ANALYSIS

The relative importance of various accounts in a company's financial statements for a single year can be highlighted by showing them as a percentage of a key financial statement figure. A financial statement that presents the various account balances as a percentage of a key figure is called a **common-size financial statement**. Sales revenue (or net sales) is the key figure used to construct a common-size income statement, whereas total assets is the key figure used to construct a common-size balance sheet.

LO3   **Explain** vertical financial statement analysis.

eLecture

MBC

    Exhibit 14-2 presents P&G's 2020 and 2019 income statement in dollars and common-size percentages. The common-size percentages show each item in the income statement as a percentage of the company's net sales.

    The common-size income statement allows financial statement users to readily compare P&G's ability to manage and control its various expenses while the level of its sales revenue changes over time. For example, P&G's net earnings increased from 5.8 percent of sales in 2019 to 18.4 percent of sales in 2020. We can observe that there are relatively small changes in almost all of the line items as a percentage of net sales with the exception of selling, general, and administrative expense, which decreased from 40.5 percent of sales in 2019 to 28.2 percent of sales in 2020. Common-size income statements are also useful when comparing across firms, especially when the firms are significantly different in size. We would expect firms of different sizes to report different levels of sales revenues and expenses on a dollar basis. But, we would expect far more similarities when the comparison is done on a common-size basis.

    Common-size percentages can also be used to analyze balance sheet data. For example, by examining a firm's current assets and long-term assets as a percentage of total assets, we can determine whether a company is becoming more or less liquid over time. Another use of common-size percentages with balance sheet data is to evaluate the changing sources of financing used by a business. For example, the proportion of total assets supplied by short-term creditors, long-term creditors, preferred stockholders, and common stockholders of P&G are shown in **Exhibit 14-3**.

    P&G's common-size balance sheets reveal relative stability between 2019 and 2020 with a few minor exceptions. P&G no longer holds short-term investments (although it holds more cash and cash equivalents) and has increased its use of long-term debt from 17.7 percent of total assets in 2019 to 19.5 percent of total assets in 2020.

The solution is on
page 14-59.

GuidedExample

MBC

*Hint: When preparing
common-size income
statements, expenses are
expressed as a positive
percentage of net sales
even though they are
subtractions on the income
statement.*

The Sanford Company reported the following income statement:

SANFORD COMPANY
Income Statement
For the Year Ended December 31

Sales revenue.	$13,500
Cost of goods sold	5,400
Gross profit.	8,100
Selling and administrative expenses	1,350
Income from operations	6,750
Interest expense.	675
Other expense	135
Income before income taxes.	5,940
Income tax expense	2,295
Net income	$ 3,645

Required
Prepare a common-size income statement for Sanford Company.

TAKEAWAY 14.2	Concept	Method	Assessment
	How do the relations within a company's income statement and balance sheet compare to those of prior years?	Income statement and balance sheet for current and prior year. Each income statement item should be presented as a percentage of sales revenue, and each balance sheet item should be presented as a percentage of total assets. Financial statements in this form are called common-size statements.	The percentages should be analyzed for differences between years, and significant changes should be analyzed to determine the reason for any change.

THINKING GLOBALLY

Financial statement analysis is executed in the same way across the world. Common-size financial statements and the financial ratios discussed below are currency neutral and can be effectively used anywhere in the world. Not all ratios are relevant, however, in all countries. For example, in emerging countries that lack the financial infrastructure to support a credit system, ratios involving accounts receivable and accounts payable are likely to be irrelevant since sales transactions in those countries are only executed on a cash basis. Similarly, solvency ratios like the times-interest-earned ratio are irrelevant since bank financing in lesser-developed countries is rare (although it is becoming more prevalent with the advent of micro-finance in these countries).

RATIO ANALYSIS

LO4 **Define** and **discuss** financial ratios for analyzing a firm.

eLecture

MBC

At this juncture, we classify ratios by their analytical objective and review their analysis and interpretation by calculating them for a single company. P&G's financial statements in **Exhibit 14-2**, **Exhibit 14-3**, and **Exhibit 14-4** provide the data for these calculations (all amounts are in millions). Also, data for industry competitor Colgate-Palmolive are presented for comparison purposes. Some of the financial ratios that are commonly calculated by investment professionals, lenders, and managers are presented and explained in **Exhibit 14-5**.

EXHIBIT 14-5	Key Financial Ratios	
Ratio	**Definition**	**Explanation**
Analyzing Firm Profitability		
• Gross profit percentage	$\dfrac{\text{Gross profit on sales}}{\text{Net sales}}$	Percentage of income generated from sales after deducting the cost of goods sold.
• Return on sales	$\dfrac{\text{Net income}}{\text{Net sales}}$	Percentage of net income remaining from a dollar of sales after subtracting all expenses.
• Asset turnover	$\dfrac{\text{Net sales}}{\text{Average total assets}}$	Amount of sales generated from each dollar invested in assets.
• Return on assets	$\dfrac{\text{Net income}}{\text{Average total assets}}$	Rate of return generated on a company's investment in assets from all sources.
• Return on equity	$\dfrac{\text{Net income}}{\text{Average stockholders' equity}}$	Rate of return generated by a business for its shareholders.
Analyzing Short-Term Firm Liquidity		
• Working capital	Current assets − Current liabilities	The difference between a firm's current assets and its current liabilities.
• Current ratio	$\dfrac{\text{Current assets}}{\text{Current liabilities}}$	Amount of current assets available to service current liabilities.
• Quick ratio	$\dfrac{\text{(Cash and cash equivalents + Short-term investments + Accounts receivable)}}{\text{Current liabilities}}$	Amount of liquid assets available to service current liabilities.
• Operating-cash-flow-to-current-liabilities ratio	$\dfrac{\text{Cash flow from operating activities}}{\text{Average current liabilities}}$	Amount of cash flow from operating activities available to service current liabilities.
• Accounts receivable turnover	$\dfrac{\text{Net sales}}{\text{Average accounts receivable (net)}}$	Number of sales/collection cycles experienced by a firm.
• Average collection period	$\dfrac{365}{\text{Accounts receivable turnover (net)}}$	Number of days required, on average, to collect an outstanding accounts receivable.
• Inventory turnover	$\dfrac{\text{Cost of goods sold}}{\text{Average inventory}}$	Number of production/sales cycles experienced by a firm.
• Days' sales in inventory	$\dfrac{365}{\text{Inventory turnover}}$	Number of days, on average, required to sell the inventory currently on hand.
Analyzing Long-Term Firm Solvency		
• Debt-to-equity ratio	$\dfrac{\text{Total liabilities}}{\text{Total stockholders' equity}}$	Percentage of total assets provided by creditors.
• Times-interest-earned ratio	$\dfrac{\text{Income before interest expense and income taxes}}{\text{Interest expense}}$	Extent to which current operating income covers current debt service charges.
• Operating-cash-flow-to-capital-expenditures ratio	$\dfrac{\text{Cash flow from operating activities}}{\text{Annual net capital expenditures}}$	The ability of a firm's operations to provide sufficient cash to replace and expand its property, plant, and equipment.
Financial Ratios for Common Stockholders		
• Earnings per share	$\dfrac{\text{(Net income − Preferred stock dividends)}}{\text{Weighted-average number of common shares outstanding}}$	The net income available to common shareholders calculated on a per share basis.
• Price-earnings ratio	$\dfrac{\text{Market price per share}}{\text{Earnings per share}}$	A measure of the price of a share of common stock relative to the share's annual earnings.
• Dividend yield	$\dfrac{\text{Annual dividend per share}}{\text{Market price per share}}$	The earnings on an investment in stock coming from dividends.
• Dividend payout ratio	$\dfrac{\text{Annual dividend per share}}{\text{Earnings per share}}$	The percentage of net income paid out to shareholders as dividends.

Analyzing Firm Profitability

Several ratios assist in evaluating how efficiently a firm has performed in its quest for profits, or what is referred to as firm profitability. These ratios include: (1) gross profit percentage, (2) return on sales, (3) asset turnover, (4) return on assets, and (5) return on equity.

Gross Profit Percentage

The **gross profit percentage** is a closely watched ratio for both retailers and manufacturers, among other industries. The ratio is calculated as:

A.K.A. Gross profit
is often referred to as *gross margin.*

$$\text{Gross profit percentage} = \frac{\text{Gross profit on sales}}{\text{Net sales}}$$

This ratio shows the effect on firm profitability of changes in a firm's product pricing structure, sales mix, and merchandise costs. **Gross profit**, or **gross profit on sales**, is defined as the difference between net sales and cost of goods sold and reveals the amount of sales revenue remaining after subtracting the cost of products sold.

P&G's common-size income statements (see **Exhibit 14-2**) reveal that its gross profit percentage increased from 48.6 percent in 2019 to 50.3 percent in 2020. These percentages are derived using the following figures:

	2020	2019
Gross profit.	$35,700	$32,916
Net sales.	70,950	67,684
Gross profit percentage.	**50.3%**	**48.6%**
Colgate-Palmolive.	60.8%	

In order to gain additional insight into P&G's computed ratios, we compare them to a competitor from the same industry, Colgate-Palmolive, a process known as **benchmarking**. We see that P&G's has a lower gross profit percentage, 55.9 percent to Colgate-Palmolive's 60.8 percent, indicating Colgate-Palmolive has better margins on their product sales.

Return on Sales (Profit Margin)

A.K.A. Return on
sales is often referred to as *profit margin.*

Another important measure of firm profitability is the **return on sales**. This ratio reveals the percentage of each dollar of net sales that remains as profit after subtracting all operating and nonoperating expenses. The return on sales is calculated as follows:

$$\text{Return on sales} = \frac{\text{Net income}}{\text{Net sales}}$$

When common-size income statements are available, the return on sales equals the net income percentage. P&G's common-size income statements in **Exhibit 14-2** reveal that its return on sales increased from 5.8 percent in 2019 to 18.4 percent in 2020. These percentages are calculated using the following figures:

	2020	2019
Net income	13,027	3,897
Net sales.	70,950	67,684
Return on sales.	**18.4%**	**5.8%**
Colgate-Palmolive.	17.4%	

The increase in the return on sales for P&G is encouraging, and as noted above, P&G's increase in its return on sales is mostly attributable to the company's cost control. Additionally, P&G's 2020 return on sales exceeds that of Colgate-Palmolive.

The return on sales and gross profit percentages should be used only when analyzing companies from the same industry or when comparing a firm's performance across multiple time periods (as we did above) since the ratio may vary widely across industries. Retail jewelers, for example, have much larger gross profit percentages than do retail grocers. Industry averages for the asset turnover ratio, discussed next, also would be expected to vary significantly from one industry to another.

Asset Turnover

The **asset turnover ratio** measures how efficiently a firm uses its assets to generate sales revenue by calculating the amount of sales dollars generated annually for each dollar of assets invested in the company. This ratio is calculated as follows:

$$\text{Asset turnover} = \frac{\text{Net sales}}{\text{Average total assets}}$$

P&G's asset turnover is calculated as (total assets were $118,310 at year-end 2018):

		2020	2019
Net sales.		$ 70,950	$ 67,684
Total assets			
Beginning of year	(a)	115,095	118,310
End of year	(b)	120,700	115,095
Average [(a + b)/2]		117,898	116,703
Asset turnover		0.60	0.58
Colgate-Palmolive.		1.06	

P&G's asset turnover increased slightly from 2019 to 2020, indicating that the company is more effective in using its assets to generate sales revenue. Specifically, the company generated $0.60 in net sales for every dollar invested in total assets in 2020, compared to $0.58 in 2019. This ratio result is, however, below the Colgate-Palmolive's asset turnover of 1.06.

Return on Assets

The rate of return on total assets, called the **return on assets**, is an overall measure of a firm's profitability. It reveals the rate of profit earned per dollar of assets under a firm's control. The return on assets is calculated as follows:

$$\text{Return on assets} = \frac{\text{Net income}}{\text{Average total assets}}$$

P&G's return on assets is calculated as:

	2020	2019
Net income	$ 13,027	$ 3,897
Average total assets	117,898	116,703
Return on assets	11.0%	3.3%
Colgate-Palmolive.	18.5%	

P&G's return on assets increased from 3.3 percent in 2019 to 11.0 percent in 2020; however, P&G's return on assets is still below Colgate-Palmolive's return on assets of 18.5 percent.

The return on assets ratio summarizes the financial impact of two component ratios: the return on sales and asset turnover; that is, the return on assets is the multiplicative product of these latter two ratios, as follows:

Ratio:	Return on sales	×	Asset turnover	=	Return on assets
Ratio calculation:	$\dfrac{\text{Net income}}{\text{Net sales}}$	×	$\dfrac{\text{Net sales}}{\text{Average total assets}}$	=	$\dfrac{\text{Net income}}{\text{Average total assets}}$
P&G:	18.4 percent	×	0.60	=	11.0 percent

Industries that are characterized by low return on sales generally have relatively high asset turnover ratios, and vice versa. Retail grocery chains, for example, typically turn over their assets five to six times per year. By way of contrast, retail jewelers average only one to two asset turnovers per year. These industry differences largely reflect the high cost of products sold by jewelers versus the low cost of products sold by retail grocers.

Return on Equity

The **return on equity** ratio measures the profitability of the ownership interest held by a company's stockholders. The ratio shows the percentage of income available to stockholders for each dollar of stockholder equity invested in a business, as follows:

$$\text{Return on equity} = \frac{\text{Net income}}{\text{Average stockholders' equity}}$$

The return on equity for P&G is calculated as (stockholders' equity was $52,883 at year-end 2018):

		2020	2019
Net income		$13,027	$ 3,897
Stockholders' equity:			
Beginning of year	(a)	47,579	52,883
End of year	(b)	46,878	47,579
Average [(a + b)/2]		47,229	50,231
Return on equity		**27.6%**	**7.8%**
Colgate-Palmolive		344.8%	

P&G's return on equity increased from 7.8 percent in 2019 to 27.6 percent in 2020. Like the return on assets, P&G's return on equity is well below that of Colgate-Palmolive, a highly leveraged company with very low stockholders' equity compared to its debt financing.

YOUR TURN! 14.4

The solution is on page 14-60.

MBC

The following data were obtained from the current financial statements for Kelly Corporation:

Net sales	$30,000
Cost of goods sold	10,500
Net income	4,500
Average total assets	50,000
Average stockholders' equity	35,000

Required

Calculate the following ratios for Kelly Corporation:

a. Gross profit percentage

b. Return on sales

c. Asset turnover

d. Return on assets

e. Return on equity

TAKEAWAY 14.3	Concept	Method	Assessment
	How much profit is a company generating relative to the amount of assets invested in the company?	Income statement and balance sheet. Calculate the return on assets by dividing net income by the average total assets for the year.	The higher the return on assets, the better a company is doing in terms of generating profits utilizing the assets under its control.

Analyzing Short-Term Firm Liquidity

A firm's **working capital** is the difference between its current assets and current liabilities. Maintaining adequate working capital enables a firm to repay its current obligations on a timely basis and to take advantage of any available purchase discounts associated with the timely payment of accounts payable. Shortages of working capital, on the other hand, can force a company into borrowing at inopportune times and unfavorable interest rates. As a consequence, many long-term debt contracts contain provisions that require the borrowing firm to maintain a specified working capital position. A firm's working capital is calculated as follows:

Working capital = Current assets − Current liabilities

Analysis of a firm's short-term liquidity utilizes several financial ratios that relate to various aspects of a company's working capital. These ratios are: (1) current ratio, (2) quick ratio, (3) operating-cash-flow-to-current-liabilities ratio, (4) accounts receivable turnover and average collection period, and (5) inventory turnover and days' sales in inventory.

Current Ratio

The **current ratio** is calculated as a firm's current assets divided by its current liabilities:

$$\text{Current ratio} = \frac{\text{Current assets}}{\text{Current liabilities}}$$

This ratio is a widely used measure of a firm's ability to meet its current obligations and to have funds available for use in daily operations. The following calculations reveal that P&G's current ratio increased from 0.75 in 2019 to 0.85 in 2020:

	2020	2019
Current assets	$27,987	$22,473
Current liabilities.	32,976	30,011
Current ratio	**0.85**	**0.75**
Colgate-Palmolive.	0.99	

In essence, P&G had $0.85 in current assets for every $1 in current liabilities at the end of 2020.

In the past, a generally accepted rule of thumb was that a firm's current ratio should be approximately 2, indicating that a company should maintain twice the dollar amount of current assets as needed to satisfy its current liabilities. Improved cash flow management techniques and alternate forms of short-term financing (such as bank lines of credit) have reduced the need for businesses to maintain such a high current ratio. Still, many creditors prefer to see a higher current ratio and consider a low ratio as a potential warning sign of short-term liquidity problems.

Evaluating the adequacy of a firm's current ratio may involve comparing it with the recent past (P&G's current ratio increased from 2019 to 2020) or with an industry peer (P&G's current ratio is below Colgate-Palmolive's current ratio of 0.99). What is considered an appropriate current ratio varies by industry. A service firm with little or no inventory, such as a car wash service, would be expected to have a smaller current ratio than would a firm carrying a large inventory, such as a hardware retailer. The composition (or mix) of a firm's current assets significantly influences any evaluation of a firm's short-term liquidity. The quick ratio, discussed next, explicitly considers the composition of a firm's current assets when evaluating short-term liquidity.

Quick Ratio

The **quick ratio** reveals the relation between a firm's liquid, or quick, assets and its current liabilities. Quick assets include cash and cash equivalents, short-term investments, and accounts receivable. The quick ratio omits a company's inventory and prepaid assets, which may

A.K.A. The quick ratio is also referred to as the *acid-test ratio*.

not be particularly liquid. Consequently, the quick ratio may give a more accurate picture of a company's ability to meet its current obligations.

Comparing the quick ratio and the current ratio indicates the financial impact of a company's inventory on its working capital. For example, a company might have an acceptable current ratio, but if its quick ratio falls to an unacceptable level, a financial analyst is likely to be concerned about the amount of inventory on hand, and consequently, analyze the company's inventory position more thoroughly.

The quick ratio is calculated as follows:

$$\text{Quick ratio} = \frac{\text{(Cash and cash equivalents + Short-term investments + Accounts receivable)}}{\text{Current liabilities}}$$

The quick ratio for P&G is calculated as:

	2020	2019
Cash and cash equivalents, short-term investments, and accounts receivable	$20,359	$15,238
Current liabilities	32,976	30,011
Quick ratio	**0.62**	**0.51**
Colgate-Palmolive	0.49	

P&G's quick ratio increased from 0.51 in 2019 to 0.85 in 2020 and is above the quick ratio of 0.49 reported by Colgate-Palmolive. P&G's increased quick ratio is mainly due to a large increase in cash and cash equivalents in 2020.

Operating-Cash-Flow-to-Current-Liabilities Ratio

Ultimately, cash will be needed to settle a business's current liabilities. Another ratio indicating a firm's ability to pay its current liabilities as they come due focuses on a company's operating cash flow. The **operating-cash-flow-to-current-liabilities ratio** is calculated as follows:

$$\text{Operating-cash-flow-to-current-liabilities ratio} = \frac{\text{Cash flow from operating activities}}{\text{Average current liabilities}}$$

The operating-cash-flow-to-current-liabilities ratio relates the net cash available as a result of operating activities to the average current liabilities outstanding during the period. A higher ratio indicates that a firm has a greater ability to settle its current liabilities using its operating cash flow.

P&G's operating-cash-flow-to-current-liabilities ratio is calculated as (current liabilities at the end of 2018 were $28,237):

		2020	2019
Cash flow from operating activities		$17,403	$15,242
Current liabilities			
Beginning of year	(a)	30,011	28,237
End of year	(b)	32,976	30,011
Average [(a + b)/2]		31,494	29,124
Operating-cash-flow-to-current-liabilities ratio		**0.55**	**0.52**
Colgate-Palmolive		0.88	

P&G's operating-cash-flow-to-current-liabilities ratio increased from 2019 to 2020 due to an increase in cash flow from operating activities. However, this ratio was lower than Colgate-Palmolive's ratio of 0.88.

Accounts Receivable Turnover

The speed with which accounts receivable are collected is of considerable interest to investment professionals when evaluating a firm's short-term liquidity. **Accounts receivable turnover** indicates how many times a year a firm collects its average outstanding accounts receivable, and thus, measures how fast a firm converts its accounts receivable into cash. The quicker a firm is able to convert its accounts receivables into cash, the less cash the company needs to keep on hand to satisfy its current liabilities. Accounts receivable turnover is calculated as follows:

$$\textbf{Accounts receivable turnover} = \frac{\textbf{Net sales}}{\textbf{Average accounts receivable}}$$

Accounts receivable less the allowance for doubtful accounts—that is, the net balance of accounts receivable—is the amount of receivables that the company expects to collect from customers. The accounts receivable turnover for P&G is calculated as (accounts receivable, net at the end of 2018 were $4,686):

		2020	2019
Net sales.		$70,950	$67,684
Average accounts receivable (net)			
Beginning of year	(a)	4,951	4,686
End of year	(b)	4,178	4,951
Average [(a + b)/2]		4,565	4,819
Accounts receivable turnover		**15.54**	**14.05**
Colgate-Palmolive.		12.18	

The higher the accounts receivable turnover, the faster a company is able to convert its accounts receivable into cash. P&G's accounts receivable turnover increased from 14.05 in 2019 to 15.54 in 2020. In addition, P&G's accounts receivable turnover is well above the 12.18 reported by Colgate-Palmolive.

Average Collection Period

An extension of the accounts receivable turnover is the **average collection period**. The average collection period reveals how many days it takes, on average, for a company to collect an account receivable. The ratio is calculated as follows:

A.K.A. The average collection period is also referred to as the days' sales outstanding, or DSO.

$$\textbf{Average collection period} = \frac{\textbf{365}}{\textbf{Accounts receivable turnover (net)}}$$

P&G's average collection period is calculated as:

	2020	2019
Days	365	365
Accounts receivable turnover	15.54	14.05
Average collection period	**23.5 days**	**26.0 days**
Colgate-Palmolive.	30.0 days	

P&G's average collection period decreased in 2020. This may have resulted from such actions as P&G tightening the credit standards it applies to its customers or reducing the allowed credit period. Alternatively, it may reflect that P&G's customers have experienced improving cash flows, and thus they are able to pay their accounts more promptly. Knowledge of P&G's credit terms would permit a more complete analysis of these results. If, for example, P&G's credit terms are n/20, then an average collection period of 23.5 days indicates that the company has a problem with slow-paying customers. If, on the other hand, P&G's credit terms are n/30, then the 2020 average collection period shows no particular problem with the company's speed of receivable collection.

Inventory Turnover

An analyst concerned about a company's inventory position is likely to evaluate the company's **inventory turnover**. This ratio indicates whether the inventory on hand is disproportionate to the amount of sales revenue. Excessive inventories not only tie up company funds and increase storage costs but may also lead to subsequent losses if the goods become outdated or unsalable. In general, a higher turnover is preferred to a lower turnover. The calculation of inventory turnover is as follows:

$$\text{Inventory turnover} = \frac{\text{Cost of goods sold}}{\text{Average inventory}}$$

P&G's inventory turnover is calculated as (inventory at the end of 2018 was $4,738):

	2020	2019
Cost of goods sold	$35,250	$34,768
Inventory		
Beginning of year . . . . (a)	5,017	4,738
End of year . . . . (b)	5,498	5,017
Average [(a + b)/2]	5,258	4,878
Inventory turnover	**6.70**	**7.13**
Colgate-Palmolive.	4.20	

P&G's inventory turnover decreased from 7.13 in 2019 to 6.70 in 2020, but remains above Colgate-Palmolive's reported inventory turnover of 4.20.

The cost of goods sold is used in the calculation of inventory turnover because the inventory measure in the denominator is a *cost* figure; consequently, it is appropriate to also use a cost figure in the numerator. By way of contrast, accounts receivable turnover uses net sales in the calculation because accounts receivable is based on sales revenue, which includes a markup for the company's expected profit.

A low inventory turnover can result from an overextended inventory position or from inadequate sales volume. For this reason, an appraisal of a firm's inventory turnover should be accompanied by a review of the quick ratio and an analysis of trends in both inventory and sales revenue.

Days' Sales in Inventory

The **days' sales in inventory** ratio is derived from a firm's inventory turnover ratio and reveals how many days it takes, on average, for a firm to sell its inventory on hand. The ratio is calculated as follows:

$$\text{Days' sales in inventory} = \frac{365}{\text{Inventory turnover}}$$

P&G's days' sales in inventory is calculated as:

	2020	2019
Days	365	365
Inventory turnover.	6.70	7.13
Days' sales in inventory	**54.5 days**	**51.2 days**
Colgate-Palmolive.	86.9 days	

P&G's days' sales in inventory reveals that the average amount of time required to sell its inventory increased by 3.3 days, from 51.2 days in 2019 to 54.5 days in 2020. However, P&G's average length of time to sell its inventory is still much lower than the 86.9 days reported by Colgate-Palmolive.

By combining the days' sales in inventory with the average collection period, it is possible to estimate the average time period from the acquisition of inventory, to the sale of inventory, to the eventual collection of cash. The sum of the days' sales in inventory plus the average collection period measures the length of the company's **operating cycle**. Although operating cycles will naturally vary across different industries, a shorter operating cycle is preferred, as it is an indicator of the operating efficiency and working capital management of the company. In 2020, for example, it took P&G 78.0 days (54.5 days' sales in inventory + 15.5 days average collection period) to sell its average inventory and collect the related cash from its customers. This operating cycle is similar to P&G's 2019 period of 77.2 days (51.2 days + 26.0 days) and significantly better than Colgate-Palmolive's 116.9 days.

YOUR TURN! 14.5

The solution is on page 14-60.

GuidedExample

MBC

The following selected data were obtained from the financial statements of Justin Corporation:

Current assets	$ 60,000
Current liabilities for both current and prior year.	40,000
Cash flow from operating activities.	55,000
Net sales.	100,000
Average accounts receivable	15,000
Cost of goods sold	70,000
Average inventory.	9,000

Required

Calculate the following financial measures and ratios for Justin Corporation:

a. Working capital

b. Current ratio

c. Operating-cash-flow-to-current-liabilities ratio

d. Accounts receivable turnover

e. Days' sales in inventory

Concept	→	Method	→	Assessment	TAKEAWAY 14.4
How financially capable is a company to pay its current liabilities as they come due?		Income statement, balance sheet, and statement of cash flows. Calculate the current ratio, the quick ratio, and the operating-cash-flow-to-current-liabilities ratio.		The higher the ratios, the higher the probability that a company will have the ability to pay its current liabilities as they become due.	

Analyzing Long-Term Firm Solvency

The preceding set of ratios examined a firm's short-term liquidity. A separate set of ratios analyzes a firm's long-term solvency, or its long-term debt repayment capability. Ratios in this latter group include: (1) debt-to-equity ratio, (2) times-interest-earned ratio, and (3) operating-cash-flow-to-capital-expenditures ratio.

Debt-to-Equity Ratio

The **debt-to-equity ratio** evaluates the financial structure of a firm by relating a company's total liabilities to its total stockholders' equity. This ratio considers the extent to which a company relies on creditors versus stockholders to provide financing. The debt-to-equity ratio is calculated as follows:

$$\text{Debt-to-equity ratio} = \frac{\text{Total liabilities}}{\text{Total stockholders' equity}}$$

This ratio uses year-end balances for the ratio's components, rather than averages, since we are interested in the firm's capital structure as of a particular point in time. The total stockholders' equity for a business is its total assets minus its total liabilities.

The debt-to-equity ratio gives creditors an indication of the margin of protection available to them (creditors' claims to assets have priority over stockholders' claims). The lower the ratio, the greater the protection being provided to creditors. A firm with a low ratio also has greater flexibility when seeking additional borrowed funds at a low rate of interest than does a firm with a high ratio.

P&G's debt-to-equity ratio is calculated as:

	2020	2019
Total liabilities (year-end)	$73,822	$67,516
Total stockholders' equity (year-end)	46,878	47,579
Debt-to-equity ratio	**1.57**	**1.42**
Colgate-Palmolive	13.46	

P&G's debt-to-equity ratio increased from 1.42 in 2019 to 1.57 in 2020, indicating an increase in reliance on debt to finance its operations. However, the ratio is well below the 13.46 debt-to-equity ratio that Colgate-Palmolive reported in 2020. Colgate-Palmolive is heavily reliant on debt financing.

Times-Interest-Earned Ratio

To evaluate the ability of a company to pay its current interest charges, an analyst may investigate the relation between the company's current interest charges and its operating income available to meet those interest charges. For example, an extremely high debt-to-equity ratio for a company may indicate extensive borrowing by the company; however, if its operating earnings are sufficient to meet the interest charges on the debt several times over, an analyst may regard the situation quite favorably.

A.K.A. The times-interest-earned ratio is also referred to as the *interest coverage ratio.*

Analysts, particularly long-term credit analysts, almost always consider the **times-interest-earned ratio** of a company with interest-bearing debt. This ratio is calculated by dividing the income before interest expense and income taxes by the annual interest expense:

$$\text{Times-interest-earned ratio} = \frac{\text{Income before interest expense and income taxes}}{\text{Interest expense}}$$

P&G's times-interest-earned ratio is calculated as:

	2020	2019
Income before interest expense and income taxes	$16,223	$6,509
Interest expense	465	509
Times-interest-earned ratio	**34.9**	**12.8**
Colgate-Palmolive	23.2	

P&G's income available to meet its interest charges increased significantly from 12.8 in 2019 to 34.9 in 2020, the result of much higher reported earnings in 2020. This ratio indicates that P&G exhibits an exceptionally good margin of safety for creditors. Generally speaking, a company that earns its interest charges several times over is regarded as a satisfactory risk by long-term creditors.

Operating-Cash-Flow-to-Capital-Expenditures Ratio

The ability of a firm's operations to provide sufficient cash to replace and expand its property, plant, and equipment is revealed by the **operating-cash-flow-to-capital-expenditures ratio**. To the extent that acquisitions of plant assets can be financed using cash provided by operating activities, a firm does not have to use other financing sources, such as long-term debt. This ratio is calculated as follows:

$$\text{Operating-cash-flow-to-capital-expenditures ratio} = \frac{\text{Cash flow from operating activities}}{\text{Annual net capital expenditures}}$$

A ratio of 1.0 indicates that a firm's current operating activities provide sufficient cash to fully fund any investment in plant capacity. A ratio in excess of 1.0 indicates that a company has sufficient operating cash flow to fund expansion in its plant capacity.

The operating-cash-flow-to-capital-expenditures ratio for P&G is:

	2020	2019
Cash flow from operating activities.	$17,403	$15,242
Annual net capital expenditures	3,073	3,347
Operating-cash-flow-to-capital-expenditures ratio	**5.7**	**4.6**
Colgate-Palmolive.	9.1	

In 2020, P&G's operating-cash-flow-to capital-expenditures ratio was 5.7, an increase from 4.6 in 2019. Although this is less than the 9.1 operating-cash-flow-to-capital-expenditures ratio reported by Colgate-Palmolive in 2020, it still appears that P&G is generating plenty of operating cash flow to cover its net capital expenditures each year.

The following selected data were obtained from the financial statements for the Hartford Corporation:

Total liabilities	$180,000
Total stockholders' equity	600,000
Cash flow from operating activities.	100,000
Annual capital expenditures	30,000
Net income	55,000
Interest expense	5,000
Income tax expense	25,000

YOUR TURN! 14.6

The solution is on page 14-60.

GuidedExample

MBC

Required
Calculate the following ratios for Hartford Corporation:
a. Debt-to-equity ratio
b. Times-interest-earned ratio
c. Operating-cash-flow-to-capital-expenditures ratio

Concept ⟶	Method ⟶	Assessment	**TAKEAWAY 14.5**
How solvent is a company?	Income statement, balance sheet, and statement of cash flows. Calculate the debt-to-equity ratio, the times-interest-earned ratio, and the operating-cash-flow-to-capital-expenditures ratio.	The higher the times-interest-earned and the operating-cash-flow-to-capital-expenditures ratios, and the lower the debt-to-equity ratio, the greater is a company's solvency.	

Financial Ratios for Common Stockholders

Present and potential common stockholders share an interest with a business's creditors in analyzing the profitability, short-term liquidity, and long-term solvency of a company. There are also other financial ratios that are primarily of interest to common stockholders. These ratios include: (1) earnings per share, (2) price-earnings ratio, (3) dividend yield, and (4) dividend payout ratio.

Earnings per Share

Because stock market prices are quoted on a per-share basis, the reporting of earnings per share of common stock is useful to investors. **Earnings per share (EPS)** is calculated by dividing the net income available to common stockholders by the weighted average number of common shares outstanding during a year. The net income available to common stockholders is a company's net income less any preferred stock dividends. Preferred stock dividends are subtracted from net income to arrive at the net income available exclusively to a company's common stock stockholders. Thus, earnings per share is calculated as follows:

$$\frac{\textbf{Earnings}}{\textbf{per share}} = \frac{\textbf{(Net income – Preferred stock dividends)}}{\textbf{Weighted-average number of common shares outstanding}}$$

Because earnings per share are a required disclosure on a company's income statement, investment professionals do not have to calculate this financial metric. P&G's income statements reveal the following earnings per share (see **Exhibit 14-2**):

	2020	2019
Earnings per share..	$5.13	$1.45
Colgate-Palmolive...	3.15	

P&G's earnings per share increased from $1.45 in 2019 to $5.13 in 2020, an increase of 254 percent. This is slightly higher than the 234 percent increase in P&G's net income over the same period. The result is due to the increase in P&G's treasury stock, which reduces the number of common shares outstanding.

Price-Earnings Ratio

A.K.A. The price-earnings ratio is also referred to as the *P/E multiple*.

The **price-earnings ratio** is calculated by dividing the market price per share of common stock by a company's earnings per share:

$$\textbf{Price-earnings ratio} = \frac{\textbf{Market price per share}}{\textbf{Earnings per share}}$$

For many analysts and investors, this ratio is an important tool for assessing a stock's valuation. For example, after evaluating the financial strengths of several comparable companies, an analyst may decide which company to invest in by comparing the price-earnings ratio of each company. Assuming that the companies have equivalent persistent earnings and financial risk profiles, the company with the lowest price-earnings ratio may represent the best investment opportunity.

When calculating the price-earnings ratio, it is customary to use the latest market price per share and the earnings per share for the last four quarters of a company's operations. P&G's price-earnings ratios as of the end of fiscal years 2019 and 2020 are:

	2020	2019
Market price per share (at year-end)	$119.57	$109.65
Earnings per share	5.13	1.45
Price-earnings ratio	**23.3**	**75.6**
Colgate-Palmolive	27.1	

The market price of a share of P&G's common stock at year-end 2020 was 23.3 times the company's 2020 earnings per share, which represents a significant improvement from the price-earnings ratio of 75.6 at the end of 2019. P&G's price-earnings ratio at the end of 2020 is somewhat lower than the 27.1 price-earnings reported by Colgate-Palmolive in 2020, suggesting that it may be a better investment opportunity than Colgate-Palmolive.

Dividend Yield

Investor expectations vary greatly with personal economic circumstances and with the overall economic outlook. Some investors are more interested in the potential share price appreciation of a stock than in any dividends that a company may pay on its outstanding shares. Other investors are more concerned with dividends than with stock price appreciation. These investors desire a high **dividend yield** on their investments. Dividend yield is calculated by dividing a company's current annual dividend per share by the current market price per share:

$$\text{Dividend yield} = \frac{\text{Annual dividend per share}}{\text{Market price per share}}$$

P&G's dividend yield per common share is calculated as (the dividend per share is disclosed in **Exhibit 14-2**):

	2020	2019
Annual dividend per share	$ 3.03	$ 2.9
Market price per share (at year-end)	119.57	109.65
Dividend yield	**2.5%**	**2.6%**
Colgate-Palmolive	2.0%	

P&G's dividend yield decreased very slightly from 2.6 percent in 2019 to 2.5 percent in 2020. This dividend yield is still above the 2.0 percent reported in 2020 by Colgate-Palmolive.

Dividend Payout Ratio

Investors who emphasize the yield on their investments may also be interested in a firm's **dividend payout ratio**—that is, the percentage of net income paid out as dividends to stockholders. The payout ratio indicates whether a firm has a conservative or a liberal dividend policy and may also indicate whether a firm is conserving funds for internal financing of its growth. The dividend payout ratio is calculated as follows:

$$\text{Dividend payout ratio} = \frac{\text{Annual dividend per share}}{\text{Earnings per share}}$$

P&G's dividend payout ratio is calculated as:

	2020	2019
Annual dividends per share	$3.03	$2.90
Earnings per share	5.13	1.45
Dividend payout ratio	**59.1%**	**200.0%**
Colgate-Palmolive	55.6%	

P&G's dividend payout ratio decreased significantly from 200 percent in 2019 to a much more reasonable 59.1 percent in 2020. The 2020 payout ratio is consistent with the payout ratio for most comparable mature U.S. industrial corporations and is slightly higher than the 55.6 percent 2020 dividend payout ratio reported by Colgate-Palmolive.

Payout ratios for mature industrial corporations vary between 40 percent and 60 percent of net income. Many corporations, however, need funds for internal financing of growth and pay out little (if any) of their net income as dividends. At the other extreme, some companies—principally utility companies—may pay out as much as 70 percent of their net income as dividends.

YOUR TURN! 14.7	The following selected data were obtained from financial statements for Baylor Corporation:
The solution is on page 14-60. MBC	Earnings per share. . . . . $ 4.50 Market price per share of common stock . . . . 54.00 Dividends per share of common stock . . . . 1.50 **Required** Calculate the following ratios for Baylor Corporation: *a.* Dividend yield *b.* Dividend payout ratio *c.* Price-earnings ratio

TAKEAWAY 14.6	Concept ➝	Method ➝	Assessment
	How much dividends are common stockholders likely to receive?	Earnings per share, dividends per share, and market price of common stock. Calculate the dividend yield and dividend payout ratio.	The higher the dividend yield and the dividend payout ratio, the more dividends a stockholder can expect to receive.

LIMITATIONS OF FINANCIAL STATEMENT ANALYSIS

LO5 **Discuss** the limitations of financial statement analysis.

eLecture
MBC

The ratios, percentages, and other relations described in this chapter reflect the analytical techniques used by investment professionals and experienced investors. Nonetheless, they must be interpreted with due consideration of the general economic conditions, the conditions of the industry in which a company operates, and the relative position of individual companies within an industry.

Financial statement users must also be aware of the inherent limitations of financial statement data. Problems of comparability are frequently encountered. Companies within the same industry may use different accounting methods that can cause problems in comparing certain key ratios. For instance, inventory turnover is likely to be quite different for a company using LIFO than for one using FIFO. Inflation may also distort certain financial data and ratios, especially those resulting from horizontal analysis. For example, trend percentages calculated from data unadjusted for inflation may be deceptive.

Financial statement users must also be careful when comparing companies within a particular industry. Factors such as firm size, diversity of product line, and mode of operations can make firms within the same industry dissimilar in their reported results. Moreover, some firms, particularly conglomerates, are difficult to classify by industry. If segment information is available, the financial statement user may compare the statistics for several industries. Often, trade associations prepare industry statistics that are stratified by size of firm or type of product, facilitating financial statement analysis.

FORENSIC ACCOUNTING

It is generally considered more difficult to deter financial statement fraud than it is to deter other types of fraud such as embezzlement. The best approach to fraud deterrence is to put into place a strong set of internal controls. Unfortunately, senior management, such as a firm's CEO and CFO, are the most likely employees to commit financial statement fraud. These individuals are able to use their position of authority to override most internal controls. Thus, it is important to consider alternative approaches to fraud deterrence. Potential alternative approaches are based on the fraud triangle concept, in which fraud is related to the interaction of three factors: (1) pressure, (2) opportunity, and (3) rationalization.

The fraud element of pressure can be reduced by avoiding the practice of setting unachievable financial goals and utilizing compensation systems that are considered fair but which do not create excessive incentives to commit fraud. Although internal controls may be circumvented by senior management, it is still important to maintain a strong system of internal controls and to establish clear and uniform accounting procedures with no exception clauses. In addition, a strong internal control department reporting to the board of directors provides further deterrence. Finally, the creation and promotion of a culture of honesty and integrity throughout an organization make the rationalization of financial statement fraud much more difficult.

COMPREHENSIVE PROBLEM

Knox Instruments, Inc., is a manufacturer of various medical and dental instruments. Financial statement data for the firm follow:

(thousands of dollars, except per-share amount)	2019
Sales revenue.	$200,000
Cost of goods sold	98,000
Net income	10,750
Dividends	4,200
Cash provided by operating activities.	7,800
Earnings per share	3.07

KNOX INSTRUMENTS, INC.
Balance Sheets

(thousands of dollars)	Current Year	Previous Year
Assets		
Cash.	$ 3,000	$ 2,900
Accounts receivable (net).	28,000	28,800
Inventory.	64,000	44,000
Total current assets.	95,000	75,700
Plant assets (net)	76,000	67,300
Total assets.	$171,000	$143,000
Liabilities and Stockholders' Equity		
Current liabilities.	$ 45,200	$ 39,750
10% bonds payable	20,000	14,000
Total liabilities	65,200	53,750
Common stock, $10 par value	40,000	30,000
Retained earnings	65,800	59,250
Total stockholders' equity	105,800	89,250
Total liabilities and stockholders' equity	$171,000	$143,000

Required

a. Using the given data, calculate the nine financial ratios below. Compare the ratio results for Knox Instruments, Inc., with the following industry medians and comment on its operations.

Median Ratios for the Industry

1.	Current ratio	2.7
2.	Quick ratio	1.6
3.	Average collection period	73 days
4.	Inventory turnover	2.3
5.	Operating-cash-flow-to-current-liabilities ratio	0.22
6.	Debt-to-equity ratio	0.50
7.	Return on assets	4.9 percent
8.	Return on equity	10.2 percent
9.	Return on sales	4.1 percent

b. Calculate the dividends paid per share of common stock. (Use the average number of shares outstanding during the year.) What was the dividend payout ratio?

c. If the year-end market price per share of Knox's common stock is $25, what is the company's (1) price-earnings ratio and (2) dividend yield?

Solution

a.

1. Current ratio = $95,000/$45,200 = 2.10
2. Quick ratio = $31,000/$45,200 = 0.69
3. Average collection period:
    Accounts receivable turnover = $200,000/($28,800 + $28,000)/2 = 7.04
    Average collection period = 365/7.04 = 51.8 days
4. Inventory turnover = $98,000/($44,000 + $64,000)/2 = 1.81
5. Operating-cash-flow-to-current-liabilities ratio = $7,800/($39,750 + $45,200)/2 = 0.18
6. Debt-to-equity ratio = $65,200/$105,800 = 0.62
7. Return on assets = $10,750/($143,000 + $171,000)/2 = 6.8 percent
8. Return on equity = $10,750/($89,250 + $105,800)/2 = 11.0 percent
9. Return on sales = $10,750/$200,000 = 5.4 percent

Although the firm's current ratio of 2.10 is below the industry median, it is still acceptable; however, the quick ratio of 0.69 is well below the industry median. This indicates that Knox's inventory (which is omitted from the quick ratio calculation) is excessive. This is also borne out by the firm's inventory turnover of 1.81 times, which compares with the industry median of 2.3 times. The firm's average collection period of 51.8 days is significantly better than the industry median of 73 days, while the operating-cash-flow-to-current-liabilities ratio is close to the industry median. Knox's debt-to-equity ratio of 0.62 indicates that the firm has proportionately more debt in its capital structure than the median industry firm, which has a debt-to-equity ratio of 0.50. Knox's operations appear efficient as its return on assets, return on equity, and return on sales all exceed the industry medians.

b. Average number of shares outstanding = (4,000,000 + 3,000,000)/2 = 3,500,000 shares.
    $4,200,000 dividends/3,500,000 shares = $1.20 dividend per share.
    Dividend payout ratio = $1.20/$3.07 = 39.1 percent.

c. Price-earnings ratio = $25/$3.07 = 8.1.
    Dividend yield = $1.20/$25 = 4.8 percent.

APPENDIX 14A: Financial Statement Disclosures

LO6   **Describe** financial statement disclosures.

Disclosures related to a company's financial statements fall into one of three categories: (1) parenthetical disclosures on the face of the financial statements, (2) notes to the financial statements, and (3) supplementary information. Most disclosures amplify or explain aggregated information contained in the financial statements. Some disclosures, however, provide additional information.

eLecture

MBC

Parenthetical Disclosures

Parenthetical disclosures are placed next to an account title or other descriptive label in the financial statements. Their purpose is to provide additional detail regarding the item or account.

An example of parenthetical disclosures indicating the amount of the allowance for doubtful accounts follows:

	2022	2021
Accounts receivable, less allowances for doubtful accounts (2022—$7,545; 2021—$7,098)...	$351,538	$300,181

Instead of using a parenthetical disclosure, companies may choose to present the additional detail in the notes to the financial statements.

Notes to the Financial Statements

Although much information is gathered, summarized, and reported in a company's financial statements, the financial statements alone are limited in their ability to convey a complete picture of a company's financial status. *Notes* are added to the financial statements to help fill in these gaps. In fact, over time, accountants have given so much attention to the financial statement notes that the notes now consume more page space in the annual report than the financial statements themselves. Notes may cover a wide variety of topics. Typically, they deal with significant accounting policies, explanations of complex or special transactions, details of reported amounts, commitments, contingencies, business segments, quarterly data, and subsequent material events.

Significant Accounting Policies

GAAP contains a number of instances for which alternative accounting procedures are equally acceptable. For example, there are several generally accepted depreciation and inventory valuation methods. The particular accounting policies selected by a company affect the financial data presented. Knowledge of a firm's specific accounting principles and methods of applying these principles helps users more fully understand a company's financial statements. Accordingly, these principles and methods are disclosed in a **summary of significant accounting policies**, which is typically the first note to the financial statements.

For example, the annual report of the **Columbia Sportswear Company** contains the following description of its inventory policy:

Inventories consist primarily of finished goods and are carried at the lower of cost or net realizable value. Cost is determined using the first-in, first-out method. The Company periodically reviews its inventories for excess, close-out or slow moving items and makes provisions as necessary to properly reflect inventory value.

Explanations of Complex or Special Transactions

The complexity of certain transactions means that not all important aspects are likely to be reflected in the accounts. Financial statement notes, therefore, report additional relevant details about such transactions. Typical examples include notes discussing the financial aspects of pension plans, profit-sharing plans, acquisitions of other companies, borrowing agreements, stock option and other incentive plans, and income taxes.

Transactions with related parties are special transactions requiring disclosure in the financial statement notes. Related party transactions include transactions between a firm and its (1) principal owners, (2) members of management, (3) subsidiary companies, or (4) affiliate companies.

Details of Reported Amounts

Financial statements often summarize several groups of accounts into a single aggregate dollar amount. For example, a balance sheet may show one asset account labeled *Property, Plant, and Equipment,* or it may list *Long-Term Debt* as a single amount among the liabilities. Notes report more detail, presenting schedules that list the types and amounts of property, plant, and equipment and long-term debt. Other items that may be summarized in the financial statements and detailed in the notes include inventories, other current assets, notes payable, accrued liabilities, stockholders' equity, and a company's income tax expense.

The notes to Columbia Sportswear Company's 2020 annual report contain several examples of financial statement items that are detailed, including revenues (**Note 3**), property, plant, and equipment (**Note 5**), short-term borrowing and credit lines (**Note 7**), accrued liabilities (**Note 8**), income taxes (**Note 10**) , and shareholders' equity (Note 13).

Commitments

A firm may have contractual arrangements existing as of a balance sheet date in which both parties to the contract still have acts yet to be completed. If performance under these **commitments** will have a significant financial impact on a firm, the existence and nature of the commitments should be disclosed in the notes to the financial statements. Examples of commitments reported in the notes include contracts to purchase materials or equipment, contracts to construct facilities, salary commitments to executives, commitments to retire or redeem stock, and commitments to deliver goods.

Columbia Sportswear Company reports the following commitments in its annual report:

During its normal course of business, the Company has made certain indemnities, commitments and guarantees under which it may be required to make payments in relation to certain transactions. These include (i) intellectual property indemnities to the Company's customers and licensees in connection with the use, sale and/or license of Company products, (ii) indemnities to various lessors in connection with facility leases for certain claims arising from such facility or lease, (iii) indemnities to customers, vendors and service providers pertaining to claims based on the negligence or willful misconduct of the Company, (iv) executive severance arrangements and (v) indemnities involving the accuracy of representations and warranties in certain contracts. The duration of these indemnities, commitments and guarantees varies, and in certain cases, may be indefinite. The majority of these indemnities, commitments and guarantees do not provide for any limitation of the maximum potential for future payments the Company could be obligated to make. The Company has not recorded any liability for these indemnities, commitments and guarantees in the accompanying Consolidated Balance Sheets.

Contingencies

If the future event that would turn a contingency into an obligation is not likely to occur, or if the liability cannot be reasonably estimated, the **contingency** is disclosed in a note to the financial statements. Typical contingencies disclosed in the notes include pending lawsuits, environmental cleanup costs, possible income tax assessments, credit guarantees, and discounted notes receivable.

Under Armour, Inc., reports the following regarding contingencies in its annual report:

From time to time, the Company is involved in litigation and other proceedings, including matters related to commercial and intellectual property disputes, as well as trade, regulatory and other claims related to its business. Other than as described below, the Company believes that all current proceedings are routine in nature and incidental to the conduct of its business, and that the ultimate resolution of any such proceedings will not have a material adverse effect on its consolidated financial position, results of operations or cash flows.

Segments

Many firms diversify their business activities and operate in several different industries. A firm's financial statements often combine information from all of a company's operations into aggregate amounts. This complicates the financial statement user's ability to analyze the statements because the interpretation of financial data is influenced by the industry in which a firm operates. Different industries face different types of risk and have different rates of profitability. In making investment and lending decisions, financial statement users evaluate risk and required rates of return. Having financial data available by industry segment is helpful to such evaluations.

The FASB recognizes the usefulness of industry data to investors and lenders. Public companies with significant operations in more than one industry must report certain financial information by industry **segment**. Typically, these disclosures are in the financial statement notes. The major disclosures by industry segment are sales revenue, operating profit or loss, identifiable assets (the assets used by the segment), capital expenditures, and depreciation.

Other types of segment data may also be disclosed. Business operations in different parts of the world are subject to different risks and opportunities for growth. Thus, public companies with significant operations in foreign countries must report selected financial data by foreign geographic area. The required data disclosures include sales revenue, operating profit or loss (or other profitability measure), and identifiable assets. Also, if a firm has export sales or sales revenue to a single customer that are ten percent or more of total sales revenue, the amount of such sales revenue must be separately disclosed.

Note 17 to **Columbia Sportswear's** financial statements in its annual report illustrates segment disclosures by foreign versus domestic segments.

Quarterly Data

Interim financial reports cover periods shorter than one year. Companies that issue interim reports generally do so quarterly. These reports provide financial statement users with more timely information on a firm's progress and are useful in predicting a company's annual financial results. The SEC requires that certain companies disclose selected quarterly financial data in their annual reports to stockholders. Included among the notes, the data reported for each quarter include sales revenue, gross profit, net income, and earnings per share. **Quarterly data** permit financial statement users to analyze such things as the seasonal nature of operations, the impact of diversification on quarterly activity, and whether the firm's activities lead or lag general economic trends.

Subsequent Events

If a company issues a large amount of securities or suffers a casualty loss after the balance sheet date, this information should be reported in a note, even though the situation arose subsequent to the balance sheet date. Firms are responsible for disclosing any significant events that occur between the balance sheet date and the date the financial statements are issued. This guideline recognizes that it takes several weeks for financial statements to be prepared and audited before they are issued. Events occurring during this period may have a material effect on a firm's operations and should be disclosed. Other examples of **subsequent events** requiring disclosure are sales of assets, significant changes in long-term debt, and acquisitions of other companies.

Supplementary Information

Supplementing the financial statements are several additional disclosures—management's discussion and analysis of the financial statements and selected financial data covering a five- to ten-year period along with possible other supplementary disclosures that are either required of certain companies by the SEC or recommended (but not required) by the FASB.

Management Discussion and Analysis

Management may increase the usefulness of financial statements by sharing some of their knowledge about a company's financial condition and operations. This is the purpose of the disclosure devoted to the management discussion and analysis. In this supplement to the financial statements, which is not audited, management identifies and comments on events and trends influencing a company's liquidity, operating results, and financial resources. Management's position within a company not only provides it with insights unavailable to outsiders, but also may introduce certain biases into the analysis. Nonetheless, management's comments, interpretations, and explanations should contribute to a better understanding of a company's financial statements.

A.K.A. The management discussion and analysis are also referred to simply as the *MD&A*.

Comparative Selected Financial Data

The analysis of a company's financial performance is enhanced when financial data for several years are available. By analyzing trends over time, it is possible for a financial statement user to learn much more about a company than would be possible by analyzing only a single year of data. Year-to-year changes may give clues as to a firm's future growth or may highlight areas for concern. Corporate annual reports to stockholders present complete financial statements in comparative form, showing the current year and one or two preceding years. Beyond this, however, the financial statements are supplemented by a summary of selected key financial statistics for a five- or ten-year period. The financial data presented in this historical summary usually include sales revenue, net income, dividends, earnings per share, working capital, and total assets.

SUMMARY OF LEARNING OBJECTIVES

Identify persistent earnings and discuss the content and format of the income statement. (p. 14-3)   **LO1**

- Persistent earnings are earnings that are likely to recur, while transitory earnings are unlikely to recur.
- The continuing income of a business may be reported in a single-step format or in a multiple-step format.
- Gains and losses from discontinued operations are reported in a special income statement section following income from continuing operations.
- The effect of most changes in accounting principle requires restatement of prior financial statements as if the new method had been applied all along.
- Companies are required to report other comprehensive income in addition to regular income in their financial statements.

Identify the sources of financial information used by investment professionals and explain horizontal financial statements analysis. (p. 14-6)   **LO2**

- Data sources for investment professionals include published financial statements, filings with the U.S. Securities and Exchange Commission, and statistics available from financial data services.
- A common form of horizontal analysis involves analyzing dollar and percentage changes in comparative financial statements for two or more years.
- Analyzing trend percentages of key figures, such as sales revenue, net income, and total assets for a number of years, related to a base year, is often useful.

LO3   **Explain vertical financial statement analysis. (p. 14-12)**

- Vertical analysis deals with the relative importance of various accounts in the financial statements for a single year.
- Common-size statements express income statement items as a percentage of sales revenue and balance sheet items as a percentage of total assets.

LO4   **Define and discuss financial ratios for analyzing a firm. (p. 14-13)**

- Ratios for analyzing firm profitability include the gross profit percentage, return on sales, asset turnover, return on assets, and return on equity.
- Ratios for analyzing short-term firm liquidity include the current ratio, quick ratio, operating-cash-flow-to-current-liabilities ratio, accounts receivable turnover, average collection period, inventory turnover, and days' sales in inventory.
- Ratios for analyzing long-term firm solvency include the debt-to-equity ratio, times-interest-earned ratio, and operating-cash-flow-to-capital-expenditures ratio.
- Ratios of particular interest to common stockholders include a company's earnings per share, the price-earnings ratio, dividend yield, and dividend payout ratio.

LO5   **Discuss the limitations of financial statement analysis. (p. 14-27)**

- When analyzing financial statements, financial statement users must be aware of a firm's accounting methods, the effects of inflation, and the difficulty of currently identifying a firm's industry classification.

LO6   **Appendix 14A: Describe financial statement disclosures. (p. 14-29)**

- Parenthetical disclosures on the face of the financial statements provide additional detail regarding the item or account.
- Notes to the financial statements provide information on significant accounting policies, explanations of complex or special transactions, details of reported amounts, commitments, contingencies, segments, quarterly data, and subsequent events.
- Supplemental information includes the management discussion and analysis and comparable selected financial information.

SUMMARY OF FINANCIAL STATEMENT RATIOS

Analyzing Firm Profitability

$$\text{Gross profit percentage} = \frac{\text{Gross profit on sales}}{\text{Net sales}}$$

$$\text{Return on sales} = \frac{\text{Net income}}{\text{Net sales}}$$

$$\text{Asset turnover} = \frac{\text{Net sales}}{\text{Average total assets}}$$

$$\text{Return on assets} = \frac{\text{Net income}}{\text{Average total assets}}$$

$$\text{Return on equity} = \frac{\text{Net income}}{\text{Average stockholders' equity}}$$

Analyzing Short-Term Firm Liquidity

$$\text{Current ratio} = \frac{\text{Current assets}}{\text{Current liabilities}}$$

$$\text{Quick ratio} = \frac{\text{(Cash and cash equivalents + Short-term investments + Accounts receivable)}}{\text{Current liabilities}}$$

$$\text{Operating-cash-flow-to-current-liabilities ratio} = \frac{\text{Cash flow from operating activities}}{\text{Average current liabilities}}$$

$$\text{Accounts receivable turnover} = \frac{\text{Net sales}}{\text{Average accounts receivable (net)}}$$

$$\text{Average collection period} = \frac{365}{\text{Accounts receivable turnover (net)}}$$

$$\text{Inventory turnover} = \frac{\text{Cost of goods sold}}{\text{Average inventory}}$$

$$\text{Days' sales in inventory} = \frac{365}{\text{Inventory turnover}}$$

Analyzing Long-Term Firm Solvency

$$\text{Debt-to-equity ratio} = \frac{\text{Total liabilities}}{\text{Total stockholders' equity}}$$

$$\text{Times-interest-earned ratio} = \frac{\text{Income before interest expense and income taxes}}{\text{Interest expense}}$$

$$\text{Operating-cash-flow-to-capital-expenditures ratio} = \frac{\text{Cash flow from operating activities}}{\text{Annual net capital expenditures}}$$

Financial Ratios for Common Stockholders

$$\text{Earnings per share} = \frac{\text{(Net income-Preferred stock dividends)}}{\text{Weighted average common shares outstanding}}$$

$$\text{Price-earnings ratio} = \frac{\text{Market price per share}}{\text{Earnings per share}}$$

$$\text{Dividend yield} = \frac{\text{Annual dividend per share}}{\text{Market price per share}}$$

$$\text{Dividend payout ratio} = \frac{\text{Annual dividend per share}}{\text{Earnings per share}}$$

Concept	Method	Assessment	SUMMARY
How does a company's current performance compare with the prior year?	Income statement, balance sheet, and statement of cash flow for current and prior year. The financial statements should be compared using the prior year as the base. Percentage changes in financial statement amounts can be computed as the change between years divided by the base year amount.	Significant changes should be analyzed to determine the reason for any change.	TAKEAWAY 14.1
How do the relations within a company's income statement and balance sheet compare to those of prior years?	Income statement and balance sheet for current and prior year. Each income statement item should be presented as a percentage of sales revenue, and each balance sheet item should be presented as a percentage of total assets. Financial statements in this form are called common-size statements.	The percentages should be analyzed for differences between years, and significant changes should be analyzed to determine the reason for any change.	TAKEAWAY 14.2
How much profit is a company generating relative to the amount of assets invested in the company?	Income statement and balance sheet. Calculate the return on assets by dividing, net income by the average total assets for the year.	The higher the return on assets, the better a company is doing with respect to generating profits utilizing the assets under its control.	TAKEAWAY 14.3
How financially capable is a company to pay its current liabilities as they come due?	Income statement, balance sheet, and statement of cash flows. Calculate the current ratio, the quick ratio, and the operating-cash-flow-to-current-liabilities ratio.	The higher the ratios, the higher the probability that a company will have the ability to pay its current liabilities as they come due.	TAKEAWAY 14.4

continued

continued from previous page

SUMMARY	Concept	➡ Method ➡	Assessment
TAKEAWAY 14.5	How solvent is a company?	Income statement, balance sheet, and statement of cash flows. Calculate the debt-to-equity ratio, the times-interest-earned ratio, and the operating-cash-flow-to-capital-expenditures ratio.	The higher the times-interest-earned and the operating-cash-flow-to-capital-expenditures ratios, and the lower the debt-to-equity ratio, the greater is a company's solvency.
TAKEAWAY 14.6	How much dividends are common stockholders likely to receive?	Earnings per share, dividends per share, and market price of common stock. Calculate the dividend yield and dividend payout ratio.	The higher the dividend yield and the dividend payout ratio, the more dividends a stockholder can expect to receive.

KEY TERMS

Accounts receivable turnover (p. 14-20)

Asset turnover ratio (p. 14-16)

Average collection period (days' sales outstanding, or DSO) (p. 14-20)

Benchmarking (p. 14-15)

Change in accounting principle (p. 14-5)

Commitments (p. 14-30)

Common-size financial statement (p. 14-12)

Comparative financial statement analysis (p. 14-7)

Comprehensive income (p. 14-5)

Contingency (p. 14-31)

Current ratio (p. 14-18)

Days' sales in inventory (p. 14-21)

Debt-to-equity ratio (p. 14-22)

Discontinued operations (p. 14-5)

Dividend payout ratio (p. 14-26)

Dividend yield (p. 14-26)

Earnings per share (EPS) (p. 14-4, 14-25)

Gross profit (Gross margin) (p. 14-15)

Gross profit on sales (p. 14-15)

Gross profit percentage (p. 14-15)

Horizontal analysis (p. 14-7)

Inventory turnover (p. 14-21)

MD&A (p. 14-32)

Multiple-step income statement (p. 14-3)

Operating-cash-flow-to-capital-expenditures ratio (p. 14-24)

Operating-cash-flow-to-current-liabilities ratio (p. 14-19)

Operating cycle (p. 14-22)

Persistent earnings (p. 14-3)

Price-earnings ratio (P/E multiple) (p. 14-25)

Quarterly data (p. 14-31)

Quick ratio (acid-test ratio) (p. 14-18)

Return on assets (p. 14-16)

Return on equity (p. 14-17)

Return on sales (profit margin) (p. 14-15)

Segment (p. 14-31)

Single-step income statement (p. 14-3)

Subsequent events (p. 14-32)

Summary of significant accounting policies (p. 14-30)

Times-interest-earned ratio (interest coverage ratio) (p. 14-23)

Transitory earnings (p. 14-3)

Trend percentages (p. 14-10)

Unusual items (p. 14-3)

Vertical analysis (p. 14-7)

Working capital (p. 14-18)

Assignments with the logo in the margin are available in *my* BusinessCourse.
See the Preface of the book for details.

SELF-STUDY QUESTIONS

(Answers to the Self-Study Questions are at the end of this chapter.)

 LO1

1. **Assume that an income statement contains each of the three sections listed below. Which will be the last section presented in the income statement?**

   a. Gross profit

   b. Income from continuing operations

   c. Discontinued operations

 LO3

2. **When constructing a common-sized income statement, all amounts are expressed as a percentage of:**

   a. net income.

   b. gross profit.

   c. net sales.

   d. income from operations.

Questions 3–9 of the Self-Study Questions are based on the following data:

HYDRO COMPANY Balance Sheet December 31			
Cash............................	$ 40,000	Current liabilities.........................	$ 80,000
Accounts receivable (net)............	80,000	10% bonds payable	120,000
Inventory........................	130,000	Common stock	200,000
Plant and equipment (net)	250,000	Retained earnings	100,000
Total assets......................	$500,000	Total liabilities and stockholders' equity	$500,000

Sales revenues were $800,000, gross profit was $320,000, and net income was $36,000. The income tax rate was 40 percent. One year ago, accounts receivable (net) were $76,000, inventory was $110,000, total assets were $460,000, and stockholders' equity was $260,000. The bonds payable were outstanding all year, and the interest expense was $12,000.

3. **The current ratio of Hydro Company at December 31 calculated using the above data was 3.13, and the company's working capital was $170,000. Which of the following would happen if the firm paid off $20,000 of its current liabilities on January 1 of the following year?**   **LO4**
   a. Both the current ratio and the working capital would decrease.
   b. Both the current ratio and the working capital would increase.
   c. The current ratio would increase, but the working capital would remain the same.
   d. The current ratio would increase, but the working capital would decrease.

4. **What was the firm's inventory turnover?**   **LO4**
   a. 6.67   c. 6
   b. 4   d. 3.69

5. **What was the firm's return on equity?**   **LO4**
   a. 25.7 percent   c. 17.1 percent
   b. 12.9 percent   d. 21.4 percent

6. **What was the firm's average collection period?**   **LO4**
   a. 36.5 days   c. 35.6 days
   b. 37.4 days   d. 18.3 days

7. **What was the firm's times-interest-earned ratio?**   **LO4**
   a. 4   c. 5
   b. 3   d. 6

8. **What was the firm's return on sales?**   **LO4**
   a. 4.0 percent   c. 5.0 percent
   b. 4.5 percent   d. 5.5 percent

9. **What was the firm's return on assets?**   **LO4**
   a. 6.0 percent   c. 7.5 percent
   b. 7.0 percent   d. 8.0 percent

10. **When performing trend analysis, each line item is expressed as a percentage of:**   **LO2**
    a. net income.   c. the prior year amount.
    b. the base year amount.   d. total assets.

11. **Recognized limitations of financial statement analysis include each of the following except:**   **LO5**
    a. companies in the same industry using different accounting methods.
    b. inflation.
    c. different levels of profitability between companies.
    d. difficulty of classifying by industry conglomerates.

12. **Financial statement disclosures include each of the following except:**   **LO6**
    (Appendix 14A)
    a. notes to the financial statements.   c. supplementary information.
    b. parenthetical disclosures.   d. promotional giveaways.

QUESTIONS

1. What is the difference between a single-step income statement and a multiple-step income statement?

2. Which of the following amounts would appear only in a multiple-step income statement?
   - a. Income from continuing operations.
   - b. Income from discontinued operations.
   - c. Gross profit on sales.
   - d. Net income.

3. What is a business segment? Why are gains and losses from a discontinued segment reported in a separate section of the income statement?

4. How do horizontal analysis and vertical analysis of financial statements differ?

5. "Financial statement users should focus attention on each item showing a large percentage change from one year to the next." Is this statement correct? Why?

6. What are trend percentages, and how are they calculated? What pitfalls must financial statement users avoid when preparing trend percentages?

7. What are common-size financial statements, and how are they used?

8. What item is the key figure (that is, 100 percent) in a common-size income statement? A common-size balance sheet?

9. During the past year, Lite Company had net income of $5 million, and Scanlon Company had net income of $8 million. Both companies manufacture electrical components for the construction industry. What additional information would you need to compare the profitability of the two companies?

10. Under what circumstances can the return on sales be used to assess the profitability of a company? Can this ratio be used to compare the profitability of companies from different industries? Explain.

11. What is the relationship between asset turnover, return on assets, and return on sales?

12. Blare Company had a return on sales of 6.5 percent and an asset turnover of 2.40. What is Blare's return on assets?

13. What does the return on equity measure?

14. How does the quick ratio differ from the current ratio?

15. For each of the following ratios, is a high ratio or low ratio considered, in general, a positive sign?
    - a. Current ratio
    - b. Quick ratio
    - c. Operating-cash-flow-to-current-liabilities ratio
    - d. Accounts receivable turnover
    - e. Average collection period
    - f. Inventory turnover
    - g. Days' sales in inventory

16. What is the significance of the debt-to-equity ratio, and how is it computed?

17. What does the times-interest-earned ratio indicate, and how is it calculated?

18. What does the operating-cash-flow-to-capital-expenditures ratio measure?

19. Clair, Inc., earned $4.50 per share of common stock in the current year and paid dividends of $2.34 per share. The most recent market price per share of the common stock is $46.80. What is the company's (a) price-earnings ratio, (b) dividend yield, and (c) dividend payout ratio?

20. What are two inherent limitations of financial statement data?

SHORT EXERCISES

Use the following financial data for Brenner Instruments to answer Short Exercises 14-1 through 14-10:

(Thousands of Dollars, except Earnings per Share)	
Sales revenue	$210,000
Cost of goods sold	125,000
Net income	8,300
Dividends	2,600
Earnings per share	4.15

BRENNER INSTRUMENTS, INC. Balance Sheets (Thousands of Dollars)	Current Year	Previous Year
Assets		
Cash.	$ 18,300	$ 18,000
Accounts receivable (net).	46,000	41,000
Inventory.	39,500	43,700
Total current assets.	103,800	102,700
Plant assets (net)	52,600	50,500
Other assets	15,600	13,800
Total assets.	$172,000	$167,000
Liabilities and Stockholders' Equity		
Notes payable—banks	$ 6,000	$ 6,000
Accounts payable	22,500	18,700
Accrued liabilities	16,500	21,000
Total current liabilities	45,000	45,700
9% bonds payable	40,000	40,000
Total liabilities	85,000	85,700
Common stock, $25 par value (2,000,000 shares).	50,000	50,000
Retained earnings	37,000	31,300
Total stockholders' equity	87,000	81,300
Total liabilities and stockholders' equity	$172,000	$167,000

Industry Average Ratios for Competitors	
Quick ratio	1.3
Current ratio	2.4
Accounts receivable turnover	5.9 times
Inventory turnover.	3.5 times
Debt-to-equity ratio.	0.73
Gross profit percentage	42.8 percent
Return on sales	4.5 percent
Return on assets	7.6 percent

SE14-1. **Quick Ratio** Calculate the company's quick ratio for the current year and compare the result to the industry average.   **LO4**

SE14-2. **Current Ratio** Calculate the company's current ratio for the current year and compare the result to the industry average.   **LO4**

SE14-3. **Accounts Receivable Turnover** Calculate the company's accounts receivable turnover for the current year and compare the result to the industry average.   **LO4**

SE14-4. **Inventory Turnover** Calculate the company's inventory turnover for the current year and compare the result to the industry average.   **LO4**

SE14-5. **Debit-to-Equity Ratio** Calculate the company's current year debt-to-equity ratio and compare the result to the industry average.   **LO4**

SE14-6. **Gross Profit Percentage** Calculate the company's current year gross profit percentage and compare the result to the industry average.   **LO4**

SE14-7. **Return on Sales** Calculate the company's return on sales for the current year and compare the result to the industry average.   **LO4**

SE14-8. **Return on Assets** Calculate the company's return on assets for the current year and compare the result to the industry average.   **LO4**

SE14-9. **Dividends per Share** Calculate the company's dividend paid per share of common stock. What was the dividend payout ratio?   **LO4**

SE14-10. **Earnings per Share** If the company's most recent price per share of common stock is $62.25, what is the company's price-earnings ratio and dividend yield?   **LO4**

LO1   **SE14-11. Persistent Earnings** Identify each of the following items as either (P) persistent or (T) transitory.

   a.   Sale of merchandise.   *c.*   Interest income.

   b.   Settlement of a lawsuit.   *d.*   Payment to vendors.

   e.   Loss from expropriations of property by a foreign government.

LO2   **SE14-12. Horizontal Analysis** Total assets were $1,000,000 in 2022, $900,000 in 2021, and $950,000 in 2020. What was the percentage change from 2020 to 2021 and from 2021 to 2022? Was the change an increase or a decrease?

LO3   **SE14-13. Common-Size Income Statement** A partial common-size income statement for Jag Company for three years is shown below.

Item	2022	2021	2020
Net sales.	100.0	100.0	100.0
Cost of goods sold	60.5	63.0	62.5
Other expenses	21.0	19.0	20.5

Did Jag's net income as a percentage of net sales increase, remain the same, or decrease over the three-year period?

LO5   **SE14-14. Financial Statement Analysis Limitations** Which of the following is not considered a limitation of financial statement analysis?

   a.   Firms may use different accounting methods.

   b.   Firms may be audited by different auditing firms.

   c.   Inflation may distort trend analysis.

   d.   It may be difficult to classify large conglomerate firms by industry.

LO6   **SE14-15. Financial Statement Disclosures** Which of the following is not a common form of financial statement disclosure?
(Appendix 14A)

   a.   Notes to financial statements.   *c.*   Parenthetical disclosure.

   b.   Supplemental information.   *d.*   Bullet points.

DATA ANALYTICS, DATA VISUALIZATION, AND EXCEL ACTIVITIES

Data Analytics, Data Visualization, and Excel Activities are available in myBusinessCourse. These assignments develop Excel, Tableau, and Data Analytics skills, which will enhance students' career readiness. These exercises are assignable and auto graded by MBC. For an overview of data analytics, see the appendix at the end of this book.

EXERCISES—SET A

LO1   **E14-1A. Income Statement Sections** During the current year, David Corporation sold a segment of its business at a gain of $210,000. Until it was sold, the segment had a current period operating loss of $75,000. The company had $700,000 income from continuing operations for the current year. Prepare the lower part of the income statement, beginning with the $700,000 income from continuing operations. Follow tax allocation procedures, assuming that all changes in income are subject to a 20 percent income tax rate. Disregard earnings per share disclosures.

LO4   **E14-2A. Earnings per Share** Myrtle Corporation began the year with a simple capital structure consisting of 480,000 shares of outstanding common stock. On April 1, 10,000 additional common shares were issued, and another 60,000 common shares were issued on August 1. The company had net income for the year of $589,375. Calculate the earnings per share of common stock.

LO2   **E14-3A. Comparative Income Statements** Consider the following income statement data from the Mono Company:

	Current Year	Previous Year
Sales revenue.	$600,000	$450,000
Cost of goods sold	336,000	279,000
Selling expenses	105,000	99,000
Administrative expenses.	60,000	50,000
Income tax expense	4,000	3,000

a.   Prepare a comparative income statement, showing increases and decreases in dollars and in percentages.

b.   Comment briefly on the changes between the two years.

E14-4A.   Common-Size Income Statements Refer to the income statement data given in Exercise E14-3A.   **LO3**

a.   Prepare common-size income statements for each year.

b.   Compare the common-size income statements and comment briefly.

E14-5A.   Ratios Analyzing Firm Profitability The following information is available for Jay Company: **LO4**

Annual Data	Current Year	Previous Year
Net sales.	$9,000,000	$8,200,000
Gross profit on sales.	3,050,000	2,736,000
Net income	567,600	500,000

Year-End Data	Dec. 31, Current Year	Dec. 31, Previous Year
Total assets.	$6,500,000	$6,000,000
Stockholders' equity	5,000,000	3,200,000

Calculate the following ratios for the current year:

a.   Gross profit percentage   d.   Return on assets

b.   Return on sales   e.   Return on equity

c.   Asset turnover

E14-6A.   Working Capital and Short-Term Liquidity Ratios Ritter Company has a current ratio of 3.00 on   **LO4**   December 31. On that date the company's current assets are as follows:

Cash.	$ 32,000
Short-term investments	49,300
Accounts receivable (net).	170,000
Inventory.	200,000
Prepaid expenses.	11,600
Current assets	$462,900

Ritter Company's current liabilities at the beginning of the year were $150,000, and during the year its operating activities provided a cash flow of $60,000.

a.   What are the firm's current liabilities on December 31?

b.   What is the firm's working capital on December 31?

c.   What is the quick ratio on December 31?

d.   What is Bell's operating-cash-flow-to-current-liabilities ratio?

E14-7A.   Accounts Receivable and Inventory Ratios Ritter Company, whose current assets at December   **LO4**   31 are shown in Exercise E14-6A, had net sales for the year of $850,000 and cost of goods sold of $550,000. At the beginning of the year, Ritter's accounts receivable (net) were $160,000, and its inventory was $175,000.

a.   What is the company's accounts receivable turnover for the year?

b.   What is the company's average collection period for the year?

c.   What is the company's inventory turnover for the year?

d.   What is the company's days' sales in inventory for the year?

E14-8A.   Ratios Analyzing Long-Term Firm Solvency The following information is available for Banner   **LO4**   Company:

Annual Data	Current Year	Previous Year
Interest expense.	$ 85,000	$ 82,000
Income tax expense	203,500	185,000
Net income.	496,500	425,000
Capital expenditures.	320,000	380,000
Cash provided by operating activities.	450,000	390,000

Year-End Data	Dec. 31, Current Year	Dec. 31, Previous Year
Total liabilities	$2,400,000	$1,900,000
Total stockholders' equity	4,200,000	3,800,000

Calculate the following:

a.   Current year debt-to-equity ratio.

b.   Current year times-interest-earned ratio.

c.   Current year operating-cash-flow-to-capital-expenditures ratio.

LO4   E14-9A.   Financial Ratios for Common Stockholders Morgan Corporation has only common stock outstanding. The firm reported earnings per share of $6.00 for the year. During the year, Morgan paid dividends of $2.10 per share. At year-end the current market price of the stock was $72 per share. Calculate the following:

a.   Price-earnings ratio   c.   Dividend payout ratio

b.   Dividend yield

LO5   E14-10A.   Financial Statement Limitations You have been asked to perform financial statement analysis on the Rush Company. The Rush Company is a large chain of retail outlets that sells a wide range of household items. Last year the company introduced its own credit card and is pleased that profit from this financing activity now accounts for over 20 percent of the company's total profit. As part of your analysis you have chosen to compare the Rush Company to Johnson Stores, a much larger chain of stores. Johnson Stores sells household items and groceries, but it does not have its own credit card. Your analysis includes both trend analysis and vertical analysis. Identify some of the limitations from the description above.

LO6   E14-11A.   Financial Statement Notes The notes to financial statements present information on significant accounting policies, complex or special transactions, details of reported amounts, commitments, contingencies, segments, quarterly data, and subsequent events. Indicate which type of note disclosure is illustrated by each of the following notes:

(Appendix 14A)

a.   The company has agreed to purchase seven EMB-120 aircraft and related spare parts. The aggregate cost of these aircraft is approximately $52,000,150, subject to a cost escalation provision. The aircraft are scheduled to be delivered over the next two fiscal years.

b.   The company has deferred certain costs related to major accounting and information systems enhancements that are anticipated to benefit future years. Upon completion, the related cost is amortized over a period not exceeding five years.

c.   The company has guaranteed loans and leases of independent distributors approximating $27,500,000 as of December 31 of the current year.

d.   An officer of the company is also a director of a major raw material supplier of the company. The amount of raw material purchases from this supplier approximated $595,000 in the current year.

EXERCISES—SET B

LO1   E14-1B.   Income Statement Sections During the current year, Ediza Corporation sold a segment of its business at a loss of $175,000. Until it was sold, the segment had a current period operating loss of $200,000. The company has $750,000 income from continuing operations for the current year. Prepare the lower part of the income statement, beginning with the $750,000 income from continuing operations. Follow tax allocation procedures, assuming that all changes in income are subject to a 20 percent income tax rate. Disregard earnings per share disclosures.

LO4   E14-2B.   Earnings per Share Heart Corporation began the year with a simple capital structure consisting of 35,000 shares of common stock outstanding. On May 1, 5,000 additional common shares were issued, and another 20,000 common shares were issued on September 1. The company had a net income for the year of $468,000. Calculate the earnings per share of common stock.

LO2   E14-3B.   Comparative Balance Sheets Consider the following balance sheet data for Davis Co., Inc., an electronics and major appliance retailer (amounts in thousands):

	Current Year	Previous Year
Cash and cash equivalents	$ 60,872	$ 7,138
Accounts receivables	52,944	37,968
Merchandise inventories.	637,950	249,991
Other current assets.	13,844	9,729
Current assets.	765,610	304,826
Property and equipment (net).	172,724	126,442
Other assets	15,160	7,774
Total assets.	$953,494	$439,042
Current liabilities.	$402,028	$186,005
Long-term liabilities	239,022	70,854
Total liabilities	641,050	256,859
Common stock	3,087	1,149
Additional paid-in-capital	224,089	137,151
Retained earnings	85,268	43,883
Total stockholders' equity	312,444	182,183
Total liabilities and stockholders' equity	$953,494	$439,042

a. Prepare a comparative balance sheet, showing increases in dollars and percentages.
b. Comment briefly on the changes between the two years.

E14-4B. Common-Size Balance Sheets Refer to the balance sheet data given in Exercise E14-3B.   **LO3**

a. Prepare common-size balance sheets for each year. (Use total assets as the base amount for computing percentages.)
b. Compare the common-size balance sheets and comment briefly.

E14-5B. Ratios Analyzing Firm Profitability The following information is available for Virginia Company: **LO4**

Annual Data	Current Year	Previous Year
Sales revenue.	$6,600,000	$6,000,000
Cost of goods sold	4,006,400	3,800,000
Net income	325,000	264,000

Year-End Data	Dec. 31, Current Year	Dec. 31, Previous Year
Total assets.	$2,850,000	$2,500,000
Stockholders' equity	1,900,000	1,700,000

Calculate the following ratios for the current year:

a. Gross profit percentage   c. Asset turnover   e. Return on equity
b. Return on sales   d. Return on assets

E14-6B. Working Capital and Short-Term Firm Liquidity Ratios Purple Company has a current ratio of 2.2 on December 31. On that date its current assets are as follows: **LO4**

Cash and cash equivalents	$ 13,000
Short-term investments	90,000
Accounts receivable (net)	125,000
Inventory.	178,500
Prepaid expenses.	11,500
Current assets	$418,000

Purple Company's current liabilities at the beginning of the year were $195,000, and during the year its operating activities provided a cash flow of $35,000.

a. What are the firm's current liabilities at December 31?
b. What is the firm's working capital on December 31?
c. What is the quick ratio on December 31?
d. What is the firm's operating-cash-flow-to-current-liabilities ratio?

LO4   **E14-7B.**   **Accounts Receivable and Inventory Ratios** Purple Company, whose current assets at December 31 are shown in Exercise E14-6B, had net sales for the year of $580,000 and cost of goods sold of $339,000. At the beginning of the year, accounts receivable (net) were $121,000 and inventory was $160,500.

a.   What is the company's accounts receivable turnover?
b.   What is the company's average collection period?
c.   What is the company's inventory turnover?
d.   What is the company's days' sales in inventory?

LO4   **E14-8B.**   **Ratios Analyzing Long-Term Firm Solvency** The following information is available for Rae Company:

Annual Data	Current Year	Previous Year
Interest expense.	$170,000	$166,000
Income tax expense	126,000	117,000
Net income	310,000	275,000
Capital expenditures.	435,000	350,000
Cash provided by operating activities.	247,000	220,000

Year-End Data	Dec. 31, Current Year	Dec. 31, Previous Year
Total liabilities	$3,400,000	$2,900,000
Total stockholders' equity	2,200,000	2,000,000

Calculate the following:

a.   Current year debt-to-equity ratio
b.   Current year times-interest-earned ratio
c.   Current year operating-cash-flow-to-capital-expenditures ratio

LO4   **E14-9B.**   **Financial Ratios for Common Stockholders** Jason Corporation has only common stock outstanding. The firm reported earnings per share of $4.00 for the year. During the year, Jason paid dividends of $0.85 per share. At year-end, the current market price of the stock was $70.30 per share.
      Calculate the following:

a.   Price-earnings ratio   c.   Dividend payout ratio
b.   Dividend yield

LO5   **E14-10B.**   **Financial Statement Limitations** You have been asked to perform financial statement analysis on the Ian Company. The Ian Company is a large manufacturer of construction machinery and vehicles. Last year the company closed down a segment of the business that produced mining equipment because it was not providing an adequate return on assets. This segment represented 15 percent of the company's total assets. As part of your analysis you have chosen to compare the Ian Company to Bertran, Inc., a much smaller manufacturer of equipment, although Bertran, Inc., also performs contract repairs for many other brands of equipment. Your analysis includes both trend analysis and vertical analysis. Identify some of the limitations from the description above.

LO6   **E14-11B.**   **Financial Statement Notes** Notes to the financial statements present information on significant
(Appendix 14A)   accounting policies, complex or special transactions, details of reported amounts, commitments, contingencies, segments, quarterly data, and subsequent events. Indicate the type of note disclosure that is illustrated by each of the following notes:

a.   Sales by the Farm and Equipment segment to independent dealers are recorded at the time of shipment to those dealers. Sales through company-owned retail stores are recorded at the time of sale to retail customers.
b.   Members of the board of directors, the advisory board, and employees are not charged the vendor's commission on property sold at auction for their benefit. (From the notes of an auctioneer company.)
c.   Sales to an airline company accounted for approximately 48 percent of the company's net sales in the current year.
d.   The company's product liability insurance coverage with respect to insured events occurring after January 1 of the current year is substantially less than the amount of that insurance available in the recent past. The company is now predominantly self-insured in this area. The reduction in insurance coverage reflects trends in the liability insurance field generally and is not unique to the company.

PROBLEMS—SET A

P14-1A. **Income Statement Format** The following information from Buchanan Company's current operations is available: **LO1**

Administrative expenses.	$ 73,000
Cost of goods sold	470,000
Sales revenue.	772,000
Selling expenses	87,000
Interest expense.	10,000
Loss from operations of discontinued segment	60,000
Gain on disposal of discontinued segment.	40,000
Income taxes:	
Amount applicable to ordinary operations.	40,000
Reduction applicable to loss from operations of discontinued segment	14,000
Amount applicable to gain on disposal of discontinued segment	8,000

Required
a.   Prepare a multiple-step income statement. (Disregard earnings per share.)
b.   Prepare a single-step income statement. (Disregard earnings per share.)

P14-2A. **Earnings per Share** Stanford Corporation began the year with 150,000 shares of common stock outstanding. On March 1, an additional 10,000 shares of common stock were issued. On August 1, another 16,000 shares of common stock were issued. On November 1, 12,000 shares of common stock were acquired as Treasury Stock. Stanford Corporation's net income for the calendar year is $489,000.   **LO4**

Required
Calculate the company's earnings per share.

P14-3A. **Earnings per Share and Multiple-Step Income Statement** The following summarized data relate to Robert Corporation's current operations: **LO1, 4**

Sales revenue.	$800,000
Cost of goods sold	460,000
Selling expenses	65,000
Administrative expenses.	72,000
Loss on sale of equipment	4,000
Income tax expense	42,000
Shares of common stock	
Outstanding at January 1	20,000 shares
Additional issued at May 1	7,000 shares
Additional issued at November 1	2,000 shares

Required
Prepare a multiple-step income statement for Robert Corporation for the year. Include earnings per share disclosure at the bottom of the income statement.

P14-4A. **Trend Percentages** Net sales, net income, and total asset figures for Janice Controls, Inc., for five consecutive years are given below. (Janice manufactures pollution controls.)   **LO2, 4**

	Annual Amounts (Thousands of Dollars)				
	Year 1	Year 2	Year 3	Year 4	Year 5
Net sales.	$72,000	$79,800	$85,275	$88,400	$94,700
Net income	3,200	3,650	4,000	4,250	4,790
Total assets.	42,500	45,000	48,700	51,000	54,900

Required
a.   Calculate trend percentages, using Year 1 as the base year.
b.   Calculate the return on sales for each year. (Rates above 2.8 percent are considered good for manufacturers of pollution controls; rates above 6.5 percent are considered very good.)
c.   Comment on the results of your analysis.

LO4   **P14-5A.**   **Changes in Various Ratios** Presented below is selected information for Turner Company:

	Current Year	Previous Year
Sales revenue.	$950,000	$850,000
Cost of goods sold	575,000	545,000
Interest expense.	20,000	20,000
Income tax expense	27,000	30,000
Net income.	65,000	55,000
Cash flow from operating activities.	70,000	60,000
Capital expenditures.	45,000	45,000
Accounts receivable (net), December 31	126,000	120,000
Inventory, December 31	196,000	160,000
Stockholders' equity, December 31	450,000	400,000
Total assets, December 31.	750,000	675,000

Required

a.   Calculate the following ratios for the current year. The previous year results are given for comparative purposes.

	Previous Year
Gross profit percentage	35.9 percent
Return on assets	8.3 percent
Return on sales	6.5 percent
Return on equity (no preferred stock was outstanding)	13.9 percent
Accounts receivable turnover	8.00
Average collection period	45.6 days
Inventory turnover.	3.61
Times-interest-earned ratio	5.25
Operating-cash-flow-to-capital-expenditures ratio	1.33

b.   Comment on the changes between the two years.

LO2, 3, 4   **P14-6A.**   **Ratios from Comparative and Common-Size Data** Consider the following financial statements for Benjamin Company.

During the current year, management obtained additional bond financing to enlarge its production facilities. The company faced higher production costs during the year for such things as fuel, materials, and freight. Because of temporary government price controls, a planned price increase on products was delayed several months.

As a holder of both common and preferred stock, you decide to analyze the financial statements:

BENJAMIN COMPANY Balance Sheets (Thousands of Dollars)	Dec. 31, Current Year	Dec. 31, Previous Year
Assets		
Cash and cash equivalents	$ 21,000	$ 12,000
Accounts receivable (net).	55,000	43,000
Inventory.	120,000	105,000
Prepaid expenses.	20,000	14,000
Plant and other assets (net)	471,000	411,000
Total assets.	$687,000	$585,000
Liabilities and Stockholders' Equity		
Current liabilities.	$ 93,000	$ 82,000
10% bonds payable.	225,000	160,000
9% Preferred stock, $50 par value	75,000	75,000
Common stock, $10 par value	200,000	200,000
Retained earnings	94,000	68,000
Total liabilities and stockholders' equity	$687,000	$585,000

BENJAMIN COMPANY Income Statements (Thousands of Dollars)		
	Current Year	**Previous Year**
Sales revenue.	$820,000	$680,000
Cost of goods sold	545,000	433,920
Gross profit on sales.	275,000	246,080
Selling and administrative expenses	175,000	149,200
Income before interest expense and income taxes	100,000	96,880
Interest expense.	23,000	16,000
Income before income taxes.	77,000	80,880
Income tax expense	15,000	19,000
Net income	$ 62,000	$ 61,880
Other financial data (thousands of dollars)		
Cash provided by operating activities	$ 65,200	$ 60,500
Preferred stock dividends	6,750	6,750

Required

a. Calculate the following for each year: current ratio, quick ratio, operating-cash-flow-to-current-liabilities ratio (current liabilities were $77,000,000 at January 1 of the previous year), inventory turnover (inventory was $87,000,000 at January 1, 2018), debt-to-equity ratio, times-interest-earned ratio, return on assets (total assets were $490,000,000 at January 1 of the previous year), and return on equity (stockholders' equity was $235,000,000 at January 1 of the previous year).

b. Calculate common-size percentages for each year's income statement.

c. Comment on the results of your analysis.

P14-7A. **Constructing Statements from Ratio Data** The following are the current year financial statements for Omni Company, with almost all dollar amounts missing: **LO4**

OMNI COMPANY Balance Sheet December 31				
Cash.	$?	Current liabilities.	$?
Accounts receivable (net).	?	8% bonds payable	?
Inventory.	?	Common stock	?
Equipment (net)	?	Retained earnings	950,000
		Total liabilities and	
Total assets.	$6,500,000	stockholders' equity.	$6,500,000

OMNI COMPANY Income Statement For the Year Ended December 31	
Sales revenue.	$?
Cost of goods sold	?
Gross profit	?
Selling and administrative expenses	?
Income before interest expense and income taxes	?
Interest expense.	80,000
Income before income taxes.	?
Income tax expense (20%).	?
Net income	$580,000

The following information is available about Omni Company's financial statements:

1. Quick ratio, 0.95.
2. Inventory turnover (inventory at January 1 was $924,000), 5 times.
3. Return on sales, 8.0 percent.

4. Accounts receivable turnover (accounts receivable (net) at January 1 were $860,000), 8 times.
5. Gross profit percentage, 32 percent.
6. Return on equity (stockholders' equity at January 1 was $3,300,000), 16 percent.
7. The interest expense relates to the bonds payable that were outstanding all year.

Required
Compute the missing amounts, and complete the financial statements of Omni Company. *Hint:* Complete the income statement first.

LO4   P14-8A.   Ratios Compared with Industry Averages Because you own the common stock of Jacob Corporation, a paper manufacturer, you decide to analyze the firm's performance for the most recent year. The following data are taken from the firm's latest annual report:

	Dec. 31, Current Year	Dec. 31, Previous Year
Quick assets.	$ 700,000	$ 552,000
Inventory and prepaid expenses.	372,000	312,000
Other assets.	4,788,000	4,200,000
Total assets.	$5,860,000	$5,064,000
Current liabilities.	$ 724,000	$ 564,000
10% bonds payable	1,440,000	1,440,000
8% Preferred stock, $100 par value	480,000	480,000
Common stock, $10 par value	2,700,000	2,160,000
Retained earnings	516,000	420,000
Total liabilities and stockholders' equity	$5,860,000	$5,064,000

For the current year, net sales amount to $12,500,000, net income is $550,000, and preferred stock dividends paid are $50,000.

Required
a. Calculate the following ratios for the current year:
   1. Return on sales
   2. Return on assets
   3. Return on equity
   4. Quick ratio
   5. Current ratio
   6. Debt-to-equity ratio
b. Trade association statistics and information provided by credit agencies reveal the following data on industry norms:

	Median	Upper Quartile
Return on sales	4.2 percent	8.6 percent
Return on assets	6.5 percent	11.2 percent
Return on equity	10.6 percent	16.3 percent
Quick ratio	1.0	1.8
Current ratio	1.8	3.0
Debt-to-equity-ratio.	1.08	0.66

Compare Jacob Corporation's performance with industry performance.

LO4   P14-9A.   Ratios Compared with Industry Averages Adams Plastics, Inc., manufactures various plastic and synthetic products. Financial statement data for the firm follow:

	Current Year (Thousands of Dollars, except Earnings per Share)
Sales revenue.	$825,000
Cost of goods sold	550,000
Net income.	50,500
Dividends.	17,500
Earnings per share.	4.04

ADAMS PLASTICS, INC. Balance Sheets (Thousands of Dollars)	Dec. 31, Current Year	Dec. 31, Previous Year
Assets		
Cash.	$ 2,100	$ 2,700
Accounts receivable (net).	66,900	60,900
Inventory.	148,000	140,000
Total current assets.	217,000	203,600
Plant assets (net)	215,000	194,000
Other assets.	13,900	4,000
Total assets.	$445,900	$401,600
Liabilities and Stockholders' Equity		
Notes payable—banks	$ 31,400	$ 25,000
Accounts payable	27,600	23,000
Accrued liabilities	25,100	24,800
Total current liabilities	84,100	72,800
10% bonds payable	150,000	150,000
Total liabilities	234,100	222,800
Common stock, $10 par value (12,500,000 shares).	125,000	125,000
Retained earnings	86,800	53,800
Total stockholders' equity	211,800	178,800
Total liabilities and stockholders' equity	$445,900	$401,600

Required

a. Using the given data, calculate items 1 through 8 below for the current year. Compare the performance of Adams Plastics, Inc., with the following industry averages and comment on its operations.

	Median Ratios for Manufacturers of Plastic and Synthetic Products
Quick ratio	1.2
Current ratio	1.9
Accounts receivable turnover	7.9 times
Inventory turnover.	7.8 times
Debt-to-equity ratio.	0.95
Gross profit percentage	32.7 percent
Return on sales	3.5 percent
Return on assets	6.3 percent

b. Calculate the dividends paid per share of common stock. What was the dividend payout ratio?

c. If the most recent price per share of common stock is $51.00, what is the price-earnings ratio? The dividend yield?

P14-10A. Financial Statement Notes: Quarterly Data Quarterly data are presented below for Company A and Company B. One of these companies is Gibson Greetings, Inc., which manufactures and sells greeting cards. The other company is Hon Industries, Inc., which manufactures and sells office furniture. Both companies are on a calendar-year basis.

LO2

	(Amounts in Thousands)				
	First Quarter	Second Quarter	Third Quarter	Fourth Quarter	Year
Company A					
Net sales.	$186,111	$177,537	$203,070	$213,608	$780,326
Gross profit	55,457	53,643	64,024	69,374	242,498
Company B					
Net sales.	$ 84,896	$ 83,796	$142,137	$235,336	$546,165
Gross profit	53,900	52,983	66,018	104,961	277,862

Required

a. Compute the percent of annual net sales generated each quarter by Company A. Round to the nearest percent.
b. Compute the percent of annual net sales generated each quarter by Company B. Round to the nearest percent.
c. Which company has the most seasonal business? Briefly explain.
d. Which company is Gibson Greetings, Inc.? Hon Industries, Inc.? Briefly explain.
e. Which company's interim quarterly data are probably most useful for predicting annual results? Briefly explain.

PROBLEMS—SET B

LO1   **P14-1B.**   **Income Statement Format** The following information from Jefferson Company's operations is available:

Administrative expenses.	$ 145,000
Cost of goods sold	928,000
Sales revenue.	1,850,000
Selling expenses	174,000
Interest expense.	14,000
Loss from operations of discontinued segment	120,000
Gain on disposal of discontinued segment.	90,000
Income taxes	
Amount applicable to ordinary operations.	125,000
Reduction applicable to loss from operations of discontinued segment	22,000
Amount applicable to gain on disposal of discontinued segment	15,000

Required

a. Prepare a multiple-step income statement. (Disregard earnings per share amounts.)
b. Prepare a single-step income statement. (Disregard earnings per share amounts.)

LO4   **P14-2B.**   **Earnings per Share** Lincoln Corporation began the year with 50,000 shares of common stock outstanding. On May 1, an additional 18,000 shares of common stock were issued. On July 1, 20,000 shares of common stock were acquired as treasury stock. On September 1, the 6,000 treasury shares of common stock were reissued. Lincoln Corporation's net income for the calendar year is $229,500.

Required

Compute earnings per share.

LO1, 4   **P14-3B.**   **Earnings per Share and Multiple-Step Income Statement** The following summarized data are related to Kennedy Corporation's operations:

Sales revenue.	$2,216,000
Cost of goods sold	1,290,000
Selling expenses	180,000
Administrative expenses.	142,800
Loss from plant strike.	95,000
Income tax expense	204,000
Shares of common stock	
Outstanding at January 1	65,000 shares
Additional issued at April 1	17,000 shares
Additional issued at August 1	3,000 shares

Required

Prepare a multiple-step income statement for Kennedy Corporation. Include an earnings per share disclosure at the bottom of the income statement. Kennedy Corporation has no preferred stock.

LO2, 4   **P14-4B.**   **Trend Percentages** Sales of automotive products for **Ford Motor Company** and **General Motors Corporation** for a five-year period are:

Net Sales of Automotive Products (Millions of Dollars)					
	Year 1	Year 2	Year 3	Year 4	Year 5
Ford Motor Company	$82,879	$81,844	$72,051	$ 84,407	$ 91,568
General Motors Corporation.	99,106	97,312	94,828	103,005	108,027

Net sales for **Pfizer Inc.** and **Abbott Laboratories** for the same five years follow:

FORD MOTOR
COMPANY

GENERAL MOTORS
CORPORATION

PFIZER INC.

ABBOTT
LABORATORIES

Net Sales (Millions of Dollars)					
	Year 1	Year 2	Year 3	Year 4	Year 5
Pfizer Inc.	$5,672	$6,406	$6,950	$7,230	$7,478
Abbott Laboratories	5,380	6,159	6,877	7,852	8,408

Required

a. Calculate trend percentages for all four companies, using Year 1 as the base year.
b. Comment on the trend percentages of Ford Motor Company and General Motors Corporation.
c. Comment on the trend percentages of Pfizer Inc. and Abbott Laboratories.

P14-5B. **Changes in Various Ratios** Selected information follow for Bush Company: **LO4**

	Current Year	Previous Year
Sales revenue.	$700,000	$520,000
Cost of goods sold	407,700	310,000
Interest expense.	22,000	14,000
Income tax expense	6,500	5,100
Net income	30,000	20,300
Cash flow from operating activities.	29,500	26,500
Capital expenditures.	42,000	25,000
Accounts receivable (net), December 31	182,000	128,000
Inventory, December 31	225,000	180,000
Stockholders' equity, December 31	205,000	165,000
Total assets, December 31.	460,000	350,000

Required

a. Calculate the following ratios for the current year. The previous year results are given for comparative purposes.

	Previous Year
Gross profit percentage	40.4 percent
Return on assets	6.5 percent
Return on sales	3.9 percent
Return on equity	14.2 percent
Accounts receivable turnover	4.77
Average collection period	76.5 days
Inventory turnover.	2.07
Times-interest-earned ratio	2.81
Operating-cash-flow-to-capital-expenditures ratio	1.06

b. Comment on the changes between the two years.

P14-6B. **Ratios from Comparative and Common-Size Data** Consider the following financial statements for Nixon Company.   **LO2, 3, 4**

During the year, management obtained additional bond financing to enlarge its production facilities. The plant addition produced a new high-margin product, which is supposed to improve the average rate of gross profit and return on sales.

As a potential investor, you decide to analyze the financial statements:

NIXON COMPANY Balance Sheets (Thousands of Dollars)	Dec. 31, Current Year	Dec. 31, Previous Year
Assets		
Cash.	$ 25,000	$ 18,100
Accounts receivable (net).	39,000	21,400
Inventory.	105,000	72,000
Prepaid expenses.	1,500	4,000
Plant and other assets (net)	463,500	427,500
Total assets.	$634,000	$543,000
Liabilities and Stockholders' Equity		
Current liabilities.	$ 80,000	$ 48,000
9% bonds payable	187,500	150,000
8% preferred stock, $50 par value	60,000	60,000
Common stock, $10 par value	225,000	225,000
Retained earnings	81,500	60,000
Total liabilities and stockholders' equity	$634,000	$543,000

NIXON COMPANY Income Statements (Thousands of Dollars)	Current Year	Previous Year
Sales revenue.	$850,000	$697,500
Cost of goods sold	552,000	465,000
Gross profit on sales.	298,000	232,500
Selling and administrative expenses	231,000	174,000
Income before interest expense and income taxes	67,000	58,500
Interest expense.	17,000	13,500
Income before income taxes.	50,000	45,000
Income tax expense	10,000	9,000
Net income	$ 40,000	$ 36,000
Other financial data (thousands of dollars):		
Cash provided by operating activities	$ 28,000	$ 24,000
Preferred stock dividends	5,000	4,800

Required

a. Calculate the following for each year: current ratio, quick ratio, operating-cash-flow-to-current-liabilities ratio (current liabilities were $40,000,000 at January 1 of the previous year), inventory turnover (inventory was $68,000,000 at January 1 of the previous year), debt-to-equity ratio, times-interest-earned ratio, return on assets (total assets were $490,000,000 at January 1 of the previous year), and return on equity (stockholders' equity was $265,000,000 at January 1 of the previous year).

b. Calculate the common-size percentage for each year's income statement.

c. Comment on the results of your analysis.

LO4   P14-7B.   Constructing Statements from Ratio Data The following are the financial statements for Truman Company, with almost all dollar amounts missing:

TRUMAN COMPANY Balance Sheet December 31			
Cash.	$?	Current liabilities.	$?
Accounts receivable (net).	?	10% bonds payable	144,000
Inventory.	?	Common stock	?
Equipment (net)	?	Retained earnings	50,000
Total assets.	$576,000	Total liabilities and stockholders' equity . . .	$576,000

TRUMAN COMPANY Income Statement For the Year Ended December 31	
Sales revenue.	$?
Cost of goods sold	?
Gross profit on sales.	?
Selling and administrative expenses	?
Income before interest expense and income taxes	?
Interest expense.	?
Income before income taxes.	?
Income tax expense (20%).	?
Net income	$70,200

The following information is available about Truman Company's financial statements:

1. Quick ratio, 2.5.
2. Current ratio, 3.0.
3. Return on sales, 8.0 percent.
4. Return on equity (stockholders' equity at January 1 was $340,000), 20 percent.
5. Gross profit percentage, 40 percent.
6. Accounts receivable turnover (accounts receivable (net) at January 1 were $97,200), 12 times.
7. The interest expense relates to the bonds payable that were outstanding all year.

Required
Compute the missing amounts, and complete the financial statements of Truman Company. (*Hint:* Complete the income statement first.)

P14-8B. **Ratios Compared with Industry Averages** You are analyzing the performance of Jackson Corpo-   **LO4** ration, a manufacturer of personal care products, for the most recent year. The following data are taken from the firm's latest annual report:

	Dec. 31, Current Year	Dec. 31, Previous Year
Quick assets.	$ 385,000	$ 350,000
Inventory and prepaid expenses.	975,000	820,000
Other assets.	4,165,000	3,700,000
Total assets.	$5,525,000	$4,870,000
Current liabilities.	$ 600,000	$ 500,000
10% bonds payable	1,300,000	1,300,000
7% preferred stock	900,000	900,000
Common stock, $5 par value	1,925,000	1,800,000
Retained earnings	800,000	370,000
Total liabilities and stockholders' equity	$5,525,000	$4,870,000

In the current year, net sales amount to $8,800,000, net income is $700,000, and preferred stock dividends paid are $70,000.

Required
a. Calculate the following for the current year:

1.	Return on sales	4.	Quick ratio
2.	Return on assets	5.	Current ratio
3.	Return on equity	6.	Debt-to-equity ratio

b. Trade association statistics and information provided by credit agencies reveal the following data on industry norms:

	Median	Upper Quartile
Return on sales	3.7 percent	10.6 percent
Return on assets	5.8 percent	14.2 percent
Return on equity	18.5 percent	34.2 percent
Quick ratio	1.0	1.8
Current ratio	2.2	3.7
Debt-to-equity ratio	1.07	0.37

Compare Jackson Corporation's performance with industry performance.

LO4   P14-9B.   Ratios Compared with Industry Averages Hardy Instruments, Inc., is a manufacturer of various measuring and controlling instruments. Financial statement data for the firm are as follows:

	Current Year (Thousands of Dollars, except Earnings per Share)
Sales revenue	$220,000
Cost of goods sold	125,000
Net income	10,000
Dividends	4,300
Earnings per share	5.00

HARDY INSTRUMENTS, INC.
Balance Sheets
(Thousands of Dollars)

	Dec. 31, Current Year	Dec. 31, Previous Year
Assets		
Cash	$ 20,000	$ 19,000
Accounts receivable (net)	46,000	43,000
Inventory	39,500	43,700
Total current assets	105,500	105,700
Plant assets (net)	52,600	51,500
Other assets	15,600	12,800
Total assets	$173,700	$170,000
Liabilities and Stockholders' Equity		
Notes payable—banks	$ 6,000	$ 6,000
Accounts payable	22,700	18,700
Accrued liabilities	18,000	24,000
Total current liabilities	46,700	48,700
9% bonds payable	40,000	40,000
Total liabilities	86,700	88,700
Common stock, $25 par value (2,000,000 shares)	50,000	50,000
Retained earnings	37,000	31,300
Total stockholders' equity	87,000	81,300
Total liabilities and stockholders' equity	$173,700	$170,000

Required

a. Using the given data, calculate ratios 1 through 8 for the current year. Compare the performance of Hardy Instruments, Inc., with the following industry averages and comment on its operations.

	Median Ratios for Manufacturers of Measuring and Controlling Instruments
Quick ratio	1.3
Current ratio	2.4
Accounts receivable turnover	5.9 times
Inventory turnover.	3.5 times
Debt-to-equity ratio.	0.73
Gross profit percentage	44.3 percent
Return on sales	4.7 percent
Return on assets	7.6 percent

b.   Calculate the dividends paid per share of common stock. What was the dividend payout ratio?

c.   If the most recent price per share of common stock is $65, what is the price-earnings ratio? The dividend yield?

P14-10B.   Financial Statement Notes: Quarterly Data   Past quarterly data are presented below for Company C and Company D. One of these companies is a children's specialty retail chain. The company's fiscal year ends on the Saturday nearest to January 31. The other company is a consumer goods company selling branded products worldwide. Their fiscal year ends on December 31.

LO2

			(Amounts in Millions)		
	First Quarter	Second Quarter	Third Quarter	Fourth Quarter	Year
Company C					
Net Sales	$1,216.6	$1,237.3	$1,339.7	$1,617.2	$5,410.8
Gross profit	753.1	773.6	839.0	1,000.8	3,366.5
Company D					
Net Sales	$1,172.5	$1,249.1	$1,345.8	$3,401.8	$7,169.2
Gross profit	362.5	384.6	423.2	1,030.3	2,200.6

Required

a.   Compute the percentage of annual net sales generated each quarter by Company C. Round to the nearest percent.

b.   Compute the percentage of annual net sales generated each quarter by Company D. Round to the nearest percent.

c.   Which company has the most seasonal business? Briefly explain.

d.   Which company is the children's specialty retail chain? The branded consumer products company? Briefly explain.

EXTENDING YOUR KNOWLEDGE

EYK14-1.   Financial Reporting Problem: Columbia Sportswear Company   The financial statements for the Columbia Sportswear Company can be found in Appendix A at the end of this book.

COLUMBIA
SPORTSWEAR
COMPANY

You are considering an investment in Columbia Sportswear after a recent outdoor trip in which you really liked some of the clothes you purchased from the company. You decide to do an analysis of the company's financial statements in order to help you make an informed decision.

Required

a.   Using the five-year selected financial data reported in the annual report, produce a five-year trend analysis, using 2016 as a base year, of (1) net sales, (2) net income, and (3) total assets. Comment on your findings.

b.   Calculate the (1) gross profit percentage, (2) return on sales, and (3) return on assets for 2019 and 2020. Comment on Columbia Sportswear's profitability. (2018 total assets = $2,368,721,000)

c.   Calculate the (1) current ratio, (2) quick ratio, and (3) operating-cash-flow-to-current liabilities ratio for 2019 and 2020 (2018 current liabilities = $572,882,000) Comment on Columbia Sportswear's liquidity.

d.   Calculate the debt-to-equity ratio for 2019 and 2020. Comment on Columbia Sportswear's solvency.

EYK14-2.   Comparative Analysis Problem: Columbia Sportswear Company vs Under Armour, Inc. The financial statements for the Columbia Sportswear Company can be found in Appendix A at the end of this book, and the financial statements of Under Armour, Inc., can be found in Appendix B. (The complete annual report is available on this book's website.)

Required
Based on the information from the financial statements of each company, do the following.

a.   Calculate the percentage change in (1) net sales, (2) net income, (3) cash flow from operating activities, and (4) total assets from 2019 to 2020.

b.   What conclusions can you draw from this analysis?

EYK14-3.   Business Decision Problem Crescent Paints, Inc., a paint manufacturer, has been in business for five years. The company has had modest profits and has experienced few operating difficulties until this year, 2022, when president Alice Becknell discussed her company's working capital problems with you, a loan officer at Granite Bank. Becknell explained that expanding her firm has created difficulties in meeting obligations when they come due and in taking advantage of cash discounts offered by manufacturers for the timely payment of the company's accounts payable. She would like to borrow $50,000 from Granite Bank. At your request, Becknell submits the following financial data for the past two years:

	2022	2021
Sales revenue.	$2,000,000	$1,750,000
Cost of goods sold	1,320,000	1,170,000
Net income	42,000	33,600
Dividends	22,000	18,000
December 31, 2017, data.		
Total assets.	1,100,000	
Accounts receivable (net).	205,000	
Inventory.	350,000	

CRESCENT PAINTS, INC. Balance Sheets	Dec. 31, 2022	Dec. 31, 2021
Assets		
Cash.	$ 31,000	$ 50,000
Accounts receivable (net).	345,000	250,000
Inventory.	525,000	425,000
Prepaid expenses.	11,000	6,000
Total current assets.	912,000	731,000
Plant assets (net)	483,000	444,000
Total assets.	$1,395,000	$ 1,175,000
Liabilities and Stockholders' Equity		
Notes payable—banks	$ 100,000	$ 35,000
Accounts payable	244,000	190,000
Accrued liabilities	96,000	85,000
Total current liabilities	440,000	310,000
10% mortgage payable.	190,000	250,000
Total liabilities	630,000	560,000
Common stock	665,000	535,000
Retained earnings	100,000	80,000
Total stockholders' equity	765,000	615,000
Total liabilities and stockholders' equity	$1,395,000	$1,175,000

Calculate the following items for both years from the given data and then compare them with the median ratios for paint manufacturers provided by a commercial credit firm:

	Median Ratios for Paint Manufacturers
Current ratio	2.5
Quick ratio	1.3
Accounts receivable turnover	8.1
Average collection period	44.9 days
Inventory turnover	4.9
Debt-to-equity ratio	0.78
Return on assets	4.8%
Return on sales	2.4%

Required

Based on your analysis, decide whether and under what circumstances you would grant Becknell's request for a loan. Explain the reasons for your decision.

EYK14-4. **Financial Analysis Problem** Listed below are selected financial data for three corporations: Honeywell International, Inc. (environmental controls), The Dow Chemical Company (chemicals and plastic products), and Abbott Laboratories (health care products). These data cover five years. (Year 5 is the most recent year; net income in thousands.)

HONEYWELL INTERNATIONAL, INC.
THE DOW CHEMICAL COMPANY
ABBOTT LABORATORIES

	Year 5	Year 4	Year 3	Year 2	Year 1
Honeywell International, Inc.					
Net income	$278,900	$322,200	$246,800	$331,100	$381,900
Earnings per common share	$2.15	$2.40	$1.78	$2.35	$2.52
Dividend per common share	$1.00	$0.91	$0.84	$0.77	$0.70
The Dow Chemical Company					
Net income	$938,000	$644,000	$276,000	$942,000	$1,384,000
Earnings per common share	$3.88	$2.33	$0.99	$3.46	$5.10
Dividend per common share	$2.60	$2.60	$2.60	$2.60	$2.60
Abbott Laboratories					
Net income*	$1,399,100	$1,239,100	$1,088,700	$965,800	$859,800
Earnings per common share*	$1.69	$1.47	$1.27	$1.11	$0.96
Dividend per common share	$0.68	$0.60	$0.50	$0.42	$0.35

*Before accounting change

Required

a. Calculate the dividend payout ratio for each company for each of the five years.
b. Companies may differ in their dividend policy; that is, they may differ in whether they emphasize a constant dividend amount per share, a steady growth in dividend amount per share, a target or constant dividend payout ratio, or some other criterion. Based on the data available, identify what appears to be each of the above firm's dividend policy over the five-year period.

EYK14-5. **Accounting Research Problem: General Mills, Inc.** The fiscal year 2020 annual report of General Mills, Inc., is available on this book's website.

GENERAL MILLS, INC.

Required

a. Calculate (or identify) the following financial ratios for 2019 and 2020:
   1. Gross profit percentage
   2. Return on sales
   3. Asset turnover (2018, total assets = $30,624.0 million)
   4. Return on assets (2018, total assets = $30,624.0 million)
   5. Return on equity (2018, total stockholders' equity = $6,141.1 million)
   6. Current ratio
   7. Quick ratio
   8. Operating-cash-flow-to-current-liabilities ratio (2018, current liabilities = $7,341.9 million)
   9. Accounts receivable turnover (2018, accounts receivable = $1,899.1 million)
   10. Average collection period

11. Inventory turnover (2018, inventory = $1,642.2 million)
12. Days' sales in inventory
13. Debt-to-equity ratio
14. Times-interest-earned ratio
15. Operating-cash-flow-to-capital-expenditures ratio
16. Earnings per share
17. Price-earnings ratio (Use year-end adjusted closing stock price of $63.04 for 2020 and $49.44 for 2019.)
18. Dividend yield
19. Dividend payout ratio

   b. Comment briefly on the changes from fiscal 2019 to fiscal 2020 in the ratios computed above.

EYK14-6. **Accounting Communication Activity** Pete Hollingsworth is currently taking an accounting course and is confused about what his professor told the class about analyzing financial statements. Pete would like you to lead a study session on the topic. In order to help everyone out, you decide to write a short memo describing some of the key points.

Required

Include the following items in your memo:

a. What is meant by trend analysis, and how is it helpful?

b. How are common-size statements constructed, and what are their uses?

c. What are a few common profitability, liquidity, and solvency ratios, and how are they interpreted?

d. What are some limitations of financial statement analysis?

EYK14-7. **Accounting Ethics Case** Chris Nelson, the new assistant controller for Grand Company, is preparing for the firm's year-end closing procedures. On December 30, 2022, a memorandum from the controller directed Nelson to make a journal entry debiting Cash and crediting Long-Term Advances to Officers for $1,000,000. Not finding the $1,000,000 in the cash deposit prepared for the bank that day, Nelson went to the controller for a further explanation. In response, the controller took from her desk drawer a check for $1,000,000 payable to Grand Company from Jason Grand, chief executive officer of the firm. Attached to the check was a note from Jason Grand saying that if this check were not needed to return it to him next week.

   "This check is paying off a $1,000,000 advance the firm made to Jason Grand six years ago," stated the controller. "Mr. Grand has done this every year since the advance; each time we have returned the check to him in January of the following year. We plan to do so again this time. In fact, when Mr. Grand retires in four years, I expect the board of directors will forgive this advance. However, if the firm really needed the cash, we would deposit the check."

   "Then why go through this charade each year?" inquired Nelson.

   "It dresses up our year-end balance sheet," replied the controller. "Certain financial statement ratios are improved significantly. Further, the notes to the financial statements don't have to reveal a related-party loan. Lots of firms engage in year-end transactions designed to dress up their financial statements."

Required

a. What financial statement ratios are improved by making the journal entry contained in the controller's memorandum?

b. Is the year-end handling of Jason Grand's advance an ethical practice? Discuss.

PROCTER & GAMBLE
COMPANY

E S G

EYK14-8. **Environmental, Social, and Governance Problem** The chapter's ESG box highlighted how Procter & Gamble (P&G) stands behind its commitment to uphold its responsibility as a good corporate citizen. Go to the P&G website and navigate to th annual citizenship report (under the Our Story tab). The report is broken into four sections: 1) Community Impact; 2) Equality & Inclusion; 3) Environmental Sustainability; and 4) Ethics & Corporate Responsibility. Choose any of these areas and report how P&G demonstrates its commitment to good corporate citizenship.

EYK14-9. **Forensic Accounting Problem** Accrual accounting is based on the principle that revenue should be reported when earned and that expenses associated with that revenue should be matched against the

revenue in the same period. Some financial statement frauds violate this fundamental concept in order to overstate net income in the current year. Provide an example of how this may be accomplished.

EYK14-10. Working with the Takeaways Below are income statements and balance sheets for the Peyton Company for 2022 and 2021:

PEYTON COMPANY Income Statement For the Years Ended December 31, 2022 and 2021		
(in millions)	2022	2021
Sales revenue.	$10,000	$9,500
Cost of goods sold	5,500	5,200
Gross profit.	4,500	4,300
Selling and administrative expenses	2,800	2,700
Income from operations	1,700	1,600
Interest expense.	300	250
Income before income taxes.	1,400	1,350
Income tax expense	420	400
Net income.	$ 980	$ 950

PEYTON COMPANY Balance Sheet December 31, 2022 and 2021		
(in millions)	2022	2021
Assets		
Current assets		
Cash and cash equivalents	$ 200	$ 400
Accounts receivable	900	800
Inventory.	700	650
Other current assets.	400	250
Total current assets	2,200	2,100
Property, plant, & equipment (net)	2,600	2,500
Other assets.	5,700	5,900
Total assets.	$10,500	$10,500
Liabilities and Stockholders' Equity		
Current liabilities.	$ 3,000	$ 2,900
Long-term liabilities	5,000	5,400
Total liabilities.	8,000	8,300
Stockholders' equity	2,500	2,200
Total liabilities and stockholders' equity	$10,500	$10,500

Required

Calculate the following ratios for the Peyton Company for 2022 and 2021 and discuss your findings:

1. Profitability
   a. Return on sales
   b. Return on equity (stockholders' equity was $2,000 on December 31, 2020)
2. Liquidity
   a. Current ratio
   b. Accounts receivable turnover (accounts receivable was $780 on December 31, 2020)
   c. Inventory turnover (inventory was $620 on December 31, 2020)
3. Solvency
   a. Debt-to-equity ratio
   b. Times-interest-earned ratio

EYK14-11. Analyzing IFRS Financial Statements The 2020 financial statements of **LVMH Moet Hennessey-Louis Vuitton S.A.** are presented in Appendix C at the end of this book. LVMH is a Paris-based holding company and one of the world's largest and best-known luxury goods companies. As a member of the European Union, French companies are required to prepare their consolidated (group) financial statements using International Financial Reporting Standards (IFRS). After reviewing LVMH's consolidated financial statements, calculate the following for 2020 and 2019:

a. Current ratio
b. Quick ratio
c. Accounts receivable turnover
d. Inventory turnover
e. Debt-to-equity ratio
f. Times-interest-earned ratio *(Hint: interest expense is called "Cost of net financial debt.")*
g. Return on sales
h. Return on assets
i. Return on equity

ANSWERS TO SELF-STUDY QUESTIONS:

1. c   2. c   3. c   4. b   5. b   6. c   7. d   8. b   9. c   10. b   11. c   12. d

YOUR TURN! SOLUTIONS

Solution 14.1

1. Persistent
2. Transitory
3. Transitory
4. Persistent
5. Transitory
6. Persistent

Solution 14.2

	Change in Current Year	
	Amount	Percent
Sales revenue............................	$50,000	6.7 percent [($800,000 − $750,000)/$750,000]
Net income.............................	20,000	20.0 percent [($120,000 − $100,000)/$100,000]
Total assets............................	10,000	3.4 percent [($300,000 − $290,000)/$290,000]

Solution 14.3

SANFORD COMPANY Income Statement For the Year Ended December 31		
	Amount	Percent
Sales revenue...	$13,500	100.0
Cost of goods sold	5,400	40.0
Gross profit..	8,100	60.0
Selling and administrative expenses	1,350	10.0
Income from operations	6,750	50.0
Interest expense..	675	5.0
Other expense	135	1.0
Income before income taxes...	5,940	44.0
Income tax expense	2,295	17.0
Net income..	$ 3,645	27.0

Solution 14.4

a. Gross profit percentage = ($30,000 − $10,500)/$30,000 = 65.0 percent
b. Return on sales = $4,500/$30,000 = 15.0 percent
c. Asset turnover = $30,000/$50,000 = 0.60
d. Return on assets = $4,500/$50,000 = 9.0 percent
e. Return on equity = $4,500/$35,000 = 12.9 percent

Solution 14.5

a. Working capital = $60,000 − $40,000 = $20,000
b. Current ratio = $60,000/$40,000 = 1.5
c. Operating-cash-flow-to-current-liabilities ratio = $55,000/$40,000 = 1.375
d. Accounts receivable turnover = $100,000/$15,000 = 6.67 times
e. Days' sales in inventory = 365/($70,000/$9,000) = 46.9 days

Solution 14.6

a. Debt-to-equity ratio = $180,000/$600,000 = 0.30
b. Times-interest-earned ratio = ($55,000 + $5,000 + $25,000)/$5,000 = 17.0 times
c. Operating-cash-flow-to-capital-expenditures ratio = $100,000/$30,000 = 3.33 times

Solution 14.7

a. Dividend yield = $1.50/$54.00 = 2.8 percent
b. Dividend payout ratio = $1.50/$4.50 = 33.3 percent
c. Price-earnings ratio = $54.00/$4.50 = 12.0

Appendix A
Accounting and the Time Value of Money

Road Map

LO	Learning Objective	Page	eLecture	Guided Example	Assignments
LO1	**Describe the nature of interest and distinguish between simple and compound interest.**	A-2	A-2	A-1	EA1A, EA1B
LO2	**Calculate future values.**	A-3	A-3	A-2, A-3	SS1, EA2A, EA3A, EA6A, EA8A, EA9A, EA11A, EA12A, EA14A, EA2B, EA3B, EA6B, EA8B, EA9B, EA11B, EA12B, EA14B
LO3	**Calculate present values.**	A-6	A-7	A-4, A-5	SS2, EA4A, EA5A, EA7A, EA10A, EA13A, EA15A, EA4B, EA5B, EA7B, EA10B, EA13B, EA15B

TIME VALUE OF MONEY CONCEPT

Would you rather receive a dollar now or a dollar one year from now? Most people would answer "a dollar now." Intuition tells us that a dollar received now is more valuable than the same amount received sometime in the future. Sound reasons exist for choosing the option of receiving the money sooner rather than later, the most obvious of which concerns risk. Because the future is always uncertain, some event may prevent you from receiving the dollar at a later date. To avoid this risk, we choose the earlier date.

LO1 Describe the nature of interest and **distinguish** between simple and compound interest.

MBC

A second reason for choosing the earlier date is that the dollar has a **time value**—that is, the dollar received now could be invested such that one year from now, you would have not only the original dollar but also the interest income on the dollar for the past year. **Interest** is a payment for the use of money, much like a rent payment for the use of an apartment. Interest is calculated by multiplying an interest rate, usually stated as an annual rate, by a principal amount for a period of time. The **principal** amount represents the amount to be repaid. The amount of interest can be computed as either a simple interest amount or a compound interest amount.

Time Value of Money: Simple Interest Model

Simple interest calculates interest on only the principal amount owed without considering any interest already earned. Simple interest is calculated using the following formula:

$$\textbf{Interest} = \textbf{p} \times \textbf{i} \times \textbf{n}$$

where

    p = principal
     i = interest rate for one period
    n = number of periods

For example, if you borrow \$3,000 for four years at a simple interest rate of 6 percent annually, the amount of simple interest would total \$720, calculated as \$3,000 × 0.06 × 4.

Time Value of Money: Compound Interest Model

Compound interest differs from simple interest because it is calculated on both the principal and any previously earned interest that has not been paid. In other words, compound interest involves computing interest on interest, along with the principal amount.

As we can see in **Exhibit A-1**, simple interest only uses the original \$3,000 principal to compute the annual interest in each of the four years. In contrast, compound interest uses the entire principal balance, including both the original \$3,000 principal and the accumulated interest to date, to compute the next year's interest. This results in increasing interest each year, with the result in **Exhibit A-1** for compound interest yielding a larger ending balance by \$67.43.

Because almost all businesses use compound interest, we will assume the use of compound interest in all of the illustrations in this appendix. Simple interest is generally only used in short-term credit arrangements, typically lasting less than a year.

EXHIBIT A-1	Illustration Comparing Simple Interest to Compound Interest					
	Simple Interest Model			**Compound Interest Model**		
	Interest Calculation	**Simple Interest**	**Principal Balance**	**Interest Calculation**	**Compound Interest**	**Principal Balance**
Year 1 ..	$3,000.00 × 6%	$180.00	$3,180.00	$3,000.00 × 6%	$180.00	$3,180.00
Year 2 ..	$3,000.00 × 6%	$180.00	$3,360.00	$3,180.00 × 6%	$190.80	$3,370.80
Year 3 ..	$3,000.00 × 6%	$180.00	$3,540.00	$3,370.80 × 6%	$202.25	$3,573.05
Year 4 ..	$3,000.00 × 6%	$180.00	$3,720.00	$3,573.05 × 6%	$214.38	$3,787.43
		$720.00			$787.43	

$720.00 ⟶ $67.43 difference ⟵ $787.43

YOUR TURN! A-1

The solution is on page A-14.

MBC

Scott Colin invests $100 in the bank for three years. Calculate the amount of interest that Scott will earn at the end of the three years assuming (1) simple interest at the annual rate of 10 percent, and (2) compound interest at the annual rate of 10 percent.

FUTURE VALUE OF AN AMOUNT

LO2 Calculate future values.

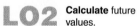

MBC

The **future value** of a single sum is the amount that a specified investment will be worth at a future date if invested at a given rate of compound interest. For example, suppose that we decide to invest $6,000 in a savings account that pays 6 percent annual interest, and that we intend to leave the principal and interest in the account for five years. Assuming that interest is credited to the account at the end of each year, the balance in the account at the end of five years is determined using the following formula:

$$FV = PV \times (1 + i)^n$$

where

FV = future value of an amount
PV = present value (today's value)
 i = interest rate for one period
 n = number of periods

The future value in this case is $8,029, computed as [$6,000 × (1.06)^5] = ($6,000 × 1.33823).

It is often easier to solve time value of money problems with the aid of a time diagram, as illustrated in **Exhibit A-2**. Time diagrams are drawn to show the timing of the various cash inflows and outflows. Note in **Exhibit A-2** that our initial $6,000 cash inflow (the amount deposited in a savings account) allows us to withdraw $8,029 (a cash outflow) at the end of five years.

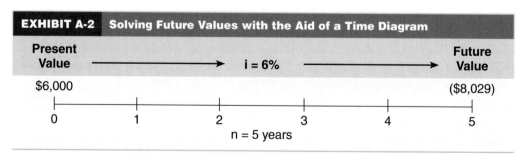

EXHIBIT A-2	Solving Future Values with the Aid of a Time Diagram

Present Value ⟶ i = 6% ⟶ Future Value

$6,000   ($8,029)

0   1   2   3   4   5

n = 5 years

We can also calculate the future value of a single amount with the use of a table like **Table I**, which presents the future value of a single dollar after a given number of time periods. Simply stated, future value tables provide a multiplier for many combinations of time periods and interest rates that, when applied to the dollar amount of a present value, determines its future value.

TABLE I	Future Value of $1											
Period	**1.0%**	**2.0%**	**3.0%**	**4.0%**	**5.0%**	**6.0%**	**7.0%**	**8.0%**	**9.0%**	**10.0%**	**11.0%**	**12.0%**
1	1.01000	1.02000	1.03000	1.04000	1.05000	1.06000	1.07000	1.08000	1.09000	1.10000	1.11000	1.12000
2	1.02010	1.04040	1.06090	1.08160	1.10250	1.12360	1.14490	1.16640	1.18810	1.21000	1.23210	1.25440
3	1.03030	1.06121	1.09273	1.12486	1.15763	1.19102	1.22504	1.25971	1.29503	1.33100	1.36763	1.40493
4	1.04060	1.08243	1.12551	1.16986	1.21551	1.26248	1.31080	1.36049	1.41158	1.46410	1.51807	1.57352
5	1.05101	1.10408	1.15927	1.21665	1.27628	1.33823	1.40255	1.46933	1.53862	1.61051	1.68506	1.76234
6	1.06152	1.12616	1.19405	1.26532	1.34010	1.41852	1.50073	1.58687	1.67710	1.77156	1.87041	1.97382
7	1.07214	1.14869	1.22987	1.31593	1.40710	1.50363	1.60578	1.71382	1.82804	1.94872	2.07616	2.21068
8	1.08286	1.17166	1.26677	1.36857	1.47746	1.59385	1.71819	1.85093	1.99256	2.14359	2.30454	2.47596
9	1.09369	1.19509	1.30477	1.42331	1.55133	1.68948	1.83846	1.99900	2.17189	2.35795	2.55804	2.77308
10	1.10462	1.21899	1.34392	1.48024	1.62889	1.79085	1.96715	2.15892	2.36736	2.59374	2.83942	3.10585
11	1.11567	1.24337	1.38423	1.53945	1.71034	1.89830	2.10485	2.33164	2.58043	2.85312	3.15176	3.47855
12	1.12683	1.26824	1.42576	1.60103	1.79586	2.01220	2.25219	2.51817	2.81266	3.13843	3.49845	3.89598
13	1.13809	1.29361	1.46853	1.66507	1.88565	2.13293	2.40985	2.71962	3.06580	3.45227	3.88328	4.36349
14	1.14947	1.31948	1.51259	1.73168	1.97993	2.26090	2.57853	2.93719	3.34173	3.79750	4.31044	4.88711
15	1.16097	1.34587	1.55797	1.80094	2.07893	2.39656	2.75903	3.17217	3.64248	4.17725	4.78459	5.47357
16	1.17258	1.37279	1.60471	1.87298	2.18287	2.54035	2.95216	3.42594	3.97031	4.59497	5.31089	6.13039
17	1.18430	1.40024	1.65285	1.94790	2.29202	2.69277	3.15882	3.70002	4.32763	5.05447	5.89509	6.86604
18	1.19615	1.42825	1.70243	2.02582	2.40662	2.85434	3.37993	3.99602	4.71712	5.55992	6.54355	7.68997
19	1.20811	1.45681	1.75351	2.10685	2.52695	3.02560	3.61653	4.31570	5.14166	6.11591	7.26334	8.61276
20	1.22019	1.48595	1.80611	2.19112	2.65330	3.20714	3.86968	4.66096	5.60441	6.72750	8.06231	9.64629
25	1.28243	1.64061	2.09378	2.66584	3.38635	4.29187	5.42743	6.84848	8.62308	10.83471	13.58546	17.00006
30	1.34785	1.81136	2.42726	3.24340	4.32194	5.74349	7.61226	10.06266	13.26768	17.44940	22.89230	29.95992
35	1.41660	1.99989	2.81386	3.94609	5.51602	7.68609	10.67658	14.78534	20.41397	28.10244	38.57485	52.79962
40	1.48886	2.20804	3.26204	4.80102	7.03999	10.28572	14.97446	21.72452	31.40942	45.25926	65.00087	93.05097
50	1.64463	2.69159	4.38391	7.10668	11.46740	18.42015	29.45703	46.90161	74.35752	117.39085	184.56483	289.00219

Future value tables are used as follows. First, determine the number of interest compounding periods involved (five years compounded annually are five periods, five years compounded semiannually are 10 periods, five years compounded quarterly are 20 periods, and so on). The extreme left-hand column indicates the number of periods covered in the table.

Second, determine the interest rate per compounding period. Note that interest rates are usually quoted on an annual or *per year* basis. Therefore, only in the case of annual compounding is the quoted interest rate the interest rate per compounding period. In other cases, the rate per compounding period is the annual rate divided by the number of compounding periods in a year. For example, an interest rate of 10 percent per year would be 10 percent for one compounding period if compounded annually, 5 percent for two compounding periods if compounded semiannually, and 2 ½ percent for four compounding periods if compounded quarterly.

Finally, locate the factor that is in the cell at the intersection of the appropriate number of compounding periods and the appropriate interest rate per compounding period. Multiply this factor by the number of dollars involved.

Note the logical progression of the multipliers in **Table I**. All values are greater than 1.0 because the future value is always greater than the $1 present amount if the interest rate is greater than zero. Also, as the interest rate increases (moving from left to right in the table) or the number of periods increases (moving from top to bottom), the multipliers become larger.

Continuing with our example of calculating the future value of a $6,000 savings account deposit earning 6 percent annual compound interest for five years, and using the multipliers from Table I, we solve for the future value of the deposit as follows:

Principal	×	Factor	=	Future Value
$6,000	×	1.33823	=	$8,029

The factor 1.33823 is in the row for five periods and the column for 6 percent. Note that this factor is the same as the multiplier we determined using the future value formula in our calculation above.

Suppose, instead, that the interest is credited to the savings account semiannually rather than annually. In this situation, there are 10 compounding periods, and we use a 3 percent rate (one-half the annual rate). The future value calculation using the **Table I** multipliers is as follows:

Principal	×	Factor	=	Future Value
$6,000	×	1.34392	=	$8,064

YOUR TURN! A-2

The solution is on page A-14.

MBC

Julie Penn invests $5,000 in the bank for four years. How much will be in her account at the end of the four years if the bank pays compound interest at the annual rate of 8 percent?

FUTURE VALUE OF AN ANNUITY

Using future value tables like **Table I**, we can calculate the future value of any single future cash flow or series of future cash flows. One frequent pattern of cash flows, however, is subject to a more convenient calculation. This pattern, known as an **annuity**, can be described as *equal amounts equally spaced over a period.*

For example, assume that $100 is to be deposited at the end of each of the next three years as an annuity into a savings account. When annuity cash flows occur at the *end* of each period, the annuity is called an **ordinary annuity**. As shown below in **Exhibit A-3**, the future value of this ordinary annuity can be calculated from **Table I** by calculating the future value of each of the three individual deposits and summing them (assuming 8 percent annual interest).

EXHIBIT A-3	**Future Value of an Ordinary Annuity**				
Future Deposits (ordinary annuity)				**FV Multiplier (Table I)**	**Future Value**
Year 1	**Year 2**	**Year 3**			
$100			×	1.16640	=	$116.64
	$100		×	1.08000	=	108.00
		$100	×	1.00000	=	100.00
				3.24640		$324.64

Table II, on the other hand, provides a single multiplier for calculating the future value of a series of future cash flows that reflect an ordinary annuity. Referring to **Table II** in the three periods row and the 8 percent interest column, we see that the multiplier is 3.24640, equal to the sum of the three future value factors in **Exhibit A-3**. When applied to the $100 annuity amount, the multiplier gives a future value of $324.64, or $100 × 3.2464. As shown above, the same future value is derived from the several multipliers of **Table I**. For annuities of 5, 10, or 20 years, numerous calculations are avoided by using annuity tables like **Table II**.

TABLE II	Future Value of an Ordinary Annuity of $1 per Period											
Period	1%	2%	3%	4%	5%	6%	7%	8%	9%	10%	11%	12%
1	1.00000	1.00000	1.00000	1.00000	1.00000	1.00000	1.00000	1.00000	1.00000	1.00000	1.00000	1.00000
2	2.01000	2.02000	2.03000	2.04000	2.05000	2.06000	2.07000	2.08000	2.09000	2.10000	2.11000	2.12000
3	3.03010	3.06040	3.09090	3.12160	3.15250	3.18360	3.21490	3.24640	3.27810	3.31000	3.34210	3.37440
4	4.06040	4.12161	4.18363	4.24646	4.31013	4.37462	4.43994	4.50611	4.57313	4.64100	4.70973	4.77933
5	5.10101	5.20404	5.30914	5.41632	5.52563	5.63709	5.75074	5.86660	5.98471	6.10510	6.22780	6.35285
6	6.15202	6.30812	6.46841	6.63298	6.80191	6.97532	7.15329	7.33593	7.52333	7.71561	7.91286	8.11519
7	7.21354	7.43428	7.66246	7.89829	8.14201	8.39384	8.65402	8.92280	9.20043	9.48717	9.78327	10.08901
8	8.28567	8.58297	8.89234	9.21423	9.54911	9.89747	10.25980	10.63663	11.02847	11.43589	11.85943	12.29969
9	9.36853	9.75463	10.15911	10.58280	11.02656	11.49132	11.97799	12.48756	13.02104	13.57948	14.16397	14.77566
10	10.46221	10.94972	11.46388	12.00611	12.57789	13.18079	13.81645	14.48656	15.19293	15.93742	16.72201	17.54874
11	11.56683	12.16872	12.80780	13.48635	14.20679	14.97164	15.78360	16.64549	17.56029	18.53117	19.56143	20.65458
12	12.68250	13.41209	14.19203	15.02581	15.91713	16.86994	17.88845	18.97713	20.14072	21.38428	22.71319	24.13313
13	13.80933	14.68033	15.61779	16.62684	17.71298	18.88214	20.14064	21.49530	22.95338	24.52271	26.21164	28.02911
14	14.94742	15.97394	17.08632	18.29191	19.59863	21.01507	22.55049	24.21492	26.01919	27.97498	30.09492	32.39260
15	16.09690	17.29342	18.59891	20.02359	21.57856	23.27597	25.12902	27.15211	29.36092	31.77248	34.40536	37.27971
16	17.25786	18.63929	20.15688	21.82453	23.65749	25.67253	27.88805	30.32428	33.00340	35.94973	39.18995	42.75328
17	18.43044	20.01207	21.76159	23.69751	25.84037	28.21288	30.84022	33.75023	36.97370	40.54470	44.50084	48.88367
18	19.61475	21.41231	23.41444	25.64541	28.13238	30.90565	33.99903	37.45024	41.30134	45.59917	50.39594	55.74971
19	20.81090	22.84056	25.11687	27.67123	30.53900	33.75999	37.37896	41.44626	46.01846	51.15909	56.93949	63.43968
20	22.01900	24.29737	26.87037	29.77808	33.06595	36.78559	40.99549	45.76196	51.16012	57.27500	64.20283	72.05244
25	28.24320	32.03030	36.45926	41.64591	47.72710	54.86451	63.24904	73.10594	84.70090	98.34706	114.41331	133.33387
30	34.78489	40.56808	47.57542	56.08494	66.43885	79.05819	94.46079	113.28321	136.30754	164.49402	199.02088	241.33268
35	41.66028	49.99448	60.46208	73.65222	90.32031	111.43478	138.23688	172.31680	215.71075	271.02437	341.58955	431.66350
40	48.88637	60.40198	75.40126	95.02552	120.79977	154.76197	199.63511	259.05652	337.88245	442.59256	581.82607	767.09142
50	64.46318	84.57940	112.79687	152.66708	209.34800	290.33590	406.52893	573.77016	815.08356	1163.90853	1668.77115	2400.01825

As another example, if we decide to invest $50 at the end of each six months for three years at an 8 percent annual rate of return, we would use the factor for six periods at 4 percent, as follows:

$$\text{Periodic Payment} \times \text{Factor} = \text{Future Value}$$
$$\$50 \times 6.63298 = \$331.65$$

Kathy Cole invests $100 monthly for 18 months at an annual rate of 12 percent. How much money will Kathy have at the end of the 18 months from her investment?	**YOUR TURN! A-3** The solution is on page A-14.

PRESENT VALUE OF AN AMOUNT

We can generalize that (1) the right to receive an amount of money now—its **present value**—is normally worth more than the right to receive the same amount later—its future value; (2) the longer we must wait to receive an amount, the less attractive the receipt is; and (3) the difference between the present value of an amount and its future value is a function of interest (Principal × Interest Rate × Time). Further, the more risk associated with any situation, the higher the appropriate interest rate.

LO3 Calculate present values.

We support these generalizations with an illustration. What amount should we accept now that would be as valuable as receiving $100 one year from now ($100 represents the future value) if the appropriate interest rate is 10 percent? We recognize intuitively that with a 10 percent interest rate, we should accept less than $100, or approximately $91. We base this estimate on the realization that the $100 received in the future must equal the present value (100 percent) plus 10 percent interest on the present value. Thus, in our example, the $100 future receipt must be 1.10 times the present value. Dividing $100 by 1.10, we obtain a present value of $90.91. In other words, under the given conditions, we would do as well to accept $90.91 now as to wait one year and receive $100. To confirm the equality of a $90.91 payment now with a $100 payment one year later, we calculate the future value of $90.91 at 10 percent for one year as follows:

$$\$90.91 \times 1.10 \times 1 \text{ year} = \$100 \text{ (rounded)}$$

Thus, we calculate the present value of a future receipt by discounting (deducting an interest factor) the future receipt back to the present at an appropriate interest rate. We present this schematically below:

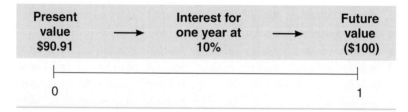

The formula for calculating the present value of a single amount is determined using the following formula:

$$PV = FV \times [1 \div (1 + i)^n]$$

where

    PV = present value of an amount
    FV = future value
      i = interest rate for one period
     n = number of periods

As can be seen from this formula, if either the number of periods (n) or the interest rate (i) is increased, the resulting present value would decrease. If more than one time period is involved, compound interest calculations are appropriate. **Exhibit A-4** illustrates the calculation of the present value of a single amount.

EXHIBIT A-4	Present Value of a Single Amount

How much must be deposited in a savings account today in order to have $1,000 in four years if the savings account pays 12 percent annual interest?

$$PV = \$1,000 \times [1 \div (1.12)^4] = (\$1,000 \times 0.63552) = \$636$$

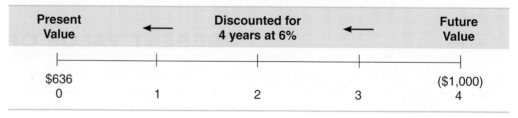

Table III can be used to calculate the present value amounts in a manner similar to the way we previously calculated future values using **Table I**. As with the future value tables, present value tables provide a multiplier for many combinations of time periods and interest rates that, when applied to the dollar amount of a future cash flow or annuity, determines its present value.

TABLE III	Present Value of $1											
Period	1%	2%	3%	4%	5%	6%	7%	8%	9%	10%	11%	12%
1	0.99010	0.98039	0.97087	0.96154	0.95238	0.94340	0.93458	0.92593	0.91743	0.90909	0.90090	0.89286
2	0.98030	0.96117	0.94260	0.92456	0.90703	0.89000	0.87344	0.85734	0.84168	0.82645	0.81162	0.79719
3	0.97059	0.94232	0.91514	0.88900	0.86384	0.83962	0.81630	0.79383	0.77218	0.75131	0.73119	0.71178
4	0.96098	0.92385	0.88849	0.85480	0.82270	0.79209	0.76290	0.73503	0.70843	0.68301	0.65873	0.63552
5	0.95147	0.90573	0.86261	0.82193	0.78353	0.74726	0.71299	0.68058	0.64993	0.62092	0.59345	0.56743
6	0.94205	0.88797	0.83748	0.79031	0.74622	0.70496	0.66634	0.63017	0.59627	0.56447	0.53464	0.50663
7	0.93272	0.87056	0.81309	0.75992	0.71068	0.66506	0.62275	0.58349	0.54703	0.51316	0.48166	0.45235
8	0.92348	0.85349	0.78941	0.73069	0.67684	0.62741	0.58201	0.54027	0.50187	0.46651	0.43393	0.40388
9	0.91434	0.83676	0.76642	0.70259	0.64461	0.59190	0.54393	0.50025	0.46043	0.42410	0.39092	0.36061
10	0.90529	0.82035	0.74409	0.67556	0.61391	0.55839	0.50835	0.46319	0.42241	0.38554	0.35218	0.32197
11	0.89632	0.80426	0.72242	0.64958	0.58468	0.52679	0.47509	0.42888	0.38753	0.35049	0.31728	0.28748
12	0.88745	0.78849	0.70138	0.62460	0.55684	0.49697	0.44401	0.39711	0.35553	0.31863	0.28584	0.25668
13	0.87866	0.77303	0.68095	0.60057	0.53032	0.46884	0.41496	0.36770	0.32618	0.28966	0.25751	0.22917
14	0.86996	0.75788	0.66112	0.57748	0.50507	0.44230	0.38782	0.34046	0.29925	0.26333	0.23199	0.20462
15	0.86135	0.74301	0.64186	0.55526	0.48102	0.41727	0.36245	0.31524	0.27454	0.23939	0.20900	0.18270
16	0.85282	0.72845	0.62317	0.53391	0.45811	0.39365	0.33873	0.29189	0.25187	0.21763	0.18829	0.16312
17	0.84438	0.71416	0.60502	0.51337	0.43630	0.37136	0.31657	0.27027	0.23107	0.19784	0.16963	0.14564
18	0.83602	0.70016	0.58739	0.49363	0.41552	0.35034	0.29586	0.25025	0.21199	0.17986	0.15282	0.13004
19	0.82774	0.68643	0.57029	0.47464	0.39573	0.33051	0.27651	0.23171	0.19449	0.16351	0.13768	0.11611
20	0.81954	0.67297	0.55368	0.45639	0.37689	0.31180	0.25842	0.21455	0.17843	0.14864	0.12403	0.10367
25	0.77977	0.60953	0.47761	0.37512	0.29530	0.23300	0.18425	0.14602	0.11597	0.09230	0.07361	0.05882
30	0.74192	0.55207	0.41199	0.30832	0.23138	0.17411	0.13137	0.09938	0.07537	0.05731	0.04368	0.03338
35	0.70591	0.50003	0.35538	0.25342	0.18129	0.13011	0.09366	0.06763	0.04899	0.03558	0.02592	0.01894
40	0.67165	0.45289	0.30656	0.20829	0.14205	0.09722	0.06678	0.04603	0.03184	0.02209	0.01538	0.01075
50	0.60804	0.37153	0.22811	0.14071	0.08720	0.05429	0.03395	0.02132	0.01345	0.00852	0.00542	0.00346

Exhibit A-5 illustrates calculations of present values using the factors in **Table III**. Note the logical progression of the multipliers in **Table III**. All values are less than 1.0 because the present value is always less than the future amount. Also, as the interest rate increases (moving from left to right in the table), or as the number of periods increases (moving from top to bottom), the multipliers become smaller.

EXHIBIT A-5	Present Value of a Single Amount Using Present Value Tables

Calculate the present value of $1,000 four years hence, at 12 percent interest compounded annually:

    Number of periods (one year, annually) = 4

    Interest rate per period (12%/1) = 12%

    Multiplier = 0.63552

    Present value = $1,000 × 0.63552 = $636

    (This result agrees with our earlier illustration.)

Calculate the present value of $116.99 two years hence, at 8 percent compounded semiannually:

    Number of periods (two years, semiannually) = 4

    Interest rate per period (8%/2) = 4%

    Multiplier = 0.85480

    Present value = $116.99 × 0.85480 = $100 (rounded)

YOUR TURN! A-4	Sabrina Flores wishes to have $2,500 in her bank account in three years. If she can earn 7 percent compounded annually, how much will she need to invest today?

The solution is on page A-14.

MBC

PRESENT VALUE OF AN ANNUITY

We can use present value tables like **Table III** to calculate the present value of any single future cash flow or series of future cash flows. For example, assume $100 is to be received at the end of each of the next three years as an annuity. As shown in **Exhibit A-6**, the present value of this ordinary annuity can be calculated from **Table III** as the present value of each of the three individual receipts and summing them (assuming 5 percent annual interest).

EXHIBIT A-6	Present Value of an Ordinary Annuity					
Future Receipts (ordinary annuity)				**PV Multiplier (Table III)**		**Present Value**
Year 1	**Year 2**	**Year 3**				
$100			×	0.95238	=	$ 95.24
	$100		×	0.90703	=	90.70
		$100	×	0.86384	=	86.38
				2.72325		$272.32

Table IV, on the other hand, provides a single multiplier for calculating the present value of a series of future cash flows that represent an ordinary annuity. Referring to **Table IV** in the three periods row and the 5 percent interest column, we see that the multiplier is 2.72325, equal to the sum of the three present value factors in **Exhibit A-6**. When applied to the $100 annuity amount, the multiplier gives a present value of $272.33 (with a $0.01 difference due to rounding).

TABLE IV	Present Value of an Ordinary Annuity of $1 per Period											
Period	1%	2%	3%	4%	5%	6%	7%	8%	9%	10%	11%	12%
1	0.99010	0.98039	0.97087	0.96154	0.95238	0.94340	0.93458	0.92593	0.91743	0.90909	0.90090	0.89286
2	1.97040	1.94156	1.91347	1.88609	1.85941	1.83339	1.80802	1.78326	1.75911	1.73554	1.71252	1.69005
3	2.94099	2.88388	2.82861	2.77509	2.72325	2.67301	2.62432	2.57710	2.53129	2.48685	2.44371	2.40183
4	3.90197	3.80773	3.71710	3.62990	3.54595	3.46511	3.38721	3.31213	3.23972	3.16987	3.10245	3.03735
5	4.85343	4.71346	4.57971	4.45182	4.32948	4.21236	4.10020	3.99271	3.88965	3.79079	3.69590	3.60478
6	5.79548	5.60143	5.41719	5.24214	5.07569	4.91732	4.76654	4.62288	4.48592	4.35526	4.23054	4.11141
7	6.72819	6.47199	6.23028	6.00205	5.78637	5.58238	5.38929	5.20637	5.03295	4.86842	4.71220	4.56376
8	7.65168	7.32548	7.01969	6.73274	6.46321	6.20979	5.97130	5.74664	5.53482	5.33493	5.14612	4.96764
9	8.56602	8.16224	7.78611	7.43533	7.10782	6.80169	6.51523	6.24689	5.99525	5.75902	5.53705	5.32825
10	9.47130	8.98259	8.53020	8.11090	7.72173	7.36009	7.02358	6.71008	6.41766	6.14457	5.88923	5.65022
11	10.36763	9.78685	9.25262	8.76048	8.30641	7.88687	7.49867	7.13896	6.80519	6.49506	6.20652	5.93770
12	11.25508	10.57534	9.95400	9.38507	8.86325	8.38384	7.94269	7.53608	7.16073	6.81369	6.49236	6.19437
13	12.13374	11.34837	10.63496	9.98565	9.39357	8.85268	8.35765	7.90378	7.48690	7.10336	6.74987	6.42355
14	13.00370	12.10625	11.29607	10.56312	9.89864	9.29498	8.74547	8.24424	7.78615	7.36669	6.98187	6.62817
15	13.86505	12.84926	11.93794	11.11839	10.37966	9.71225	9.10791	8.55948	8.06069	7.60608	7.19087	6.81086
16	14.71787	13.57771	12.56110	11.65230	10.83777	10.10590	9.44665	8.85137	8.31256	7.82371	7.37916	6.97399
17	15.56225	14.29187	13.16612	12.16567	11.27407	10.47726	9.76322	9.12164	8.54363	8.02155	7.54879	7.11963
18	16.39827	14.99203	13.75351	12.65930	11.68959	10.82760	10.05909	9.37189	8.75563	8.20141	7.70162	7.24967
19	17.22601	15.67846	14.32380	13.13394	12.08532	11.15812	10.33560	9.60360	8.95011	8.36492	7.83929	7.36578
20	18.04555	16.35143	14.87747	13.59033	12.46221	11.46992	10.59401	9.81815	9.12855	8.51356	7.96333	7.46944
25	22.02316	19.52346	17.41315	15.62208	14.09394	12.78336	11.65358	10.67478	9.82258	9.07704	8.42174	7.84314
30	25.80771	22.39646	19.60044	17.29203	15.37245	13.76483	12.40904	11.25778	10.27365	9.42691	8.69379	8.05518
35	29.40858	24.99862	21.48722	18.66461	16.37419	14.49825	12.94767	11.65457	10.56682	9.64416	8.85524	8.17550
40	32.83469	27.35548	23.11477	19.79277	17.15909	15.04630	13.33171	11.92461	10.75736	9.77905	8.95105	8.24378
50	39.19612	31.42361	25.72976	21.48218	18.25593	15.76186	13.80075	12.23348	10.96168	9.91481	9.04165	8.30450

Jamal Turner is planning to attend a four-year university. He hopes to save money from his current job so that he will have enough in the bank account when he starts college to allow him to withdraw $10,000 at the end of each of the four years. He expects to earn 6 percent compounded annually on his investment. How much money will he need in his bank account when he starts college?

YOUR TURN! A-5

The solution is on page A-14.

GuidedExample

MBC

CALCULATIONS USING A CALCULATOR AND A SPREADSHEET

While present value tables can provide a handy method to solve some time value of money problems, they are not suitable for many real-world situations. For example, many real-world interest rates are not even integers like those appearing in **Table I** through **Table IV**, nor are many problems limited to the number of time periods appearing in the tables. While it is still possible to solve these problems with the provided formulas, financial calculators and spreadsheet programs provide a much quicker solution. Financial calculators can be distinguished from other calculators by the presence of dedicated keys for present and future values, along with keys for the number of periods, interest rates, and annuity payments. There are many brands of financial calculators; however, all of them work in much the same way.[1]

---

[1] It is usually necessary to do some preliminary setup on a financial calculator before performing time value of money calculations. For example, the HP 10BII calculator has a default setting of monthly compounding. This may need to be changed if the problem calls for a different number of compounding periods, such as annual. In addition, the calculator assumes annuity payments occur at the end of each period. This will need to be changed if the problem requires beginning of period payments. See your calculator manual to determine how to make these setting changes.

SUMMARY OF LEARNING OBJECTIVES

LO1   **Describe the nature of interest and distinguish between simple and compound interest. (p. A-2)**
- Interest is payment for the use of money over time.
- Simple interest is computed only on the principal.
- Compound interest is computed on the accumulated principal including any earned interest that has not been paid.

LO2   **Calculate future values. (p. A-3)**
- The future value of a single amount is the amount that a specified investment will be worth at a future date if invested at a given rate of compound interest.
- The formula for calculating the future value of a single amount is $FV = PV \times (1 + i)^n$.
- Future value tables provide a multiplier for many combinations of time periods and interest rates that, when applied to the dollar amount of a present value, determines its future value.
- An annuity represents a special case of a pattern of cash flows where the cash flow amounts are of equal amounts and equally spaced over time.
- A separate table is available that provides a multiplier for the future value of an annuity rather than using separate multipliers from the future value of $1 table.

LO3   **Calculate present values. (p. A-7)**
- The right to receive an amount of money now—its present value—is normally worth more than the right to receive the same amount later—its future value.
- The formula for calculating the present value of a single amount is $PV = FV \times [1 \div (1 + i)^n]$.
- A separate table is available that provides a multiplier for the present value of an annuity rather than using separate multipliers from the present value of $1 table.

KEY TERMS

Annuity (p. A-5)	Interest (p. A-2)	Principal (p. A-2)
Compound interest (p. A-2)	Ordinary annuity (p. A-5)	Simple interest (p. A-2)
Future value (p. A-3)	Present value (p. A-7)	Time value (p. A-2)

Assignments with the ⬤ logo in the margin are available in BusinessCourse.
See the Preface of the book for details.

SELF-STUDY QUESTIONS

(Answers to Self-Study Questions are at the end of this appendix.)

LO2   1. **Calculate the future value of each of the following items.**
   a. $10,000 deposited in a savings account for ten years if the annual interest rate is
      1. Twelve percent compounded annually.
      2. Twelve percent compounded semiannually.
      3. Twelve percent compounded quarterly.
   b. $4,000 received at the end of each year for the next 10 years if the money earns interest at the rate of 4 percent compounded annually.
   c. $2,000 received semiannually for the next five years if the money earns interest at the rate of 8 percent compounded semiannually.
   d. $3,000 deposited each year for the next 10 years plus a single sum of $17,000 deposited today if the interest rate is 10 percent per year compounded annually.

LO3   2. **Calculate the present value of each of the following items.**
   a. $75,000 10 years hence if the annual interest rate is
      1. Eight percent compounded annually.
      2. Eight percent compounded semiannually.
      3. Eight percent compounded quarterly.
   b. $2,000 received at the end of each year for the next eight years if money is worth 10 percent per year compounded annually.

c. $500 received at the end of each six months for the next 15 years if the interest rate is 8 percent per year compounded semiannually.

d. $200,000 inheritance 10 years hence if money is worth 10 percent per year compounded annually.

e. $3,000 received each half year for the next 10 years plus a single sum of $60,000 at the end of 10 years if the interest rate is 12 percent per year compounded semiannually.

EXERCISES—SET A

EA-1A. Simple and Compound Interest   LO1

a. For each of the following notes, calculate the simple interest due at the end of the term.

Note	Principal	Rate	Term
1	$20,000	2%	6 years
2	$20,000	4%	4 years
3	$20,000	6%	3 years

b. Compute the amount of interest due at the end of the term for each of the above notes assuming interest is compounded annually.

EA-2A. Future Value Computation At the beginning of the year you deposit $5,000 in a savings account. How much will accumulate in three years if you earn 8 percent compounded annually?   LO2

EA-3A. Future Value Computation You deposit $5,000 at the end of every year for three years. How much will accumulate in three years if you earn 8 percent compounded annually?   LO2

EA-4A. Present Value Computation You will receive $5,000 in three years. What is the present value if you can earn 8 percent interest compounded annually?   LO3

EA-5A. Present Value Computation You receive $5,000 at the end of every year for three years. What is the present value of these receipts if you earn 8 percent compounded annually?   LO3

EA-6A. Future Value Computation What amount will be accumulated in four years if $10,000 is invested today at 6 percent interest compounded annually?   LO2

EA-7A. Present Value Computation You are scheduled to be paid $10,000 in four years. What amount today is equivalent to the $10,000 to be received in four years assuming interest is compounded annually at 6 percent?   LO3

EA-8A. Future Value Computation What amount will be accumulated in four years if $10,000 is invested every six months beginning in six months and ending four years from today? Interest will accumulate at an annual rate of 10 percent compounded semiannually.   LO2

EA-9A. Future Value Computation You are scheduled to receive $10,000 every six months for eight periods beginning in six months. What amount in four years is equivalent to the future series of payments assuming interest compounds at the annual rate of 8 percent compounded semiannually?   LO2

EA-10A. Present Value Computation Savanna, Inc., believes it will need $150,000 in five years to expand its operations. Savanna can earn 5 percent, compounded annually, if it deposits its money right now. How large of a deposit must Savanna make in order to have the necessary $150,000 in five years?   LO3

EA-11A. Future Value Computation Kate Company deposited $12,000 in the bank today, earning 8 percent interest. Kate plans to withdraw the money in five years. How much money will be available to withdraw assuming that interest is compounded (a) annually, (b) semiannually, and (c) quarterly?   LO2

EA-12A. Future Value Computation Stan Smith deposited $5,000 in a savings account today. The deposit will earn interest at the rate of 8 percent. How much will be available for Stan to withdraw in four years, assuming interest is compounded (a) annually, (b) semiannually, and (c) quarterly?   LO2

EA-13A. Present Value Computation Paul Jefferson made a deposit into his savings account three years ago, and earned interest at an annual rate of 8 percent. The deposit accumulated to $30,000. How much was initially deposited assuming that the interest was compounded (a) annually, (b) semiannually, and (c) quarterly?   LO3

LO2   **EA-14A. Future Value Computation** Kendal Jennings has decided to start saving for his daughter's college education by depositing $3,200 at the end of every year for 18 years. He has determined that he will be able to earn 6 percent interest compounded annually. He hopes to have at least $90,000 when his daughter starts college in 18 years. Will his savings plan be successful?

LO3   **EA-15A. Present Value Computation** Kershaw Bales won the state lottery and was given four choices for receiving her winnings.

1. Receive $500,000 right now.
2. Receive $540,000 in one year.
3. Receive $50,000 at the end of each year for 20 years.
4. Receive $45,000 at the end of each year for 30 years.

Assuming Kershaw can earn interest of 8 percent compounded annually, which option should Kershaw choose?

EXERCISES—SET B

LO1   **EA-1B. Simple and Compound Interest**

    a.   For each of the following notes, calculate the simple interest due at the end of the term.

Note	Principal	Rate	Term
1	$6,000	8%	8 years
2	$6,000	12%	5 years
3	$6,000	4%	2 years

    b.   Compute the amount of interest due at the end of the term for each of the above notes assuming interest is compounded annually.

LO2   **EA-2B. Future Value Computation** At the beginning of the year you deposit $1,500 in a savings account. How much will accumulate in four years if you earn 6 percent compounded annually?

LO2   **EA-3B. Future Value Computation** You deposit $1,500 at the end of every year for four years. How much will accumulate in four years if you earn 6 percent compounded annually?

LO3   **EA-4B. Present Value Computation** You will receive $1,500 in four years. What is the present value if you can earn 6 percent interest compounded annually?

LO3   **EA-5B. Present Value Computation** You receive $1,500 at the end of every year for four years. What is the present value of these receipts if you earn 6 percent compounded annually?

LO2   **EA-6B. Future Value Computation** What amount will be accumulated in six years if $5,000 is invested today at 4 percent interest compounded annually?

LO3   **EA-7B. Present Value Computation** You are scheduled to be paid $5,000 in 10 years. What amount today is equivalent to the $5,000 to be received in 10 years assuming interest is compounded annually at 6 percent?

LO2   **EA-8B. Future Value Computation** What amount will be accumulated in five years if $4,000 is invested every six months beginning in six months and ending five years from today? Interest will accumulate at an annual rate of 4 percent compounded semiannually.

LO2   **EA-9B. Future Value Computation** You are scheduled to receive $5,000 every six months for 12 periods beginning in six months. What amount in six years is equivalent to the future series of payments assuming interest compounds at the annual rate of 8 percent compounded semiannually?

LO3   **EA-10B. Present Value Computation** Mimi, Inc., believes it will need $150,000 in 10 years to expand its operations. Mimi can earn 8 percent, compounded annually, if it deposits its money right now. How large of a deposit must Mimi make in order to have the necessary $150,000 in 10 years?

LO2   **EA-11B. Future Value Computation** Zeus Company deposited $10,250 in the bank today, earning 8 percent interest. Zeus plans to withdraw the money in five years. How much money will be available to withdraw assuming that interest is compounded (a) annually, (b) semiannually, and (c) quarterly?

EA-12B. Future Value Computation Jason Smithton deposited $2,500 in a savings account today. The deposit will earn interest at the rate of 12 percent. How much will be available for Jason to withdraw in three years, assuming interest is compounded (a) annually, (b) semiannually, and (c) quarterly?   **LO2**

EA-13B. Present Value Computation Rose Gomez made a deposit into her savings account four years ago and earned interest at an annual rate of 12 percent. The deposit accumulated to $60,000. How much was initially deposited assuming that the interest was compounded (a) annually, (b) semiannually, and (c) quarterly?   **LO3**

EA-14B. Future Value Computation Herman Lett has decided to start saving for his daughter's college education by depositing $3,000 at the end of every year for 15 years. He has determined that he will be able to earn 6 percent interest compounded annually. He hopes to have at least $65,000 when his daughter starts college in 15 years. Will his savings plan be successful?   **LO2**

EA-15B. Present Value Computation Kelly Fullerton won the state lottery and was given four choices for receiving her winnings.   **LO3**

1. Receive $800,000 right now.
2. Receive $832,000 in one year.
3. Receive $120,000 at the end of each year for eight years.
4. Receive $46,400 at the end of each year for 30 years.

Assuming Kelly can earn interest of 4 percent compounded annually, which option should Kelly choose?

ANSWERS TO SELF-STUDY QUESTIONS:

1. *a.* 1. $10,000 × 3.10585 = $31,059
     2. $10,000 × 3.20714 = $32,071
     3. $10,000 × 3.26204 = $32,620

b. $ 4,000 × 12.00611 = $48,024

c. $ 2,000 × 12.00611 = $24,012

d. $ 3,000 × 15.93742 = $47,812
     $17,000 × 2.59374 = $44,094
                 $91,906

2. *a.* 1. $ 75,000 × 0.46319 = $34,739
     2. $ 75,000 × 0.45639 = $34,229
     3. $ 75,000 × 0.45289 = $33,967

b. $ 2,000 × 5.33493 = $10,670

c. $ 500 × 17.29203 = $ 8,646

d. $200,000 × 0.38554 = $77,108

e. $ 3,000 × 11.46992 = $34,410
     $ 60,000 × 0.31180 = $18,708
                  $53,118

YOUR TURN! SOLUTIONS

Solution A-1

(1)
Year	Calculation	Interest
1	$100 × 0.10 =	$10.00
2	$100 × 0.10 =	$10.00
3	$100 × 0.10 =	$10.00
Total		$30.00

(2)
Year	Calculation	Interest
1	$100 × 0.10 =	$10.00
2	$110 × 0.10 =	$11.00
3	$121 × 0.10 =	$12.10
Total		$33.10

Solution A-2
$5,000 × 1.36049 = $6,802.45

Solution A-3
$100 × 19.61475 = $1,961.48

Solution A-4
$2,500 × 0.81630 = $2,040.75

Solution A-5
$10,000 × 3.46511 = $34,651.10

Appendix B
Data Analytics

Road Map

LO	Learning Objective	Page	eLecture	Guided Example	Assignments
LO1	**Define Big Data and describe its four attributes.**	B-2	B-1		SS1
LO2	**Identify and define the four types of data analytics.**	B-3	B-1		SS2, EB6, EB7, EB8, EB9
LO3	**Describe the use of data analytics within the accounting profession.**	B-3	B-2		EB6, EB7, EB8, EB9, PB11, PB12, PB13, PB14, PB15, PB16, PB17, PB18, PB19, PB20, PB21, PB22, PB23, PB24, PB25
LO4	**Describe the analytics mindset.**	B-5	B-3		SS3, PB10, PB11, PB12, PB13, PB14, PB15, PB16, PB17, PB18, PB19, PB20, PB21, PB22, PB23, PB24, PB25
LO5	**Describe data visualization best practices.**	B-7	B-4		SS4, SS5, PB10, PB11, PB12, PB14, PB15, PB17, PB19, PB20, PB21, PB22

DATA ANALYTICS

Data analytics can broadly be defined as the process of examining sets of data with the goal of discovering useful information from patterns found in the data. Increasingly, this process is aided by computers running programs ranging from basic spreadsheet software, such as **Microsoft Excel** and **Google Sheets**, to specialized software, such as **Tableau** or **Power BI**. This technology can reveal trends and insights that would otherwise be lost in the overwhelming amount of data.

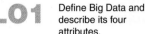

Define Big Data and describe its four attributes.

Big Data

The concept of data analytics is intertwined with the concept of **big data**. While no precise definition exists for big data, a commonly accepted definition is that big data is a collection of data that is both extremely large and also extremely complex, thus making its analysis beyond the scope of traditional tools. Important attributes of big data, commonly referred to as the four V's, are Volume, Variety, Velocity, and Veracity. **Volume** refers to the amount of data. According to IDC (a market intelligence company), there were 33 available zettabytes of data globally in 2018. IDC predicted that the amount of data would increase to 175 zettabytes by 2025. (Just so you know, there are 21 zeros in one zettabyte.) Total amounts of data are growing because we are creating more data (through new technologies) and because we are able to store more data (using cloud storage services like Amazon Web Services [AWS] and Microsoft Azure). Massive data sets can't be managed on a single machine. They must be stored in clusters over multiple physical or virtual machines.

Variety refers to the source of data. Data can be structured, semi-structured, or unstructured. Structured data can be contained in rows and columns and stored in spreadsheets or relational databases. Although most accounting data is structured, it is estimated that less than 20 percent of all data is structured.

Unstructured data cannot be easily contained in rows and columns and is therefore difficult to search and analyze. Photos, video and audio files, and social media content are examples of unstructured data.

Semi-structured data has characteristics of both structured and unstructured data. It may include some defining details but doesn't completely conform to a rigid structure. For example, the words in an email are unstructured data. The email date and the addresses of the sender and the recipient are structured data. Artificial intelligence algorithms are used to process unstructured and semi-structured data in a way that makes the information useable.

Velocity refers to the speed at which the data is being produced. The amount of data is not only growing; it's growing exponentially as more people gain internet access, and more technology is created that connects humans to machines and machines to machines. Collecting and translating data (especially unstructured data) into usable information is complicated by how quickly new data is generated.

Veracity refers to the quality of the data. Data quality can be negatively affected by untrustworthy data sources, inconsistent or missing data, statistical biases, and human error. The veracity of unstructured data is especially difficult to determine. Machine learning, a type of artificial intelligence based on the idea that systems can learn from data and can identify patterns, is often used to assess data quality.

In summary, a set of data would be considered "big data" if:

- The data set is too large to be managed by traditional methods.
- The data set includes a variety of types of data (structured, semi-structured, and unstructured).
- The amount of data in the data set is expanding rapidly.
- The accuracy and reliability of the data may be uncertain.

Types of Data Analytics

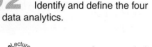

LO2 Identify and define the four types of data analytics.

eLecture MBC

Data analytics can be categorized into four main types, ranging in sophistication from relatively straightforward to very complex. The first category is **descriptive analytics**, which describes what has happened over a given period of time. Simple examples include determining sales trends over a period of time and the relative effectiveness of various social media promotions based on click-through rates. Microsoft Excel and other spreadsheet programs include built-in functions that greatly simplify performing descriptive analytics.

Diagnostic analytics focuses more on why something occurred. This data analytics technique is used to monitor changes in data and often includes a certain amount of hypothesizing: Did the marketing campaign lead to the increase in sales? Did changing the beverage items affect food choices? Did the opening of competing restaurants negatively impact sales growth? Diagnostic analytics is useful because past performance is often a reliable predictor of future outcomes and can greatly aid in planning and forecasting.

Whereas descriptive and diagnostic analytics use data to try to understand what happened and why, **predictive analytics** uses data to try to determine what *will* happen. The movie ***Moneyball*** made the general manager of the **Oakland Athletics**, Billy Beane, famous for using predictive analytics to make personnel decisions in professional baseball. In his evaluation of baseball players, Beane used data to predict player performance so he could assemble the team with the greatest likelihood of winning the World Series. Banks also use predictive analytics to identify and prevent fraudulent transactions by monitoring customer credit card transactions and red flagging those that deviate from a customer behavior profile that was developed from previous transaction and geographic data.

Prescriptive analytics moves beyond what is going to happen to suggesting a course of action for what *should* happen to optimize outcomes. The forecasts created using predictive analytics can be used to make recommendations for future courses of action. For example, if we own a sports bar and determine there is a high likelihood of our local sports team winning the championship this year, we should expand the bar area and add more big-screen televisions to maximize revenues. **Exhibit B.1** summarizes the four types of data analytics.

EXHIBIT B-1 The Four Types of Data Analytics

Type of Data Analytics	Purpose	Example
Descriptive	To explain what happened	What were sales by month last year?
Diagnostic	To understand why it happened	Did the new advertising campaign cause sales to increase last quarter?
Predictive	To predict what will happen	Does this credit card charge deviate (amount, location, etc.) from past purchases by this credit card holder?
Prescriptive	To determine what should happen	How many servers should be on the schedule for game nights?

Data Analytics in the Accounting Profession

LO3 Describe the use of data analytics within the accounting profession.

eLecture MBC

Accountants are already preparing descriptive analytic reports regularly. Comparative income statements, sales reports by location, inventory valuation reports, and ratio calculations (average collection periods, days' sales in inventory, etc.) are all examples of descriptive analytics.

Budget variance reports and segment reports by region or product line prepared by accountants can be used for diagnostic analytics. Accountants may also work with sales and production managers to analyze the reasons behind changes in operating results. A distributor might want to know how much of the increase in overall sales last year was caused by the transfer of two of its representatives to other sales regions. A grocery store manager might want to know if the winter storm last month impacted sales in all or just some of the various departments. A production manager might work with the accounting department to determine any correlation between equipment repair costs and the number of units produced over the last two years.

Data analytics should not be limited to only descriptive and diagnostic analysis. Accountants can provide even more value by employing predictive and prescriptive analytics. Accountants can obtain data from a variety of company sources, including enterprise resource planning systems, customer relationship management systems, and point-of-sale systems, to aid them in obtaining insight into future outcomes and providing guidance for future actions. The area of credit granting provides an example. Predictive analytics can help compute credit scores to predict the likelihood of future payments. As a result, prescriptive analytics can aid in suggesting terms for granting credit. Predictive analytics can also be used to help analyze outstanding accounts receivables and determine estimated credit losses based on how much time has elapsed since the credit sale took place.

Many other opportunities exist for accountants to utilize data analytics. Tax accountants can apply data analysis to unique tax issues to suggest optimal tax strategies. Accountants serving as investment advisors can use big data to find patterns in consumer behavior that others can use to build analytic models for identifying investment opportunities.

Perhaps no area of accounting can benefit more from an understanding of data analytics than auditing. Auditors employ data analytics to shift from the sample-based audit model to one based on continuous modeling of much larger data sets. This allows auditors to identify the riskiest areas of an audit by focusing on outliers and exceptions.

The major accounting firms have fully embraced the power of data analytics. **PricewaterhouseCoopers** (PWC), **Deloitte**, **Ernst & Young** (EY), and **KPMG** all devote significant staffing resources to provide data analytics services to their clients. These firms claim they can help their clients optimize their data assets to aid in faster and better decisions. For example, PWC provides a flowchart starting with the building of a data foundation and applies advanced analytics to improving business performance, ultimately leading to opportunities for innovation.

While computers and software are instrumental in the entire process, the human element is the most critical factor in the success of any data analytics program. One commonality among surveys of top company managers is the value placed on data analytics for the company's future. Another commonality is the need for professionals trained in data analytics to help the company attain its goals.

DATA ANALYTICS IN ACCOUNTING

Data Analytics

Benford's Law provides an example of how data analytics has been used to uncover fraud in a national call center. Forensic accountants utilized their knowledge of Benford's Law to form evidence of a problem by observing patterns in the data. According to Benford's Law, in any list of financial transactions, the number one should occur as the first digit 30.1 percent of the time, with each successive number occurring as the first digit in lesser percentages, with the number nine occurring less than 5 percent of the time. Forensic accountants examined issued refunds and noticed an excessively high occurrence of the number four. The forensic accountants learned that the company had a policy that required supervisor approval of refunds that exceeded $50. The accountants were able to identify a small group of operators who had been issuing fraudulent refunds to family, friends, and themselves. These fraudulent $40 refunds totaled several hundred thousand dollars.

In order to be useful, data needs to be analyzed. Technology has provided the analyst with powerful tools that allow big data to provide insights that would not have been possible in the past. Still, the most important tool in the analytics toolkit comes from the analyst. Without critical thinking and good judgement, the value would remain locked within the data.

The Analytics Mindset[1]

 Describe the analytics mindset.

The analytics mindset consists of a four-step process of (1) asking the right questions; (2) extracting, transforming, and loading the necessary data; (3) applying appropriate data analytics techniques; and (4) interpreting and presenting the results. **Exhibit B.2** summarizes the steps and requirements of an analytics mindset.

EXHIBIT B-2	Steps of an Analytics Mindset
Steps in the Analytics Mindset	**Requirements**
Ask the right questions	Understand the objectives of the end user Understand the underlying business processes
Extract, transform, and load the data	Know what to ask for Manage the data security Transform the data into the required format Cleanse the data for completeness and accuracy
Apply the appropriate analytics techniques	Determine if the need is for a confirmatory or an exploratory approach
Interpret and present the results	Use appropriate critical judgement regarding what you see Visually display the results in a format that is easy to understand without unnecessary clutter

Note that while technology is imbedded in this process, the process still begins and ends with the human element of asking the right questions and interpreting the results. Nothing is more critical than the first step of knowing what to ask. The right questions guide the process to find the right data to analyze and interpret.

Asking the right questions requires a few prerequisites. First, you need to know the audience that the analysis is for and what their objectives are. Next, you need to understand the context underlying the problem. For example, to analyze a marketing question you should understand the industry characteristics and the consumer demographics. Without this knowledge you may not select the correct indicators to analyze.

Along with knowing the right questions to ask, an analytical mindset requires you to form an idea of what to expect from the data. For example, when analyzing inventory salability, you would expect to see certain associated movements in sales and receivables.

After your questions are formed, you need to determine the data needed to aid in finding answers to those questions. This requires a knowledge of the data characteristics of the four V's previously mentioned. With this knowledge you can begin the data extraction process. Here you will need to know what data to ask for, how to manage data security, and what form the data will take.

Once you have the data, you will need to transform it into a format suitable for analysis. This is often referred to as data cleaning. Data is rarely found in the form of a nicely organized Excel spreadsheet. Rather, the data will often need to be converted into a proper format and tested for completeness and accuracy. Further, unnecessary data should be removed from the data set.

The data should then be loaded into the proper analysis tool, such as **Tableau** or Microsoft's **Power BI**. Once loaded, the data should again be cleansed to be sure it is ready for analysis in the chosen software.

It is necessary to determine the appropriate technique to analyze the data within the analysis tool. There are a multitude of ways that the data can be analyzed. Possible choices include

---

[1] The analytics mindset discussed here is an approach developed by the Ernst & Young Foundation.

computing ratios between associated measures, identifying trends among various measures, creating comparisons between dates, and sorting measures. The proper technique to use will be guided by the questions being asked.

In your interpretation of the data, you should ask yourself what do you see and is this what you expected? In other words, do these results make sense or did the results create new questions that require further analysis?

Eventually, the results must be packaged into a presentation that can be shared with the intended audience. Software such as Tableau, Power BI, or Excel can greatly enhance these presentations through their ability to create **visualizations** and **dashboards**. These visualizations can take many forms, from simple tables to bar or pie charts, to more sophisticated scatter plots, map charts, heat maps and more. Dashboards are created by combining multiple visualizations. Interactive dashboards allow users to filter out or drill down on content included in the charts and tables, on demand.

Data Analytic Tools

Technologies used by organizations to analyze data and communicate information to users are known as Business Intelligence (BI) tools. Data warehousing (data storage), data mining (extracting usable insights from data), and reporting and querying software are all BI tools.

Excel and Tableau are two popular BI tools that you will be using in the exercises and problems at the end of this Appendix.

Although Excel and Tableau can be used in similar ways, there are some important differences. Excel is a software application that is used for creating, organizing, and analyzing data. Tableau is a data visualization tool. Although calculations can be performed in Tableau, those calculations are made to create new fields for use in visualizations, not as support for accounting transactions. For example, Excel might be used to calculate sales commission amounts, which are then inputted into the accounting system. Tableau would not be used for that purpose.

Users in both Excel[2] and Tableau can

- Connect with different data sources
- Create visualizations and dashboards
- Work with big data sets

Tableau has much stronger interactivity tools and a more comprehensive selection of chart options. Excel generally has more flexibility and more extensive analytics tools.[3]

ACCESSING EXCEL AND TABLEAU

Excel, if not available to you through your school, can be accessed for free by creating a Microsoft account at https://office.live.com/start/Excel.aspx. A free version of Tableau (Tableau Public) is available to you at https://public.tableau.com/en-us/s/. Tableau Public has most of the functions of Tableau Desktop (the full version). However, you can't save your workbooks locally if you're using Tableau Public. Instead, all workbooks are saved online and are accessible to any Tableau user unless you elect to hide your visualizations. Hiding visualizations is done in Settings once you've registered for Tableau on the Tableau website. Walk-through videos are available for every exercise and problem at cambridgepub.com. Tableau tutorial videos are available at https://www.tableau.com/learn/training/.

Python and **R** are popular programming languages that are used for data analysis, particularly when working with big data sets. Although these are programming languages and not application software (Business Intelligence tools), they are relatively easy to code compared

---

[2] Full functionality in Excel is only available if you have Excel 2010 or newer and you are running a 64-bit version of Windows. To determine the version of Windows on your computer, go to Settings>System>About. The version will be listed in the Device specifications section.

[3] Pan and Blankley, Excel vs. Tableau: See your data differently, *Journal of Accountancy*, February 29, 2020.

to other languages and can be used to write software programs that perform powerful data analyses and visualizations.

Data Visualization

LO5 Describe data visualization best practices.

eLecture

MBC

As noted above, the final step in the analytics mindset is to present your results. This is often done in the form of a visualization. While it is possible to present results as a bunch of tables full of numbers, visualizations with imagery are often a far better means to convey the raw numbers. Visualizations can be thought of as a blending of the art of design with the science of data.

There is an unlimited number of ways that data can be presented; however, certain best practices exist that can serve as a guide when building a visualization. For example, the exact same data on GDP levels are shown in the three charts in **Exhibit B.3**, but each displays the data differently. The table presents the raw data; however, the reader cannot easily rank the different economies. The two bar charts both show the same data, however the one all in blue makes it far easier to compare economies by showing the data in sorted order. Also, note that adding multiple colors to the other bar chart does nothing to aid the reader, rather it just adds confusion.

Visualizations can be divided into two primary categories, exploratory and explanatory. **Exploratory visualizations** are meant to allow the reader to explore the data presented in order to do additional analysis. Exploratory visualizations would normally include interactive tools like filters that allow the user to change the level of data displayed. This can be useful when the problem is not clearly defined, and the reader wishes to gain a further understanding of the data.

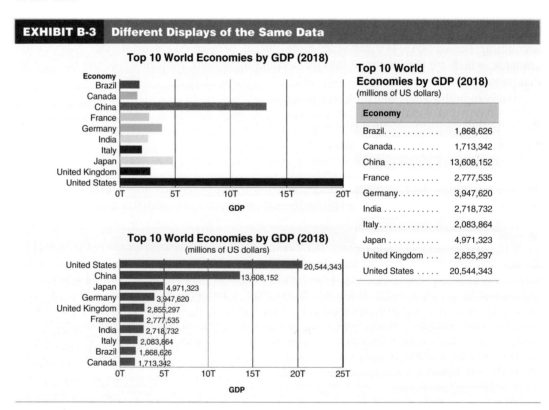

EXHIBIT B-3   Different Displays of the Same Data

In contrast to exploratory visualizations, **explanatory visualizations** are used to convey information to the audience. A classic example of such a visualization was prepared in 1854 by the British physician Dr. John Snow. Dr. Snow plotted cholera deaths in central London on a map that also showed the location of water pumps. The visualization identified the relationship between these deaths and the Broad Street water pump and lead to a change in the water and waste systems. Dr. Snow's visualization is shown in **Exhibit B.4**.

EXHIBIT B-4   **Cholera Deaths in London in 1854**

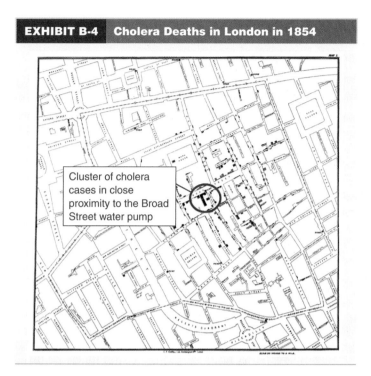

Good visualization design can be enhanced by considering how our brains process visual details such as form, position, and color.

For example, items that are different from the rest become the focus of attention as shown in **Exhibit B.5**. An item that is longer, wider, or in a different orientation will stand out, as will an item that is of a different size, shape, in a different position, or has a different hue or intensity of color.

EXHIBIT B-5   **Displays that Emphasize How Differences Focus Our Attention**

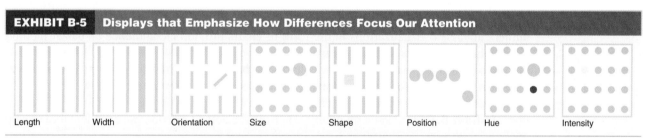

While the use of color can help an item to stand out, it is important to use color correctly. The use of too much color can add to visual clutter. And it's important that color is used consistently, such as always representing a certain year or category. The choice of color is also important since color can convey meanings that differ from one culture to another. For example, red may mean good luck and green may mean jealousy.

Good visualization design requires the removal of items that detract from the message that we are trying to communicate. **Visual clutter** confuses the audience and lessens the chance that they will be able to easily understand the information that is being conveyed. The concept that less is more is the essence of the visualization design principles developed by Edward Tufte, a statistician and professor emeritus at Yale University. Tufte uses the term chart-junk to refer to any unnecessary or confusing elements included in information displays. His principles show that "excellence in statistical graphics consists of ideas communicated with clarity, precision and efficiency."[4]

Exhibit B.6 illustrates **Tufte's principles**. Note in the first visualization all of the visual clutter only serves to distract the audience from seeing the main point that the U.S. is the largest

---

[4] E.R. Tufte, *The Visual Display of Quantitative Information* (Graphics Press, Cheshire, CT 2001).

economy based on its GDP. Now notice how much cleaner the second visualization is after removing the distracting yellow background, the color coding of each economy, the redundant labeling, and the unnecessary grid lines.

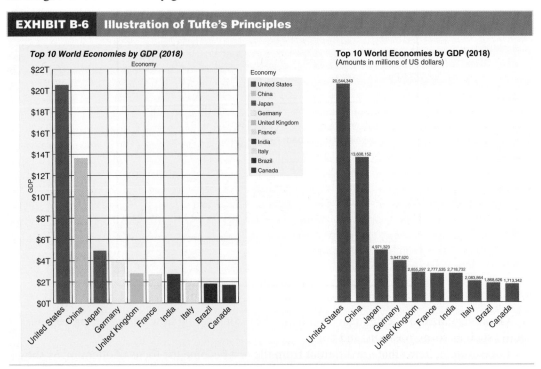

EXHIBIT B-6   Illustration of Tufte's Principles

Good visualization construction also involves choosing the most effective chart type depending on what information is being presented.

The starting point for all of the visualizations we will be discussing is a simple table of data. While the table is excellent for looking up values and can precisely communicate numerical values, visualizations in the form of charts provide the audience an easier method to see what the analyst is attempting to convey.

Among the most used chart types, column and bar charts are best for showing comparisons, line charts are useful for showing trends, pie charts are typically used for showing how individual parts make up a whole, and scatter plots are best for showing relationships and distributions. **Exhibit B.7**, reprinted with permission from the author, provides an excellent tool to help in choosing the correct chart type.[5]

Column (vertical) charts and **bar** (horizontal) charts are best used to compare different categories. Adding labels to the bars rather than just having values showing on the axes makes it easier for the audience to determine these values. Finally, avoid using too many colors that just add to visual clutter.

As a general rule, **line charts** are best for illustrating changes over time and work best with continuous data. Best practices include clearly labeling the axes so the audience knows what is being shown, removing excess clutter such as grid lines and redundant labeling, and avoiding comparing more than five to seven lines.

Pie charts are best used to show parts of a whole. Be sure the parts add up to 100 percent. Pie charts work best when there are just a few categories. If there are many categories of similar size, consider using a bar or column chart instead. Finally, avoid the temptation to get "fancy" with 3-D imagery and tilting the pie chart.

Scatter plots are useful if the goal is to show correlations between two variables. They are also useful for showing data distributions and clustering, which can identify anomalies

---

[5] Abela, Andrew V. (2013). *Advanced Presentations by Design: Creating Communication that Drives Action*. John Wiley & Sons.

EXHIBIT B-7 Chart Types

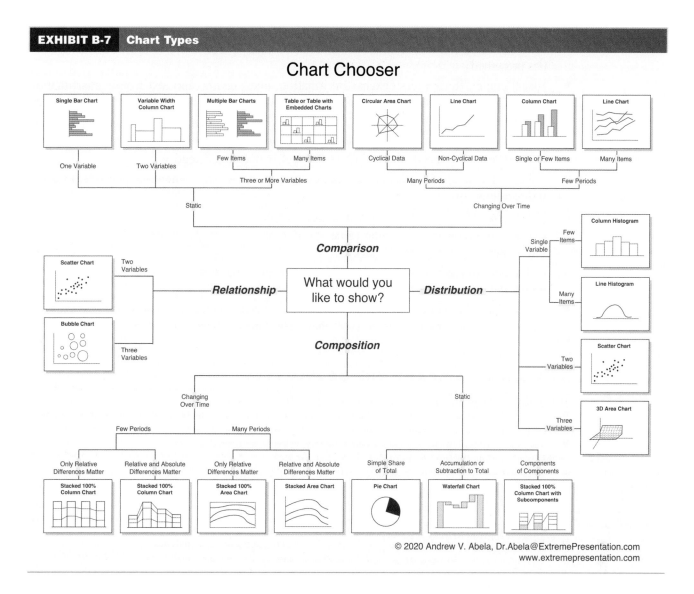

Chart Chooser

© 2020 Andrew V. Abela, Dr.Abela@ExtremePresentation.com
www.extremepresentation.com

and outliers. A **bubble chart** can extend the capability of a scatter plot by adding an additional dimension through changing the size of each bubble in the scatter plot. The more data that is included in a scatter plot or bubble chart, the better are the comparisons that can be made. If the elements being graphed are distributed over a very wide range, the horizontal axis can be converted from a linear to a logarithmic scale (where the numbers on the horizontal axis increase by multiples of a number). Bubble charts should use only circles rather than other shapes. Bubble charts should be scaled based on the area of the circle and not the diameter.

A **map chart** is a good choice if the data being conveyed in the visualization includes geographic locations. Map charts are best at showing relative differences in numerical values among geographic locations rather than precise differences since the values are usually portrayed as differences in a color gradient.

There are several general rules to follow regardless of the chart type. The following list was found from a search of best practices for data visualization charts.[6]

■ Time axis. When using time in charts, set it on the horizontal axis. Time should run from left to right. Do not skip values (time periods), even if there are no values.

[6] https://eazybi.com/blog/data_visualization_and_chart_types/

- Proportional values. The numbers in a chart (displayed as bar, area, bubble, or other physically measured element in the chart) should be directly proportional to the numerical quantities presented.
- Visual clutter. Remove any excess information, lines, colors, and text from a chart that do not add value.
- Sorting. For column and bar charts, to enable easier comparison, sort your data in ascending or descending order by the value, not alphabetically. This applies also to pie charts.
- Legend. You don't need a legend if you have only one data category.
- Labels. Use labels directly on the line, column, bar, pie, etc., whenever possible, to avoid indirect look-up.
- Colors. In any chart, don't use more than six colors.
- Colors. For comparing the same value at different time periods, use the same color in a different intensity (from light to dark).
- Colors. For different categories, use different colors. The most widely used colors are black, white, red, green, blue, and yellow.
- Colors. Keep the same color palette or style for all charts in the series and the same axes and labels for similar charts to make your charts consistent and easy to compare.

SUMMARY OF LEARNING OBJECTIVES

LO1 **Define Big Data and describe its four attributes. (p. B-2)**
- Big data is a collection of data that is both extremely large and also extremely complex, thus making its analysis beyond the scope of traditional tools.
- The four attributes of Big Data are volume, variety, velocity, and veracity.

LO2 **Identify and define the four types of data analytics. (p. B-3)**
- Data analytics can broadly be defined as the process of examining sets of data with the goal of discovering useful information from patterns found in the data.
- Data analytics can be categorized into four types: descriptive, diagnostic, predictive, and prescriptive.

LO3 **Describe the use of data analytics within the accounting profession. (p. B-3)**
- Many accountants are already performing descriptive and diagnositc data analytics.
- Accountants can add value by performing predictive and prescriptive data analytics.
- The large accounting firms have devoted large resources to data analytics.
- Being well trained in data analytics is important for future accountants.

LO4 **Describe the analytics mindset. (p. B-4)**
- Analytics is the process of deriving value from the data.
- An analytics mindset requires critical thinking and judgement.
- The four steps of the analytics mindset include (1) asking the right questions; (2) extracting, transforming, and loading the data; (3) applying the proper analytics techniques; and (4) interpreting and presenting the results.

LO5 **Describe data visualization best practices. (p. B-7)**
- Form, position, and color can be used to have elements stand out without any conscious effort by the audience.
- Tufte's principles of design emphasize the elimination of visual clutter that serves to distract from the ability of a visualization to convey its message.
- Use of the proper chart type can help the intended audience to visualize comparisons, compositions, distributions, and relationships in the data.

KEY TERMS

Bar (p. B-9)	Bubble chart (p. B-10)	Data analytics (p. B-2)
Benford's Law (p. B-4)	Column chart (p. B-9)	Descriptive analytics (p. B-3)
Big data (p. B-2)	Dashboards (p. B-6)	Diagnostic analytics (p. B-3)

Assignments with the ⓂⒷⒸ logo in the margin are available in ᵐʸBusinessCourse.
See the Preface of the book for details.

QUESTIONS

1. **Which of the following are four characteristics of big data?**   LO1
   a. Volume, variety, vagueness, veracity
   b. Volume, variety, velocity, veracity
   c. Volume, validate, velocity, veracity
   d. Volume, variety, velocity, vulnerability

2. **Which of the following are the four categories of data analytics?**   LO2
   a. Descriptive, diagnostic, predictive, prescriptive
   b. Expressive, diagnostic, predictive, prescriptive
   c. Descriptive, analytical, predictive, prescriptive
   d. Descriptive, diagnostic, prognostic, prescriptive

3. **What is the correct order of the steps in the analytics mindset?**   LO4
   a. Extract, transform, and load the data; ask the right questions; apply the proper analytics techniques; interpret and present the results.
   b. Ask the right questions; extract, transform, and load the data; apply the proper analytics techniques; interpret and present the results.
   c. Ask the right questions; extract, transform, and load the data; interpret and present the results; apply the proper analytics techniques.
   d. Ask the right questions; apply the proper analytics techniques; extract, transform, and load the data; interpret and present the results.

4. **Charts are used in visualizations to convey the following primary types of information:**   LO5
   a. comparisons, compositions, distributions, and relationships.
   b. comparisons, historical, distributions, and relationships.
   c. comparisons, compositions, forecasts, and relationships.
   d. geographical, compositions, distributions, and relationships.

5. **Which of the following statements is not true regarding the use of color in a chart?**   LO5
   a. Use at most six different colors in a chart.
   b. To show changes in an item over time use a color gradient rather than different colors.
   c. Always use color in a chart to differentiate items.
   d. Use the same color palette in a chart series.

EXERCISES

EB-6. **Public Accounting Firms and Data Analytics** Go to PWC.com and select "Services" and then "Data and Analytics." Choose a topic and write about how PWC is using data analytics to help its clients.   LO2, 3

EB-7. **Public Accounting Firms and Data Analytics** Go to KPMG.com and select "Insights." Under "Areas of interest," select "Special Attention" and then "Data and Analytics." Choose a topic and write about how KPMG is using data analytics to help its clients.   LO2, 3

EB-8. **Public Accounting Firms and Data Analytics** Go to Deloitte.com and select "Services" and then "Analytics." Choose a topic and write about how Deloitte is using data analytics to help its clients.   LO2, 3

LO2, 3   **EB-9.**   **Public Accounting Firms and Data Analytics** Go to EY.com and enter Big data and analytics in the search bar. Choose a topic and write about how Ernst & Young is using data analytics to help its clients.

PROBLEMS

Problems PB-10 through PB-12 use financial statement data for S&P 500 companies for the years 2015 through 2019. The Excel file Compustat SP500 2015_2019.xlsx is accessible on the textbook's website. A video demonstrating Tableau tools used to answer the questions in the next two problems is also available on the website.

LO4, 5   **PB-10.**   **Building Basic Tableau Visualizations**

a.   Connect the Tableau software to the Excel file Compustat SP500 2015_2019.xlsx. This file consists of four workbooks. First bring in the Balance sheet workbook and then join both the cash flow statement and the income statement workbook to the balance sheet workbook using both of the fields company name and year.

b.   What is the sum of net income for all firms in the database for all years combined? One way to determine this is to drag the measure Net income to the canvas.

c.   How many unique companies are included in the database? One way to determine this is to drag the dimension Company name to the rows shelf and then select Measure Count(Distinct) from the pull down menu on the Company name pill.

d.   How many distinct firms are there in each segment? One way to determine this is to drag the dimension Segment to the Columns shelf in the visualization created in part *c*. The totals for each segment will appear if the Show marks label is checked in the Label card.

e.   What is the sum of total assets for all companies in each segment for the year 2018? One way to determine this is to drag the dimension Segment to the Columns shelf and then drag the Total Assets measure to the Rows shelf. Next drag the Year dimension to the filters shelf, select year as the filter, click next and then check 2018. Totals for total assets can be seen in the tool tip by hovering over any bar or by checking Show marks label in the Label card.

f.   What firm had the most sales in 2018? What segment was this firm in? One way to determine this is to drag the dimension Company name to the rows shelf and drag the measure Sales to the columns shelf. Next drag the Year dimension to the filters shelf, select year as the filter, click next and then check 2018. Segments can be highlighted by dragging the dimension Segment over the color card. Finally sort the Company names by Sales by clicking the sort icon in the tool bar.

g.   Save the file for future use.

LO3, 4, 5   **PB-11.**   **Tableau Visualizations to Analyze Accounting Performance Measures** You recently joined a firm as a junior financial analyst, and you would like to make a good impression by showing your manager the power of visualizations for analyzing data. In order to get a feel for the Tableau software and the dataset you created of financial statement data for S&P 500 firms, you decided to create a few very basic visualizations. Two widely used ratios to analyze company performance are gross profit percentage and return on sales. You decide to create a visualization that compares these two ratios by segment and further compares segment performance to the median values of these ratios for the entire database of companies.

a.   Because of the way cost of goods sold is reported for companies in the real estate segment you decide to exclude this segment from the visualization. After excluding real estate, for the year 2017, which segment reported the highest median value for gross profit percentage and for return on sales?

b.   Did any segment report a higher median return on sales than the upper band of the 95 percent confidence interval of overall median return on sales in 2015?

c.   What company had the highest gross profit percentage in 2018 for the segment with the highest median gross profit percentage?

LO3, 4   **PB-12.**   **Using Tableau to Analyze Inventory** You have learned of the importance of a company being able to sell its products in a timely fashion, and that the ratio of days sales in inventory provides this useful information. You decide a dashboard would be helpful in seeing if this ratio is improving or declining in the consumer discretionary and the consumer staples segments between 2017 and 2018. You build two sheets that are included in the dashboard. The first sheet shows the level of the ratio for each segment for the two years in question. The second sheet shows the change in the ratio between the two years.

Has the ratio days sales in inventory improved or declined in the consumer discretionary and the consumer staples segments between 2017 and 2018. By how much?

PB-13. **Using Tableau for Fraud Detection** Benford's Law represents a powerful tool in the forensic accountant's toolkit to aid in the detection of fraud. Benford's Law is a mathematical law that recognizes the leading (first) digit in many real-life number sets is distributed in a certain manner, and often not in the manner that a fraudster would expect. Specifically the number 1 occurs as the first digit approximately 30 percent of the time, with each succeeding digit appearing less often as follows: 1–30%, 2–18%, 3–12%, 4–10%, 5–8%, 6–7%, 7–6%, 8–5%, and 9–5%. Fraudsters who are unaware of this natural ordering will often arrange digits in a random order that deviates from Benford's Law.

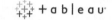

LO3, 4

In Part A of this problem you will use Tableau to show how a natural data set of GDP by country conforms to Benford's Law and how a random set of numbers does not. In Part B you will use the same data used in an actual court case to convict a fraudster of embezzlement. Finally, in Part C you will use Benford's Law to test a new reimbursement procedure for possible fraud. A video demonstrating the Tableau tools used in this problem is available on this textbook's website.

Part A Use Tableau to show how a natural data set of GDP by country conforms to Benford's Law and how a random set of numbers does not.

- Download the file **GDP Tableau.xlsx** from the textbook website. The file contains World Bank GDP data by country for 2018, along with a separate column of random numbers that was generated in Excel using the command =RAND()*1000.
- After you have uploaded the workbook to Tableau, create two calculated fields.
- The first calculated field will pull the first digit from each country's GDP amount. Choose Analysis > Create Calculated Field and name the calculation First Integer. Then either type or paste the following formula in the formula area: LEFT(STR([GDP]),1)
- Next create a second calculated field named Benfords Law by typing or pasting the following in the formula area: LOG(INT([First Integer])+1)- LOG(INT([First Integer]))
- To create the visualization, drag First Integer from the Dimensions area to Columns and drag Number of Records from the Measures area to Rows. Click Sum(Number of Records) on Rows to show the pull-down menu and choose Quick Table Calculation > Percent of Total. The visualization should now show a bar chart with the bars conforming to Benford's Law.
- While it is relatively easy to see that the data conforms to Benford's Law, with a little more work the visualization can be significantly enhanced. To do this, drag Benfords Law from the Measures area of the Data pane to Detail on the Marks card, and then click Benfords Law on the Marks card and choose Measure > Minimum.
- Next switch from the current Data pane to the Analytics pane and then drag Distribution Band over the chart and drop it on the cell icon in the pop-up. A dialog box will appear. Under computation change the value to percentages of 90,100,110 and select Percent of to be Min(Benfords Law). Choose a fill line as the thick black line and then click OK.
- Finally click on the Label icon in the Marks section and select the Show marks labels box.

a. Does the GDP data appear to conform to Benford's Law?

Now return to the Data pane and create a new calculated field for the random numbers by naming the calculation Random Values and typing or pasting the following formula in the formula area: LEFT(STR([Random]),1)

- Drag the Min(Benfords Law) pill out of the Marks area to remove the bands and drag Random Values from the Dimensions area on top of First Integer to replace it in the visualization. If both pills remain in the columns section, simply drag First Integer away.

b. Do the random values appear to conform with Benford's Law?

Part B Use the same data used in an actual court case to convict a fraudster of embezzlement.

In the 1993 court case *State of Arizona v. Wayne James Nelson* Benford's Law was used to convict the defendant of defrauding the state of nearly $2 million by diverting money to a nonexistent vendor. Nelson tried to make the checks appear random; however, he was unaware that these check amounts should actually follow Benford's Law much closer than the random distribution he created. Download the file **Arizona Fraud.xlsx** from the textbook website and follow the same procedure as you did in Part A above and use Tableau to show how the data conforms to Benford's Law.

a.   From a casual observation of the checks, can you detect anything suspect?

b.   After using Benford's Law, does the list of checks appear suspect?

Part C Use Benford's Law to test a new reimbursement procedure for possible fraud.

Wally's Enterprises has been reimbursing its employees for business expenses after the employee submits detailed evidence of the expense, such as paid receipts. Management has recently changed the reimbursement policy because of the time spent checking all the submitted evidence, with an especially high volume of smaller reimbursement requests. The new policy only requires evidence be submitted if the reimbursement request exceeds $50. As the company's internal auditor, you are concerned that this policy change may result in fraudulent reimbursement requests. In order to test the new policy, you have gathered a random sample of 100 reimbursement requests from both before and after the policy change. This data is located in the file **Expense Reimbursement.xlsx** on the textbook's web page. Download this file and using Tableau, apply Benford's Law to test whether the new policy appears to have resulted in any fraud.

a.   Do the reimbursement requests prior to the policy change appear to follow Benford's Law?

b.   Do the reimbursement requests occurring after the policy change appear to follow Benford's Law?

c.   What, if anything, leads you to believe that fraud may be occurring?

LO3, 4, 5   PB-14.   Segment Reports Using Tableau (Descriptive and Diagnostic Analytics) Southern Comforts, Inc. is a department store chain with stores in North Carolina, Tennessee, Kentucky, and West Virginia. Its corporate headquarters are located in Charlotte, North Carolina.

In the past, the store owners only received financial reports for the company operations overall. They have recently asked for reports of costs and profitability by segment (Location and department). Southern Comforts' locations include the four stores (Charlotte, Nashville, Virginia Beach, and Louisville) and the corporate office (Charlotte HQ). Departments include the product lines (Mens, Womens, Kids, Shoes, and Home) and the overhead expense types (Facilities, Labor, and Other).

They have provided you with an Excel workbook that includes Southern Comfort transactions for 2020. (The workbook, **Segment Report Data Set Tableau.xlsx**, is accessible on the textbook's website. A video demonstrating Tableau tools used to answer the questions in this problem is also available on the website.)

The first step is to make sure the data is in the form needed.

- Convert the data to a table.

- Check each column to make sure there is no missing or inconsistent data. Make any corrections necessary. *HINT:* There are two errors. One error is in the Month column. The other is in the State column.

- All transactions are included in the Transactions column. You will need to separate revenue transactions from expense transactions. Use the IF function to create a Revenues column and an Expenses column. (All positive numbers in the Transactions columns are Revenues; all negative numbers are expenses. You may want to change the sign of the amounts in the Expense column to positives.)

- Add a column after Month and call it Month Name. Use the TEXT function to convert the date format to a text format (name of the month).

Save the file with a new name. Open Tableau and import the workbook.

1.   Create Sheets in Tableau to answer the following questions:

a.   Which store was the most profitable (in dollars)? What was that store's profit? Which store had the most revenue? How much?

b.   Which month had the highest revenue? How much? What percentage of total sales occurred during that month? (Round % to two decimals.) Which month was the least **profitable** (in dollars)? What was the net profit that month? *HINT:* You will need to include the corporate costs to determine net profit.

c.   What was the total gross margin (in dollars) for 2020? Which store had the highest gross margin? How much? *HINT:* You will need to filter out the overhead expense categories (Facilities, Labor, and Other).

    d. What was the total gross profit ratio for 2020? (Round % to two decimals.) Which store had the lowest gross profit ratio? Which product line (department) had the highest gross profit ratio?

2. The store with the highest sales (b.) and the highest gross margin (d.) was not the most profitable (a.). Why? Look at the revenues, gross profit margins and ratios, and the overhead expenses for both stores.

3. Create charts on your Sheets and use them to create an interactive dashboard. Include filters to allow users to look at selected data.

PB-15. Job Profitability Using Tableau (Descriptive and Diagnostic Analytics)   Harvard Products is a job shop (a company that manufactures custom products in small batches). Each batch is managed by one of Harvard's four project managers. Manufacturing facilities are located in Illinois, Wisconsin, Michigan, and Indiana.

LO3, 4, 5

    The President of Harvard Products has asked for information about costs and profits by job, Location, customer, and project manager. A summary of costs (by job) is included in the **Job Order Data Set-Tableau.xlsx** file available on the textbook's website. A video demonstrating Tableau tools used to answer the questions in this problem is also available on the website.

    Before uploading the workbook to Tableau, add columns to the Data sheet to separate out account amounts (revenue, direct material, etc.). The IF function is useful here.

    Once you've uploaded the workbook to Tableau, change the data type for Job # to text. (It should be a Dimension, not a Measure.) Give Location a geographic role.

    Create sheets in Tableau to answer the following questions:

1. Which customer was the most profitable for Harvard? What was the job number for the most profitable job for that customer? What was the average revenue on jobs for that customer ? What was the average revenue for all jobs?

2. Which Location was the least profitable (in dollars) for Harvard? What appears to have contributed more to the lower profits at that Location—size of jobs (average revenue) or profit margin ratios? Which Location had the highest average revenue per job?

HINT: To answer the next three questions, you will need to create four new fields. One for the gross profit ratio and one for the three expense ratios.

3. Which Location had the highest gross profit ratio? Which cost element had the highest expense ratio in that Location? What Location had the lowest gross profit ratio? Which cost element had the highest expense ratio in that Location? Which cost element had the largest expense ratio difference between Locations? What factors might be causing those differences?

4. The President of Harvard Products has decided to give performance bonuses to project managers. Determine which project manager will receive the highest bonus if performance is based on:
    a. Average revenue per job?
    b. Number of jobs? *HINT:* You'll need to duplicate Job # to get a count. (Counts would be Measures.)
    c. Total profit?
    d. Profit margin ratios?

5. Create a Dashboard the president could use when evaluating different bonus calculation performance measures. Use a map for one of the sheets included in the dashboard.

6. Based solely on the information you have available, would you encourage management to close the facility with the lowest profit margin? Why or why not? Include in your answer the information you might need to have before making a final decision.

PB-16. Determining Fixed vs. Variable Cost Components Using Tableau (Diagnostic Analytics)   Genessee Industries introduced a new product last year (6582-D). Although it was very popular, it wasn't very profitable. Management has asked you to provide them with information to help them set a new sales price.

LO3, 4

    You know that the direct costs per unit are $25 for direct materials and $5 for direct labor. You are given information about last year's monthly production levels and manufacturing overhead costs (indirect materials, indirect labor, and other). (That information is included in the **Fixed and Variable Data Set Tableau.xlsx** file available on the textbook's website. A video demonstrating Tableau tools used to answer the questions in this problem is also available on the website.)

1. Use the Trendline tool in Tableau to determine the fixed and variable components for each of the three manufacturing overhead components. Use the default model type (linear). (Round all amounts to two decimals.)

    a. What is the cost formula for indirect materials?

    b. What is the cost formula for indirect labor?

    c. What is the cost formula for other manufacturing overhead?

2. What is the cost formula for 6582-D (per month)?

3. Determine the minimum sales price Genessee could charge to achieve a monthly gross profit of $7,500 next year. Management expects unit sales will average 1,500 per month. *HINT:* You won't be able to use Tableau for this. Start by determining the CVP formula.

LO3, 4, 5 **PB-17.** **Forecasting Using Tableau (Predictive Analytics)**

Melton Manufacturing opened in January 2019. Sales have increased significantly in the first two years of operations, and management is now looking to expand production capacity. To finance the purchase of a new factory, they would need to either raise capital or borrow funds.

They have asked you to make some projections for the next year of operations. They intend to share these with potential investors and lenders.

Information about unit sales, sales revenues, and net profits for the past two years is included in the **Forecasting Data Set Tableau.xlsx** file available on the textbook's website. (A video demonstrating Tableau tools used to answer the questions in this problem is also available on the website.)

1. Create a worksheet that shows revenues, net operating income, and units sold by month. Add a Forecast. *HINT:* There will be three graphs

    a. Extend the trendline out for one full year. Since you have complete data for each month, do not ignore the last month of 2020.

    b. Use a prediction interval of 95%

2. Use the forecasts to determine:

    a. Expected unit sales in October 2021

    b. Expected sales revenue in June 2021

    c. Expected net operating income in December 2021

3. Open the Describe Forecast screen. Use the Summary tab to determine:

    a. What percent of the forecast was attributed to seasonality for net operating income?

    b. What was the range given for number of units sold for January 2021?

5. Duplicate the worksheet as a cross-tab and swap the axes. Filter out details for net operating income and units sold. For December 2021, what is Tableau's:

    a. estimate?

    b. lower prediction interval?

    c. upper prediction interval?

6. How could Melton use forecasts to manage or expand the business?

A video demonstrating the use of Microsoft Excel to use Benford's Law in the detection of fraud is available on the textbook's website to assist in solving problem PB-18.

LO3, 4 **PB-18.** **Using Excel for Fraud Detection**

Benford's Law represents a powerful tool in the forensic accountant's toolkit to aid in the detection of fraud. Benford's Law is a mathematical law that recognizes the leading (first) digit in many real-life number sets is distributed in a certain manner, and often not in the manner that a fraudster would expect. Specifically the number 1 occurs as the first digit approximately 30 percent of the time, with each succeeding digit appearing less often as follows: 1–30%, 2–18%, 3–12%, 4–10%, 5–8%, 6–7%, 7–6%, 8–5%, and 9–5%. Fraudsters who are unaware of this natural ordering will often arrange digits in a random order that deviates from Benford's Law.

In Part A of this problem you will use Microsoft Excel to show how a natural data set of GDP by country conforms to Benford's Law and how a random set of numbers does not. In Part B you will use the same data used in an actual court case to convict a fraudster of embezzlement. Finally, in Part C you will use Benford's Law to test a new reimbursement procedure for possible fraud. A video demonstrating the Excel tools used in this problem is available on the textbook's website.

Part A Use Microsoft Excel to show how a natural data set of GDP by country conforms to Benford's Law and how a random set of numbers does not.

- Download the file **GDP.xlsx** from the textbook website. The file contains World Bank GDP data by country for 2018.

- In order to use Benford's Law you need to first extract the leading digit from each country's GDP amount. To do this, place the cursor in cell C2 and input the formula =Left(B2,1). Copy this formula down column C for each country.
- Next in cells F2 through F10 input the numbers 1 through 9. In cell G2 input the formula =COUNTIF(c2:C205,F2) and copy the formula down for each number 1 through 9. This formula goes through the entire range of extracted first digits in column C and records the count of these digits in the cell if it matches the number in column F.
- Sum the column total in cell G11.
- Next determine the percentage that each leading digit appears by dividing the amount in column G by the total of these amounts in cell G11 and place this figure in column H.
- In column I, compute the predicted occurrences of each digit (given above) by placing the formula =Log10(1/F2+1) in cell I2 and copying the formula down the column.
- Finally create a Combo chart to visualize these results by highlighting cells H1:I10 and selecting Combo chart.

a. Do the naturally occurring GDP amounts appear to follow Benford's Law?

- Next replace the GDP amounts with random numbers to see if random numbers also obey Benford's Law.
- Input the formula =Rand()*1000 in cell B2 and copy this formula down the column.
- Observe the results in the table and the chart. Try to recalculate the spreadsheet several times to obtain different sets of random numbers.

b. Do random numbers appear to follow Benford's Law?

Part B Use the same data used in an actual court case to convict a fraudster of embezzlement.

In the 1993 court case *State of Arizona v. Wayne James Nelson* Benford's Law was used to convict the defendant of defrauding the state of nearly $2 million by diverting money to a nonexistent vendor. Nelson tried to make the checks appear random; however, he was unaware that these check amounts should actually follow Benford's Law much closer than the distribution he created. Download the file **Arizona fraud.xlsx** from the textbook website and follow the same procedure as you did in Part A above.

a. From a casual observation of the checks, can you detect anything suspect?
b. After using Benford's Law, does the list of checks appear suspect?

Part C Use Benford's Law to test a new reimbursement procedure for possible fraud.

Jimmy's Enterprises has been reimbursing its employees for business expenses after the employee submits detailed evidence of the expense, such as paid receipts. Management has recently changed the reimbursement policy because of the time spent checking all the submitted evidence, with an especially high volume of smaller reimbursement requests. The new policy requires evidence be submitted only if the reimbursement request exceeds $50. As the company's internal auditor, you are concerned that this policy change may result in fraudulent reimbursement requests. In order to test the new policy, you have gathered a random sample of 100 reimbursement requests from both before and after the policy change. This data is located in the file **Expense Reimbursement Excel.xlsx** on the textbook's web page. Download this file and use Benford's Law to test whether the new policy appears to have resulted in any fraud.

a. Do the reimbursement requests prior to the policy change appear to follow Benford's Law?
b. Do the reimbursement requests occurring after the policy change appear to follow Benford's Law?
c. What, if anything, leads you to believe that fraud may be occurring?

PB-19. **Segment Reports Using Excel (Descriptive and Diagnostic Analytics)**   **LO3, 4, 5**

Southern Comforts, Inc. is a department store chain with stores in North Carolina, Tennessee, Kentucky, and West Virginia. Its corporate headquarters are located in Charlotte, North Carolina.

In the past, the store owners only received financial reports for the company operations overall. They have recently asked for reports of costs and profitability by segment (location and department). Southern Comforts' locations include the four stores (Charlotte, Nashville, Virginia Beach, and Louisville) and the corporate office (Charlotte HQ). Departments include the product lines (Mens, Womens, Kids, Shoes, and Home) and the overhead expense types (Facilities, Labor, and Other).

They have provided you with an Excel workbook that includes Southern Comfort transactions for 2020. (The workbook, **Segment Report Data Set.xlsx**, is accessible on the textbook's website. A video demonstrating Excel tools used to answer the questions in this problem is also available on the website.). The first step is to make sure the data is in the form needed.

- All transactions are included in the Transactions column. You will need to separate revenue transactions from expense transactions. Add two columns to the table. Use the IF function to create a Revenues column and an Expenses column. (All positive numbers in the Transactions columns are Revenues; all negative numbers are expenses.) *HINT:* To save some time, convert the data to a Table.

- Add a column after Month and call it Month Name. Use the TEXT function to convert the date format to a text format.

1. Use pivot tables to answer the following questions:
   a. Which store was the most profitable (in dollars)? What was the store's profit?
   b. Which store had the most revenue? How much? Which month had the highest revenue? How much? What percentage of total sales occurred during that month? (Round % to two decimals.)
   c. Which month was the least **profitable** (in dollars)? What was the net profit that month?
   d. What was the total gross margin (in dollars) for 2020? Which store had the highest gross margin? How much? *HINT:* Consider creating a calculated field using the Revenues and Expenses columns in the data sheet. Slicers can be used to filter out the overhead expense categories (Facilities, Labor, and Other).
   e. What was the total gross profit ratio for 2020? (Round % to two decimals.) *HINT:* You can create another calculated field using the gross margin field from d. Which store had the lowest gross profit ratio? What was it? Which product line (department) had the highest gross profit ratio? What was it?

2. The store with the highest sales (b.) and the highest gross margin (d.) was not the most profitable (a.). Why? Look at the revenues, gross profit margins and ratios, and the overhead expenses for both stores.

3. Create pivot charts from some of your pivot tables and use them to create an interactive dashboard. Include slicers on the dashboard that allow management to filter by location or month.

LO3, 4, 5   **PB-20.**   **Job Profitability Using Excel (Descriptive and Diagnostic Analytics)**

Harvard Products is a job shop (a company that manufactures custom products in small batches). Each batch is managed by one of Harvard's four project managers. Manufacturing facilities are located in Illinois, Wisconsin, Michigan, and Indiana.

The President of Harvard Products has asked for information about costs and profits by job, location, customer, and project manager. A summary of costs (by job) is included in the **Job Order Data Set.xlsx** file available on the textbook's website. A video demonstrating Excel tools used to answer the questions in this problem is also available on the website. *HINT:* Add columns to the Data sheet to separate out account amounts (revenue, direct material, etc.). The IF function is useful here.

Create PivotTables to answer the following questions:

1. Which customer was the most profitable for Harvard? What was the job number for the most profitable job for that customer? What was the average revenue on jobs for that customer? What was the average revenue for all jobs?

2. Which location was the least profitable (in dollars) for Harvard? What appears to have contributed more to the lower profits at that location – size of jobs (average revenue) or profit margin ratios? Which location had the highest average revenue per job?

3. The President of Harvard Products has decided to give performance bonuses to project managers. Determine which project manager will receive the highest bonus if performance is based on:
   a. Average revenue per job?
   b. Number of jobs?
   c. Total profit?
   d. Profit margin ratios?

4. Based solely on the information you have available, would you encourage management to close the facility with the lowest profit margin? Why or why not? Include in your answer the information you might need to have before making a final decision.

PB-21. **Determining Fixed vs. Variable Cost Components Using Excel (Diagnostic Analytics)**   Genessee   **LO3, 4**
Industries introduced a new product last year (6582-D). Although it was very popular, it wasn't very
profitable. Management has asked you to provide them with information to help them set a sales price
that will provide them with a monthly gross profit of $7,500. (Last year's sales price was $75 per
unit.)

You know that the direct costs per unit are $25 for direct materials and $5 for direct labor. You
are given information about last year's monthly production levels and manufacturing overhead costs
(indirect materials, indirect labor, and other). (That information is included in the **Fixed and Variable
Data Set.xlsx** file available on the textbook's website. A video demonstrating Excel tools used to answer
the questions in this problem is also available on the website.)

1. Determine the cost formula for 6582-D. Use Excel's regression analysis tool to calculate the fixed
   and variable manufacturing overhead costs. Round elements to two decimal places.
   a. Check the 95% confidence level. Consider checking the box to add a line fit plot for each indirect
   cost element to show the relationship in chart form. (You may need to change the minimum bound
   on the horizontal axis to 700 to see the line clearly.)
2. Use the prior year data to create a graph of the various overhead costs by month.
   a. Create a combo chart as follows:
      i. The primary vertical axis in dollars, and the secondary vertical axis is units of production.
      ii. The horizontal axis is Months.
      iii. Units produced should be a clustered column type; the overhead cost elements should be line
          type. (Units produced would be linked to the secondary vertical axis.)
3. Use Excel's Goal Seek tool to determine the sales price required to meet the $7,500 gross profit
   goal. Management believes monthly sales will average 1,500 next year. Assume the company will
   not maintain any inventory of finished goods.
4. Discuss how Goal Seek (or any other Excel tool) might help management with CVP Analysis.

PB-22. **Forecasting Using Excel (Predictive Analytics)**   **LO3, 4, 5**
Melton Manufacturing opened in January 2019. Sales have increased significantly in the first two years
of operations, and management is now looking to expand production capacity. To finance the purchase
of a new factory, they would need to either raise capital or borrow funds.

They have asked you to make some projections for the next year of operations. They intend to share
these with potential investors and lenders.

Information about unit sales, sales revenues, and net profits for the past two years is included in
the **Forecasting Data Set.xlsx** file available on the textbook's website. A video demonstrating Excel
tools used to answer the questions in this problem is also available on the website.

1. Create three line graphs in Excel (one for units sold, one for sales revenue, and one for net operating income). Add trendlines to all graphs.
   a. Extend the trendline out for 12 months.
   b. Use the Polynomial (Order 2) trendline option for all charts
   c. To see how closely the trendline matches the data, check the *Display R-squared value on chart*
   box. The closer the R-square value is to 1, the better the match.
2. Create the same three graphs using the Forecast Sheet tool (line charts) in Excel.
   a. Set the *Forecast End* to 12/1/2021.
   b. Use an 85% *Confidence Interval.*
   c. Check the *Include forecast statistics* box.
   d. Leave remaining defaults as is.
3. Use the trendline graphs to determine: (*HINT:* To help identify the answers, display gridlines.
   Consider changing vertical axis bounds.)
   a. Expected unit sales in October 2021
   b. Expected sales revenue in June 2021
   c. Expected net profits in December 2021
4. Use the Forecast sheets to determine:
   a. Range of expected unit sales in October 2021 (Upper to lower Confidence bounds)
   b. Expected sales revenue in June 2021 (Upper to lower Confidence bounds)
   c. Range of expected net profits in December 2021 (Upper to lower Confidence bounds)
5. To evaluate the Forecast sheets, rerun the forecasts. This time change the *Forecast Start* date to
   1/1/2020 to see what the model would have predicted for 2020. (Leave all other options the same

as B. above.) Were the predictions higher or lower than the actual results? What could have caused the differences?

LO3, 4   PB-23. Utilization of Constrained Resources Using Excel (Prescriptive analytics)

Backyard Helpers, Inc. is a small manufacturing company with 18 different gardening tools in its product line. All of the products are fabricated using the same equipment.

Recently, sales demand has increased. Unfortunately, Backyard Helpers cannot produce enough products with existing equipment to meet that demand. Facilities can be expanded, and new equipment purchased, but it will be at least two years before that happens. The production manager needs to make production scheduling decisions now.

The **Constrained Resource Data Set.xlsx** file available on the textbook's website includes information about demand, sales price, cost, and fabrication time on the shared equipment for each of Backyard Helpers' products. A video demonstrating Excel tools used to answer the questions in this problem is also available at cambridgepub.com.

Maximum machine time is 40,500 minutes per month. The demand for all products is spread equally throughout the month. Fixed costs (manufacturing, selling, and administrative) total $755,750 per month. Backyard Helpers maintains no inventory of finished goods. (All units produced are sold during the month.)

1. Ignore machine time limits in answering the following:
   a. Which product has the highest contribution margin per unit? How many units of that product should be produced each month?
   b. If Backyard could meet demand, what would be the total net operating income per month?
2. If demand was unlimited for all products, which products should Backyard Helpers produce?
3. Given the maximum number of machine minutes per month, use Solver in Excel to answer the following:
   a. How many of the following products should be produced each month?
      i. R25
      ii. JK369
   b. Which products would be temporarily eliminated from Backyard Helpers product line under the Excel solution?
   c. What is the total net operating income per month given the machine time constraints and the quantities determined by Solver?
   d. What is the **maximum** amount Backyard Helpers should be willing to pay to rent fabrication time from another company? (Assume transportation and other costs would total $50,000.)
4. In Questions 3b, you identified products that would be temporarily eliminated if Backyard followed the Excel solution. What reasons, if any, might management have for continuing to produce some of those products even if it means reducing the supply of some of the other products?

LO3, 4   PB-24. Budget Variance Analysis Using Excel (Descriptive and Diagnostic Analytics)

Preston Township's City Council will be evaluating costs incurred in the various city departments at its next meeting. In total, costs exceeded budgeted amounts in the prior year by $576,277. The Council president has asked for information about actual vs. budgeted costs by department and by expense type to help in the evaluation process. Transaction and budget information is included in the **Budget Variance Data Set.xlsx** file available on the textbook's website. A video demonstrating Excel tools used to answer the questions in this problem is also available on the website.

1. Create two PivotTables.
   a. One for actual costs by department and expense type.
   b. One for budgeted costs by department and expense type.
2. Create two Budget Variance reports (one for variances by department and one for variances by expense type). Both reports should link actual and budget data from the PivotTables.
   a. The report should include columns for budgeted amounts, actual amounts, variance (in dollars), and variance (in percent). Show the unfavorable dollar variances as negative numbers, favorable variances as positive numbers. Show all percent variances as positive numbers. *HINT:* Use the ABS function in Excel in the formula to calculate percent variances.
3. Use the PivotTable and the variance reports to answer the following questions:
   a. Which department experienced the greatest variance between budgeted and actual cost (in dollars)? Which expense type in that department accounted for the largest share of the variance? *HINT:* Filter your PivotTables to update the variance reports.

      b. Which expense type had the highest unfavorable variance (in dollars)? Which department had the highest unfavorable variance in that expense type? Which expense type had the highest favorable variance (in dollars)? Which department had the highest favorable variance in that expense type?

      c. Which department had the highest percentage variance? Which type of expense was most over or under budget in that department? Which expense type had the highest percentage variance? Which department was most over or under budget in that expense type?

      d. Schools had the largest budget. Does it appear that the budget dollars were well managed? Explain your answer.

4. In general, should the council members be more concerned about the departments or expense types with the highest unfavorable dollar variances or the highest unfavorable percentage variances? Should the council members be concerned about departments or expense types with favorable variances? Explain your answers.

PB-25. Activity-Based Costing Using Excel (Predictive Analytics)   **LO3, 4**

Kirkland Industries (a contract assembly manufacturer) has decided to adopt activity-based costing techniques to determine its manufacturing overhead rates. The production manager has identified three activities (materials movement, assembly, and packaging/shipping) and a number of possible activity measures (# of jobs, direct labor hours, machine hours, # of boxes shipped, and # of components used). Working together, the production and accounting managers have used historical data from 2014 to 2021 to determine total activity costs by month. Those results are included in the **ABC Cost Drivers Data Set.xlsx** file available on the textbook's website. The workbook also includes totals for the various activity measures from the same 2014-2021 period. (A video demonstrating Excel tools used to answer the questions in this problem is available on the website.)

      Budgeted overhead dollars and activities are:

Budgeted Overhead		Budgeted Measures	
Materials movement	$1,080,000	# of jobs	480
Assembly	$1,950,000	Direct labor hours	16,000
Packaging/Shipping	$1,584,000	Machine hours	7,800
		# of boxes shipped	48,000
		# of components used	4,000,000

1. Use the correlation tool in Excel to determine which measure should be used for each activity. *HINT:* The correlation tool can be found on the *Analyze* menu on the Data tab in Excel. If the *Analyze* section does not appear, you will need to load the *Analysis ToolPak*. Click the *File* tab, click *Options*, and click *Add-Ins*. Make sure Excel *Add-ins* appears in the *Manage* field. Check the *Analysis ToolPak* option and click *OK*.

2. Using the measures identified in 1., determine the activity rates for allocating manufacturing overhead to jobs.

3. What would the predetermined rate be if direct labor hours were used to allocate all manufacturing overhead costs?

4. Assume Kirkland had a job that required 36 direct labor hours, 16 machine hours, 1,875 components, and 68 boxes. How much manufacturing overhead would be applied to that job under ABC? How does that compare to the amount applied if direct labor hours were used to allocate overhead? What might account for the difference?

Index

Exhibits and notes are included in the index with a corresponding *e* or *n* following the page numbers.

Exhibits and notes are included in the index with a corresponding *e* or *n* following the page numbers.

Exhibits and notes are included in the index with a corresponding *e* or *n* following the page numbers.

Exhibits and notes are included in the index with a corresponding *e* or *n* following the page numbers.

Exhibits and notes are included in the index with a corresponding *e* or *n* following the page numbers.